The Cultural Front

The Laboring of American Culture
in the Twentieth Century

◆

MICHAEL   DENNING

VERSO
London • New York

THE HAYMARKET SERIES

Editors: Mike Davis and Michael Sprinker

The Haymarket Series offers original studies in politics, history and culture, with a focus on North America. Representing views across the American left on a wide range of subjects, the series will be of interest to socialists both in the USA and throughout the world. A century after the first May Day, the American left remains in the shadow of those martyrs whom the Haymarket Series honors and commemorates. These studies testify to the living legacy of political activism and commitment for which they gave their lives.

First published by Verso 1997
© Michael Denning 1997
Paperback edition first published by Verso 1998
© Michael Denning 1998
All rights reserved

The right of Michael Denning to be identified as the author
of this work has been asserted by him in accordance with
the Copyright, Designs and Patents Act 1988

Verso
UK: 6 Meard Street, London W1V 3HR
USA: 180 Varick Street, New York NY 10014–4606

Verso is the imprint of New Left Books

ISBN 1–85984–170–8

British Library Cataloguing in Publication Data
A catalogue record for this book is available from the British Library

Library of Congress Cataloging-in-Publication Data
A catalog record for this book is available from the Library of Congress

Typeset by SetSystems, Saffron Walden, Essex, UK
Printed and bound in the USA by
R.R. Donnelly & Sons

The Cultural Front

Michael Denning was born in Vermont in 1954 and grew up in New York state, the child of school teachers. After studying at Dartmouth, the Birmingham Centre for Contemporary Cultural Studies, and Yale, he taught at Columbia and Wesleyan and now works as Professor of American Studies at Yale University. The author of *Mechanic Accents: Dime Novels and Working-Class Culture in America* and *Cover Stories: Narrative and Ideology in the British Spy Thriller*, he has written on American culture and politics for the *Village Voice*, *Social Text*, *Radical History Review*, *Socialist Review* and *History Workshop*. Long active in union campaigns, he is a member of the National Writers Union. He lives in Guilford, Connecticut with Hazel Carby and their son Nicholas.

Contents

for Edwina, and in memory of Bill,
for my parents,
and, for Nicholas

Acknowledgments

My parents grew up during the depression and World War II, but I was not a red diaper baby. Like many Americans, I inherited the Popular Front's laboring of American culture without knowing it; Cold War repression had left a cultural amnesia. It was not until I was working on this book that I learned, in a historical study, that a neighbor during my childhood had been a veteran of the Lincoln Brigade. For my education in the Popular Front, I am indebted to my high school history teachers, Sam Michelson and Jack Leshner, who, I now realize, continued the arguments between New York's American Labor Party and Liberal Party into the 1960s; to the librarian at Sullivan County Community College, who assembled the collection of Folkways records I devoured; to Michael Harrington and the DSOC members who told stories of Shachtmanites and Cannonites late into the night at socialist youth conferences; to Stanley Aronowitz, whose stories began for me twenty years ago in St Cloud and whose influence on this book is much greater than the footnotes indicate; to Paul Joseph for many years of conversation about the left old and new; and especially to Edwina Hammond Pomerance and the late Bill Pomerance for embodying the art, thought, and activism of the Popular Front. The long friendly argument in Killingworth between Bill and Perry Anderson over the meaning of the American Labor Party was one of the sources of this book.

I am also indebted to my colleagues in Yale's American Studies Program (and particularly to the teaching assistants in the Formation of Modern American Culture and to the members of the various "1930s" seminars I have taught), to the brothers and sisters in GESO (Graduate Employees and Students Organization) and Locals 34 and 35 of the Federation of University Employees, and to the informal left academy that took shape as the Southern New England Left Triangle and the What's Left group.

Michael Sprinker was once again a great editor, sticking with this project through many changes, past many deadlines, and offering encouragement and criticism. Dolores Hayden, Rachel Rubin, Tina Klein, Kathy Newman, and Jean-Christophe Agnew read and commented helpfully on the manuscript. Kathy Newman's research assistance was crucial in the final stages.

I am particularly grateful to Holly Allen, who co-authored the original version of the chapter on the cartoonists, and Paul Buhle, who invited me along for interviews with Ring Lardner Jr, Abraham Polonsky, and Paul Jarrico, and lent me notes and transcripts of his other interviews. Thanks also to David Montgomery, Paul Gilroy, Vron Ware, Jim Fisher, Laura Wexler, Judy Smith, Eric Lott, Alan Trachtenberg, George Lipsitz, Alan Wald, Paula Rabinowitz, Cary Nelson, Bryan Wolf, Faith Hubley, Lou Renza, Carlo Rotella, David Stowe, Dorothy Rony, Xiao Hong Shen, Michelle Stephens, Benjamin Filene, Bill Lowe, Cora Kaplan, Joe Tinari, Tony Lombardozzi, Sandhya Shukla, Nikhil Singh, Joe Entin, Rebecca Schreiber, Tom Thurston, Dan Belgrad, Cynthia Young, Sonya Michel, Stephen Shapiro, Barbara Savage, Gloria Monti, Margaret McFadden, David Phillips, Trysh Travis, Suzanne Smith, Gaspar González, Debra Nicolis Thurston, Ingrid Baumgartner, and Fred Jameson for offering help and suggestions.

A section of the proletarian literature chapter was delivered to the "Reading in America" conference at the University of Paris and appeared in *Cahiers Charles V*.

The chapter about the cartoonists was originally written with Holly Allen for a special issue of *South Atlantic Quarterly*. We are indebted to the issue's editor, Susan Willis, and to Mary Eastman, Edwina Hammond Pomerance, and the late Bill Pomerance for their interviews.

An earlier form of the chapter about Orson Welles was written and delivered at the Wesleyan Center for the Humanities, then at New York University's Welles Retrospective, and published in *Persistence of Vision*. Noel Carroll and Richard Slotkin spurred the work on Welles, and I am grateful to Richard Vann, Richard Ohmann, and Elizabeth Traube of the Humanities Center both for the Mellon fellowship and the Center's lively intellectual life. Thanks also to William Simon, Jane Levey, and James Naremore for help in the Welles research.

Sections of the final chapter first appeared in different forms in David Bennett, ed., *Cultural Studies: Pluralism and Theory*; and Cary Nelson and Dilip Gaonkar, eds, *Disciplinarity and Dissent in Cultural Studies*.

A National Endowment for the Humanities Summer Stipend helped support the final work on the book.

Hazel Carby was a constant collaborator on the cultural (and other) fronts. Her work on blues-women and race men has been a counterpoint to this one, as Paul Robeson wandered out of this book and into hers, and Billie Holiday migrated from hers (temporarily) into this one. From the vague origins of the project a decade ago to her patient help laboring over the copyedited endnotes, this book would not have been possible without her.

Introduction

"Do not ask me to write of the strike and the terror," the young Tillie Lerner (later Olsen) wrote of San Francisco's General Strike in 1934. "I am on a battlefield, and the increasing stench and smoke sting the eyes so it is impossible to turn them back into the past. [. . .] The rest, the General Strike, the terror, arrests and jail, the songs in the night, must be written some other time, must be written later. . . . But there is so much happening now. . . ." The long strike of longshoremen for union recognition in the spring of 1934 had culminated in the violent attempt by shipowners to reopen San Francisco's docks on 5 July, the "Bloody Thursday" during which two workers were killed, thirty were treated for bullet wounds, and many more were clubbed, gassed, and stoned. The general strike that shut down San Francisco the following week marked the birth of a new social movement—the Popular Front—out of the depths of the depression.[1]

"The city became a camp, a battlefield," Lerner wrote, "the screams of ambulances sent the day reeling, class lines fell sharply—everywhere, on streetcars, on corners, in stores, people talked, cursing, stirred with something strange in their breasts, incomprehensible, shaken with fury at the police, the papers, the shipowners . . . going down to the waterfront, not curious spectators, but to stand there, watching, silent, trying to read the lesson the moving bodies underneath were writing, trying to grope to the meaning of it all." Lerner herself was trying to read the lesson the moving bodies were writing, but she was also one of those moving bodies.

The daughter of Russian immigrants, she had grown up in working-class Omaha and had never completed high school. After joining the Young Communist League at the age of eighteen, she moved to California and became active in the 1934 waterfront struggles; her work for the *Waterfront Worker* led to her arrest for vagrancy. Her arrest and imprisonment drew national attention because she had published a remarkable short story about a mining camp, "The Iron Throat," in the proletarian literary magazine, *Partisan Review*. Robert Cantwell told her story in the *New Republic* as an example of "The Literary Life in California," and the following week the *New Republic* carried her own account of the arrest, "Thousand-Dollar Vagrant." But Lerner's promise to write about "the rest" was not kept until forty years later when her "lost" novel, *Yonnondio: From the Thirties* (1974), was reconstructed from old manuscripts, emerging as the lyric masterpiece of the Popular Front. Opening with her mining-camp tale, "The Iron Throat," the novel ends amidst stench and smoke when a steam pipe explodes in a packinghouse, a figure for "the fists of strike" and "the pickax of revolution."[2]

If 1929 became a symbol of despair and ruin, an emblem of the crash of an economy and a way of life, 1934 stands as one of the lyric years in American history. Along with 1848, 1886, and 1968, 1934 is an emblem of insurgency, upheaval, and hope. A new militancy and solidarity among American working people appeared as the battles of San Francisco's longshoremen, Minneapolis's teamsters, and Toledo's auto-parts workers won the allegiance of citizens and neighbors. General strikes brought each city to a halt, figuring, however briefly, a cooperative commonwealth.

In September 1934, a national textile strike became the largest strike in a single industry in American history, involving 400,000 workers from Maine to Alabama. Strikes in California's factories in the fields were the largest agricultural strikes in American history. These strikes seared the imaginations of young writers and artists. "I have never been in a strike before," Meridel Le Sueur wrote of the Minneapolis General Strike. "I felt my feet join in that strange shuffle of thousands of bodies moving with direction, of thousands of feet, and my own breath. As if an electric charge had passed through me, my hair stood on end. I was marching." "The strike taught me that I was definitely a part of the labor movement," the Filipino poet Carlos Bulosan later wrote of a lettuce strike in Lompoc. "From this day onward my life became one long conspiracy . . . I was so intensely fired by this dream of a better America that I had completely forgotten myself." A year later, in the fall of 1935, the leader of the United Mine Workers, John L. Lewis, responded to the labor uprisings by forming the CIO (Committee for, later Congress of, Industrial Organizations). The next two decades were the age of the CIO.[3]

At the same time, a new radical culture was taking shape. On 6 January 1935, the audience at New York's Civic Repertory Theatre, 1,400 strong, chanted "Strike! Strike!" at the end of the first performance of *Waiting for Lefty*. An unknown one-act play about a taxi strike by an unknown playwright, performed by Group Theatre actors to benefit the left-wing magazine *New Theatre, Waiting for Lefty* captured the imagination of this movement; theater groups across the country produced it. By the end of the year, *Waiting for Lefty* was "the most widely performed play in America—and the most widely banned." America, it seemed, was waiting for lefty.[4]

The heart of this cultural front was a new generation of plebeian artists and intellectuals who had grown up in the immigrant and black working-class neighborhoods of the modernist metropolis. They were the second generation of the second wave of immigration: ethnic Italians, Jews, Poles, Mexicans, Serbians, Croatians, Slovaks, Japanese, Chinese, and Filipinos along with African Americans who had migrated north. The children of public education, they were caught between the memories and stories of their parents and the realities of urban streets and shops. Some joined the small and militant Young Communist League; others joined the tiny revolutionary parties that had split from the Communists; many belonged to no political group but simply adopted the name: they were all "communists." All three general strikes had been led by these young communists: in San Francisco by members of the Communist Party like Lerner herself; in Minneapolis by the Trotskyists of the Communist League of America; and in Toledo by A. J. Muste's American Workers Party. The artists and writers among them formed proletarian literary clubs, workers theaters, camera clubs, film and photo leagues, composers collectives, Red dance troupes, and revolutionary choruses: the proletarian avant-garde of the depression. Nineteen thirty-four saw a flowering of little magazines that published proletarian stories, poems, songs, and cartoons: *Blast, Anvil, Dynamo, Partisan Review, Left Front*. In October 1935, an anthology entitled *Proletarian Literature in the United States* gathered together the stories, poems, plays, reportage, and criticism of this avant-garde: it included Lerner's "The Iron Throat" as well as *Waiting for Lefty*.

These young plebeian artists found allies among the older generation of American modernists drawn to the Popular Front. In March 1935, *Waiting for Lefty* was followed by *Panic*, an agitprop verse drama written by Archibald MacLeish, starring a nineteen-year-old Orson Welles playing the ruined capitalist McGafferty. MacLeish, a well-known poet, was only one of the writers and artists of the modernist generation who turned to the left. John Dos Passos, in the midst of writing his radical trilogy, *U.S.A.*, led a delegation of writers to investigate the repression of miners in Harlan County, Kentucky. Langston Hughes wrote a play and poems about the Scottsboro Nine, and Duke Ellington performed at Scottsboro benefits. Malcolm Cowley's influential chronicle of the moderns, *Exile's Return* (1934), ended by calling on artists to "take the workers' side" in the class struggle. "So far as I can see," Kenneth Burke wrote in *Permanence and Change* (1935), "the only coherent and organized movement making for the subjection of the technological genius to humane ends is that of Communism, by whatever name it may finally prevail." In 1932, a number of these modernist intellectuals, including Dos Passos, Cowley, Hughes,

Edmund Wilson, and Lincoln Steffens, had issued a manifesto, *Culture and the Crisis,* announcing their support for the Communist Party candidates "in the interests of a truly human society in which all forms of exploitation have been abolished; in behalf of a new cultural renaissance."[5]

They also found allies among the anti-fascist émigrés fleeing Hitler. Bertolt Brecht, Hanns Eisler, and Kurt Weill all first came to the United States in 1935, transplanting Weimar's radical music and theatre to New York. Hollywood was infused with the talents of German film. The muralists of the Mexican revolution—José Clemente Orozco, Diego Rivera, and David Alfaro Siqueiros—painted murals in the United States and exercised a powerful political and artistic influence: the whitewashing of Rivera's Rockefeller Center mural was a major political controversy in 1933. All three groups—the young plebeians, the radical moderns, and the anti-fascist émigrés—came together in the cultural front, the extraordinary flowering of arts, entertainment, and thought based on the broad social movement that came to be known as the Popular Front.

At the end of the century, what is left? For most critics and historians of American culture, not much. "To this day," one of our finest historians has written, "when I hear the words Pop Front I think of atrocious art." The post-war Red scare and anti-communist purge combined with the Cold War to eradicate much of the radical culture of the Popular Front. The "thirties" became an icon, the brief moment when "politics" captured the arts, when writers went left, Hollywood turned Red, and painters, musicians, and photographers were "social-minded." The left turn of the depression is usually seen as a detour if not a wrong turn. But were the 1930s merely a "Red decade" or were they, as Michael Gold claimed, a "second American Renaissance"? In the pages that follow, I hope to persuade you that the cultural front reshaped American culture. Just as the radical movements of abolition, utopian socialism, and women's rights sparked the antebellum American Renaissance, so the communisms of the depression triggered a deep and lasting transformation of American modernism and mass culture, what I will call the *laboring* of American culture.[6]

What is the laboring of American culture? What does it mean to labor a culture? In this book, I use the phrase to sum up a number of interrelated arguments, and, at the risk of belaboring it, I will outline those meanings and those arguments. First, the laboring of American culture refers to the pervasive use of "labor" and its synonyms in the rhetoric of the period. It includes the common reference to the "labor movement" and a "labor party," as well as the use of the term "proletarian" by the young militants in the early days of the movement. Together with the various forms of "work," "industry," and "toil," these were key words in the vocabulary of the cultural front: the language itself was "labored." Second, it refers to what a more technical usage would call the "proletarianization" of American culture, the increased influence on and participation of working-class Americans in the world of culture and the arts. As I shall argue, this was largely the result of a remarkable expansion of what is usually called mass culture: on the one hand, secondary and higher education; and on the other, the industries of entertainment and amusement. In this sense, there was a laboring of American culture as children from working-class families grew up to become artists in the culture industries, and American workers became the primary audience for those industries.

Third, the laboring of American culture refers to the new visibility of the labor of cultural production. Culture had become an industry in the early twentieth century, and artists, musicians, and writers were laborers in that industry. As a result, one of the central stories of the cultural front is the organization of unions by these workers, including screenwriters, cartoonists, journalists, and teachers. Fourth, the phrase reminds us that the culture and politics of the Popular Front were not simply New Deal liberalism and populism. It was a social democratic culture, a culture of "industrial democracy" and "industrial unionism." In England, the culture and politics of social democracy and the post-World War II Labour Party is often called "labourism"; the Popular Front was in this sense "laborist," and fought for the laboring—the social democratization—of American culture.

Finally, the laboring of American culture connotes a birthing of a new American culture, a second American Renaissance. But it was also a laboring in that this birth was painstaking and difficult. This was neither a revolution nor a coup d'état; it was not even a transformation. To labor is to plod, to be hampered, to pitch and roll in a storm. In all these senses, the cultural front was a laboring, an incomplete and unfinished struggle to rework American culture, with hesitations, pauses, defeats, and failures.

This book is a history of the cultural front and an interpretation of the artistic and intellectual formations it fostered. I begin with the question that has long dominated the cultural history of the depression: Why did the left have a powerful, indeed an unprecedented, impact on US culture in the 1930s? For most critics and historians, the answer is embodied in the image of the "fellow traveler," the individual artist or intellectual attracted to the Communist Party and the Soviet Union in the face of a collapsing economy and a rising fascism. The history of the "commitment" of these "fellow travelers" is commonly told as a morality tale of seduction and betrayal, utopian dreams and Cold War disenchantment. However, the narrative of the "fellow traveler" is misleading and does not capture the full significance of the cultural front. For the cultural front was not simply the product of individual political commitment: it was, I will argue in part one, the result of the encounter between a powerful democratic social movement—the Popular Front—and the modern cultural apparatuses of mass entertainment and education.

The broad social movement known as the Popular Front was the ground on which the workers theaters, proletarian literary magazines, and film industry unions stood: it was, I will argue, a radical social-democratic movement forged around anti-fascism, anti-lynching, and the industrial unionism of the CIO. The Popular Front emerged out of the crisis of 1929, and it remained the central popular democratic movement over the following three decades, the years I will call the age of the CIO. Here I take issue with most accounts of the Popular Front, sympathetic or hostile, which have seen it through a core-periphery model, in which the core was the Communist Party and the periphery was the surrounding circles of "fellow travelers" with greater or lesser degrees of affiliation to the Party. This view leads to a remarkably inadequate understanding of the depth and breadth of the social movement, as well as a disproportionate emphasis on central Party leaders, an over-reading of the significance of pronouncements in Communist Party journals, and, in some cases, a search for the Moscow gold that kept it all running.

In cultural studies, this has often led to a fetishization of Party membership, and an overemphasis on the narrative of affiliation and disaffiliation. However, Party membership was not that central; many people passed through the Party at different times, and the large majority of Popular Front radicals were never members. Indeed, many figures thought of themselves as generic "communists," using the term with a small *c*, the way earlier and later generations thought of themselves as generic "socialists," "feminists," or "radicals." "I cannot help calling myself a communist," Lewis Mumford wrote to Van Wyck Brooks, "for that points to the fundamental demand." "Most of us down here consider ourselves pretty good communists, you know," the secretary of the Arkansas labor school, Commonwealth College, wrote to Jack Conroy, "but we can't work with the party. It's the old question of tactics again." As Kenneth Burke wrote to Malcolm Cowley, "my book will have the communist objectives, and the communist tenor, but the approach will be the approach that seems significant to me."[7]

Thus, in part one, "The Left and American Culture," I sketch an alternative view of the Popular Front, seeing it as a historical bloc: I begin with its base in the industrial unions of the CIO, then move to its political superstructures, and finally turn to its cultural formations. I then outline the history of the Popular Front, its rise and fall through the age of the CIO. The impact of the Popular Front on American culture was magnified by the rise of what C. Wright Mills was to call the "cultural apparatus." I conclude part one by arguing that this modern cultural apparatus not only found its audience among the ethnic working classes of the modern metropolis, but recruited its artists and intellectuals from those urban working classes. A generation of plebeian artists and intellectuals came to staff the agencies of the federal government and the studios of the culture industries. With the emergence of the Popular Front social movement, these "hacks" and "stars" of the cultural apparatus became the moving spirits of the cultural front.

Part two, "Anatomy of the Cultural Front," is an overview of the cultural politics and aesthetic ideologies of the cultural front. The cultural front was a common metaphor of the time, combining two meanings of the word "front": the military metaphor designating a place, a site of struggle or battlefront; and the political metaphor designating a group, a coalition with a common purpose. Thus, the "cultural front" referred both to the cultural industries and apparatuses—a "front" or terrain of cultural struggle—and to the alliance of radical artists and intellectuals who made up the "cultural" part of the Popular Front. It is perhaps not surprising that the term often appeared as the title of a newspaper or magazine column, for the column was a place where one spoke out, took a stand, and mobilized an audience. As early as 1932, "The Cultural Front" was the title of a column in the mimeographed *Baltimore John Reed Club Bulletin*. And by 1938 there was a regular column in the glossy photomagazine *Direction*, "the lively, entertaining and crusading magazine of the People's Front in the Arts," entitled "Cultural Front," which listed current performances and exhibitions of interest to the left (Figure 1). Michael Gold, a columnist for the *Daily Worker*, called one of his columns "Notes on the Cultural Front." Even vehement left-wing critics of the Communist Party used the phrase: James Farrell's literary columns in *Socialist Call* and *Partisan Review* were both called "The Cultural Front"; and Dwight Macdonald titled a section of his *Memoirs of a Revolutionist*, "The Cultural Front."[8]

To understand the cultural front, I will distinguish two notions of the politics of art: "cultural politics," the politics of allegiances and affiliations, and "aesthetic ideologies," the politics of form. The first, cultural politics, is at one level simply the politics of letterheads and petitions, the stances taken by artists and intellectuals, the pledges of allegiance and declarations of dissent. But it is also the politics of the cultural field itself, the history of the institutions and apparatuses in which artists and intellectuals work. For the kinds of political stances artists and intellectuals take depend upon their understanding of the ground on which they work. The notion of the cultural front itself was an attempt to theorize the relation of culture to politics. Chapter two, "Marching on May Day," will explore the ways the cultural front inflected the movement culture of the CIO, the state cultural institutions of the New Deal order, and the studios of the culture industry.[9]

But if these allegiances and affiliations represent the "social consciousness" of the cultural front, the works produced by the communist artists and intellectuals also bear the traces of a "political unconscious." The cultural front embodied a politics of form, an aesthetic ideology. The novels, plays, films, and musicals written and performed by the radical artists within and without the cultural apparatus used a repertoire of forms and styles, genres and conventions; and the critical controversies and debates that surrounded them established ways of seeing and judging, canons of value. So chapter three, "Ballads for Americans," looks at the popular aesthetics and ideologies that informed the cultural front, their revolutionary symbolisms, ethnic Americanisms, and labor feminisms.[10]

Part three, "Formations of the Cultural Front," takes up what Raymond Williams called "the most central and practical element in cultural analysis: the exploration and specification of distinguishable cultural formations." Cultural formations, he suggested, "are simultaneously artistic forms and social locations." Each of the chapters of part three explores an artistic form that was also a social location: the narrative of the decline and fall of the Lincoln republic in John Dos Passos's *U.S.A.*; the "literary class war" of the proletarian literature movement; the genre of ghetto or tenement pastorals that came to dominate American literature through the works of novelists like Richard Wright and Tillie Olsen; the migrant narratives of California's factories in the fields composed by Woody Guthrie, Carlos Bulosan, and Ernesto Galarza; the experiments in musical theater represented by Marc Blitzstein's *The Cradle Will Rock*, the Labor Stage's *Pins and Needles*, and Duke Ellington's *Jump for Joy*; the cabaret blues of Billie Holiday and Josh White; the theater, radio, and film of Orson Welles and his Mercury Theatre; the strikes and cartoons of Disney's radical animators; and the encounter between American culture and socialist theory that reshaped American thought in the works of figures like Kenneth Burke, Carey McWilliams, and Elizabeth Hawes.[11]

Although the Popular Front was defeated by the forces of the "American Century," and the "thirties" seemed to be over by 1948, the works of the cultural front had a profound impact on American culture, informing the life-work of two generations of artists and intellectuals. For the first time in the history of the United States, a working-class culture had made a significant imprint on the dominant cultural institutions. Both high culture and mass culture took on a distinctly plebeian accent. Black and ethnic writers, descendants of the proletarian avant-garde, dominated twentieth-century American literature. Vernacular musics like jazz, blues, and country resonated around the world. Gangster movies and *films noir* had founded the "American" look in film. The cultural front had begun a laboring of American culture.

PART I

The Left and American Culture

1

Waiting for Lefty

"In any view of the American cultural situation, the importance of the radical movement of the Thirties cannot be overestimated. It may be said to have created the American intellectual class as we now know it in its great size and influence." Lionel Trilling's retrospective observation remains a starting point for understanding the importance of the cultural front. For the age of the Congress of Industrial Organizations (CIO) marked the first time in the history of the United States that the left—the tradition of radical democratic movements for social transformation—had a central, indeed shaping, impact on American culture. Whether we think of culture as the norms, values, beliefs, and ways of life of particular groups of people, or, in a more limited sense, as the texts, artifacts, and performances produced by a variety of artists, entertainers, and cultural craftworkers, the left had had little influence on the cultures of the United States in the nineteenth and early twentieth centuries. There were of course particular immigrant and ethnic communities in which the left—whether socialist, anarchist, or communist—was influential in shaping daily life and popular entertainments; and certain radicalisms—feminism, abolition, and populism—had mobilized large numbers of Americans, creating alternative movement cultures of solidarity. But the world of culture in the more limited sense—that part of the social surplus devoted to the arts and entertainment—had few ties to the left. There were exceptions—one thinks of the labor radicalism of the dime novelist George Lippard, of Margaret Fuller's feminism, or of William Dean Howells's defense of the Haymarket anarchists—but their iconoclasm and idiosyncrasy stands out.[1]

The "little renaissance" of the 1910s signaled a more sustained connection between the arts communities and the left, between the bohemia of Greenwich Village and the movement cultures of the Debsian Socialist Party and the Wobblies. Indeed, the legendary Paterson Pageant of June

3

1913, which brought together striking silkworkers of Paterson, New Jersey, and Greenwich Village writers and artists at Madison Square Garden, inaugurated a new relation between the left and the producers of culture; it was the first great "benefit concert." Nevertheless, the radical culture of the 1910s, of Greenwich Village and Provincetown, was only a harbinger of the left culture of the depression. For by the late 1930s, a remarkable range of writers, intellectuals, and artists had some connection to the left and its cultural initiatives.

The usual account of this turn to the left in the 1930s gestures to the Great Depression and the rise of fascism, to the sight of breadlines and the fear of jackboots; the radicalism of the artists, we are told, was a response to a particular moment, and it evaporated with the defeat of fascism and the return of prosperity. Though the depression and the rise of fascism were surely triggers for many individuals, the emergence of a left culture in the age of the CIO was the result of two larger transformations in American life: the appearance of a powerful mass social movement, the Popular Front, based on the unprecedented organization of industrial workers into the new unions of the CIO; and the remarkable development of the modern "cultural apparatus," to adopt a phrase of C. Wright Mills, consisting of the culture industries of mass entertainment and the state cultural institutions. Thus, this chapter has three parts: a sketch of the lineaments of the Popular Front social movement, an outline of its history, and an account of the emergence of the cultural apparatus.

1. The Popular Front as a Social Movement

The Popular Front was the insurgent social movement forged from the labor militancy of the fledgling CIO, the anti-fascist solidarity with Spain, Ethiopia, China, and the refugees from Hitler, and the political struggles on the left wing of the New Deal. Born out of the social upheavals of 1934 and coinciding with the Communist Party's period of greatest influence in US society, the Popular Front became a radical historical bloc uniting industrial unionists, Communists, independent socialists, community activists, and émigré anti-fascists around laborist social democracy, anti-fascism, and anti-lynching. Along with the Socialist, feminist, and syndicalist insurgencies of the early 1910s (represented by Eugene Debs's Socialist Party, the women's suffrage movement, the IWW, and the *Masses* magazine), and the New Left, black liberation, and feminist movements of the 1960s and 1970s, the moment of the Popular Front stands as a central instance of radical insurgency in modern US history. Indeed, Popular Front attitudes so impressed themselves on the American people that a 1942 *Fortune* poll found that 25 percent of Americans favored socialism and another 35 percent had an open mind about it.[2]

As a result, the politics of the Popular Front haunts all the periodic debates over the meaning and legacy of the 1930s. Unfortunately, the legacy of the anti-Communist crusade of the late 1940s and 1950s has placed the Communist issue at the heart of virtually all considerations of the Popular Front. Whether the subject is the American Writers' Congress or the United Automobile Workers, the first question about the protagonists remains that of the House Committee on Un-American Activities: Are you now or have you ever been a member of the Communist Party? As a result, the politics of the period have a spurious simplicity: Was she or wasn't she? The Popular Front, we are told, was made up of Communists and fellow-traveling liberals; the center was red, the periphery, shades of pink. This model not only informs the anti-Communist historiography, but also the liberal defenses of non-Communist fellow travelers and the recent revisionist histories of the Communist Party. "A fixation on the Party, in both memoirs of members and ex-members and in the work of historians, has left enormous gaps in our knowledge of the radical past," David Roediger has recently noted.

> Moreover, the assumption of too many Communists, ex-Communists, and historians is that those labeled "fellow travelers" were superficial, easily misled, and reactive in their politics and were seekers of vicarious pleasure through identification with the Russian Revolution. . . . Oddly, a historical literature bitterly denouncing fellow travelers coexists with a growing body of scholarship sympathetic to longtime Party leaders. Perhaps one way to move the history of communism beyond the rather arid current debates within the field would be to focus on the tens of thousands of fellow travelers, rank-and-file workers in Communist-led unions, and persons who left the Party without great hostility. This periphery, far larger than the Party, voted with its feet by supporting some Party activities in some periods and refusing to support other causes at other times.[3]

Indeed, any examination of the Popular Front, particularly its cultural front, supports Roediger's suggestion: the rank and file of the Popular Front were the fellow travelers, the large periphery. But even this terminology is misleading; the periphery was in many cases the center, the "fellow travelers" *were* the Popular Front. It is mistaken to see the Popular Front as a marriage of Communists and liberals. The heart of the Popular Front as a social movement lay among those who were non-Communist socialists and independent leftists, working with Communists and with liberals, but marking out a culture that was neither a Party nor a liberal New Deal culture. Many of the key figures of the cultural front—Orson Welles, F.O. Matthiessen, Elizabeth Hawes, Carey McWilliams, Louis Adamic, John Hammond, and Kenneth Burke—were independent leftists who worked with Party members like Marc Blitzstein, Tillie Olsen, John Howard

Lawson, Granville Hicks, and Richard Wright. Any history of the Popular Front must give the Communist Party its due—it was without doubt the most influential left organization in the period and its members were central activists in a range of formations and institutions—while recognizing that the Popular Front was more a historical bloc, in Gramsci's sense, than a party, a broad and tenuous left-wing alliance of fractions of the subaltern classes.

What would it mean to think of the Popular Front social movement as a historical bloc? Like many useful theoretical terms, Gramsci's notion of an historical bloc has two senses: it connotes both an alliance of social forces and a specific social formation. The connection between the two lies in the concept of hegemony: a moment of hegemony is when a historical bloc (in the sense of a particular alliance of class fractions and social forces) is able to lead a society for a period of time, winning consent through a form of representation, and thereby establishing a historical bloc (in the sense of a social formation). In such moments, one often finds the historical period taking its name from the social alliance. The New Deal was such a historical bloc, at once a particular alliance of political actors and the ruling force in the society.[4]

In analyzing a historical bloc, Gramsci turns to the dialectic of base and superstructure, seeing social movements and alliances as microcosms of the social order as a whole. This offers a more powerful model for analyzing the Popular Front than the center-periphery model that has dominated most histories. For though the social alliance represented by the Popular Front historical bloc never achieved national power or hegemony, remaining an unruly part of Roosevelt's New Deal alliance, its economic, political, and cultural authority among the ethnic working classes of the great metropolises and industrial towns of North America was far reaching. To understand the Popular Front we must look at its material base as well as its political and cultural superstructures, its social content as well as its ideological forms.[5]

The base of the Popular Front was the labor movement, the organization of millions of industrial workers into the new unions of the CIO. For this was the age of the CIO, the years that saw what one historian has called "the largest sustained surge of worker organization in American history." Technically, the CIO began as a dissident group of industrial unionists within the American Federation of Labor in the fall of 1935; the largest participating unions were the mineworkers led by John L. Lewis and the two major needle trades unions (the Amalgamated Clothing Workers of America (ACWA) led by Sidney Hillman and the International Ladies' Garment Workers Union (ILGWU) led by David Dubinsky). But this initiative itself was a response to the tremendous surge of worker organization that had followed the 16 June 1933 signing of the National Industrial

Recovery Act, which led to the general strikes of 1934. Workers flocked into the federal unions of the AFL and the Communist-led unions of the Trade Union Unity League (TUUL). In some industries, the fledgling CIO issued charters to these emerging rank-and-file unions; in other industries, they sent in organizing committees to form unions. After the remarkable success of the sit-down strikes of the Akron rubberworkers (in February and March 1936) and the Flint autoworkers (between December 1936 and February 1937), the CIO became a federation of industrial unions, backed largely by the power of John L. Lewis's United Mine Workers. By the early 1940s, the CIO was dominated by new unions in the metalworking industries—the United Auto Workers, the United Steel Workers, and the United Electrical Workers—and "industrial unionism" was not simply a kind of unionism but a vision of social reconstruction.[6]

As a result, the CIO stands for more than the labor federation itself; as Len De Caux later wrote, "unorganized workers of all kinds tried to get into the nearest CIO union, regardless of name or industry. They just wanted to 'join the CIO.' It was a mass movement with a message, revivalistic in fervor, militant in mood, joined together by class solidarity." The CIO marks the emergence of a new working class, what I will call the CIO working class. This new working class had been created by the migration of millions of people from an agricultural periphery that included Quebec, Scandinavia, European Russia, Hungary, Croatia-Slovenia, Greece, Italy, Sicily, the defeated Confederate States of America, central and northern Mexico, and parts of Japan and China to an industrial core in the Northeast and Middle West of the United States. This "proletarian globe-hopping" had created the multi-racial, multi-ethnic metropolises of modernism. By 1930, two-thirds of the people in the great cities of the United States were foreign-born or the children of the foreign-born; and the "black metropolises" within those cities had formed as many black Americans migrated from the segregated, sharecropping South to the northern cities of industry.[7]

The children of these proletarian migrants, the second-generation ethnic workers, were the rank and file of the new CIO unions. And they were also the creators of a new militant working-class culture that was no longer marginalized in the "foreign" ghettoes. The famous Section 7-A of the National Industrial Recovery Act of 1933 had established "the right of labor to representatives of its own choosing"; in its wake, workers found economic representatives in the mass CIO unions and political representatives in Roosevelt's New Deal Democratic Party, Earl Browder's Communist Party, and the state labor parties. But these second-generation workers who created the CIO also found cultural representatives, as a host of organic intellectuals ranging from actors to novelists, popular singers to Marxist theorists, began to reshape American culture. Moreover, this new working-class culture was, as I shall argue, the foundation of the cultural front, nurturing many of its plebeian writers and artists, and becoming subject and audience of many of its works.[8]

But if the young second-generation workers coming of age during the depression were in many ways responsible for the workplace and neighborhood militance that formed the new industrial unions, they were in turn reshaped by the CIO's movement culture and by the Popular Front. In grasping this dialectic, a number of recent labor historians have been able to escape the old arguments about whether the CIO was "radical" or "conservative," whether a militant rank and file was restrained or betrayed by its conservative leaders, or whether the CIO radicalism was simply a few militants trying to rouse essentially conservative working-class masses. For if the pioneers of industrial unionism were often skilled workers with radical politics—"sparkplug unionists"—the success of the unions depended on their alliance with the second-generation ethnic machine tenders. "Virtually every industrial union that arose in the United States in the 1930s," labor historian Gary Gerstle has written, "depended on the same alliance of radical and ethnic workers that propelled the ITU [Independent Textile Union] into being." This alliance was built on a wide-ranging shift in workers' orientations in the 1920s and 1930s, a transformation in what Lizabeth Cohen calls "patterns of loyalty and . . . allegiance" to ethnic organizations, welfare agencies, stores, theaters, political parties, and unions.[9]

It is clear that the stark opposition of revolutionary socialism and middle-class liberalism or consumerism does not adequately grasp the subtleties of this new working-class culture, these new patterns of loyalty and allegiance, these new ideologies. To say that most workers were not communists surely does not mean that their values and beliefs were shaped by the languages and symbols of liberalism or mass consumerism. Rather, the culture of the CIO working class was marked by a sustained sense of class consciousness and a new rhetoric of class, by a new moral economy, and by the emergence of a working-class ethnic Americanism.[10]

As Vanneman and Cannon's persuasive study of class perception and identification shows, the depression generation—the cohort born between 1904 and 1923—was "the most working-class cohort in American history": it had the highest number of people identifying themselves as working class. This was not the result of shifts in the social structure; rather, they conclude that "it is the trauma of the Depression that solidifies working-class perceptions and changes the way Americans think about class." Moreover, as a number of historians have demonstrated, this was embodied in a new iconography and rhetoric of class.[11]

This pronounced class awareness or consciousness framed many of the working-class ideologies that developed in the age of the CIO. "Most working- and middle-class Americans in the Depression were not socialists in any strict ideological sense," Robert McElvaine concludes from a study of public opinion polls, "but they were certainly leaning to the left." Though these working-class ideologies often took incompatible forms, all projected a "moral economy" that would temper the ravages of capitalism: the Catholic corporatism with its organic conception of the body politic that deeply influenced CIO leaders like Philip Murray; the anti-Semitic Catholic fascism of Father Coughlin; the revolutionary syndicalism whose roots lay in the Wobblies; the American versions of social democracy developed around a notion of "industrial democracy"; and the socialist and communist visions of social transformation, of a cooperative commonwealth or a Soviet America.[12]

Along with these moral economies, there emerged a paradoxical synthesis of competing nationalisms—pride in ethnic heritage and identity combined with an assertive Americanism—that might be called "ethnic Americanism." This dominates much of the culture of the second-generation ethnic workers, who Louis Adamic called the "new Americans." This combination created a potent ideological constellation, sustaining both the radical "cultural pluralism" of the left-wing Popular Front and the white ethnic nationalism that characterized the anti-communist anti-capitalism of the CIO's right wing.[13]

It was this new working-class culture of the second-generation machine tenders that sustained the CIO and provided the base for the Popular Front social movement. For the Popular Front became the attempt to unite these millions of industrial workers with the "middle classes"—white-collar workers, professionals, and shopkeepers—in powerful urban alliances, building what one historian has called "an all-embracing Popular Front civic culture." Under the sign of the "people," this Popular Front public culture sought to forge ethnic and racial alliances, mediating between Anglo American culture, the culture of the ethnic workers, and African American culture, in part by reclaiming the figure of "America" itself, imagining an Americanism that would provide a usable past for ethnic workers, who were thought of as foreigners, in terms of a series of ethnic slurs. Its anthem, as we shall see later, was Paul Robeson's version of Earl Robinson's cantata, "Ballad for Americans," with its invocation of "everybody who's nobody . . . an Irish, Negro, Jewish, Italian, French and English, Spanish, Russian, Chinese, Polish, Scotch, Hungarian, Litvak, Swedish, Finnish, Canadian, Greek and Turk, and Czech and double Czech American."[14]

This Popular Front public culture took three political forms: a social democratic electoral politics; a politics of anti-fascist and anti-imperialist solidarity; and a civil liberties campaign against lynching and labor repression. The first of these, the electoral politics of the Popular Front, included both halves of the continuing antinomy in left electoral strategies in the US: the hope and desire for a genuine "third party," a farmer-labor party (a hope that contributed to the 1948 Progressive Party campaign of Henry Wallace); and the vision of a "realignment" whereby the New Deal Democratic Party created by Roosevelt might contain within it the seeds of a social democratic labor party—the dream of the 1944 CIO-PAC (Political Action Committee) campaign.[15]

Neither of these fully succeeded. On the one hand, in some places, the Popular Front social movement did become the basis for state and local political formations like New York's American Labor Party, Minnesota's Farmer-Labor Party, Wisconsin's Progressive Party, Upton Sinclair's End Poverty in California (EPIC) campaign, and Washington's Commonwealth Federation (which the journalist John Gunther characterized as "the first effective popular front in America"). At the local level, political figures like New York's Vito Marcantonio and Benjamin Davis, Jr, Washington's Hugh DeLacy, and Minnesota's Floyd Olson became tribunes of the Popular Front. However, at the national level, the Popular Front had no independent political vehicle. Not only did the giant figure of Franklin Roosevelt dominate the Popular Front imagination, but the only national *political* figure who represented the Popular Front was a New Deal Democrat, Henry Wallace: Wallace's "Century of the Common Man" speech was the Popular Front response to Henry Luce's "The American Century," and he became the movement's standard-bearer in the disastrous 1948 Progressive Party presidential campaign. But neither Wallace nor Earl Browder, the Popular Front leader of the Communist Party, ever achieved the symbolic stature of Eugene Debs or Jesse Jackson, two other presidential standard-bearers of the twentieth-century left. And in many places, the Popular Front supported New Deal Democratic governors, California's Culbert Olsen, Pennsylvania's George Earle, and Michigan's Frank Murphy, for example. Thus, in some ways, the US Popular Front was *not* a Popular Front at all; unlike the Front Populaire in France, in which the union of Socialists and Communists was a single, if short-lived, political force, the Popular Front in the US was largely an alliance of the social movement with Roosevelt's Democratic Party.[16]

Thus, many historians have seen the Popular Front as nothing more than New Deal liberalism, with the Communist Party a "fellow traveler" of the New Deal. However, this is misleading; as Ira Katznelson has persuasively argued, the alliance of the Popular Front social movement with the New Deal Democratic Party became the American equivalent of European social democracy. "That labor had the ability to lead a social democratic breakthrough in American politics that could build on the achievements of the New Deal and radicalize them was a commonplace of the early 1940s," Katznelson argues, "one that appeared to be affirmed during

World War II by such achievements as the organization by the CIO of Ford and Bethlehem Steel, the growth in the size of organized labor, the incorporation within labor's embrace of the previously unorganized female and black members of the labor force, and an extraordinary wave of strikes in the aftermath of the war." One can see the outlines of this social democratic politics in the organization of the CIO Political Action Committee in 1943 and its comprehensive "People's Program for 1944." If the Popular Front was not a revolutionary movement, neither was it merely an extension of US liberalism. Rather, the earlier collapse of the Debsian Socialist Party meant that US social democracy was the product not of a Second International labor or Socialist party but of the alliance of the New Deal and the Communist Party. As a result, the defeat of the Popular Front social movement in the Cold War years meant the defeat of a US social democracy.[17]

The second form of Popular Front public culture was the politics of international solidarity. Much of the energy of the Popular Front social movement—the "premature anti-fascists" as the witchhunters would later call them—went into the struggle to mobilize Americans to stand with the Spanish Republic besieged by the fascist Franco, to support Ethiopia invaded by Mussolini, to defend China against imperial Japan, and to aid the victims of and refugees from Hitler's Third Reich. Though none of these campaigns changed state policy, the Nazi invasion of the Soviet Union in June 1941 and the attack on Pearl Harbor in December 1941 inaugurated an official anti-fascist alliance between the US and the USSR, and the anti-fascist politics of the Popular Front merged with the politics of war mobilization, the struggles to define the aims and objectives of the war. Moreover, the politics of anti-fascism incorporated many refugee writers and artists into the Popular Front social movement in the US, making it as internationalist a culture as any to have appeared in US history. Both before and during the war, the Popular Front against fascism became a broad and deep political and cultural movement among Americans; it not only contributed to the defeat of fascism in the 1940s, it created an anti-fascist common sense in American culture.[18]

But the politics of international solidarity also meant solidarity with the socialist experiment in the Soviet Union. This has led many historians to see the Popular Front, not as a social movement, but simply as a strategy of the Communist Party, a political line dictated by the Moscow-controlled Communist International to the various national Communist Parties to accommodate the foreign policy of Stalin's USSR. In the face of Hitler's rise to power in Germany, Communists around the world tempered their anti-capitalist and anti-imperialist struggles against the capitalist democracies and their sectarian attacks on Socialist, social democratic, and liberal organizations (though not their attacks on anti-Stalinist parties and individuals associated with Trotsky) in order to forge a united front against fascism domestically and internationally. The revelations of the Moscow purge trials and the Communist attacks on anarchists, socialists, and syndicalists in Spain fractured the alliances between left anti-fascists; Popular Front anti-fascism had a near fatal shock when the Soviet Union signed a non-aggression pact with the Nazis on 23 August 1939, and Communist Parties around the world supported the Soviets' "neutrality." This ended when the Soviet Union was invaded by Germany in June 1941, and the wartime alliance between the US and the USSR redefined international solidarity, as the Communist Party subordinated everything to the war effort. However, this wartime front collapsed in 1945 with the onset of the Cold War, with its proxy wars and battles in Eastern and Southern Europe and in the decolonizing Third World.

In this view, the central issue of the Popular Front remains Stalinism, and the litmus test for US intellectual and cultural figures is their attitude towards and statements about the USSR. For historians like William O'Neill, the cultural significance of Paul Robeson is summed up in his "Stalinism" and that of Dwight Macdonald in his "anti-Stalinism." Indeed, the "lessons" of the dangers of fellow traveling remained a leitmotif in the attacks on left-wing solidarity movements from the 1960s to the 1980s. However, this narrative only illustrates the well-known contradictions of any politics of international solidarity: on the one hand, it is built on powerful ways of imagining the globe, narratives of the world system that make sense of an incomprehensible totality; and, on the other hand, it is subject to the twists and turns of international diplomacy and to the internal crises of foreign movements, parties, and regimes. To focus on the zigzags of international diplomacy is to misunderstand the larger significance of Popular Front solidarity.

For the culture of the Popular Front transformed the ways people imagined the globe. It did this in its daily work of helping refugees, organizing tours, and holding benefit performances and dances for Spanish and Russian war relief. But it also did this through the international stories dramatized in the works of the cultural front. The campaigns of solidarity for Ethiopia and the Spanish Republic depended on a larger narrative of anti-fascism and anti-imperialism that can be glimpsed in the retellings of the Haitian revolution (ranging from C.L.R James's history *The Black Jacobins* and the novels of Arna Bontemps and Guy Endore, to Jacob Lawrence's *Toussaint L'Ouverture* paintings and the Federal Theater productions of *Black Empire*, *Haiti*, and the "voodoo" *Macbeth*), in the allegories of fascist invasion (from MacLeish's *Fall of the City* and Langston Hughes's *Air Raid* to Picasso's *Guernica*), and in the anti-fascist espionage thrillers. And the romance of revolution was manifested not only in the popularity of the Soviet films of Eisenstein and Pudovkin, but also in the romance of the Mexican revolution, embodied in the grand murals of Diego Rivera and José Clemente Orozco, the novels of B. Traven, and the films *Juarez* and *Viva Zapata*. The success of the Popular Front politics of international solidarity lay in the ability of these narratives to displace the imperial fantasies of race war that dominated American popular culture.[19]

Perhaps the most effective part of Popular Front public culture was its third form, the mobilization around civil liberties and the struggle against lynching and labor repression. The "mass" or "labor" defense developed by the International Labor Defense (ILD) combined legal action with a mass protest campaign, building popular support for jailed unionists, political prisoners, immigrant radicals facing deportation, and black defendants facing racist trials. Founded in 1925, the ILD can be seen as the earliest Popular Front organization, and, as we will see, its campaign to free Sacco and Vanzetti was the first act of the new left of the depression. The ILD's photomagazine, *Labor Defender*, was probably the most important left-wing magazine of the late 1920s and early 1930s. For it was the *Labor Defender*'s photomontages, reportage, and testimonies that turned the obscure local strikes and trials of Gastonia, Harlan, and Scottsboro into national conflicts: Theodore Dreiser wrote articles for it on Scottsboro and Harlan and John Dos Passos wrote about Gastonia and Scottsboro. The ILD took the lead in the defense of the Scottsboro Nine (arrested and sentenced to death on rape charges in 1931) and it helped organize the National Committee for the Defense of Political Prisoners, which sent a delegation of writers and intellectuals led by Dreiser to Harlan County, Kentucky, in 1931 and 1932, publicizing the repression of union activists. The politics of labor defense, creating national movements in support of celebrated political defendants and prisoners, remained at the heart of the Popular Front social movement for three decades, extending to the defense of the young Chicano defendants in the 1943 Sleepy Lagoon case and eventually to the support of defendants in Cold War trials, deportations, and congressional hearings.

The other side of the labor defense was the legislative campaigns against labor repression and lynching. The hearings before the La Follette Civil Liberties Committee between 1936 and 1940 brought national attention to the use of spies, munitions, strikebreakers, and private police forces against workers organizing unions; though the La Follette Committee failed to enact legislation against repressive labor practices, its hearings became part of the common sense of the Popular Front social movement, retold in popular books like Leo Huberman's *The Labor Spy Racket* and dramatized in films like *Native Land*. Similarly, though the campaign to enact federal anti-lynching legislation never succeeded, it remained a central part of

Popular Front culture, figured in Billie Holiday's classic performance of "Strange Fruit."[20]

All three of these forms of Popular Front public culture—the social democratic electoral politics, the politics of international solidarity, and the campaigns against lynching and labor repression—were national in ambition, attempting to organize and re-imagine what Gramsci called the national-popular, the American people. However, as with many American social movements, the strength of the Popular Front was regional and local, rooted in particular cities and industrial towns. These urban Popular Fronts were the products of distinct political histories, and had a variety of class, ethnic, and racial complexions. A key institution of the urban Popular Front was the CIO's Industrial Union Council (IUC), which brought together representatives of CIO unions in a particular city or region. The IUCs coordinated strikes and organizing campaigns, took part in political campaigns, and were a forum for statements on civil rights and social justice. Thus, much of the movement's national visibility derived from the influence of the urban Popular Fronts of New York, San Francisco, and Los Angeles on the culture industries located in those cities.[21]

In New York, there were three bases of the Popular Front: the garment and needle trades, the white-collar unions, and the Harlem community organizations. Predominantly Jewish and Italian women, the needle trades workers not only made up a large part of New York's ethnic working class, but were well-organized and militant. Sidney Hillman's Amalgamated Clothing Workers of America (ACWA) and David Dubinsky's International Ladies' Garment Workers Union (ILGWU) were, along with the United Mine Workers, the original backbone of the CIO, and were committed to organizing textile workers across the nation and extending labor's political and cultural power. The needle trades unions helped organize and fund the political manifestation of New York's Popular Front, the American Labor Party, an attempt to build a labor party without abandoning political figures from the major parties who supported labor: as a result, the ALP was able to cross-endorse Democrats like Franklin Roosevelt and Republicans like Fiorello La Guardia and Vito Marcantonio, as well as electing city council members of their own, including Mike Quill, the leader of the largely Irish American Transport Workers Union. An alliance of the needle trades unions founded the Labor Stage, which eventually became the ILGWU's theater: their production of the show *Pins and Needles*, as I will show later, was one of the great accomplishments of the cultural front.[22]

The growing white-collar unions made up the second wing of New York's Popular Front. Perhaps the most visible was the Newspaper Guild, organized in 1933 and led by the radical journalist Heywood Broun. Broun was one of New York's most famous and most controversial columnists: he had been fired by the New York *World* in 1927 for his columns protesting the execution of Sacco and Vanzetti and had run unsuccessfully for Congress as a Socialist in 1930 before putting his energies into the organization of the Guild. Throughout the 1930s, his widely read column in the New York *World-Telegram,* "It Seems to Me," was a mainstay of the Popular Front. The less visible white-collar unions—the American Communications Association, the United Office and Professional Workers of America (UOPWA), and the teachers union (Local 555, affiliated with the United Public Workers)—provided many of the activists of the Popular Front. "Many of the women who were active in the UOPWA," one historian writes, "came from working class families where reading and intellectual improvement were a part of growing up.... [They] had put themselves through city colleges or night school to become teachers, librarians, economists and social workers, but could find nothing other than office work." Those who found work as teachers and social workers were the rank and file of the teachers union and the UOPWA's social service locals.[23]

The Harlem left was the third wing of New York's Popular Front, and New York was the site of some of the most visible alliances across racial lines of the period. The Harlem left had two sources: the long struggle to organize the Brotherhood of Sleeping Car Porters, beginning in 1925, and the campaign to free the Scottsboro Nine in the years following their conviction in 1931. The sleeping car porters were led by A. Philip Randolph, who had been part of the group of radical intellectuals who had founded the *Messenger* in 1917; the Scottsboro campaign was led by two black Communist lawyers, William Patterson and Benjamin Davis. In 1936, the Harlem Popular Front took institutional form in the National Negro Congress, a coalition of 585 organizations with a membership of 1.2 million, which depended on a prickly and often fragile alliance between Randolph's Brotherhood, the largest black union in the country, Adam Clayton Powell's Abyssinian Baptist Church (Powell was elected to the city council in 1941 on the American Labor Party ticket, and to Congress in 1944), and the Harlem Communist Party, whose standard-bearer, Benjamin Davis, was elected to Powell's city council seat in 1943. Political organizing by Randolph, Powell, and Davis sustained the Harlem social movement through periodic crises, and the left-wing Harlem newspaper, the *People's Voice,* served as its principal organ. The Harlem Popular Front also had deep roots in African American cultural circles: the prominence of Paul Robeson, Langston Hughes, and the young Richard Wright, combined with the cultural organizing of Louise Thompson, brought many performers and artists into the Harlem movement.[24]

Because of the concentration of cultural institutions in New York, the city's Popular Front always had a strong cultural superstructure. The left had a substantial presence in New York's theaters, including Broadway, the alternative theater, and the units of the Federal Theatre Project. The City

University, the "working-class Harvard," was the center of the student left; its "alcoves" are often recalled as the battlegrounds where the myriad tendencies of the Marxist left competed. The proletarian avant-garde was represented in New York's "coffee-pots" and small galleries, and in the networks made up of the John Reed Club, the Composers Collective, the Film and Photo League, and the Artists Union. The grand conventions of the cultural front took place largely in New York: the biannual American Writers' Congresses, the American Artists' Congress, the famous Spirituals to Swing concerts of 1938 and 1939. There were also several attempts to create a Popular Front photomagazine: the short-lived *Ken* and *Friday* were both attempts to create weeklies on the model of *Life*, and *TAC* and *Direction* were glossy monthly magazines of arts and culture. Perhaps the most successful organ of the New York Popular Front was *PM*, the afternoon tabloid newspaper that appeared throughout the 1940s, featuring extensive labor reporting, the "News for Living" section of Elizabeth Hawes, and Weegee's photographs of the "naked city."[25]

The New York Popular Front was always deeply divided between Communists and non-Communist leftists. New York was the center of Communist Party strength: half of the Party's total national membership was in New York, and, under the editorship of Clarence Hathaway, the *Daily Worker* had been transformed from a simple Party organ into a semblance of a metropolitan newspaper with columnists, comic strips, and Lester Rodney's sportswriting. Communists led a number of unions, and Party activists could be found throughout the labor movement, the American Labor Party, and the cultural organizations. But the old social democratic left remained powerful in the garment unions, and the newer formations of dissident communists including the Trotskyists and Lovestoneites had significant influence. The ACWA's Sidney Hillman, like John L. Lewis, was willing to work with the Communist left, but Dubinsky's ILGWU, influenced by the expelled Communist leader Jay Lovestone, grew increasingly hostile to the Communists. In 1938, the ILGWU left the CIO and returned to the AFL, and in 1944 Dubinsky left the American Labor Party to form New York's Liberal Party. Similarly, the divisions between the NAACP and the Communist Party, which had grown out of their conflict over the handling of the Scottsboro case, were never settled. Harlem's leading labor leader, A. Philip Randolph, was deeply suspicious of the Communist Party, having been periodically attacked by them. As a result, the history of the New York Popular Front is a zigzag of temporary alliances and broken coalitions, of denunciations and reconciliations, splits and mergers.[26]

The California Popular Front was less divided. Its base was the longshoremen's union, led by Harry Bridges, that had grown out of the 1934 San Francisco General Strike. "We take the stand that we as workers have nothing in common with the employers," Bridges told a University of

Washington student. "We are in a class struggle, and we subscribe to the belief that if the employer is not in business his products will still be necessary and we still will be providing them when there is no employing class. We frankly believe that day is coming."[27]

After taking the Pacific Coast District of the AFL's International Longshoremen's Association into the CIO in August 1937 (becoming the International Longshoremen's and Warehousemen's Union [ILWU]), Bridges became the CIO's West Coast regional director, and the longshoremen's union became the base for a "march inland," organizing warehousing, packing-shed, food-processing, and agricultural workers. Linking up with the Communist-led union of agricultural and cannery workers, and the new West Coast locals of the United Automobile Workers (UAW) (led in part by the Communist unionist Wyndham Mortimer), Bridges's West Coast CIO served as the heart of the California Popular Front; indeed, as the US government embarked on a long attempt to deport Bridges, an Australian, he became a folk hero, an emblem of the militant and incorruptible labor leader. Woody Guthrie wrote two ballads of Harry Bridges, and the leaders of the Citizen's Committee for Harry Bridges are a microcosm of the cultural front: the Harvard literary critic F.O. Matthiessen, the jazz critic and producer John Hammond, and the theater and film director Orson Welles.[28]

The "march inland" forged an alliance between the longshoremen and the Mexican American and Asian American workers in the fields and canneries of California's agricultural factories. The formation of the United Cannery, Agricultural, Packing, and Allied Workers of America (UCAPAWA) in 1937 was the result of a decade of agricultural strikes and organizing, which I discuss in chapter 7. Filipino, Japanese, and Chinese workers traveled throughout the West and Northwest working the fields, fisheries, and canneries; and the independent unions organized by figures like Chris Mensalvas, Carlos Bulosan, and Karl Yoneda joined UCAPAWA in San Francisco, Seattle, and Portland. In Southern California, UCAPAWA began organizing the workers in California's canneries and food-processing plants, three-quarters of whom were women, under the leadership of the Guatemalan immigrant Luisa Moreno. Moreno, who became the state CIO vice president, was also a moving force behind El Congreso del Pueblo de Habla Española (the Congress of Spanish-Speaking Peoples), the main vehicle of the Mexican American Popular Front. El Congreso brought together figures like Josefina Fierro de Bright, a young Mexican activist who had worked in support of the farmworkers, and Bert Corona, the president of Los Angeles's Local 26 of the ILWU. Though El Congreso was short lived, it was, as one historian concludes, "a crucial training ground for a generation of Mexican American and immigrant political and social activists."[29]

The political roots of the California Popular Front lay in Upton Sinclair's historic, if unsuccessful, 1934 EPIC (End Poverty in California) campaign for governor; the legacy of the EPIC campaign was the Democratic Federation for Political Unity which was formed to support the successful gubernatorial campaign of Culbert Olsen, a left-wing New Dealer. In an important symbolic gesture, Olsen freed labor radicals Tom Mooney and Warren Billings, who had been framed for a 1916 San Francisco bombing, after more than twenty years in prison. The years of the Olsen administration, 1938–42, were in many ways the high point of the California Popular Front. The voices of the West Coast Popular Front were the *Pacific Weekly*, a lively magazine edited by Ella Winter and Lincoln Steffens out of Carmel in the mid 1930s, and the *People's World*, the Communist newspaper edited by Al Richmond, which featured popular vernacular columns of humor and politics by Woody Guthrie and Mike Quin.[30]

The August 1942 arrest and subsequent conviction for murder of seventeen young Chicanos galvanized the California Popular Front: Sleepy Lagoon became the West Coast equivalent of Scottsboro. Josefina Fierro de Bright organized the Sleepy Lagoon Defense Committee, which united the activists of El Congreso with Popular Front figures like writer and lawyer Carey McWilliams. By 1944, the convictions had been reversed, but the two years of the defense campaign coincided with a moral panic about "Mexican crime" that swept Southern California, culminating in the "zoot suit" race riots of June 1943. Conflicts over race and ethnicity grew increasingly central to the California Popular Front in these years, and Carey McWilliams became one of its most eloquent voices. McWilliams had led the Steinbeck Committee in support of the struggles of migrant farmworkers in the late 1930s; during the war years he chaired the Sleepy Lagoon Defense Committee and spoke out against the internment of Japanese Americans. McWilliams's series of books on race and the peoples of the United States, which I discuss in the final chapter, stands as one of the major intellectual accomplishments of the cultural front.

Both San Francisco and Los Angeles had, as we will see, a network of avant-garde proletarian artists and writers, but the Hollywood studios were without doubt the central cultural apparatus on the West Coast. So it is not surprising that the story of the California cultural front is in large part the story of the links between the left-wing labor movement of Bridges's CIO and the left-wing artists, writers, and craftspeople in the Hollywood studios, many of whom were veterans of New York's left-wing theater and Weimar's left-wing cinema. This alliance created many of the key Popular Front cultural organizations of the depression and war years: the Hollywood Anti-Nazi League, the Hollywood Writers' Mobilization, the magazines *Black and White* (which became *The Clipper*), *Equality*, and *Hollywood Quarterly*, and the California Labor Schools. Indeed, Chicana activist Josefina Fierro de Bright was married to the radical screenwriter John Bright, and the Hollywood left, including Orson Welles and the Mexican American actors Rita Hayworth and Anthony Quinn, was active in the Sleepy Lagoon Defense Committee.

The Hollywood Popular Front was also the product of the drive to unionize the film industry's crafts, culminating in the bitter strikes by the Conference of Studio Unions in 1945 and 1946. The screenwriters were the leaders of the studio unions, and the 1947 investigation of the Hollywood Ten came to mark the beginning of the post-war attack on the Popular Front. If the garment workers' musical comedy, *Pins and Needles*, stands as an emblem of the New York Popular Front, the *noir* thrillers written by the studio's contract writers might be taken as the emblem of the Los Angeles Popular Front: for *noir* was, in Mike Davis's brilliant summary, a "fantastic convergence of American 'tough-guy' realism, Weimar expressionism, and existentialized Marxism—all focused on unmasking a 'bright, guilty place' (Welles) called Los Angeles."[31]

Since the major CIO unions hostile to the Communists had few West Coast members, and since the Communist Party was smaller, the California Popular Front was less divided internally; one finds fewer denunciations and recriminations among both Communists and non-Communist leftists on the West Coast than in New York. However, the California right was very powerful, and a state senate committee on un-American activities chaired by Jack Tenney launched a decade-long attack on the California left in 1941. By 1949, Harry Bridges was on trial for a third time, and a number of Latina and Filipino labor leaders faced deportation, including Luisa Moreno, Josefina Fierro de Bright, and Chris Mensalvas.[32]

In the industrial cities of the Northeast and Midwest, the heartland of the largest CIO unions—the United Automobile Workers (UAW), the United Steel Workers of America (USWA), the United Mine Workers (UMW), and the United Electrical Workers (UE)—the Popular Front was largely a community-based unionism uniting CIO locals, ethnic fraternal organizations, and women's consumer activism. These cities included the eastern electrical cities, like Lynn, Massachusetts, and Schenectady, New York, where there were key UE locals at General Electric plants, and Philadelphia, home of UE locals at Philco, Westinghouse in South Philadelphia, and RCA across the river in Camden, New Jersey. Pittsburgh and the steel towns of the Monongahela Valley were the center of the USWA's strength, as well as of UE at Westinghouse in East Pittsburgh. Youngstown, Cleveland, Gary, and the Calumet region of southeast Chicago were centers of steelworker organization. Toledo had been the site of a general strike in 1934, and Akron was the center of the United Rubber Workers. The Michigan auto towns included Detroit, with Ford's River Rouge plant outside the city limits in Dearborn, and Flint, home of General Motors.

The left was particularly strong in Milwaukee, with its UAW local at Allis-Chalmers, and in Minneapolis, where teamsters had ignited a general strike in 1934. In these cities, as in the tobacco towns of the Piedmont and the mining towns of West Virginia, Kentucky, and the Southwest, the Popular Front was less a cross-class cultural alliance than the shape that working-class politics and culture took, united by what Lizabeth Cohen has called the CIO's "culture of unity." Unlike the cultures of the skilled trades, whose focus was the workplace, the CIO's culture of unity was built on leisure and recreation, sponsoring labor radio stations, dances, picnics, summer camps, softball teams, and bowling leagues.[33]

The Popular Front in the mining and metalworking cities and towns was a multi-ethnic and multi-racial movement, but it had a substantial Eastern European base. By World War II, 51 percent of the workers in heavy industry were Slavic, and Pittsburgh, Cleveland, Chicago, and Detroit all had large Slovenian, Croatian, Slovak, Hungarian, and Polish communities. As a result, the infrastructure of the Popular Front social movement lay in the ethnic fraternal associations, like the Slovene National Benefit Society and the national sections of the International Workers Order (a federation of left-wing orders including the Polonia Society, the Hungarian Brotherhood, the Slovak Workers' Society, the Croatian Benevolent Fraternity, and the Serbian-American Fraternal Society). The ethnic lodges provided meeting places for the CIO organizing committees and supported ethnic language newspapers, theater groups, mandolin orchestras, and singing societies. A group of activists, editors, and intellectuals—figures like the Slovenian writer Louis Adamic, the Polish Communist CIO organizers from Detroit Stanley Nowak and Boleslaw "Bill" Gebert, and the Polish Socialist Leo Krzycki, the vice president of the ACWA—were the moving forces behind the wartime American Slav Congress, an influential Popular Front alliance of twelve Eastern European ethnic groups, not unlike the National Negro Congress and El Congreso del Pueblo de Habla Española.[34]

For the most part, the Popular Front of the metalworking cities had few connections to the national culture industries and institutions of New York and California. Though the heroic conflicts of Little Steel and Flint were often represented in the labor reportage and novels of the Popular Front, there were relatively few young artists and intellectuals of the Slavic working class recruited from the local theaters, newspapers, and polka bands into the national industries of film, publishing, and music. One exception was the Group Theatre actor Karl Malden, who appeared in the Group's production of Clifford Odets's *Golden Boy* and was best known for his work in Elia Kazan's productions of *A Streetcar Named Desire* and *On the Waterfront*. Malden, born Mladen Sekulovich, first appeared on stage in the Serbian theater of Gary, Indiana, where his father, Peter Sekulovich, was a leading performer. Similarly, the anti-Communist purges in Hollywood,

New York, and Washington have received far more attention than the purge of the steel industry in 1950; however, as David Caute has noted, "the violent epicenter of the anti-Communist eruption in postwar America was the steel city of Pittsburgh," where the paid informer Matthew Cvetic fingered hundreds of workers to HUAC, becoming the basis for the 1951 Hollywood film, *I Was a Communist for the FBI.*[35]

This picture of the Popular Front in New York, California, and the metalworking Midwest illuminates the difficulties of offering a unified history of this social movement, for the Popular Front was a product of unequal developments across North America: particular histories of union successes or failures, the local balance of political forces, and regional formations of race and ethnicity.[36] Nevertheless, the life of the Popular Front social movement coincided with a particular history, which can be viewed as a conjuncture, a generation, and a transition between two epochs. That moment might be called the age of the CIO.

2.   The Age of the CIO

To name a period—the "depression," the "thirties," the "New Deal," the "age of Roosevelt," "modernism," the "streamlined years," the "age of the CIO"—is already to argue about it. Much of the argument about this period has revolved around the issue of periodization itself. If the crash of 1929 is widely accepted as the beginning of the crisis, the "end" of the "thirties" is hotly disputed. W. H. Auden dated the end of the "low dishonest decade" in his famous poem "September 1, 1939," and many literary and cultural historians critical of the Popular Front have followed suit. Within five short years, they argue, the left cultural renaissance was over, lost in the betrayals of the Moscow Trials, the Nazi-Soviet Pact, and the onset of global war. For these memoirists and historians, the thirties tell a cautionary tale: a story of impetuous youthful radicalism, of seduction and betrayal, of a "god that failed."

For others, more sympathetic to thirties radicalism, the glory days were already over by the time *Waiting for Lefty* hit Broadway in the spring of 1935. For these critics, the 1935 American Writers' Congress betrayed the young writers of the John Reed Clubs; the documentaries of Frontier Films failed to carry out the radical promise of the Workers Film and Photo League; and the Popular Front was a liberal sentimental façade replacing the radical vigor of the early 1930s. Malcolm Cowley's memoir of the 1930s ends in the summer of 1935, summarizing the last half of the decade in twenty pages; similarly, Daniel Aaron's durable history abandons its narrative in 1935 and concludes by looking at the disenchantment of half a dozen figures.[37]

For a third group, closer to the perspectives of the Popular Front itself,

the thirties ended with the Henry Wallace campaign of 1948 and the onset
of the Cold War. For them, the rise of McCarthy, the Hollywood blacklist,
and the execution of the Rosenbergs mark the end of the period as clearly
as the Moscow Trials, the Spanish Civil War, and the Nazi-Soviet Pact did
for the various anti-Communists.[38]

All of these attempts to date the end, to mark the betrayal of the hopes
born out of the depression, remain tied to the time of biography, the
scarring of private lives by public events. However, to begin to capture the
complexities of this period, we need several time frames: the conjunctural,
the generational, and the epochal. A "conjuncture" was Gramsci's useful
term for the immediate terrain of struggle: "[W]hen an historical period
comes to be studied," Gramsci notes, "the great importance of this
distinction becomes clear. A crisis occurs, sometimes lasting for decades.
This exceptional duration means that incurable structural contradictions
have revealed themselves ... and that, despite this, the political forces
which are struggling to conserve and defend the existing structure itself
are making every effort to cure them, within certain limits, and to
overcome them. These incessant and persistent efforts ... form the terrain
of the 'conjunctural,' and it is upon this terrain that the forces of
opposition organise."[39]

The decades following 1929—the age of the CIO— are just such a crisis.
The crash of 1929 triggered what Gramsci called a "crisis of hegemony" in
the United States, a moment when social classes became detached from
their traditional parties, a "situation of conflict between 'represented and
representatives'." The years of depression and war saw a prolonged "war of
position" between political forces trying to conserve the existing structures
of society and the forces of opposition, including the Popular Front social
movement, who were trying to create a new historical bloc, a new balance
of forces. The eventual post-war "settlement," marked by the famous 1950
General Motors-UAW contract, which *Fortune* called the "Treaty of Detroit,"
depended on the defeat of the Popular Front and the post-war purge of
the left from the CIO and the cultural apparatus. If the metaphor of the
front suggests a place where contending forces meet, the complementary
metaphor of the conjuncture suggests the time of the battle.[40]

From this point of view, the history of the Popular Front might be seen
as a series of offensives and retreats on the "terrain of the conjunctural."
The first great surge was the revolutionary season from the summer of
1933 through 1934, with remarkable unrest among the unemployed,
veterans (the Bonus Army march), and farmers (the Farmer's Holiday
movement), culminating in a wave of strikes following the National
Industrial Recovery Act, including the left-led general strikes of 1934 in
Toledo, Minneapolis, and San Francisco. Though Hitler's rise to power in
Germany in early 1933 and the fascist destruction of Vienna's Socialists in

early 1934 were ominous developments, they too seemed to be signs of the disintegration of the old order. Even in the United States, the propertied classes genuinely feared insurrection and revolution, and young radicals imagined a Soviet America. This was the moment of the "proletarian avant-garde" as young communist writers and artists produced a wave of little magazines and exhibitions.[41]

The second great surge began in the fall of 1936 and continued through the spring and summer of 1937: kicked off by the CIO victories in Akron and Flint, it was the year of "sit-down fever." The elections of Popular Front governments in Spain (February 1936) and France (May 1936) raised the hopes of socialists around the world; Franco's revolt against the Spanish Republic in July 1936 led to two years of US organizing in solidarity with the Spanish Loyalist government. These were the years when the term "Popular Front" emerged as the characteristic name of the movement. Nineteen thirty-seven was the year of the great Popular Front theatrical events: the Mercury Theatre's musical of Steeltown, USA, *The Cradle Will Rock*; the musical revue staged by New York garment workers, *Pins and Needles*; and the documentary film of the Spanish Civil War, *The Spanish Earth*. The summer of 1937 was one of the most violent in the history of American workers: eighteen workers were killed that summer, beginning with the Memorial Day Massacre, when Chicago police killed ten steelworkers and wounded dozens at Republic Steel. The defeat at Little Steel, and mounting unemployment in the fall of 1937, dampened the movement. If the August 1936 hearings of Senator La Follette's Civil Liberties Committee on labor espionage and strikebreaking mark the beginning of this wave, the August 1938 hearings of Congressman Dies's Un-American Activities Committee mark its end.

The defeat of the Spanish Republic in early 1939, the Nazi-Soviet Pact of August 1939, and the onset of war in Europe were deeply discouraging, and marked a crisis for the Popular Front. Nevertheless, during the fall of 1940 and the spring and summer of 1941, there was an often-overlooked resurgence. Although it had made little headway since 1937, the CIO led one of the largest strike waves in US history in 1941, winning both at Ford's River Rouge plant and against the firms that made up Little Steel. "The year 1940 had been one of UE success," a UE leader later wrote. "But 1941 topped everything ... [it was] UE's peak year for organization and economic gains." Nineteen forty-one also marked the beginning of the modern civil rights movement: the March on Washington Movement, led by A. Philip Randolph, won black workers jobs in the defense industries and led to the creation of the FEPC (Fair Employment Practices Commission). In 1941, the New York Popular Front elected the first black city council member, Adam Clayton Powell, and the first Communist city council member, Pete Cacchione. The spring of 1941 saw the opening of the Mercury Theatre's production of Richard Wright's *Native Son*, as well as the release of *Citizen Kane*. Duke Ellington's "socially conscious" revue, *Jump for Joy*, played in Los Angeles through the summer of 1941. In June 1941, the Nazis invaded the Soviet Union, and in December the Japanese bombed Pearl Harbor, bringing the US into the war; very quickly, the social struggle was subordinated to war mobilization.[42]

The fourth surge was from the summer of 1943 through the election of 1944: the wartime Popular Front. In the face of a summer of hate strikes and race riots in 1943, the "labor victory front" linked the call for a second front in the anti-fascist war to a vision of post-war decolonization and a social democratic "century of the common man." The formation of CIO-PAC to support Roosevelt marked the labor movement's most ambitious electoral campaign, outlining a "people's platform" for the post-war world. In New York, Powell was elected to Congress, and Benjamin Davis was elected to the city council in his place. An important defeat at this stage was Roosevelt's choice of Truman over Henry Wallace for vice president.

The Popular Front's final offensive was from V-J Day in August 1945 through 1946, when the CIO launched a massive strike wave: by 1 February, 1946 over a quarter of the CIO's membership was on strike in what was the "most massive strike episode in American history." There were general strikes in a half-dozen US cities, including Houston, Pittsburgh, and Oakland, and a series of bitter strikes in the Hollywood studios. The CIO launched Operation Dixie, an attempt to organize the South, and the Popular Front social movement seemed to be moving again. But the fall of 1946 saw the beginning of the end: the first Republican Congress since 1932 was elected, and Truman dismissed Henry Wallace as secretary of commerce. With the announcement of the Truman Doctrine and the Marshall Plan in the spring of 1947, the Cold War had begun in earnest. Within a year, the anti-labor Taft-Hartley Act was passed (June 1947), repealing the rights labor had won during the New Deal and requiring a non-Communist affidavit from union officers; and a revived House Committee on Un-American Activities called the Hollywood Ten to testify (fall 1947). When the Communists staged a coup against the Popular Front government in Czechoslovakia in February 1948, all hopes of an alternative to the Cold War seemed futile. Though Henry Wallace's Progressive Party presidential campaign in 1948 brought together some fractions of the Popular Front, the campaign was a disaster, and the CIO's leadership used it as a way of beginning its purge of Communist-led unions, removing Harry Bridges from his position as regional director. Within the next two years, eleven unions and a million members were driven out of the CIO as a result of the anti-Communist purge; the southern organizing drive failed. By 1949, a Gallup Poll found that support for socialism had dropped to 15 percent. Though a Popular Front subculture persisted through the 1950s, blacklisted and in internal disarray, the backbone of the Popular Front social movement was broken.[43]

In another sense, however, the culture of the Popular Front, the culture of the "thirties," lasted well into the post-war era. The divisions—both political and cultural—on the American left at midcentury seem, to a historian's eye, less absolute. As I will argue, there is more continuity between the "proletarian culture movement" and the "Popular Front" than appeared to the advocates of one or the other. The traumatic rifts between Stalinists and anti-Stalinists, between the literary figures of the *New Masses* and those of *Partisan Review*, even between the Hollywood Communists and the New York intellectuals, often conceal deeper continuities. In 1947, Richard Hofstadter, himself one of the New York intellectuals, saw his study of *The American Political Tradition* as a response to and critique of Popular Front versions of American history, and it surely was. But a preface he wrote twenty years later suggests another way of looking at his own book:

[I]t seemed to me that I had been looking at certain characters in American political history not only somewhat from the political left but also from outside the tradition itself, and that from this external angle of vision the differences that seemed very sharp and decisive to those who dwelt altogether within it had begun to lose their distinctness, and that men on different sides of a number of questions appeared as having more in common, in the end, than one originally imagined.[44]

One can say as much of the "Old Left," particularly in the world of culture. "Despite the sharp political differences that separated us from the Communists," the Trotskyist activist Paul Jacobs recalled,

we were culturally dependent upon the Communists and their web of peripheral and supporting organizations, for the American Trotskyist movement had no folk-singing groups, no foreign-language associations, no fraternal orders, no hiking clubs, no classes in drama, nor any of the varied other activities which made the "What's Doing" column in the *Daily Worker* so long every day.

The "What's Doing" column was an important part of our daily reading, even though we were Trotskyists. If we wanted to see a movie about the Russian Revolution, we had to go to the Cameo Theatre on Fourteenth Street, where we would sit in the balcony, cracking sunflower seeds with our teeth, and giggle at the more blatant examples of Stalinist propaganda. Sometimes, as when the screen showed a Russian girl falling asleep to dream of a luminous, fatherly Stalin tossing her baby high in his arms and chucking it under the chin, we would laugh—but always surreptitiously, lest some of the Stalinist faithful in the downstairs section hear us and come up to start a fight. But we thrilled at the heroics in Eisenstein's *Potemkin* and, no matter how often I saw it, the scene in *Chapayev* when the Red Army finally overcomes the White Russians always sent shivers through my body. So, too, when the proletarian heroes, the union members and organizers, rushed out onto the stage in the last scene of the plays presented by the New Theatre League at the old Civic Repertory Theatre, I responded just as viscerally as did any Communist.

Thus mine is less a story of political divisions than of cultural continuities; the culture of the Popular Front represented a larger laboring of American culture, which political adversaries often shared in shaping.[45]

The Popular Front might in this way be seen as a structure of feeling, to use Raymond Williams's phrase. This concept reminds us that decades are by no means the most adequate way of periodizing cultural history; between the punctual events of a decade and the wider horizon of an epoch (modernism or Fordism) lies the generation. Williams himself suggested the affinity between a structure of feeling and a generation when he argued that "one generation may train its successor, with reasonable success, in the social character or the general cultural pattern, but the new generation will have its own structure of feeling. . . . [T]he new generation responds in its own ways to the unique world it is inheriting." To see the Popular Front as a structure of feeling is thus to see it as a political and cultural charter for a generation. This is why many figures who broke decisively with the Communist Party, like Richard Wright or Elia Kazan, did not really break with the Popular Front, and continued to produce works within a Popular Front structure of feeling: there is a clear continuity between Kazan's minor acting role in *Waiting for Lefty* and his direction of the 1954 film *On the Waterfront*, one of the greatest "proletarian" dramas.[46]

From this generational point of view, the end of the Popular Front is neither 1939 nor 1948. Rather, it has two ends. The first is in the early 1960s when a "New Left" appears; from the beginning, the New Left was understood not only as a break with earlier ideologies and organizations, but as a new structure of feeling characterizing a post-war generation. Henceforth, both protagonists and antagonists of the Popular Front would be called the "Old Left." Nevertheless, the figures of the Old Left continued to work through the 1960s and 1970s, and many of the most interesting works of the cultural front are products of the second half of the century, as artists and writers formed in the age of the CIO embodied its concerns, its narratives, and its icons in works of a postmodern epoch. The films directed by Martin Ritt (like *Norma Rae* [1979] or *The Molly Maguires* [1970]) and Sidney Lumet (particularly *Serpico* [1973], *Daniel* [1983], and *Q&A* [1990]) and those written by Waldo Salt (*Serpico*) and Ring Lardner, Jr (*M.A.S.H.* [1970]) are, like the writings of Tillie Olsen, E.L. Doctorow, and Ernesto Galarza, embodiments of a Popular Front structure of feeling. Thus, the second end of the Popular Front is the result of the gradual death of the depression cohort in the last decades of the twentieth century.[47]

However, if the notion of a structure of feeling is to be more than a way of characterizing the mood of a generation, the fundamental task remains, as Fredric Jameson has noted, "that of coordinating new forms of practice and social and mental habits (this is . . . what . . . Williams . . . had in mind by the notion of a 'structure of feeling') with the new forms of economic production and organization thrown up by the modification of capitalism." Thus, in order to understand the rise and fall of the Popular Front social movement, the conjunctural and generational frames must be accompanied by an epochal one: one must triangulate the conjuncture and the generation with those larger narratives that make up our sense of cultural history, in this case the narratives of modernism and postmodernism, Fordism and post-Fordism. That the moment of the Popular Front—the age of the CIO—is usually visible only as an interregnum, a dead end, the "thirties," is a result, I suggest, of its seeming to fall outside those larger stories of modernism and postmodernism, Fordism and post-Fordism. However, the Popular Front, the age of the CIO, stands, not as another epoch, but as the promise of a different road beyond modernism, a road not taken, a vanishing mediator. It was a moment of transition between the Fordist modernism that reigned before the crash, and the postmodernism of the American Century that emerged from the ruins of Hiroshima.[48]

"Modern times," the half-century between the 1890s and the 1940s, were what economic historians have called a "long wave" in capitalist development, comprising a period of growth and expansion from the late 1890s to World War I and a period of stagnation and contraction from World War I to World War II. "In a purely economic sense, capitalism seemed set for a long and untroubled future around 1900," Eric Hobsbawm writes. "The international capitalist economy . . . had, by and large, . . . an astonishing run for its money . . . until 1914." These "modern times" that emerged from the deep depression of the 1890s had been built on the defeat of the Populists and Knights of Labor; on a racial regime of segregation and sharecropping based on black disenfranchisement, Jim Crow legislation, and lynching; on the massive importation of migrant laborers from Southern and Eastern Europe; and on the exercise of imperial muscle in the Caribbean and the Pacific. Politically, the Republican Party dominated the nation, holding the White House from the McKinley election of 1896 until 1932, with the brief interlude of Woodrow Wilson, who came to power only when Taft and Theodore Roosevelt split the Republican Party.[49]

This economy was built on the technologies of oil, rubber, and steel fabricated into the automobile, and on the patterns of work and leisure to which Ford gave his name: the reorganization of work by the assembly line and the remaking of leisure by the family car and the five-dollar day. The opening of the Highland Park assembly line in 1915 stands as the symbolic inauguration of the Fordist labor process, combining the production of standardized parts using standardized machine tools, a continuous assembly line which brought the work to the worker in massive plants, and a workforce of semiskilled machine operators controlled by engineers and designers, embodying the Taylorist dream of separating conception from execution. The announcement of the five-dollar, eight-hour day for all workers who could pass Ford's Sociological Department's examination of "the clean and wholesome life" on 1 January 1914 marked the symbolic initiation of Fordist mass consumption, the sense that mass production requires a working-class consumer.

Thus, modernism itself might be understood as the culture of Fordism, schizophrenically divided between the functionalist machine aesthetic of Ford himself, who wished to produce one generic car, reduced to essentials, without frills or useless parts, in any color the customer wanted "as long as it is black," and the aesthetic of packaging pioneered by Alfred Sloan of General Motors, who captured Ford's market by offering new styles, new models, new colors. But modernism also became the name of the cultural ferment of the early decades of the century. The experimental avant-gardes mixed sexual and artistic radicalism with sympathies for the revolutions in Mexico and Czarist Russia, and had a lasting impact on the more widespread youth countercultures of the 1910s and 1920s, what Malcolm Cowley later called a "revolution in morals which began as a middle class children's revolt." For modernism marked a transformation of gender relations: part of the generational revolt against the "Victorian" was a refusal of the patriarch. The first two decades of the century were a high point of the woman's movement: these years were dominated by the struggle for women's suffrage, by the emergence of a "new woman," and by the invention of a new term—"feminism." There were close connections between women's rights, sexual radicalism, and the artistic renaissance: indeed, in 1917, the New York *Evening Sun* was noting that "some people think women are the cause of modernism, whatever that is."[50]

Thus, modernism came to be the expression of the dreams, discontents, and cultural contradictions of the disaffected young people of the predominantly Anglo bourgeoisie as they came to grips with the changes in the corporate economy and the changes in proper sexuality and gender roles, with the new imperialism, with the "foreign hordes" of immigrant workers. They had broken from the genteel tradition because they were caught directly between capital and labor: they were the settlement house activists, the social scientists like Walter Wykcoff who disguised themselves to see how the other half lives, the journalists like John Reed and Mary Heaton Vorse who went from Harvard and Provincetown to witness revolutionary struggles in Paterson, New Jersey, Lawrence, Massachusetts, Mexico, and

Russia, and the experimental, expatriate writers and artists like Ernest Hemingway, Gertrude Stein and T.S. Eliot. They dominated the renaissance in American culture because they attempted to represent the world of Fordism, to capture the new.

The age of the CIO grew out of the crisis of this modernism, a crisis figured by the crash of 1929. The CIO had itself emerged in the heartland of the Fordist economy and culture, in the industries that mass-produced automobiles and radios. Its unions were built by the children of the modernist migration, challenging the strikebreakers and private police of Ford, General Motors, US Steel, General Electric, and Westinghouse. The Liberty League, the now largely forgotten alliance of capitalists led by the Du Ponts, dominated the Popular Front imagination, as did the giant fortunes of J.P. Morgan, Henry Ford, William Randolph Hearst, and the Mellons. The culture of the age of the CIO was built by the children of the modernist arts, struggling to assimilate and transcend its legacy of formalist experiment. The opening shots of the cultural front were the narratives of modernist disenchantment, like Malcolm Cowley's *Exile's Return* and Caroline Ware's *Greenwich Village*. The young artists and intellectuals of the age of the CIO inherited the mantle of modernism, naming their clubs for the legendary John Reed, but, as I will argue later, they sought to create a new social modernism, a "revolutionary symbolism."

Nevertheless, the success of the CIO and the Popular Front social movement depended on the world of Fordism and modernism; and as the continental shelf of Fordism and modernism began to slip in the midst of the Second World War, revealing the first glimpses of the world we now call post-Fordism or postmodernism, the fault lines in the Popular Front social movement began to appear, cracks first evident in the 1943 riots in the war-boom cities across the continent. By the time these fault lines had entirely reshaped US society, the Popular Front social movement had vanished, together with its vision of a social democracy.

There were four aspects of this midcentury earthquake: the shift from modern to postmodern gender relations and household formations; a racial revolution that inaugurated a postmodern racial regime; the largest internal migration in US history, a migration of black and white southerners to the North, remaking the industrial working class; and the "third technological revolution" and the emergence of a post-Fordist economy. Despite the attempts by Popular Front activists to respond to these changes, each dis-organized the Popular Front social movement.

The question of whether the Second World War was a watershed in the history of US gender relations and household formations remains a contentious point among historians of women: the very visibility of the recruitment of women workers into the war industries, and the popular iconography of Rosie the Riveter that accompanied that recruitment, has made it difficult to assess whether the changes that took place were superficial or lasting.[51] Moreover, changes in the social organization of sex and gender are hard to register by decades or even by generations; conceptions of manhood and womanhood, of parenting and growing up, change slowly, even glacially. So it is difficult to correlate these changes with changes in culture and the arts, let alone with changes in political regimes.

Nevertheless, there are periods of intensified conflict between men and women, children and parents, periods of gender strife—which the early part of the century called "sex antagonism," the middle part of the century, the "battle of the sexes," and the end of the century, "sexual politics"— rooted in changes in the sexual division of labor. As the literary historians Sandra Gilbert and Susan Gubar put it: "the sexes battle because sex roles change, but, when the sexes battle, sex itself (that is, eroticism) changes." Transformations in the way work is done and divided, whether wage work, childrearing work, the work of consumption, or the unwaged work of maintaining a household, lead to an unsettling of customary stories of manhood and womanhood, in forms and ideologies of sexuality.[52]

Thus, whether or not the changes wrought by Rosie the Riveter have been overemphasized, it seems clear that the period between 1929 and 1948 marked a moment of crisis and transformation in the sexual organiz- ation of work, in gender relations, and in household formations. The modernist gender system, forged from the revolt of young women and young men against Victorian patriarchy and manifest in the emergence of what Lois Banner has called "fashion culture," was rocked by the crash of 1929. If the depression years were not a moment of feminist militancy, they were surely a time of gender strife and change: many commentators at the time noted the crisis in masculinity that accompanied the massive unem- ployment of the depression; the birthrate "dropped precipitously" by 1933; there was a renewed ideological attack on married women workers, who became a scapegoat for the depression; and there was a national outcry about the state of mothering and the evils of "momism" during the war years. These two decades saw the beginnings of what might be seen as the shift from a modern to a postmodern gender formation.[53]

First, there was a remarkable increase in the proportion of *married* women working for wages. Despite the depression campaign to eliminate married women from the labor force and to strengthen the "marriage bar," the percentage of married women in the wage-labor force increased between 1930 and 1940; and by 1950, the rate was twice what it had been in 1930. As one historian has noted, "it is no wonder that even as early as the 1920's, social commentators shifted their attention from the plight of the single working woman to that of the married woman." In large part, this increase in married women workers was a consequence of the shifts in the overall occupational structure; it was not that women joined men in occupations, but that sectors of the economy employing women grew in the midcentury decades. As several studies have shown, even in the wartime mass-production industries, job segregation by sex continued, as women worked in women's departments and in jobs newly defined as "women's jobs," and those gains did not, for the most part, survive the war. Thus, the lifting of the marriage bar in teaching and clerical work by about 1950 was responsible for much of the increase in married women workers.[54]

Second, there was a marked decrease in domestic service. In the early part of the century, more women worked in domestic service than in any other occupation, and domestic service was racially and ethnically structured: in the Northeast, most domestic workers were European immigrant women; in the South, most were African Americans; in the Southwest, most were Chicanas; and in the West, most were Asian. The Second World War marked a dramatic decline in domestic service, particularly among white women. The major growth in women's employment came in clerical work and in commercial services. By 1930, clerical work was already the single most important occupational group for white women, despite the fact that married women were largely excluded from it. With the disappearance of the marriage bar by 1950, women of the depression cohort who had had greater high-school education swelled the ranks of clerical workers (women of color remained excluded from clerical work until the 1960s).[55]

These changes in women's employment were part of far-reaching shifts in household structure. If the household is the basic unit of social reproduction, the transformation from Fordism to post-Fordism has seen the growing commercialization of the household's reproductive functions; as a result, there have been remarkable shifts in the kinds of households and in the relations within households. With the decline in child labor and the rise in schooling in the first half of the century, relations between parents and children altered, as children were less a resource, contributing to the household budget, than an investment requiring resources: this paralleled a long-term decline in the birth rate. The decline in domestic service was matched by a rise in commercial services, particularly food service: the 1930s mark both the growth and feminization of commercial food service.[56]

Moreover, the expansion of the state apparatuses in this period is in large part due to the increasing involvement of the state in the household: the early welfare state was in part devised by "progressive maternalists," and the conflict between mothers and social workers runs throughout the working-class fiction of the period. The WPA day nurseries, established to provide relief work for teachers, nurses, and nutritionists, marked the first federal support of child care, and the 1941 Lanham Act funded the construction of child-care centers for war workers.[57]

These commercial and state interventions in the household accompanied the rise of a new sexual economy. The "companionate marriage," a phrase that dates from the mid 1920s, was built around birth control and the right of divorce, and placed an "unprecedented emphasis on the importance of sexual gratification in marriage." In turn, new households based on gay and lesbian sexual ties emerged, and the Second World War saw the development of an urban gay and lesbian subculture which would become a fundamental part of the postmodern household formation.[58]

These changes in work patterns and household structures had profound consequences for the Popular Front social movement, which remained closely linked to the characteristic household form of the mass-production industries, with its emphasis on the "family wage" of the male worker. This is not to say that women were not central to the Popular Front: in New York, the women workers of the garment trades were at the heart of the Popular Front, and this was, as we shall see, why *Pins and Needles* became a key cultural icon of the moment. Moreover, since the Popular Front was in many ways a community-based social movement—epitomized perhaps in the citywide general strikes of 1934 and 1946—the key community organizers were often women. Finally, though the entry of women into the wartime mass-production industries was often tense and difficult, it rarely manifested itself in anti-women hate strikes. For the most part, the CIO unions actively recruited and supported women workers.[59]

Nevertheless, the forms of organizing that would come to dominate post-Fordism—the organization of clerical and service workers, and the sexual politics of the women's movement and the gay and lesbian movements—did not emerge in the Popular Front. Women were usually imagined as "auxiliaries" in the struggle, and only rarely did a Popular Front feminism develop. Perhaps the first explicit Popular Front feminism appeared in the work of Mary Inman and Elizabeth Hawes. Inman's controversial study of women's oppression, *In Woman's Defense*, was serialized in the *People's World*, the voice of the California Popular Front in 1939 and 1940; and Elizabeth Hawes's labor feminism, which I will discuss at length later, took shape in her "News for Living" columns in *PM*, the New York Popular Front tabloid. The first organizational forms of Popular Front feminism came after the Second World War: the Congress of American Women was formed in November 1945 and the 1945 equal pay bill became a key focus for both the CIO and womens groups. But these initiatives fell victim to the Cold War. Similarly, the Popular Front social movement never developed a self-conscious political struggle for gay or lesbian rights; however, when the first gay political organization, the Mattachine Society, was formed in 1950, all its founders, most notably its early leader Harry Hay, were Popular Front activists who had met through the left-wing labor school, the People's Educational Center, where Hay taught courses in music.[60]

The second aspect of the midcentury earthquake that shook the Popular Front was the racial revolution of the 1940s, the transition from a modern racial regime to a postmodern one. The racialization of peoples had long been a fundamental aspect of settler colonial societies like the United States. Since land was cheap and labor expensive, various forms of forced and imported labor reigned, class structures were racialized, and the white settlers developed racial ideologies of creole exceptionalism. Nevertheless, as Stuart Hall reminds us, this history is not a single, uninterrupted story: there is no racism, only *racisms*. In the United States, the modern racial formation emerged in the years after the Civil War. The end of the systems of forced labor in the 1860s—US slavery, Russian serfdom, and Australian transportation—marked not only a remarkable expansion of global labor migration and the rise of the "new imperialism" in the late nineteenth century, but also the birth of the modern racial systems with their legal codes of segregation, exclusion, reservations, and anti-miscegenation. In the United States, the end of Reconstruction and the restoration of white supremacy in the South were accompanied by the Chinese Exclusion Act of 1882, the Dawes Act of 1887, which undermined the tribal land ownership of Americans Indians, and the colonial conquests of Hawaii, Puerto Rico, and the Philippines.[61]

This racial regime of modernism began to unravel in the midst of World War II. Nineteen forty-two and 1943 were years of exceptional racial conflict. In early 1942, 110,000 Japanese Americans were evacuated to assembly centers at racetracks and fairgrounds and were then interned in camps in remote desert areas of the West. In the spring and summer of 1942, race riots over public housing and "hate strikes"—white workers refusing to work with black workers—broke out throughout Detroit. Similar hate strikes occurred in Mobile, Baltimore, and Gary in 1943, culminating in the long transitworkers strike in Philadelphia in the summer of 1944, in which white streetcar employees walked out to protest the upgrading of black workers: 5,000 federal troops were called in to restore order. In June 1943, young Chicanos, Filipinos, and African Americans wearing zoot suits were stopped, stripped, and beaten by white servicemen in Los Angeles. These "zoot-suit riots" went on for a week and spread across the country in cities where servicemen were stationed: in Philadelphia, twenty-five whites attacked four blacks wearing zoot suits on 12 June. The zoot-suit riots triggered a wave of race riots throughout the summer of 1943: in San Diego, Philadelphia, Chicago, Evansville, Beaumont, Detroit, and Harlem.[62]

The internment camps, hate strikes, and race riots were symptoms of a dramatic reshaping of the American racial regime, a postmodern rewriting of the color line that derived from new relations to Asia and Latin America and the emergence of a powerful civil rights movement. The war with

Japan marked the beginning of thirty-five years of war in Asia, as the
United States was covertly or overtly involved in wars and insurrections in
the Philippines, Korea, Indonesia, Vietnam, Cambodia, and Laos. The
Asian American communities were deeply affected by the mobilizations
and migrations that accompanied these wars. During the Second World
War, while Japanese and Korean Americans were regarded as enemy
aliens, Filipinos were allowed to become citizens for the first time, and the
Chinese Exclusion Acts were repealed.[63]

The war was also a watershed in hemispheric relations. The 1942 Bracero
Program recruited thousands of Mexican agricultural workers to release
US farmworkers for the war plants and military; and by 1956 Mexican
Americans made up a quarter of all US farmworkers. Puerto Rico's
"Operation Bootstrap" of 1945 marked the beginning of the major
migration of Puerto Ricans to the mainland.

Meanwhile, the national March on Washington Movement to protest the
racist hiring practices of the new defense industries marked the beginning
of a powerful new African American civil rights movement. Organized by
the foremost black labor leader, A. Philip Randolph, the March on
Washington Movement held demonstrations across the country to prepare
for the 1 July 1941 march. Though the march was called off when Roosevelt
met with Randolph and agreed to outlaw discrimination in the defense
industries, the organization and militancy of African Americans continued
to grow: the NAACP's membership multiplied ninefold during the war and
the Congress on Racial Equality (CORE) was founded in 1943.[64]

In many ways, the Popular Front was more prepared for the racial
realignments of the war years than for the gender realignments. The
Popular Front social movement had been built around a politics of anti-
racism and anti-imperialism and had struggled for an interracial movement. Moreover, the infrastructure of the Popular Front was made up of
an intricate network of ethnic fraternal associations, foreign-language
newspapers, and arts clubs that supported a kind of "cultural nationalism,"
emphasizing the distinctive histories of the peoples of the United States.
The CIO unions, particularly the left-led unions, had actively worked to
organize African American, Asian American, and Latino workers, and
fought against the hate strikes and zoot-suit riots. One of the major
successes of the wartime CIO was the ILWU's organization of Filipino and
Japanese American plantation workers in Hawaii. The campaign to
strengthen and enforce the Fair Employment Practices Commission
(FEPC) continued throughout the war years. Though the Communist Party
did not protest the internment of Japanese Americans and even suspended
their Japanese American members, the West Coast Popular Front spoke
out against the camps: Louis Goldblatt, the secretary-treasurer of the
California CIO and Harry Bridges's right-hand man, was one of the few

who testified against the internment order at the start, and Carey McWilliams, perhaps the leading intellectual of the California Popular Front, became one of the few white critics of the camps, spending three years visiting them, writing about them, and speaking against them on the radio. From Paul Robeson's 1939 version of Earl Robinson's "Ballad for Americans" to Frank Sinatra's 1945 version of Earl Robinson's "The House I Live In," the anthems of the Popular Front were pleas for racial and ethnic tolerance.[65]

Nevertheless, the Popular Front was dramatically dis-organized by the central cause of the racial realignment of the 1940s: the massive migration of white and black southerners to the war-industry cities of the North and West, a migration that remade the working classes. It was the largest internal migration in US history: not only did southwesterners—"Okies" and "Arkies"—continue to pour into California, but a million people left the southern Appalachians in each of the two decades of the 1940s and 1950s. One historian has estimated that between 8 and 12 million white southerners left the South in the quarter century after 1945. In addition, 4.5 million black southerners left the South's Black Belt between 1940 and 1970, between 12 and 15 percent of the South's black population; 90 percent of black southerners moved to six states: California, Illinois, Michigan, Pennsylvania, Ohio, and New York. In some ways, the full extent of the black migration is disguised by the additional migration to cities within the South. At the peak of southern sharecropping in 1920, half of all black Americans lived on farms; by 1984, that had dropped to 1 percent.[66]

The effect of the migration on US national culture was tremendous; the years after midcentury saw a "southernization" of American culture. Before 1954, the South was another country, another people, the land of the defeated Confederacy, ruled by large landowners and home to a system of sharecropping and segregation. One of the characteristic forms of pre-World War II national culture was the "southern", as much a genre as the western, including mythical tales of the Civil War like *Gone with the Wind* and sensational fictions of sharecropper life like Erskine Caldwell's salacious bestsellers. The migration of millions of southerners transformed the national culture. The most successful popular musics in the post-war years were those that had been called "race" and "hillbilly" and were now renamed "rhythm and blues" and "country." Similarly, a southern "regional" writer whose works were largely out of print at the end of the war, William Faulkner, became recognized as the leading "national" novelist, winning a Nobel Prize. In part, this was because Faulkner was one of the few white writers who dealt with the legacy of slavery and the racial divide. As I shall argue later, most of his white contemporaries who had been highly regarded—Hemingway, Fitzgerald, and Dos Passos—had evaded the issue of race, or, to put it slightly differently, had been unable to imagine a racial story.[67]

The relations between black and white Americans took on a dramatic new centrality in the culture as a whole; what had earlier often seemed to be a problem of the Jim Crow South was now a national divide. The cities that emerged from the migration were extremely segregated: sociologists who study residential segregation by statistical measures of "relative isolation" have found that the highest rate of isolation ever recorded for an ethnic group—Milwaukee's Italians in 1910—was the same as the lowest rate for black Americans in 1970 (in San Francisco). A history of urban disinvestment, slum clearance in neighborhoods adjoining white neighborhoods, and the construction of high-density public housing to contain the black population, combined with the government subsidy of mortgages and highways to build white suburbs, created a new Black Belt Nation, not the Black Belt of the cotton South, but an archipelago of cities across the continent: this *de facto* apartheid became the dominant social fact of American social life in the second half of the twentieth century.[68]

The South-to-North migration and the world it created dis-organized the Popular Front social movement. The race riots and the hate strikes of the war years were emblems of these tensions, as the CIO unions, which had signed a no-strike pledge for the duration of the war, were experienced by the new workers as an alien power: not their representatives, but part of the discipline of the workplace. Just at the moment when the CIO working class, those Italian, Polish, Slavic, and Jewish ethnics of whom Robeson and Sinatra sang, gained a measure of cultural, political, and economic power, they were faced with a new working class. Whereas the CIO working class had deep roots in European radicalisms—Jewish socialism and communism, Italian anarchism, and Finnish communism, among others—the southern migrants came with little history of left-wing radicalism. The white populism of the South and Southwest was in some cases inflected by the residual socialism of the Debsian party—Woody Guthrie is an emblem of that tradition—but more often tinged with the Klan. There were exceptions, but even the militant unionism and underground Communism of rural sharecroppers, miners, and textileworkers was based in a cultural world foreign to the urban Popular Fronts of the North. If the ethnic fraternal lodges of the IWO served as a seed bed for the CIO and the Popular Front, the black and white holiness and Pentecostal churches of the southern and southwestern migrants rarely became part of the Popular Front social movement.[69]

Moreover, the cultural divide between the predominantly Catholic and Jewish workers of the CIO generation and the new southerners, black and white, was tremendous; this conflict stood at the center of the great proletarian novel of midcentury, Harriette Arnow's epic narrative of the migration of the Nevels family from Kentucky to Detroit, *The Dollmaker*. It could also be seen in the divide between the swing of Frank Sinatra, Benny Goodman, and Count Basie, and the rhythm and blues of Hank Williams, Muddy Waters, and Elvis Presley. By the 1960s, an anthem written by the Oklahoma migrant Woody Guthrie, "This Land Is Your Land," had not only displaced the Earl Robinson anthems sung by Paul Robeson and Frank Sinatra, but Irving Berlin's "God Bless America" as well. The failure of the CIO's southern initiatives—both the pre-war Textile Workers Organizing Committee aimed at the largest group of southern industrial workers, and the post-war Operation Dixie—loomed larger and larger as Dixie became America.[70]

If this religious, ethnic, and cultural divide within the working classes broke up the fragile alliances built by the Popular Front, the emerging labor processes of post-Fordism weakened the industrial home of the CIO unions. As Robert Hill has noted, "the word 'automation' was coined around 1946 by the automobile industry to describe the introduction of automatic devices and controls to mechanize production." The development of these computer-controlled machine tools transformed the labor process of the semiskilled machine operatives, who were the heart of the CIO mass-production unions, weakening the shop-floor systems of power that industrial unionism had won and reducing the size of the labor force. As industrial production shifted from economies of scale to economies of scope, avoiding the rigidities of large-scale production by subcontracting and small-batch production, employment shifted away from goods production: in 1947, there was an even balance between employment in goods and services; by 1981, two-thirds of all workers were in services. Nineteen fifty-six was the first year when white-collar workers outnumbered blue-collar workers. The CIO's inability to organize clerical and service workers, and to invent a labor feminism that spoke to the women working in the new offices, the "factories" of post-Fordism's information industries, was to weaken the Popular Front social movement.[71]

The Popular Front social movement grew out of the crisis of Fordist modernism, and it built a remarkable coalition for economic justice and civil rights and liberties. Its political defeat in the post-war settlement was due both to the dis-organizing social transformations of midcentury and the strength of its adversaries. The capitalist revival in the years after the war sustained the anti-Communist crusade at home and abroad, and clinched the victory of Henry Luce's vision of an American Century over Henry Wallace's social democratic vision of a People's Century. Nevertheless, as Stuart Hall reminds us, "social forces which lose out in any particular historical period do not thereby disappear from the terrain of struggle; nor is struggle in such circumstances suspended." If the Popular Front was defeated on the political terrain, and the age of the CIO gave way to the American Century, it nevertheless continued to have a deep influence on US culture.[72]

For the Popular Front social movement had created and nurtured a new culture, a distinctive sensibility, aesthetic, and ideology, embodied in stories that were told again and again. It did not represent the entire US culture, nor did it ever become a dominant culture. But it left its mark on the institutions of American culture—from broadcasting and Hollywood to the novel and the universities—and it influenced those who grew up among the subaltern classes of US society. The most important legacy of the Popular Front may have been this culture. Even critics saw its power: "The Popular Front was not merely a political tactic," Irving Howe and Lewis Coser wrote, "it was also, and in the United States even more importantly, a kind of culture. . . . The phenomenon of mass culture is pervasive in modern industrial society, but there can be little doubt that at least part of its contemporary American flavor is a heritage of the Popular Front." The reasons for the Popular Front "flavor" of US mass culture lie in another central social transformation of modernity, the rise of what C. Wright Mills called the "cultural apparatus."[73]

3. The Cultural Apparatus

The "cultural apparatus," the radical social theorist C. Wright Mills wrote in 1959, as the age of the CIO was coming to an end, "is composed of all the organizations and *milieux* in which artistic, intellectual and scientific work goes on, and of the means by which such work is made available to circles, publics, and masses. In the cultural apparatus art, science, and learning, entertainment, malarkey and information are produced and distributed." "It contains an elaborate set of institutions," he continued, "schools and theaters, newspapers and census bureaus, studios, laboratories, museums, little magazines, radio networks. It contains truly fabulous agencies of exact information and of trivial distraction, exciting objects, lazy escapes, strident advice." The development of this cultural apparatus was one of the central aspects of Fordism and modernism. Not only did the Taylorism of modernity accentuate the division between design and execution, mental and manual labor, but it created entire industries and classes built on "mental labor" and the appropriation of the skills of the craftworker. The rise of the great corporate and university research laboratories and the professionalization of engineering and science are of course the most direct instances of capitalist "mental labor." But the mental labor and performing skills of the arts were also appropriated and reorganized in the first half of the twentieth century. This took two principal forms: a culture industry of leisure and entertainment built on the new technologies of motion pictures, recorded sound, and broadcasting; and a state cultural bureaucracy collecting, subsidizing, and distributing arts, information, and education through a variety of schools and agencies.[74]

The CIO working class—the plebeian communities of second-generation ethnic workers—became the new mass audience for the popular arts and entertainment, and the source of the new mass labor force that staffed the studios and agencies of these cultural industries and state institutions. The new left of 1934 was in many ways the child of these cultural apparatuses, and it left its mark—the Popular Front "flavor" of US mass culture—on them. In this section, I will briefly look at the rise of the culture industries and the state cultural institutions, and then consider the meaning of their mass audience and mass labor force.

One of the most striking changes in American life between the Paterson pageant of 1913 and *Waiting for Lefty* in 1935, between the bohemian left of the *Masses* and the communist left of the *New Masses*, was the growth and maturity of the culture industries. Those two decades had witnessed the emergence of narrative feature films (generally dated from 1915's *Birth of a Nation*) and the Hollywood studio system that manufactured them. They had seen the invention of broadcasting, the unprecedented provision of free mass entertainment in the home, paid for by incessant advertising, a form that was entirely unexpected by the inventors and developers of radio communication and that would come to dominate television communication as well. The development of sound recording had put popular musics not only on the radio but in the home and on the local jukebox, transforming an industry that had been based on the sale of sheet music into one based on the sale of 78s. The tabloid, the weekly newsmagazine, and the newsreel transformed mass journalism, with Henry Luce's empire—the weekly national newsmagazine *Time*, the photojournalism of *Life*, and the radio and film newsreels *The March of Time*—leading the way. Popular fiction came to be dominated by the symbiotic relation between the pulp magazines and radio serials and soap operas. And mass spectator sports, led by the baseball reinvented by Babe Ruth and housed in the new urban ballparks of steel and concrete (Yankee Stadium was "the house that Ruth built"), became a "national pastime."

Perhaps the earliest attempt to deal with these new popular arts appeared a quarter of a century before Mills's exploration of the cultural apparatus: Gilbert Seldes's pathbreaking book of 1924, *The Seven Lively Arts*. Seldes's book, with its impassioned claim that Charlie Chaplin and George Herriman, the creator of the comic strip *Krazy Kat*, were the only great American artists of the day, was a manifesto of the young modernist intellectuals who used and celebrated the popular cultures of the early decades of the twentieth century, including comic strips, jazz, vaudeville, newspaper humor, and the movies, particularly slapstick comedy, as weapons against the genteel tradition. But Seldes's book is also generally taken as the first in what is now a long line of treatises participating in the intellectual debate about American popular culture, and as such it marks the moment when mass-produced entertainments assume a central place in considerations of "civilization in the United States."

Why did mass-produced entertainments assume this new importance? Before the epoch of Fordism and modernism, the popular arts were generally ignored by the "educated classes," the "cultured classes," the "leisure class," the various parts of the American bourgeoisie. The popular arts—dime novels, melodramas and vaudeville acts, blues singers and string bands, traveling circuses, minstrel shows, and tent shows, as well as the foreign-language cultures of immigrant neighborhoods—inhabited a different universe from the budding metropolitan high culture—"legitimate" theater, symphony orchestras, universities, art museums, the publishers and magazines like Charles Scribners and the *Atlantic Monthly* that published the novels and stories of Howells, James, and Wharton. The only times the "high" culture concerned itself with the "low" were when reformers of various sorts attempted to censor, police, or uplift the "vulgar" and "immoral" entertainments of the people. It is telling that the title of one of the earliest accounts of American popular culture by an intellectual was *Certain Dangerous Tendencies in American Life* (1880); this book by the Rev. Jonathan Baxter Harrison had been originally published in the *Atlantic Monthly*.

But this situation changed in the early part of the twentieth century when the production of cultural entertainments was industrialized and cheap cultural artifacts were mass-produced and distributed. There had been precedents, of course: the book itself is one of the earliest mass-produced commodities. The technological transformations in printing in the early nineteenth century together with the transportation revolution of steam, railroads, and canals had created the cheap nickel and dime novels and penny newspapers in the 1830s and 1840s; chromolithography and photography brought cheap visual images into homes across the country. Nevertheless, books and newspapers always had a hidden cost: the years of labor that it takes to learn to read, for without literacy, books are a relatively inert commodity. Here the world of modernism marked a watershed: the inventions of motion pictures, sound recording, and radio broadcasting all made relatively direct appeals to sight and hearing and could be easily decoded. Moreover, the hardware and software of these new devices could be mass-produced and sold relatively cheaply.[75]

The marketing of motion picture projectors in 1896 gave birth to the nickelodeon, a storefront theater, popular in immigrant, working-class neighborhoods, that ran continuous shows combining live entertainments—comedy acts, jugglers, illustrated lectures—with short silent films featuring skits, slapstick, special events, and natural wonders. By the mid 1910s, the beginning of the modern film industry was taking shape, based on the studio production of feature-length fiction films, marketed by a star system, and exhibited through nationwide theater chains. By 1937, movies accounted for three-quarters of America's dollars spent on leisure, and the country's leading writers, actors, musicians, composers, and designers were finding their way to Hollywood. The movies centralized and homogenized US culture; five firms—Paramount, Loew's MGM, Warner Brothers, Twentieth Century Fox, and RKO—dominated the industry, owning production studios in California, worldwide distribution networks, and national chains of theaters.[76]

The results of sound recording were somewhat different, however. Music "became a thing" in 1877, and, though Edison meant his invention for business uses, by the turn of the century the phonograph was being sold as a household appliance. By the 1910s, the popular music industry began to change as sales of sheet music plummeted and sales of records and phonographs skyrocketed; popular songs became shorter to fit the three-minute playing time of records, but they grew more complex musically. The dance musics of the 1910s, set to the rhythms of ragtime and the tango, were difficult to play on the piano but easy to play on the phonograph. By the early 1920s, recording companies began to record and market regional, ethnic, and racial musics; as a result, the phonograph, together with the relatively low capital requirements of making records, not only helped keep traditional cultures alive and developing but provided the foundation for a new urban music. From the combination of these recorded racial and ethnic musics and a popular songwriting aimed at an audience of record players rather than piano players emerged modern American vernacular musics. When Louis Armstrong first recorded a Tin Pan Alley song in 1928, "I Must Have That Man," he embodied the dialectic that was to dominate American music for a generation, a dialectic between the blues and the Tin Pan Alley "standard," between the neighboring urban communities of working-class African Americans and working-class Jews, Italians, and Poles, between the blues scales of African American music, the *frigish* scales of Yiddish popular music, and the pentatonic scales of Eastern European folk musics.[77]

The depression rocked the music industry: the phonograph had remained expensive throughout the 1920s and 1930s, and record sales crashed from 100 million in 1927 to 6 million in 1932. By the time sales recovered in the late 1930s, three major record companies dominated the industry: RCA Victor, Decca, and Columbia/ARC (American Record Company). The music industry had found new forms in the rise of the public phonograph, the jukebox (which took 60 percent of record sales in 1939), in the coming of sound to motion pictures, and in the emergence of radio broadcasting with its constant flow of music. Radio broadcasting had begun in the wake of the radio fad of 1922 as a way of encouraging the sales of radio receivers, but it quickly developed into a national system of networks with corporate sponsors in control of programming. The National Broadcasting Corporation (NBC) made its debut as a national network in 1926, broadcasting on 26 stations to 12 million people; in 1929, *Amos 'n' Andy*, a situation comedy built on the foundations of the black-face minstrel show, became broadcasting's *Birth of a Nation*, pioneering the narrative form that would dominate radio and television. By the early 1930s, an estimated 40 million people—1 in 3 Americans—listened to *Amos 'n' Andy*; and in its wake advertising agencies came to serve as the Hollywood studios of the airwaves, producing the situation comedies, adventure serials, and soap operas that NBC "Blue," NBC "Red," and CBS broadcast.[78]

The emergence of this new commercial culture had several major consequences, all of which made the "popular arts" the new center of American culture. First, the capitalist culture industries, unlike the cultural institutions of the nineteenth century, were built on profit, not taste. Though many compromises with the forces of good taste were made in order to stay profitable—one thinks of the self-censorship codes in Hollywood, the highbrow "sustaining" radio programs, and the separate "luxury" markets of higher-priced goods—nevertheless the overall tendency of the culture industries was to make what sold, to build on popular taste. As a result, many more people experienced various kinds of cultural entertainments in contexts far from the original venues. Forms which had had a local base traveled far and wide; the "classics," once owned and preserved by the cultured and leisured classes, were now cheaply available, and the working-class entertainments of black and ethnic neighborhoods were available to the educated classes. Much of the "cultural front," as we shall see, was built on this "popularization" of high culture and diffusion of "proletarian" and "folk" culture.

Second, because of the size of the mass audiences and the capital invested in production, the popular arts achieved a technical accomplishment and brilliance that had never before been possible. This is not an absolute rule by any means: for one thing, for all their poverty of resources, traditional folk arts can and have reached extraordinary levels of accomplishment. Moreover, as the critics of the culture industry have long argued, the assembly-line production of mass entertainment has meant that much of the standardized product that was shipped out had little aesthetic or cultural value. It is clear that the desire to reach the largest audience by avoiding controversy and complexity has produced some materials that deserve the rich vocabulary of derision that has developed to describe them. Nevertheless, the new industries of culture made possible remarkable achievements that have, for all practical purposes, broken down the line between the high, learned arts and the popular arts, as the work of such figures as Dashiell Hammett, Orson Welles, Duke Ellington, and Billie Holiday demonstrates. As a result, the popular arts no longer seemed a sometimes quaint, sometimes vulgar enclave that could be safely ignored. The state of popular culture was the state of the culture generally, particularly in the United States, which had an overdeveloped set of culture industries and an underdeveloped established high culture: indeed, for Europeans, Americanism was mass culture.

Third, if the new culture industries produced some remarkable works of popular art, the rise of broadcasting also made them an elaborate front for the advertisements of national corporations. "It is inconceivable," Commerce Secretary Herbert Hoover said of radio in 1922, "that we should allow so great a possibility for service, for news, for entertainment, for education to be drowned in advertising chatter"; nevertheless, within a few years, radio broadcasting adopted the mixture of advertising and programming that the "magazine revolution" of the 1890s had pioneered. The programs, like the magazine's features, were a way of attracting an audience to the advertisements: they were, in a way, advertisements for the advertisements. The radio programs of the 1930s and 1940s were not only sponsored by advertisers, but were produced by advertising agencies, and their success or failure was tracked by the radio rating services pioneered by Archibald Crossley in 1930.

Thus, the growing advertising industry was the backbone of the new culture industries, attracting the investments of other industrial sectors in culture and entertainment. The culture industries took the lead in developing a new capitalist political agenda in the years following the crash of 1929. In some cases, their actions were ordinary power politics, as when the Hollywood studios organized an extraordinary campaign to defeat Upton Sinclair's EPIC campaign in 1934. But in other cases, culture industry executives realized the consequences of the crisis and attempted to rebuild a hegemonic historical bloc. In 1935, Bruce Barton, the head of Batten, Barton, Durstine & Osborne (BBDO), a leading advertising agency handling the accounts of General Motors and General Electric, told the National Association of Manufacturers that industry needed a "new vocabulary" to win the hearts and minds of Americans: "business must regain its rightful position of social and political leadership lost to the New Deal." Barton's advice was heeded by his friend Henry Luce, who had invented modern news coverage with his magazines *Time*, *Life*, and *Fortune*, and his radio and film newsreels, the *March of Time*. In 1941, Luce published an influential manifesto in *Life* entitled "The American Century." In the years that followed, Luce's brief essay and its title became a kind of shorthand for corporate America's vision of the world that was to emerge from the war, a world dominated by American commercial entertainments: "American jazz, Hollywood movies, American slang, American machines and patented products, are in fact the only things that every community in the world from Zanzibar to Hamburg, recognizes in common." Luce's manifesto is only the most striking example of the new corporate aesthetic, embodied in the work of advertising agencies and industrial designers.[79]

For other culture industry leaders, however, the solution lay in the New Deal itself: the new historical bloc that Roosevelt assembled in 1936 depended on an important group of internationalist and capital-intensive corporations who dominated the major American foundations and had close ties to the cultural apparatus. This corporate liberalism was secured, the historian Thomas Ferguson argues, "by the spread of liberal Protestantism; by a newspaper stratification that brought *the* free-trade organ of international finance, the *New York Times*, to the top; by the growth of capital-intensive network radio in the dominant Eastern, internationally-oriented environment; and by the rise of the major news magazines." Media corporations—newspapers, film and magazine companies—were significantly more likely to support Roosevelt than other industries: Warner Brothers, for example, famously became the "New Deal" studio.[80]

If the commercial cultural industries developed a new self-consciousness in the years after the crash, the public cultural apparatus was virtually invented by the New Deal. The two decades after *Waiting for Lefty* saw an unprecedented involvement of the federal government in culture. The state sponsorship of writers, artists, theaters, and musicians that began in the spring of 1935 under the Works Progress Administration as relief from the economic crisis became an attempt to redefine American culture and to create a "cultural democracy" by establishing a bureaucracy that would provide "culture" for the people. Though the specific WPA cultural "projects" were disbanded during the war, their goals and personnel were shifted first into the wartime propaganda agencies and then into the permanent "arts projects," the vastly expanded post-war university systems, which were to reshape dramatically intellectual and artistic life in the United States. Thus, federal interventions in culture took three principal forms: direct funding of the arts in the relief apparatus of the depression; development of international cultural exchange and diplomacy out of the wartime propaganda agencies; and state sponsorship of higher education.

The first of these, the federal relief projects for artists, remains a central icon of the New Deal: as *Fortune* magazine put it in 1937, "whatever else may be said of the Government's flyer in art, one statement is incontrovertible. It has produced, one way or another, a greater human response than anything the government has done in generations." After a couple of initial efforts at white-collar relief under the Civil Works Administration (notably the Public Works of Art Project [PWAP] in the winter of 1933–34), the

Works Progress Administration (WPA), a national employment program established in the spring of 1935, organized relief for artists under Federal Project Number One, including art (directed by Holger Cahill), music (directed by Nikolai Sokoloff), drama (directed by Hallie Flanagan), writers (directed by Henry Alsberg), and, somewhat later, historical records.[81]

The cultural projects ran orchestras, theaters, and community art centers, and produced thousands of public murals and radio programs, over eight hundred plays, and the famous *American Guide* series of tour books. For the most part, the cultural work of the projects was closely monitored, particularly the theater productions and public murals. The writers were generally not allowed to pursue their own work but were hired to write for particular projects, like the guidebooks. As Roosevelt himself said, "I can't have a lot of young enthusiasts painting Lenin's head on the Justice Building." Nevertheless, the WPA arts projects were a constant subject of controversy: individual murals and theater productions provoked political battles, and the House Committee on Un-American Activities, chaired by Martin Dies, launched an investigation of Federal One in August 1938 that led to the abolition of the Federal Theatre Project and the transfer of the other projects to the states in 1939. By the spring of 1942, all cultural activities that did not relate to the war effort were eliminated.[82]

Though the WPA arts projects did not prove to be a model for future government support for the arts, they were a vanishing mediator, leaving an indelible imprint on the modern cultural apparatus. Their demise meant that the federal government would not compete with the culture industries in providing popular entertainment. No state broadcasting system like the BBC emerged from the New Deal, no state film studio, no state recording company. Moreover, despite their genuine aesthetic and popular successes, the *productions* of the WPA arts projects did not finally compete with the culture industries: the easel paintings did not have the impact of *Life*'s photographs; the murals did not reclaim the landscape from the omnipresent billboard; the federal theaters did not reverse live theater's losses to Hollywood; neither the federal symphonies nor the folk-music collections displaced the swing of the big bands; and the *American Guides* faded in the face of the 25-cent Pocket Books.

Nonetheless, the WPA arts projects left their mark on the development of a semipublic institutional culture of foundations, museums, and universities in the years after the war. The first link was with the wartime propaganda agencies that had emerged from the New Deal state: the State Department's Division of Cultural Relations was formed in June 1938 to handle cultural exchanges with Latin America; it was joined by the CIAA (Coordinator of Inter-American Affairs) under Nelson Rockefeller in

August 1940. The Coordinator of Information, founded in July 1941, gave way to the Office of War Information and the Office of Strategic Services in June 1942. With the elimination of the WPA projects during the Second World War, many arts projects participants moved into the war information agencies. Under Robert Sherwood, the OWI brought figures like John Houseman, who had been a director of two Federal Theatre units in New York, to head the government's radio broadcast, "Voice of America." Malcolm Cowley, who was recruited into the Office of Facts and Figures, wrote to his friend Kenneth Burke that "you can get a vague picture of a government agency by imagining the business of General Motors being run by the faculty of . . . Columbia." Indeed, the battles within the New Deal state apparatus continued through the war years, as Sherwood's people were eventually forced out of the OWI. Nevertheless, the post-war years saw the continuation and expansion of federal cultural programs, some overt, like the State Department's support of art exhibitions and concert tours, and others covert, like the CIA's funding of the magazine *Encounter.*[83]

Perhaps the most important federal intervention in culture was the building of the postwar university system, supported by government research and development funds and by the GI Bill of 1944, which financed higher education for 8 million veterans. "From the end of the war and for the next two decades," Daniel Bell writes, "R & D expenditures in America multiplied by 15 times, and the total expenditure on education by six." Colleges and universities, which had been the preserve of an elite, achieved a mass "audience" in the decades after the war, enrolling students from working-class families in large numbers for the first time. If universities were not exactly mass entertainment in the way that film studios were, they nonetheless were a central part of American mass culture.[84]

The specter of these cultural apparatuses of commercial entertainment and state information haunted the activists and intellectuals of the left: from James Rorty's path-breaking 1934 critique of advertising, *Our Master's Voice*, to the 1945 analysis of the "culture industry" by the émigré Marxists of the Frankfurt School, Theodor Adorno and Max Horkheimer, to C. Wright Mills's unfinished project of the late 1950s, *The Cultural Apparatus.* For many of them, as we shall see, these technologies of communication degraded aesthetic perception and overwhelmed both learned and folk cultures, reducing their audiences to distracted, resigned consumers of escapist fantasy: "Both escape and elopement," Adorno and Horkheimer wrote, "are predesigned to lead back to the starting point. Pleasure promotes the resignation which it ought to help to forget." For others, however, the dialectic of distraction was itself part of the political struggle. "It is one of the most astonishing things about the modern American film," C.L.R. James wrote in 1950, "that it does not treat of the Great Depression,

the pervading fear of another economic collapse, the birth and development of the union movement, the fear of war, the fundamental social and
political issues of the day." "It might seem," he goes on,

> that this is deliberate sabotage by those who control the economic life of the
> country. That is quite false. The industrial magnates, a movie producer so anti-
> union as De Mille, and great numbers of people in authority would wish nothing
> better than to employ the finest available talent in order to impose *their* view of
> the great political and social questions of the day upon the mass. *They dare not do
> it.* The general public accepts, or to be more precise, appears to accept the
> general political ideas, standards, social ethics, etc., of the society which is the
> natural framework of the films as they are produced today. Whenever possible a
> piece of direct propaganda is injected, but the C.I.O., the great strikes, capital
> and labor, war and peace, these are left out by mutual understanding, a sort of
> armed neutrality.[85]

The other side of this "armed neutrality" of mass entertainment was its
adoption of popular accents. Since the heart of the new mass audience was
the urban working class, living and working in the multi-racial, multi-
ethnic metropolises of modernism, the songs and stories, the hacks and
stars, of the cultural apparatus often assumed the accents of the urban
streets and tenements. Many of the culture industries grew out of the
commercial amusements of the cities, the world of vaudeville theaters,
nightclubs and dance halls, amusement parks like Coney Island, baseball
parks, penny arcades. The early moving pictures and phonographs were
not in the home but were part of the "automatic amusement machines" at
arcades. In the long run, of course, the culture industries were to break
the tie between the city and culture; movies, records, and broadcasting did
not need the city's audience and did not want the city's labor-intensive live
performances, for which the actors, musicians, and stage hands had to be
paid every night. When the film industry moved to Hollywood to find
sunshine and a non-union labor force, it created another of the mythical
places—Tin Pan Alley, Motown, Madison Avenue, the Super Bowl—where
mass entertainments are fabricated and then reproduced in every Main
Street and Middletown. Nevertheless, the early entrepreneurs of leisure
often had experience in the less respectable urban amusements and
recruited performers and technicians from the world of vaudeville, thus
giving a plebeian, ethnic accent to mass entertainment.[86]

As a result, the cultural apparatus became a contested terrain between
the Popular Front and the Advertising Front, as working-class styles, stars,
and characters emerged alongside the sales plug. Indeed, as Lizabeth
Cohen argues, young workers "used mass culture to create a second-
generation ethnic working-class culture that preserved the boundaries
between themselves and others. That they felt alienated from their parents'

world did not necessarily mean that they forsook it for a nonethnic, middle-class one." Summarizing the place of radio broadcasting, filmgoing, and chain stores in working-class neighborhoods, she argues that

> contrary to the usual assumption that mass culture was depoliticizing, the experience of industrial workers in the 1930s suggests that even as workers shared more in national commerical culture, integration enabled them to mount more effective political action, specifically to overcome the cultural fragmentation that had hindered them earlier. . . . At a time when they were all suffering from the depression and searching for collective solutions, talking about a boxing match on the radio or the latest bargain at the A&P helped workers to maintain their group identity. Ironically, the broader dissemination of commercial culture that accompanied its consolidation in the 1930s may have done more to create an integrated working-class culture than a classless American one.

Rather than simply eroding earlier working-class cultures, mass consumer culture became a common ground of a new working-class culture.[87]

If the modern cultural apparatus created a new mass audience, it also required a new labor force, a huge number of "cultural workmen," as Mills called them. Not only was it now possible to make a living as a popular artist, writing, composing, performing, designing, but these artists were not live performers for local audiences: they were laborers in large industrial studios. Here again the WPA arts projects were a crucial mediator; they had a labor force of 30–40,000 throughout the late 1930s, and they proved to be a way-station for the young plebeian artists and intellectuals of ethnic working-class backgrounds who would go on to careers in the federal bureaucracies, the culture industries, and the universities. As Harold Rosenberg noted in his introduction to a collection of the "spare time work" by WPA writers and artists, these young artists shared less an "esthetic unity" than a "common social experience": "the present selection," he wrote, "differs from earlier little magazine issues in that it came into being not as the result of a theoretical or esthetic grouping, but through an economic predicament. But if the employment of all its contributors on Federal Project No. 1 does not confer upon them an esthetic unity, it does immerse them in a common social experience." Later, Rosenberg argued that the influence of the arts projects lay less in their productions than in the ways they contributed to the professionalization of the arts.[88]

As early as 1937, Edward Lindeman had suggested that federal support allowed artists to say "farewell to bohemia," and as the post-war universities increasingly became a major center of American cultural life, employing intellectuals, sponsoring theaters and orchestras, and providing a place where writers, artists, and musicians worked "in residence," they further displaced urban bohemias, professionalizing and bureaucratizing the arts.

The culture industries also professionalized and bureaucratized the arts; Hollywood, radio, and the illustrated magazine were magnets for writers, actors, composers, photographers, and painters. Moreover, those artists who were not employed by the new mass media found themselves competing with them. The older notions of the bohemian artist and freelance intellectual were no longer adequate to the new armies of white-collar and professional workers in the cultural bureaucracies that Daniel Bell named the "cultural mass"—"those persons in the knowledge and communications industries who, with their families, would number several million persons."[89]

Occupational statistics are notoriously inexact, but they offer a sense of the shift. From 1920 to 1950, the labor force grew by 40 percent, from 42 million to 59 million. In the same years, the number of teachers grew by 53 percent (from 752,000 to 1,149,000) and the number of photographers by 93 percent (from 29,000 to 56,000). A number of groups more than doubled: artists and art teachers increased by 137 percent (from 35,000 to 83,000); editors and reporters by 138 percent (from 39,000 to 93,000); athletes, dancers, and entertainers by 140 percent (from 48,000 to 115,000); and authors by 143 percent (from 7,000 to 17,000). Two categories almost quadrupled: librarians grew by 280 percent (from 15,000 to 57,000) and college professors by 285 percent (from 33,000 to 127,000). Moreover, a category of miscellaneous intellectuals, including social scientists, labor-relations workers, and natural scientists, multiplied by fifteen (from 20,000 to 302,000). Only one group of cultural workers failed to keep pace with the overall labor force: musicians and music teachers, challenged by the rise of recorded music, grew by only 28 percent (from 130,000 to 166,000), though they remained the largest single group of artists. All in all, the "cultural mass" of 1950 was roughly 2 million people.[90]

For the most part, work in the cultural trades became increasingly standardized during these years; as C. Wright Mills wrote, "mass culture . . . rests on the ascendency of the commercial distributor" who hires and manages a "stable of cultural workmen." "The search goes on for 'fresh ideas,' for exciting notions, for more luring models; in brief: for the innovator. But in the meantime, back at the studio, the laboratory, the research bureau, the writer's factory—the distributor manages many producers who become the rank-and-file workmen of the commercially established cultural apparatus." Nevertheless, one of the remarkable aspects of the cultural apparatus during these years is that the "rank-and-file workmen" began to organize themselves into culture industry unions and guilds. There were some long-standing AFL unions, including the American Federation of Musicians, Actors' Equity, and the IATSE (International Alliance of Theatrical Stage Employees). But the revival of the labor movement after 1934 saw the emergence of the new Hollywood unions—the Screen Actors, Screen Directors, Screen Cartoonists, and Screen Writers' Guilds—the broadcasting unions including the Radio Writers' Guild, an Artists Union (which became United American Artists, Local 60 of UOPWA-CIO), and the CIO's Newspaper Guild, led by Heywood Broun.[91]

The new left of 1934 was entangled in this apparatus, this industrial form of modern mental labor, in three ways. First, the young radicals and communists were themselves the mass audience of the culture industries, having grown up with the movies, jazz, and the cheap amusements of the modernist metropolis. Second, as we shall see, they went to work in the culture industries, writing copy for Luce's publishing empire and the advertising agencies, making movies in the Hollywood studios, and producing records in the music industry. They found relief work in the WPA projects; enlisted in the wartime propaganda agencies; and were hired as teachers and artists in the post-war universities. They were often catalysts in organizing the culture industry unions, and they were the targets of the periodic legislative red scares. Finally, these same mental workers offered a powerful analysis of these new "mass communications" and the "new class" that operated them. Beginning with the League of Professionals' 1932 manifesto "Culture and the Crisis: An Open Letter to the Writers, Artists, Teachers, Physicians, Engineers, Scientists, and Other Professional Workers of America," and continuing through C. Wright Mills's 1959 anatomy of the "cultural apparatus," the new left of 1934 was obsessed with the meaning of the economic changes in culture itself: as I will suggest below, the term "cultural front" itself is an attempt to name that new situation.

The cultural front is thus the terrain where the Popular Front social movement met the cultural apparatus during the age of the CIO. From that conflict and conjuncture came the Popular Front "flavor" of American mass culture, what I will call the laboring of American culture.

PART II

Anatomy of the
Cultural Front

Every revolutionary class must wage war on the cultural front.

Lewis Corey, *The Decline of American Capitalism*, 1934

The most important problem to discuss in this paragraph is this: whether the philosophy of praxis excludes ethico-political history, whether it fails to recognize the reality of a moment of hegemony, treats moral and cultural leadership as unimportant and really judges superstructural facts as "appearances." One can say that not only does the philosophy of praxis not exclude ethico-political history but that, indeed, in its most recent stage of development, it consists precisely in asserting the moment of hegemony as essential to its conception of the state and to the "accrediting" of the cultural fact, of cultural activity, of a cultural front as necessary alongside the merely economic and political ones.

Antonio Gramsci

2

Marching on May Day: Cultural Politics

Unlike the musician, who is a union man and a petty bourgeois with an organized orientation in class-struggle tactics and consequently a tendency toward political affiliations (he is usually either a Third-International Communist or an extreme-right reactionary); unlike the poet, who has an over-elaborate education and no economic place in society at all and who tends hence to shoot the works politically by attaching his unrequited social passions to some desperate and recondite cause like Catalan autonomy, Anglo-Catholicism, or the justification of Leon Trotsky; unlike the sculptors and the architects, who in order to function at all must pass their lives in submission among politicos and plutocrats; unlike the doctors, the scholars, and the men of science, who are a whole social class to themselves, and who function as a united political party for the maintenance of that strangle-hold on the educational system which they acquired during the nineteenth century; unlike the manufacturers and the merchants, who know their cops and their aldermen and who always vote (to say the least); unlike actors and theater people, who, whether poor or prosperous, are irresponsible vagabonds, but who do have a trade-union of sorts and an enormous class solidarity; the painter is a man of no fixed economic orientation, no class feeling, and very little professional organization of any kind.

Virgil Thomson, 1939[1]

"I remember," the painter Stuart Davis later told an interviewer, "that I got out of bed on May Day when they used to have a May Day parade. I never thought of the May Day parade, or any other parade so far as that goes, but it was right in front of the house. I came down about noontime in a stupor out of bed, and here was this tremendous parade going on. That must have been in 1934 and then the next year I was marching in it."

53

"It wasn't a choice," Davis went on, "it was a necessity to be involved in what was going on, and since it had a specific artist section connected with it—I mean it may have happened before to a lesser degree, but for the first time I know of, the artists felt themselves part of everything else, general depression, the needs of money and food and everything else." Stories of May Day parades are a common narrative in memoirs of the cultural front. The May Day marches of the age of the CIO were the visible signs of the Popular Front, the massed forces of the city's people marching under banners of unions, mutual benefit associations, and organized fronts. Ralph Fasanella's painting, *May Day*, captures the parade's pageantry and solidarity; Davis's own famous drawing for the cover of the May 1935 issue of *Art Front* is an abstract representation of a May Day parade, complete with banners (Figure 2). Dorothea Lange's earliest social photographs were her shots of San Francisco's May Day parades: "I said, 'I will set myself a big problem. I will go down there, I will photograph this thing, I will come back and develop it. I will print it and I will mount it and I will put it on the wall, all in 24 hours. I will do this to see if I can grab a hunk of lightning.'" She did grab a hunk of lightning in the famous photograph, "May Day Listener" (Figure 4).[2]

The May Day parade in New York "was so big in 1933," Malcolm Cowley recalled, "that it had to be divided into two sections, one starting from near the Battery and marching north, the other from midtown and marching south, with the two sections converging in Union Square. The John Reed contingent, with which I marched again—this time recognizing many more faces and singing 'The International' as loudly as the others— was part of the southbound column. . . . The whole New York police force of nineteen thousand men was on duty to suppress a riot. . . . But the sun was bright, the crowd was good-humored, and nobody wanted a riot. . . . I didn't stay for the speeches, since I had to pack before leaving early in the morning" to visit Zelda and Scott Fitzgerald. Cowley, at thirty-five, was the literary editor of the *New Republic* and about to publish his first major book, *Exile's Return*. Jack Conroy, also born in 1898, had just published the most acclaimed proletarian novel of the time, *The Disinherited*, when he came to New York for the 1935 American Writers' Congress and marched in the May Day parade. "It was the time of the United Front," he later recalled, "with the Irish Workers Clubs brandishing shillelahs and shouting 'Free Tom Mooney and the Scottsboro Boys!' as they marched just before the resplendent white limousine of Father Divine, in which he sat regally. Flanking the limousine on foot was a bevy of angels clad in heavenly robes and banging tambourines. It reminded me of Vachel Lindsay's poem 'General William Booth Enters Heaven': 'The banjos rattled, and the tambourines jing, jing jingled in the hands of queens.' To the shouts of the Irish Workers 'Free Tom Mooney and the Scottsboro Boys' the angels chanted without missing a beat on their tambourines: 'Tell 'em to pray and get right with God.'"[3]

"'FelLOW WORkers, join our RANKS!' It was 1936 and there I was, Mary Johnsrud, marching down lower Broadway in a May day parade, chanting that slogan at the crowds watching on the sidewalk. 'FelLOW WORkers!' Nobody, I think, joined us; they just watched. We were having fun." So opens Mary McCarthy's comic memoir of New York in the 1930s, recounting "the high point of the slight attraction [she] felt toward Communism." But if McCarthy depicts the May Day parade as farce, Richard Wright narrates it as tragedy: the 1936 May Day parade in Chicago is the final episode of his memoir, *American Hunger*. Arriving late for his union local, which had already begun marching, he is invited to march in the Communist Party ranks by an old Party friend; but two white Communists object and throw him out of the parade. The incident marks his separation from the Party, the end of his "passionate hope," and his sense of being "really alone."[4]

These May Day parades serve as emblems of commitment and disenchantment, of solidarity and separation; they offer a way into the controversies over the relations between political engagement and artistic practice. Perhaps the most illuminating May Day story was an exchange that took place between the cultural theorist Kenneth Burke and the *Partisan Review* editor William Phillips at a 1965 symposium: Phillips, a long-time critic of the Popular Front, argued that "we have to recognize some of the nonsense in it. I remember one incident, Kenneth Burke, when you and I, and a lot of other people, were marching in a May Day parade. I've told this story a lot of times and I think it illustrates a lot of things. I remember your joining in the shout, 'We write for the working class.' And I remember wondering whether Kenneth Burke really thought he wrote for the working class. How many workers read Kenneth Burke?"

"I do not remember the incident," Burke replied, "but I couldn't deny that it is possible. Few can subscribe to all the slogans printed or shouted in a parade, but I probably joined in the shouting."

Phillips persisted: "I've thought of the story many times when I give graduate courses in criticism, and assign something by Kenneth Burke. Some of my graduate students have a little difficulty understanding you, and I have to explain the text to them."

To which Burke then elaborated his reply: "That was the basis of my talk at the first Writers' Congress. That's precisely what they got after me for: I said I couldn't write for the working class. That was the irony of the case. You remember it, I've forgotten it, but I'll take your word for it. I'm sure I paraded, I know once—," at which point he was interrupted and the conversation took another direction.[5]

In his reply to Phillips, Burke recognized the inherent comedy in the spectacle of artists and intellectuals taking a stand, parading and joining in the shouting. But unlike Phillips, who saw a simple contradiction between the parade's slogans and Burke's theoretical writing, Burke understood the complex relations between slogans, public speeches, and theoretical writing, all of which share the inherent ambiguities of symbolic action. For Burke, unlike Phillips, the issue was not whether workers read Kenneth Burke; it was whether the artists and intellectuals allied themselves with the social movement of working people: "the future is really disclosed *by finding out what people can sing about.* What values can enlist the most vigorous and original craftsmen? And what values, on the other hand, can merely enlist the public relations counsel?" The fact that Burke did not write for workers was, as he recalled, the point of his 1935 Writers' Congress speech, in which he argued for an inclusive populist rhetoric because it was "vitally important to enlist the allegiance" of the petty bourgeoisie. Indeed, Burke's Writers' Congress speech, with its outline of the "complete propagandist," stands, as we shall see, as one of the clearest formulations of the strategy of the cultural front.[6]

Nevertheless, Burke, who never renounced his participation in the Popular Front social movement, recognized that marching in parades and shouting slogans was an important form of symbolic action which had consequences for the work of artists and intellectuals. As he wrote in 1941, if we consider a work in its historical context, "we might well find that the given philosopher, by manipulating the possibilities of emphasis in one way rather than another, was able symbolically to enroll himself in one social alliance, with its peculiar set of expectancies, rather than another. Here we should see what participation in a Cause caused his work, by what Movement it was motivated, on what sub-stance it made its stand." In chapter 12, I will reconsider Burke's own cultural theory, and explore the ways he symbolically enrolled himself in the Popular Front social alliance. Here I simply want to suggest that Burke's model of symbolic enrollment offers a powerful way to understand the cultural politics of the age of the CIO.[7]

One can see this if one looks briefly at the two notions that have dominated considerations of political art in this period: the notion of "commitment" and the mechanism of the "front." Commitment was the rubric used to sum up the "political" aspect of the career of writers and artists. It was rooted, as Raymond Williams has argued, in the Romantic notion of the artist as the epitome of the free individual, and it viewed the politics of art as an individual act, an almost heroic choice. There is no question that the problematic of commitment saturated the literary world of the time: there were endless symposia in *Partisan Review* and *Modern Quarterly* on the writer's responsibility and the role of the intellectual.

Writers Take Sides was the title of a League of American Writers pamphlet on the Spanish Civil War. As a result, political art came to be seen in either of two apparently opposed guises: "agitprop" and "fellow traveling." Both of these are rooted in the act of will associated with the notion of commitment, the decision to take a stand, to speak out, and both tend to pay more attention to the speaking out than to what is said, to the cultural achievement itself. As a result, the discussion of political art as either agitprop or fellow traveling tends to reduce it to nonsense, in William Phillips's word, or the chanting of slogans.[8]

Agitprop—the contraction of *agitation* and *propaganda* in political jargon—is the name for a variety of forms of directly political art: topical songs and poems, street theater, manifestos, works of journalistic and documentary immediacy. There is no question that much of the art of the cultural front fell into this category, but its role and place must be understood. Like topical works of any moment of insurgency, one must recreate the moment in order to give them life. Otherwise they appear as dead letters, the ephemera of cultural history. If such works rarely evoke responses in other times and places, if they do not in themselves constitute a political culture, nevertheless one cannot imagine radical culture, indeed any cultural flowering at all, without them; they are the crocuses of a radical culture.

The other side of agitprop—its unlikeable face—is the face of cultural prescription: every moment of political art, indeed every cultural initiative, has its apologetics and denunciations. Too often, the vitriolic denunciations of renegade writers by a Michael Gold or the Olympian dismissals of expressionism and modernism by a Georg Lukács are taken as the preeminent examples of the cultural politics of the Popular Front. Together, the limits of agitprop productions and a prescriptive aesthetics have seemed, to many critics, to sum up Popular Front culture: all politics and no art.

For other critics of Popular Front culture, its failings are captured in the notion of fellow traveling, which places a different twist on the formula of all politics and no art. Here, commitment seems to amount to nothing more than speaking out, and the history of the cultural politics of the Popular Front appears to be a history of letterheads. Liberal and left-wing critiques of the Hollywood screenwriters have often sounded this note: though they may have been Communists when they raised money for the Spanish Republic, they were merely screenwriters when they worked for the studios (for the most part, the right was more convinced that they had actually corrupted Hollywood). This has been a leitmotif of the criticism of many other cultural figures as well, a sense that though an Orson Welles, a Kenneth Burke, or a Langston Hughes may have taken public stands on the left, their work was never really affected by it: Arnold Rampersad follows an account of Langston Hughes's left-wing affiliations with the comment that "the fact that there was now more shadow than substance to his socialism escaped almost everyone, including his enemies." As a result, the history of "writers on the left" remains a history of literary journalism, congresses, and commitments, a bizarre inversion of the blacklisters' *Red Channels*, that compilation of organizations joined, petitions signed, marches marched in, and benefits attended.[9]

Again, though the phenomenon of fellow traveling was certainly real in the age of the CIO—there were artists and writers who occasionally took left-wing stands but were in no sense part of a left-wing culture—this view of commitment has obscured our understanding of Popular Front culture. If a history of the relations between the left and American culture is to be more than the historian "naming names," more than the "finagling among literary politicians" that Kenneth Burke accused his friend Malcolm Cowley of writing, we need a better sense of the meaning of cultural politics and a political art than is offered by the notion of commitment.[10]

Here, Raymond Williams's notion of alignment is suggestive, since it reverses the voluntarism of commitment: "born into a social situation with all its specific perspectives, and into a language, the writer begins by being aligned." Thus commitment, Williams suggests, lies in "becoming conscious of our own alignments." Though "some of the most publicized cases of 'commitment' are when people shift ... from one set of beliefs and assumptions to another, and this can involve a quite radical shift in real practice," commitment may also involve confirming one's own alignments, "because really to have understood the social pressures on our own thinking, or when we come to that wonderful although at first terrible realization that what we are thinking is what a lot of other people have thought, that what we are seeing is what a lot of other people have seen, that is an extraordinary experience." Williams's attention to unconscious, involuntary alignments, and to the ways we become conscious of them, brings together the "socially conscious" and the "political unconscious," and unites social and aesthetic alignments. "When I hear people talk about literature," Williams continues, "describing what so-and-so did with that form—how did he handle the short novel?—I often think that we should reverse the question and ask, how did the short novel handle him."[11] Williams's notion of alignment shifts the analysis of the artistic career from an individual narrative of commitment to an account of the ways the social and formal alignments that produce artists and intellectuals are reshaped and transformed. Thus, I would suggest that the melodramas of commitment that dominate the cultural history of this period are better understood as three kinds of alignment, three distinct social and aesthetic situations: that of the *moderns*, the *émigrés*, and the *plebeians*. Indeed, the cultural front might be understood as the uneasy but powerful alliance between these three groups of artists and intellectuals.

The *moderns* were generally well-established before their association with the left, and their work was transformed as a result. Their break with previous alignments, with earlier genres and forms, often looked like a "conversion," the metaphor often invoked to "explain" the political sea change.[12] The radical moderns had been part of that extraordinary flowering of writers and artists, born in the last decade of the nineteenth century and coming of age during the First World War, who had adopted the European avant-gardes: cubism, surrealism, futurism, and many others. For the most part, the US modernists were Anglos from established bourgeois backgrounds: many of the men had Ivy League educations. As Malcolm Cowley, their foremost chronicler, noted, they had a complex relation to the emerging consumer culture of Fordism with its elaborate marketing and advertising of consumer goods. Though the most experimental artists depended on wealthy patrons, many worked in the growing advertising agencies, and the most successful supplied illustrations and stories for the expensive "slick" magazines like *Vanity Fair* and the *New Yorker*, which flourished on advertising revenues in the 1920s.[13]

Though a few had had ties to the Greenwich Village radicalism of the *Masses*, most of the moderns were apolitical. If they were critical of the commercialism and Babbittry of US culture, their alienation was expressed in expatriation to Europe and avant-garde formal experiment. The turning point came in the late 1920s: for some, as we shall see, it was the execution of Sacco and Vanzetti in 1927; for others, it was the crash of 1929 and the depression that ensued. "It would be three years," Josephine Herbst wrote in her memoir of 1927, "before we took down a volume of *Kunstgeschichte* from our shelves, to be replaced by a thin narrow book in red entitled *What Is to Be Done?*, by V. I. Lenin." Perhaps the most celebrated turns to the left were made by Edmund Wilson and Malcolm Cowley, whose personal biographies would later seem to themselves and to others to mirror the lives of their generation.[14]

If Wilson and Cowley were the most visible radical moderns, one can see similar inclinations among novelists like Ernest Hemingway, F. Scott Fitzgerald, Sherwood Anderson, and Josephine Herbst, photographers like Paul Strand, poets like Langston Hughes, composers like Aaron Copland and Duke Ellington, filmmakers like Charlie Chaplin, painters like Stuart Davis, fashion designers like Elizabeth Hawes, critics like Kenneth Burke, and playwrights like John Howard Lawson. However, the turn to the left by the American modernists was not simply a shift in political opinion, nor was it a retreat from modernism to a Victorian realism. As I will argue below, in almost every case, writers and artists of the modernist generation attempted to reconstruct modernism, to tie their formal experimentation to a new social and historical vision, to invent a "social modernism," a "revolutionary symbolism."

If the left-wing moderns of the depression sometimes looked like a revival of the pre-World War I Greenwich Village radicals, with the *New Masses* claiming the legacy of the *Masses*, the other two forces in the cultural front, the *émigrés* and the *plebeians*, were distinctively new formations in American culture. The *émigrés*, the artists and intellectuals who fled fascism, were often products of the Marxist modernisms of Europe, Asia, and Latin America, and producers like John Houseman (Jacques Haussemann), actors like Bela Lugosi, filmmakers like Fritz Lang, Jean Renoir, and William Dieterle, writers like Bertolt Brecht, Christina Stead, Ayako Ishigaki, André Breton, Anna Seghers, and Franz Werfel, Marxist theorists like Theodor Adorno, Karl Korsch, C.L.R. James, and Paul Mattick, and composers like Hanns Eisler, Kurt Weill, and Béla Bartók, exercised a profound influence on US culture during the age of the CIO. Many of them had been left-wing activists in Europe, part of the European cultural front, organized by the impresario Willi Münzenberg. Others were drawn to the Popular Front only through the experience of fascism.

The makeshift salons of the exiled artists in New York and Southern California—perhaps most famously that of Salka Viertel—became critical meeting places of the cultural front. Much of the day-to-day work of the cultural front was raising funds and negotiating visas and work permits for the refugees, and they in turn became vital members of the Anti-Nazi Leagues of the Popular Front. Moreover, the émigrés often became catalysts in the reconstruction of American modernism, as personal ties transformed their American collaborators. But if the influx of European artists and intellectuals revolutionized the US cultural apparatus, from Broadway and Hollywood to the foundations and universities, the US sojourn often left an imprint on the émigrés themselves, producing a distinctive "American" moment in their work.[15]

The other new force in the cultural front was the emergence of the *plebeians*, a generation of artists and intellectuals from working-class families, writers like Richard Wright, Thomas Bell, Carlos Bulosan, Tillie Olsen, Toshio Mori, Clifford Odets, Henry Roth, and Pietro di Donato, singers like Billie Holiday, Josh White, and Frank Sinatra, bandleaders like Artie Shaw, Benny Goodman, and Count Basie, filmmakers like Elia Kazan, Abraham Polonsky, Edward Dmytryk, James Wong Howe, and Leo Hurwitz, philosophers like Sidney Hook, critics like Philip Rahv, Alfred Kazin, and Irving Howe, photographers like Aaron Siskind and Weegee, artists like Jacob Lawrence, Ralph Fasanella, and Miné Okubo, songwriters like Yip Harburg, and actors like John Garfield and Canada Lee. They were "new Americans," as Louis Adamic called them, the second generation of the second wave of immigration. They were children of the public library and public education, for it was only in the early twentieth century that workers' children began to receive secondary education. For them, the expansion of the culture industries and the state cultural apparatuses meant that they could make a living as writers or artists; they could move out of their parents' world of manual labor into that uncertain terrain of the white-collar proletariat, apparently middle class, but still working for wages and with little job security. Their aspirations were supported by the government relief agencies for writers and artists, and many went on to radio, recording and film studios, as well as to the post-war universities.[16]

The term "plebeian" is their own; Mary McCarthy recalled that *Partisan Review* editor Philip Rahv "was a partisan of what he called 'plebeian' values—he loved that word." Indeed, Rahv was an embodiment of the plebeian: born Ivan (or Ilya) Greenberg in the Ukraine, he came to the United States at fourteen and never finished high school. He was an autodidact—his alma mater, Fred Dupee quipped, was the Forty-second Street Library—and he first worked as an advertising copywriter and a Hebrew teacher. He joined the New York John Reed Club in 1932, edited its journal, *Partisan Review*, and worked on the Federal Writers Project; by 1957, he was not only a leading critic and intellectual, but had become a professor at Brandeis. For these writers and artists, the association with the left was less a conversion to than an affiliation with a movement that enabled both an artistic and a political vocation or career. "Who had ever . . . offered to young writers an audience so vast?" Richard Wright asked in *American Hunger*. "Out of the magazines I read came a passionate call for the experiences of the disinherited, and there were none of the same lispings of the missionary in it. It did not say: 'Be like us and we will like you, maybe.' It said: 'If you possess enough courage to speak out what you are, you will find that you are not alone.'" The cultural front and the Communist arts movement enfranchised these young artists, and their proletarian avant-garde created a flurry of journals, manifestos, debates, and icons. They were of the left as they were becoming artists and intellectuals.[17]

The generational differences between the moderns and the plebeians are not, of course, absolute. There were a few plebeian figures of the modernist generation, notably Anzia Yezierska, Langston Hughes, Lewis Corey/Louis Fraina, and Michael Gold; and there were depression-generation figures from established Anglo middle-class families who were part of the cultural front, notably Orson Welles, Joseph Losey, Alexander Saxton, and Pete Seeger. Nonetheless, the overall contrast between the older Anglo moderns and the younger ethnic plebeians is striking: as I shall argue later, part of Michael Gold's cultural importance lay in the fact that he was one of the few "new Americans" in the circles around the *Masses* and the Provincetown Players. Similarly, in an essay on the way

Orson Welles was seen as a "boy genius," Robert Sklar has suggested that the modernist "lost generation," who received widespread youthful recognition, had few inheritors in the next generation.[18]

Moreover, the tensions among the moderns, the émigrés, and the plebeians were the source of many of the controversies and splits of the period. The hostility to Popular Front figures like Malcolm Cowley, Granville Hicks, and F.O. Matthiessen on the part of Alfred Kazin, Irving Howe, and the *Partisan Review* circle was not entirely determined by the divide between Stalinists and anti-Stalinists. Rather, the young New York Jewish intellectuals saw Cowley, Hicks, and Matthiessen as provincial and middlebrow, too enamoured of English culture, and out of touch with the modernisms of the Continent. Similarly, the young working-class writer Tillie Olsen recalled feeling out of place among the Hollywood left and the "Carmel crowd." On the other hand, the moderns were often suspicious of the young Jewish leftists: literary controversies broke out over Archibald MacLeish's caricature of "Comrade Levine" and over anti-Semitic remarks by Dreiser. Moreover, the letters and diaries of John Dos Passos and Edmund Wilson show that their alienation from the Communist Party was as much a consequence of the Jewishness as of the Stalinism of the Communists: "The Jews," Wilson wrote, "have no sense of the American revolutionary tradition." The cultural front is thus less the spectacle of commitment, either the momentary flurries of committed agitprop art or the public stances of committed artists, than the often unstable alliance of cultural figures with distinct alignments: modernist, émigré, or plebeian.[19]

The second metaphor that runs throughout discussions of the politics of culture in the age of the CIO is that of the "front." For its anti-Communist critics, the Popular Front was a façade, a Potemkin Village, a false front. In his 1941 attack on *The Red Decade*, Eugene Lyons called the front a "Trojan Horse trick," and Irving Howe was later to characterize it as a "brilliant masquerade." For these critics, the front groups were "innocents clubs," manipulated by the Communist Party. Thus, the cultural politics of the period come to be explained by tropes like seduction or manipulation, whereby the innocent artist succumbs to the wiles of the Party working under the disguise of the "front." Artists, we are told, have little or no political sense; and their eventual break with the front groups is a recognition of having been duped, a recovery of the artist's true vocation. This story of outraged innocence was the story told again and again by the "friendly" witnesses before the House Committee on Un-American Activities. Humphrey Bogart claimed to be a "dope" in his famous 1948 *Photoplay* article separating himself from the left, "I'm No Communist." Indeed, after the decade of congressional investigations and blacklists, it was hard to see the "front" as anything other than a façade. Even one of finest reflections on it, Martin Ritt's 1976 film, *The Front*, starring Zero Mostel and Woody

Allen, plays with this sense: the "front" in the film is the innocent friend who agrees to take credit for the screenplays written by the blacklisted writers. However, as the "front man" gets involved in the world of the radicals themselves, he moves from being a "front," in the sense of a façade, to becoming part of the "front," in the sense of a political alliance with the blacklisted radicals.[20]

However, the "front" organizations were not mere façades; their remarkable successes resulted from the ways in which they built on the characteristic form of American radical politics, the voluntary reform association. Though insurgent political parties, "third parties," have had little success in US history, single-issue reform groups have organized large numbers of people and won powerful victories. The "front" groups belonged to this tradition of reform organizing: coalitions assembled to contest a particular "front," whether by field or occupation (magazines like *Art Front* and *Film Front*, the League of American Writers, the League of Women Shoppers), by gender or nationality (the Congress of American Women, the National Negro Congress, the American-Slav Congress, El Congreso del Pueblo de Habla Española), or by international solidarity (the American Friends of Spanish Democracy, the Hollywood Anti-Nazi League), as well as many ad hoc organizations and coalitions which were forgotten until they were indexed as "subversive" by the attorney general.

Here, the notion of a front is not far from that of hegemony which the Italian Marxist Antonio Gramsci was developing in this period. For Gramsci's concept of hegemony begins not with the question of individual "commitment" but with the question of how social movements are organized among both the dominant and subordinate groups, how social formations are led. The building of hegemony is not only a matter of "ideas," of winning hearts and minds, but also of participation, as people are mobilized in cultural institutions—schools, churches, sporting events—and in long-term historic projects—waging wars, establishing colonies, gentrifying a city, developing a regional economy. This participation depends on reorganizing patterns of loyalty and allegiance, articulating cultural practices in a new historical bloc. Such a historical bloc attempts to forge an alliance of social groups and class fractions: by offering a new culture, a way of life, a conception of the universe, it creates the conditions for a political use or reading of cultural performances and artifacts, the conditions for symbolizing class conflict.[21]

Thus, the politics of affiliation and the politics of form may come together at moments when a historical bloc coalesces, when political sentiments and opinions are transformed into ways of living and ways of seeing; at times, the cultural front succeeded in constituting such an alternative hegemony. In such moments, the forms and genres one works in, the audiences one addresses, and the aesthetic choices one makes are,

as Kenneth Burke suggested, intimately related to the apparently unconnected affiliations and allegiances one announces as a political citizen.
Indeed, it is precisely because the Popular Front deeply affected patterns
of life in the United States that so many commentators—even those hostile
to the Popular Front—have seen it as a form of culture.

The cultural front succeeded in establishing what Raymond Williams has
called a "structure of feeling." It did this not only by attracting "the most
accomplished craftsmen" in the arts, to use Burke's standard, but by
organizing and mobilizing audiences. If audiences are not the passive,
manipulated consumers depicted in early critiques of mass culture, neither
are they the unruly, resisting readers imagined by more recent celebrants
of popular culture. Though it is true that people make all sorts of bizarre
and unintended uses of popular texts, and that virtually any cultural
commodity can become a private scripture, licensing oppositional and
utopian desires, drives, and actions, not to mention anti-social and patho-
logical behaviors, these "readings" rarely have much historical significance.
Subaltern experience does not necessarily generate social criticism and
cultural resistance; the possibility of popular political readings of cultural
commodities depends on the cultivation, organization, and mobilization of
audiences by oppositional subcultures and social movements.[22]

So an accurate sense of the cultural politics of the age of the CIO would
begin not with the tired rhetoric of commitment and the hackneyed story
of innocents' clubs, but with an exploration of the sites and institutions,
the networks and associations, built out of the alliance of the radical
moderns, the émigré Marxists, and the young plebeians. These formations
organized and mobilized their rank-and-file audiences in several ways, for
the cultural front was, at different moments, a proletarian avant-garde, a
movement culture, an aspect of state culture, and a part of mass culture
itself.

1. Proletarian Avant-Garde

The cultural front began as an avant-garde culture, as young writers and
artists formed dozens of proletarian literary clubs, workers theaters, camera
clubs, dance troupes, choruses, and composers collectives in the late 1920s
and early 1930s. Some of these young artists were scattered across the
continent, writing letters and exchanging mimeographed magazines;
others lived together in "shock troupes," communal households of artists.
In cities across the country, they met in "coffee pots" and created the
transient institutions of an avant-garde culture: little magazines, alternative
galleries, theaters, and art schools that offered training, support, and
exposure for young working-class artists.[23]

There were many groups of worker writers and rebel poets around the country, some of which became chapters of the John Reed Club. The Reed clubs included not only writers, but painters: the famous New York John Reed Club show of 1933—"The Social Viewpoint in Art"—which included works by Stuart Davis, Ben Shahn, Anton Refregier, Kathe Kollwitz, José Clemente Orozco, and Thomas Hart Benton, was hailed as being "as significant as the historic Armory exhibit." Though the Reed clubs, with their national conferences, became one of the most visible manifestations of this avant-garde, there were many other local formations. In Harlem, Louise Thompson and the sculptor Augusta Savage organized Vanguard, which sponsored dance and theater groups, a summer musical program, and a Marxist study group; in Los Angeles, a Japanese Proletarian Artists' League was formed by Japanese American Communists, publishing a magazine, *Proletarian Art*, until its editor was deported after a Red Squad raid.[24]

The Workers Film and Photo League, which had grown out of the Workers Camera Club in New York, supplied photographs to radical labor magazines, shot newsreels of strikes, May Day parades, and unemployment demonstrations, ran the Harry Potamkin Film School (named for the young Marxist film critic who had died in 1933), and distributed the Soviet films of Eisenstein, Vertov, and Pudovkin; members published *Film Front*, *Experimental Cinema*, and *Photo Notes*, and branches of the Film and Photo League grew up in Chicago, Philadelphia, Boston, Los Angeles, San Francisco, Laredo, Texas, and Newark, New Jersey.[25] The workers theater movement was made up of amateur groups, mobile troupes who played on street corners and flatbed trucks, at factory gates, docks, and ethnic fraternal halls. Their agitprop skits consisted of allegorical characters, dressed alike, chanting, miming, and dancing in unison or antiphony, accompanied by drums, gongs, and hand-held posters. The form was pioneered by the German-language group Prolet-Buhne and was adopted by the influential Workers Laboratory Theatre (later known as the Theatre of Action) in New York, and by the Solidarity Players in Boston, the New Theatre in Philadelphia, the Blue Blouses in Chicago, and the Rebel Players in Los Angeles. By 1933, the League of Workers Theatres had 250 affiliates, and a national magazine, *Workers Theatre*, was being published. The young members of the Theatre of Action included three major post-war film directors: Elia Kazan, Nicholas Ray, and Martin Ritt.[26] Young modern dancers influenced by Martha Graham, Doris Humphreys, and Helen Tamiris formed more than a dozen radical dance groups around the country, including the Red Dancers and the Rebel Dance Group.[27]

These groups often grew out of the existing cultural institutions of the immigrant working class. The Yiddish-language theater group, Artef (Arbeiter Teater Verband), saw itself as a radical alternative to the mainstream Yiddish theater; similarly, the foreign-language choruses, bands, and orchestras that made up the Workers Music League were a left-wing version of the long tradition of working-class musical groups. One branch of the Workers Music League was the Pierre Degeyter Club (named after the composer of the "International"), which included choruses and an orchestra: it also included a Composers Collective made up of emerging American modernists like Charles Seeger, Henry Cowell, Aaron Copland, and Marc Blitzstein as well as the leader of the famous Freiheit chorus, Jacob Schaefer. They published magazines (*Music Front* was the Pierre Degeyter Club journal, and *Music Vanguard* that of the Composers Collective), songbooks, and opened the Downtown Music School.[28]

Since the young artists and writers were themselves often unemployed, they were active in the unemployed councils and relief demonstrations: in New York, an Unemployed Artists' Group and an Unemployed Writers' Group emerged out of the John Reed Club.[29] But the heart of the political and artistic energies of the proletarian avant-garde was probably the International Labor Defense (ILD). The ILD was a radical legal-action group built by the Communist Party to defend jailed unionists, immigrants facing deportation, and African Americans facing southern terror. With its theory of the "labor" or "mass" defense which sought to support court action with public protest, and its pioneering photomagazine, *Labor Defender*, the ILD led the campaigns to free Sacco and Vanzetti, Tom Mooney, and the Scottsboro Nine. The "labor defense" became central to the proletarian avant-garde, and many of the poems, stories, dances, songs, and street theater sketches invoked the martyrs made famous by the ILD.[30]

Not surprisingly, theirs was an experimental and iconoclastic aesthetic, breaking with the conventions of the established culture. If they have often been seen as anti-modernist—and their self-assured dismissals of Proust and Stein have often been cited—it was because European modernisms already represented an orthodoxy. Their rhetoric invoked the people, though their work was rarely popular in any market sense; they proclaimed their "realism," but compared to the canons of realism operating in mainstream film, fiction, and painting, theirs was more a "proletarian grotesque." "We took it out on the goddamn streets," the Theater of Action's Earl Robinson recalled. "Agitprop, that was an honourable word. We never even thought of anything else in the world except that, agitation and propaganda." As the groups developed, however, controversies broke out in each of the proletarian avant-gardes over issues of form and function, as those who preferred the immediacy and militant amateurism of agitprop—the defenders of street theater, newsreels, newsphotos, picket-line ballads, and poster making—debated those who wanted to develop professional productions and modernist craftsmanship, and were somewhat more skeptical of political immediacy and mass popularity. Thus, the Nykino production group seceded from the Film and Photo League in order to make more ambitious and technically proficient films; the Composers Collective gradually split from the Pierre Degeyter Club in order to concentrate on more complex music than songs for May Day parades; and professional theater companies like the Theater Union emerged out of the workers theater movement.[31]

Like all avant-gardes, the proletarian avant-garde was short-lived; it coincided with the upheavals of 1934 and 1935, and then collapsed. As we shall see, many of its young artists and writers went on to succeed in the movement culture of the Popular Front, in the New Deal arts projects, and in the culture industries. However, the majority of the proletarian artists never left the factories, shops and households of working-class life: their patron saint is Tillie Lerner Olsen. Immediately recognized as one of the most powerful voices of the proletarian movement on the basis of a single story published in *Partisan Review* (and reprinted in the *Proletarian Literature in the United States* anthology), she achieved a minor celebrity when the publisher Bennett Cerf found her in jail in San Francisco, arrested in the 1934 general strike. But Olsen abandoned her writing as she returned to work and raised her children. Her "lost" novel of the depression, *Yonnondio: From the Thirties*, was not published until 1974, and her collection of essays, *Silences*, is a classic analysis and evocation of voluntary and involuntary literary silences, an elegy for many of the young writers and artists of the proletarian avant-garde. In chapter 5, I will look more closely at the dynamics of this proletarian avant-garde by focusing on the literary movement.[32]

2. Movement Culture

By the mid 1930s, the cultural front was sustained by a movement culture, a world of working-class education, recreation, and entertainment built by the Communist Party, the new industrial unions, and the fraternal benefit lodges, particularly those of the International Workers Order (IWO). In this world, the proletarian artists found an enthusiastic and sympathetic audience, one for whom their works and performances became emblems of solidarity and self-affirmation. As the social movement grew from relief demonstrations, hunger marches, and eviction protests to sit-down strikes, rent strikes, and meat boycotts across the country, the proletarian avant-garde became its troubadours, particularly in the performance arts. If movement cultures are often stigmatized as "preaching to the converted," it is worth recalling that *most* preaching is to the converted, that the power of any political or religious movement lies in its ability to sustain, inspire, and console its adherents.[33]

One half of this movement culture was sponsored by the labor unions themselves. At the beginning of the depression, few unions had developed educational or recreational programs. "Speaking with ... CIO union leaders during 1936–37," Louis Adamic wrote, "I felt that, outside of the predominantly Jewish garment workers' unions whose headquarters are in New York and whose interest in education is already a matter of decades, none had any real idea of the new labor movement's educational needs." Indeed, the garment unions had pioneered a notion of union culture, developing health and credit services as well as education and recreation activities; as one historian has noted, this "social democratic approach" of "having the union itself provide quasi-economic benefits unachieved in collective bargaining" was "particularly suited to well-organized unions in poorly paid industries." The ILGWU had created the first full-scale union educational program in 1915; its Unity Center, founded in 1917, offered gyms, dancing, sports, lectures, and music for urban workers, and its Unity House was a summer vacation camp in the Poconos. By 1934, the ILGWU had established a Cultural and Recreational Division, which sponsored mandolin orchestras, theater groups, choruses, and sports teams.[34]

Despite Adamic's concerns, however, many of the new industrial unions of the CIO adopted the social democratic approach to unionism, creating what Lizabeth Cohen has called the CIO's "culture of unity." In some cases, they did this by taking over the "welfare capitalist" programs of employers, turning the sports and recreation programs of company unions into CIO activities. But in cities with a strong Popular Front social movement like New York, Philadelphia, and Minneapolis, the needle trades unions offered both an example of and support for a citywide labor culture. In Philadelphia, the garment and textile unions, together with the Philco local of the United Electrical Workers, created a citywide labor movement culture, with labor-backed theaters, a CIO Labor Sports League, and dances at the Labor Lyceum. In Minneapolis, the ILGWU helped found the Minnesota Labor School in 1934; both the ILGWU and the militant General Drivers' Local 574 formed drama groups. The New York–based Transport Workers Union developed an education program with courses in photography, dancing, singing, and creative writing as well as public speaking and parliamentary procedure; it also had an extensive sports program, annual dances, an art exhibit—Art for the Subway—and a drama group, which produced a play written by a subway worker. The young writers and artists of the proletarian avant-garde were often prominent in these local labor schools and theater groups. The proletarian writer Meridel Le Sueur taught in the Minnesota Labor School, and veterans of the Workers Laboratory Theatre like Earl Robinson and Charles Friedman taught and directed at the ILGWU's Labor Stage.[35]

The workers schools that were created by the Communist Party and the labor unions were crucial to the development of young working-class activists and intellectuals. The Communist Party itself served, as Richard

Flacks has suggested, as "the functional equivalent of a university for working-class young people." "If you were a working-class youth who was interested in the world of ideas," Flacks writes, "the Party ... provided opportunity for intellectual development, for the acquisition of skills, and the establishment of a vocation ... In the twenties and thirties, thousands of young men and women, drawn from steel towns and ghettos, from auto plants and sweat shops, from mines and docks, were schooled in this way." One of these working-class youths, a Croatian immigrant named Stjepan Mesaroš (later, Steve Nelson), recalled that "my experience with the Workers' School was fairly typical of that of a large number of young workers, many of whom were foreign-born and poorly educated like myself. The radical movement was our teacher. It was a great step forward to be drawn together in a group to talk and listen, to be induced to read and study. Where else could we get that opportunity?" There were two main types of labor school that came to serve as an infrastructure for the Popular Front social movement: the urban night schools sponsored by central labor councils and the Communist Party; and the residential labor colleges and summer schools, which trained activists.[36]

The urban night schools had been pioneered by the ILGWU's Workers University, established by Fannia Cohn in 1918 and drawing on New York City college teachers, including the historian Charles Beard. They began to get federal support between 1933 and 1942 through the Workers' Education Project (renamed the Workers' Service Program in 1939), which had been created by the New Deal relief programs, FERA (Federal Emergency Relief Administration) and WPA (Works Progress Administration), and was directed by Hilda Smith, who had founded and directed the Byrn Mawr Summer School for Women Workers. Local unions and community groups could request classes through a government sponsor— a state university or a department of education or labor—and hire unemployed teachers from relief rolls to teach them. Many local unions and labor councils took advantage of the program, and at its peak in 1936 there was "an enrollment of over 65,000 workers in 3,000 classes, using about 1,000 instructors drawn from relief rolls in thirty-three states." The most popular classes were in the social sciences, economics, and labor history; about half the classes were held in union halls, the other half in public schools. In Philadelphia, the Workers' Education Project became a key part of the city's labor culture; and in Minneapolis, the existing Minnesota Labor School received WPA backing in these years.[37]

When the WPA was closed down in 1942, the labor movement began a long and unsuccessful attempt to pass a labor extension education service; at the same time, the Popular Front left established a series of labor schools to pick up from the Workers' Service Program. The California Labor School in San Francisco, the Jefferson School of Social Science and the

George Washington Carver School in New York, the Samuel Adams School in Boston, the Abraham Lincoln School in Chicago, and the People's Educational Center in Los Angeles were the best-known of these Popular Front labor schools, all of which offered low-tuition night courses and lectures. The California Labor School, founded in 1942 with the backing of local unions, had 2,600 students a semester by 1946; and veterans could use their GI Bill benefits to study there. The school had four departments: labor organization (including labor history, economics, and journalism); social sciences; creative writing; and industrial arts (with training in photography and graphic arts). The teachers were mainly union officials and local college teachers, but filmmaker Orson Welles, poet Muriel Rukeyser, and architect Frank Lloyd Wright all spoke at the school, Leadbelly performed there, and monies from Frank Sinatra's short film *The House I Live In* were contributed to the school. Probationary members of Local 10 of the longshoremen's union (ILWU) were required to take classes at the school to become full members of the union. "I knew nothin' about trade unions before I went into the ILWU," the longshoreman Cleophas Williams recalled. "Once you went to the California Labor School and were among other workers, hearing different talk, different rhetoric, you began to question, you began to see. It was a conversion."[38]

New York's Jefferson School, founded in 1943, drew some of its faculty from the teachers dismissed from City College in the Rapp-Coudert purge of 1940–41; it had 5,000 students a term by its peak in 1947–48. In the years after the war, Dashiell Hammett regularly taught a course on mystery writing and Pete Seeger taught a course in folk music. Uptown in Harlem, the George Washington Carver School was led by Gwendolyn Bennett, the Harlem Renaissance poet and painter who had been dismissed from the WPA Harlem Community Arts Center in the Rapp-Coudert red scare. Chicago's Abraham Lincoln School was organized by the radical lawyer William L. Patterson: both Josephine Herbst and Jack Conroy taught there in the early 1940s, and Willard Motley, Nelson Algren, and Richard Wright all spoke at the school.[39]

The People's Educational Center in Los Angeles, established in 1943, was sponsored by three dozen affiliated AFL and CIO unions; its executive secretary, William Wolff, was a long-time activist in labor education and had been the ILGWU's Pacific Coast education director. The faculty at both the downtown and Hollywood branches included the UCLA film scholar Kenneth MacGowan, screenwriter John Howard Lawson, composer Earl Robinson, and People's Songs activist Harry Hay. One of the founders and trustees of the Samuel Adams School in Boston was the literary critic F.O. Matthiessen. Paul Sweezy later recalled that "during its first year, Matty taught a course in the major American literary masters he had studied in *American Renaissance* . . . thanks more to Matty than to any other individual, [the school] was able to maintain a remarkably high educational level" until its demise in 1947 when it, along with the other Popular Front labor schools, was put on the Attorney General's list of subversive organizations.[40]

The residential labor colleges were also a crucial institutional framework for the Popular Front's movement culture. In the Northeast, the most important ones were the Bryn Mawr Summer School for Women Workers (which became the Hudson Shore Labor School) and the Brookwood Labor College. The Bryn Mawr Summer School for Women Workers was directed by Hilda Worthington Smith from 1921 to 1933 with the support of the Women's Trade Union League, the YWCA Industrial Department, and the needle trades unions: it brought young women factory workers to Bryn Mawr in the summer for courses in history, literature, and economics. Though it was committed to an ideal of liberal education for factory workers, it became increasingly a program for women union activists, leading it to sever its ties with Bryn Mawr in 1938 and become the Hudson Shore Labor School in West Park, New York. The Brookwood Labor College in Katonah, New York, was directed by A.J. Muste from 1921 to 1933; most of its students were trades unionists from the garment industry and the coal mines, and Brookwood alumni were to serve as key organizers and intellectuals for the CIO, even though the school itself closed in 1937, in large part a victim of the political upheavals of the middle 1930s. Though Brookwood was more an organizers school than a part of the cultural front—indeed, the writer and editor V.F. Calverton was turned down because his interests were "primarily cultural or scholarly"—nevertheless, it had its links to the cultural front. In 1936, two young veterans of the Workers Laboratory Theatre, Nicholas Ray and Earl Robinson, were hired by Brookwood to direct a labor theater. Moreover, an important Brookwood teacher was the young miner/writer Tom Tippett. Not only did Tippett write a book on southern textiles strikes, *When Southern Labor Stirs* (1931), and a proletarian novel drawing on his working days in Illinois coal-mines, *Horse Shoe Bottoms* (1935), he was a key figure in forging the link between rural folk musics and the labor movement: as Archie Green wrote, "in his constant travel between southern textile and mining areas and Brookwood Labor College, Tippett carried hillbilly discs north and union songbooks south."[41]

In the South, two other labor colleges were central to Popular Front culture: the Commonwealth Labor College and the Highlander Folk School. Commonwealth Labor College had been founded as a labor school in the cooperative Socialist community of New Llano, Louisiana, in 1923 and had then moved to a farm in Mena, Arkansas. The college offered workshops in labor organizing and was active in organizing black and white sharecroppers, but it was also a center for the proletarian literature movement: the little magazine *Windsor Quarterly* was published there, and Jack Conroy taught there in the summer of 1935. In 1937, Claude Williams and Lee Hays arrived there to build the Commonwealth Players, who used drama and spirituals as organizing devices. Their "zipper" songs and plays— constructed so the contents of a local struggle could be "zipped" into the basic framework—became the aesthetic form for the singing groups Lee Hays was later to join, the Almanac Singers and the Weavers. In 1940, the school was raided and its property seized and auctioned under Arkansas's sedition laws.

The Highlander Folk School was founded in 1932 in Monteagle, Tennessee, by Myles Horton and Donald West, southerners who had met at Union Theological Seminary. Modeled on the Danish folk schools and sponsoring folk festivals, it quickly became involved in the upheavals of 1933 and 1934; the leader of a miners strike in Wilder, Tennessee, who had been teaching at Highlander, was shot by thugs in May 1933. Highlander became a crucial center for young southern organizers: "workers who show promise of becoming active in the labor movement as organizers or local leaders are selected as resident students," Louis Adamic noted after a mid-1930s visit. "Their number is between one and two dozen. Most of them are from the mills and sharecropper families." In 1937, after local organizers had been killed and kidnapped, Elia Kazan and Ralph Steiner of Frontier Films went to Highlander and made *People of the Cumberlands*, perhaps the most successful independent Popular Front film of the period. Highlander became an important part of the Popular Front through its music, dance, and drama program, directed by the young Arkansas radical Zilphia Johnson Horton, who attempted to fuse southern vernacular culture with the avant-garde workers theater of the Northeast. She put on plays like Lee Hays's *Gumbo*, the story of a murdered black sharecropper, and collected folk and labor songs for the school's eleven songbooks: it was she who learned the great anthem "We Shall Overcome" from the activists of the Food, Tobacco, and Allied Workers Union and spread it through the movement. Highlander was also the only major labor school to survive the period. If Brookwood and the Bryn Mawr Summer School of the 1920s laid the ground for the CIO generation, Highlander was to lay the ground work for the civil rights movement: Rosa Parks, Fannie Lou Hamer, and Stokely Carmichael were all students at Highlander.[42]

Nonetheless, the urban night schools remained local, and the labor colleges trained a relatively small number of activists and organizers. Thus, in the wake of the defeats of 1937, the CIO sought to build a national movement culture. Gardner Jackson, one of John L. Lewis's key aides, outlined a program aimed at both CIO members and the non-labor population which involved cultivating key newspaper columnists, recruiting sympathetic artists to prepare pamphlets, distributing radio programs like the CIO's newspaper of the air, "Our Daily Bread," and working with the left-wing Frontier Films to produce films portraying the "working man's life against the stark cruelty of the greed-run machine." By the time the CIO's Political Action Committee (CIO-PAC) was founded in 1943, the CIO's cultural offensive was in full swing: the painter and photographer Ben Shahn was hired as the chief artist in CIO-PAC's graphics division, and he produced a series of powerful posters, including the famous image of two welders, *For Full Employment after the War* (Figure 11). At the same time, the UAW, which had taken the lead in producing labor films, cartoons, and radio programs, sponsored the production of a campaign cartoon, *Hell-Bent for Election*, made by former Disney animators.[43]

By 1942, after a long struggle by the labor movement for network radio time, NBC set up a weekly fifteen-minute program called "Labor for Victory", which alternated between the AFL and the CIO. The series told stories of various unions, spoke out against racism, and presented labor's platforms. Whereas the AFL programs favored interviews and round tables, the CIO programs used the techniques of radio drama and drew on Popular Front radio writers and actors. Mike Quin, whose sarcasm and "crisp machine-gun diction" had made his San Francisco ILWU radio show "like a religion all over the waterfront," became the "CIO Reporter on the Air" between 1943 and 1945. Indeed, in the decade between 1937 and 1947, the CIO, together with the education departments of the major industrial unions, began to develop an alternative intellectual world in the United States, a proletarian public sphere.[44]

This proletarian public sphere created the space for labor movement intellectuals; and these figures are in many ways as central to the Popular Front as the more celebrated novelists and literary critics. They included union education staff like Lawrence Rogin and Joe Glazer of the textile workers, Agnes Martocci of the ACWA, Mark Starr and Fannia Cohn of the ILGWU, Tom Tippett (the Brookwood teacher) of the Machinists, Tillie Olsen (like Tippett, a proletarian fiction writer) of the ILWU, and Elizabeth Hawes of the UAW; and labor journalists like Mary Heaton Vorse, Harvey O'Connor of the Federated Press (the author of popular histories of the house of Morgan and of the oil industry), David Erdman of the UAW's *Ammunition* (later a leading Blake scholar), and Len De Caux of the *CIO News*.[45]

Leo Huberman might be taken as an emblem of this group: born in 1903 in Newark, he was a plebeian youth who graduated from high school and normal school and began teaching elementary school at eighteen. Over the next two decades, he traveled, wrote, attended New York University, and worked as an editor. In the early 1940s, he was the labor editor for the Popular Front tabloid, *PM*; a columnist for *U.S. Week*, a short-lived weekly; and, in 1942, the director of education and public relations for the National Maritime Union. The "NMU's apparatus includes some of the slickest trade union literature in the world," *Time* magazine reported of the NMU's bookstore (the first union bookstore in the US), "most of it the work of Leo Huberman." Huberman's lucid books and pamphlets were CIO and Popular Front best sellers, used in union night schools and summer programs: *We, the People,* a popular history of the United States, illustrated by Thomas Hart Benton; *Man's Worldly Goods,* an introduction to socialist economics; *The Labor Spy Racket,* the popularization of the La Follette Committee hearings published in the innovative paper-back series of Modern Age books; *America, Incorporated,* an economic history of the United States; and *The Truth about Unions,* a popular introduction to unionism used by organizers.[46]

These union intellectuals forged links between the labor movement and the cultural organizations of artists and intellectuals. As we shall see, one of the most important consequences of the anti-Communist purge of the unions for American cultural life generally was the collapse of the very notion of a labor intellectual: many of the figures with Popular Front affiliations were forced out of the labor movement, and the links between unions and cultural formations dissolved, as when one of the founders of People's Songs, CIO education director Palmer Webber, quietly cut his ties to the organization in 1947.[47]

If the educational and recreational activities of the industrial unions made up one half of the Popular Front movement culture, the other half was sustained by the fraternal benefit associations, particularly the IWO, the International Workers Order. The IWO grew out of the socialist Jewish subculture that had blossomed in the immigrant ghettoes in the early decades of the century, particularly among garment workers, and that was represented by the Workmen's Circle, a Jewish mutual aid society. The Workmen's Circle was divided between Socialists and Communists through-out the 1920s; and the secession of the left-wing in 1930 led to the creation of the IWO. Like other benefit societies, the IWO was an insurance organization offering sickness, disability, and death benefits; from that base it created a network of lodges, vacation camps, and schools that were centers of culture and recreation in Jewish working-class communities. There were about a hundred elementary schools and three secondary schools that taught Yiddish as well as Jewish culture and the populist, progressive traditions of social justice; at their peak in 1947 they had seven thousand students. Its summer camps—Camp Kinderland for children and Camp Lakeland for adults in upstate New York—where labor activists came to speak and singers and musicians like Pete Seeger, Leadbelly, and Paul Robeson performed, became an important part of the socialization into the Popular Front social movement and its culture. In some cases, entire cooperative housing projects were part of the Popular Front culture: the famous United Workers Cooperative Colony, the "Coops," housed several thousand Yiddish-speaking immigrant workers—mostly Communist or pro-Communist garment workers—on Allerton Avenue in the Bronx.[48]

Though ethnic benefit societies and insurance organizations suffered and often collapsed in the depression, the IWO became the fastest growing fraternal benefit society in the United States in the 1930s, from about 3,000 members in 1930 to 165,000 in 1940.[49] Its success had three sources: its low-cost insurance; its pan-ethnic organization; and its Popular Front anti-Fascist political culture. The costs of the IWO's insurance were very low; moreover, the IWO offered insurance to all working people at the same rate, regardless of occupation or race. Thus, the IWO became strong among workers in high-risk occupations, like coal-miners, and among black Americans, because it was one of the few national insurance carriers that did not charge blacks higher rates than whites. Moreover, unlike earlier ethnic benefit societies, including the Workmen's Circle, from which it had split, the IWO quickly became a federation of allied ethnic benefit societies. In some cases, existing nationality societies merged into the IWO: the Hungarian Workingmen's Sick Benefit and Educational Association joined in 1932; the Slovak Workers' Society in 1933; the Russian National Mutual Aid Society in 1935; and the Finnish Workers' Federation in 1941. In other cases, the IWO's leaders built new nationality sections: the Garibaldi-American Fraternal Society in 1931; the Ukrainian-American Fraternal Union and the Polonia Society in 1932; the Rumanian-American Fraternal Society in 1934; the Croatian Benevolent Fraternity in 1935; the Serbian-American Fraternal Society and the Cervantes Fraternal Society (a Latino section that was largely Puerto Rican) in 1938; the Carpatho-Russian Peoples Society in 1939; and the Hellenic-American Brotherhood in 1942. However, not all IWO lodges were organized by nationality: the English or General section, which included black members, was the second-largest section.

Indeed, throughout its history, the IWO wrestled with the conflicting demands of ethnic autonomy and working-class universalism. The IWO's general secretary, Max Bedacht, had led the attempt to transform the organization from a Jewish fraternal order into a multi-national organiz-ation, and he encouraged the growth of the English-language General sections: Bedacht saw the IWO as an increasingly "American" working-class organization. But the section leaders fought for greater independence in order both to work in ethnic alliances (like the American Slav Congress, the National Negro Congress, El Congreso del Pueblo de Habla Española, and the American Jewish Congress) and to compete with conservative church-based nationalist associations. The IWO had long opposed segre-gated Jim Crow lodges, but by the mid 1940s black members were calling for greater autonomy. In 1944, the section leaders succeeded in gaining greater autonomy for the nationality groups and in instituting the Lincoln-Douglass Society for black members.[50]

Though these tensions between ethnic nationalism and working-class internationalism often led to internal conflicts, the IWO's symbolic fusion of ethnicity and Americanism was responsible for its success. For the pan-ethnic internationalism of the IWO allowed second-generation ethnic workers to preserve their own language and cultural traditions while participating in an interracial and multi-national federation defined by its labor radicalism and its opposition to fascism. The IWO developed alongside the CIO and the Popular Front. In the steel towns of Ohio and Pennsylvania, the IWO lodge hall not only provided meeting places and mobilized support for the Steel Workers Organizing Committee, but, with its Hungarian, Yiddish, Slovak, Polish, and Croatian language newspapers, successfully united steelworkers across national and racial boundaries. The IWO lodges in Flint and Detroit provided a base in the Southern and Eastern European communities for the UAW organizers at General Motors and Ford. And the IWO lodges mobilized anti-Fascist opposition not only to Hitler and Franco but also to the Horthy regime in Hungary and to Mussolini's invasion of Ethiopia.[51]

This labor and anti-Fascist activism was tied to the cultural life of the communities. IWO lodges held dances and picnics, basketball and softball tournaments, concerts and folk festivals, film showings and pageants. They sponsored schools, choral groups, dance groups, theater groups, and literary study circles. The Order's newspaper, *New Order* (and later *Fraternal Outlook*), was published in every language of the federation, and several sections had their own newspapers. Books of poetry and prose—notably Langston Hughes's poetry collection, *A New Song*—were published and distributed. An IWO concert and lecture bureau organized programs for lodges, and figures like Langston Hughes, Paul Robeson, and Rockwell Kent (the painter and book illustrator who served as president of the IWO) toured the country for the IWO. Carleton Moss's 1941 pageant, "The Negro in American Life," featured Paul Robeson in a dramatization of major events in African American history. The Harlem branch of the IWO, Lodge 691, led by Louise Thompson, was a particularly active one; it sponsored the Harlem Suitcase Theater, directed by Langston Hughes, which met in the IWO Community Center at 317 West 125th Street and produced Hughes's *Don't You Want to Be Free.*[52]

The Puerto Rican lodges in New York—including the Mutualista Obrera Puertorriqueña, IWO Lodge 4792, and the Club Obrero Español, IWO Lodge 4763—were crucial supporters of the Hispanic political theater, which flourished under the leadership of the actress, director, and playwright Marita Reid. They also sponsored their own amateur companies, which performed to raise funds for ambulances and medical aid for the Spanish Republicans. The Cervantes Fraternal Society, led in New York by Jesus Colon, organized a Puerto Rican People's Chorus and childrens dance ensembles. In general, however, the IWO was strongest in the Northeast and in the heavily Slavic and Eastern European steel towns of the Great Lakes industrial corridor. With the exception of Los Angeles, where the IWO thrived among Jewish garment workers and where there was a Mexican American lodge, the Lázaro Cárdenas Society, there were few lodges in the South and West, and no Asian American lodges.[53]

Like the Popular Front labor schools, the IWO reached its peak in the two years after World War II; indeed, though most historians continue to see the Nazi-Soviet Pact of 1939 as the end of the Popular Front, it is clear that the movement culture of the Popular Front sustained itself through the war years and into the immediate post-war period, with its hopes for a "people's century." There were challenges to the IWO in the post-war years, both from conservative church-oriented ethnic associations and from the new state entitlements that returning veterans received in the GI Bill. But it was the right-wing attack on this movement culture that destroyed it. The labor schools and the IWO lodges were included on the Attorney General's list of "subversive organizations" and were investigated and raided; members could no longer expect to hold federal jobs. The IWO, which was "the largest, most successful left-wing organization in modern American history," was a particular target; and in the only court case in American history in which an insurance company was prosecuted for its political views (there was never any question about its financial health or practices), the IWO was liquidated and its assets taken over by the state of New York.[54]

But the cultural front was not only the movement culture of the Popular Front social movement; it was also, as I have suggested, a child of the federal government and the culture industries, and this is why it moved from the precincts of the avant-garde and the labor movement to reshape United States culture generally. Indeed, it was the growing influence of the cultural front in the state cultural apparatuses and the major cultural industries that provoked the cultural civil war known as the "red scare" or "McCarthyism."

3. The State Apparatus

The development of relief projects for artists and teachers during the first New Deal meant that many plebeian artists found work writing, painting, and performing for the federal government, and they brought the aesthetics and politics of the proletarian avant-garde and the labor movement culture into the arts projects of Federal One. I have already noted how local unions made use of the WPA's Workers' Education Project to develop night schools. The creation of the Federal Theater in 1935 drained much of the talent of the impoverished workers theater movement, as the Theatre Union disbanded and Artef lost members. The Theatre of Action (the Workers Laboratory Theatre) was incorporated directly into the FTP as the One-Act Experimental Theatre; Alfred Saxe and Nicholas Ray of the Shock Troupe went to the FTP's Living Newspaper; the Harlem theater group around Rose McClendon became part of the Federal Negro Theatre; the dancers of the New Dance League dominated the Federal Theatre Dance Project in New York; and Orson Welles assembled a number of young radicals in the FTP's Project 891.[55]

The poets and fiction writers who had published in the proletarian magazines wrote tour guides and collected folklore on the Writers Project: Jack Conroy, whose *Disinherited* was perhaps the most successful radical novel, is a good example. Conroy worked on four different writers projects: in 1936 and 1937, he worked in St Louis on the state guidebook of the Missouri Writers Project, though his contributions on the Ozarks and Cape Girardeau were eventually cut. In 1938, he moved to Chicago and worked on the industrial folklore project inspired by radical folklorist Benjamin A. Botkin; along with Nelson Algren, he collected a number of railroad stories, mining narratives, and factory tall tales, some of which appeared in Botkin's popular *Treasury of American Folklore* (1944), and others of which grew into the children's stories he wrote with Arna Bontemps. When the folklore project folded in 1939, Conroy joined a group, led by the dancer and anthropologist Katherine Dunham, which was exploring black storefront religions; and when Dunham left, Conroy was assigned to Horace Cayton's Project 30068, where he worked with Arna Bontemps on a study of "The Negro in Illinois." Though it was shut down in 1941, this work provided the basis for two major studies of black migration, both published in 1945: St Clair Drake and Horace Cayton's *Black Metropolis*, and Conroy and Arna Bontemps's *They Seek a City*.[56]

A number of the young proletarian painters of the John Reed Clubs became muralists decorating federal buildings for the Treasury Department and the Federal Art Project: William Gropper painted a Department of Interior mural, *Reclamation*, in Washington; Stuart Davis painted the abstract mural, *Swing Landscape*, for the Williamsburg Housing Project; and Philip Guston and Anton Refregier did WPA murals at the 1939 New York World's Fair. Many other young radical painters worked for the Federal Art Project producing easel paintings: Jack Levine's *The Feast of Pure Reason* (1937), Jacob Lawrence's *The Life of Harriet Tubman* (1939), and Jackson Pollock's *Man, Bull, Bird* (1938–41) were all painted for the FAP. And several of the young camera workers of the Film and Photo League got jobs making photographs and films for various parts of Federal One.[57]

Some radical young orchestral musicians found work on the Federal Music Project, but very few composers were employed; nevertheless, the FMP's Composers' Forum-Laboratory did premier the work of several radical composers, including Marc Blitzstein, Hanns Eisler, and Ruth Crawford. Charles Seeger, who had been active in the Composers Collective, was hired as assistant to the director of the Federal Music Project, and he initiated the collecting and recording of folk musics, particularly of Mexican American musics in the Southwest. Other members of the Composers Collective, including Blitzstein and Earl Robinson, were hired to compose music for Federal Theatre Project productions.[58]

The employment of young radical plebeian artists and writers by the relief projects had profound effects, greater than might be imagined given the relatively short life of Federal One. Though the project directors who sympathized with the radical artists were rare—Hallie Flanagan, the Vassar theater professor, had sponsored the radical theater at Vassar and continued to foster it in the projects; and the aristocratic painter George Biddle (of the Treasury Department's PWAP program) hoped the muralists would do for Roosevelt what the Mexican muralists had done for Obregon—many of the lower-level supervisors and directors, the 10 percent of WPA employees who were "non-relief," had been drawn to the projects because of their own populist and radical sentiments. So figures like Orson Welles, John Houseman, and Joseph Losey in the Federal Theatre Project, Benjamin Botkin in the Federal Writers Project, Charles Seeger in the Federal Music Project, photographer Berenice Abbott, who supervised the photographic division of the Art Project, and cultural historian Constance Rourke, who was the editor of the Index of American Design, actively supported the work of the radical young artists on relief. Thus, the federal arts projects became a crucial site where alliances were formed between the plebeian radicals and the established artists and intellectuals who dominated the non-relief personnel.

However, by no means were all of Federal One's supervisors sympathetic to the left: Federal Art Project director Edward Bruce wanted to stop the "Mexican invasion on the border" (referring to the influence of the muralists); and Federal Music Project director Nikolai Sokoloff maintained that "skits of the John Reed Club" had no place in federally sponsored concerts. As a result, many battles over the politics of project productions erupted, particularly in the closely watched worlds of theater and mural painting. As we shall see, the Federal Theatre's production of *The Cradle Will Rock* was halted, and its unofficial production was a celebrated event. There were several battles with state and city administrators: Chicago's mayor halted a production of Meyer Levin's *Model Tenements*; a California administrator stopped a production of *Stevedore*; and the Harlem Community Arts Center, directed by Gwendolyn Bennett, was shut down.

Moreover, there were many less visible incidents as well: an unknown young radical painter, Jackson Pollock, was fired for being a Communist sympathizer. When the Dies Committee began its hearings into un-American activities in the fall of 1938, the theater and writers projects were early targets, and the negative publicity resulted in the closure of the Federal Theatres in 1939.[59]

In an understandable reaction to the Dies Committee's exaggerations about both the numbers of Communists in Federal One and the political radicalism of its productions, recent historians have generally emphasized Federal One's overall *lack* of radicalism. And it is surely true that the great majority of project productions—murals, plays, guidebooks, concerts, and radio shows—were not radical, but shared the middlebrow nationalism and domesticity of the aesthetics of regionalism and the "American scene." Since the arts projects were locally based, the presence of the left in particular arts projects depended on the strength of the Popular Front social movement in particular cities and towns. But it is worth recalling the importance of the young plebeian radicals who produced the most lasting productions of the arts projects—the Negro *Macbeth*, *The Cradle Will Rock*, the murals of Stuart Davis, and the paintings of Jacob Lawrence, among others—and the influence of left-wing politics and aesthetics on the young artists and intellectuals of the projects.[60]

The relief projects were a remarkable version of government-sponsored culture because the employees were recruited from the relief rolls; they were not ordinary government workers. However, as I suggested earlier, the New Deal expansion of the state apparatuses extended far beyond the relief projects, and, as radical young lawyers, labor activists, and intellectuals were hired by government bureaucracies, political and cultural battles increasingly took place within, as well as outside and against, federal agencies and departments. For the cultural left, the experience of the Resettlement Administration and the Office of War Information was particularly important. The Resettlement Administration, directed by Rexford Tugwell, was, along with Jerome Frank's Agricultural Adjustment Administration, one of the more radical New Deal programs housed in Henry Wallace's Department of Agriculture. The Resettlement Administration attempted to address rural poverty by setting up experimental communal farms, by establishing green-belt model communities for unemployed workers, and by building housing for migrants. The Resettlement Administration (later renamed the Farm Security Administration [FSA]) hired photographers, filmmakers, artists, and musicians to work on these projects: their most celebrated accomplishment was, of course, the vast archive of documentary photographs of sharecroppers and migrant workers taken by such figures as Ben Shahn, Dorothea Lange, Walker Evans, Marion Post Walcott, and Gordon Parks, under the direction of Roy

Stryker. However, the Resettlement Administration also hired Pare Lorentz, an established film critic, to make two successful documentary films, *The Plow That Broke the Plains* and *The River*, the first of which employed the radical filmmakers of Nykino as cameramen. Charles Seeger became the music program director for the RA, placing musicians in the new communities in an attempt to build community through music and recreation; and Nicholas Ray became the director of theater activities, staging community pageants and recording music in Arkansas, North Carolina, Tennessee, and Pennsylvania. Similarly, Ben Shahn painted a mural for the Hightstown, New Jersey, homestead for garment workers. As the sculptor Lenore Thomas later recalled, "the planning wasn't formal. . . . Each of us decided what he wanted to do and did it. Charles Seeger travelled through the country making recordings and studying folk songs, Ben Shahn travelled through the country with his camera and painted frescoes in certain communities, I did sculptures for different communities, and lived in one of them, in Tennessee, for several months. That gives the impression of an artists' paradise, and I suppose it was one."[61]

In 1941, the Resettlement Administration's Historical Unit was transferred to the Office of War Information, and this shift paralleled that of a number of the New Deal cultural radicals. Though the anti-fascist Popular Front had been split by the Nazi-Soviet Pact and the beginning of the war in Europe, with pro-Soviet leftists and anti-war activists at odds with Popular Front interventionists, the invasion of the Soviet Union and the attack on Pearl Harbor led most of the left to see the war as an anti-fascist struggle that would eventually strengthen Popular Front and anti-imperialist resistance movements throughout the world. Thus, when Roosevelt created the federal information agencies, the domestic Office of Facts and Figures (OFF) and the overseas Office of the Coordinator of Information (OCI)— (both of which were incorporated into the Office of War Information (OWI])—a number of Popular Front and émigré anti-fascists were brought in to mount the wartime propaganda effort, particularly under Archibald MacLeish, director of OFF, and Robert Sherwood, director of the OCI's Foreign Information Service.

Ben Shahn worked for the OWI throughout 1942 and 1943 designing posters, only two of which were ever printed. Dorothea Lange, who had been laid off by the FSA several times, was hired by the War Relocation Agency to document the internment of Japanese Americans and later worked for the OWI, photographing ethnic and racial minority communities in the Bay Area. John Houseman, who, together with Orson Welles, had gone from the Federal Theatre to produce the radio Mercury Theatre of the Air, was brought in by Sherwood to create overseas radio propaganda: the result, the "Voice of America", drew on a number of Popular Front and émigré radicals. Nicholas Ray, who had worked with Alan Lomax on folk-music radio programs, directed the music programs, featuring Woody Guthrie, Josh White, Leadbelly, and the Almanac Singers. Howard Fast worked for "Voice of America"'s English feature desk; André Breton worked on the French desk; and Bertolt Brecht on the German desk. The Japanese American radical writer Ayako Ishigaki and painter Eitaro Ishigaki both worked for the OWI.[62]

Throughout the war, however, battles raged within and without the federal government over the Popular Front figures in the OFF, the OCI, and the OWI. Not only was there congressional opposition from Republicans, who felt that the information agencies were simply propaganda for the New Deal itself, but there were also struggles within the Roosevelt administration between the corporate war aims of the military and the State Department and the Popular Front liberal anti-fascism. Whereas the State Department was unwilling to support the French resistance, the information agency anti-fascists supported the European resistance movements and Popular Front coalitions, and opposed the US collaboration with the Vichy government. These ideological and strategic controversies lay beneath the continual battles over the left-wing affiliations of information agency employees. One of the early battles involved the critic and editor Malcolm Cowley, who was appointed to the Office of Facts and Figures by Archibald MacLeish in 1942; after Martin Dies led a campaign against Cowley's Popular Front connections, Cowley resigned. The novelist Josephine Herbst was fired from the German desk of the Office of the Coordinator of Information in early 1942. The Almanac Singers, the Popular Front folk group including Pete Seeger, Woody Guthrie, and Lee Hays, were part of a national OFF radio broadcast, "This Is War", in early 1942, and were attacked in the press and dropped from the OWI. By 1944, Houseman and Ray themselves were forced out of "Voice of America."[63]

Although the federally supported "people's theaters" and Living Newspapers were closed down, and many of the murals painted over, and the Popular Front vision of the anti-fascist war was defeated by the corporate vision of an American Century in the OWI (and in its successor, the USIA), nevertheless the cultural front in the state apparatus had significant effects. There is no doubt that the avant-garde iconoclasm of the proletarian moment was tempered; if traces of the proletarian aesthetic remain in San Francisco's Coit Tower murals and in the Living Newspapers, for the most part, the arts projects and federal information agencies changed the work of the radical artists, reinforcing populist iconography and diluting experimental forms and techniques. On the other hand, the audiences attracted by the arts projects and the information agencies were wider than those the radical theaters had ever achieved, and they were more working class than those of the mainstream Broadway theater. Perhaps more significantly, the contradictory and embattled place of cultural radicals in government agencies, including the state university systems, was to become a fundamental part of cultural politics in the second half of the century.

4. The Culture Industries

The most controversial legacy of the cultural front lay in its impact on the culture industries, on mass culture. On the one hand, the right wing in the United States—the alliance of nativists, Catholic fascists, southern white supremacists, and nationalist, labor-intensive corporations—denounced the Popular Front "infiltration" of the mass media as a conspiracy orchestrated by the Communist Party and supplemented the congressional investigations of film, broadcasting, and recording with scores of newsletters and pamphlets "exposing" the red menace in the mass media. Curiously, however, many on the left also denounced the unholy alliance between the Popular Front and the image factories and celebrity machines of Hollywood and Tin Pan Alley as a betrayal of a radical culture, a betrayal of either working-class and folk authenticity or of modernist experiment and aesthetic integrity.

However, neither the tales of Communist commissars in Hollywood nor the aesthetic and political handwringing over the moral bankruptcy of Hollywood radicals explains the successes and failures of the cultural front in mass culture. Rather, it was the peculiar combination of the corporate liberalism of the media corporations, the internal labor relations of the culture industries, and the working-class audience of the film, broadcasting, and music industries that resulted in a remarkable and contradictory politics of mass culture, producing the phenomena of left-wing "stars" and "socially conscious" nightclubs, radio broadcasts, and picture magazines.

Two developments within the culture industry allowed the emergence of this laborist, social democratic left with its "aesthetics of social significance." On the one hand, the private industries that manufactured culture, and the private foundations that subsidized culture, became a center for the emerging "multi-national liberalism" or "corporate liberalism," the loose ideology that united those investment bankers and capital-intensive industries that came to support Roosevelt's new historical bloc; this enabled the emergence of a number of left-wing "producers" in the culture industries. On the other hand, a new culture industry unionism emerged among the plebeian workforce of the factories of news and entertainment, bringing both "hacks" and "stars" into the social movement of the Popular Front.[64]

One can see both of these forces at work in the peculiar history of Henry Luce's magazine and newsreel empire, in which a surprising number of Popular Front figures found work. Some were recruited at the top; others were part of the magazine's rank and file. The figures at the top—the equivalents of Hollywood's "producers"—included Luce's Yale friends, the poet Archibald MacLeish and the *New Yorker* journalist Ralph Ingersoll, both of whom were hired to run *Fortune*, a magazine devoted to American business, established in 1929. Luce was a self-conscious propagandist for American business, celebrating investment bankers and corporate leaders on the covers of *Time*. Almost a third of *Time* covers in 1929 were businessmen, including NBC's David Sarnoff, Standard Oil's Walter Teagle, and Thomas Lamont of the Morgan banks; General Electric's Owen Young was *Time*'s Man of the Year. Many of these, moreover, were the leaders of the multi-national bloc that would move toward Roosevelt's Democratic Party by 1936; and Luce's magazines, like the Astor/Harriman *Newsweek*, as well as the radio networks and the major foundations, were the public face of this multi-national bloc. But if Luce's intentions were hagiographic—his own *Fortune* article on Pittsburgh was a paean to the gentle industrial paternalism of the Mellons—MacLeish and Ingersoll assembled a group of young Ivy-League writers, including James Agee and Dwight Macdonald, who moved to the left during the depression and produced a host of serious, critical portraits of American capitalism. "Luce was divided between his pro-business convictions and his journalistic instinct, which told him the CIO was news and that the wonders of American Cyanamid Co. weren't," Dwight Macdonald later wrote. "He compromised (as did we) and for a few years *Fortune* was a pastiche of mildly liberal articles on 'social' themes and reluctantly written 'corporation pieces'."[65]

By the mid 1930s, conflicts had broken out on *Fortune* and within Time Inc. Dwight Macdonald resigned in 1936 when Luce objected to his four-part series on US Steel; Macdonald went on to write an exposé of the "Lucepapers" for the *Nation*. Luce himself announced in a series of internal memos that in the struggle between labor and capital, *Fortune* was on the side of capital. In late 1936, a profile of southern sharecroppers by James Agee and Walker Evans was rejected by *Fortune*; it later became *Let Us Now Praise Famous Men*. A major struggle took place over *Time*'s coverage of the Spanish Civil War; MacLeish had become an active figure in the Popular Front and objected to *Time*'s support for the fascists. By the summer of 1938, MacLeish had quit, and Ralph Ingersoll followed in the spring of 1939, going on to establish the Popular Front tabloid, *PM*.[66]

However, one cannot underestimate the importance of the moment of corporate liberalism in the culture industries and the foundations; though it was surely never radical or anti-capitalist, the competitions and internal struggles between capitalists nevertheless allowed a space—always compromised and always under siege—in which populist, laborist, and anti-fascist productions appeared. Indeed, despite Luce's own conservative politics, the innovations in mass journalism his magazines and newsreels pioneered—the techniques of documentary reenactment in the radio and film *March of Time*, the photojournalism of *Life*, and the investigative journalism of *Fortune*—led him to recruit the very artists, writers, and photographers who were drawn to the Popular Front social movement. The young proletarian novelist Robert Cantwell wrote for *Time* and *Fortune*, and several of Orson Welles's Mercury Theatre group, including Welles, had been anonymous actors for the *March of Time*, dramatically recreating news events on the radio. Through the 1940s, the art editors of *Fortune* featured the works of such Popular Front artists as Jacob Lawrence (reproducing his *Migration of the Negro* series), Ben Shahn, and Miné Okubo.[67]

If the MacLeish-Ingersoll *Fortune* represents the cultural front at the top, the emergence of the Time Inc. unit of the Newspaper Guild represents the rank-and-file cultural front. The Newspaper Guild was one of the new culture industry unions to emerge in 1933 and 1934, and a group of Communists and leftists (including Dwight Macdonald) organized a Time Inc. unit, fighting through 1937 and 1938 to gain recognition: "the *Time* unit of the Guild," as Whittaker Chambers later wrote with disdain, "was made up of a proletariat of file clerks, office boys, and other unskilled intellectuals whose interests the Communists were peculiarly solicitous of, for their numbers gave the Communists control. . . . [T]he unit also included a sizable group of responsible writers and researchers, most of them college graduates." In 1939, the Communists at *Time* published a shop paper, *High Time*, criticizing Luce's authoritarianism and *Time*'s pro-fascist foreign coverage.[68]

It was these rank-and-file culture industry workers—"unskilled intellectuals" in Whittaker Chambers's curious formulation—who were largely responsible for the Popular Front's influence on mass culture. These writers, actors, photographers, and artists had escaped the shops and factories in which their parents had labored, and found work in advertising, the mass magazines, and the radio and film industries, bringing their Popular Front politics with them. "Never as in the Thirties, when history proclaimed itself every day in the significances of daily struggle, could a story in *Time* have seemed so significant to a writer," Alfred Kazin wrote in his acid portrait of "Harriet," a young Marxist active in the campaign to support the Spanish Loyalists who worked for *Time*. Harriet had started as a researcher at *Time*, "an enterprise where women alone could be depended on to organize facts for a 'story' and then check their accuracy, putting a dot over each word, after the writer, who had to be male, had handed in *his* copy." After talking herself into a writer's job, "the writing of a story . . . became to Harriet a scholarly feat because of the masses of uncollected facts that had to be collected, and a literary feat because of the harsh stylistic frame to which a story had to be fitted. But if you pleased the row of bosses waiting to pass on your copy, you got paid well, praised as only great writers are ever praised, and felt that you were an artist, of sorts." Though Kazin's portrait reeks of a condescension—"she could never forgive me for not regarding her as an artist"—all too typical of the New York intellectuals, it nevertheless gives a sense of the contradictions faced by the young employees of the culture industry studios.[69]

Like the radicals in government agencies, the artists of the culture industries saw their work cut, cropped, and censored: "it was worse than going to jail," screenwriter Lester Cole recalled, "the evisceration of a politically meaningful script cut right into my soul." And just as many historians have come to minimize the radicalism of the New Deal arts projects, so many historians of the Hollywood studios have concluded that the studio radicals had little influence on the movies: "if the majority of the films made from their scripts seem politically indistinguishable from the films made from the scripts of non-radical screenwriters," Larry Ceplair and Steven Englund conclude, "it is not necessarily because they lacked skill or determination, but because the studio executives were more skilled and determined—and by far more powerful." However, this generalization about "the majority of films" misses the continual battle by studio radicals to make films of "social significance." As several recent critics have shown, that battle took place in the internal bureaucratic struggles over scripts and final cuts, as gestures and lines, characters and endings, were challenged by producers and the Breen censorship office. There were successes, particularly among the anti-fascist war films and the B-movie genres of crime and horror melodramas, but for the most part the released films are compromise formations that need to be read against the archive of treatments, rewrites, and script conferences. Indeed, perhaps the most lasting emblems of the culture industry radicals are the *noir* thrillers they wrote: "the *noir* of the 1930s and 1940s," Mike Davis has argued, "became a conduit for the resentments of writers in the velvet trap of the studio system . . . [and] repainted the image of Los Angeles as a deracinated urban hell." It is perhaps not surprising that the studio system of *Time* and *Life* produced its own *noir* classic when Kenneth Fearing, a proletarian poet who had worked in the Luce empire, imagined the murder of a Luce-like figure in the 1946 thriller, *The Big Clock*.[70]

But if the impact of the studio radicals on the cultural commodities they produced is hard to judge, their impact on the new unionism of the culture industries is much clearer. Several culture industry unions had formed in the early part of the century, particularly among theater workers, musicians, and teachers, but few of them were thriving by the early years of the depression. The International Alliance of Theatrical Stage Employees and Moving Picture Operators (IATSE), organized in 1893, was a powerful alliance of stagecraft workers, but it had come under the control of Chicago gangsters in the early 1930s. Actors' Equity, formed in 1913 and affiliated with the AFL in 1919, was a union of theater actors, which had won a historic strike in August 1919 with the support of IATSE and the musicians union. It achieved an Equity shop in the theater industry by 1924, but its attempts to organize screen actors had failed. The success of the actors in 1919 led playwrights to form the successful Dramatists' Guild in 1920, as a branch of the Authors' League of America.[71]

Musicians had been organized since the late nineteenth century, and the AFL's American Federation of Musicians, formed in 1896, had grown into a large and powerful union. But its gains were threatened by the challenge talking pictures and sound recording represented to live music, and by 1934, membership had declined dramatically from its peak in 1929. Teachers unions also went back to the turn of the century in Chicago, and the American Federation of Teachers had been organized in 1916; but it too had shrunk by the early years of the depression.

It was the prairie fire of union organizing sparked by Roosevelt's National Industrial Recovery Act of 1933, with its declaration of labor's right to representatives of its own choosing, that rekindled culture industry unionism. In some cases, the unions grew out of campaigns for relief for unemployed artists and writers. The young activists of New York's John Reed Club helped form an Unemployed Writers' Group and an Unemployed Artists' Group in 1933; they were soon transformed into the Writers Union and the Artists Union. The Writers Union, led by the left-wing writer, Robert Whitcomb, whose *Talk United States* was one of the most interesting experimental radical works of the time, was most active in New York, attracting two hundred aspiring unemployed writers to its weekly meetings; in the winter of 1935, it organized picket lines around New York and a Conference of Professional, Cultural and White Collar Workers, which called for white-collar relief programs. The Writers Union went on to represent writers on the Federal Writers Project, organizing sit-ins and strikes in 1936 and 1937; however, like many efforts to organize writers, it remained weak. The Artists Union was more successful, forming locals in a number of cities, bargaining for artists working on the Federal Art Projects and campaigning for the unsuccessful Federal Arts Bill. In 1937, the Artists Union, together with the Commercial Artists and Designers Union, an AFL federal union, and the independent Cartoonists Guild, affiliated with the CIO's new white-collar union, the United Office and Professional Workers of America (UOPWA-CIO), as United American Artists, Local 60 of UOPWA-CIO, with the illustrator and painter Rockwell Kent as president.[72]

The organization of writers and artists was closely tied to white-collar organizing generally; the first successful strike in the publishing industry was the 1934 Macaulay strike, led by the Office Workers Union, an independent left-wing union. It was, according to the *New Masses* labor reporter, "one of the first white-collar strikes to rally professionals to assist clerical workers." The Office Workers Union was one of several independent unions that joined Lewis Merrill's New York local of the Bookkeepers, Stenographers and Accountants Union (BSAU-AFL) to form the CIO's UOPWA in 1937. The mainstays of the Communist-led UOPWA were the insurance agents and office workers in the big three of Metropolitan Life, Prudential, and John Hancock; but it also organized stenographers, bank clerks, bookkeepers, typists, artists, engineers, architects, and the office employees of CBS Radio.[73]

Perhaps the most successful of the NIRA white-collar unions was the Newspaper Guild, which was summoned into existence by Heywood Broun's famous call for a union of newspaper writers in his 7 August 1933 New York *World Telegram* column: "Beginning at nine o'clock on the morning of October 1," Broun wrote, "I am going to do the best I can to help in getting one [a newspaper writers union] up. I think I could die happy on the opening day of the general strike if I had the privilege of watching Walter Lippman heave half a brick through a *Tribune* window at a non-union operative who had been called in to write the current Today and Tomorrow column on the gold standard." Broun never got to see Lippman heave that brick, but, by the end of 1933, the Newspaper Guild had been organized with Broun as its first president. After major strikes in Newark, Milwaukee, and Seattle between 1934 and 1936, the militant guild had made important inroads in the Hearst and Scripps-Howard chains, and, as we have seen, in Time Inc; in 1937, the Guild affiliated with the fledgling CIO. The Newspaper Guild was a crucial part of the Popular Front social movement in a number of cities, and Broun became a key spokesman of the Popular Front in the years before his death in 1939.[74]

Unions also made some headway in the broadcasting industry. NBC organized a company union of technical employees in 1933 and 1934, but it broke away from the company with organizing drives in the late 1930s; by 1940, it had renamed itself the National Association of Broadcast Engineers and Technicians (NABET), and it joined the CIO in 1951. Radio performers in New York and Los Angeles came together in the spring of 1937 to form the American Federation of Radio Artists (later, with the addition of television performers, AFTRA). Chartered by the AFL, it organized both local stations, beginning with KMOX in St Louis, and the networks themselves. The Radio Writers' Guild was formed in 1937 under the auspices of the Authors' League of America, but it remained the weakest of the four writers' guilds (authors, dramatists, screen, and radio).[75]

However, the most dramatic union struggles in the culture industry took place in the film industry. The Hollywood studio unions were also a product of the NRA period. The Screen Actors' Guild was formed in 1933 with Eddie Cantor as its president; it affiliated with the AFL in 1934 and was recognized by the producers in May 1937, after the threat of strike. The moribund Screen Writers' Guild was revived in 1933 with the left-wing playwright John Howard Lawson as its president; but the writers' struggle for recognition met the determined opposition of both the studios and a rival organization, the Screen Playwrights, as well as the domination of Hollywood labor by the gangster-led IATSE. The SWG won a National Labor Relations Board election in 1938, but it was not until 1941, the year of the Hollywood cartoonists strike discussed below, that the producers signed an agreement with the SWG. The long battle to organize the screen guilds was a central part of the Hollywood Popular Front, radicalizing the writers, artists, and musicians who worked in the studios. The screen guilds also supported the wartime Hollywood Writers Mobilization and the Los Angeles labor school, the People's Educational Center. After the war, the Conference of Studio Unions brought together an alliance of AFL, CIO, and independent unions in a powerful united front against the studios, resulting in a successful eight-month strike in 1945, part of the massive post-war strike wave in the fall and winter of 1945–46.[76]

The Hollywood and broadcasting blacklists and the state and federal legislative investigations were as much about the growing powers of these new unions as about the contents of movies or music. The 1947 congressional investigations of Hollywood (which led to the imprisonment of the Hollywood Ten) were largely provoked by the post-war strikes led by the Conference of Studio Unions; and the red scare in Hollywood did eventually destroy the CSU. At the same time, the 1947 congressional investigation of James Petrillo's powerful American Federation of Musicians was provoked less by the presence of Communists in New York's Local 802 than by the success of the recording ban of 1942–44. The musicians union had rebuilt itself in the late 1930s and early 1940s and had responded to the use of recorded music in broadcasting with a 27-month ban on recording, winning a record royalty to go to a relief fund for unemployed musicians. The Lea Act of 1946, which attempted to curb the effectiveness of the musicians union, was the beginning of the anti-union legislation that culminated in the Taft-Hartley Act of 1947.[77]

As in the CIO's mass-production unions, the investigations of union Communists came to dominate internal union struggles, particularly after the Taft-Hartley Act's imposition of the non-Communist affidavit for union officials. The left-wing of the Screen Writers' Guild, represented by the editors of *The Screen Writer*, Dalton Trumbo and Gordon Kahn, was removed in 1947 as the HUAC hearings began. The American Federation of Teachers had grown rapidly in the Popular Front years (from 13,700 in 1935 to 32,000 in 1939) under the presidency of Jerome Davis, who had been fired from Yale University for his support of labor unions and for his Popular Front book, *Capitalism and its Culture*. In 1939, New York's version of HUAC, the Rapp-Coudert committee, began its attack on the teachers union and City College; in its aftermath, an anti-Communist alliance took over the AFT and expelled the Communist-led locals in New York and Philadelphia. In the years after the war, similar struggles took place within the Newspaper Guild, the New York Local 802 of the AFM, and the American Federation of Radio Artists, as left-wing leaders and activists were defeated or forced out. The unions in which the left remained strong—notably the United Office and Professional Workers—were expelled in the CIO's purge of left-wing unions.[78]

It is difficult to overstate the importance of the new unions for the cultural front. Though their strength and numbers never rivaled those of the CIO's industrial unions, and they were not successful in organizing the great mass of office workers, school teachers, and government employees (that was not to happen until the great white-collar and public-employee drives of the 1960s and 1970s), they had a disproportionate effect on performers and artists, who came to feel directly connected to the union struggles of American working people. Moreover, since the idea of white-collar and professional unionism had been largely confined to the left, and since the union activists were often the alumni of the proletarian avant-garde, the culture industry unions were often led by Communists and Popular Front leftists. As a result, the struggle to organize and maintain these culture industry unions radicalized and mobilized the rank and file of the cultural front.

The ability of these rank-and-file studio workers in the recording, broadcasting, and film industries to create works of popular art that embodied their laborist, social democratic values depended on two other components of the cultural front: Popular Front producers in the studios; and independent production companies and institutions. Producers were key figures in the culture industry, mediating between the studio executives and financiers on the one hand, and the contract writers and performers on the other. In some cases, these producers forged alliances between star performers and the Popular Front social movement through benefit performances; in other cases, they enabled the work of radical writers and artists to be produced and distributed. The most important left-wing producers in the recording industry, John Hammond and Norman Granz, were examples of the first type. Hammond not only produced the successful records of jazz musicians like Teddy Wilson, Benny Goodman, Count Basie, and Billie Holiday, but he helped organize benefit concerts for the Scottsboro Nine and the Spanish Loyalists. Hammond was one of the first producers to record racially integrated bands; he wrote pseudony-mous attacks on the exploitation of recording artists for the *New Masses*; and he produced the landmark Spirituals to Swing concerts of 1938 and 1939 that presented a remarkable range of African American vernacular musics and brought musicians like Sonny Terry, Meade Lux Lewis, and the Golden Gate Quartet to national attention. Similarly, Norman Granz not only produced the recordings of many bebop musicians but organized the famous 1944 benefit concert for the Sleepy Lagoon defendants, the first Jazz at the Philharmonic.

Though radio broadcasting remains the least explored and most anonymous wing of the culture industry, it may have been the site of the left's greatest success in the culture industry, largely because of the Popular Front producers. Though most of radio's programming was produced directly by advertising agencies and avoided anything with a political or social content, the non-commercial "sustaining" programs, sponsored directly by the networks as part of the legislative compromise embodied in the Communications Act of 1934, became vehicles of political and aesthetic innovation.

Popular Front producers developed sustaining programs like CBS's "Columbia Workshop" (under Irving Reis and William Robson), "The Pursuit of Happiness" (Norman Corwin), and the "Mercury Theatre on the Air" (Orson Welles), which featured left-wing writers, actors, and musicians in radio plays like Archibald MacLeish's anti-Fascist "The Fall of the City" (1937), starring Orson Welles, and Norman Corwin's "Ballad for Americans" (1939), sung by Paul Robeson. An "unpaid, unsponsored and uncontrolled" group of Popular Front radio writers and directors were brought together by James Boyd in 1941 to make up "The Free Company", which presented a "series of plays about our basic liberties" over CBS; the series included Orson Welles's drama about freedom of assembly, "His Honor, the Mayor." Two years later, the left-wing Hollywood Writers Mobilization sponsored the "Free World Theatre", produced by Arch Oboler on NBC's Blue Network; it included Milton Merlin and Clarence Muse's drama about black soldiers, "Something about Joe" (1943), starring Hazel Scott and Lena Horne.[79]

The Popular Front folklorist Alan Lomax was running the Archive of American Folk Song at the Library of Congress when CBS asked him to do a radio series on folk music. "I thought this was a joke," he later recalled. "I didn't know that anybody could be seriously interested in working on the radio, a pile of crap. Then I heard Corwin's broadcasts and I did a flip, I realized that radio was a great art of the time." Together with Nicholas Ray, Lomax produced a morning show, "The American School of the Air," in 1939 and the ambitious and successful prime-time sustaining show, "Back Where I Come From" in 1940, which featured Leadbelly, Josh White, the Golden Gate Quartet, and Woody Guthrie.[80]

Most of the successes of the Hollywood left were also the result of alliances between liberal producers and left-wing writers and directors. The one Popular Front film on the Spanish Civil War, *Blockade*, written by

John Howard Lawson and directed by émigré William Dieterle, was produced for United Artists by the liberal independent Walter Wanger. Hal Wallis and Jerry Wald produced Warner Brothers' series of populist urban thrillers and anti-fascist films, which were built around the acting of James Cagney, Bette Davis, and Humphrey Bogart and the writing of radicals like Lawson, Robert Rossen, Howard Koch, and John Wexley. Several of the post-war *film gris* of Edward Dmytryk, Joseph Losey, and Nicholas Ray were the products of Dore Shary's brief reign at RKO; and Darryl Zanuck, who had produced *The Grapes of Wrath* at Twentieth Century Fox in 1940, sponsored a series of "social problem" films after the war. But only two Hollywood radicals had independent control: one was Charlie Chaplin, who had built on his own stardom to develop an independent production company, part of United Artists, which allowed him to make his Popular Front classics, *Modern Times* (1936), *The Great Dictator* (1940), and *Monsieur Verdoux* (1947); the other was Orson Welles, who came to RKO Studios with an unprecedented degree of independence for his Mercury Productions, an independence that allowed the making of *Citizen Kane* (1941), but which was subsequently lost.

The rise of independent producers in post-war Hollywood also opened a space for radical writers and directors just as the Red Scare was beginning. Universal International became a home for independent producers like Mark Hellinger (who produced Jules Dassin's political thrillers) and Diana Productions (the alliance of Wanger, Fritz Lang, and Joan Bennett). Stanley Kramer's Screen Plays, Inc., John Huston's Horizon, Jerry Wald/Norman Krasna (which made *Clash by Night*), and Enterprise Studios (which made Abraham Polonsky's *Body and Soul* and *Force of Evil*) produced many of the social melodramas that have come to be called *film gris*. Few of these independents survived the political and economic crises of Cold War Hollywood; the blacklist and the new competition of television doomed their political, aesthetic, and economic innovations.[81]

Nevertheless, these attempts to create independent production companies were among the most ambitious projects of the cultural front; along with a number of independent theater companies, nightclubs, newspapers, photomagazines, publishing houses, record companies, and galleries, they constituted the beginnings of a Popular Front mass media. These were not the same as the alternative institutions of the movement culture. Though the boundary is vague and one might dispute particular examples, in general the institutions of the movement culture—the labor schools, workers theaters, and IWO lodges—depended on long hours of volunteer labor and were aimed at a local movement audience. The independent production companies attempted to compete with the major culture industries, using their forms and techniques. The most successful were those in industries with small, highly competitive firms, and a live audience.

Thus, the ACA Gallery (American Contemporary Art Gallery), founded by Herman Baron, and the Downtown Gallery, directed by Edith Gregor Halpert, became important New York galleries, featuring the works of Popular Front artists like Philip Evergood and William Gropper (at the ACA) and Jacob Lawrence and Ben Shahn (at the Downtown). The productions of the Group Theatre, directed by Harold Clurman, and the Mercury Theatre, directed by Orson Welles, were able to challenge Broadway theater. Barney Josephson's racially integrated nightclub, Café Society, became a major venue for jazz and comedy, featuring Billie Holiday, Lena Horne, and Josh White.[82]

Publishing ventures were less successful and rarely survived. There were several short-lived attempts to create a left-wing equivalent of the tremendously successful Book-of-the-Month Club, including the Book Union, the Book Find Club, and the Labor Book Club. One of the first experiments with paperback books was Modern Age Books, backed by Richard Storrs Child, which featured both mystery novels and popular political works like Bruce Minton and John Stuart's *Men Who Lead Labor* and Leo Huberman's *The Labor Spy Racket*. Modern Age also published *Photo-History*, a short-lived but exceptionally powerful photomagazine which documented contemporary history, selling popular illustrated accounts of the war in Spain and the rise of the CIO for a quarter (Figure 10).

Photo-History was only one of several attempts to create a Popular Front picture magazine. The longest lived was *Direction*, which became a glossy arts monthly and perhaps the most interesting of all Popular Front cultural journals. Beginning as a "non-profit magazine devoted to American arts and letters of the left," it was launched with the celebrity of Theodore Dreiser, and Dreiser's long-time literary secretary Marguerite Tjader Harris was its guiding spirit from December 1937 to its demise in 1944. *Direction* saw itself as a "progressive 'slick'," and it featured illustrated reviews of theater, dance, and film, as well as reproductions of the work of Popular Front painters, muralists and photographers. *Direction* covered both the WPA arts projects—the collection of WPA writing and prints, *American Stuff*, first appeared as a special issue—and the culture industries, with a special issue on Hollywood and regular coverage of radio drama. By the early 1940s, it had a remarkable array of advisory editors, including Richard Wright and Kenneth Burke for fiction, Jay Leyda for film, William Gropper for art, John Gassner for theater, Catherine Littlefield for dance, Elie Siegmeister for music, and Arch Oboler for radio. Perhaps more than any other magazine, *Direction* embodied the alliance of the moderns, the plebeians, and the émigrés. An out-take from Dos Passos's *U.S.A.*, "Tin Can Tourist," appeared in the inaugural issue, and Ralph Ellison's first published story, "Slick Gonna Learn," appeared in September 1939. An "exiled German writers" issue featured Thomas Mann, Bertolt Brecht, and Ernst

Bloch, as well as a photomontage by John Heartfield. Though most literary historians claim that the commitment to "proletarian literature" vanished with the coming of the Popular Front in 1935, the fiction issues of *Direction* regularly published young worker/writers (there were special issues devoted to "documentary" writing and to fiction by workers in the war industries). Though *Direction* was close to the League of American Writers, publishing the program of the 1939 American Writers' Congress as a special issue, it remained an independent magazine, operated on a shoestring by Marguerite Tjader Harris out of Darien, Connecticut. With its monthly column, "Cultural Front," which listed exhibitions, readings, and benefit performances, *Direction* came to stand as a representation of the cultural front (Figure 1).[83]

If *Direction* was aimed primarily at readers interested in the world of the arts, both of the other picture magazines were more ambitious, seeking to compete directly with Luce's *Life*. *Ken* was a project of Arnold Gingrich, the successful editor of *Esquire*; it was a biweekly political magazine born out of Gingrich's anti-fascism and sympathy for the Spanish Loyalists. It was to be, as George Seldes recalled, "the first mass-circulation, public-opinion-forming magazine in history on the liberal side," and its editors included Seldes and Ernest Hemingway. Launched in April 1938, *Ken* staggered through a year and a half of controversy, supported by *Esquire*. Seldes left after his muckraking investigation of the American Legion was suppressed; he went on to found his influential newsletter, *In Fact*. Hemingway continued to contribute articles on the Spanish Republicans, but many on the left attacked Gingrich's mixture of anti-fascism and anti-Communism. Soon after *Ken*'s demise in the fall of 1939, a wealthy young radical, Daniel Gillmor, founded *Friday*, an illustrated weekly modeled on the French Popular Front magazine *Vendredi*.[84]

Staffed by left-wing *New Yorker* writers like Ruth McKenney and Richard O. Boyer, *Friday* began in March 1940 as an anti-fascist, pro-labor version of *Life*. "*Friday* believes in trade unions and believes in them hard," it announced in its first issue. "You'll find lots of articles about CIO and AF of L leaders in our magazine." But *Friday* also adopted the pin-up aesthetic of the picture magazines: "We like to look at a pretty girl all dressed up in a brand new bathing suit, and we laugh with Fred Allen." So *Friday* combined the investigative labor photojournalism that had been pioneered in the late 1920s by the *Labor Defender*—the cover of its second issue featured the murder of a 25-year-old union leader, Laura Law—with steady coverage of baseball, jazz, and Hollywood stars, particularly ones associated with the Popular Front.[85]

Though *Friday* lasted only from March 1940 to September 1941, it gives, as we will see, a rare glimpse into the Popular Front common sense of its audience, the second-generation ethnic workers of the CIO. A longer-lived version of this Popular Front popular culture was *PM*, the pioneering New York tabloid launched in June 1940 and surviving until 1949 (in its last year as the *Star*). Its founder was Ralph Ingersoll, who had joined Henry Luce from the *New Yorker* in 1930, first as managing editor of *Fortune*, and then as publisher of *Time*. He left *Time* in 1939, having been unsuccessful in his attempts to reshape it. For *PM*, Ingersoll created an alliance of professional journalists (many of whom were active in the Newspaper Guild), writers from Time Inc., and Popular Front intellectuals, particularly the circle around Dashiell Hammett and Lillian Hellman. Though histories of *PM* are dominated by the internal battles between communists and anti-communist social democrats, *PM* proved to be a popular and innovative daily, with first-rate labor coverage by Leo Huberman, excellent sports pages, and the remarkable "News for Living" section, run by Elizabeth Hawes. Its editorial page was run by Max Lerner, who became one of the Popular Front's most visible commentators. I.F. Stone was one of its investigative reporters, and Theodor Geisel, who later created the Dr Seuss children's books, was a *PM* cartoonist. The *PM* photographs of Weegee made up the classic *Naked City* of 1946, and Dr Benjamin Spock's series on baby and child care led to his post-war classic *Baby and Child Care*.[86]

The industries of film, recording, and broadcasting were much more centralized and there were few successful alternatives to the "majors." Outside Hollywood, the most important Popular Front independent was Frontier Films, which made a number of films, including *Native Land*, one of the greatest Popular Front productions. There were several attempts by Hollywood professionals to produce independent left-wing films, including American Labor Films, Inc., which made *Millions of Us*; the unsuccessful Motion Picture Guild Inc. of 1939; and the post-war Xanadu Films. The most successful, however, was a product of the blacklist: the 1953 film of a strike by Mexican American miners, *Salt of the Earth*, made by Herbert Biberman, Paul Jarrico, and Michael Wilson.[87]

The recording industry was even more concentrated than the film industry, and the three majors offered few openings to the left. Nevertheless, there were a few alternative record companies, precursors of the great explosion of independent labels in the years after the war. The most important was perhaps Keynote Records, established in 1940 by Eric Bernay, a former publisher of the *New Masses*. Keynote began as a small left-wing folk and jazz label, releasing Marc Blitzstein's *No for an Answer*, the Almanac Singers' *Talking Union*, and Josh White's *Southern Exposure*, as well as small sessions with Lester Young, Teddy Wilson, and Count Basie; in 1946, John Hammond took over as president and he brought it into Mercury Records.[88]

Together, the two halves of the mass-culture front—the unionism of rank-and-file studio workers and the development of Popular Front companies and productions by radical producers—had a powerful impact on the styles and forms of American mass culture in the age of the CIO. Moreover, the interconnections between the proletarian avant-garde, the CIO movement culture, the WPA arts projects, and the studio radicals provoked a remarkable debate about the nature of American mass culture, a debate that attempted to theorize the cultural front.

5. Theories of the Cultural Front

i. The emergence of modern mental labor

If this overview of the various formations that made up the cultural front demonstrates the ways in which it was itself the product of the new cultural apparatuses of the state and industry, it is worth considering the ways in which the figures in and around the Popular Front social movement made sense of their situation. For much of the debate within and about the "Old Left" was, I will suggest, a debate about how these cultural apparatuses were to be understood. It was a debate about "mass culture," "consumerism," and the "new class." Indeed, the principal reason that the 1930s, the Hollywood blacklist, the Hiss and Rosenberg cases, and the Popular Front remain alive and controversial today is that the "mass culture" and the "new class" they encountered and named continues to be at the heart of our political and ideological controversies. For all of these terms—mass culture, the new class, the culture industry, the cultural apparatus, the cultural front—are attempts to understand the emergence of modern mental labor.

The division between mental and manual labor is one of the founding oppositions of all socialist thought, and it lurks behind many of the classic "problems" of socialist theory and politics. The relation between workers and intellectuals in socialist movements; the debates over the relation between "economic forces" and "ideology," and the metaphor of "base" and "superstructure"; the polemics over "vulgar materialism" and "idealism," as well as the more subtle explorations of the relations between social being and social consciousness; the controversies over the "deskilling" of work: these questions which haunt the socialist and Marxist traditions are all elaborations of a fundamental antinomy of mental and manual labor.

In particular, the division between mental and manual labor remains the starting point for any Marxist *cultural* theory: for "culture" in its modern sense is another name for accumulated mental labor, and the emergence of "culture" as a distinct region depends on a social surplus, extracted through exploitative labor relations. As Terry Eagleton has put it, "men and women do not live by culture alone; the vast majority of them throughout history have been deprived of the chance of living by it at all, and those few who are fortunate enough to live by it now are able to do so because of the labour of those who do not. Any cultural or critical theory which does not begin from this single most important fact, and hold it steadily in mind in its activities, is . . . unlikely to be worth very much." The Marxist cultural theories that emerged in the era of the Popular Front were attempts to come to grips with the forms of modern mental labor— mass education, industries of culture and entertainment, state cultural bureaucracies, and white-collar employment; and the notion of the "cultural front" was an attempt to imagine a politics of mental labor.[89]

ii. A league of professionals

Paradoxically, the notion of the cultural front was not a product of mainstream Communist thought. For the American Communist tradition, the emergence of modern *manual* labor was the central story, and their distinctive traditions of thought were geared to understanding and organizing the industrial working classes, the proletariat. The US Communist movement was the heir to a long American tradition of revolutionary syndicalism, which stressed industrial unionism, direct action, factory councils, and workers control. That tradition of revolutionary industrial unionism grew out of the syndicalism of the IWW and the theoretical writings of Austin Lewis and Daniel DeLeon, the American Marxist leader of the Socialist Labor Party, and it became, as Paul Buhle has argued, "the most internationally recognized theoretical or strategic perspective developed in the USA." "Its popularization coincided with the great international revolts of the unskilled proletariat, from Glasgow to Berlin, Turin and Petrograd," Buhle notes. "Revolutionary industrial unionism was . . . the first American doctrine to win *political* adherents in virtually every large-scale industrial center." Its foremost spokesman in the Communist movement was William Z. Foster, and Foster's leadership and influence contributed to the Communist Party's dedication to building the industrial unions of the CIO.[90]

Culture, for most of the early Communists, as for the socialists of the Second International, meant high European culture, the inheritance of Goethe, Schiller, Heine, and Beethoven, which would rightfully belong to the socialist future. There were, of course, a number of radical young Communists drawn to the avant-garde and iconoclastic visions of "proletarian culture" emerging from Germany and the Soviet Union, and most of the early cultural controversies were conflicts between the advocates of a proletarian culture and the defenders of the nineteenth-century inheritance.[91] The notion of the cultural front was not part of either vision: it grew out of the reflections on the "new" middle class and the new means of communication by a number of intellectuals who made up the tradition that has come to be known as Western Marxism.

Western Marxism was, as Perry Anderson has suggested, the product of defeat, the product of the failure of the revolutionary upheavals in Europe after the First World War. The Western Marxists were intellectuals of the modernist generation drawn to the revolutionary struggles of workers, but generally outside the official Communist Parties. They sought to renew historical materialism through an engagement with the modern philosophical and intellectual work of Croce, Weber, Freud, Durkheim, and Dewey. "The result," Anderson notes, "was that Western Marxism as a whole . . . came to concentrate overwhelmingly on study of *superstructures*. . . . It was culture that held the central focus of its attention." However, it is worth recalling that the Western Marxist focus on culture was not only a concern for aesthetics and philosophy, but also a concern for the economic and political meanings of the cultural apparatus.[92]

The European Western Marxists, the tradition from Gramsci, Lukács, and Korsch through Benjamin, Adorno, and Sartre, are well known; the US Western Marxists—figures like Lewis Corey/Louis Fraina, James Rorty, Kenneth Burke, Sidney Hook, C.L.R. James, and C. Wright Mills—remain less visible. Nevertheless, they are key figures in theorizing the cultural front. The origins of this US Western Marxism lie in the 1932 pamphlet, *Culture and the Crisis: An Open Letter to the Writers, Artists, Teachers, Physicians, Engineers, Scientists, and Other Professional Workers of America.* Written by a group of left-wing intellectuals who organized the League of Professional Groups for Foster and Ford to endorse the Communist Party's 1932 presidential candidates, the pamphlet was an explicit appeal to the "brain workers" of the United States to join the "muscle workers" in building a new civilization: it marks the first, relatively crude, attempt by the left to theorize the social and political significance of modern mental labor. In contrast to the proletarian art controversies of the same time, *Culture and the Crisis* began not with questions of the form and content of revolutionary works of art, but with the economic crisis of professional workers. The cultural crisis is defined as the unemployment of cultural workers:

> There are teachers on the bread lines, engineers patching the sheet-iron sheds in the "Hooversvilles," musicians fiddling in the "jungles." . . . All this unemployment and misery, all this training and talent thrown away, not because there are too many doctors, teachers, artists, writers and the like, but despite the fact that this country has never yet been able to provide its population with a sufficiently large body of trained intellectuals and professionals to satisfy its cultural needs.[93]

Thus, the choice facing professional workers "is between serving either as the cultural lieutenants of the capitalist class or as allies and fellow travelers of the working class." "Under Socialism," the pamphlet argues, the professional workers, whom capitalism either exploits or forces to become exploiters, are liberated to perform freely and creatively their particular craft function—the engineer need consider only the efficiency of his work, the economist and statistician can purposively plan the organization, management and social objectives of industry, the architect is released from profit and speculative motives and may express his finest aspirations in buildings of social utility and beauty, the physician becomes the unfettered organizer of social preventive medicine, the teacher, writer, and artist fashion the creative ideology of a new world and a new culture.

This craft vision of professionals, intellectuals, and artists was a crucial element of the depression left; it informed the Conference of Professional, Cultural and White Collar Workers, which called for white-collar relief programs in the spring of 1935 as well as the post-1933 wave of culture-industry unionism.[94]

The main writer of *Culture and the Crisis* was Lewis Corey (known earlier as Louis Fraina), one of the most important Western Marxists in the United States. Corey is a remarkable figure because he united the radical industrial unionism of DeLeon and Foster with an attention to the new middle classes and the cultural front. As a result he is the great theorist of the Popular Front social movement, the American Antonio Gramsci. Indeed, the parallels between Corey/Fraina and Gramsci are remarkable. Both were born in southern Italy, Gramsci in Sardinia in 1891, and Corey (born Luigi Carlo Fraina) in Salerno in 1892. Both moved to industrial cities and became active socialist journalists in their teens. Gramsci went to the industrial city of Turin, a center of Italian socialism, in 1911, and he was a full-time journalist for the Socialist Party weekly, *Il Grido del Popolo*, by 1915. Fraina's parents took him to New York, a center of US socialism, at the age of three; by 1909 he was writing for the *Weekly People*, the newspaper of Daniel DeLeon's Socialist Labor Party, and he covered the 1912 Lawrence textile strike. Both were deeply influenced by the revolutionary industrial unionism of DeLeon and were active in the upheavals of World War I. In 1919, Gramsci, influenced by DeLeon's ideas, founded a left-wing socialist weekly, *Ordine Nuovo*, which became the voice of the Italian factory councils, and he was a founder of the Italian Communist Party in 1921. Fraina, having met Trotsky, Bukharin, and Kollontai in New York in 1917, helped found the journals of the left-wing American socialists, *Revolutionary Age* and *Class Struggle*; he was jailed for war resistance in 1919, and was a founder of the US Communist Party in 1919.

Both Gramsci and Fraina spent time in Moscow working for the Comintern; both married women they met in Moscow (Gramsci was in Moscow from the summer of 1922 to the spring of 1924 and married Julia Schucht; Fraina was in Moscow from 1921 to 1922 and married a Comintern translator). Gramsci became a leader of the Italian Communist

Party, was arrested by Mussolini in 1926 and spent the rest of his life in prison, dying in 1937; it was during these years that he composed the prison notebooks that became his enduring legacy to socialist thought. Fraina left his Comintern work in Mexico and resigned from the factionalized and underground American Communist Party; he worked as a proofreader in New York, and began writing in the middle 1920s under the name Lewis Corey. At this point his career dramatically diverges from that of Gramsci: over the next quarter-century he became a typical figure of the cultural front, working in the cultural apparatuses of the state, the universities, and the unions. From 1931 to 1934, he worked for the *Encyclopedia of the Social Sciences*; in 1937, he worked as a WPA economist; he was a professor of economics at Antioch College between 1942 and 1951; and he was an education director for the ILGWU's Local 22 (1937–39) and for the Amalgamated Meat Cutters and Butcher Workmen (1951–52). He helped organize the League of Professionals in 1932, edited the short-lived *Marxist Quarterly* in 1937, and wrote two major works, *The Decline of American Capitalism* (1934) and *The Crisis of the Middle Class* (1935), both of which were widely read in the Popular Front social movement. Though he became increasingly critical of the Communist Party, he was a target of the anti-Communist purge; he was served with deportation papers in late 1952, and died in 1953.[95]

The biographical parallels between Corey/Fraina and Gramsci are echoed in their political and theoretical writings. Both began as revolutionary syndicalists, advocates of mass action and factory councils in the upheavals of 1919. By the 1930s, however, their writings combined this revolutionary industrial unionism with a new analysis of the role of intellectuals and the middle classes; they turned increasingly to what they called the "cultural front." The question of "whether the philosophy of praxis [Marxism] excludes ethico-political history, whether it fails to recognize the reality of a moment of hegemony, [and] treats moral and cultural leadership as unimportant" becomes increasingly important to Gramsci as he writes his prison notebooks in the early 1930s. "One can say," he concludes, "that not only does the philosophy of praxis not exclude ethico-political history but that, indeed, in its most recent stage of development, it consists precisely in asserting the moment of hegemony as essential to its conception of the state and to the 'accrediting' of the cultural fact, of cultural activity, of a cultural front as necessary alongside the merely economic and political ones." Gramsci's sense of the importance of the cultural front in understanding social struggles has a remarkable echo in Corey's major work of 1934, *The Decline of American Capitalism*. "Every revolutionary class must wage war on the cultural front," Corey maintains. "The university, science, technology, and learning were in general manifestations of bourgeois development, under bourgeois control, waging the bourgeois cultural struggle against the feudal order. But now all these forces, in their dominant institutional forms, are opposed to the proletariat; its revolutionary culture, while it includes many concrete achievements, is necessarily and mainly potential, a culture of revolutionary criticism and ideological struggle, interpreting, clarifying, projecting, capable of becoming dominant only after the revolution." For Gramsci, attention to the cultural front meant a rethinking of the role of intellectuals; for Corey, it meant a rethinking of the "new" middle class.[96]

Corey's next work, *The Crisis of the Middle Class* (1935), opens, like the earlier *Culture and the Crisis*, with the specter of "unprecedented unemployment among salaried employees"; it then offers a powerful social and historical account of this "new" middle class. If the old middle class was built on the ownership of independent small property, the "new" middle class has no such identity: its upper layer of corporate managers and supervisors are "institutional capitalists"; its large lower-salaried layers are "economically and functionally a part of the working class: a 'new' proletariat." Unlike the earlier pamphlet, which called on professionals to become "allies" of the working class, Corey now argues that "the mass of lower salaried employees and professionals are not 'allies' of the working class, they are part of the working class and its struggle for socialism because of their economically proletarian condition, their identification with collectivism [by which he means their work within the large bureaucratic structures of the corporation], and the necessity of their labor under socialism. (Only a minority of salaried employees and professionals are socially useless and parasitic.)" For Corey, salaried employees and professionals would come to adopt proletarian forms of action—strikes, unions, mass demonstrations; together with the "radicalization of intellectuals" who would "carry on the class war on the cultural field," this would bring a "cultural revolution."[97]

Corey's analysis of the "new" middle class was particularly influential for the group of radical modernist intellectuals who gathered at V.F. Calverton's legendary New York open houses and published in his *Modern Quarterly*. *Modern Quarterly* was a center for political, sexual, and aesthetic radicalism, and brought together all factions of the left in freewheeling and often acrimonious debates. Soon after Corey and the League of Professionals issued *Culture and the Crisis*, Calverton reshaped his magazine into a monthly aimed explicitly at the "professional workers." "There are a number of papers and periodicals which make their appeal to the industrial workers," Calverton wrote, "while there is none dedicated to the interests of the professional workers—none, at least, with any radical vision or conception of a new society . . . We shall specifically be concerned with the problems of the American school teacher today, the American doctor, the American engineer, the American writer, the American artist."[98]

The impact of Corey's work on the "new" middle class and the significance of *Culture and the Crisis* has often been missed because memoirists and historians alike have been distracted by the details of sectarian quarrels. It is true that the ad hoc alliance that produced the League of Professionals and *Culture and the Crisis* was brief and unstable; it included figures moving toward the Communist Party, like Malcolm Cowley and Matthew Josephson, who became mainstays of the Popular Front social movement, and figures moving away from the party, like Sidney Hook and James Rorty, who became critics of the Popular Front. Moreover, both Corey and Calverton were closely associated with the group of dissident communists led by Jay Lovestone and Bertram Wolfe; as a result, Calverton's *Modern Monthly* was attacked by Communist Party leaders. Ironically, however, the group of radicals around Corey and Calverton pioneered the major themes of the Popular Front social movement before the Communist Party itself adopted them: the stress on American exceptionalism and on "Americanizing" Marxism; the appeal to radicalized white-collar workers; and the turn from a rhetoric of "proletarian culture" to a notion of a "cultural front." When the Popular Front social movement took shape in the mid 1930s, many of the figures around *Modern Monthly*, including Calverton, remained suspicious of the Communist Party and attacked the Popular Front. However, others who had been influenced by Corey and Calverton—Kenneth Burke and Louis Adamic, for example—became important Popular Front activists.[99]

Indeed, Kenneth Burke's portrait of the "complete propagandist" in his address to the 1935 American Writers' Congress stands as another key formulation of the theory of the cultural front. Burke was a modernist critic drawn to the left in 1932 by his friend Malcolm Cowley, one of the authors of *Culture and the Crisis.* By the time of the 1935 American Writers' Congress, Burke had published one of the classics of Western Marxism, *Permanence and Change*, an "account of the devices whereby Marxian and psychoanalytic fields can be brought together." Unfortunately, the controversy surrounding Burke's speech at the American Writers' Congress has usually overshadowed its substance, as critics have interpreted the quarrel as a morality play in which Burke is shouted down by philistine Communist "functionaries." In fact, Burke's essay, "Revolutionary Symbolism in America," stands as a central document in the developing notion of a cultural front.[100]

If Corey's contribution lay in his analysis of the cultural crisis as a crisis of the "new" middle class, the cultural workers, Burke outlined a politics of culture to that "new" middle class. Though most discussions of the essay have focused on his first argument—that the symbol of the "people" ought to be adopted by the left since it was a more inclusive symbol than that of the "worker"—Burke himself noted that his second argument was more important and was not dependent on the first: "the second was that the imaginative writer seek to propagandize his cause by surrounding it with as full a cultural texture as he can manage, thus thinking of propaganda not as an over-simplified, literal, explicit writing of lawyer's briefs, but as a process of broadly and generally associating his political alignment with cultural awareness in general." The "complete propagandist," Burke suggested, "would take an interest in as many imaginative, aesthetic and speculative fields as he can handle—and into this breadth of his concerns he would interweave a general attitude of sympathy for the oppressed and antipathy towards our oppressive institutions . . . In a rudimentary way, this is what our advertisers do when they recommend a particular brand of cigarette by picturing it as being smoked under desirable conditions; it is the way in which the best artists of the religious era recommended or glorified their Faith." In the final chapter, I will untangle the cultural theory that Burke builds to support this notion of the "complete propagandist," the remarkable account of culture as "symbolic action." Here, I want to suggest that Burke's "complete propagandist" was the working model for the intellectual of the "cultural front."[101]

Moreover, like Corey's account of the radicalized intellectual and Dos Passos's account of the writer as technician (which I will discuss below), Burke's portrait of the "complete propagandist" finds mirror images in the works of the European Western Marxists, particularly in Walter Benjamin's discussion of the "author as producer." In the face of "a vast process in which literary forms are being melted down," Benjamin wrote, the "place of the intellectual in the class struggle can only be determined, or better still chosen, on the basis of his position in the production process." One position was that of the "hack," the writer "who refuses as a matter of principle to improve the production apparatus and so prise it away from the ruling class for the benefit of Socialism." Against this, Benjamin adopted Brecht's notion of "refunctioning" to describe "the transformation of forms and instruments of production by a progressive intelligentsia." This "refunctioning" of the "apparatus" was both institutional and formal: "Does he see ways of organizing the intellectual workers within their actual production process? Has he suggestions for changing the function of the novel, of drama, of poetry?"[102]

The similarities between Burke and Benjamin, Gramsci and Corey, derive from a common historical project: all of them were attempting to theorize a new cultural politics, a politics summed up in the phrase "the cultural front." This politics broke not only with the German *Kultur* associated with social democracy and communism as far back as Marx himself, but with the avant-garde politics of proletarian culture. Dos Passos's earliest description of the "word-slinging organisms" occurs in a 1926 response to his friend Michael Gold's call for a proletarian literature;

Burke's 1935 speech was explicitly posed against the rhetoric of proletarianism; Gramsci's important note on the struggle for a new culture was
written as a response to the proletarianism of Paul Nizan; and Benjamin's
1934 lecture on "the author as producer" was a response to Johannes
Becher's conception of the proletarian writer. However, unlike many
critics of the proletarian culture movement, they did not turn to an ideal
of the autonomous intellectual or writer, but rather attempted to theorize
the general role of symbol producers in a society dominated by mass
communications. In so doing, they shaped the cultural theory of the
Popular Front social movement.[103]

In order to see the stakes in this conception of the cultural front more
clearly, it is worth contrasting the positions of Corey, Burke, Gramsci, and
Benjamin with their critics. In what follows I want to look briefly at two
very different sorts of critics: the half-century-long controversy over Popular
Front espionage; and the impressive, though to my mind flawed, critique
of the cultural front developed in the 1940s by a group of anti-bureaucratic
Marxists.

iii. Spies and propaganda

The crudest and most lurid attack on the cultural front has been the
recurring accusation that it was a cover for Soviet espionage. From the
Soviet defector Walter Krivitsky's 1939 book, *In Stalin's Secret Service*, to the
recent "exposé" of *The Secret World of American Communism*, spy stories
circulated around the Popular Front. There are three reasons for this
continuing fascination. First, as I have argued in a previous book, spy
narratives became a powerful and popular way of comprehending the
global struggles of the twentieth century: the defeat of the old empires, the
rise of communism and fascism, two world wars, and a half-century of Cold
War. The anti-fascist spy thriller invented by Eric Ambler and Graham
Greene became one of the classic genres of the Popular Front itself.
Moreover, revelations of domestic espionage were a central part of Popular
Front politics: the hearings of the La Follette Committee between 1937
and 1939 revealed the widespread use of private espionage agencies by the
large industrial corporations to infiltrate and undermine labor organiz-
ations. One purpose of the 1938 Dies Committee hearings on un-American
activities was to draw attention away from the La Follette investigations.
Popular Front stories of stool pigeons and informers stretch from Frontier
Film's *Native Land* to Elia Kazan's *On the Waterfront*.[104]

Second, the three great spy cases offered more than spies: they stood as
an inverted image of the alliance that made up the Popular Front social
movement. Alger Hiss was immediately recognized as an emblem of the
Ivy League–educated modern, from an established Anglo family; Julius and

Ethel Rosenberg were the epitome of the young ethnic plebeians coming of age in the depression; and Klaus Fuchs symbolized the émigré intellectual. Admittedly, Fuchs has not had the same mythic significance as Hiss and the Rosenbergs. Nonetheless, the spy stories always require their émigré character: think only of the role of Gerhardt Eisler, the brother of the composer Hanns, or of the shadowy Comintern agent J. Peters in other accounts. The political attack on the radical émigrés was most clearly demonstrated in the HUAC questioning of Bertolt Brecht and the exile of Charlie Chaplin. Thus, it is not surprising that these narratives have been so powerful and so controversial throughout the second half of the twentieth century: if the British fascination with the Kim Philby case and the Cambridge University spies spoke to anxieties and resentments about the loss of Empire, the Hiss, Rosenberg, and Fuchs cases were a map of the anxieties and resentments provoked by the reconstruction of the US in the age of the CIO.[105]

Finally, the espionage narratives gained power because the spy was an emblem of the white-collar employees of the culture industry and the state apparatus, the bureaucrat. The "general spirit of bureaucracy," the young Marx wrote, "is the official secret ... Its hierarchy is a *hierarchy of information.*" The melodramas about Popular Front spies often take their logic from a distorted understanding of the cultural front. The classic argument is that of Whittaker Chambers. "These were the years," he writes in *Witness,*

> that floated Alger Hiss into the party and made possible the big undergrounds, the infiltration of the Government, science, education and all branches of communication, but especially radio, motion pictures, book, magazine and newspaper publishing ... From 1930 onward, a small intellectual army passed over to the Communist Party.... Within a decade, *simply by pursuing the careers that ordinarily lay open to them,* these newcomers would carry the weak and stumbling American Communist Party directly into the highest councils of the nation. (my emphasis)

But can one characterize the ordinary pursuit of a career as "infiltration"? The great weakness of the spy chasers was that they understood the world of culture simply as propaganda, and the politics of the cultural apparatuses simply as infiltration. Thus, since the cultural front was built on the radical activism of the government and the culture-industry workers, who Chambers himself, unconsciously echoing Lewis Corey, called "a proletariat of ... unskilled intellectuals," every Popular Front activist was imagined as a spy, as one of "the party's agents, working in the communications field."[106]

Chambers's vision lies behind Stephen Koch's recent *Double Agents,* with its ludicrous argument that the Popular Front was an elaborate cover for

Soviet secret-service recruitment, and that such political activities as "the founding of the Screen Writers Guild" were "pseudo-missions." One could just as well say that Yale University was an elaborate cover for US intelligence recruitment: it is, after all, well documented that particular members of the Yale faculty have been involved in such recruitment with the knowledge of administrators. But only the adepts of secret-service history (who imagine that spies rather than multi-national corporations, political parties, armies, or social classes are the primary actors in history) would think that secret-service recruitment explained much about the social and political functions of Yale University. No one doubts that Soviet intelligence agencies used the left-wing networks of the Popular Front to recruit agents and gather information; nor is it a surprise that US intelligence agencies, notably the OSS, used those same left-wing networks to recruit agents and gather information. But the intelligence agencies sought to use those networks precisely because the Popular Front was a powerful and influential social movement: that movement, not the machinations of intelligence agencies, is what is historically significant.[107]

Nevertheless, Koch's book is interesting, for his spy melodrama depends on an account of the cultural front: a narrative of the international network of cultural organizations orchestrated by the German publisher, Willi Munzenberg. Munzenberg owned two daily newspapers in Germany as well as the pioneering photomagazine, the *Arbeiter Illustrierte Zeitung*, and he built his ownership of the Soviet distribution rights of German films into a Moscow film-production studio, Mezhropohmfilm, and into the film-distribution companies, Prometheus and Welt Film, which brought the pathbreaking Soviet films of Eisenstein, Pudovkin, and Vertov to Europe and America. Munzenberg had also organized the Workers International Relief to raise famine relief for the Soviet Union in the early 1920s, and, as I suggested earlier, many of the early Communist cultural organizations—particularly those of photographers and filmmakers—were organized not by the Communist Party itself, but by the various branches of the Workers International Relief: the American branch was the International Labor Defense. Koch overstates Munzenberg's originality, claiming that he invented everything "from the protest march to the mock-trial to the politicized writers' congress to the politicized arts festival to the celebrity letterhead to the ad hoc committee for numberless causes"; nevertheless, Munzenberg was indeed one of the great entrepreneurs of the cultural front. Though Koch's melodrama turns Munzenberg's entire "apparatus" into a vehicle for Soviet espionage, he is more accurate when he notes in passing that Munzenberg makes "one think less of le Carre's Karla than of Henry Luce."[108]

For both Munzenberg and Luce represented a new kind of politics of culture, and it is perhaps no accident that Whittaker Chambers himself was an important figure in Luce's apparatus for almost a decade, rising from a "third-string book reviewer" in 1939 to *Time*'s foreign-news editor. And to a degree, that new politics of culture did see itself through the lens of propaganda. There was a tremendous outpouring of studies of propaganda and the manipulation of the mass media. The Institute for Propaganda Analysis was founded in 1937 by a number of liberal sociologists and issued a series of studies. Munzenberg himself wrote a study of Nazi propaganda, *Propaganda as Weapon*. Perhaps the finest of these propaganda studies was Kenneth Burke's "The Rhetoric of Hitler's *Battle*," delivered to the 1937 American Writers' Congress. One of the earliest full-length studies of the American Communist Party was Harold Lasswell's sociological account of left-wing propaganda, *World Revolutionary Propaganda*. Most Communist activists shared some of the vocabulary of the ex-Communist Chambers, thinking of their work as agitation and propaganda; and there was often a tendency to see all cultural activity as a form of agitprop. Indeed, the fascination with the new and frightening powers of mass communications was captured in the debate over the great Martian panic caused by the Mercury Theatre radio show.[109]

Nevertheless, the real story of the period is not captured by these lurid images of espionage, infiltration, and propaganda; the politics of the cultural apparatus is less the story of "sleepers" infiltrating the government and propagandists manipulating the masses than the story of modern forms of political struggle within state agencies and cultural institutions. This was seen most clearly by a group of left anti-Stalinists who developed a thorough-going critique of Popular Front culture in journals like *New International*, *Partisan Review*, *Politics*, *Commentary*, and *Dissent* between 1940 and the early 1950s. For these figures—they include James Farrell, Clement Greenberg, Harold Rosenberg, Dwight Macdonald, Robert Warshow, Irving Howe, Lionel Trilling, and C.L.R. James—the critique of the Popular Front went well beyond the critique of Stalinism; they saw the Popular Front as the other face of Henry Luce, as an acceptance of both the "kitsch" of the culture industries and the "official" art of the state apparatus.

iv. A league of frightened philistines

The earliest and perhaps most powerful of these anti-bureaucratic Marxists was the novelist James T. Farrell, himself a product of the proletarian renaissance. For Farrell, the Popular Front was made up of the hacks and stars of the culture industries, encompassing "nearly everyone *but* radicals." "The new 'cultural front,'" he wrote in 1939 in *American Mercury*, "hastily enlisted commercial writers, high-priced Hollywood scenarists, a motley assortment of mystery-plot mechanics, humorists, newspaper columnists, stripteasers, band leaders, glamour girls, actors, press agents, Broadway producers, aging wives with thwarted literary ambitions, and other such ornaments of American culture." Farrell's bitter diatribes against this "league of frightened philistines" grew out of his own truculent radicalism and a plebeian defense of an uncompromising aesthetic of seriousness and realism. For Farrell, American commercial culture was a wasteland "owned and operated by finance capital." "A large proportion of the literary talent of America is now diverted to Hollywood and to radio writing," Farrell wrote. "This is a positive and incalculable social loss . . . consider how many lives, how much labor power, how much talent, how much of social goods is poured not only into Hollywood but into American commercial culture as a whole. The social cost is fabulous."[110]

Farrell's 1944 attack on the "counterfeit culture" and "inner emptiness" of Hollywood, like Dwight Macdonald's "A Theory of Popular Culture" (published in the first issue of his magazine *Politics* in 1944) and Theodor Adorno and Max Horkheimer's "The Culture Industry: Enlightenment as Mass Deception" (in *Dialectic of Enlightenment*, written in 1944), saw no possibility of compromise with the culture industries. If Farrell went after Hollywood's "liberal" producers, Darryl Zanuck and Walter Wanger, Adorno and Horkheimer did not even spare the Popular Front icons, Orson Welles and Charlie Chaplin. Welles's "departures from the norm . . . serve all the more strongly to confirm the validity of the system"; "the ears of corn blowing in the wind at the end of Chaplin's *The Great Dictator* give the lie to the anti-Fascist plea for freedom." As a result, the Popular Front notion of a culture-industry politics, "refunctioning" the apparatus by the "complete propagandist," was seen as a capitulation to the apparatus. Farrell's hostility to the industrialization of writing extended to the trades union responses of the "mystery-plot mechanics" and Hollywood scenarists. When the mystery novelist James M. Cain, together with the left-wing of the Screen Writers' Guild, led a campaign in 1946 to create an American Authors' Authority to protect the copyrights of all writers in all fields, Farrell became its most visible and vocal opponent, seeing it as a bureaucratic and Stalinist threat to the freedom of writers.[111]

Both Farrell and Macdonald had been active in the small Trotskyist movement of the late 1930s and early 1940s, and their critique of mass culture owes much to the anti-Stalinist debates over the nature of modern political and cultural bureacracies, debates that had developed out of the critique of Stalin's dictatorship. Indeed, the distinctive contribution of left anti-Stalinism in the United States was its deep suspicion of the huge new state and corporate apparatuses, with their "new class" of state administrators, personnel managers, cultural bureaucrats, and labor leaders. The anti-bureaucratic Marxism that emerges in C.L.R. James's notion of "state capitalism," Max Shachtman's account of "bureaucratic collectivism," and even in James Burnham's theory of a "managerial revolution," saw uncanny resemblances among corporate liberals, social democrats, and Stalinists. "The inevitable direction of society," C.L.R. James wrote in his 1950 manuscript, *American Civilization*, "... is towards the vast centralized bureaucratic state in which labor leaders and intellectuals of all types will form a solid governmental mass, controlling labor in the factories, administering the state, with vast resources and power to influence press and radio, controlling the armed forces and the F.B.I." Thus, the battle between labor and capital is increasingly seen as a "world-wide conflict *between the workers and the bureaucratic-administrative-supervising castes.*" James's image grows directly out of the experience of the wartime state, with its alliance between Roosevelt's US and Stalin's USSR, its vast propaganda agencies, often staffed by Popular Front cultural figures, and, most clearly, its no-strike pledge, enforced by both the leaders of CIO industrial unions and the Communist Party. Thus, for the left anti-Stalinist critics, the theory and practice of the cultural front was a collaboration with this bureaucratic apparatus of propaganda and entertainment, a betrayal of the function of the radical intellectual.[112]

Though the left anti-Stalinist critique of the "new class" of state administrators and labor bureaucrats was powerful, it tended to fall back on two older notions of the avant-garde or vanguard intellectual which ignored the very changes in cultural organization that they criticized. The first was the classic modernist notion of the intellectual as an unattached, avant-garde, and anti-bourgeois sensibility. The second was the Leninist notion of the intellectual as a vanguard intellectual, part of a party cadre. The Leninist conception had been particularly relevant to societies made up of a mass of workers and peasants with little formal schooling and a very small intellectual elite, a "talented tenth" in Du Bois's famous metaphor, some of whom might be drawn into workers and peasants movements. However, neither of these conceptions addressed the "new class" of intellectual workers created by mass education and mass culture. Indeed, as the American Trotskyists came to break with their Leninist parties in the 1940s, most began to use the term "intellectual" simply as an honorific to distinguish the "creative" or "authentic" intellectual from what Daniel Bell was to call the "cultural mass," the large number of educated workers engaging in selling, packaging, and transmitting culture.

This ideology of the "intellectual" became the badge of the post-war New York intellectuals, many of whom cut their teeth on these Trotskyist debates; a number of figures, including Richard Hofstadter, Irving Howe, Gertrude Himmelfarb, Irving Kristol, and Seymour Martin Lipset, had been members of the Workers Party—the small Trotskyist group led by Max Shachtman, James, and Macdonald—and many others were formed in the intellectual milieu of *Partisan Review* and Dwight Macdonald's *Politics*. For them, the "intellectual" had to take a stand against mass culture, kitsch, and middlebrow taste, and the popular cultural initiatives of the Popular Front were seen as more pernicious than even the ordinary products of the culture industry. Far from being a genuine experiment in a democratic, people's culture, the Popular Front's popularizations of high culture and urbanizations of rural folk cultures were simply capitulations to the middlebrow tendencies of a culture industry that debased the fine arts, defanged the avant-garde, and turned the folk arts into a processed kitsch.

Moreover, in a theme developed at length by the *Partisan* art and literary critics like Clement Greenberg, Lionel Trilling, and Robert Warshow, these "second-hand" products did not create a popular, democratic audience; rather, they embodied a middlebrow notion of art "appreciation" that offered an easy escape from "the shock of experience": "the chief function of mass culture," Warshow wrote, "is to relieve one of the necessity of experiencing one's life directly." It destroys "the emotional and moral content of experience, putting in its place a system of conventionalized 'responses.'" By the early 1950s, the demonization of Popular Front culture as a "second-hand" culture, the product of corrupt hacks and stars, was itself a "second-hand" theme in Cold War magazine journalism, as Murray Kempton, Leslie Fiedler, and Richard Rovere attacked eveything from the prison letters of the Rosenbergs to the screenplays of the Hollywood Ten. "In the last analysis," Warshow concluded, "the intellectual had sold out . . . And he lived surrounded by the evidence of his betrayal: a culture solidifying in vulgarity and dishonesty, of which he was a part."[113]

Paradoxically, the New York intellectuals themselves became celebrated neither as tribunes of the immigrant working class from which they came nor as avant-garde iconoclasts but as the theorists, novelists, teachers, aesthetic consultants, ideologues, and Jeremiahs of the "new class." Their history is intertwined with the institutions of this "new class", with book clubs, magazine journalism, and the politics of universities, foundations, publishing corporations, and government agencies. Despite their nostalgia for the "advanced" intellectual of Leninism and modernism, they were not only critics of the cultural front, they were a part of the cultural front.[114]

v. Repossessing the apparatus: hacks, stars, and the New Left

The figure who best understood these contradictions was C. Wright Mills, who might be seen as either the last thinker of the Old Left or the first of the New. For Mills adopted the left anti-Stalinist critique of the new administrative order while seeing the genuine contradictions within the new class itself. Mills, born in 1916, was of the depression generation and he combined three formative intellectual associations: the progressive and

Popular Front social science and history at Wisconsin's graduate school, represented by such figures as Selig Perlman and Hans Gerth; the Trotskyist-inflected milieu of the New York intellectuals—his friends Richard Hofstadter and Harvey Swados had been in the Workers Party and he wrote for Daniel Bell's *New Leader*, Dwight Macdonald's *Politics*, the social democratic labor journal, *Labor and Nation*, and Irving Howe's *Dissent*; and the administrative social research of Paul Lazarsfeld's Bureau of Applied Social Research—like Theodor Adorno, Mills labored discontentedly on Lazarsfeld's grand empirical studies of radio, public opinion, and mass communications.

After publishing three major books, all of which investigate aspects of the new class of professionals and managers—labor leaders in *The New Men of Power* (1948), middle managers in *White Collar* (1951), and political, corporate, and military executives in *The Power Elite* (1956)—Mills contemplated a study of what he called the "cultural apparatus," the world of mass culture and the new class of intellectuals. Though the book was never completed, the essays he wrote offer a powerful account of both the forms of cultural organization *and* the possibilities they offer for a politics of culture. The fact that the project gradually changed from a book entitled *The Cultural Apparatus* to one entitled *The New Left* (neither completed) indicates the way Mills's reflections on the cultural apparatus generated an account of the possibilities of political transformation.[115]

Mills's argument begins with a portrait of the "post-modern period" (one of the early uses of the phrase): it is characterized by the collapse of liberalism and socialism in the face of bureaucratic one-party and two-party states where "rationally organized social arrangements" have become "a means of tyranny and manipulation," where democracy and workers control are fictions, and the "marketing apparatus transforms the human being into . . . the cheerful robot." The diagnosis is the culmination of two decades of the anti-bureaucratic Marxism of Trotskyists like Macdonald and James, dissident communists like Lewis Corey, and Frankfurt intellectuals like Adorno and Horkheimer.[116]

But Mills then offers a remarkably different account of "mass culture" or the culture industry. He begins by refusing the art and literary critics' condemnation of the "second-hand" world of mass culture. Drawing on the pragmatic theorists of culture from Mead to Kenneth Burke, he insists that all culture is second-hand—"the first rule for understanding the human condition is that men live in second-hand worlds"—and that all experience is shaped by symbols, the product of a society's cultural apparatus. "In the cultural apparatus, art, science, and learning, entertainment, malarkey, and information are produced and distributed . . . Taken as a whole, the cultural apparatus is the lens of mankind through which men see; the medium by which they interpret and report what they see."

He also refuses the heroic "myth of the intellectual." Offering a brief "natural history of modern culture," he argues that "the models of the cultural creator that still prevail among us: the inherently and necessarily free man, and the cherished and heroic notion of advance-guard" are actually the products of a particular historical moment when "the cultural workman becomes an entrepreneur."[117]

That moment has passed: the cultural workman has become part of "a set of bureaucracies" and "a great salesroom," in which there is little control over the means of cultural distribution. As Mills tells the story: "The distributor—along with his market researcher—'establishes a market' and monopolizes access to it. Then he claims to 'know what they want.' The orders he gives, even to the free-lance, become more explicit and detailed. The price he offers may be quite high—perhaps too high, he comes to think, and perhaps he is right. So he begins to hire and in varying degree to manage a stable of cultural workmen."[118]

"In this situation," Mills argues, "the cultural workman tends to become either a commercial hack or a commercial star." The commercial hack is the rank and file of the studio, the laboratory, the research bureau, the writers factory; the star, on the other hand, is the "person whose productions are so much in demand that, to some extent at least, he is able to use distributors as his adjuncts." Nevertheless, the star is "culturally trapped by his own success," a subject of the market's fashions. In many ways, Mills's vision is bleaker than that of Trilling, Greenberg, and Warshow: he holds out no place for the autonomous avant-garde or intellectual. But neither does he hold the hacks and stars responsible for the situation; the "ambiguous position of the cultural workman in America" is not the result of selling out, of a betrayal by the intellectuals.[119]

Instead, Mills sees the hacks and stars of the cultural apparatus as agents for change; and he calls on cultural workmen to "repossess" the "cultural apparatus." Mills's formulations are sketchy, merely suggestions and exhortations. In the famous "Letter to the New Left," he oversimplifies his own arguments: rejecting what he calls the "labor metaphysic," the notion that the working class would be the primary agent of historical change, he writes that "it is with this problem of agency in mind that I have been studying, for several years now, the cultural apparatus, the intellectuals— as a possible, immediate, radical agency of change. For a long time I was not much happier with this idea than were many of you; but it turns out now, in the spring of 1960, that it may be a very relevant idea indeed." It was indeed relevant, and became a powerful New Left ideology of the radical intelligentsia: indeed, there is a link between the League of Professional's *Culture and the Crisis* pamphlet of 1932 and the *Port Huron Statement* of the Students for a Democratic Society.[120]

But the strength of Mills's analysis of the cultural apparatus was that he did *not* abandon the "labor metaphysic": he consistently tried to replace the older "intellectual" with his phrase "cultural workman." Indeed, he rejected the notion of the "committed intellectual," replacing it with a sense of the politics of cultural work: "the politics of cultural work is not to be identified with the explicit political views or activities of the cultural workman . . . The political choices of individuals must be distinguished from the political functions, uses and consequences of the cultural work they do." Thus, his call to repossess the cultural apparatus was based on an ideal of workers' control: the "cardinal value" of "art, science and learning" was, for Mills, "craftsmanship." "The writers among us bemoan the triviality of the mass media, but why . . . do they allow themselves to be used in its silly routines by its silly managers? These media are part of *our* means of work, which have been expropriated from us . . . we ought to repossess *our* cultural apparatus and use it for our own purposes."[121]

If the specter of the new mass communications controlled by a new class of administrators and bureaucrats led many of the anti-bureaucratic Marxists to miss the contradictions within the state apparatuses and culture industries, Mills's reflections on the cultural apparatus grew out of a moment when its social and political contradictions were becoming visible. So Mills's work was not only a kind of synthesis of two decades of debate over the cultural front, fusing Burke's account of symbolic action and Corey's account of the new middle classes with the experience of the CIO and Popular Front intellectuals; it was also part of a new "cultural turn" in left-wing theory and practice. He was not alone: in a 1959 review of the "new generation" of radical thinkers, Daniel Bell noted that "the problem of radical thought today is to reconsider the relation of culture to society." Thus, there are clear parallels between Mills's work on the cultural apparatus and that of others who straddle the Popular Front and the New Left, including Raymond Williams, whose *The Long Revolution* of 1961 offered a not dissimilar account of the development of the cultural apparatus in Great Britain, and Leo Marx, whose "Notes on the Culture of the New Capitalism" in a 1959 *Monthly Review* called for an analysis of a capitalism based on consumption and advertising.[122]

Perhaps the most striking example was Harold Cruse's *The Crisis of the Negro Intellectual* (1967). Cruse had been part of the Popular Front social movement in the 1940s and 1950s, reviewing films for the *Daily Worker* and chairing the Harlem Writers' Club, a group of dissidents within Harlem's cultural front. The vitriolic nature of his history and critique of the Harlem Popular Front and its leading figures—Richard Wright, Paul Robeson, Lorraine Hansberry, and his old adversaries in the Committee for the Negro in the Arts (CNA)—has often overshadowed the fact that his analysis is rooted in a theory of what he himself calls the cultural front. Unlike the New York intellectuals, Cruse's critique of Popular Front culture is not a rejection of the mass media and the new class; it is an attempt to take Mills's analysis of the cultural apparatus as the basis for a more thorough-going cultural politics, one in which "the key idea is cultural institutions (theaters, halls, club sites, and movie houses) *owned and administered* by the people of Harlem." Writing of the 1926 Lafayette Theater strike, Cruse argues that "this profound conflict, that touched on practically every aspect of community life and its relationships to white society, was the result of a controversy that started *on the cultural plane.* It was not police brutality, or high rents, or bad schools—but *the impact of the developing American cultural apparatus* on the economics, the politics, the creative and social develop-ment of the black community—that sparked this conflict." "To democratize the cultural apparatus is tantamount to revolutionizing American society," Cruse argues, "to revolutionize the cultural apparatus is to deal fundamen-tally with the unsolved American question of nationality."[123]

The importance of Cruse's work in the midst of the cultural upheavals of the 1960s reminds us that, in many ways, the culmination of the cultural front—its culture-industry unions, its attempt to "refunction" the forms and media of the culture industry and the state to create a new "national-popular" culture—is found in the years after the anti-Communist purges. The vast white-collar workforce, often the children of the CIO's industrial workers, became the base for the wave of unionization between 1960 and 1980; the huge educational system created at mid-century was the seedbed for massive student movements; and the struggles within the music industry and Hollywood resulted in a remarkable flowering of vernacular American cultures. And the various stances taken by the Western Marxists—Benjamin and Burke, Corey and Gramsci, Adorno and James, Farrell and Howe, Mills and Cruse—are less interesting for their moral judgements on "mass culture" than as seismic readings of the fault lines in the cultural front.

3

Ballads for Americans: Aesthetic Ideologies

If marching in the May Day parade served as a metaphor for the political affiliations and allegiances of artists and intellectuals of the Popular Front, Paul Robeson's rendition of the song "Ballad for Americans" has come to stand for the aesthetic forms and ideologies of the Popular Front. "Ballad for Americans" was written by Earl Robinson, a 29-year-old composer who had been part of the Shock Troupe of the Workers Laboratory Theatre and the Composers Collective, and John LaTouche, a young lyricist who had written for the left-wing cabarets sponsored by TAC (the Theatre Arts Committee). Robinson and LaTouche came together to write a cantata, "The Ballad of Uncle Sam," for one of the Federal Theatre Project's most elaborate and controversial productions, the musical revue *Sing for Your Supper*. After eighteen months of rehearsals, *Sing for Your Supper* opened successfully in the spring of 1939, but its run was interrupted when the Federal Theatre Project was shut down. After the show closed, the radio writer Norman Corwin turned this "musical history of the United States" into a short "ballad opera," renaming it "Ballad for Americans," and broadcast it on his CBS network series, "The Pursuit of Happiness." The singer was Paul Robeson, who had recently returned to the United States after a number of years abroad, and the 5 November 1939 broadcast was such a success that Robeson repeated the broadcast on New Year's Day 1940. In early 1940, Robeson recorded "Ballad for Americans" with the American Peoples Chorus, an amateur working-class chorus directed by Earl Robinson; the Victor record was a great success and the song was featured throughout Robeson's triumphant cross-country concert tour in the summer of 1940.[1]

In the years that followed, Robeson sang "Ballad for Americans" to many CIO and Popular Front audiences, and it became an unofficial anthem of the movement. But it also became a target for critics of Popular Front culture. In an influential 1947 essay on "The Legacy of the Thirties," the young *Commentary* critic Robert Warshow attacked the "tradition of middle-class 'popular front' culture" which thought that "*Confessions of a Nazi Spy* was a serious movie and 'Ballad for Americans' was an inspired song": this "mass culture of the educated classes—the culture of the 'middle-brow,' as it has sometimes been called," was, Warshow maintained, a "disastrous vulgarization of intellectual life." Six years later, in an essay on the prison letters of Ethel and Julius Rosenberg, Warshow used Ethel Rosenberg's account of being inspired by hearing "Ballad for Americans" as an example of the "awkwardness and falsity of the Rosenbergs' relations to culture" and of Popular Front culture generally. Warshow was the Charlie Parker of the New York intellectuals, dying in 1955 at the age of thirty-seven, and his essays served as a touchstone for a generation of New York intellectuals whose critical platform in post-war America was built on their opposition to the politics and culture of the Popular Front. These critics, including Irving Howe, Dwight Macdonald, and Lionel Trilling, named "Popular Front culture," detecting a Popular Front sensibility and deploring its effects on American culture; for them, the cultural consequences of the Popular Front were deeper and more pernicious than its immediate political consequences. Though they argued that the styles and tastes of Popular Front culture had infected much of US culture, particularly in music, film, and broadcasting, they insisted that few if any lasting works of art or intellect emerged from it.[2]

A generation later, New Left critics were no less harsh, and again "Ballad for Americans" took its blows. If the New York intellectuals objected primarily to its "middlebrow" aesthetic, the New Left critics objected to its sentimental nationalism. Stanley Aronowitz mocked the "execrable 'prole-tarian' novels" of the depression left and saw the "appearance of such musical political tracts as Earl Robinson's cantatas, *Ballad for Americans* and *Lonesome Train*" as the "apogee" of an easy-listening music that made the left "the vanguard of commercial culture": "its tenor was a fair imitation of the joyfulness and optimism that marked the popular front aims of the left." "The cantata form," Aronowitz argued, "with its combination of words and music, provided the perfect opportunity to present the new democratic ideology of the popular front in the context of a musical style that conformed to the demand for the popularization of 'serious music.'" Christopher Lasch wrote of the "excesses and absurdities" of Popular Front culture; and Warren Susman summed up the case against the Popular Front most completely: "out of it came an absurd vision of the American past, a peculiar notion of American society in the present, a ludicrous attitude toward American culture in general. At a most critical juncture in our history American socialists helped us little in understanding ourselves or the world." Susman characterized "Ballad for Americans" as a "pseudo-folk ballad"; it "represents the kind of new 'folk' material being created in the Jungian age ... a testament—as sentimental as Norman Rockwell's *Saturday Evening Post* covers—to the unity in a way of life that involved all ethnic groups, creeds, colors." Like virtually all subsequent historians, Susman noted the ironic postscript that "Ballad for Americans" was used as the theme song for the *Republican* National Convention in the fall of 1940.[3]

By the 1980s, this caricature of Popular Front culture was so ingrained that a liberal political commentator—in the cruelest cut of all—suggested that it culminated in Ronald Reagan. Reagan embodied

> the last recapitulation of the popular liberal esthetic of the Depression and war years: *The people, yes.* He still inhabited the mood of Frank Capra's populist movies, Archibald MacLeish's poetic tributes to the brotherhood of the common people, the uplifting social realism of WPA post-office murals. Reagan echoed the spirit of "Ballad for Americans," the Popular Front pseudo-folk song about "nobody who was anybody" and "anybody who was everybody"—"You know who I am: the people!" His mass cultural style of democratic schwärmerei, like that of the old liberal left he once championed, was pitched for ideological advantage. *Let America Be America Again.* Conservatism is twentieth-century Americanism.

As we shall see, this writer gets the lyrics to "Ballad for Americans" wrong; nevertheless, he captures all of the key objections to Popular Front culture: its commitment to the "folk idiom and the documentary aesthetic," its social realism, its sentimental populism and narrow nationalism, its masculine brotherhood, and its fundamental conservatism.[4]

Even historians sympathetic to the Popular Front share this image: "Popular Front culture offered a sentimental, egalitarian, and schematic world view," Maurice Isserman writes, embodied in "such popular works as Steinbeck's *Grapes of Wrath* ... or in Paul Robeson's rendition of Earl Robinson's choral 'Ballad for Americans'." "The Popular Front in culture," the biographer of Woody Guthrie writes, "was an attempt to create a mythology of 'the people' using the guise of realism." If this is an adequate account of Popular Front culture, one can see why the "thirties" are more often seen as a moment of cultural degradation, vulgarization, and decadence than a renaissance.[5]

In the pages that follow, I will reconsider the aesthetic ideologies of the Popular Front, challenging the accepted wisdom that its aesthetic legacy is a handful of insipid ballads for Americans. Indeed, by reconsidering the crucial issues of "social realism" and "documentary," as well as its apparent populism, nationalism, and masculinism, I will argue that the aesthetic innovations of the cultural front wrestled with the cultural contradictions of modernity, and led to a laboring of American culture. The characteristic narratives, tropes, and forms of the cultural front—the satiric newsreels, ghetto pastorals, proletarian grotesques, and cabaret blues—informed the most powerful and lasting works of twentieth-century American fiction, music, theater, and film, as well as the cultural criticism and theory that surrounded them. Many of these works are ruins, unfinished and collapsing, and the laboring of American culture was no doubt a failure, pummeled by the new postmodern forms of commodity fetishism. "History progresses by failure rather than by success," Fredric Jameson reminds us, "and it would be better to think of Lenin or Brecht (to pick a few illustrious names at random) as failures—that is, as actors and agents constrained by their own ideological limits and those of their moment of history—than as triumphant examples and models in some hagiographic or celebratory sense." However if we begin to understand the lineaments of those failures, we may even be able to hear Robeson's "Ballad for Americans" with new ears.[6]

1. Toward a Revolutionary Symbolism: The Proletarian Grotesque

Nothing is more firmly established than the perception that the "thirties" was a time of social realism. "Social Realism became not *a* style of the period," Tom Wolfe has written, "but *the* style of the period." Social realism in this sense has come to mean three things: the documentary aesthetic, a rearguard opposition to modernism, and a relatively straightforward representationalism in the arts. In fact, all three aspects are misunderstood: the documentary aesthetic was actually a central modernist innovation; the cultural front was *not* characterized by an opposition to modernism; and the crucial aesthetic forms and ideologies of the cultural front were not simple representationalism. Indeed, the aesthetic manifestos of the cultural front regularly sought a "revolutionary symbolism," and the styles and forms that resulted might be better characterized as a "proletarian grotesque."[7]

The argument that "documentary expression" distinguishes the culture of "thirties America"—first elaborated in Alfred Kazin's discussion of "documentary literature" in his 1942 literary history, *On Native Grounds*— has dominated American cultural studies since William Stott's 1973 study, *Documentary Expression and Thirties America.* Stott's book was a breakthrough in understanding depression culture: it cut across the Communist/anti-Communist divide that had dominated the 1950s and 1960s, and it crossed the boundaries between intellectual and popular culture. By focusing on the voracious appetite for documentary journalism, particularly the documentary book, that hybrid of photographs and text epitomized by Erskine Caldwell and Margaret Bourke-White's *You Have Seen Their Faces*, Stott persuasively documented the documentary impulse as it infiltrated radio news, film newsreels, novels, sociology, reportage, and even the American

Guide books of the Federal Writers Project. He explicitly turned his gaze away from the "proletarian novel" and recast left culture in the documentary mold: *The Grapes of Wrath*, we were reminded, began as a documentary book.

The documentary synthesis reoriented cultural history and criticism by changing the objects of study, making photography, and particularly the photographs of the Farm Security Administration, the central depression genre, and by turning critical debate to the formal and political issues raised by documentary: the problematics of capturing the "real," the desire for the objectivity and immediacy of "experience," the dangers of manipulation and propaganda. Not only did the documentary synthesis bring together the culture in a comprehensible whole, it provided a framework for understanding the book that had emerged in the 1960s as the masterwork of the depression, James Agee and Walker Evans's *Let Us Now Praise Famous Men*. It was, in Kazin's words, a "documentary book written to end all documentary books." Embodying and at the same time transcending the documentary genre, it became both a witness to depression America's desire to see the "real" and a cautionary tale of documentary's tragic superficiality.[8]

In retrospect, however, the success and influence of Stott's documentary synthesis seems as much a product of the 1960s as of the 1930s. After all, the revival of *Let Us Now Praise Famous Men* was part of the 1960s obsession with documentary and folk authenticity that produced the folk and blues purism of the "folk revival" (quite unlike the agitprop "impurity" of Popular Front singers like Josh White), the "new journalism," and cinéma verité. Though the focus on depression documentary does illuminate the middle-class attempts to visualize the depression, to give a face to economic crisis by collecting, classifying, and presenting images of the nation, it fails to capture the complexity of the aesthetic ideologies of the cultural front, leading us to imagine that Richard Wright and Edwin Rosskam's documentary book, *12 Million Black Voices*, is somehow more representative than Wright's novel, *Native Son*. Moreover, it tends to reinforce the sense that social realism was the dominant tendency, rather than seeing that the documentary impulse itself was less a triumph of realism than a sign of the failures of narrative imagination.[9]

Indeed, as we shall see in part three, nothing characterizes the works of the cultural front so much as the inability to imagine a completed narrative. The knowable communities and settled social relations that provide the underpinning for realist narrative were themselves in crisis. The documentary impulse was a peculiarly modernist solution to this crisis: the word "documentary" itself was coined in 1926 by the film critic John Grierson and the form was adopted by experimental writers and filmmakers. One can see this in the modernist aesthetic of the radical documentary filmmaker Leo Hurwitz. Hurwitz, who later wrote that he came "to hate the word documentary (though I never devised a better)," suggested that "the documentary film was anything but a document." "It did not 'document' reality at all," he wrote. "Its tiny documents in the form of shots and sounds bore the same relation to the film as the small pieces of colored stone and glass to the mosaic mural, the brush-strokes to the painting, the individual words and phrases to the novel. The stuff was document, but the construction was invented, a time-collage." To characterize film montage as "time-collage" directly echoes the spatial collages of modern painting. Moreover, much of the "documentary" work of the cultural front actually involved the experimental incorporation of news genres into art works: one sees this in Dos Passos's Newsreels, the theatrical Living Newspapers, and in Orson Welles's parodies of film newsreels and radio news coverage. Again, these "documentaries" are less a form of social realism than formal experiments.[10]

The second meaning of "social realism" is a negative one: it is understood as a rearguard opposition to modernism. "Even the most dedicated Modernists were intimidated," Tom Wolfe writes. "For more than ten years from about 1930 to 1941, the artists themselves, in Europe and America, suspended the Modern movement . . . Left politics did that for them." The depression is usually marked as an interregnum between modernism and postmodernism, the last hurrah of a lost nineteenth-century realism. With a few exceptions, we are told, the artists and critics of the left waved the banners of 1848, touting a middlebrow humanist cousin to Stalinist socialist realism. In this story, it is not surprising that the Popular Front appears as a cultural as well as a political failure; if the era belonged to the modernists, and the future—the American Century after the war—belonged to a still unnamed postmodernism, the moment of "social realism" was a lamentable, if understandable, detour. Even Fredric Jameson suggests as much when he speaks of "late modernism" as "the last survival of a properly modernist view of art and the world after the great political and economic break of the Depression, where, under Stalinism or the Popular Front, Hitler or the New Deal, some new conception of social realism achieves the status of momentary cultural dominance by way of collective anxiety and world war." For many cultural historians, only the *Partisan Review* heroically defended the modern and the modernists; a philistine anti-modernism ruled the rest of the old left. In this account, the post-war world restored cultural history to its main line: the triumph of abstract expressionism consigned the figurative social realists to the dustbin of history, and, as the tradition of the American romance was discovered to be the genius of American literature, the plebeian naturalism of left-wing fiction was forgotten.[11]

This history of the "modern" is flawed both in its sense of modernism in the United States and in its projection of the other of "social realism." Modernism in Europe was already staggering from the carnage of the Great War; the rise of European fascisms, the crash of 1929, and the worldwide depression left the various avant-gardes and modernisms in profound crisis. This was even more striking in the United States, where modernism had hardly emerged as an oppositional or avant-garde culture. Despite the blasts at the "genteel tradition," and the totemic figure of the "censored" and "suppressed" Dreiser, modernism in the United States was less the bohemian outrage against a nineteenth-century bourgeois culture than the cultural logic of Fordist capitalism, the soundtrack to the "roaring" twenties. By the late 1920s, this was evident to the preeminent ideologues of the modern in the United States; it is what makes Malcolm Cowley look so prescient, as he anticipates postmodernist critiques of modernism by arguing in 1934 that the modern and the bohemian were uncanny doubles of the culture of consumption, advertising, and marketing. The distinction between modernism and the avant-garde is nowhere more important than in America; for the US was, as Andreas Huyssen has argued, notoriously a place with a developed modernist culture and relatively few avant-gardes.[12]

The "proletarian" movement in culture was in fact one of the few important avant-gardes in US culture, and it attracted many of the artists whose careers had begun under the sign of an oppositional European modernism, the "exiles" who returned. Their return, and the simultaneous emergence of a generation of depression artists, produced a counterculture to Fordism and its nascent machinery of mass advertising, journalism, and broadcasting, a counterculture whose powerful emblems—*U.S.A., Citizen Kane, Modern Times, The Cradle Will Rock, Black, Brown, and Beige*— can hardly be grasped by the term "social realism." This is not to deny that the term "realism" offered a powerful attraction, reviving the inaugural American modernisms that were, after all, the naturalism of Dreiser and Norris and the "ashcan" figuralism of Sloan and the Eight. But the "realisms" of the cultural front were modified in oxymoronic fashion.

A remarkable cluster of aesthetic terms emerged in the years of the cultural front: new realism, dynamic realism, magic realism, social surrealism, proletarian surrealism, epic theater, and revolutionary symbolism. The "new realism" was Fernand Leger's name for a modern art based on "montage and closeups of commonplace objects"; the concept attracted the painter Stuart Davis, who featured Leger's essay in *Art Front*. Many subsequent "new" or "neo" realisms followed, including the "dynamic realism" of the photographer Paul Strand. "Magic realism" was coined in 1942 to characterize the left-wing painters like Peter Blume who were influenced by the Mexican modernism of the muralists and who "by means of an exact realistic technique try to make plausible and convincing their improbable, dreamlike or fantastic visions." In a similar vein, the Marxist art historian Oliver Larkin noted the "social surrealism" of the painter Walter Quirt and the sculptor David Smith; and *Direction* featured the paintings of James Guy and Louis Guglielmi under the title "Proletarian Surrealism"—"a style of painting usually identified with extreme individ- ualism and decadence takes on new vigor and meaning when it is used to express the moods and emotions of the dispossessed." "Epic theater," Brecht's theory and practice of a non-illusionist theater, found a number of US advocates, including Mordecai Gorelik, whose *New Theatres for Old* stands as the finest and most influential work of theatrical theory in the period. Almost all of the great Popular Front theatrical productions—from the Living Newspaper, to the Mercury's *Julius Caesar*, to Marc Blitzstein's operas—set themselves against theatrical naturalism.[13]

All of these terms are contradictory fusions. Some attempt to fuse a precapitalist mode—magic or the epic—with realism, imagining that this hybrid would enable access to forms outside capitalist rationalization, forms that could figure a collective life, forms that promised a genuine "socialist realism." Others attempt to fuse the energies of modernism, the "new," with a recognition of the social and political crisis. Thus, one might accurately call the work of the cultural front a "social modernism," a third wave of the modernist movement. This "social modernism" is embodied in the title of Kenneth Burke's 1935 address to the American Writers' Congress, "Revolutionary Symbolism in America." The title carries two meanings: it is both a discussion of the role of symbols in revolutionary politics *and* a juxtaposition of "symbolism"—the word that had become the shorthand for the arts of the modern—with "revolution," thus figuring a "revolutionary modernism." The trope of "revolutionary symbolism" is an inversion of the trope of "magic realism"; however, both signal the double sense of rupture and continuity with the modernist project. The project to transcend and rebuild modernism, often associated with Brecht and Benjamin, will, I suggest, yield a richer view of the culture of the Popular Front than any notion that the Popular Front aesthetic is an embodiment of "social realism." The very redundancy of "social realism" (imagine its opposite, a "magic symbolism," the apolitical modernism that Edmund Wilson broke from in *Axel's Castle*) stands in contrast to the oxymorons by which the cultural front attempted to name its aesthetic.[14]

The oxymoron—the apparent contradiction—is, Kenneth Burke argued, the characteristic trope of the grotesque, and the grotesque is the poetic form most appropriate to moments of crisis and transition, a form in which "the perception of discordancies is perceived without smile or laughter." "Humor tends to be conservative," Burke suggests, "the grotesque tends to be revolutionary." The grotesque creates gargoyles that violate accepted classifications, human heads on the bodies of birds. For Burke, the grotesque way of seeing characterizes both communism and surrealism, both Marx's account of class consciousness, which grotesquely realigns our categories of allegiance, and the "modern linguistic gargoyles" of Joyce. Indeed, Burke characterizes two of the young proletarian writers of the time, Robert Cantwell and Erskine Caldwell, as instances of the grotesque imagination. One could take Burke's suggestions further: in retrospect, the arts of the cultural front are better characterized as a "proletarian grotesque" than as any kind of social realism. The twisted figures of Philip Evergood's *American Tragedy* or *Dance Marathon*, the distended vowels of Billie Holiday's "Strange Fruit," the gargoyles that open *Citizen Kane*, the accident-victim photographs in Weegee's *Naked City*, the inventories of the Gudgers' belongings in *Let Us Now Praise Famous Men*, the gigantic head of Mussolini in Peter Blume's *Eternal City*, the political caricatures of Ollie Harrington and William Gropper: all echo the moment in Tillie Olsen's *Yonnondio* when the narrator interrupts the tale of a mine explosion for an extraordinary and grotesque lyric: "And could you not make a cameo of this and pin it onto your aesthetic hearts? . . . Surely it is original enough— these grotesques, this thing with the foot missing, this gargoyle with half the face gone and the arm . . . You will have the cameo? Call it Rascoe, Wyoming, any of a thousand mine towns in America, the night of a mine blowup."[15]

These "grotesques" are an attempt to wrench us out of the repose and distance of the "aesthetic." Olsen's taunting refusal of the aesthetic response to the mine explosion—"Surely it is classical enough for you— the Greek marble of the women, the simple flowing lines of sorrow, carved so rigid and eternal"—can also be heard in James Agee's passionate outburst against aestheticizing the lives of the Gudgers in *Let Us Now Praise Famous Men*, and in Billie Holiday's vocalization of the lynched body as a grotesque fruit, a chilling cameo of a "pastoral scene of the gallant South." This proletarian grotesque is a plebeian appropriation of the avant-garde hostility to "art," the anti-aesthetic of dada and surrealism. Moreover, it characterizes many of the "magic realisms" and "revolutionary symbolisms" that the artists and intellectuals of the cultural front imagined as a solution to the crisis of modernism and Fordism. The proletarian grotesque was an unstable, transitional modernism. On the one hand, its strange beasts did not have the classical repose of high modernism; on the other hand, its grim refusal of smiles and laughter continues to make it unpalatable to the playful mixes of postmodernism.

2. The People, Yes?

The symbol I should plead for, as more basic, more of an ideal incentive, than that of the worker, is that of "the people."

Kenneth Burke

Kenneth Burke provoked a famous controversy at the 1935 American Writers' Congress with his proposal to shift the rhetoric of the left from the "worker" to the "people"; in doing so he inadvertently became the foremost rhetorical theorist of the Popular Front. Though Burke was challenged by a number of critics at the Writers' Congress, he spoke for the vast majority of the depression left, the rank and file who would make up the Popular Front social movement that emerged when the Communist Party itself shifted to a populist rhetoric after the Seventh Congress of the Communist International in the summer of 1935. "The people" became the central trope of left culture in this period, the imagined ground of political and cultural activity, the rhetorical stake in ideological battle. The cultural front imagined itself as a "people's culture."[16]

"The people . . . are the heroes of our most gratifying books," the literary critic Samuel Sillen wrote in a *New Masses* essay called "The People, Yes": "of Elliot Paul's *The Stars and Stripes Forever*, of Ruth McKenney's *Industrial Valley*, of Richard Wright's *Uncle Tom's Children*, of Josephine Herbst's trilogy. The people, yes: in Margaret Bourke-White's and Erskine Caldwell's *You Have Seen Their Faces*, in Archibald MacLeish's *Land of the Free . . .* They have been successful in the measure that they have been faithful to the people." Sillen's litany was repeated in calls for a people's theater, people's songs, a People's Front. Indeed, nothing seems more obvious than the "populism" of the Popular Front. Moreover, this turn to the "people" is generally understood to be a retreat from the radical "proletarianism" of the early 1930s, as a sentimental liberalism which dissolved a politics of class conflict, of workers mobilization and self-organization, and obscured the divisions of ethnicity, race, and gender in an imagined unity of the "people" and the "people's culture." For most historians, the populism of the Popular Front is only a minor aspect of the wider populism that dominated American culture. "Certainly during the period from 1935 until the end of World War II," Warren Susman writes, "there was one phrase, one sentiment, one special call on the emotions that appeared everywhere in America's popular language: the people."[17]

If this populism was a rhetorical success, few have defended its intellectual and aesthetic consequences. Sillen's simple assertions that the "people" are the heroes of the "most gratifying" books, and that the books are successful insofar as they have been "faithful" to the people seem to justify Leslie Fiedler's claim that this was "a new middlebrow literature, no longer sentimentally Christian and pro-feminist like the best sellers of pre-World War I days, but sentimentally liberal and pro-'little people'—the maudlin tradition carried on by such Forties-Fifties writers of the second rank as James Michener, John Hersey and Irwin Shaw."[18]

However, this account of the "populism" of the age of the CIO is profoundly misleading on several counts. First, it confuses a populist *rhetoric* with a populist *politics*. There was *not* a radical break between the "proletarian moment" of the early 1930s and the Popular Front; the politics of the Popular Front was *not* populist, but remained a class-based labor politics. Second, the populist rhetoric of the Popular Front was not merely one voice harmonizing in a grand New Deal chorus. Rather, it was a response to the explosion of discordant "populisms" that emerged in the wake of the crisis of 1929. Third, the engagement with the rhetoric of the "people" by artists and intellectuals of the cultural front was less an imaginary solution than a formal and aesthetic problem. "The people," Jed Leland jeers at Kane in Welles's *Citizen Kane*, "your precious people. You talk as if you owned them." The question of "representing" the people—to depict and to speak for the people—lies at the center of the artistic and intellectual works of the cultural front, and, more often than not, it is the *absence* of the people that characterizes the works of the Popular Front.

If one defined political movements and parties by their rhetoric, virtually all of the political actors in modern mass democracies could be called "populist." The language of "we, the people" is a central part of twentieth-century political rhetoric and mobilization: if language were politics, we would all be populists. However, political movements are built on more than rhetoric, and populism, as a recurring form of social movements, is better understood as the politics of rent, credit, and taxes. The struggle over rent, credit, and taxes is what unites the populist farmers of the late nineteenth century and the neighborhood populisms of the 1970s and 1980s. Populism is usually a territorial politics, stressing issues of land, tenancy, and community: the Marx of populism is Henry George.[19]

By this measure, the politics of the Popular Front social movement were rarely populist; rather, the Popular Front combined three distinctive political tendencies: a social democratic laborism based on a militant industrial unionism; an anti-racist ethnic pluralism imagining the United States as a "nation of nations"; and an anti-fascist politics of international solidarity. Each of these was rooted in the politics of the early Communist Party and the International Labor Defense, and continued in different forms throughout the age of the CIO. The dramatic change in rhetoric from the Third Period's "Toward Soviet America" to the Popular Front's "Communism is Twentieth-Century Americanism" has often obscured the deeper continuities in left-wing activism. The desperate, apocalyptic rhetoric of the unemployed young radicals of the early 1930s was less a description of political strategies than a measure of the depths of the depression; as Walter Kalaidjian shrewdly notes, "the typical symbols of proletarian solidarity—the vertical red banner of class brotherhood, the assertive upraised fist (often clenching a weighty tool such as a wrench, sledgehammer or sickle), the contractual handshake, the muscle-bound torso, the strained but determined visage—stand not so much as phallic

icons of working-class hegemony but as uncanny symptoms of its absence."
The emergence of a populist rhetoric was not a retreat from revolution,
but a response to the growing power of the movement, and to the
competing populist rhetorics of the time.[20]

The extraordinary proliferation of populist rhetorics in the depression
was itself a symptom of the crisis. The crisis of 1929 was a crisis of
representation, a moment when social groups became detached from their
traditional parties. "These situations of conflict between 'represented' and
'representatives'," Gramsci suggested in his notes on periods of crisis,
"reverberate out from the terrain of the parties," creating a "crisis of
authority." This disarray in political and cultural representation generated
new forms of politics and culture, each attempting to reconstruct the
nation by representing the "people," to speak for the people by depicting
the people. There is no question that, as Warren Susman noted, "the idea
of the people is in abundant evidence in the rhetoric of the period"; the
novels, films, plays, and paintings of the "thirties" were dominated by
representations of the "people": a gallery of allegorical icons of victimiza-
tion, innocence, and resilience, ranging from Franklin Roosevelt's "forgotten man" to Steinbeck's Ma Joad, from Dorothea Lange's Migrant Mother
to Frank Capra's Mr Smith. But these representations should not be
lumped together into an undifferentiated "populism"; the apparent consensus of the "thirties"—the shared rhetoric of the people—obscures
deeper divisions and conflicts.[21]

In the wake of the Bolshevik revolution and the mass strikes and
uprisings of 1919, conservative and authoritarian mass movements had
grown in Europe and North America: fascism had become a serious mass
movement in Germany, Italy, Austria, Romania, and Hungary; moreover,
as Michael Mann has suggested, "fascism was only the most radical version
of a broader interwar movement rejecting democracy in favour of rightist
authoritarianism." In the United States, a number of authoritarian movements had emerged by the middle of the depression. The modern Ku Klux
Klan organized significant support in the Middle West and Southwest in
the 1920s, taking power in Texas and Arkansas. It became, in the words of
one historian, "the most powerful movement of the far right that America
has yet produced"; and both Klan leaders and contemporary critics saw the
Klan as the US variant of European fascism.[22]

Though the Klan's strength peaked before the crash of 1929, four
distinct kinds of authoritarian mass mobilizations followed. The first were
the relatively minor US supporters of European fascism, like the American
Order of Fascisti, or Black Shirts, and the German-American Bund; though
they gained few adherents, they served an important ideological role in
circulating European fascist ideologies in the United States. Second, there
were the various corporate populisms where business leaders sought to

address and mobilize popular constituencies directly, as in the case of Hearst's newspaper empire and the Du Pont-sponsored Liberty League; the American Liberty League was particularly important in mobilizing significant sectors of American capital against the New Deal in general and the federal labor relations machinery in particular.[23]

Third, there were several regional grass-roots movements, including Huey Long's Share Our Wealth movement, Father Coughlin's National Union for Social Justice, Francis Townsend's Old Age Revolving Pension organization, and William Dudley Pelley's Silver Shirts; these groups were contradictory mass movements combining popular hostility to corporate power with a variety of right-wing appeals to race and nation. Though some of these movements had seemed to be part of the left-wing insurgency of 1933 and 1934, calling for social justice and the redistribution of wealth, they turned markedly to the right when faced with the success of the New Deal and the Popular Front–backed CIO. After Long's assassination in 1935, anti-Semitism, anti-Communism, and racism came to dominate the rhetoric of his follower Gerald L. K. Smith; at the same time, Father Coughlin's Christian Front emerged in a number of cities as a significant form of Catholic fascism. Finally, there were a number of quasi-secret vigilante groups, like the Black Legion in Detroit, which were organized to combat labor unions; though they never had the national presence of the Liberty League or Father Coughlin, they were always a significant force in industrial cities, the source of labor spies and thugs. Though the national alliance of several of these figures in the Union Party campaign of 1936 was unsuccessful, the social movements of the right continued throughout the age of the CIO with substantial local support in Chicago, Detroit, Indianapolis, Brooklyn, and Los Angeles.[24]

Each of these authoritarian movements used images of class, race, religion, nation, and gender to define and organize the "people." In the populist rhetoric of the right, the "people" were generally the white American plain people, threatened by an underclass of "foreigners", blacks, and "fallen" women, provoked by Communist agitators. There were distinct clashes between different elements of the right: Father Coughlin had been a target of Detroit's Klan, and Huey Long's appeals to "share the wealth" seemed as dangerous to the Du Ponts' Liberty League as the CIO. Moreover, in response to these social movements, an official, mainstream populist rhetoric emerged in the New Deal state and in the culture industry, perhaps best represented by the fireside chats of Franklin Roosevelt and the films of Frank Capra. This populism might well be called sentimental, for, unlike the populisms of the right and the left, its narratives avoided the depiction of enemies, villains, or scapegoats. The people were not oppressed or exploited, they were merely "forgotten." They had only fear itself to fear; with confidence and faith, adversity could be conquered.[25]

The populist rhetoric of the Popular Front social movement must be understood as a political and ideological response both to the social movements of the right and to the official populism of the New Deal. On the one hand, the fact that US fascists achieved only local and regional power should not blind us to the genuine threat they represented to the left-wing labor and community movements; on the other hand, the left quickly saw the ways the popular response to the New Deal opened up new possibilities for mobilization and organization. The turn to a populist rhetoric was less a retreat from radicalism than an emblem of the shift from an embattled subculture to a significant mass social movement. Moreover, the "people" invoked by the left-wing Popular Front were neither the vast "middle" between the economic royalists and the foreign "lower classes" nor the white, ethnically unmarked, forgotten men: they were working men and women of many races and nationalities.

One can see this even in the relatively simple "Ballad for Americans." In a powerful and influential essay, Warren Susman argued that "Ballad for Americans" was about "the role of belief, about 'nobody who was anybody' and the 'anybody who was everybody,' about the ultimate identification: 'You know who I am: the people!'" Unfortunately, Susman got the lyrics to "Ballad for Americans" wrong. There is no "ultimate identification": the song is a continual deferral and refusal of a single identification. "Who are you?" the chorus asks; the reply—"I'm the everybody who's nobody. I'm the nobody who's everybody"—is followed not by "the people" but by two lyric catalogs. The first is a definition by class: "I'm an engineer, musician, street cleaner, carpenter, teacher." And, the chorus adds, "farmer . . . office clerk . . . mechanic . . . house wife . . . factory worker . . . stenographer . . . beauty specialist . . . bartender . . . truck driver . . . seamstress . . . ditch digger." "I am the et ceteras. And the and so forths that do the work." The second catalog is a definition by ethnicity, nationality, race: "Are you an American?" the chorus asks, to which the singer replies: "Am I an American? I'm just an Irish, Negro, Jewish, Italian, French and English, Spanish, Russian, Chinese, Polish, Scotch, Hungarian, Litvak, Swedish, Finnish, Canadian, Greek and Turk, and Czech and double Czech American." John LaTouche's lyrics are precisely about the difficulty of representing the people; though the singer says "I represent the WHOLE," that whole is made up of "nobodies," "et ceteras," and "and so forths." The drama of the cantata is the continual questioning: Who are you? What's your name, Buddy? What's your racket?[26]

Nevertheless, the cantata does invoke the figure of America; it is a ballad for "Americans" and the singer ends by repeatedly singing the word "America." Is this not an emblem of what literary critic Jonathan Arac has called the "euphoria of America" and historian Gary Gerstle has called "the politics of patriotism," the Popular Front nationalism that has warmed the hearts of liberal historians and dismayed radical critics? A number of recent interpretations of the "rise and fall of the New Deal Order" have argued that the populist and Americanist Roosevelt coalition was fractured by a turn to the politics of race and to an "anti-American" politics of anti-imperialism; and many radical critics of the Popular Front have argued that it ignored issues of race and ethnicity in the pursuit of a nationalist rhetoric. Though these two interpretations of the Popular Front come from opposed political perspectives, they both take the Communist Party's Popular Front slogan—"Communism is twentieth-century Americanism"— as an accurate summation of Popular Front ideology and aesthetics.[27]

There is no question that the politics and poetics of Americanism lay at the center of the Popular Front social movement. But it is a mistake to see it simply as a "politics of patriotism," a rhetorical invocation of unity and harmony which, in Gerstle's words, "made workers receptive to patriotic appeals," and whose "decisive feature . . . was a reverence for the country's political heritage, values and institutions." Rather, as Matthew Josephson put it in 1936, "'Americanism'—Heaven preserve us—is any man's battle." The figure of "America" became a locus for ideological battles over the trajectory of US history, the meaning of race, ethnicity, and region in the United States, and the relation between ethnic nationalism, Americanism, and internationalism. Indeed, the ubiquity of "America" in the rhetoric of the period is less a sign of "deep reverence" or "harmony" than a sign of the crisis of Americanism, provoked by the crash of 1929 and the social conflicts of the depression, not least the violent suppression of the "Bonus Marchers," the World War I Veterans, in 1932.[28]

The debate over Americanism on the cultural left can be seen in the 1936 *Partisan Review and Anvil* symposium, "What is Americanism?", in which Josephson's comment appeared. The symposium focused on the issues of American exceptionalism and the nature of the American tradition: Was there a "distinct native revolutionary heritage" or was "the brutal struggle for individual riches" the "essence of Americanism"? Was the culture of the United States separate from and opposed to that of Western Europe? What was the relation of Marxism to the American tradition? These questions had been debated on the left for a number of years, particularly by the dissident communist intellectuals around Calverton's *Modern Monthly*, who felt that the Communist Party had ignored the specificities of US experience. In the spring of 1930, Calverton had brought together a group of radical intellectuals to collaborate on a Marxist study of the United States, "America at the Crossroads"; two years later, a similar attempt to produce a Marxist version of the famous 1922 *Civilization in the United States* was mounted by Granville Hicks, Newton Arvin, and Bernard

Smith. Though neither of these anthologies was produced, they marked
the beginning of a wave of left-wing reflections on the meaning of
American history and culture, which included the *Partisan Review and Anvil*
symposium of 1936.[29]

Most of the participants in the *Partisan Review and Anvil* symposium were
established modernist writers, including Theodore Dreiser, Josephine
Herbst, Kenneth Burke, William Carlos Williams, Newton Arvin, and Waldo
Frank. For them the figure of "America" was embodied in the promise of
the Lincoln republic; "the old democratic radicals—Paine, Samuel Adams,
Freneau, and their like," Newton Arvin wrote, "had envisioned an individ-
ualistic, but quite classless, republican society." The moderns imagined
themselves as the inheritors of those democratic radicals; Josephine Herbst
made the case most directly by telling the history of her own family from a
colonial land grant from William Penn to landlessness. But the promise of
what Josephson called the "free (petty bourgeois) citizen's Republic" had
been betrayed by the rise of the "robber barons," the "big money": after
the "full flowering" of the "bourgeois-capitalist perspective," Kenneth
Burke wryly noted, "there was nothing left to do but go in for a series of
real estate booms." This narrative of the decline and fall of the Lincoln
republic informed many of the works of the radical moderns, ranging from
Matthew Josephson's trilogy of popular historical works, *The Robber Barons*,
The Politicos, and *The President Makers*, to Josephine Herbst's grand trilogy
of novels about the Trexler family.[30]

One writer, however, took a distinctly different tack. "If you lose an arm,
you are likely to think a great deal about arms," Joseph Freeman wrote,
"and if you are born into an oppressed nationality you are likely to think a
great deal about oppression and about nationalism." Freeman had arrived
in the slums of New York from the Ukraine at the age of seven, and his
conception of Americanism and nationalism was shared by many of the
first- and second-generation plebeian artists and intellectuals who made up
the cultural left. "The native-born American," he wrote, "takes his Americanism for granted; the 'alien,' absorbing America into his heart, being
absorbed into its culture, thinks about the meaning of America day and
night." The result was a paradoxical synthesis of competing nationalisms
and internationalism—pride in ethnic heritage and identity combined with
an assertive Americanism and a popular internationalism—which dominated much of the culture of those Louis Adamic called the "new
Americans." This "pan-ethnic Americanism" is perhaps the most powerful
working-class ideology of the age of the CIO, and it significantly reshaped
the contours of official US nationalism.[31]

Many of the new forms and styles of Popular Front culture were attempts
to figure this pan-ethnic Americanism, which was a complex and contradictory amalgam of three different tendencies. First of all, it included a

fascination with the grand narratives—the tall tales—of the American past. Howard Fast's historical novels like *Citizen Tom Paine* and *Freedom Road* became perennial favorites of the ethnic rank and file of the Popular Front. Moreover, the anxiety that one was not part of "America" led to the exaggerated "Americanism" that later historians and critics have mocked, like the Communist Party's resurrection of Earl Browder's Virginian ancestor, Littleberry Browder, who had fought in the Revolution. But it is worth noting that this appropriation of American mythologies had a more radical edge than is usually admitted. Whereas the official Americanisms of the Depression usually invoked the figure of Lincoln, the Popular Front was more likely to invoke John Brown.[32]

However, this attraction to American mythologies was accompanied by a second tendency, an accentuation of nationality. Far from ignoring the ethnic and racial divisions of the United States, the writers and artists of the cultural front continually questioned what Richard Wright called the "nationalist implications of their lives." Like Joseph Freeman, Wright had been drawn to Marxism in part through the writings of Lenin and Stalin on oppressed nationalities. Indeed, the notion of a working-class federation of nationalities was a vital part of American Communist theory and practice, the other side of its revolutionary industrial unionism. Since much of the strength of the early Communist Party lay in its foreign-language federations, the great political and theoretical divide within the Party had always been between those in trades-union work, organizing largely inside the existing AFL craft unions and guided by Foster's revolutionary syndicalism, and those in nationality work, organizing in the foreign-language associations of working-class immigrants who labored in non-union industries.[33]

Nevertheless, there was a significant decline in ethnic cohesion during the age of the CIO, and the second-generation Americans, the heroes of labor history, are often cast as the villains of ethnic history. Many Popular Front figures distanced themselves from forms of racial or ethnic national-ism and challenged conservative religious and entrepreneurial leaders in ethnic communities: "Negro writers," Richard Wright argued, "must accept the nationalist implications of their lives, not in order to encourage them, but in order to change and transcend them. They must accept the concept of nationalism because, in order to transcend it, they must *possess* and *understand* it." Both the Americanism and the nationalism of the Popular Front was inflected with a popular *internationalism.* "Perhaps we should not use the same term 'nationalism' which the capitalists use," wrote the left-wing Chinatown writer Wenquan; his alternative, "ethnicism," was "an ethnic perspective of the internationalist proletariat," encompassing both "our warm love for the language and cultural tradition of our ancestral country . . . [and] a respect for racial equality, the love for, and the unity among all peoples of all nations." This pan-ethnic appeal to a federation of nationalities both within the United States and around the globe was a powerful part of Popular Front culture; one can see it in the federal structure of the IWO, in the solidarity campaigns for Spain, Ethiopia, and China, and in the sense of a kinship between the two great continental federations of nationalities, the United States and the Soviet Union. The success of the Popular Front social movement was in part the result of the alliance between the left-wing nationality orders of the IWO and the new unions of the CIO. In a similar way, the labor stories of Popular Front culture—the proletarian novels and strike dramas—are almost always nationality stories: narratives of ethnic and racial communities stand at the heart of the Popular Front aesthetic. Some take the form of the migration narrative; others take the form of the ghetto or tenement pastoral. Virtually all claim to be ballads for Americans, alternately cursing Columbus and eulogizing Lincoln.[34]

This pan-ethnic internationalism was always an unstable combination, challenged by official Americanisms, conservative anti-Communist ethnic nationalisms, and persistent racism and ethnic antagonism. "Our most solemn duty," Wenquan wrote, "is to purify our corrupted souls. We must be honest with ourselves in order to reform and re-educate ourselves on the meaning of 'we the people.'" Often, the federation of nationalities seemed only a rhetorical unity, as writers and artists grasped for adequate metaphors. Using a common trope, the artist Rockwell Kent, president of the IWO, testified that the IWO rejected the image of the "melting pot," seeing the "culture of America" as "more like a tapestry, woven of brilliant colored threads, every one of which can be distinguished, and keep its own characteristics." In her novel *Yonnondio*, Tillie Olsen has the child Mazie reading names on the blackboard: "Na-tion-al-it-ies American Armenian Bohemian Chinese Croatian (Croatian—that was what ol' man Kvaternick was, ol' man Kvaternick in the mine and he was dead now, dead. Worms . . . no don't think of ol' man Kvaternick) Irish French Italian Jewish Lith . . . A face was black, black like when the men come up from the mine; lots of faces were black. [. . .] Mexican Negro Polish Portuguese." Mazie's revery on black faces in the midst of the catalog is itself a figure of the way that African American culture often became the touchstone for this new "American" culture. Indeed, Paul Robeson's concerts were, for his audiences, an embodiment of this Popular Front vision. By singing songs from around the world, he created a symbolic federation of national folk musics anchored in the African American spiritual.[35]

If the modernist lament for the betrayal of the Lincoln republic and the plebeian invention of a pan-ethnic Americanism mark two crucial forms of Popular Front "Americanism," the rise of a "proletarian regionalism" provided a third kind of "national" thinking on the cultural left. "Regionalism," like populism, was a multi-accented slogan in early years of the depression, encompassing the white supremacist nostalgia of the southern Agrarians, the remarkable historical murals of Thomas Hart Benton, and the new social science of "regions," developed by figures like Lewis Mumford and Howard Odum. A "new regionalism in American literature," as the young California writer Carey McWilliams called it, had emerged in late 1920s and early 1930s in small magazines like Benjamin Botkin's *Folk-Say* and *Space*, and it often overlapped with the proletarian culture avant-garde. For many of the young midwestern, southwestern, and western writers collecting folklore and contributing stories to the little magazines, the "regionalist" banner was adopted in the face of the metropolitan cultural left, and the "proletarian" banner was adopted in opposition to the forms of reactionary and racist regionalism epitomized by the southern Agrarians.

The New York cultural left often ignored or rejected this radical regionalism: "'Regional'," the left-wing regionalist Sanora Babb recalled, "was the stinging word used by certain influential New York groups to try to keep writers outside NY in their places." Cultural historian Constance Rourke opened her influential 1933 discussion of the "significance of sections" by criticizing the metropolitan Marxist critics V.F. Calverton and Granville Hicks for ignoring and denying the importance of regionalism: "Even if revolution starts in a tenth-floor loft in New York," Rourke argued, "or in the textile mills of a Southern village or a plant on the River Rouge, a knowledge of these regional differences would seem essential for the enterprise of initiating the class struggle on any broad scale." Rourke went on to argue that the United States had a "deeply rooted, widespread folk expression—regional in character, some of it quite proletarian in sentiment."[36]

However, as the controversies over regionalism developed, this "proletarian regionalism," as Benjamin Botkin called it, was primarily aimed at conservative and reactionary regionalisms. These regionalisms, Botkin argued, identified regional culture with a particular way of life, and thus took "a certain social background for granted and a certain social order as final." This was particularly true, he continued, of the southern Agrarians, whose picture of an organic agrarian culture was based on the social order of white supremacy and ended up excusing the "regrettably violent" practice of lynching. Indeed, whereas conservative regionalists nostalgically evoked past ways of life, radical regionalists paradoxically pointed to the absence of culture, the lack of roots. "Nothing has ever been rooted there," the Communist regionalist Meridel Le Sueur wrote of the Plains. "We have never, in the Middle West, had ease or an indigenous culture. We have been starved since our birth." As a result, the left-wing regionalists hailed the novelists who wrote of regional transitions from agriculture to industry (the proletarian novelist Grace Lumpkin is cited by both Constance Rourke and B.A. Botkin) and emphasized new forms of industrial folklore. This had a powerful institutional impact on the New Deal cultural apparatuses: Rourke became the editor of the Federal Art Project's *Index of American Design* and Botkin served as the national folklore editor of the Federal Writers Project, the chair of the WPA's Joint Committee on the Folk Arts, and the head of the Library of Congress Archive of American Folk Song.[37]

Rourke and Botkin were both important Popular Front intellectuals, in their affiliations (both were members of the League of American Writers) and in their cultural and aesthetic ideologies. Their work on the popular arts, industrial folklore, and regional cultures became central to the Popular Front exploration of what Gramsci called the "national-popular." Indeed, if we translate the categories that have dominated considerations of the age of the CIO—"populism" and "nationalism"—into Gramsci's notion of the "national-popular," we might better see the complex and often contradictory meaning of Popular Front "populism" and "national-ism." These were not the sentimental invocations of a people without race or ethnicity, nor were they the "politics of patriotism," resolving all conflicts in the harmony of "Americanism." Rather, they were attempts to imagine a new culture, a new way of life, a revolution.[38]

Consider the parallels between the 1933 arguments of Gramsci and Rourke. Both were provoked by the contemporary arguments over a revolutionary or proletarian literature. In a critique of Paul Nizan's account of revolutionary literature, Gramsci challenged the avant-garde sense that a "new literature has to identify itself with an artistic school of intellectual origins, as was the case with Futurism." On the contrary, a new literature must "sink its roots into the humus of popular culture as it is, with its tastes and tendencies and with its moral and intellectual world, even if it is backward and conventional." Similarly, Rourke argued that folk expression is "the basis from which . . . a revolutionary literature can develop." The "mistake" of Calverton and Hicks, she argues, "is to consider that a literature—and perhaps a revolution—can take flight from an intellectual synthesis, and to ignore humble influences of place and kinship and common emotion that accumulate through generations to shape and condition a distinctive native consciousness."[39]

Both Gramsci and Rourke wished to recast the argument about a new art as an argument about a new culture. "It seems evident," Gramsci argued in his prison notebooks,

> that . . . one should speak of a struggle for a "new culture" and not for a "new art." . . . To fight for a new art would mean to fight to create new individual artists, which is absurd since artists cannot be created artificially. One must speak of a struggle for a new culture, that is, for a new moral life that cannot but be

intimately connected to a new intuition of life, until it becomes a new way of feeling and seeing reality and, therefore, a world intimately ingrained in "possible artists" and "possible works of art." . . . A new social group that enters history with a hegemonic attitude, with a self-confidence which it initially did not have, cannot but stir up from deep within it personalities who would not previously have found sufficient strength to express themselves fully in a particular direction.

Gramsci's unfinished notebooks on folklore, serial novels, and popular culture are echoed by Rourke's pioneering studies of American humor, vaudeville, and vernacular art.[40]

Much of the "populist" and "nationalist" cultural work inspired by the Popular Front social movement might be seen as an attempt to answer the question Gramsci poses time and again: "When can the conditions for awakening and developing a national-popular collective will be said to exist?" The answers were not, as Warren Susman charged, "an absurd vision of the American past, a peculiar notion of American society in the present, [and] a ludicrous attitude toward American culture in general." Rather, they were the extraordinary series of "ballads for Americans": the cultural histories of Constance Rourke; the pioneering studies of American capitalist development by Lewis Corey, Louis Hacker, Matthew Josephson, and Paul Sweezy; the literary histories of Granville Hicks, F.O. Matthiessen, Alfred Kazin, Leo Marx, William Charvat, and Leslie Fiedler; the studies of race and ethnicity by Carey McWilliams, Louis Adamic, and Oliver Cromwell Cox; the histories of slave rebellion and resistance by C.L.R. James, W.E.B. Du Bois, and Herbert Aptheker; the histories of American women's movements by Eleanor Flexner and Gerda Lerner, the studies of jazz and black vernacular musics by Sidney Finkelstein, Eric Hobsbawm, and Leroi Jones; the intellectual histories of Merle Curti and Richard Hofstadter, not to mention the grand syntheses in C.L.R. James's *American Civilization* and Max Lerner's *America as a Civilization*. Indeed, as I have argued elsewhere, the development of the academic field of "American studies" in the age of the CIO has its roots in the Popular Front explorations of the "national-popular."[41]

Thus, Paul Robeson's "Ballad for Americans" should be understand not as an emblem of middlebrow patriotism, but as a synecdoche for the extraordinary flowering of the historical imagination in Popular Front fiction, film, music, and art. Dos Passos's *U.S.A.* and Josephine Herbst's Trexler trilogy; Orson Welles's *Citizen Kane* and *The Magnificent Ambersons*; the reinvention of history painting in Jacob Lawrence's sequences about Harriet Tubman, Frederick Douglass, and Toussiant L'Ouverture, Ben Shahn's *Passion of Sacco and Vanzetti,* and Philip Evergood's *American Tragedy*; Paul Strand's work of historical photography, *Time in New England*;

Duke Ellington's musical history of black America, *Black, Brown and Beige*; the historical novels of the Rosenberg trial by E.L. Doctorow and Robert Coover: none of these end like the Hollywood *Grapes of Wrath*, with Jane Darwell's Ma Joad insisting, "Can't nobody lick us. We'll go on forever. We're the people." Rather, they meditate on the absence of the people: on the martyrs, the losses, the betrayals, the disinherited.

3. Panther Women of the Needle Trades

The age of the CIO lay between the two great waves of US feminism in the twentieth century, and most historians have concluded that, despite the importance of radical women activists and intellectuals, no explicit feminist aesthetic or ideology emerged in the Popular Front social movement. Moreover, over the last two decades, a powerful feminist critique of Popular Front culture has emerged, a critique markedly different from both the New York intellectuals' attack on Stalinist kitsch and the New Left's critique of uncritical populism and nationalism.

The feminist critique of the Popular Front social movement takes two forms: a critique of the sexual politics of the movement, and a critique of the gender unconscious of its culture. The first part is largely persuasive: the leaderships of the left, the labor movement, and the organizations of the cultural front were dominated by men, and they set its priorities. Nevertheless, as several recent historians have argued, there was a rank-and-file "left feminism" in these years that has been obscured both by the marginalization of women on the left and by the antagonism between Popular Front women activists and the self-conscious "feminists" of the National Women's Party. This left feminism had a number of sources, including the neighborhood and community councils of housewives which organized consumer boycotts, housing protests, and strike support; the growing numbers of women in the cultural apparatus, particularly those in the left-wing locals of the teachers union; the dramatic increase in the numbers of women in the Communist Party itself; and, of course, the wartime employment of women in the metalworking industries. By the end of the war, this Popular Front feminism was at the core of the Congress of American Women, a national feminist organization founded in 1946 which united activists for peace, social justice, and women's rights until it was attacked by HUAC in 1948.[42]

However, the feminist critique of Popular Front culture goes beyond the sexual politics of the movement, arguing that the symbolic systems and aesthetic ideologies of the Popular Front were inscribed with what might be called a "gender unconscious". "During the 1930s," Paula Rabinowitz writes, "class struggle in the United States was metaphorically engendered through a discourse that re-presented class conflict through the language of sexual difference." Moreover, the symbolic systems of the Popular Front drew on a traditional iconography and rhetoric of manhood and woman-hood that was at odds with the utopian and emancipatory hopes of the movement. "Women remained in a marginal and subordinated position in that movement," Elizabeth Faue concludes, "excluded both from the arrangements of power and from the symbolic system of labor." As a result, Wendy Kozol writes, "American radicalism remained a guardian of male sexual authority."[43]

Two aspects of this gender unconscious have drawn most attention: the belligerent masculinism of the proletarian avant-garde and the militant labor movement; and the sentimental maternalism of Popular Front representations of women. The cult of the virile male working-class body is without a doubt a major element of the early proletarian avant-garde, which, like many of the modernist avant-gardes, invoked masculinist metaphors of sexual conflict in their manifestos. Figures like Michael Gold and Philip Rahv saw themselves threatened by both a "feminine" genteel tradition and a "feminine" mass culture. Cartoon images of giant male workers pervaded union newspapers and radical magazines; as Elizabeth Faue has argued, militant labor unions "forged a web of symbols which romanticized violence, rooted solidarity in metaphors of struggle, and constructed work and workers as male." However, as the cultural front became less an embattled avant-garde and more the culture of a social movement, this masculinist rhetoric was contested, and new representa-tions of women began to emerge in the years of the Popular Front.[44]

However, several critics and historians have argued that these new images of womanhood were dominated by "icons of militant motherhood." "As proletarianism gave way to populism," Paula Rabinowitz writes, "revol-utionary girls became partisan mothers." Maternity became a powerful political force, she argues, and feminism receded in the face of a left-wing pronatalism. Though Rabinowitz offers nuanced readings of the radical novels that invoke the "great mother," she suggests that these works still carry "traces of the bourgeois motherhood depicted in domestic fiction." "Without a[n] . . . aesthetic and political culture of feminism, [the writers] remained stuck in traditional renderings of femininity."[45]

Perhaps the most famous image that emerged from the Popular Front was an icon of motherhood, Dorothea Lange's photograph, "Migrant Mother" (Figure 7). Drawing on a long tradition of portraits of Madonna and child, its power lies largely in its iconic, non-narrative stasis, its sense of presence and being. The title seems an oxymoron, as if migrant and mother were contradictory; indeed, there is little sense of migration or movement in the photograph. Though recent critics have attempted to recover its hidden narrative by identifying the woman, Florence Thomp-son, and situating the photograph as part of a series of photographs that

Lange took of Thompson, the image resists history. Moreover, it is striking that most of the crucial women characters in the "grapes of wrath" narrative are these migrant mothers, whom Wendy Kozol called "Madonnas of the Fields": one thinks particularly of Ma Joad in *The Grapes of Wrath*, memorably played by Jane Darwell in the film, but also of Doña Henriqua in Ernesto Galarza's *Barrio Boy*. In most of the migrant narratives, the mother of the young male protagonist is vividly depicted but remains a static figure of tradition and family.[46]

Nevertheless, the gender unconscious of the Popular Front was more complex than these icons of motherhood would indicate. Though the "revolutionary girl" did disappear from left iconography, her place was taken by a contradictory figure who was not a traditional rendering of femininity: the figure of the young woman garment worker who produces and consumes the fashions of the clothing trades. This "panther woman of the needle trades," to borrow the title of an experimental film about the Popular Front feminist Elizabeth Hawes, not only stands at the heart of the Popular Front social movement but is found throughout its stories, not only as a character in its musicals and films but as an emblem of a contradictory world of work and fashion, feminism and femininity, in the autobiographical narratives of the Popular Front left feminists.

The symbolic center of Popular Front womanhood was the garment industry. The majority of workers in the needle trades were women, largely immigrants or the children of immigrants, and women were the rank and file of the Amalgamated Clothing Workers of America (ACWA) and the International Ladies' Garment Workers Union (ILGWU). In a series of dramatic strikes in 1933 and 1934, the organization of women dressmakers had resurrected the divided and demoralized ILGWU, and the ACWA also grew rapidly in the wake of the NIRA of 1933. The social democratic unionism of the needle trades unions put them at the forefront of the emerging industrial unionism of the CIO, and, as I argued above, they had developed pioneering cultural, educational, and recreational wings.[47]

There is no doubt that the needle trades unions reflected the masculinism of the labor movement generally: as one historian has written of the ACWA, "the nearly complete male dominance of a union at least half female was never seriously challenged." Rose Pesotta, who served for a decade as the only woman vice president of the ILGWU, stepped down in 1944 after deciding that "a lone woman vice-president could not adequately represent the women who now make up 85 per cent of the International's membership." Moreover, as Elizabeth Faue has argued, the iconography of the ILGWU's newspaper, *Justice*, was dominated by images of male workers. Nevertheless, the radical young women of the needles trades found other ways to represent themselves, stitching their work lives together with a popular culture of fashion, romance, and celebrity to create a distinctive figure of the modern working woman. Perhaps the most famous self-representation was that of Ruth Rubinstein, who sang the lyric lament of a department-store worker, "Chain Store Daisy," in *Pins and Needles* (Figure 8). *Pins and Needles*, which I shall look at closely in chapter 8, was a musical revue staged by young garment workers; it became the longest-running Broadway show in history and toured the US for four years.[48]

"Ruth Rubinstein," according to the description in the *Pins and Needles* program, "the little girl who 'used to be on the daisy chain and now she's a chain store daisy,' is a crackjack brassiere operator. She can turn out twenty-five dozen a day, no mean achievement." Ruth Rubinstein was an emblem of the young working women caught between the world of wage labor and a popular culture saturated with fashion, consumer cosmetics and beauty products, Hollywood stars, romance magazines, and the love songs of Tin Pan Alley. They were not the "rebel girls" of the 1910s, the avant-garde, self-conscious feminists epitomized for a generation by the figures of Elizabeth Gurley Flynn, Emma Goldman, and the 1909 Uprising of the Ten Thousand: that revolutionary girl predated the Hollywood star system. The "NRA babies" who joined the depression ILGWU and ACWA had grown up under the sign of the flapper, and during the thoroughgoing transformation of the feminist culture of the 1910s into what Lois Banner has usefully termed "fashion culture." As early as 1927, the "industrial feminists" of the earlier generation were asking themselves: "Can we organize the flapper?" The Popular Front activism of these young women workers was, one might say, a combination of industrial feminism and the flapper.[49]

"The girls came dressed in their best dresses, made by themselves, and reflecting the latest styles," ILGWU organizer Rose Pesotta wrote of the 1933 picket line of Mexican American dressmakers in Los Angeles. "Many of them were beauties, and marched on the sidewalks like models in a modiste's salon." By 1940, Pesotta was organizing "a dozen union girls in evening dress" to picket Hollywood's Spring Style Pageant: the "local papers carried pictures of our picket line in evening garb, alongside those of Hollywood models wearing gowns our members had made." The union held fashion shows at the Biltmore and sponsored style-show floats at Labor Day parades.[50]

This culture of fashion and beauty pervaded the world of working women. There was, one historian writes, "avid support among waitresses for beauty contests" sponsored by their unions. Among California cannery workers—like those in the garment trade, young immigrant and ethnic women—movie stars and romance magazines like *True Story* were a shared idiom; a Chicana UCAPAWA activist recalled that she "broke the ice" with a Jewish workmate "by talking about Clark Gable . . . I loved *True Story*, and

she did, too. We'd discuss every little story." The combination of labor
feminism and Hollywood lay at the heart of the Popular Front picture
magazine, *Friday*, which, as I noted earlier, had been launched in the
spring of 1940 as an anti-fascist, pro-labor version of *Life*. Photo essays on
ordinary women workers—like the ones on Laura Law, a murdered union
activist, and hotel worker Marie Crane, the 21-year-old daughter of a
Pittsburgh steelworker, visiting the New York World's Fair—ran next to
features on Popular Front stars, including the dancer Katherine Dunham,
Rita Hayworth, Dorothy Comingore ("Mrs Citizen Kane"), and the young
Café Society singer, Helena (later, Lena) Horne.[51]

The response of left-wing artists and intellectuals in the cultural front to
this working-class culture of fashion and beauty was contradictory, at times
refusing its false promises and at other times trying to capture its mythic
power. The proletarian avant-garde tended to be hostile to the culture of
the love story and screen magazines, explicitly imagining itself as an
alternative: *Working Woman* and the *New Masses* were to take the place of
True Story. There were several experiments in collective writing by women
workers: "Stockyard Stella," the "first American proletarian love story," was
written by women meatpackers and published in the Communist Party's
Working Woman in 1935; *I Am a Woman Worker* was a collection of
anonymous autobiographies published by the social democratic women
activists of the Affiliated Schools for Workers in 1936. The work of the
young proletarian writer, Tillie Lerner Olsen, gives a sense of these
tensions. Olsen, born around 1913 in Nebraska, was the daughter of
working-class Russian Jewish immigrants; she never completed high school,
going to work and joining the Young Communist League while in her
teens. Part of the proletarian avant-garde of the early 1930s, her first
publication was a poem about garment workers in a 1934 issue of *The
Partisan*, the magazine of the West Coast John Reed Club. The *New Masses*
and the little magazines of the proletarian avant-garde sought letters from
workers about their lives, and a number of proletarian poets crafted verse
based on this "workers correspondence." Olsen's poem, "I Want You
Women Up North to Know," is one of these, reworking a letter to the *New
Masses* by Felipe Ibarro.[52]

The poem, like the letter, explicitly links the dresses of the department
stores with the labor of Chicana garment workers in San Antonio in a
"grotesque act:"

> I want you women up north to know
> how those dainty children's dresses you buy
> at macy's, wanamakers, gimbels, marshall fields,
> are dyed in blood, are stitched in wasting flesh,
> down in San Antonio, "where sunshine spends the winter."

The poem dissolves the "salesladies trill / 'exquisite work, madame'" into the "cough" of the consumptive Catalina. Its central conceit, "the esthetic dance of her fingers," rhymes the "needle pocked fingers" of "maria, ambrosa, catalina" with both the "feverish dawn" whose "malignant fingers . . . jerk them to work," and the women up North who "finger the exquisite hand made dresses." The poem sets itself against the fashions of the North—the "exquisite pleats"—offering as an alternative the "designs, multitudinous, complex and handmade by Poverty / herself," "more intricate than any a thousand hands could fashion." This exorcism of the culture of fashion and sweatshops—the last lines are "I tell you this can't last forever. / I swear it won't."—is built on the opposition of North and South.[53]

In Olsen's novel *Yonnondio*, however, the culture of fashion has come to inhabit the sweatshop itself, figured as the dump in which the children of the packinghouse play. Jinella collects her "'properties': blond wood-shaving curls, moldering hats, raggy teddies, torn lace curtains (for trains and wedding dresses), fringes, tassels, stubs of lipstick, wrecks of high-heeled shoes and boots, lavish jewelry Tiffany would never recognize," all in order to act out "[t]welve-year-old Jinella's text: the movies, selected . . . *Sheik of Araby. Broken Blossoms. Slave of Love. She Stopped at Nothing. The Fast Life. The Easiest Way.*" "The conjurer magic of a shining screen in darkness Saturdays" not only effaces the books the librarian offers the children, but stands as a constant challenge to the proletarian writer herself: "On a little table there were a lot of magazines," the narrator of *Yonnondio* tells us, "*Screen Star* and *True Confession*. Mazie turned the pages—there were pictures in them of men and ladies smiling, or kissing." The lure of the romance and screen magazines haunted the proletarian avant-garde.[54]

Moreover, a significant group of left-wing writers—figures like Hope Hale, Ruth McKenney, and Vera Caspary—worked for the slick and pulp women's magazines. Entangled directly in the culture of fashion and romance, they attempted to reconcile their commercial writing with their political affiliations. Hope Hale, born in Iowa in 1903, the daughter of a midwestern high-school principal, was, as she later wrote, one of the young women of the 1920s in New York who "spent our days pursuing success and our nights gaining what we thought of as experience." She worked in magazine advertising; by 1930 she was the promotions manager of the popular humor weekly *Life*, and in 1931 created a briefly successful romance magazine sold in department stores, *Love Mirror*. After *Love Mirror* folded, she became a free-lance writer of magazine stories for pulps like *Snappy Stories* and *Modern Romances* and slicks like the *New Yorker*. She also wrote for the *New Masses*, was active in the League of American Writers, and was a member of the secret branch of the Communist Party in Washington that included a number of New Deal government employees.[55]

Hale spoke at the 1939 American Writers' Congress, and criticized the avant-gardism of the proletarian literature movement. "We have started 'little' magazines, one after another," she said, "to be read by dutiful fellow writers for the few months necessary ... [U]ntil lately we have been too hypocritical or unrealistic in our devotion to proletarian literature to make any attempt to discover what workers really like to read and do read." "The very biggest single group of readers in the world," she went on, "are those who literally wear out the more than two million copies of *True Story* printed every month." McFadden's *True Story*—which indeed was the most widely read magazine among young working-class women and men— recognized "the demand for realistic fiction." "Up to that time popular magazines dealt with only the most superficial, decorative aspects of human emotions. From the slicks on down through the love story pulps, the regular fare was escape fiction in which the heroine lived on air and walked on clouds and did her suffering only over such problems as whether to stow away on a millionaire's yacht." *True Story*, on the other hand, did admit that "crime, cruelty, disease, and even the sacred course of true love might be affected by economic problems. Sex played a big part in this new realism, probably almost as big as in life, and very elaborate formulas were necessary to break the old taboos which still hamper realistic writers for almost all other markets."[56]

Hale herself wrote first-person "confessions" for *True Story*, based on La Follette Committee testimonies as well as her own visits to southern sharecropper strikes and mining towns in Harlan County. Though she often had to follow what she called the "'sin and pay' formula," her stories attempted to "show the dreams of a working-class girl and her meager choices for fulfillment, with an honesty ruled out by the taboos of proper women's magazines."[57]

Ruth McKenney, on the other hand, seems to have been more divided about her writing, at least by the evidence of her disguised autobiography, *Love Story*, and the *roman à clef* based on her written by her friend, the novelist Christina Stead. Born in 1911, McKenney, the college-educated daughter of a Cleveland factory manager, became a newspaper reporter in Akron and New York. She achieved national celebrity with her humorous *New Yorker* stories about her childhood, collected as the best-selling *My Sister Eileen* (1938) and turned into a successful Broadway show. At the same time, she became an editor of the *New Masses* and wrote one of the classic works of CIO reportage, *Industrial Valley* (1939), a narrative of the United Rubber Workers in Akron. McKenney was a comic writer, and her narrative of life in the "movement" in *Love Story* remains the funniest account of the cultural front; its satiric portraits of *New Masses* writers and the Hollywood left are intertwined with slapstick tales of her labor-journalist husband, forced into an impromptu speech to a membership meeting of the National Maritime Union (NMU), and of her attempts to solve "the whole problem of the Modern American Marriage, the Emancipated Female (me) and the Working Mother (ditto)."[58]

Her discussions of writing are characteristically self-mocking, as when she sobs, "I don't want to be a humorist. I want to be a *p-p-p-p-roletarian writer.*" "Here I was," she writes of a publisher's cocktail party, "purporting to be the author of careless comic fiction; whereas all the time, in real life, I was an embattled, blazing-eyed partisan of the CIO, with 312,000 fierce, unfunny, and militant words about rubber workers at home." "My sturdy associates in the labor movement—poets, members of Local 65, subway conductors, union organizers, and other big eaters—came up to the castle on week ends in droves, and while making cruel havoc of the Saturday-night corned beef hash, denounced the trivial, bourgeois bits of fluff I composed for the decadent middle classes. I felt humiliated, betraying my exploited rubber workers, but what could I do? Diaper service does not come free in this wicked world, and *The New Yorker* paid cash on acceptance, a stuffy middle-class practice unknown in left-wing circles."[59]

The portrait of McKenney in Christina Stead's novel, *I'm Dying Laughing,* is, however, far bleaker. Not only does the character based on McKenney, Emily Wilkes, feel that her "Toonerville tales, short amusing anecdotes, in simple language, recollections, stories about uncles, parents, cousins, grocers, mailmen, townspeople of the small towns" are simply a way of making a living, drawing attention away from her serious labor books, but the novel relentlessly dramatizes her alienation from her husband and her Party comrades, who refuse to recognize her serious work. "They just want me, like you, to keep on writing belly-laughs," she tells her husband. "I'm dying laughing." Stead's novel is an indirect form of evidence, no doubt, and the portrait of Emily is filtered through the eyes of Christina Stead, herself a left-wing woman novelist. But the picture of the conflict between commercial writing and political writing in McKenney's career is probably accurate. Indeed, in a 1940 *New Masses* essay, "Women Are Human Beings," McKenney attacked "the immense body of propaganda for the dream world of romantic love" in which "Greta Garbo either dies for love or gives up an important job for ditto." Nevertheless, although McKenney thought that her narrative of the Akron rubber workers, *Industrial Valley,* was her most lasting work, the 1950 narrative of a marriage, *Love Story,* written from Europe at "the end of our long, long years in the radical movement," is a comic antidote to the "dream world of romantic love," a reconciliation of private and public, humor and politics.[60]

Between Hope Hale's desire to use *True Story* to reach working-class women readers and Ruth McKenney's alienation from her own popular writing, one might put the work of Vera Caspary, a more successful popular novelist than either Hale or McKenney. Caspary, born in 1899, grew up in a middle-class German Jewish Chicago family and began working as an advertising copywriter in the 1920s, eventually editing one of the Mac-Fadden magazines, *Dance Magazine*. Her 1929 novel, *The White Girl*, was a popular success, and she went on to write stories for Street and Smith and *Good Housekeeping*, and screenplays in Hollywood. Her greatest success was the fine thriller *Laura* (1942), which became a classic *film noir*. Caspary was very active in the Popular Front, spending two and a half years in the Communist Party in New York and Connecticut before moving to Holly-wood at the beginning of the war. Though she left the Party, she "kept up membership in the Anti-Nazi League, the League Against War and Fascism and the League of American Writers, [and] taught classes on the writing of movie originals to raise money to bring refugee writers to America . . . For the Left, these were fruitful years . . . Almost every night there were fund-raising parties, benefits and concerts. There was a steady influx of new people coming to work in the studios—actors, writers, directors from New York, refugees from Europe."[61]

In her autobiography, Caspary satirized her own desire to write a proletarian novel. "How could I write a proletarian novel when I had never known a proletarian? Were the girls who worked in factories different from those I'd known in offices? Were the dreams of a girl who fed a machine unlike those of a secretary or saleswoman?" Caspary never completed her "proletarian" novel; instead, she wrote the classic murder mystery *Laura*, whose title character is an advertising copywriter who plans campaigns for "Lady Lilith Face Powder" and "Jix Soap Flakes." But the unwritten "working girl" does appear in the character of Diane Redfern, the struggling model who is murdered by mistake. Diane's boarding-house room is filled with movie magazines and confession magazines, "the sort that told stories of girls who had sinned, suffered, and been reclaimed by the love of good men." Her real name proves to be Jennie Swobodo: she "hadn't been so long away from Paterson and the silk mills."[62]

However, a crucial section of Caspary's autobiography is the story of her attempt to cross the boundaries of class when she is introduced to a group of Norwalk, Connecticut, garment workers by an Amalgamated Clothing Workers organizer. "Once a week," she writes, "my house became a recreation center. There was no other place in town where girls of Italian, Polish and Hungarian descent could engage in organized recreation . . . Our discussions ranged from the correct attire for a morning wedding to the importance of belonging to a union; from the recipes of their mothers to the exploitation of workers; from the latest fashion to the courage of workers and farmers who were Loyalists in Spain." Caspary's story of this club of working women, the Confidences Club, begins with talk of "John

Garfield, Carole Lombard and Hedy Lamar" over hot dogs and deviled eggs, and ends with a discussion of birth control.[63]

Caspary's brief alliance with the young garment workers of Norwalk, built on a mixture of Hollywood stars and union politics, fashion and birth control, may be taken as an emblem of the labor feminism of the Popular Front. This alliance appears not only in these reflections of popular women novelists on their relation to working-class women readers, but in the emergence of a Popular Front labor feminism in 1939 and 1940. In the fall of 1939, the California Popular Front newspaper, *People's World*, began serializing Mary Inman's *In Woman's Defense*, the most ambitious Marxist analysis of women's oppression of the period; in February 1940, the left-wing Modern Age Books published *Restless Wave*, the autobiography of émigré Japanese feminist Ayako Ishigaki, under the pen name Haru Matsui; and in the spring of 1940, the New York tabloid *PM* was featuring "News for Living," Elizabeth Hawes's reconstruction of the "outworn Woman's Page and household features in the standard newspaper." In the writings of both Ishigaki and Hawes, the story of sewing and the garment trades becomes the locus for a rethinking of women's experience and the politics of labor.[64]

Ayako Ishigaki was born in 1903, the daughter of a college professor. She had come to the United States in 1930, after being arrested and detained in Japan, and she soon became active in the New York left. Like many immigrant radicals, much of her work concerned her homeland; a member of the Japanese Workers' Club, she wrote for Japanese-language newspapers and spoke publicly against the Japanese invasion of Manchuria and for the boycott of Japanese goods. However, she was also a member of the New York John Reed Club and, together with her husband, the painter Eitaro Ishigaki, was active in left cultural circles. She published *Restless Wave* in 1940, before the US entry into the war and the internment of Japanese Americans. Both Ayako and Eitaro Ishigaki worked for the Office of War Information during the Second World War, but their friendship with Agnes Smedley led to their deportation in the early 1950s. Ishigaki returned to Japan and became a well-known feminist writer.[65]

Restless Wave opens with a classic instance of what I will call the proletarian sublime: in what she calls her first memory as a child, she is frightened by the sight of women workers building their house. "They frightened me, these women. I ran, afraid, to my father. Are these strange people who work with men, banter their men, roll up their sleeves—are they women?" In a way, the entire narrative that follows is an unraveling of its opening scene, a transformation of that class fear of childhood into a new hope. "These women are no longer strange to me," she writes. "These women no longer make me fear. I can see them occupying the house whose foundation they make firm. These women give me hope." The first two sections of *Restless Wave* are the story of Matsui's childhood in Japan. Though she is rebuked for imitating street performers and taking an interest in the "new women," she dreams of herself as an obedient bride, sewing like her mother. "To sew well was considered one of woman's chief accomplishments," she recalls. "As a child, tirelessly I had watched my mother's hands as she sewed my clothes. Then I had prayed that I would soon be able to do sewing."[66]

The narrative's crucial turning point takes place in 1919, as two scenes of sewing come together: she watches a group of mill girls laboring in a Tokyo textile factory during a school trip "as though we were watching a play," and she watches her elder sister sewing as they argue over her sister's arranged marriage. The two scenes of cloth-making and sewing leave her "with thoughts so stormy and agitating that to sew quietly was wearisome." The third part of *Restless Wave* thus becomes a narrative of her political activities in Japan in the 1920s, attending a women's college, writing for women's suffrage, visiting Tokyo's slums, and working for *Women and Labor*, "a magazine published by a feminist agitator." It ends with her arrest and her departure for the United States. The fourth and final section is a brief account of her decade in the United States. It repeats the narrative of isolation and recognition. Her life among strangers in New York is marked by her break with her father and the death of her child; she then moves west to discover the Japanese American community of Los Angeles. Traveling with a woman who sells cosmetics, she visits the Japanese farmhouses and fishing villages, meeting the Japanese women who work in the fish canneries of San Pedro and wear the "blue American trade-union buttons." Though Matsui's narrative remains that of the exiled émigré intellectual, tactful and cautious in its mention of the "fences of prejudice" and "social ostracism" that face the US-born second generation of Little Tokyo, it stands as a remarkable account of the intertwining of feminism, labor radicalism, and émigré anti-fascism in the Popular Front social movement.[67]

Perhaps the most imaginative and important exponent of this labor feminist aesthetic was Elizabeth Hawes. Hawes emerged as a leading Popular Front social critic in 1940 when she closed her dress designing business and became the editor of the "News for Living" section of the newly launched left-wing New York tabloid, *PM*. Over the previous decade, Hawes had established herself as one of the leading US dress designers, a well-known critic of Parisian fashion, and a part of New York's avant-garde art and theatre circles. For her 1933 show, the photographer and film-maker Ralph Steiner had made a fifteen-minute silent comedy, *The Panther Woman of the Needle Trades*; and Hawes designed the costumes for the Federal Theatre Project's famous Living Newspaper, *Triple A Plowed Under*. However, her experiments in mass-producing her dress designs led her out of the world of made-to-order couture and into the garment industry, visiting the Carolina fabric mills of Marshall Fields in 1934 and the Soviet Dress Trust in 1935. She came to think that her attempts to combine good design and mass-production were unsuccessful, and by 1940 she left her design business and turned to writing, addressing the working-class readers of *PM*.[68]

The "News for Living" section was a cross between the traditional women's page of newspapers and the consumer activism of the Popular Front that had given birth to the Consumers Union in 1936. Since *PM* carried no advertising, the "News for Living" offered a digest of the advertising in the other New York papers; it also covered food, clothing, beauty, housing, and education, each from the "paper's conception of a better life—a less expensive life with more for your money and more fun in it." Hawes's weekly columns offered a populist, feminist criticism of clothing. Like many of the Popular Front feminists, Hawes initially imagined the audience for her clothes and her writings to be the young white-collar women working in offices. "There are in the United States thousands of secretaries between the ages of eighteen and twenty-five who must dress every day for work," she wrote in *Why Is a Dress?* "What are they to wear?" This is, she argued, the central question for dress design, and it informed her own designs. Moreover, Hawes's concern for a democratic dress design in "popular-priced" clothes grew into a wider concern with the lives of working women. "If you are going to design clothes for white-collar girls," Hawes wrote to the aspiring dress designer, "you will study them, know their offices, where they eat, live, dance, where they go for vacations . . . If you find that they care what Deanna Durbin thinks, then you have to care too." Hawes became active in a left-wing consumers group, the League of Women Shoppers, and helped organize the Committee for the Care of Young Children in Wartime, a cross-class alliance of left-wing women and philanthropists like Elinore Gimbel working for government-funded child care. In 1943, Hawes organized a benefit show for the child-care committee, A Gallery of American Women, at the Associated American Artists Gallery.[69]

These two concerns—women's work clothes and child care for women workers—led Hawes to go to work in a wartime airplane engine factory in 1943: "everything I'd ever been interested in, from child care to clothes, landed me up against the factory gate." Out of that experience she wrote *Why Women Cry; or Wenches with Wrenches* (1943) and was recruited into the education department of the United Auto Workers, writing a weekly column in the *Detroit Free Press* (the first of which called for public nurseries and a thirty-hour work week), editing pamphlets and a special issue of the UAW's magazine, *Ammunition* (Figure 12), and traveling the country visiting UAW locals. Hawes's books—*Why Is a Dress?* (1942), *Why Women*

Cry; or Wenches with Wrenches (1943), and *Hurry Up Please Its Time* (1946)—
were widely read in the labor movement and in the Popular Front social
movement generally.[70]

As its title indicates, *Why Women Cry; or Wenches with Wrenches* is a divided
book, and its fault line is the consequence of the earthquake in household
structures and gender relations that Hawes was trying to measure. The first
and third sections of the book, which might be called "Why Women Cry,"
are a powerful but somewhat abstract feminist manifesto. We have all been
notified that "the day of the Common Man is coming up," she writes,
alluding to the Popular Front rhetoric of Henry Wallace, "[d]on't think
the Common Woman is just sitting around preparing to spend the whole
of that day in the kitchen." A revolution is in progress, "brewing right in
your kitchen." The purpose of the war is "to abolish all servants—the
servants of Hitler and Hirohito, of the British, Dutch, French and other
empires—and our personal servants . . . But as most people never had a
servant, the major problem is really how to run a home without turning
the wife into a servant." After attacking the myth of the "contented cow"—
"I have never met a contented housewife"—she offers a satirical typology
of American women: "les riches bitches," the "equal righters," the "clubwomen," the "womenworkers," and the "she-wolves." Not surprisingly, given
the symbolic centrality of garment workers in Popular Front culture, Hawes
sees "Miss Garment Worker" as "the freest of the Workingwomen," since she
is "not generally confused by the social questions of whether she is a Lady
and never bothered about what kind of neckline her boss prefers her to
wear at the sewing machine"; unhampered by the "clothes-consciousness"
of Miss White Collar, she can "make efforts, sometimes very unladylike
efforts, to improve her wages so she can live better."[71]

Hawes then goes on to outline a socialist vision of "sex education and
contraceptives for everyone," housing projects with community restaurants
and public nurseries, and a "mass medical care" that includes "gymnasiums
and beauty parlors and hairdressers" so as to make the "body beautiful" a
democratic right. Cast in the form of conversations with fictional friends
Amanda and Janet, and written in the style of women's magazine journalism, this part of Hawes's book stands in the long tradition of feminist
thought which has united child care, dress reform, cooperative housekeeping, and physical culture with social reconstruction.[72]

In the midst of this satirical manifesto lies a long section entitled
"Wenches with Wrenches." This narrative of Wright Plant Seven is a
powerful war-plant diary, the story of learning to run machines and acquire
tools, of shop-floor conflicts and union politics, of sexual tensions and
racial conflicts in the plant. Here the allegorical "Miss White Collar" and
"Miss Garment Worker" give way to a novelistic rendering of the individuals
who are her co-workers on the night shift. The two halves of the book

never fully cohere; indeed, Hawes's own solution—working for the UAW's education department—is the genesis of her next book, a kind of sequel to *Why Women Cry, Hurry Up Please Its Time*.

Hurry Up Please Its Time is a narrative of Hawes's work in the UAW; a more coherent book than its predecessor, it sacrifices satiric portraits and visionary utopias. Hawes had been hired to develop educational programs and literature for the new women workers in the war plants. "Nobody knew what to do about the women," she comments, "which was the only comforting thing about my early work." The narrative takes shape around a series of organizing drives between 1944 and 1946, narrated in letters and dialogues between her and Eve, a shopworker and UAW organizer: the drive in Flint, "the malest town in the whole USA"; the women's meeting in Columbus; the Baltimore organizing drive; the brief visit to the California locals; Eve's account of the campaign in Elmira; and their work together in Cleveland (where the book opens and ends). It is not a story of epic triumphs; nothing could be further from the heroic CIO reportage of the sit-down era by Ruth McKenney, Edward Levinson, and Mary Heaton Vorse. Rather, it is a tale of arbitration cases over sexual harassment, conflicts with union men over sex, and battles for seats and better cafeteria food for women workers: "the position of the female in the USA was getting me down quite a bit those days."[73]

No longer is the issue of innovative dress design for working women at the forefront. Rather, Hawes's eye for clothing notes the way women's clothing for leisure obscures class. "Something interesting about a group of shop workers dressed for nonworking life is that anyone can tell the men are 'workers,' but it's impossible to put your finger on the women." Make-up, clothes, and hands have a regional look rather than a class look. Moreover, her own clothes became an issue: "dressing for trade union work is a frightful problem for all women union representatives," she writes, since men unionists felt that "the female organizer or representative of the union should uphold the sartorial reputation of the union and . . . this meant looking as near like a live fashion illustration as possible." There is a growing sense of desperation in Hawes's narrative, captured in the title itself, *Hurry Up Please Its Time*. She left the UAW as the anti-Communist purge was beginning; though she was not a Communist Party member, the education department had been a stronghold of the left-wing of the union, and she had been a vocal critic of red-baiting. Union red-baiting, she had argued earlier, was often a cover for attacking women activists.[74]

Hawes never resolved the contradictions at the heart of her work, and at the heart of Popular Front labor feminism. As she became increasingly active in the day-to-day shop struggles, she found herself drawn away from the "clothes consciousness" of the fashion industry and the condescending philanthropy of clubwomen. "After a decade or so of worrying about the

White-Collar girl's work clothes," she wrote in 1943, "it has become quite a simple matter to keep the conversation concerning these womenworkers on sartorial matters and ignore the basic fact that most White-Collar girls are terribly underpaid in relation to what they do." Her 1948 book, *Anything but Love*, was a bitter satiric attack on women's magazines and their "rules for feminine behavior." "During the research for and the writing of this book," Hawes wrote, "the author often felt she had either strayed into or was creating a madhouse." Nevertheless, she insisted that it was important to stay in touch with the popular culture of romance and fashion, to know what the Deanna Durbins were thinking. "A large number of people shun this material completely," she noted of the true romance and screen magazines, "and many of those who expose themselves to it have never bothered to analyze the full content." But "no one in the United States, male or female, is exempt from the effects of the rules and advice we will summarize." Hawes never gave up her sense of the importance of good design and even returned to dress designing with a well-received 1948 show.[75]

The contradictions in Hawes's work might also be taken as an emblem of the fault lines in the fragile but extraordinary Popular Front "clothes" alliance, which encompassed the liberal entrepreneurs and foundations based on department-store fortunes, including Elinore Gimbel, Marshall Field (both of whom invested in *PM*), and the Rosenwald Foundation; the Popular Front Hollywood stars who lent support like Helen Gahagan Douglas (recruited to speak to garment workers by the ILGWU's Rose Pesotta), and those like Ginger Rogers, Jean Arthur, and Deanna Durbin, who played working girls on screen in scripts often written by Hollywood reds; the fashion designers and critics like Hawes; and the women of the ILGWU and the ACWA who worked in the garment shops, textile mills, and department stores and wore the ready-to-wear fashions and watched the films.[76]

Moreover, Hawes's increasing concern with issues of child care for married women in the workforce offers a different perspective on the question of Popular Front "motherhood." Though the "Madonnas of the fields" of the late 1930s may well call on traditional notions of family to narrate the agonies of migrant farm labor, the maternal melodramas that characterize the cultural front in the 1940s and 1950s—from Joan Crawford's role in *Mildred Pierce*, a film produced by Jerry Wald at Warner Brothers with the assistance of left-wing writer Albert Maltz, to Billie Holiday's story of the genesis of her song "God Bless the Child" in a fight over her mother's restaurant, to Harriette Arnow's extraordinary portrait of Gertie Nevels, a "migrant mother" in the warplant housing of Detroit, in *The Dollmaker*—stand as powerful attempts to narrate the contradictions involved in the transformation from a modern to a postmodern gender formation. The popular stories of women who sacrificed themselves for the success of their children came in two forms: the sentimental ones were tear-jerkers in which the tragedy of the woman's sacrifice is transcended in her final happiness at the child's success; but the melodramatic and *noir*-ish versions—like *Mildred Pierce*—show the sacrifice to be in vain as ungrateful and unworthy children make a mockery of it. However, both forms of the maternal melodrama were reflections on the move of married women into the wage-labor force, the decline in domestic service, and the transformation in what parents and children owe each other. Perhaps the briefest and most powerful of these maternal melodramas is the 1955 short story, "I Stand Here Ironing," which marked Tillie Olsen's return to fiction writing after almost two decades of work and mothering. It is the maternal melodrama in a minor key, the thoughts of a woman about her daughter, provoked by a teacher or social worker who wants to help. The story ends, as so often in Popular Front feminism, with pins and needles, with a dress: "Only help her to know—help make it so there is cause for her to know—that she is more than this dress on the ironing board, helpless before the iron." From her early poem about a garment worker to her story about a mother ironing, Olsen embodies the labor feminist aesthetic of the Popular Front.[77]

4. The Laboring of American Culture

"There is a tendency," Warren Susman remarked of studies of the Great Depression, "for historians suddenly to switch their focus and concentrate on the newly discovered poor, the marginal men and women, migrant workers, hobos, various ethnic minorities deprived of a place in the American sun ... and to see the period in terms of the most radical responses to its problems, to see a Red Decade in which cultural as well as political life is somehow dominated by the Left." "Yet the fact remains," he insisted, "... that the period ... is one in which American culture continues to be largely middle class culture." "The story of American culture," Susman argued, is the story of "the enormous American middle class."[78]

"If we keep our focus on the middle class," he maintained, "we may better understand why some shifts to the Left proved so temporary or even why the period proved in the end so fundamentally conservative as it concentrated on finding and glorifying an American Way of Life." Susman agreed with those who suggested that "the Popular Front ... helped shape that Americanism," but argued that "few would be willing to suggest that the kind of society and kind of culture that resulted could in any legitimate sense be designated as socialist."[79]

Susman was a crucial New Left intellectual and one of the finest US cultural historians, but his interpretation of the conservative, middle-class nature of the age of the CIO is fundamentally mistaken. He poses two stark and unnecessary oppositions: "conservative" versus "socialist"; and "marginal men and women" versus "middle class." Few would be willing to suggest that the society and culture that emerged from the depression was socialist: I certainly wouldn't. But that doesn't mean that the only alternative characterization is conservative. Similarly, to suggest that the "marginal men and women" were not the main story of American culture does not mean that it remained a "middle class culture." Susman's influential portrait of the "culture of the thirties" entirely ignores the industrial unions of the CIO and the culture of the men and women who built them. He misses the laboring of American culture.

In fact, American culture was transformed by the CIO working classes, by those Tillie Olsen called "the nameless FrankLloydWrights of the proletariat." A Popular Front labor sensibility scarred the dominant culture in these decades. It did not result in a socialist culture; rather, its imprint was social democratic and laborist. It labored hard to survive: the three decades after 1929 were a constant cultural war. The years of the depression and the Second World War saw the plebeian sensibility confident, almost hegemonic; the years of the cultural Cold War saw it under a state of siege. Nevertheless, the American culture that resulted was hardly "middle class": vernacular musics like jazz, rhythm and blues, and country dominated national tastes; the major post-war writers were black or ethnic, products of the Popular Front; and gangster movies and *film noir* had created the "American" look in film. Tillie Olsen's child did not become, as Olsen's 1934 *Partisan Review* author's note promised, a "citizen of Soviet America"; nevertheless, Olsen's narratives of working-class life became classics, part of the "selective tradition" that, as Raymond Williams always reminded us, is the product of continual struggle.[80]

It is easy to see why this laboring of American culture has so often been overlooked. Just as no Labor Party emerged in the US, so the institutions of a labor culture were weak and underdeveloped. The studio radicals, the rank-and-file workers of the culture industries, rarely succeeded in making radical, avant-garde productions. "There were no films made in Hollywood that had any real left-wing impact at all," the Popular Front director Joseph Losey later recalled, "with the possible exception of *The Grapes of Wrath*." Moreover, the dramatic purge of the Popular Front from the state and the culture industries during the Cold War aborted many initiatives. Nevertheless, if there were few radical works, clear examples of a left aesthetic or politics, a Popular Front sensibility inflected many culture industry productions.[81]

This laboring of popular culture was in large part a consequence of the growth of a working-class audience. Not only did swing, baseball, radio soap operas, and the talkies change the patterns of working-class leisure, but, in the curious dialectic that has always characterized US mass culture, these forms and media adopted the styles and accents of the second-generation ethnic workers who joined the CIO unions and the IWO lodges. This dialectic is often missed because the popular arts of the age of the CIO, like most of the successful forms and genres of US mass culture, had developed out of "lowbrow" working-class cultures and were sanitized, Americanized, and whitened to attract a "respectable" middle-class audience, an audience with substantial resources for amusement, entertainment, and culture. Thus, on the surface, the mass culture of the 1930s and 1940s seems to be a "classless" and "American" culture, with white covers of black music, and Jewish and Italian stars with anglicized stage names.

However, like the Christianization of pagan gods and holidays, this Americanization cut both ways. If the Anglo middle classes watched a celebration of an ethnically unmarked middle-class American people, in which the attenuated ethnicity of figures like Artie Shaw, John Garfield, Lena Horne, or Rita Hayworth fit effortlessly beside the Mr Smiths and John Does of Jimmy Stewart, the young ethnic workers of the CIO recognized Shaw, Garfield, Horne, and Hayworth as their own. They were working-class ethnic stars precisely *because* they were "American." They were tricksters, as Shaw himself recognized: "It was a zigzag path indeed," he later wrote, "that brought about the curious metamorphosis of a shy, introspective little Jewish kid named Arthur Arshawsky into a sort of weird, jazz-band-leading, clarinet-tooting, jitterbug-surrounded Symbol of American Youth." As with the ethnic Communists who took "American" names— Stjepan Mesaroš becoming Steve Nelson—the metamorphosis of Arthur Arshawsky into Artie Shaw was less a "passing" from the foreign-language working class to an English-language middle class than a forging of a "new American" people, in Louis Adamic's phrase. Perhaps the most powerful and symptomatic name-change was that of the writer Itzok Granich, who renamed himself Mike Gold, a name that announced itself as American and Jewish, an inoculation with the very anti-Semitic slurs he was to attack in the opening of his novel, *Jews without Money*, a Gold without gold.[82]

At the heart of this plebeian popular culture were the Popular Front stars, the city boys and working girls whose voices and images pervaded radio, screen, records, and photomagazines. These stars affiliated themselves with the Popular Front social movement in a variety of symbolic ways, appearing at benefit performances, signing celebrity letterheads, and speaking out on the issues that were mobilizing their audiences. Many left activists and intellectuals were ambivalent about this celebrity politics, and historians have tended to discount it. Many of the Popular Front stars were hardly radical, let alone communist; the sybaritic lifestyles of the "left-wing" stars were far from working-class daily life; and many quickly distanced

themselves from their political allegiances when the red scare threatened
their livelihoods. But none of this lessens the cultural importance of the
political stars, as two figures of the cultural front, C.L.R. James and Eric
Hobsbawm, recognized.

"For the last twenty years," James wrote in 1950, ". . . the most outstanding feature of the American movie is the complete domination of the star
system ... whereby a certain selected few individuals symbolize in their
film existence *and in their private and public existence* the revolt against the
general conditions. If the great body of the public did not need stars, there
would be no stars." Thus, Rita Hayworth "is in no sense a mere creation of
predatory industrialists for stupid masses," James argued, "but is a product
of the age." "No publicity in the world can create a great star, the mass
chooses its major stars with remarkable judgment." How the masses choose
their stars remains a difficult question in cultural history, but two aspects
seem clear. First, the star, like the politician, wins the loyalty and allegiance
of audiences through an implicit or explicit claim to represent them. Often
this derives from the symbolic weight of the star's social origin. "The artist
sprung from the unskilled poor, and playing for the poor," Eric Hobsbawm
has written, "is in a peculiar social position . . . The star musician, dancer,
singer, comedian, boxer, or bullfighter is not merely a success among this
sporting or artist public, but the potential first citizen of his community or
his people. A Caruso among the poor of Naples, a Marie Lloyd in the East
End, a Gracie Fields in Rochdale, a Jack Johnson, Joe Louis or Sugar Ray
in Harlem, a Louis Armstrong occupy a position far more eminent among
'their' people than a Picasso or Fonteyn in orthodox society . . . For the
star was what every slum child and drudge might become: the king or
queen of the poor, because the poor person writ large." Many of the
Popular Front stars were themselves of ethnic, working-class, and plebeian
origins, including Benny Goodman, Artie Shaw, Frank Sinatra, Billie
Holiday, Count Basie, Paul Muni (Muni Weisenfreund), Rita Hayworth
(Margarita Carmen Cansino), Sylvia Sidney (Sophia Kosow), Charlie
Chaplin, John Garfield (Julius Garfinkle), Joan Crawford (Lucille Le
Sueur), and Susan Hayward, and they became the kings and queens of the
CIO working classes.[83]

However, the star need not come from the "people" to represent them.
Many of the stars of the age of the CIO won the loyalty of their audiences
by enacting plebeian roles or styles, including the "city boys" like Humphrey Bogart, Marlon Brando, and Robert Ryan ("a special favorite," Paul
Buhle notes, "of the Hollywood Left"). Stardom is part of the struggle for
hegemony, part of the way social institutions and movements win consent.
This does not simply mean that stars tend "to reinforce the dominant
ideology of the culture ... or to conceal important cultural tensions."
Though that may often be true, it underestimates not only the fragility of

stardom— as one critic has noted, "because stardom depends on winning and maintaining the good graces of an audience and because public taste and cultural values shift over time, nearly every star's career is a story of his or her rise and fall"—but also its place in popular struggles.[84]

The implicit and explicit politics of the star are a crucial part of the "star image," the product of the roles played by the star, the persona created by the studio's publicity, and the critical discourses about the star. In some cases the roles played by the star reinforced the star's political affiliations: this was true of John Garfield and Canada Lee, co-stars in the Rossen/Polonsky *Body and Soul* (1947). Garfield had gone from the Group Theatre to Warner Brothers' thrillers and war films, playing tough, working-class outsiders; Lee was a star of Harlem's left-wing theater (acting in *Macbeth*, *Haiti*, and *Native Son*), and he appeared in several of Hollywood's post-war racial dramas. Both were visible figures in the Popular Front, and their careers and lives were destroyed by the Hollywood inquisition: both died in 1952.[85]

The dialectic between star roles and politics often drew relatively non-political stars into the Popular Front. Loyal to their audience, film stars like Paul Muni, Joan Crawford, Bette Davis, Humphrey Bogart, and Rita Hayworth, musicians like Benny Goodman, Count Basie, and Frank Sinatra, baseball players like Satchel Paige, Josh Gibson, Red Rolfe, and Ripper Collins, and the boxer Joe Louis found themselves supporting the Spanish Loyalists, raising money for anti-fascist refugees, playing benefits for Popular Front politicians, and promoting themselves in the *Daily Worker* as part of their implicit contract with their audience. A few stars, most notably Paul Robeson, explicitly used their celebrity to build the social movement. However, the majority of the actors most involved in the Popular Front social movement—like the majority of actors generally— were character actors, like Howard da Silva, Will Geer, Anne Revere, and Gale Sondergaard, and minor stars like Frances Farmer, Dorothy Comingore, Karen Morley, and Judy Holliday.[86]

Ironically, a number of Hollywood's "working-girl" films were the products of studio marriages between left-wing screenwriters and conservative stars like Barbara Stanwyck and Ginger Rogers, both of whom were founders of the right-wing Motion Picture Alliance for the Preservation of American Ideals in 1944. Stanwyck's combination of streetwise toughness and humor made her a favorite of Popular Front audiences, despite her politics. She starred in film versions of two Odets plays, *Golden Boy* (1939) and Fritz Lang's *Clash by Night* (1952); *You Belong to Me* (1941) was written by Dalton Trumbo and *The Strange Love of Martha Ivers* (1946) was written by Robert Rossen. "Not only had she worked with many of the Hollywood Ten," her biographer notes, but "she continued to do so" even after her husband, Robert Taylor, became the most visible anti-Communist star,

naming names. Similarly, several of Ginger Rogers's most successful films
were written by Popular Front screenwriters, including *Kitty Foyle* (1940),
by Dalton Trumbo and Donald Ogden Stewart, *Tom, Dick and Harry* (1941),
by Paul Jarrico, and *Tender Comrade* (1943), by Trumbo. By 1947, Rogers's
mother, Lela Rogers, was telling HUAC that "her daughter had bravely
refused to speak a typical piece of Communist propaganda, 'Share and
share alike—that's democracy,' which had appeared in Dalton Trumbo's
script for *Tender Comrade*."[87]

What one sees in these peculiar alliances is the emergence of genres
inflected by the laborist sensibility of the Popular Front: the working-girl
women's films like *Kitty Foyle, Tender Comrade*, and *The Devil and Miss Jones*;
anti-Fascist romances like *Casablanca*; war films like John Howard Lawson's
trilogy, *Action in the North Atlantic* (1943), *Sahara* (1943), and *Counterattack*
(1945), the first two starring Bogart and the third, Muni; and the post-war
social melodramas and thrillers which have come to be called *film gris*, and
which culminate in two classic tales of the proletarian waterfront, Kazan's
On the Waterfront (1954) and Martin Ritt's *Edge of the City* (1957). Though
few of these films could be seen as "radical," and few had the direct topical
impact of *The Grapes of Wrath*, nevertheless they marked a new attention to
working-class daily life and styles. In this they were not unlike the rise of
the ghetto pastorals on radio and television, which set domestic dramas
about family struggles over scarce resources in sentimental and humorous
ethnic working-class "situations." This genre began with the pioneering
depression radio serials *Amos 'n' Andy*, the controversial minstrel show
about black migrants to the North, and *The Rise of the Goldbergs*, starring
Gertrude Berg and Popular Front activist Philip Loeb and based on the
daily life of a Jewish immigrant family on New York's Lower East Side. Both
went on to television, where they were joined by broadcast versions of the
films *I Remember Mama* and *A Tree Grows in Brooklyn*. One sees a similar
laboring of popular culture in the post-war integration of white professional baseball, and in the rise of post-war vernacular musics—country,
rhythm and blues, and rock and roll—which were deeply indebted to the
innovations of Popular Front singers like Josh White, Woody Guthrie,
Leadbelly, Brownie McGhee, and Sonny Terry.[88]

Perhaps the best picture of this laborist Popular Front popular culture
can be glimpsed in the pages of the illustrated weekly, *Friday*. "The only
national picture magazine that covers labor," *Friday* represented the
Popular Front politics and laborist popular culture of the CIO working
classes through the medium of the mass magazine, and captured the
common sense of its audience, the second-generation blue-collar and
white-collar ethnic workers. From its first issue on 15 March 1940, *Friday*
linked politics and popular culture, defending James Cagney, Joan Crawford, Irving Berlin, and Bette Davis against the attack by right-wing

congressman Martin Dies. Over the next two years, *Friday* covered the waterfront. Not only did it cover the docks, comparing the New York and West Coast shapeups and getting Theodore Dreiser to interview Harry Bridges, but it followed the struggles of transport workers, Woolworth counter waitresses, and the successful battle in the spring of 1941 to unionize Ford. The Ford narrative offers a microcosm of the magazine's style. In January 1941, *Friday* ran an exposé of Henry Ford's anti-Semitism, which continued the magazine's regular coverage of anti-Semitism. A month later, there was an article on Ford's "fascism," covering Harry Bennett's notorious Service Department of thugs, spies, and secret police; this was followed by an exposé of Ford's exploitation of agricultural workers on "Ford's Tobacco Row." Meanwhile, there was a large spread on the UAW's Ford Organizing Committee, and color photographs of the Ford strike appeared on the magazine's cover. The success of the organizing campaign was celebrated with an article on "Ford with a Union Label," featuring an autoworkers' jazz band and a Dearborn tournament of union baseball teams.[89]

Jazz bands and baseball teams were fitting emblems, since *Friday*'s cultural front was dominated by jazz, baseball, popular amusements, ethnic traditions, and, of course, the movies. At a time when the big swing bands were rarely integrated and when middle-class magazines featured the white bands, *Friday*'s "All American Jazz Band" was an emblem of plebeian taste; featuring the stars of the Basie band—Lester Young, Walter Page, Jo Jones, Buck Clayton—as well as Armstrong, Coleman Hawkins, Johnny Hodges, Charlie Spivak, Eddie Condon, and Jack Teagarden. A year later, in an interview about his new band, Benny Goodman captured the Popular Front sense of jazz: "Jazz isn't changing; it's just being recognized as fine music at last. It was perfected by all of the 'foreigners' who make up America, particularly the Negroes." *Friday*'s baseball coverage included not only a forecast of the 1941 season but accounts of the lives of "baseball's migratory workers"—players in the minor league farm system—and a feature on the Negro League stars Satchel Paige and Josh Gibson.[90]

There were regular features on popular amusements like the pinball craze and Coney Island, and continuing coverage of ethnic and racial traditions, with articles on Irish American labor history, Jews celebrating Passover, Amateur Night at Harlem's Apollo, and the Chinese opera at New York's Canton Theatre. An article on the anti-alien bills being considered by Congress was headlined with President Roosevelt's "We are all immigrants." *Friday* also featured leading African American artists, including the painter Horace Pippin, the dancer Katherine Dunham, and the novelist Richard Wright: Wright's *Native Son* was given out free with trial subscriptions. Paul Robeson contributed an article, "In What Direction Are We Going?"[91]

Hollywood film was, of course, everywhere. Readers followed the story of Orson Welles's *Citizen Kane* (which included a letter from Welles and a feature on Dorothy Comingore, who played Susan Alexander), and new films like the John Garfield vehicle *Saturday's Children*, and the Paramount comedy about a Detroit auto plant, *Reaching for the Sun*, were summarized in two-page sequences of stills. "Jean Arthur Joins the Union and Signs Up the Devil," the headline read over *Friday*'s feature on the Norman Krasna production *The Devil and Miss Jones*. "Miss Jones is a plucky clerk in a department store. Her boyfriend is a union organizer," *Friday*'s reviewer wrote in a playful and ironic account. "There are enough stones in their pathway to throw a tank but Mary Jones gets Joe O'Brien when the union conquers the obstinate store management." *Friday*'s review offers a glimpse of the way working-class Americans made sense of films like *The Devil and Miss Jones*:

> The Devil is J.P. Merrick, the Richest Man in the World, who starts out to spy on his disgruntled employees and ends up as Santa Claus to the union leading a demonstration against himself. When J.P., the reformed employer, gives the union ten times what it asks, you will have to pinch yourself because such events are hard to find in the newspapers. Real life perversely refuses to conform with Hollywood's occasional attempts to picture it.

Friday's readers did not expect social realism or even political coherence; but the combination of Jean Arthur's screwball romance and the comic inversion that introduced the department store tycoon to the daily work of the store made the film part of their lives.[92]

Friday's success and failure is an emblem of the laboring of American culture generally. It lasted through 1940 and 1941 and died with the outbreak of the war, a victim of its anti-war, anti-interventionist stance. Moreover, since it, unlike Luce's *Life*, has been almost completely forgotten, one might conclude that *Life*, not *Friday*, more accurately "represented" the culture of the time. But this is misleading. First, the success of *Friday* and the tabloid *PM* in 1940 brought alarmed attacks from the right. "It is a smooth-coat journal, does an excellent two-color job, and is full of expensive art layouts," Benjamin Stolberg wrote of *Friday* in the *Saturday Evening Post*, before "exposing" it and *PM* as the contributions of "millionaire playboys"—like the young editor and publisher of *Friday*, Daniel Gillmor—to "American Communism." Despite his reductive view of the Popular Front as a "transmission belt" of the Communist Party, Stolberg does understand that the existence of illustrated weeklies like *Friday* and tabloids like *PM* marked a new popularity for left political culture, beyond both the movement culture and the arts world. Second, the failure of *Friday* was due to the economics of the mass illustrated magazine: they depended on advertising not circulation for their revenues. Thus *Life* and *Look* did turn to the middle classes for their readers. Not only were advertisers unwilling to support a mass magazine that supported labor— that had been demonstrated by the failure of Gingrich's *Ken* a year earlier—but they did not see the working-class audience of *Friday* as a significant market. To advertisers, *Friday* may have had the surface of a "smooth-coat journal" but it had the demographics of a pulp, the working-class fiction magazines that carried no consumer advertising, used cheap paper and penny-a-word hacks, and did not include "expensive art layouts." Indeed, most of the advertisements *Friday* carried were for the pulps: *Argosy* and *Detective Fiction Weekly* sought readers in the pages of *Friday*.[93]

So *Friday*'s lack of *commercial* success should not be taken as a judgement of its *cultural* success. For a brief moment, it represented the laborist popular culture of the young ethnic workers who built the CIO, danced to the sounds of Basie and Shaw, followed Joe DiMaggio and Josh Gibson, listened to Robeson's "Ballad for Americans," and watched Jean Arthur find love and the union in a screwball comedy. The moment of *Friday* passed, but the culture it captured did not. The common sense of the Popular Front had taken root among American working people, and it took a cultural civil war, an anti-communist crusade, to eradicate it. Unfortunately, even our best critics and historians repeat the bromides about the nationalist, sentimental, and fundamentally conservative nature of the Popular Front and its "ballads for Americans," and seem to believe that the vision of Paul Robeson was little different from that of Ronald Reagan. Actually, the oft-repeated anecdote about the 1940 Republican Convention adopting "Ballad for Americans" as its theme song is not an emblem of the conservatism of the song, but of the power of Popular Front culture: it is an example of what Kenneth Burke called "the stealing back and forth of symbols." It is time to reclaim those symbols and do justice to the difficult, unfinished, and almost forgotten laboring of American culture.

PART III

Formations of the Cultural Front

What then emerges as the most central and practical element in cultural analysis is what also marks the most significant cultural theory: the exploration and specification of distinguishable cultural formations... It is the steady discovery of genuine formations which are simultaneously artistic forms and social locations...

Raymond Williams

4

The Decline and Fall
of the Lincoln Republic:
Dos Passos's *U.S.A.*

1. From the Cubist Barricades

One of the roots of the cultural front was the crisis of modernism triggered by the Wall Street crash of 1929 and the Great Depression that ensued, a crisis that reshaped the careers and works of the moderns, transforming their experiments in form and their pursuit of the new. "The stock market crash," Edmund Wilson wrote in an account of the "literary consequences of the crash," "was to count for us [the modernist writers, artists, and intellectuals] almost like a rending of the earth in preparation for the Day of Judgment." For many, it marked a turn to the left, as they took on a variety of symbolic affiliations and allegiances. Since then, critics and historians have lamented this leftward swerve, seeing it as an uncritical and quasi-religious conversion that yoked them to a conventional social realism and sapped the originality and rigor of their work. However, the story of the left-wing modernists is more complex than these tales of seduction and betrayal, conversion and apostasy, suggest. For the attempt to imagine the crash and the depression, to figure that rending of the earth, to narrate the crisis of the new, produced a series of powerful meditations on the history of the United States, including works of social and literary history, a new "history painting" in the visual arts, and several vast fictional trilogies. Together they constituted a modernist counterepic, the story of the decline and fall of the Lincoln republic.[1]

The group of writers, artists, and intellectuals whom I will call the radical modernists were only one part of the cultural front, but their symbolic presence was vital. Born around the turn of the century, they had already emerged as the leading young writers, artists, and intellectuals in the decade after the First World War. Though they had little connection to the left, they were allied with the iconoclastic and experimental European modernisms. They were not of plebeian background; most were young

men from established Anglo families, educated in preparatory schools and
Ivy League colleges. They had met each other in school, worked together
on little magazines and in little theaters, socialized and corresponded with
each other. Most were based in New York, retreating in summer to the
beaches of Provincetown or the farms of Connecticut, the Hudson Valley,
and Bucks County, Pennsylvania. There were several overlapping but
distinct groups. The oldest and most established was the circle of novelists
and writers that included John Dos Passos, F. Scott Fitzgerald, Ernest
Hemingway, Edmund Wilson, Josephine Herbst, and John Howard Lawson;
a second group formed around the writers Kenneth Burke, Malcolm
Cowley, Matthew Josephson, and the painter Peter Blume; a more academic circle in the Connecticut River Valley included the literary critics
Granville Hicks, Newton Arvin, and Robert Gorham Smith; and the circle
that included the director Harold Clurman, the composer Aaron Copland,
and the photographer Paul Strand was the genesis of the Group Theatre.

Perhaps the most important and influential figure among the modernists
who affiliated themselves with the left was the writer John Dos Passos. Dos
Passos entered the left in the spring of 1926 when he joined the executive
board of the newly launched magazine *New Masses* and became a director
of the radical New Playwrights' Theatre. He was thirty years old and his
fourth novel, *Manhattan Transfer,* had just appeared to wide acclaim: in a
landmark review, Sinclair Lewis suggested that it was "the first book to
catch Manhattan" and "the foundation of a whole new school of novel-
writing." In April 1926, Dos Passos joined the picket lines of a textile strike
in Passaic, New Jersey, and in June, he visited the Italian immigrant
anarchists Nicola Sacco and Bartolomeo Vanzetti in prison; over the next
year, he worked with the Sacco and Vanzetti Defense Committee, publishing open letters, covering the protests for the *Daily Worker,* getting arrested
in the protests (Figure 5), and writing a pamphlet on the case, *Facing the
Chair: Story of the Americanization of Two Foreignborn Workmen.* Though Sacco
and Vanzetti were executed in August 1927, Dos Passos went on to become
the most visible radical novelist, campaigning for political prisoners,
supporting striking miners, and writing accounts of his travels to Mexico
and the Soviet Union. "Responding to Dos Passos's call," Matthew Josephson recalled, "many of us now returned to reading *Das Kapital* and the
brilliant historical analysis of *The Eighteenth Brumaire of Louis Napoleon*...
By his courageous example and his eloquent reports from the field, Dos
Passos pointed to the mission of leadership in the social struggle to which
writers in the thirties might be called."[2]

However, Dos Passos's importance for the moderns was not simply a
function of his activism: he was one of them, part of their social and literary
circles in New York and Paris, a close friend of Ernest Hemingway, F. Scott
Fitzgerald, Edmund Wilson, Hart Crane, John Howard Lawson, Josephine

Herbst, and e.e. cummings, among others. He had made his literary mark at Harvard, one of a group of young aesthetes who collaborated on the volume, *Eight Harvard Poets*; he had served as a gentleman volunteer in the ambulance corps of the Great War. He was in many ways the rightful heir of John Reed, the Harvard poet turned literary radical who had died at the age of thirty-two in 1920. Dos Passos's work was a part of what was coming to be known as "modernism," what he himself called "the creative tidal wave that spread over the world from the Paris of before the last European war." "Under various tags: futurism, cubism, vorticism, modernism," Dos Passos wrote in 1931,

> most of the best work in the arts in our time has been the direct product of this explosion, that had an influence in its sphere comparable with that of the October revolution in social organization and politics and the Einstein formula in physics. Cendrars and Apollinaire, poets, were on the first cubist barricades with the group that included Picasso, Modigliani, Marinetti, Chagall; that profoundly influenced Maiakovsky, Meyerhold, Eisenstein; whose ideas carom through Joyce, Gertrude Stein, T.S. Eliot (first published in Wyndham Lewis's *Blast*). The music of Stravinski and Prokofieff and Diageleff's Ballet hail from this same Paris already in the disintegration of victory, as do the windows of Saks Fifth Avenue, skyscraper furniture, the Lenin Memorial in Moscow, the painting of Diego Rivera in Mexico City and the newritz styles of advertising in American magazines.

Since the "cubist barricades" in New York had been built with Dos Passos's *Manhattan Transfer* and the expressionist productions of the New Playwrights' Theater's two seasons, including Lawson's *Loud Speaker* and Dos Passos's *Airways, Inc.*, Dos Passos's example—both as activist and artist— was crucial when the economic crisis of 1929 became a cultural crisis, a crisis of the "new," of the "modern" itself. As the depression challenged the aesthetic ideologies and expatriate experimentalism of the modernist generation, many, including Lawson, Herbst, Cowley, Burke, Josephson, and Wilson, followed the path Dos Passos had marked.[3]

For Dos Passos, however, the crash and the depression were not the "rending of the earth" that they were for his friends, including Edmund Wilson. "The Great Depression . . . didn't affect me very much personally," Dos Passos later wrote, ". . . I used to tell people I had been just as broke before the stockmarket crash as after it . . . It was what I saw of other people's lives that brought home the failure of New Era capitalism." The Sacco and Vanzetti case had already split open Dos Passos's world: the night of the execution—22 August 1927—would remain a more important marker for Dos Passos than the October days of the 1929 Wall Street crash. "It is up to the writers now to see to it that America does not forget Sacco and Vanzetti," he wrote in the *New Masses* soon after the execution. In the face of industrial society's "idiot lack of memory," "we must have writing so fiery and accurate that it will sear through the pall of numb imbecility that we are again swaddled in after the few moments of sane awakening that followed the shock of the executions." By the following spring, Dos Passos had begun a novel—soon to become a trilogy—that was to ensure that Americans did not forget Sacco and Vanzetti.[4]

The first volume of the *U.S.A.* trilogy, *The 42nd Parallel*, was completed a few weeks before the Wall Street crash and appeared in February 1930. The second volume, *Nineteen-Nineteen*, was written over the next two years, with sections appearing in both left-wing magazines like the *New Masses* and in small literary magazines like *Hound and Horn* and *Pagany*. Finished in September 1931, it was published in March 1932, with the country deep in depression and before the election of Roosevelt. Though neither sold well, both novels were critical successes. Mapping a vast social and historical landscape from the cubist barricades, they were one of the earliest attempts to synthesize the legacy of Joyce and Picasso with that of the October Revolution, to create a "revolutionary symbolism."

The final volume, *The Big Money*, took much longer to write, and did not appear until August 1936. Though some sections were published in Arnold Gingrich's new magazine, *Esquire*, Dos Passos remained unable to break into the popular magazines: sections of the novel were rejected by *Redbook*, *Cosmopolitan*, *Story*, and *The New Yorker*. However, the four years between *Nineteen-Nineteen* and *The Big Money* had seen the radical insurgencies of 1934 and the emergence of the Popular Front social movement. Among these readers, Dos Passos's reputation had grown steadily and *The Big Money* was eagerly awaited. When it appeared, the novel proved to be his most successful, and Dos Passos was featured on the cover of *Time*. In early 1938, the three volumes were issued together as *U.S.A.*, and the trilogy was immediately recognized as a landmark in American fiction: major critical essays appeared in 1938 by Lionel Trilling, T. K. Whipple, Granville Hicks, Delmore Schwartz, and Jean-Paul Sartre, who declared Dos Passos "the greatest writer of our time."[5]

In many ways, *U.S.A.* remains the ur-text of the Popular Front; at the Second American Writers' Congress in 1937, *The Big Money* was voted the best novel of the year, receiving the votes of 350 of the 500 delegates, even though Dos Passos was in the process of breaking with the left. Dos Passos had moved away from the Communist Party in 1934 and had become deeply skeptical of Popular Front politics, attending neither the 1935 nor the 1937 American Writers' Congresses (though he did contribute an essay to the 1935 congress). I am not suggesting that *U.S.A.* comes out of the Popular Front; on the contrary, it could be argued that Dos Passos's subsequent novels of the 1940s and 1950s, satirizing the Communist Party, the New Deal, the Hollywood left, and the labor unions, are his Popular

Front "epic," a scathingly hostile portrait of a left he felt had betrayed him. Rather, *U.S.A.* served as the charter for the Popular Front, its starting point, its founding mythology. *U.S.A.*'s nostalgic invocation of the pre-war world of Wobblies, anarchists, Eugene Debs, and Jack Reed, and its rendition of the decline and fall of the Lincoln republic, became the master narrative, the tall tale, for a generation. As a result, it was immediately acclaimed as the great American novel.[6]

U.S.A.'s great reputation at the time is particularly curious because it must be admitted that the book no longer lives for American readers. It remains in print, and has a place in American literary history, but it is not the focus of critical debates, nor is it a founding text for contemporary cultural formations. After the 1940s, no one argued about Dos Passos. He stands in inverse relation to Faulkner: as Dos Passos's reputation waned, Faulkner's waxed. Faulkner remains a "contemporary," in the sense that critics and readers still argue over his work. One can understand why people would dislike *U.S.A.*; but why does it provoke indifference, boredom?

In part, Dos Passos's decline was a result of his political trajectory: to put it crudely, his move to the radical right lost him his left-wing admirers, while the undisputed sense that his early works are his finest has made him a difficult icon for the right. Moreover, despite the reversal in his political affiliations, the *political* never left the foreground of his work. Unlike many of his contemporaries, he did not move from a radical political art to an apolitical formalism, and thus never won the allegiance of formalist or aestheticist critics. As a result, the history of Dos Passos's political opinions has tended to overshadow his fiction. There are far more biographical accounts of Dos Passos than critical accounts, and one of the few critical controversies about *U.S.A.* revolves around its political complexion: whether the work is informed by his "Marxism" or his "Veblenism." But the politics of literary reputation does not fully explain the eclipse of *U.S.A.* Rather, what makes the work "historical" in the negative sense is precisely the source of the trilogy's original power—the tale of the decline and fall of the Lincoln republic. The tall tale he told is no longer ours; far from being a foundational epic, *U.S.A.* now stands, like *The Education of Henry Adams*, as a tombstone for an America that no longer exists.[7]

For Dos Passos's generation, the Civil War had been, as Charles Beard put it, the "Second American Revolution": it founded a new nation. It is not an accident that one of the few films Dos Passos's characters see is D.W. Griffith's *Birth of a Nation*. If the southern tale of the defeated Confederacy lay beneath the genealogies of Faulkner and the romance of *Gone with the Wind*, the northern tale of how the winning side lost—how the promise of the Lincoln republic was betrayed—lay beneath the work of the radical moderns. One sees it at its grandest in the fictional trilogies:

Dos Passos's *U.S.A.*, Josephine Herbst's Trexler trilogy, W.E.B. Du Bois's
Mansart trilogy, and Orson Welles's Mercury "trilogy," *Citizen Kane, The
Magnificent Ambersons,* and *The Stranger.* But it also informs the Popular
Front historical trilogy of Matthew Josephson (*The Robber Barons, The
Politicos,* and *The President Makers*), the literary histories of Granville Hicks
and Alfred Kazin, musical compositions like Aaron Copland's *Lincoln
Portrait* and Duke Ellington's *Black, Brown, and Beige,* and visual works like
Paul Strand's film *Native Land* and his photohistory *Time in New England.*
The culmination of this tradition may well be the historical novels of Gore
Vidal (who was a young radical in the 1940s): *Burr, Lincoln, 1876, Empire,*
and *Hollywood.* The great reputation and standing of *U.S.A.* derives from
its role in formulating this story.[8]

In a way, the story of the decline and fall of the Lincoln republic is not
dissimilar to the great cycle of British spy novels in the decades after the
Second World War, reflections on the irony of apparent victory, of winning
the war and losing the peace. These narratives return to the years after the
Civil War to tell a tale of the "big money," of lost opportunities, of a
republic that became an empire. The Lincoln republic, redeemed from
the sin of slavery, had been lost to the great robber barons, to Mr
McKinley's wars in the Caribbean and the Pacific, and to Mr Wilson's war
in Europe. The republic of the "producing classes" had been crucified on
a cross of gold.

It is striking, however, that this northern story only became a "story" with
a symbolic defeat, the crash of 1929. Only a few years earlier, the
characteristic mode for invoking the American past had been elegiac, not
epic. Willa Cather's *A Lost Lady* and F. Scott Fitzgerald's *The Great Gatsby*
were lyric elegies for a simpler past, a lost time when giants walked the
earth, a time of the pioneers. They were not histories as much as reflections
on past and present, innocence and experience. However, the depression
made possible a new way of understanding American history and society, a
new kind of historical fiction. Not only did the crash coincide with the
celebrated return of the expatriate artists, the "exile's return" Malcolm
Cowley chronicled, but many of them took up American subjects and
themes, laboring with the inheritance of the continent. The changes
worked on the chords "native" and "ground" in these years are remarkable:
Dos Passos's *The Ground We Stand On,* Kazin's *On Native Grounds,* Wright's
Native Son, Strand's *Native Land,* Adamic's journal, *Common Ground,* and his
memoir, *The Native's Return.* But this was not simply a rhetoric of Americanism adopted as an antidote to "Europe." The trauma of the depression—
and, for some, the execution of Sacco and Vanzetti—punctuated the
history of the Lincoln republic; it gave the story a beginning, middle, and
end.

The formal problem in each of these narratives of the decline and fall of the Lincoln republic is straightforward: How does one narrate this history? Whose lives embody the Lincoln republic? Whose voice can tell its story? Along what parallel can one chart a map of the continent, the nation? Dos Passos's solutions made him not only the representative novelist of the Popular Front social movement, but, for a time, the most acclaimed and respected American writer.

2.   Dos Passos's "New Clean Construction"

There is, I believe, only one explicit figure of the novelist in the *U.S.A.* trilogy, and it is a telling one. When Mary French goes to Boston to work for the Sacco and Vanzetti Defense Committee, she decides "that when the case was won, she'd write a novel about Boston. She bought some school copybooks in a little musty stationers' shop and started right away taking notes for the novel." The case was not won, and we hear no more of Mary French's novel of Boston. Moreover, though Dos Passos's own novel came directly from his work for the Sacco-Vanzetti defense, it is not a story of Boston nor a story of Sacco and Vanzetti: Upton Sinclair used the trial transcripts to write that novel, *Boston.* Nor is *U.S.A.* the story Mary French would have told. Frankly, it is difficult to imagine the author of *U.S.A.*: Dos Passos's work does not seem to originate from a storyteller. "I've always been a frustrated architect," Dos Passos told an interviewer in 1962, and *U.S.A.* at first glance seems more a building than an epic, more the work of an architect than of a historian.[9]

A more apt emblem of Dos Passos's own project is the architect Frank Lloyd Wright, the "patriarch of the new building," a "preacher in blue-prints." "Building a building," Dos Passos writes in his prose portrait of Wright, "is building the lives of the workers and dwellers in the building. The buildings determine civilization as the cells in the honeycomb the functions of bees." Wright's life was a call for "a new clean construction, from the ground up, based on uses and needs," and *U.S.A.* was a writer's response, an "effort to intersect word with word to dovetail clause with clause to rebuild out of mangled memories unshakably (Old Pontius Pilate) the truth." "The writer who writes straight," Dos Passos maintained in a 1932 account of his own work, "is the architect of history."[10]

Dos Passos's trilogy can be seen as a "new clean construction," a series of formal solutions to the problem of building a novel that culminates in the magical unity of the title itself, *U.S.A.* First, Dos Passos unites fiction, history, and autobiography in the very architecture of the novel, juxtaposing different modes of writing to tell the history of the "big money." Second, *U.S.A.* imagines the United States as the "speech of the people," and invents a modern vernacular in order to "rebuild the ruined words worn slimy in the mouths of lawyers districtattorneys collegepresidents judges." Finally, *U.S.A.* encompasses the lives of the nation by becoming a library of American novels: a war novel, a Hollywood novel, a novel of the returning vet, a working-girl romance, a proletarian novel. Each of these, however, depends on three fundamental narratives: the cocktail party as a narrative kernel and the quintessential social form; the narrative of the road, embodied in the ur-character, Vag; and the narrative of slumming, the story of the proletarian sublime. By exploring these elements of *U.S.A.* we can begin to see the power and limits of both Dos Passos's "new clean construction" and the tale of the decline and fall of the Lincoln republic.[11]

i. "The great imperial steamroller of American finance"

Dos Passos's experiment in uniting history, fiction, and memoir in a new type of "historical novel" was immediately apparent in the division of the novels into four distinct types of writing: the sixty-eight Newsreels; the fifty-one Camera Eyes; the twenty-seven biographical portraits; and the fictional narratives organized around twelve major characters. In retrospect, however, these experimental devices seem less a cure than a symptom, one of a variety of modernist attempts to square the circle of personal memory and public history, to capture private consciousness and the vast overarching social forces of modernity in a single form. However, it is not the success of the synthesis that we are struck by; rather, the Camera Eyes and the Newsreels stand, like the interchapters of Hemingway's *in our time*, as stark and arbitrary testimonies to an aesthetic Taylorism, a divided and rationalized labor. Perhaps Dos Passos's self-mocking reference to the trilogy's structure as his "four-way conveyor system" was an acknowledgement that he may have built an assembly line rather than a skyscraper.

Nevertheless, whether assembly line or skyscraper, the trilogy is a remarkable instance of modernist history-writing. "The only excuse for a novelist," Dos Passos wrote in a 1928 "Statement of Belief," "aside from the entertainment and vicarious living his books give the people who read them, is as a sort of second-class historian of the age he lives in." Dos Passos is more than a "second-class historian," but the "four-way conveyor system" of *U.S.A.* produces a complex and contradictory kind of historical narrative. Not only is each of the conveyors clocked at a different speed, but each presents a different history, even a different conception of history.[12]

The work of public history is at first glance the job of the Newsreels, Dos Passos's collages of newspaper headlines and popular song lyrics. They serve as a kind of historical chorus, answering the fictional events with a cacophony of wars, strikes, and revolutions. They open by heralding the New Century and end with the Wall Street crash. However, despite attempts to locate the Newsreels' "sources" in specific songs or newspapers, few critics have found any coherent historical narrative in them; undated and unauthored, they remain less a firm grounding in the spirit of the time or even an evocation of historical color than a repetitive and finally ahistorical serial, establishing the always already contemporary, an emblem of industrial society's "idiot lack of memory."

The work of memory, on the other hand, is the labor of the Camera Eye, the dreamwork of the trilogy, a series of symbolist prose poems swirling around unnamed lyric shifters—I, He, She—and invoking a time "Longago Beforetheworldsfair Beforeyouwereborn." The Camera Eye passages are, as critics have shown, autobiographical evocations of Dos Passos's own experiences. Thus, they not only stand outside the fictional world of the novel, but are intentionally private and enigmatic. Nevertheless, in many ways, they are more deeply historical than the apparently historical Newsreels, as they seek to unite private memory and public history. "Who were the Molly Maguires?" is the reiterated refrain of the early Camera Eye of a Presbyterian church service in Pennsylvania. Though the reader never gets a direct answer, the Camera Eye stands as a memorial connecting the Molly Maguires, coal-miners martyred in 1877, and Sacco and Vanzetti, the fish peddlar and shoemaker martyred in 1927.[13]

If the Newsreels offer the official history of the New Century, and the Camera Eye offers a memorial to its victims, the grand narrative of the Lincoln republic is outlined in the twenty-seven biographical portraits of actual historical figures. More than any other part of the book, the portraits embody the history Dos Passos wanted to tell, chronicling the republic from the year of Buchanan's election (when, we are told, both Woodrow Wilson and Frederick Winslow Taylor were born) to 1929, the symbolic year in which both Thorstein Veblen and Paxton Hibben die.[14]

Dos Passos's portrait of Paxton Hibben—"A Hoosier Quixote"—could stand as an allegory for the entire work. Hibben's biography of Henry Ward Beecher had been a model for Dos Passos at the moment he was conceiving *U.S.A.*, and he reviewed it in the *New Masses* in 1927. "History is always more alive and more interesting than fiction," Dos Passos wrote in the review, ". . . because a story is the day-dream of a single man, while history is a mass-invention, the day-dream of a race." Moreover, Hibben's history of the Beechers captured for Dos Passos the trajectory of the American past: "From Lyman Beecher to Henry Ward you have the break in the American mind that came when a farmers' and traders' democracy began to founder in a flood of gilt-edged securities . . . In those two men you have the whole disintegration of the American mind." The review concluded with a call for more books like Hibben's, "more accurate and imaginative studies of the American past to set our compasses by." When Dos Passos included a portrait of Hibben in *Nineteen-Nineteen*, he used Hibben's career to chart the disintegration of the American republic. Hibben had grown up with the middle western sense that "something was wrong with the American Republic," and he had tried to revive its ideals. He "believed passionately" in the republic, in "righteousness and reform," in Roosevelt's "Big Stick that was going to scare away the grafters and malefactors of great wealth and get the common man his due," in Wilson's War to End War. But he was betrayed by Roosevelt, by Wilson, by his Princeton classmates. The mock lynching of Hibben at a class reunion is a farcical rendition of the actual lynching of the Wobbly Wesley Everest in a subsequent portrait.[15]

Unlike the Newsreels and the Camera Eye, which have often mystified readers—when they were excerpted in *Esquire*, readers were instructed how to read them—the biographical portraits were a great popular and critical success: most had been published separately in magazines, and Dos Passos and his publishers considered publishing them as a separate volume. T. K. Whipple noted in 1938 that "on one point at least everyone probably agrees: that the biographical portraits are magnificent, and are the best part of the book." The imaginative power of Dos Passos's portraits have made him one of the great, if unacknowledged, historians of his day, the equal of Beard or Hofstadter in shaping our imagination of Debs, Veblen, Ford, and the others. The portraits also became the center of the controversy over Dos Passos's explanatory system. After Whipple argued that "the biographical portraits are the best part of his book because they are the most nearly Marxist, showing the dynamic contradictions of our time ... in the minds and lives of whole men," the question of whether Dos Passos was a Marxist, a Veblenite, a Beardian, a technocrat, a Binghamite, an anarchist, or a Whitmanian democrat dominated critical debates. In retrospect, the answer to this question is less significant than the debate itself. The interest and power of Dos Passos's explanatory system lies not in the way his "ideas" matched any of these imagined positions, but in the fact that he was saturated in the peculiar mixture of Marx and Veblen, Whitman and Beard, anarchism and populism, that made up American radicalism at the time. The peculiar blindness and insight of his portraits are echoed throughout Popular Front history-writing.[16]

The heart of Dos Passos's history was the story of the "big money," of "the great imperial steamroller of American finance." "It's about time that American writers showed up in the industrial field where something is really going on, instead of tackling the tired strawmen of art and culture," Dos Passos wrote in 1929; however, when he "showed up in the industrial field," he did not write narratives of factory labor. Dos Passos was always uncomfortable with the slogan of "proletarian literature": his was more a tale of capital. He shared this with many other radical modernists. Most of the significant Marxist histories of the United States—including Lewis Corey's *The Decline of American Capitalism* and Matthew Josephson's *The Robber Barons: The Great American Capitalists, 1861–1901*—were histories of capital rather than labor. Corey's *The Decline of American Capitalism*, written in the depths of the depression and published in the midst of the uprisings of 1934, was a massive study of American accumulation, wealth, and monopoly. "It is one of the best introductions to Marxism that has appeared in the English language," the young Columbia historian Louis Hacker wrote in *Scribner's*, ". . . and it is a brilliant appendix, drawn entirely from American experience, to Marx's *Capital.*" It was probably the most influential US Marxist work of the period, widely reviewed and read among left and liberal intellectuals.[17]

If Corey documented the crisis in an array of tables, graphs, and statistics, Matthew Josephson's *The Robber Barons* became the most widely read work of radical history by retelling the stories of Rockefeller, Carnegie, and Morgan. Josephson was the former editor of the modernist little magazines, *Broom* and *Secession*, and a close friend of Malcolm Cowley and Kenneth Burke. After working for a stock exchange firm in the mid 1920s, he had published a series of journalistic reports on "the bulls and bears of Wall Street" before deciding "to make a large gallery of historical portraits" of "men of fortune" and "the post-Civil War era in which they thrived, when America was the paradise of the freebooting entrepreneurs." Fusing Marx, Veblen, and Charles Beard (Josephson's neighbor at the time) in a dramatic and satirical narrative, *The Robber Barons* was an immediate best seller and a choice of the Book of the Month Club. The figure of the robber baron, revived from an 1880 antimonopoly pamphlet of Kansas farmers, proved a popular and lasting image of American capitalism, and the fascination with robber barons past and present extended well beyond Josephson's book. Probably more of the young depression radicals had read Gustavus Myers's three-volume classic, *History of the Great American Fortunes* (1910) than had read Marx's *Capital*; and Lewis Corey's *The House of Morgan* (1930), Harvey O'Connor's *Mellon's Millions* (1933), and Ferdinand Lundberg's *Imperial Hearst* (1936) were only the best known of many Popular Front studies of tycoons. The giant figures of the robber baron and the tycoon haunted Popular Front works of art: William Randolph Hearst is portrayed in Dos Passos's *U.S.A.* and in Welles's *Citizen Kane.*[18]

In a 1929 review of biographies of Edison and Steinmetz (both of whom were subjects of portraits in *The 42nd Parallel*), Dos Passos wrote of his "great many futile hours spent grubbing in the literature of the last fifty years of American industrial development." He, like Josephson and Welles, was drawn to individual figures; though there is a record of his reading Lewis Corey's *Decline of American Capitalism* as well as Veblen's *Absentee Ownership*, the heart of his research lay in biography. From these studies came his modern Plutarch, the twenty-seven portraits of the republic's usurpers and defenders.[19]

Two grand conflicts structure the portraits: the conflict of labor and capital, and the conflict of the engineers and the price system, in short, Marx and Veblen. Both narratives share one cluster of characters: the robber barons—Minor Keith, Andrew Carnegie, J. P. Morgan, Henry Ford, William Randolph Hearst, and Samuel Insull—and the politicians who served them—Theodore Roosevelt and Woodrow Wilson. In the conflict between labor and capital, they thrive on "wars and panics on the stock exchange ... good growing weather for the House of Morgan." Against them are set a gallery of martyrs for the republic, including the lynched Wobbly Wesley Everest and the Unknown Soldier, and defenders of the republic, the leaders of the "plain people" and the "workingman," including Eugene Debs, Big Bill Haywood, William Jennings Bryan, and Robert La Follette.

In the parallel conflict of the engineers and the price system, the robber barons—here epitomized by Samuel Insull, whose "engineering" was "largely concerned with engineering all I could out of the dollar"—are set against a gallery of inventors and engineers, torn between an ideal of craft and the demands of profit: Luther Burbank, the Wright brothers, Thomas Edison, Frank Lloyd Wright, Frederick Winslow Taylor, and Charles Steinmetz—"the most valuable piece of apparatus General Electric had." In both conflicts, Dos Passos's story is one of defeat at the hands of capital: he writes of Eugene Debs abandoned by his brothers—"where were the locomotive firemen and engineers when they hustled him off to Atlanta Penitentiary?"; of Haywood dying in Moscow; of Steinmetz worn out by GE; and of Frank Lloyd Wright "without honor ... in his own country."[20]

The very success of Dos Passos's historical portraits has often overshadowed the fourth of *U.S.A.*'s conveyor belts: the fictional narratives organized around twelve major characters. Despite the counterpoint of fictional and historical characters, of Mac to Big Bill Haywood, Margo to Isadora Duncan, and Charley Anderson to Henry Ford, the incommensurability of the fictional creations and the historical figures seems to mark a fault line in the trilogy. "There is more human reality in the 10 pages given to Henry Ford than in the 220 given to Charley Anderson," T.K. Whipple argued in a famous critical response; the historical figures are portrayed with "ruling passions" and "motive powers," while the fictional characters and the Camera Eye persona are "devoid of will or purpose." The novel seems caught in the formal trap that Lukács identified: the "real" historical characters in a historical novel must be kept firmly in the background or they will take over, outshining the mere fictional creations.[21]

There are two reasons for this discrepancy between the historical portraits and the fictional narratives. First, whereas the historical miniatures of the portraits explicitly parallel the arc of individual lives with the arc of the republic, the continuous present of the fictional narratives obscures those relations. The fictional narratives do span an epoch: they open in the bleak winter that followed the Panic of 1893, with the young Fenian McCreary leaving Middletown, Connecticut, his father having lost his job in a strike and his mother having died; they end a generation later with the killing of a young labor organizer and the suicide of an interior decorator in the winter of 1927–28. But the haphazard and accidental relations between the characters—the story of McCreary, "Mac," is simply abandoned—and the various time warps—what Barbara Foley has called the text's "chronological distortions"—block any sense of a linear history or overall narrative; one hardly imagines that a generation has passed in the course of the trilogy.[22]

Moreover, the protagonists of the biographies are absent from the fictional narratives. Curiously, one finds no characters drawn from the robber barons and tycoons themselves, no Hearsts or Insulls. There is neither Citizen Kane nor Dreiser's Charles Yerkes. Nor are there any characters that look like Debs, Haywood, Steinmetz, or Frank Lloyd Wright. Rather, the fiction is dominated by figures not represented in the biographies: public relations executives, interior designers, newspaper correspondents, Hollywood actresses, and social workers. This disjunction is particularly striking because there were historical sources for many of Dos Passos's major characters: J. Ward Moorehouse was drawn in part from the public relations man Ivy Lee; Ben Compton was drawn from the radical labor leader Albert Weisbord; Mary French was based in part on the writer and activist Mary Heaton Vorse; and Doc Bingham was based on the *True Story* publisher Bernarr MacFadden. The sorts of characters that seem central to the historical epic of the Lincoln republic—the subjects of the biographies—are somehow not the stuff of fiction; and, inversely, the sorts of characters whose lives are traced in *U.S.A.*'s narratives are not the subjects of the grand design.[23]

As many critics have noted, the social range of Dos Passos's fictional characters is more limited than that of the biographies. The fictional narratives of *U.S.A.* are neither *The Robber Barons* nor a "proletarian novel"; they appear to be a "middle-class" epic. But it is misleading to see this as Dos Passos's particular blindness, simply a class provincialism that restricts his canvas. Dos Passos's choice of characters—his focus on people in the "trades that deal with words"—is a result of a second great unifying structure: his attempt to invent a modern vernacular, to capture the continent in its language.

ii. "But mostly *U.S.A.* is the speech of the people"

When Dos Passos came to publish *U.S.A.* as a trilogy in 1938, he added a brief introduction that ended with the line "mostly *U.S.A.* is the speech of the people." If the experiment of the "four-way conveyor belt" seems less a formal solution than a symptom of the problem, Dos Passos's invention of a modern vernacular remains one of his most striking, if contradictory, accomplishments, a strange synthesis of the word-experiments that had been conducted in the laboratories of Gertrude Stein and the populist lexicography embodied in H.L. Mencken's *The American Language.*

Dos Passos's kinship to modernist prose is readily apparent; an early reviewer noted that *The 42nd Parallel* was told "in that carefully naive condensed, colloquial style that Ernest Hemingway, among the followers of Stein and Joyce, has most successfully affected." Dos Passos built paratactic sentences, linked with ands, and ran words together in unortho- dox compounds. But Edmund Wilson shrewdly noted in his 1930 *New Republic* review that "Dos Passos has studied Anita Loos and Ring Lardner for the method of *The 42nd Parallel,* and he is perhaps the first really important writer to have succeeded in using colloquial American for a novel of the highest artistic seriousness." To link Dos Passos to Loos and Lardner seems odd at first; though they were as much satirists as Dos Passos, the characters they created have an innocence, humor, and sympathy that few of Dos Passos's creations share. However, Wilson is right: if at first it seems odd to link Charley Anderson to Lardner's Jack Keefe, one can hear the accents of the Busher in a classic "big money" passage:

> Bill, goddam it, we'll be in the money. How about another bottle? . . . Good old Bill, the pilot's nothin' without his mechanic, the promoter's nothin' without production . . . You and me, Bill, we're in production, and by God I'm goin' to see that we don't lose out. If they try to rook us we'll fight, already I've had offers, big offers from Detroit . . . in five years now we'll be in the money and I'll see you're in the big money too.

Similarly, one can often hear the voice of Anita Loos's Lorelei in the words of Margo Dowling: "Honest, Tad, I like you fine . . . but you know . . . Heaven won't protect a working-girl unless she protects herself."[24]

Nevertheless, Dos Passos's vernacular would not be confused with that of Lardner and Loos, nor would his sentences be confused with the machined periods of Stein or Hemingway. In part, this is because Dos Passos's modernist colloquialism derived from an aesthetic ideology that differed from both the rich linguistic populism that underlies Lardner and Loos and the pure distillation and renovation of perception aimed at by Stein and Hemingway. All of those writers shared a linguistic romanticism, a belief that a purer or more popular style could redeem modernity and its debased languages. One part of Dos Passos believed it as well, as Fred Pfeil has pointed out. An organic conception of language can be seen in the opening metaphor of speech as a vine—"the ears are caught tight, linked tight by the tendrils of phrased words, the turn of a joke, the singsong fade of a story, the gruff fall of a sentence: linking tendrils of speech twine through the city blocks, spread over pavements, grow out along broad parked avenues"—and the modernist hope for a purified language surges up in the three final Camera Eye passages (numbers 49, 50 and 51) which set the "clean words our fathers spoke" against the "slimy and foul" words of America's "betrayers" and oppressors, imagining language as a weapon of the oppressed: "we have only words against" is the final line of the last Camera Eye.[25]

But, for the most part, Dos Passos's vernacular is resolutely anti-populist; if *U.S.A.* is the speech of the people, the speech of the people is mostly headlines, popular songs, and advertising slogans, the colloquialisms of the commercial culture that addresses Vag on the final page: "books said opportunity, ads promised speed, own your home, shine bigger than your neighbor, the radiocrooner whispered girls, ghosts of platinum girls coaxed from the screen ... the cleared desk of an executive with three telephones on it." The sentence production of *U.S.A.* is less a renewal of perception than a Tayloring of the novel: Dos Passos's compound words are not a device of defamiliarization but a streamlined and efficient elimination of unnecessary parts and motions.[26]

This anti-populist, Taylorized colloquialism led Edmund Wilson to complain to Dos Passos that "you tend to make your characters talk clichés." And this impulse manifests itself in the narrative discourse as well: unlike the great first-person vernaculars of Twain, Lardner, and Loos, Dos Passos distances his "speech of the people" as well as his characters through an indirect narrative that, as Jean-Paul Sartre put it, "reports [the] characters' utterances to us in the style of a statement to the Press." Storytelling itself is radically reduced to the "about how" construction: "Agnes had told her all about how getting drunk was something that men did and that they hadn't ought to"; "he tried to break it up by telling about how he'd been taken for Charles Edward Holden in that saloon that time, but nobody listened." The text creates a kind of continuous present, a constant ticking of the clock, so regular that you hardly notice it, with little use of flashbacks, internal monologues, or disrupted time sequences: its storytelling is as regular and relentless as an assembly line.[27]

It is not sufficient, however, to see Dos Passos's colloquialism as entirely satirical, as a cynical, even misanthropic, manifestation of Dos Passos's "naturalism," "determinism," or "behaviorism." True, *U.S.A.* is not a redemption of storytelling and orality in the manner of Faulkner or Hurston. Whereas these two share an agrarian modernism—defined by the impossible project of recreating oral storytelling between the covers of the book—Dos Passos is resolutely anti-agrarian. Leaving the farm is the desire that drives several characters and runs through many of the biographies. His America is a continent with the agrarian parts left out; even the South is the Florida of the real-estate boom, not the land of cotton and sharecropping. And if Dos Passos did not share the redemptive ideologies of the populist vernaculars, neither did he share the redemptive modernism of the "revolution of the word."

Rather, he fashioned an aesthetic ideology around the figure of the writer as "technician," the writer as engineer or machinist: "a writer is after all only a machine for absorbing and arranging certain sequences of words out of the lives of the people round him." When Edmund Wilson accused Dos Passos of believing that "the language of everybody . . . is a tissue of the ready-made phrases that go with his profession or milieu," he was right: early on, Dos Passos had written that "people are formed by their trades and occupations much more than by their opinions. The fact that a man is a shoesalesman or a butcher is in every respect more important than that he's a republican or a theosophist." But, unlike Wilson, Dos Passos did not entirely scorn the "ready-made phrases" of the "profession." Recall the account of Veblen in *The Big Money*: "his language was a mixture of mechanics' terms, scientific latinity, slang and Roget's Thesaurus"—a relatively good description of *U.S.A.* itself.[28]

But if the "speech of the people" consists of the "ready-made phrases" of a "profession or mileu," the scraps of headlines, song lyrics, advertising slogans, and mechanics' terms, it is deeply influenced by what Dos Passos called "the great semi-parasitic class that includes all the trades that deal with words from advertising and the Christian ministry to song writing . . . the word-slinging organism." Thus, it is perhaps less surprising that *U.S.A.* is not a story of robber barons and proletarians, nor even of engineers and profiteers, but a tale of journalists, advertisers, and songwriters. Characters who seem unconnected are united by the "trades that deal with words." Not only are the Newsreels made up largely of newspaper headlines and clippings, it seems that everyone has done a stint working for a newspaper: Mac works for the San Francisco *Bulletin*, the Nevada *Workman*, and the Mexican *Herald*; J. Ward Moorehouse works for the *Herald* in Paris and for the Pittsburgh *Times Dispatch*; and Mary French works for the Pittsburgh *Times-Sentinel*. Many of the recurring characters are correspondents: Jerry Burnham works for UP; Al Johnson for the *World*; Don Stevens for the *Call* and *Metropolitan*. Other types of word-slinging turn up as well: both Mac and J. Ward Moorehouse get their start as traveling booksellers; Mac ends up running a bookstore in Mexico City. Janey Williams takes typing as the way to a desk job; her brother Joe has a stint as a Western Union messenger. Even Charley Anderson becomes a word-slinger when, in one of the running jokes of *The Big Money*, he is mistakenly introduced at a party as Charles Edward Holden, a writer whom Eveline will call the "real poet of modern New York."[29]

This linguistic totality explains the absence of the robber barons from the novels. The industrial tycoons, the capitalists who embody the "big money," finally resist Dos Passos's totality because they resist language itself. Dos Passos himself suggested as much in his explanation of the dismal quality of the writing about American business: "you have to read these books [the biographies of Edison and Steinmetz and Broderick's *Forty Years with General Electric*] to believe how muddle-headed, ill-written, and flatly meaningless they can be." One reason, Dos Passos suggested, is that "the writing was usually left to hired hacks and publicity men. The people who were actually doing the work had no time and no inclination to put themselves down on paper." But this is not all, he continued:

> Good writing is the reflection of an intense and organized viewpoint towards something, usually towards the values and processes of human life. The fact that the writing that emanates even from such a powerful institution as General Electric is so childish is a measure of proof that the men directing it are muddled and unclear about their human aims.

For Dos Passos, the use of words becomes a quintessential human act, and his fictional characters—more often than not the "hired hacks and publicity men"—are defined by their uses and abuses of language.[30]

In the course of writing *U.S.A.*, Dos Passos developed a rough theory about this "great semi-parasitic class" that is interesting both as an explanation system for the novel and as an account of the cultural front itself. In a 1930 contribution to a *New Masses* discussion of intellectuals, Dos Passos wrote that:

> there is a layer: engineers, scientists, independent manual craftsmen, writers, artists, actors, technicians of one sort or another, who insofar as they are good at their jobs are a necessary part of any industrial society . . . As a writer I belong to that class whether I like it or not, and I think most men who graduate from working with their hands into desk jobs eventually belong to it, no matter what their ideas are. You can call 'em intellectuals or liberals or petty bourgeoisie or any other dirty name but it won't change 'em any. What you've got to do is convince the technicians and white collar workers that they have nothing to lose . . . The most difficult thing you have to buck is the fact that along with the technical education that makes them valuable to the community they have taken in a subconscious political education that makes them servants of the owners . . . It's the job of people of all the professions in the radical fringe of the middle class to try to influence this middle class, that most of them would rather not belong to, so that at least some of its weight shall be thrown on the side of what I've been calling civilization. It's a tough job, but somebody's got to do it.

This is perhaps the clearest statement of Dos Passos's own political stance in the years he was writing *U.S.A.*, contributing political essays to journals of opinion, and organizing support for striking workers and political prisoners.[31]

Moreover, it became the political stance of radicalized artists, writers, and professionals in the years that followed, in the Popular Front organizations, campaigns, and cultural activities. One of the precursors of the cultural front was the League of Professional Groups for Foster and Ford, an ad hoc alliance supporting the Communist Party presidential ticket in 1932: Dos Passos was one of fifty writers and critics—including Edmund Wilson and Matthew Josephson—who joined in signing their pamphlet, *Culture and the Crisis: An Open Letter to the Writers, Artists, Teachers, Physicians, Engineers, Scientists, and Other Professional Workers of America.* Though the attempt to turn the league into a permanent organization floundered on the battles over its connection to the Communist Party, it proved to be a model for the white-collar Popular Front.

U.S.A. grew out of Dos Passos's ambivalence about the word-slinging organisms, the desk workers, and his own work. On the one hand, he believed in the crafts themselves, that the work the technicians did was valuable to the community; on the other hand, he had a deep suspicion of the culture of the technicians, of their education, their values, their ability to serve any master. *U.S.A.*'s gallery of word-slingers was an attempt not only to capture the "speech of the people," but to imagine the contradictory lives of those who traded in the speech of the people. We can see this by juxtaposing two pairs of characters: Mac and Richard Ellsworth Savage; and Mary French and J. Ward Moorehouse.

The only link between Mac, the migrant worker who drifts from Middletown to Mexico, and Richard Ellsworth Savage, the Harvard-educated poet turned advertising man, is the figure of Doc Bingham, but the contrast between the worker-printer and poet-advertiser is central to the trilogy. At the beginning of the trilogy, Mac gets his first job with Doc Bingham's Truth Seeker, Inc. as a traveling salesman, selling pamphlet pornography and Bible stories out of the back of a wagon; a quarter of a century later, Dick Savage's one creative act comes in an advertising campaign for Doc Bingham's patent medicines. For Mac, the episode with Bingham is part of a picaresque education in rogues and scoundrels; his place among the "trades dealing with words" had already been established as an apprentice printer, learning the trade from his socialist uncle. For Savage, on the other hand, the work for Bingham is the culmination of a long betrayal of his "daydream of ... sending out flaming poems and manifestos, calling young men to revolt against their butchers, poems that would be published by secret presses all over the world." If the figure of worker-printer serves as an emblem of craft and intelligence throughout Dos Passos's trilogy, Savage stands as Dos Passos's version of a characteristic obsession of the radical modernists, the tale of the poet-advertiser. "After the suppression of *Broom*," Malcolm Cowley writes in *Exile's Return*, "I had no energy for new undertakings and for a time I was simply another advertising copywriter who hated his job." Cowley's account of "the advertising men who served as priests and poets of American prosperity" was published in the same year—1934—as James Rorty's pathbreaking anatomy of "the apparatus of advertising": both Cowley and Rorty had contributed to the *Culture and the Crisis* pamphlet.[32]

J. Ward Moorehouse, the advertising executive for whom Savage works, and Mary French, the radical activist who organizes the defense of Sacco and Vanzetti, never meet in the trilogy, and their narratives rarely overlap. However, there is a remarkable parallel in their stories, figured in their arrivals in Pittsburgh, the city of their initial triumphs. Moorehouse arrives there by train: "here he was twentythree years old and he hadn't a college degree and he didn't know any trade and he'd given up the hope of being a songwriter . . . Through the window he could see black hills powdered with snow, an occasional coaltipple, rows of gray shacks all alike . . . Stragglings of darkfaced men in dark clothes stood in the slush at the crossings." He gets a job as a reporter on the *Times Dispatch*, "writing up Italian weddings, local conventions of Elks, obscure deaths, murders and suicides among Lithuanians, Albanians, Croats, Poles . . . never to get an assignment that wasn't connected with working people or foreigners or criminals: he hated it." In a Homestead strike, Moorehouse finds his vocation and his livelihood: he founds a publicity agency to explain and advertise the steel industry's views.[33]

Moorehouse's story has an unlikely echo in that of Mary French, who arrives in Pittsburgh, having dropped out of Vassar and "graduated" from Hull House. "I just can't imagine anyone coming to Pittsburgh for their vacation," her librarian friend tells her, "you know they don't employ Vassar graduates in the open-hearth furnaces." She too gets a newspaper job, with the *Times-Sentinel*. And she too discovers a vocation: she is fired by the paper for an article about a union, and she goes to work doing publicity for the Amalgamated during the strike of 1919. Like Moorehouse, she is in publicity, but she chooses the other side: the foreigners and working people he hated. The opposite choices Ward and Mary make are crucial to Dos Passos: as he wrote at the time, "as a producer and worker, any writer who's not a paid propagandist for the exploiting group (and most of them will be) will naturally find his lot with the producers." But the lives on either side of the fence are not dissimilar: "the word-slinging organism is substantially the same whether it sucks its blood from Park Avenue or Flatbush," Dos Passos wrote, "whether his aims are KKK or Communist he takes on the mind and functional deformities of his trade."[34]

The trilogy ends with Mary French's return to Pittsburgh after the death of an organizer. "We ought to have been in Pittsburgh all along," she says, and one senses that part of Dos Passos felt that the novels themselves ought to have been in Pittsburgh, a place people wouldn't go for vacation, the scene of the battle for both Moorehouse and French. But the novels are not set in Pittsburgh, and Mary French's final scene takes place not in union headquarters but at Eveline's cocktail party. The cocktail party—a place of talk, of the "speech of the people"—is a fitting conclusion; it is Dos Passos's "Pittsburgh," the stage for most of *U.S.A.*'s stories.[35]

iii. The world a cocktail party

"You know it does seem too silly to spend your life filling up rooms with illassorted people who really hate each other," Eveline Hutchins Johnson tells her friend just before committing suicide at the end of the trilogy. If the line is an epitaph for Eveline and her social world, a world Mary French characterizes with the Veblenesque word "waste," it is also uncomfortably close to the novelist's own work: *U.S.A.* might easily be seen as a series of rooms filled with "illassorted people who really hate each other." Perhaps the most striking and unsettling aspect of *U.S.A.* is the lack of any coherent connection between the characters: no family or set of families constitutes the world of the novel; no town, neighborhood, or city serves as a knowable community; no industry or business, no university or film colony unites public and private lives; and no plot, murder, or inheritance links the separate destinies. When Dos Passos drew a "geography" of *Nineteen-Nineteen*, it looked nothing like Faulkner's map of Yoknapatawpha County. It was a circle labeled Paris surrounded by four circles labeled New York, Alsace, Rome, and Constantinople. Dos Passos's lists of characters are just that, not the genealogies that epic novelists ordinarily create. The characters in *U.S.A.* come together by accident, usually at cocktail parties.[36]

Cocktail parties are the climax of each of the three volumes, as the unrelated main characters are thrown together: the Mexican party at which Mac meets J. Ward Moorehouse and Janey Williams (and the recurring minor character George Barrow) in *The 42nd Parallel*; the Paris dinner at the Hermitage where Daughter and Eveline Hutchins (and George Barrow) find Moorehouse, Richard Ellsworth Savage, and Eleanor Stoddard at the next table in *Nineteen-Nineteen*; and Eveline's final New York cocktail party, where the Hollywood film star Margo Dowling is pointed out to the labor activist Mary French (by George Barrow) in *The Big Money*. But these are only the most "illassorted" mixtures in a constant series of parties at hotels, apartments, restaurants, bistros, bars, and dives. In one sense, the endless round of drinks is the object of Dos Passos's satire, an emblem of the decadence and decay at the end of the Lincoln republic, a modernist motif that echoes Fitzgerald's *The Great Gatsby* and can also be seen in Malcolm Cowley's tale of the suicide of Harry Crosby in *Exile's Return.*

However, the cocktail parties of *U.S.A.* are more than a satire of the "Roaring Twenties," more than an indictment of conspicuous waste. Everyone parties in these books: the party becomes the quintessential social form in *U.S.A.*, the necessary, if arbitrary, assembling of "the changeable the multitudinous lives" into the "fiveoclock drama," as it is put in the meditation on the cocktail party in the Camera Eye (45). The party is first and foremost a place of talk—"the narrow yellow room teems with talk"—and thus a principal locus of *U.S.A.*'s invention of a vernacular. Moreover, the cocktail party is a space where meetings occur across class lines; it serves as a stage not only for the young men and women on the way up, out for the "big money," but for those slumming, seeking another world. Finally, the cocktail party is the place of "sex antagonism," bringing women and men together in a dance of desire and boredom, sex and death.[37]

Thus, the cocktail party stands as a substitute for narratives of home and family, an alternative to the domestic space that usually organizes the novel. Dos Passos's cocktail parties mediate between public and private spaces: the rooms of apartments and homes are interchangeable with those of restaurants and bars. In *U.S.A.*, the party is not only a social structure and a symbolic space, it is a narrative kernel, one of the basic building blocks of the novel, developing from the rituals of anticipation—dressing, arriving, or waiting for guests to arrive—to the frenzy and seductions of smoke, alcohol, bodies, and talk, punctuated by a sexual encounter, and completed by the inevitable retribution, the hangover (*The Big Money* opens with a hangover). Moreover, all the major deaths are the result of parties: Eveline's suicide follows a party; Charley Anderson and Daughter leave drunken parties to die in a car and a plane crash, respectively; and Joe Williams is killed in a drunken brawl at a party celebrating the armistice.

It is this vision of the world as an endless and repetitive cocktail party that makes Dos Passos's characters so unsympathetic and his universe so bleak; Alfred Kazin called it "one of the saddest books ever written by an American." The war, politics, business, art, even the demonstrations and meetings of the radicals: all are cocktail parties. Dos Passos's cocktail parties are not unlike the dance marathons depicted by depression radicals like Philip Evergood, in his 1934 painting, *Dance Marathon,* and Horace McCoy, in his 1935 novel, *They Shoot Horses, Don't They?* In these remarkable proletarian grotesques, the dance marathon becomes an allegory of an American capitalism in which endless, repetitive amusement and entertainment is oppressive, consuming the dreams of its youth, turning dance into wage slavery.[38]

The sex that punctuates Dos Passos's parties is as mechanical as the dance marathon. Whereas Hemingway, Dos Passos recalled, "was *always* concerned with four-letter words," he was "never bothered." "Sex can be indicated with asterisks," he concluded. The sexual encounters in *U.S.A.* have little need for much more than asterisks; for Charley Anderson, they tend to be entirely monosyllabic: "It made Charley feel bad having her talk like that and he had to pet her a little to make her stop crying. Then he got hot and had to make love to her. When he left he promised to call her up next week." For Mary French, they are more technical: "He talked and talked about love and the importance of a healthy sexlife for men and women, so that at last she let him. He was so tender and gentle that for a while she thought maybe she really loved him. He knew all about contraceptives and was very nice and humorous about them. Sleeping with a man didn't make as much difference in her life as she'd expected it would." The only consequences of sex are, for the most part, the biological ones: pregnancy and venereal disease.[39]

The two come together in Margo Dowling's story: raped by her step-father, she gives birth to a baby blinded by venereal disease. The child dies, and Margo is left unable to have children. The absence of any generational story is surely one of the oddest aspects of Dos Passos's "epic." Though the childhoods of each of the characters are narrated, we never see one of their children grow up and take a place in the novel. Nor does the conflict between parents and children really structure any of the narratives. There seem to be more abortions than births in the trilogy: this *U.S.A.* has no future. Nor does it have a past. The only grandparent in the trilogy is Richard Ellsworth Savage's grandfather, a legendary Civil War general, whose memory is invoked to facilitate a farcical military pro-motion. *U.S.A.* eschews the genealogical ambitions of virtually every epic; there are no "begats" in this America. The novels take us from 1893 to 1929, yet one rarely has a sense of the passing of time, the changing of a guard. This is a tale of contemporaries, of a single generation and their encounters with each other at parties.[40]

At the center of *U.S.A.*'s parties are the novels' working women. One of the most striking differences between *U.S.A.*'s historical portraits and its fictional narratives is the place of women. Only one of the twenty-seven portraits is of a woman—Isadora Duncan—whereas half of the dozen fictional narratives are women's narratives. The "working-girl" novel is one of the genres within *U.S.A.*, and *U.S.A.*'s stenographers and department-store clerks are Dos Passos's revisions of Dreiser's *Sister Carrie.* Janey Williams, the stenographer who ends up working for J. Ward Moorehouse, is the most prosaic version. Though her white-collar success is contrasted to the failure of her working-stiff brother Joe, she becomes the "inevitable Miss Williams," completely in the shadow of J.W., whose initials she shares. An inverse trajectory is taken by Mary French, the doctor's daughter who refuses the "position ... among the better element" to which her mother aspires. "I'm not a Vassar graduate," she shouts, "I'm just like any other workinggirl." Mary French abandons her bourgeois background, going to work as a counter waitress in Cleveland and as a clerk "in the ladies' and misses' clothing department at Bloomingdale's." Her "article about depart-mentstore workers for the *Freeman*" gets her a "job doing research on wages, living costs and the spread between wholesale and retail prices in the dress industry for the International Ladies' Garment Workers," and she becomes the trilogy's central embodiment of the radical "writer as technician."[41]

If Mary French embodies one aspect of the "dress front"—the recurring Popular Front narrative of fashion, department stores, and garment workers—the friendship of Eleanor Stoddard and Eveline Hutchins repre-sents another. Both are from Chicago—they meet at the Art Institute—and their friendship is one of the major axes of the trilogy. Eleanor, whose name echoes Chicago's Eleanor Association residential clubs for white-collar women, is escaping the world of the stockyards for a world of fashion and art by working first in a small lace-shop and then at Marshall Fields. She hates the stench of the stockyards on her father's clothes and hates the "Italian families with squalling brats that filled the air with a reek of wine and garlic" that she meets when visiting her working-class uncle and aunt in Pullman. Eveline is a clergyman's daughter who attends art classes, travels to Florence, and works at Hull House. With Eleanor's skills and Eveline's money, they open an interior-decorating business.[42]

Though the business does not survive, it is an emblem of their sub-sequent lives, as they design theater sets and costumes, decorate houses, and orchestrate a series of parties, teas, and liaisons in apartments in Paris and New York. Like Carrie, Eleanor is a success. From the time she tells Eveline that her father is a painter in Florence, she continually reinvents herself; by the end, her decorating business has made her wealthy and she is about to marry an exiled aristocrat, Prince Mingraziali. Eveline, on the other hand, drifts from affair to affair, party to party, eventually committing suicide. Her final conversation is with Mary French, by now a communist labor activist: "Oh, Miss French, I so wanted to talk to you about the miners ... I never get a chance to talk about things I'm really interested in any more ... I don't think I'll ever do this again ... It's just too boring."[43]

Eveline figures a world of boredom and "waste" which Dos Passos both depicted and resented. He remained deeply ambivalent about *U.S.A.*'s world of cocktail parties and about the women at their center. The "whole trouble with the opus," he wrote to Hemingway in 1932, "is too many drawing room bitches—never again—it's like fairies getting into a bar—ruin it in no time." The rest of the letter to Hemingway is an account of his travels: "we detrained in Tucson and bought us a very old Chrysler roadster (wait till they hear that on union square) and drove to Yuma and then to Santa Monica, back across the Mojave Desert to Flagstaff." The gesture is a classic one—Huck Finn leaving Aunt Sally "to light out for the Territory"—and Dos Passos repeats it throughout *U.S.A.*, leaving the cocktail party to hit the road and tell the story of Vag.[44]

iv. Vag; or, The proletarian on the road

At the end of the trilogy, Dos Passos added a curious coda, a section entitled "Vag," a brief sketch of a young man hitchhiking, which combines the narrative mode of the fictions (Is Vag the trilogy's thirteenth character?), the lyricism of the Camera Eye (Is Vag the "I" of the Camera Eye?), and the format of the historical portraits (Is Vag the final biography, sharing the anonymity of the Unknown Soldier biography that ends *Nineteen-Nineteen*?). None of these readings of Vag is really persuasive. Vag remains a final, somewhat desperate, attempt to bring it all back home, to figure the continent in a kind of ur-character, the young man on the road. As such, Vag is a revealing symptom of one of the trilogy's unresolved stories. For Vag marks the return of Mac, the first character in the trilogy, as well as of Joe and Ike and the other working stiffs with monosyllabic names who appear in the first half of *U.S.A.*. The origin of the trilogy lay in this character, in the figure of an itinerant former Wobbly, Gladwin Bland, whom Dos Passos had met in Mexico during the winter of 1926–27. The tales Bland told Dos Passos were the basis for Mac's narrative; and this masculine romance of the migratory workers who made up the Wobblies always hovers on the edges of *U.S.A.*, a world apart from the "word-slinging organism" and "drawing room bitches."

Not only were Mac and Joe and Vag the ideal characters at the roots of the trilogy, they were Dos Passos's ideal readers, represented perhaps by one James McCann, an inmate at San Quentin who corresponded with Dos Passos:

> *1919* is the most realistic piece of writing that has ever crossed my bows … [Y]ou may rest assured that this dingbat convict read every word, was admirably entertained in some places, amazed at your temerity in others, and burnt up in still other spots when you skated along giving fact after fact … Joe Williams, I know hundreds of them, have eaten with them, worked alongside them on tankers, cargo ships and got drunk with them in France, Germany, England, Holland … John Reed is excellently done … Not for nothing did they select you as one of the bigshots of the J.R. Clubs … This last work makes you stand alone, the greatest of America's proletarian writers, fit to head the John Reed club … On behalf of those workers and criminals incarcerated I want to thank you for a piece of literature that has never been approached in this land. Carry on, comrade.

In a subsequent letter, McCann asked, "[A]re you going to make a trilogy of *42nd* and *1919*? It appears to me that another one, giving all the dope on the depression would be very appropriate . . . Sinclair has gone haywire, Lewis is not interested, Dreiser lives in the past, and London is dead. It's up to you, me lad." That Dos Passos in some ways shared McCann's masculinist and Americanist proletarian aesthetic can be seen in his reply to a *Modern Quarterly* question about "proletarian literature" in 1932:

> Theodore Dreiser is, and has been for many years, a great American proletarian writer. He has the world picture, the limitations, and the soundness of the average American worker, and expresses them darn well. Sherwood Anderson does too. So did Jack London. We have had a proletarian literature for years, and are about the only country that has. It hasn't been a revolutionary literature, exactly, though it seems to me that Walt Whitman's a hell of a lot more revolutionary than any Russian poet I've ever heard of.

In the character of Mac, Dos Passos had assumed "the world picture, limitations, and the soundness of the average American worker"; his success in creating a Wobbly Huck Finn led many critics to lament Mac's disappearance from the trilogy.[45]

Dos Passos could have written a novel entitled *Vag* in which the picaresque adventures of Mac and Joe Williams stand alone; several such works came out of the proletarian literature movement and remain classics of the period, including Tom Kromer's *Waiting for Nothing*, Edward Dahlberg's *Bottom Dogs*, and Woody Guthrie's *Bound for Glory*. Each is a remarkable work of vernacular writing; all share the glories and the limits of the masculine romance of the road. Thus, when the drifting working stiff reappears as the hitchhiking Vag at the trilogy's end, we wonder again why he had disappeared, why his story had been obscured by the tales of advertisers and interior decorators, film stars and Communist militants, why the figures of Mac, Joe, and Vag remain ciphers. In fact, Dos Passos had planned to return to the working stiff by making Ike Hall—a minor character from Mac's narrative in *The 42nd Parallel*—central to *The Big Money*. Ike and Mac had bummed across Canada and the Northwest together, until Mac fell off a freight that Ike caught: "That was the last he saw of Ike Hall." Dos Passos intended to pick up Ike's story in *The Big Money*, making him an assembly-line worker at Ford. Right up to the penultimate draft table of contents, the entire trilogy was to end with Ike Hall.[46]

However, Dos Passos decided to eliminate the Ike Hall narrative in his last revisions of *The Big Money*. His reasons remain unclear, though Donald Pizer suggests that Dos Passos saw him as having an "extremely limited life." Two sections of the Ike Hall narrative were published in left-wing magazines a year after *The Big Money*, and they, together with the unfinished tale of Mac, make up Dos Passos's incomplete, repressed "proletarian novel." In "Migratory Worker," published in *Partisan Review*, an unemployed and desperate Ike takes a scab job to support his pregnant wife, Jinny; in "Tin Can Tourist," published in *Direction*, Ike is laid off from Ford after the war, Jinny dies after a miscarriage, and Ike and his two boys hit the road, working in the rubber plants of Akron, at a garage in Jacksonville, and ending on "the long graywhite ribbon of Route 1." If the hitchhiking Vag is the trilogy's thirteenth character, it is because he is all that remains of the repressed Ike Hall.[47]

The displacement of Mac and the excision of Ike Hall reveal the formal and ideological difficulties of turning the ur-character Vag into a narrative of the world of Fords and films. If Vag and the story of "on the road" remain the trilogy's source, they proved incapable of generating the stories and lives of the continent for four reasons. First, the figure of Vag resisted the narrative of the Fordist assembly line and the Taylorized factory. *U.S.A.*'s depictions of the working stiff depend largely on the road narrative, on stories of movement, hitching rides, catching freights, and tramping. Work is always a break, an interruption, in the narrative, never its source. Though Dos Passos wanted to make Ike Hall his "Ford worker," the assembly lines are never the stuff of storytelling. In the Ike Hall segments that were published, Ike's jobs are way-stations as the narrative drifts from Detroit to Toledo to Akron to Jacksonville, just as Joe Williams's narrative was organized by his shipboard movements. This is true of the other left-wing road narratives as well: they rarely made the link between the travel narratives of tramps and the social novel of the factory town. The contrary legacy of Ike Hall can be seen in the gap between two great short works of the middle 1950s: Jack Kerouac's story of driving cars, *On the Road*, and Harvey Swados's story of making cars, *On the Line*.

Moreover, when Dos Passos did imagine the work of his plebeian heroes, more often than not they turned out to be word-workers. Mac begins peddling books from the back of a wagon and ends running a bookstore in Mexico; in between he works on newspapers. The young Benny Compton gives up the road and manual labor to go to City College and become a union speechmaker. One of *U.S.A.*'s recurring utopian spaces is the print shop, where working with words is not mere talk, but a craft, a union of mental and manual labor. They include Uncle Tim's jobprinting shop in Chicago, where Mac imbibes the religion of labor and social democracy; the San Francisco print shop run by the Italian anarchist Bonello; the office of the *Nevada Workman*, a Wobbly paper; and the union publicity offices where Mary French works: "she liked the long hours digging out statistics, the talk with the organizers, the wisecracking radicals, the working men and girls who came into the crowded dingy office she shared with two or three other researchworkers." The narrative energy of Dos Passos's working stiff depends on the complementary spaces of the road and the print shop; any story that would put Vag on the assembly line eluded Dos Passos.[48]

The second formal and ideological problem of the Vag narrative emerges clearly in Mac's narrative: the novel of the road and the drifting migrant could not imagine a domestic space that was not a prison. All the women in Mac's story are versions of Tom Sawyer's Aunt Polly, missionaries of respectability and settling down. Mac is torn between his wife, Maisie, who burns his socialist and Wobbly papers and wants him to join her brother in the bungalow-owning class of southern California, and his Wobbly friends who tell him that "a wobbly oughtn't to have any wife or children, not till after the revolution." In one of the most successful intertwinings of fictional and historical characters, Mac hears Big Bill Haywood speak and imagines Haywood in his own dilemma: "Big Bill talked about solidarity and sticking together in the face of the masterclass and Mac kept wondering what Big Bill would do if he'd got a girl in trouble like that." Throughout the trilogy, the Wobbly narrative is a story of how, in the words of Ben Compton's friend, women "were the main seduction of capitalist society." We see this in Ike Hall's story as well: Ike is "sick and tired of the whole woman business," and his marriage to Jinny forces him to abandon his values, take a scab job, and tear up his red card: "He looked himself right in the eye and whispered 'Ike Hall, you're a married man and a skunk.'" Though Dos Passos was clearly attracted to this ideology of masculine rebellion (witness his remark about *U.S.A.*'s "drawing room bitches"), *U.S.A.* is not primarily a version of the American masculine romance, not a celebration of the road. Rather, *U.S.A.* became a novel neither of the home nor of the road, but of the cocktail party. It is finally a lament for the destruction of domestic life, a bitter satire of the sacrifices made in the name of revolution, art, patriotism, or the big money, which yield the ruined private lives of J. Ward Moorehouse as well as Mary French, of Eveline Hutchins as well as Charley Anderson.[49]

The third reason for the eclipse of Mac's narrative can be seen in the differences between the early versions of Vag, Mac, and Joe Williams, and the later figures of Charley Anderson and Margo Dowling. All are plebeian characters, and the tale of Charley's youth at the end of *The 42nd Parallel* echoes Mac's story. Charley imbibes Debsian socialism from old man Vogel, and befriends the Farmer-Labor radical Michaelson and the Wobbly Monte Davis. Like Mac, he is torn between the road and settling down with Emiscah and a job as a mechanic. But whereas Mac and Joe Williams are constantly moving, the Charley and Margo of *The Big Money* are men and women on the move. Drifting turns to desiring; Huck Finn gives way to Sister Carrie. One can see this shift in Dos Passos's titles. The first two are markers in space and time, geographical and chronological numbers to which Dos Passos imparts a symbolic charge. *The 42nd Parallel* took its title from an 1865 book, *American Climatology*, which suggested that North American storms followed the 42nd parallel. The novel seemed to follow its characters as if they were so many storms crossing the continent. *Nineteen-Nineteen* took a single explosive year as its imaginative whole. *The Big Money*, on the other hand, suggests an organizing social logic, a master narrative.[50]

The phrase, "the big money," comes to have at least three meanings in Dos Passos's work. From the beginning, it stands for American capital, for the narrative of the robber barons themselves, those who engineer profits. It is also part of Dos Passos's narrative of the technicians: the big money is the constant temptation to betray one's craft and cash in, to become a hack, a servant of power. Finally, it comes to sum up the logic of American mass culture, the Dreiserian drive and desire that animates Charley Anderson and Margo Dowling. It is the logic of the big money that makes the drifters, the working stiffs like Mac, anachronisms. "Suppose a feller didn't want to get rich," Mac says to Maisie and her brother, Bill, "you know what Gene Debs said, 'I want to rise with the ranks, not from the ranks.'" To which Bill replies, "when a guy talks like that he's ripe for the nuthouse." The young Charley Anderson once shared Mac's sentiment, and right to his death he dreams of giving up the "racket," the big money; nevertheless, "he had a grand in bills in his pocket and that made him feel good, anyway. Gosh, money's a great thing, he said to himself." Mac begins as a tramp bookseller; Charley Anderson begins by running a roller coaster at an amusement park. And for Dos Passos, the story of *U.S.A.* is no longer the story of tramps on the road, but of the roller coasters of the American amusement park.[51]

The quintessential amusement park was Hollywood, and it is perhaps not surprising that the phrase "the big money" came out of Dos Passos's unhappy stint working in Hollywood during the summer of 1934. One biographer notes that the phrase "appeared in almost every letter he wrote during this period." In a pattern that will be repeated throughout the course of the Popular Front, the proletarian road novel in *U.S.A.* is displaced by a Hollywood novel. The vernacular energies represented by Mac and Joe Williams are resurrected in the character of Margo Dowling. Margo is Dos Passos's grandest revision of *Sister Carrie*, and the romance between Margo and Charley Anderson is a rewriting of the romance between Carrie and Hurstwood. Margo's mother and stepmother had been "salesladies at Siegel Cooper's at the artificialflower counter," and Margo, "a mick and a Catholic," inherits the world of artificial flowers. She is a child star on the vaudeville stage, a dancer on the Ziegfeld chorus line, a model in Jules Piquot's French gown-shop, and a Hollywood extra, eventually becoming a film star, "the nation's newest sweetheart," married to her director, Sam Margolies. But Hollywood, for Dos Passos, was neither a heroic print shop nor an experimental theater. The director Sam Margolies, who begins as a young Jewish photographer who sees "motion-pictures" as "the real art of the future," might have become a heroic figure, a Chaplin, the embodiment of the Camera Eye; however, he is one of the trilogy's villains, reminding Charley Anderson "of a pimp" and manufacturing films that are, in his own words, "nonsense." Moreover, Margo's stardom is fleeting: "she's no good for talkingpictures," George Barrow gossips at Eveline's final party, "voice sounds like the croaking of an old crow over the loudspeaker."[52]

If architects and engineers are heroic figures in *U.S.A.*, the technicians of the culture industries are little better than advertisers. The culture industries are, for Dos Passos, a "new El Dorado / where the warmedover daydreams of all the ghettos / are churned into an opiate haze" by "screenstars, admen, screenwriters, publicitymen, columnists, millionaire editors." Indeed, Dos Passos's hostility to Hollywood was the source of much of his hostility to the Popular Front. Even though his own notion of the "writer as technician" deeply influenced the studio radicals, not least his friend John Howard Lawson, Dos Passos shared Farrell's contempt for them. Whereas the studio radicals embraced the culture industry in one way or another, and celebrated the work of Chaplin, Welles, Ellington, and Basie, Dos Passos resisted it. At one point, Lawson, who had gone from collaborating with Dos Passos in the New Playwrights' Theatre to screenwriting in Hollywood, attempted to write a film script of *The Big Money*, but Dos Passos was skeptical. "Certain vital things could come out of it," Lawson maintained, "I don't agree with you about the movies." The friendship between Lawson and Dos Passos fell victim to their political differences, and Dos Passos later wrote a bitter satire of Lawson and the Hollywood left, *Most Likely to Succeed*, the title itself a parody of Lawson's Group Theatre play, *Success Story*.[53]

Nevertheless, Dos Passos's "Hollywood novel"—the Margo Dowling narrative in *The Big Money*—does displace the "proletarian novel" of Vag, taking its place next to the Hollywood dystopias written by the studio radicals like Nathanael West and Horace McCoy. The figure of Vag, the Wobbly narrative of the road, was unable to represent the Fordist assembly line, the working-class bungalow, and the new mass culture of Hollywood films. There is, however, a fourth reason why the narrative of Vag fails to unify the trilogy and fails to solve the formal and ideological problems Dos Passos set himself: Vag is not an adequate figure for the shoemaker and fishpeddler at the heart of *U.S.A.*, Nicola Sacco and Bartolomeo Vanzetti.

v. The proletarian sublime

The project of *U.S.A.* began with the execution of Sacco and Vanzetti, and with Dos Passos's resolution to keep their memory alive. In some ways, the central formal problem of the trilogy always remained how to represent Sacco and Vanzetti, or, perhaps better, how to represent the nation and its people in a narrative that culminates in the passion of Sacco and Vanzetti. Dos Passos chose not to write a topical novel, the novel that Mary French imagined and Upton Sinclair wrote: he had, after all, published a long pamphlet on the case, *Facing the Chair*. Rather, during his trip to Mexico, Dos Passos met the former Wobbly whose story would provide a starting point, the tale of Mac. The entire trilogy might be seen as nothing but a way of getting from Mac to Sacco and Vanzetti. But Dos Passos doesn't quite get there. Though the trilogy approaches Sacco and Vanzetti in several ways, they are never directly represented. Sacco and Vanzetti were listed as subjects for a biographical portrait in an early plan of *The Big Money*, but that was cut. The men in the death house remain the necessary absence that produces *U.S.A.* But precisely because the passion of Sacco and Vanzetti resists figuration, the three places where the trilogy comes closest to representing it—the recurring figure of the Italian American anarchist; the story of Mary French's work for the Sacco-Vanzetti Defense Committee; and the prophetic Camera Eyes at the end of the trilogy—reveal the historical limits of the narrative of the decline and fall of the Lincoln republic.

From the time Mac gets work "in a small print-shop run and owned by a baldheaded Italian . . . named Bonello . . . [who] had been a redshirt with Garibaldi and was now an anarchist," the figure of the Italian American anarchist is a recurring part of *U.S.A.*'s landscape. There is Grassi, whom Charley Anderson meets in Louisville: an accordion-playing anarchist who had worked in the Fiat factories in Torino, he teaches Charley "to eat spaghetti and drink red wine" and accompanies him to New Orleans before taking off for Argentina, leaving Charley with the gift of an accordion. There is the Greenwich Village waiter, Giovanni, a "maximalist" who is introduced to Eveline Hutchins by Don Stevens. And there is Nick Gigli, the young anarchist construction worker who befriends Ben Compton and teaches him about Bakunin, Malatesta, and rolling cigarettes.[54]

None of these characters develops into a major figure in the trilogy; none of them even takes a place with Doc Bingham, Jerry Burnham, and George Barrow in *U.S.A.*'s gallery of minor characters who circulate throughout the trilogy. Rather, the Italian American anarchists, like the novels' itinerant Wobblies, Mexican anarchists, and German American socialists, serve a key function in the novels' road narratives: they are the donors, to borrow a term from Propp's analysis of folktales, the figures who give the hero—the avatars of Vag—the secret weapons and magic amulets necessary to his quest. They are the repository of traditions of rebellion and solidarity, of the crafts of work and the arts of living, the keepers of red wine and accordions. But they are also always "the foreigners," Vag's Other. Dos Passos's plebeian drifters are always "Americans," "white men." Indeed, the unrepresentability of Sacco and Vanzetti—whose story Dos Passos had once called "the Americanization of Two Foreignborn Workmen"—lies both in Dos Passos's deep ambivalence about the racial fault lines that run through *U.S.A.* and in the inability of the tall tale of the Lincoln republic to incorporate the story of immigrant workers.

This emerges in a slightly different way in the explicit narrativization of the Sacco-Vanzetti case in the Mary French segments. Mary French goes to Boston to join the Sacco and Vanzetti Defense Committee, and the narrative of meetings, demonstrations, and drinking sessions culminates in her arrest at the deathwatch protest. Curiously, however, Mary French's visits to Sacco in Dedham jail and to Vanzetti in Charlestown jail are related in half a sentence, immediately displaced by narratives of her meals with the alcoholic journalist Jerry Burnham and the lecherous union bureaucrat G.H. Barrow. This imbalance is particularly striking because Dos Passos himself had visited Sacco and Vanzetti in jail, and had written an account of the visit and his impressions of the condemned men for the *New Masses.*

Not only are the visits to Sacco and Vanzetti passed over in Mary French's narrative, but they are passed over in the two Camera Eye passages devoted to Sacco and Vanzetti, which is particularly curious since the Camera Eye is generally autobiographical. The Camera Eye (49) recounts a walk from Plymouth to North Plymouth (where Vanzetti lived and worked) to link the seventeenth-century settlers ("the roundheads the sackers of castles the kingkillers haters of oppression") with the twentieth-century immigrant workers ("or that this fishpeddler you have in Charlestown Jail is one of your founders Massachusetts?"); while the Camera Eye (50) recounts the deathwatch vigil in the rain: though America stands defeated and "clubbed off the streets," "the old American speech of the haters of oppression is new tonight . . . the men in the deathhouse made the old words new before they died." In both, the voice of the Camera Eye—the mixed metaphor a just corollary of the tension between observation and prophesy in these final passages—attempts to dovetail the passion of the new immigrants with the chronicle of the old republic, a construction that otherwise eludes *U.S.A.*'s narrative.[55]

Though these final prophetic Camera Eye passages stand among the great lyrics of American writing and are the climax of *U.S.A.*'s *writing,* they remain, as Fred Pfeil writes, "the most amazing and scandalous passage[s] in all of *U.S.A.*" because "the *U.S.A* machine" has been "unable to narrate any story of how the fragmented, passively percipient, detached subject of the Camera Eye became a historically informed, politically engaged moral

center speaking out in a unified prophetic voice." For it is not the
vernacular voice of Vag who comes to say "all right we are two nations"
and to memorialize Sacco and Vanzetti: unlike many of the proletarian
romances, Dos Passos's *Vag* is not a tale of plebeian political awakening.
On the contrary, the difficulty of imagining a figure who can tell the stories
that make up *U.S.A.* is conflated with the difficulty of representing Sacco
and Vanzetti, since the deathwatch is shared by the two likeliest "authors"
of *U.S.A.*—the Camera Eye persona and Mary French herself.[56]

What the Camera Eye persona and Mary French share, what enables
them to *witness*, if not narrate, the passion of Sacco and Vanzetti, is the
experience of what might be called the proletarian sublime. If the sublime
is traditionally understood as the aesthetic experience of awe and fear
provoked by the incomprehensible and inhuman scale and power of the
natural world, the proletarian sublime might be understood as the aesthetic
awe and fear provoked by the emergence of a class of despised laborers, a
social Other: we see a classic instance in an early Camera Eye:

> but you're peeking out of the window into the black rumbling dark suddenly
> ranked with squat chimneys and you're scared of the black smoke and the puffs
> of flame that flare and fade out of the squat chimneys Potteries dearie they work
> there all night Who works there all night? Workingmen and people like that
> laborers travailleurs greasers
> you were scared

Throughout the early Camera Eyes, the mills and their workers lurk on
the edge of consciousness, just over the horizon, provoking fear, dread,
and awe, a magnet that alternately repels and attracts. In Camera Eye (7),
"we clean young American Rover Boys" are "skating on the pond next the
silver company's mills," looking out for the "bohunk and polak kids" who
"put stones in their snowballs write dirty words up on walls do dirty things
up alleys." A turning point comes in Camera Eye (20), which tells of the
death of the Harvard student who went to Lawrence to break a strike of
"wops" and "damned Dagoes"; by Camera Eye (25), the mills and the
"millworkers marching with a red brass band through the streets of
Lawrence Massachusetts" have become a force of attraction.[57]

Mary French's childhood is marked by a similar consciousness, caught
between her mother's social ambitions and her father's social medicine,
between Denver and the mining town of Trinidad. Mary's mother won't
let her play with the mine children, and Mary hears her "muttering . . .
that if poor Daddy ever took half the trouble with his paying patients that
he did with those miserable foreigners and miners he would be a rich man
today and she wouldn't be killing herself with housework." Mary learns a
symbolic geography not unlike the Harvard/Lawrence of the Camera Eye:

Whenever anybody said Denver it made her think of sunny. Now they lived in Trinidad where everything was black like coal, the scrawny hills tall, darkening the valley full of rows of sooty shanties, the minetipples, the miners most of them greasers and hunkies and the awful saloons and the choky smeltersmoke and the little black trains. In Denver it was sunny, and white people lived there, real clean American children.

The proletarian sublime is built on the symbolic oppositions of "clean" and "dirty," "American" and "foreigner," "white" and "black," and these oppositions structure the magnetic field of the trilogy.[58]

In the final Camera Eyes, the poles are reversed: the "dirty words" are no longer those written on walls by the "bohunk and polak kids," but the "slimy and foul" words of the businessmen, politicians, and college presidents. It is the men in the death house, the "damned Dagoes," who clean and renew the old words. Similarly, the "foreigners" become "Americans," as the word "immigrant" serves to unite the Italian workers of Plymouth with the founders of Plymouth. Moreover, in the final Camera Eye, set in a mining town, the "Americans" are made foreigners: "they [the robber barons and their hired guns] have made us foreigners in the land where we were born."[59]

But these rhetorical reversals are not reflected in *U.S.A.*'s narrative, which remains caught in an ambivalent dialectic of attraction and repulsion. Nowhere is this clearer than in the novels' rhetoric of "whiteness." If *U.S.A.* is an encyclopedia of ideological stock phrases and clichés, the common coin of self-justification and rationalization, none is more insistent than "this was still a white man's country," and the "real clean Americans" are "white people." One hears it in the accents of Mary French's Colorado mother quoted above, in the words of the American oil prospector in Mexico who tells Mac that it "ain't fit for a white man down here," and in the Camera Eye account of the Harvard strikebreakers who go "to man the streetcars and show the foreign agitators this was still a white man's . . .," the phrase so familiar it is left unfinished.[60]

The color line is drawn across the entire trilogy: the novels' non-white peoples encompass black Americans, the Southern and Eastern European immigrants and ethnics, Asian Americans, and Latinos, as well as the continental Europeans the characters meet during the war, and the Mexicans, Cubans, and Caribbeans encountered when the narratives of Mac, Margo, and Joe leave the United States. National identity is racial identity; the non-white peoples are summed up in the trilogy's catalog of racial and ethnic slurs. The proletarian sublime in *U.S.A.* is always already a racial sublime: the same early Camera Eyes that recall the child's fear of the mills and their workers summon up his mother's fear and dread of "colored" peoples: "He kept saying What would you do Lucy if I were to invite one of them to my table? They're very lovely people the colored people and." Indeed, it is clear that the basis of the color line lies in the demarcation between whites and blacks: the story of Janey Williams's childhood begins with the moment she is forbidden to play with Pearl, the black girl across the street.[61]

Perhaps the keenest barometer of whiteness is Anne Elizabeth Trent, who comes to New York from Texas, which "had the blackest soil and the whitest people." After being taken on a tour of New York's immigrant neighborhoods by a Columbia student, she argues that "we oughtn't to let all these foreigners come over and mess up our country . . . [T]hey're not white people and they never will be. They're just like Mexicans or somethin', or niggers." Later, when she is in post-war Italy with Near East Relief, she tells Dick Savage, "all these foreigners make me kinder lonesome. . . . I'm glad I got a white man with me." However, Dos Passos's working stiffs are equally entangled in the codes of white supremacy. Both Mac and Charley Anderson encounter figures who appeal to white solidarity, like Doc, who opposes the war because he "didn't believe in white men shootin' each other up, only niggers." Joe Williams gets into a barroom quarrel over the "whiteness" of the Wobblies: "Joe said that that stuff was only for foreigners, but if somebody started a white man's party to fight the profiteers and the goddamn bankers he'd be with 'em. The guys from Chicago began to get sore and said that the wobblies were just as much white men as he." Indeed, Joe's narrative, an aimless traversing of the Atlantic as a merchant marine and sailor, has a racial subtext throughout, punctuated as it is by his sexual encounters with black and Latin women in Caribbean ports. And it ends with a racial brawl: on Armistice Day, Joe punches a black Senegalese officer who is dancing with a white woman, and Joe is killed in the fight that follows.[62]

There is no question that *U.S.A.* stands as a powerful satire of the "white man's country." The tales of racial and imperial warfare are consistently rendered as farce. We see this not only in the story of Joe Williams's death, but in the allegory of the Spanish-American war: a drunken Delaware state militia imagined they saw the Spanish fleet invading and "immediately opened fire on an old colored man crabbing out in the river . . . When the old colored man had hauled in his last crabline he sculled back to shore and exhibited to his cronies several splintery bulletholes in the side of his skiff." Moreover, insofar as the trilogy can be seen as Dos Passos's meditation on the failure of American socialists, anarchists, and Wobblies to win over American workers to a vision of a cooperative commonwealth, the jingoism and racism of native-born white Americans is held largely responsible (his other main "explanation" is the lure of the "big money"). This is why Dos Passos's Vag narratives never turn into heroic proletarian romances of political awakening.[63]

But if the novel satirizes the shibboleths of white supremacy and imperial destiny, insisting that "America was hybrid," Dos Passos's own sentiments on race and nationality remained deeply ambivalent. "It would be funny," Dos Passos wrote to Edmund Wilson in 1934, "if I ended up an Anglo Saxon chauvinist—Did you ever read my father's Anglo Saxon Century? We are now getting to the age when papa's shoes yawn wide." The elder Dos Passos's 1903 book was a significant part of the racial literature at the turn of the century, arguing for a "common citizenship for every member of the Anglo-Saxon race," and imagining that "the twentieth century is *par excellence* 'The Anglo-Saxon Century,' in which the English-speaking peoples may lead and predominate the world." Though much of Dos Passos's work can be understood as a reply to his father, a prominent corporation lawyer who had also written major works on stockbroking and commercial trusts, Dos Passos's letters demonstrate how much he shared his father's Anglo-Saxon chauvinism: they are filled with casual racial and ethnic slurs. His break with Communism had more to do with the Communists' Jewishness than with their Stalinism: "what I mean by harping on the jewish note," he writes to John Howard Lawson, "is that I am just beginning to realize how much of New York rebellious mentality is a jewish European import." And, asking Edmund Wilson about the Scottsboro case, he concludes that "the poor devils of nigs are done for." Like his father, he is ambivalent about his own Portuguese heritage (his grandfather had come to the US from Portugal in 1830) and is both fascinated and repelled by the Latin cultures he often visited. When he writes "Cubans . . . are generally louses" in a 1934 letter from Havana, his sentiments seem close to those he gives Margo Dowling in *The Big Money*.[64]

Though *U.S.A.* will ironically take its distance from these sentiments, putting them in the mouths of characters it satirizes, the racial narrative of the Anglo-Saxon century permeates the trilogy. As has often been noted, the biographies tell no story of race and Jim Crow. And there is only one story of the "new" immigration: the brutally satirical portrait of Rudolph Valentino. If the deathwatch for Sacco and Vanzetti is the trilogy's tragedy, the funeral of Valentino is its farce. The "wops," the "greasers," the "nigs" have no independent narratives. Of the twelve major characters, only Ben Compton, the son of immigrant Jews, is on the "other" side of the color line, and his story opens with a renunciation: "The old people were Jews but at school Benny always said no he wasn't a Jew he was an American." For the most part, the racial landscape of *U.S.A.* is less "a slice of a continent" than an ordinary Hollywood production. The "colored people" of the novel are servants, barely visible: Charley Anderson's "Japanese houseboy," Taki; the Filipino butler in Hollywood; Eleanor's "Martinique maid"; and a series of African American maids and chauffeurs—Augustine, Raymond, Eliza, and Cynthia.[65]

If the proletarian sublime is essentially a poetic trope, the momentary recognition of the laboring Other through fear and awe, the narrative form it takes is the all-too-common story of slumming, the search for the exotic, the lower depths. *U.S.A.* is constantly on the brink of slumming. The temptation is so great that Dos Passos includes an analysis and critique of the "slummer" in his portrait of William Randolph Hearst: Hearst "had a knack for using his own prurient hanker after the lusts and envies of plain unmonied lowlife men and women (the slummer sees only the streetwalkers, the dopeparlors, the strip acts and goes back uptown saying he knows the working class districts); the lowest common denominator; manure to grow a career in, the rot of democracy. Out of it grew rankly an empire of print." But Dos Passos's own "empire of print," which often seems to grow out of the "lusts and envies of plain unmonied lowlife men and women," is not finally a depiction of the working-class districts; it is a depiction of those who seek them out.[66]

The narrative of Anne Trent is surely the most compact story of slumming, as she is led through New York's ghettoes by her radical lovers. But the key figure here is the Harvard aesthete, Richard Ellsworth Savage, whose slumming begins in the wartime ambulance corps and ends in Harlem. In one of the several endings to the trilogy, Savage becomes the classic slummer, searching for an anonymous club in Harlem, a place where "there were no white people ... at all." Here the trilogy's long flirtation with homosexuality culminates in Savage's dance with a black male prostitute who calls himself Gloria Swanson; at the end of the night, he is slugged and robbed by Gloria Swanson and his boyfriend Florence. Savage's story is one of many racial "romances" that run through *U.S.A.*, ranging from Eleanor's Mexican affair with José O'Reily, to Margo's Cuban sojourn with Tony Garrido, to Mary French's affair with Ben Compton. However, we always see that narrative through "white" eyes.[67]

The story of the decline and fall of the Lincoln republic is fundamentally the story of the *discovery* of classes in a place where they were not meant to exist: "all right we are two nations." That narrative was unable to tell the story of the other nation, the ghettoes themselves. That became the task of the plebeian writers who created the great ghetto pastorals I will look at in the next chapters. The narrative of the decline and fall of the Lincoln republic may mark the starting point of the Popular Front imagination of the American past, but its inability to imagine the racial and ethnic transformations of the twentieth century led to the invention of new narratives, new tales. The ghetto pastorals and gangster stories are the other side of *U.S.A.*'s stories. If *U.S.A.* sees the mining town through the eyes of the doctor's daughter, Mary French, Tillie Olsen's *Yonnondio* sees it through the eyes of the miner's daughter. Ben Compton's story is a pale imitation of Mike Gold's *Jews without Money* or Henry Roth's *Call It Sleep*.

Dos Passos himself recognized the difference in a review of Mike Gold's stories:

> Mike Gold is very lucky to have been born when he was and where he was. The New York East Side before the war was one of the most remarkable phenomena in history, a germ of an ancient eastern-european culture transplanted pure into the body of America . . . To have been able to live from its beginning the growth of the leaven of Jewish culture in American life may not seem so important now, but from a vantagepoint of twenty-five years I think it will seem tremendously important.[68]

This is why *U.S.A.* is no longer a contemporary novel, no longer important to readers and critics. It is an epitaph for an America that no longer exists. Its greatness at the time of its publication was that it narrated in a powerful and convincing way the history of its present: the history of the Lincoln republic, of how the promise of a continental nation of small producers, full of Yankee ingenuity, tinkerers like the Wright brothers and even Henry Ford, was betrayed by the "big money," ending in the Wall Street crash and the depression. But it was a tombstone, ending in death, abortion, and suicide. Unlike Fitzgerald's *The Great Gatsby*, which retains its hold on the American imagination, *U.S.A.* is relentlessly anti-mythical. Despite its size, it is not finally an epic. Epics are stories of origins, of the birth of nations. Epics may have sacrificial and redemptive deaths, but someone—some Ishmael, some Nick—is left to tell the tale. *U.S.A.* glimpses no future: Charley's death is a drunken accident, not an encounter with a white whale; unlike Carrie, Margo is not bound for stardom, but becomes one of the freaks of film history whose voices betrayed them when talkies emerged.

The only myth left is the passion of Sacco and Vanzetti. Perhaps this is why the book is built on an implicit taboo against representing them. Those who stand in the drizzling rain at the deathwatch are not slummers: they do not go back "knowing" the working-class districts. Here lies the difference between Hearst's empire of print and Dos Passos's, the difference between the slumming Savage's final trip to Harlem and Mary French's final trip to Pittsburgh. It is a difference many critics who see *U.S.A.* as a bitter and cynical attack on the left miss. The deathwatch is the culmination of *U.S.A.*'s story of Sacco and Vanzetti, the passion story so sacred that it refuses the profanity of a graven image; it marks the politicization of slumming, the truth of Dos Passos's proletarian sublime.

5

"The Literary Class War": Rethinking Proletarian Literature

The year of the general strikes—1934—was also the year young poets and writers proclaimed themselves "proletarians" and "revolutionaries," the year when dozens of experimental magazines publishing proletarian stories, poems, and manifestos were suddenly recognized by mainstream publishers and the established reviews. The proletarian avant-garde had spread like prairie fire across the continent in the few years since the crash; for a brief moment, it dominated the American literary world. Like earlier modernist avant-gardes—cubism, dada, and the others—the proletarian avant-garde was met with hurrahs, denunciations, and ridicule, and provoked what was called the "literary class war." The phrase captures both its narrower and wider significances: it was at once a war among the "literary class" and a "class war" in literature. As a war among the literary class, the proletarian avant-garde shared the fate of other avant-gardes, burning itself out in a flurry of manifestos and polemics. By the fall of 1935, when a hefty anthology of stories, poems, plays, essays, and reportage appeared under the title *Proletarian Literature in the United States*, it seemed already more a monument than a manifesto; a year later, in the winter of 1936, *Literary America* announced that "The great proletarian novel has been shelved. Whereas last year there was an abundance of books dealing with the working class and whereas heroes and heroines were concerned with finding their place in the economic world, novelists this year seem to have abandoned these characters to an unsolved limbo and have turned to less depressing subjects."[1]

But "proletarian literature" was not merely a war among the literary class, a moment when poets and novelists adopted a rhetoric of class and revolution, that passed as the revolutionary fervors of 1934 gave way to the laborist and anti-fascist rhetorics of the Popular Front. Nor did it consist only of the politically inspired writings of figures attracted to the Communist Party in the early 1930s—a handful of largely forgotten novels, poems, and agitprop plays. Rather, it marked the opening of a class war in literature, the first act in a larger proletarian renaissance that stamped an indelible working-class imprint on American culture.

The proletarian literature movement left a profound and lasting mark on American literature. The writers who emerged from the movement have proved to be the central figures of their generation, and the formal and aesthetic issues with which they grappled inflected the work of many other writers of their generation as well. The gravitational force exerted by the magazines, conferences, alliances, and debates of the proletarian literature movement was similar to that exerted by the magazines and controversies of the avant-garde modernists of the previous generation. Moreover, the movement produced at least as many enduring and valuable works of fiction as any other literary movement or school in the twentieth century. If we fail to understand the proletarian literature movement, its contradictory successes and failures, its conscious aesthetic goals and its often ironic results, then we fail to understand much of American fiction from John Dos Passos, Richard Wright, and Tillie Olsen to Toni Morrison and E.L. Doctorow. For the proletarian literature movement has had far greater influence on the subsequent half century of American fiction than the experimental modernism of Stein and Hemingway.

Just as the American renaissance grew out of the radical movements and ideologies of the 1840s and 1850s—abolitionism, utopian socialism, women's rights, and transcendentalism—so the proletarian renaissance grew out of the radical movements and ideologies of the 1930s. In the next two chapters, I will argue that the renaissance ignited by the proletarian avant-garde was responsible for two key developments in American literary history: the emergence of a generation of plebeian ethnic writers who represented—in several senses of the word—the new working-class cultures of America and who were to transform American letters in the decades to follow; and the creation of a genre—the ghetto or tenement pastoral—that is still at the heart of the American novel.[2]

1. Proletarian Literature as a Formation

Not surprisingly, many of the manifestos and polemics of the proletarian avant-garde attempted to define "proletarian" literature: the centerpiece of a *Partisan Review* symposium in the spring of 1935, intended to provoke debate at the American Writers' Congress, was Edwin Seaver's "What Is a Proletarian Novel? Notes toward a Definition." Too often critics and historians have begun with the same question: Does one define proletarian literature by author, audience, subject matter, or political perspective? Is it literature by workers, for workers, or about workers? Or is it simply revolutionary literature? But these critical attempts to define "proletarian literature" as a genre all fail because they treat genres as abstract and ahistorical ideal types; they forget that genres are literary institutions that have grown out of particular social formations and must be understood not as a class of objects but as the products of those formations.[3]

A similar difficulty plagues attempts to answer the question that novelist William Rollins posed in a 1935 *New Masses* article, "What Is a Proletarian Writer?" Critics and historians have argued over definitions based on family origins, work experience, and political affiliation, including and excluding various writers, often resulting in crude and reductive "labels." Writers, like genres, are products of literary formations and institutions; they choose to write, what to write, and how to write in a particular situation. Thus, rather than ask "What is proletarian literature?" or "What is a proletarian writer?" one would better ask "What was the proletarian literary formation?" What kinds of writers did it produce? What effects did it have on the writers who were drawn to it? And what kinds of writing, what genres, forms, and formulas did those writers produce?[4]

Proletarian literature was a formation in Raymond Williams's sense, an alliance of writers, editors, agents, publishers, reviewers, political activists, and readers who came together in formal and informal clubs, magazines, contests, conferences, schools, and public lectures, as well as at political rallies, in May Day parades, and on picket lines. They shared slogans—revolution, communism, the proletariat, the cultural front—and a sense of common political and artistic struggle; but they argued vehemently over the meanings of those slogans and the means of that struggle. Some were deeply committed to the movement; others aligned themselves with it only briefly. Such a cultural formation may be seen as the combination of a cultural politics and an aesthetic ideology. By a cultural politics, I mean the infrastructure of any cultural initiative, the necessary world of publishers, galleries, salons, patrons, and reviewers by which artists and audiences are recruited and mobilized, and without which no cultural formation can take root. By aesthetic ideology, I mean the conscious and unconscious ways of valuing that a cultural formation develops and inculcates, its "aesthetic," its sense of what is good, true, and beautiful. This aesthetic ideology is rarely straightforward and uncomplicated. One usually finds a contradictory juxtaposition of explicitly formulated values and prescriptions, a selected tradition of valuable precursors, a hierarchy of more or less important forms and genres, a few highly regarded contemporary works, and the traces of established tastes, acquired in a particular habitus, marked by class, ethnic, and gender distinctions.[5]

As a result, the symposia that abstractly defined and debated "proletarian writing" are often misleading. Though Michael Gold is usually remembered for the manifestos that outlined his own proletarian aesthetic, it is worth recalling that he also maintained that "proletarian literature is taking many forms. There is not a standard model which all writers must imitate, or even a standard set of thoughts. There are no precedents. Each writer has to find his own way. All that unites us, and all we have for a guide, is the revolutionary spirit." The arrogance and self-righteousness of the young polemicists often masks the flux and contradictions of the movement. To gain a better sense of the cultural politics and aesthetic ideologies that gave proletarian literature its meaning, one must look at the variety of little magazines and literary circles it produced and at the writers who were emblems and models of proletarian literature. There is no doubt that Mike Gold and his *New Masses* was one of these, but his influence was ballasted by the John Reed Clubs, by the "mushroom mags" that sprang up across the country in the early 1930s, and by a host of styles which embodied proletarian literature: the surgical experimentalism of William Carlos Williams; the worker narratives and industrial lore of Jack Conroy; the blues vernacular and racial romances of Langston Hughes; the lyric feminist regionalism of Meridel Le Sueur; and the gangster melodramas of Benjamin Appel.[6]

2. "Revelations by Rebel Chambermaids"

There is no question that Mike Gold's *New Masses* was a central magazine. Founded in 1926, the *New Masses* began by invoking the Greenwich Village radicalism of the *Masses* and including its editors, Max Eastman and Floyd Dell, on the new editorial board. The first years were marked by editorial struggles and financial crisis. Mike Gold became the sole editor in May 1928, transforming it into a magazine for the writings of young workers. His July 1928 editorial called for "worker-correspondents" to send

> Confessions—diaries—documents
> Letters from hoboes, peddlars, small town atheists, unfrocked clergymen and schoolteachers—
> Revelations by rebel chambermaids and night club waiters—
> The sobs of driven stenographers—
> The poetry of steelworkers—
> The wrath of miners—the laughter of sailors—
> Strike stories, prison stories, work stories—
> Stories by Communist, I.W.W. and other revolutionary workers.

At the beginning of 1929, Gold repeated his appeal in an editorial, "Go Left, Young Writers!," a key manifesto of the proletarian literary movement. "In the past eight months," Gold wrote,

> the *New Masses* has been slowly finding its path toward the goal of a proletarian literature in America. A new writer has been appearing; a wild youth of about

twenty-two, the son of working-class parents, who himself works in the lumber camps, coal mines and steel mills, harvest fields and mountain camps of America . . . A Jack London or a Walt Whitman will come out of this new crop of young workers who write in the *New Masses* . . . Once more we appeal to our readers: Do not be passive. Write. Your life in mine, mill and farm is of deathless significance in the history of the world. Tell us about it in the same language you use in writing a letter. It may be literature—it often is. Write. Persist. Struggle.

For the next five years, Gold's *New Masses* persisted in its struggle to find and publish the revelations, sobs, poetry, and wrath of American workers.[7]

Gold's project combined several elements in American culture at the time of the crash. In part, it was imagined after the examples of proletarian literature in the Soviet Union. From the original Proletcult groups that Gold had hailed in a lyric manifesto of 1921 entitled "Toward Proletarian Art," to the November 1927 assembly of writers and artists from fourteen countries at the First International Conference of Proletarian and Revolutionary Writers in Moscow, the cultural initiatives and ferment that had followed the Bolshevik Revolution were watched by American writers and intellectuals; they were part of the European modernisms that so profoundly reshaped American culture at this time. Gold had visited the Soviet Union in 1925, and just as the constructivist theater of Meyerhold had prompted him to join Dos Passos and John Howard Lawson in the New Playwrights' Theatre, so the worker-correspondents and literary studios of the Proletcult movement were the inspiration for his rebuilt *New Masses*.[8]

However, Gold's *New Masses* was not, as it has often been portrayed, simply an unlikely Russian transplant, doomed to failure in the United States, a caricature of the innovative *Masses*. The *New Masses* was also a child of the mass culture of the 1920s, adopting a formula that had created the most successful new magazine of the time, the "true confession" of Bernarr MacFadden's *True Story*. Beginning in 1919, MacFadden had turned a magazine of readers' stories into the most popular reading matter among working-class Americans. Like Gold, MacFadden held that "every man and woman has lived at least one big story which has that ring of truth for which authors of fictions strive with might and main." "Tell it naturally, simply, in your own words," *True Story* told its readers, "and the judges will consider it entirely upon its qualities as a story." Gold's vision of the *New Masses* can be seen as a radical mutation of *True Story*, an attempt to build a new culture out of the stories and confessions of ordinary workers.[9]

Behind the models of the Proletcult and *True Story*, there also lay the Yiddish working-class culture in which Gold had grown up. He himself had heard and heeded an earlier call for stories of working-class life. "Under your tenement roofs are stories of the real life-stuff; the very stuff of which

Loan Receipt
Liverpool John Moores University
Library Services

Borrower Name: Sam Oultram
Borrower ID: ******

Cultural front : the laboring of American
culture in the twentieth century /
31111009351212
Due Date: 17/03/2018 15:09:52 GMT

Total Items: 1
03/03/2018 15:10

Please keep your receipt in case of
dispute.

great literature can be made," the Yiddish-language *Forward* had written to its readers in 1910, when Gold was seventeen. "Send them to us. Write them any way you can. Come and bring them, or tell them to us." A decade later, as he struggled with his "East Side Novel" and formulated his first vision of "proletariat art," he echoed the *Forward*'s rhetoric: "When I think it is the tenement thinking ... Art is the tenement pouring out its soul through us." Thus, Mike Gold stood at the center of the proletarian literary movement and the cultural front because he united its two halves: on the one hand, he was one of the modernist generation, part of the *Masses* circle and the Provincetown Players, a friend and collaborator of Dos Passos and Lawson; on the other hand, he was the eldest of the plebeians, the first of the writers who grew up in the tenements, the young Jews, Italians, blacks, and Poles who answered his call to "Go Left, Young Writers!"[10]

For his contemporary Dos Passos, Gold represented "thirty years of raw history, the East Side growing up, Jewish life bursting the shell of its old ossified culture, bringing forth flowers in the rank soil of American slums; gangsters, songwriters, scientists—and the helterskelter lives of millions of Mexicans, Negroes, Bohunks, Wops, Hungarians, Albanians, Polacks building a continent out of their sweat." But for the young Joseph North, the son of Ukrainian Jewish immigrants, "Mike Gold was Isaiah ... The monthly *New Masses* arrived at my mailbox in a Pennsylvania city and I could not wait until I tore the wrapper off ... My father was a blacksmith who had never mastered the reading or writing of English; my mother a seamstress who taught herself to read and write; I, myself, a rivet-passer in the shipyard when I wasn't in the books." North was one of the many young writers who answered Mike Gold's call, sending stories and sketches to the *New Masses* and setting up little magazines across the country.[11]

3. "These Clubs of Often Famished and Angry Youth"

If the *New Masses* was the national magazine for young radicals like North, the John Reed Clubs and their magazines became the local organizations for the worker-correspondents. The *New Masses* had established a John Reed Club for writers and artists in New York in 1929, but it was not until the spring of 1932 that John Reed Clubs appeared across the country. A national convention was held in New York in May, bringing together writers and artists from Boston, Newark, New York, Philadelphia, Detroit, Chicago, Seattle, Portland, Hollywood, and San Francisco. Soon after, clubs began publishing small magazines. By the time of the second national convention in September 1934, after the summer of the general strikes, there were 30 clubs with 1,200 members.[12]

There has been some debate about the members of the John Reed

Clubs; Paula Rabinowitz has argued that the clubs "were conceived as a training ground for young, gifted writers from the working class but were actually composed of committed intellectuals from the middle class." This was true of a few of the more celebrated chapters, notably the one in Carmel, California, where Lincoln Steffens was the *éminence grise*. Tillie Olsen, a member of the San Francisco Reed club, recalled feeling out of place among the "Carmel crowd" when she was invited to the home of Steffens and Ella Winter. But in general Rabinowitz's argument is misleading. First, the Reed clubs were not really the Communist Party's "training ground" for writers; they never had the structure or coherence of the Party's schools for organizers. Rather, they were informal and self-organized clubs of young writers, supported by the Party but at some distance. "I find in the party," Chicago Reed club member Abe Aaron wrote to Jack Conroy, "that the J.R.C. is regarded disdainfully and with tolerant amusement by a great number of comrades." Moreover, though the Reed club members were not adult factory workers or working-class housewives, they were hardly established middle-class intellectuals. Virtually all accounts indicate that they were young, unemployed, and unpublished. Though some had attended college and had held white-collar jobs, most were young high-school graduates from ethnic working-class backgrounds, who hoped to break into journalism.[13]

Even in New York, where more established intellectuals were associated with the John Reed Clubs, those older left-wing moderns saw the clubs as haunts of young militants fond of revolutionary rhetoric and arcane argument. Though "there was some talent to be found in these clubs of often famished and angry youth," Matthew Josephson wrote, they were mainly "social gathering places of mostly unemployed young men who neither wrote nor painted anything." In a similar tone, Joseph Freeman condemned the Reed club members as "bohemians," neither workers nor intellectuals, but "hangers on of the art world": "many of the people in the writers' group do not write and cannot write; they do not read; they do not know what is going on in the intellectual field and it is impossible to struggle with them on the basis of ideas . . . not being Party members, these elements cannot be disciplined by the needs of the economic struggle; not being intellectuals, they cannot be reasoned with." There is no doubt much truth in Freeman's observations. The rank and file of any artistic subculture are bohemians—"a person," in Freeman's useful definition, "who has broken with his social class; hence he has no social roots; the old ideology is gone and no new ideology has taken its place." But Freeman's analysis misses the importance of these bohemian subcultures, which have historically offered a place for young people to abandon class roots and experiment with other social forms, forms of utopian reconstruction as well as of personal disintegration. Moreover, the heat of those bohemian subcultures has forged oppositional artists, intellectuals, and activists.[14]

Malcolm Cowley's essay, "From a Coffee Pot," remains the best account of the Reed clubs by one of the older moderns precisely because he recognized their importance as a bohemian subculture. Cowley begins by recalling his impressions of a visit to the New York Reed club, who had invited him to a discussion of one of his articles: there were no women, he recalls, they drank only coffee in paper cups, and they criticized his article from the left. Nevertheless, after quoting Freeman's remarks of 1932, Cowley reminds us that many of the writers and artists in the clubs did produce significant work in their careers, and that the Proletcult slogans of the clubs served as a "vocabulary for attacking established writers" in a battle of literary generations. "Coming of age in 1920, they would have been Dadaists; ... in the late 1940s, Existentialists; in the 1950s, Beats." However, the depression generation was, Cowley suggests, the "least fortunate" of literary generations. "The artists among them had almost no hope of selling or even exhibiting their pictures ... Book publishers, whose volume of business had been reduced by 60 percent in three years, no longer offered advances against royalties to unknown authors." Just as people of the depression cohort were more likely to identify themselves as working class than their parents or children, so the artists of that cohort were more likely to see themselves as proletarians than were their Dadaist forbears and Beat progeny. For those who came from working-class neighborhoods, the Reed clubs, Cowley writes, "became not only a meeting place but a career," writing stories and poems, editing magazines, making posters, and organizing lectures.[15]

Those who belonged to the clubs and did the unpaid work of the cultural front recall "passionate disputations on literature in a big blowy loft on Sixth Avenue that was heated by a pot-bellied stove." "Argumentation," Jerre Mangione wrote of the New York club, "was the John Reed Club's chief activity. The debates usually centered on differences of Marxist interpretation as precipitated by recently published books and articles." Though not a Communist and, by his own account, skeptical of Marxism, he sporadically attended meetings for two years, "drawn by the companionship of writers" and "welcomed as a contributor to left-wing periodicals at a time when few publications were accepting the work of new writers." But Mangione also recalls the "business of promoting the revolution": distributing leaflets, soapbox speaking, marches and demonstrations, and a writers' school. "I don't think any of us would have survived without the Reed Clubs and our bond with each other," Meridel Le Sueur later recalled. "It was a very hard time to live to be a writer. The left was very severe on you. It had its own orthodoxy ... But it also summoned us forth ... We wouldn't have tried without them ... the Communists gave us light and even love."[16]

The John Reed Clubs helped to organize a radical subculture in cities across the United States. From the beginning, the clubs were an alliance of different kinds of artists and intellectuals—painters, writers, critics, dancers, sculptors, filmmakers and photographers—and they engaged in two kinds of activities: on the one hand, a variety of cultural events including lectures, writers workshops, art exhibits, dance performances, and plays; on the other hand, support work for labor struggles and political trials, like the Scottsboro case. In New York, which had the first and largest John Reed Club, there was a writers school with courses on poetry (taught by Horace Gregory), fiction (taught by Edward Dahlberg), English prose (taught by Kenneth Burke), and literary criticism (taught by Philip Rahv, Jerre Mangione, and William Phillips), and there were regular lectures on Marxism and literature. The artists' section sponsored a celebrated February 1933 exhibit, "The Social Viewpoint in Art."[17]

Moreover, the New York Reed club spawned more specialized organizations of radical artists. Two early members of the Reed club, Harry Potamkin and Sam Brody, joined other photographers and filmmakers in the Workers Film and Photo League in 1930; they shared space with the left-wing Japanese Workers Camera Club. John Reed Club member Philip Rahv was part of the New York chapter of Rebel Poets; the Workers Laboratory Theatre had preceded the Reed clubs by a few months in 1929, but Reed club members were part of the New York Suitcase Theatre in 1931. Indeed, by 1934, the John Reed Club of New York was challenged by the Socialist Party's Rebel Arts Group, which included groups for dancers, musicians, writers, and artists, as well as a drama group, a puppet group, a chess club, a camera club, and the Rebel Arts Radio Players on WEVD.[18]

Though the New York John Reed Club has received most attention, it was probably not the most representative. There were several active Reed clubs on the West Coast. The San Francisco John Reed Club was formed in 1931 by the poet Kenneth Rexroth, who wanted to create "a genuine organization of intellectuals who had been radicalized by the world economic crisis." An anarcho-syndicalist with an attachment to the Wobblies, Rexroth staged agitprop skits and poetry readings from a flatbed truck in San Francisco, and fought with the New Yorkers at Reed club conventions. In Carmel, California, a small group including the photographer Edward Weston, the sculptor Jo Davidson, the playwright Orrick Johns, and, while he was living there, Langston Hughes, gathered around Ella Winter and Lincoln Steffens. They sponsored lectures by visiting radical intellectuals and local labor leaders, and lent support to struggles by cannery workers and migrant farm laborers and to the longshoremen's strike of the spring and summer of 1934.[19]

In Los Angeles, the John Reed club, which included fiction writer Sanora Babb, sponsored lectures by the Mexican muralist David Alfaro Siqueiros; Siqueiros also painted a mural in the Reed club auditorium. Japanese American artists formed the Japanese Proletarian Artists' League, which published *Proletarian Art* and *Hataraku Hito* (Workingman). The LA Reed club also mounted an exhibition of works by black painters to benefit the Scottsboro defendants; it was broken up by the police, who also prevented their production of Langston Hughes's *Scottsboro Limited.*[20]

In other cities, the Reed clubs included different mixtures of artists and activists. In Boston, the Reed club was led in part by Eugene Gordon (who had been a central figure in the group of black writers who put out the *Saturday Evening Quill* from 1928 to 1930), and they covered the Scottsboro case regularly in their monthly magazine, *Leftward.* In the Midwest, the strongest club was in Chicago, where it was dominated by painters and artists, who sponsored exhibits of "proletarian art," anti-war paintings, and the drawings of Kathe Kollwitz. The writers, who included Richard Wright and Nelson Algren, were dubbed the "Chicago Post Office school of writers" by Jack Conroy because a number of them had met while working in the post office. Conroy himself attended meetings of the St Louis Reed club, which had been organized with the help of the Chicago branch.[21]

Clubs sprang up throughout the industrial corridor of the Northeast and Midwest, and many published little mimeographed magazines in 1932 and 1933. For the most part, they were not really literary magazines: the occasional poems, stories, and short plays were outweighed by reportage of local labor disputes, political prisoners and legal cases, autobiographical accounts of "turning leftward" by young workers, and listings of club meetings, lectures and dances. For example, *Leftward* published special issues on the Tom Mooney case and on the deportation of radical textile organizer Edith Berkman; it also published life stories by an immigrant machinist turned accountant, Philip Goldberg, and the son of a South Braintree shoemaker, Charles Kendall. The young writers of the clubs often attempted to attach themselves to a local industry so they could learn about it and write about it. The Reed club magazines included *Red Boston* (which became *Leftward*); the *Hammer* from Hartford; *Revolt* from Paterson, New Jersey; the *Red Pen* and *Left Review* from Philadelphia; the *Baltimore John Reed Club Bulletin*; the *John Reed Review* from Washington, D.C.; *Red Spark* from Cleveland; *Midland Left* from Indianapolis; *New Force* from Detroit; *War* (which was largely an anti-war publication) from Milwaukee; the *Cauldron* from Grand Rapids; *Proletcult* from Seattle and Portland; and the *Partisan* from Hollywood. As far as I can tell, only two of the Reed club magazines, New York's *Partisan Review* and Chicago's *Left Front*, survived past the spring of 1933 and developed into more than mimeographed bulletins.

Perhaps the most illuminating narrative of the John Reed Clubs remains
that of Richard Wright in his memoir, *American Hunger*. Wright was the
epitome of the famished and angry young men who joined the Reed clubs
in the early 1930s; his narrative avoids both the nostalgia and the
condescension that mark many of the more casual accounts. Though
Wright was skeptical and suspicious of the clubs' crossing of the color line,
he was impressed by the "scope and seriousness" of the clubs' activities.
"The club," Wright recalls, "was demanding that the government create
jobs for unemployed artists; it planned and organized art exhibits; it raised
funds for the publication of *Left Front*; and it sent scores of speakers to
trade-union meetings." But the ambition and hope of its members—
"fervent, democratic, restless, eager, self-sacrificing"—always vied with the
debilitating sectarianism and factionalism that haunt powerless and marginal radical groups, culminating, for Wright, in the peculiar story of
Comrade Young from Detroit, who denounced traitors in the club, only to
prove to be an escapee from a mental institution. "Were we all so mad that
we could not detect a madman when we saw one?"[22]

In a way, Wright suggests, they were all mad, necessarily mad: his mother
thinks the pictures in the *New Masses* are "enough to drive a body crazy"
and asks if he is ill. But from the *New Masses* Wright hears "a passionate call
for the experiences of the disinherited," with none of the "lispings of the
missionary in it." "Feeling for the first time that there were listening ears,"
he writes a poem, "I Have Seen Black Hands," which was published in the
New Masses. He decides to write biographical sketches of black Communists,
"while mopping the operating rooms of the medical research institute."
Out of the club came the relationships Wright would sustain for years:
"The club was my first contact with the modern world. I had lived so utterly
isolated a life that the club filled for me a need that could not be imagined
by the white members who were becoming disgusted with it."[23]

American Hunger is built around Wright's tormented relationship to
Chicago's Communists: the black Communists in the South Side Party unit,
the white Reed club radicals, the Communists in the Federal Theatre and
Writers Project, as well as the national Party leaders. Its anecdotal episodes
are, in his words, at once "spectacles of glory" and "spectacles of horror."
And the well-rehearsed tale of the end of the Reed clubs is one of these
spectacles: Wright bitterly opposed the Communist Party's decision to
withdraw support from the clubs. However, in the midst of his account,
there is a soliloquy in parentheses, reflecting on the meaning of the
experience:

(Indeed we felt that we were lucky. Why cower in towers of ivory and squeeze
out private words when we had only to speak and millions listened? Our writing
was translated in French, German, Russian, Chinese, Spanish, Japanese ... Who

had ever, in all human history, offered to young writers an audience so vast? True, our royalties were small, or less than small, but that did not matter.
(We wrote what we felt. Confronted with a picture of a revolutionary and changing world, there spilled out of our hearts our reaction to that world, our hope, our anger at oppression, our dreams of a new life; it spilled without coercion, without the pleading of anyone.)

In that sense of a vast audience sharing an anger at oppression and a dream of a new life, Wright captures the meaning of proletarian literature for the young plebeian writers of the time.[24]

4. "Mushroom Mags": Modes of Proletarian Writing

But the Reed clubs touched only a fraction of the plebeian writers attracted to proletarian literature. For many, the literary subculture of the left existed in the mails, and the heart of the proletarian literary formation lay in the dozens of proletarian little magazines with idiosyncratic and independent politics that sprang up across the country in the early 1930s. These "mushroom mags" were almost all better produced than the mimeographed Reed club bulletins, and all were primarily literary magazines, printing stories, poems, plays, and literary criticism. Many of the readers and contributors to these magazines knew each other through the mail, not through meetings and coffee pots. Whereas the Reed club bulletins offered lists of events and news of local strikes and political rallies, these proletarian literary magazines featured ads for each other's journals and for current books. Thus, if the Reed club bulletins are a good index to the cultural politics of the proletarian avant-garde—the meetings, lectures, and performances taking place in various cities—the proletarian little magazines are a better index to the aesthetic ideologies that shaped the movement. Moreover, the writers who are featured in the magazines are in some ways more representative of the aesthetic models of proletarian literature than any of the prescriptions made by critics and writers in symposia and manifestos.[25]

There were basically two kinds of little magazines: the radical modernist magazines that appeared in the wake of the crash; and the "classic" proletarian magazines that followed the appearance of *Anvil* and *Broom* in 1933. The radical modernist magazines attempted to rekindle the flame of the avant-garde, and they were descendants of the little magazines of modernism like *Broom, Fire!,* and *Secession.* Perhaps the most ambitious was Richard Johns's *Pagany,* founded in the winter of 1930. It was the most established of the new journals, and the least connected to the proletarian aesthetic. It published many of the moderns who were turning leftward—Dos Passos, Herbst, William Carlos Williams, Kenneth Burke, and Edwin

Seaver—as well as younger writers like Farrell, Conroy, Meridel Le Sueur, and Erskine Caldwell. *Blues: A Magazine of New Rhythms*, edited by Charles Henri Ford out of Columbus, Mississippi, beginning in 1929, was similar in spirit: its contributing editors included William Carlos Williams and the *transition* experimentalist Eugène Jolas, whose "Revolution of the Word" manifesto had provoked great controversy with its anti-political modernism. Most of *Blues*'s contributors were young radicals in their mid twenties who would become part of the cultural front: Kenneth Rexroth, Kay Boyle, Jay Leyda, Louis Zukofsky, and Parker Tyler.[26]

The Saturday Evening Quill, an annual published by a group of black writers in Boston, was modeled on the short-lived Harlem magazine *Fire!*; its two central figures, Eugene Gordon and Dorothy West, both subsequently became allied with the cultural front. Both *Contempo*, which was published in Chapel Hill beginning in 1931, and *Trend*, an arts magazine published in New York beginning in 1932, found themselves attracted to the emerging proletarian movement, as were the short-lived little magazines out of Albuquerque edited by the southwestern modernist poet Norman MacLeod—*Jackass*, *Palo Verde* (both in 1928), *Morada* (1929–30), and *Front* (1930–31). These began in the orbit of Paris modernism—there was a memorial issue for Harry Crosby and contributions from Pound and Jolas—but they were soon drawn into the proletarian debate: an issue of *Morada* featured Ezra Pound's critique of Mike Gold, and the trilingual *Front* published the young American radicals associated with Rebel Poets and the New York John Reed Club, as well as the Japanese proletarian poet Kei Mariyama and the Peruvian Marxist José Carlos Mariátegui. By the final issue in 1931, when the money ran out, the editors wanted to turn it into a "radical proletarian magazine."[27]

Perhaps the most interesting of these radical modernist magazines were *The Left*, whose two issues were published in Davenport, Iowa in 1931, and *Contact*, whose three issues were edited by William Carlos Williams and Nathaniel West in 1932. *The Left: A Quarterly Review of Radical and Experimental Art* was deeply indebted to Soviet modernism, using Soviet film stills for its cover and featuring a unique cinema section with the young Lewis Jacobs. *Contact*, on the other hand, envisioned a distinctively American modernism: its first cover promised that "Contact will attempt to cut a trail through the American jungle without the use of a European compass." Williams's history of US literary magazines and West's bibliography of the little magazines of the previous three decades claimed the inheritance of the American avant-garde, but they too were drawn to the left. They considered an issue devoted to communism, and Williams's valedictory essay defended the link between poetry and communism.

The figure who best exemplifies this radical modernism is William Carlos Williams. Though Williams is rarely mentioned in histories of proletarian literature, he is a ubiquitous figure in the mushroom mags. He was, as a contributor's note in a 1934 issue of *The Magazine* put it, "one of the best known writers in the 'left-wing' camp of American literature." Williams's connection to the proletarian literary movement is the result not only of his commitment to the little magazine, but of his idiosyncratic communism and his decade-long attempt to portray working-class life on the Passaic.

Williams's communism was a poet's communism, not an organizer's communism. "I cannot swallow the half-alive poetry which knows nothing of totality," he wrote in a brief comment in *Contact.* "It is one of the reasons to welcome communism. Never, may it be said, has there ever been great poetry that was not born out of a communist intelligence. They have all been rebels... The unchristian sweep of Shakespeare, the cantless, unsectarian bitterness of Dante against his time, this is what is best in communism." Williams's essay on the farmer poet H.H. Lewis in the *New Masses* remains one of the unlikeliest celebrations of a worker-writer in American letters. Nevertheless, he always remained as skeptical of Marxism as he was of other European philosophies and aesthetics: "My opinion," he wrote in a 1936 *Partisan Review and Anvil* symposium on Marxism and the American tradition, "is that the American tradition is completely opposed to Marxism. America is progressing through difficult mechanistic readjustments which it is confident it can take care of. But Marxism is a static philosophy of a hundred years ago which has not yet kept up—as the democratic spirit has—through the stresses of an actual trial." However, Williams's iconoclastic communism was more typical of figures in the proletarian literature movement than historians have realized: though perhaps no one shared Williams's particular blend of communism, Americanism, and populist rhetoric, analogous amalgams can be found everywhere.[28]

Moreover, Williams's fiction had a profound impact on the proletarian movement. "When somebody writes the future history of the pioneer beginnings of proletarian literature in America," Mike Gold suggested, "I am sure W.C. Williams will be somewhere large in the table of contents... Williams has never written about a strike or a labor union. What he has done, however, is to reflect as in a faithful mirror the raw powerful force of the unorganized American worker, and the horrors of the slum life he leads." Gold was referring to Williams's "proletarian portraits": the stories collected in *The Knife of the Times* (1932), *Life along the Passaic River* (1938), and the novel *White Mule* (1937). In some ways, Williams's stories are miniature versions of Dos Passos's *U.S.A.*, implicitly narrating the decline and fall of the Lincoln republic. "Makes me think," one story ends, "of an old man I knew, when they'd ask him how far back he could remember he'd say, I can remember back to when the U.S. was a republic." But whereas Dos Passos rarely represented the "new" Americans of the ethnic ghettoes, Williams depicts working-class Jews, Hungarians, Poles, Italians, and African Americans as patients under the clinical eye of a doctor. The stories are staccato bursts of vernacular speech and medical jargon, anecdotes of birth, autopsy, and sick children. One critic said of *White Mule* that it was as if James Joyce had written *Studs Lonigan*, and Williams's combination of experimental modernism and proletarian portraiture made him a model for younger radical writers.[29]

A number of Williams's stories appeared in *Blast* and *Anvil*, which together created the style and rhetoric of the second kind of radical little magazine. *Blast—Proletarian Short Stories* began in September 1933, edited by an impoverished and unemployed young tool maker, Fred C. Miller: Williams contributed not only stories, but money and his name, as associate editor. Unlike the John Reed Club magazines, *Blast* had no news, no rhetoric, no manifestos, just stories. *Anvil*, edited by Jack Conroy in Moberly, Missouri, was similar: its first subtitle was "Stories for Workers." Conroy had grown up in a family of coal-miners in Moberly, worked in Moberly's railroad shops, and returned there after working in the auto plants of Detroit and Toledo through the 1920s. *Anvil* began in May of 1933 as a fifteen-cent pulp, a result of a split in the Rebel Poets group; over the next three years it became the leading proletarian literary magazine. Both magazines received national attention when the *New Republic* reviewed them as "mouthpieces of proletarian literature." "Their first issues will hardly excite the enthusiasm of lovers of prose or lovers of fine printing," the anonymous reviewer (most likely Malcolm Cowley) wrote,

> but they are respectable efforts and they are almost entirely given to the work of young and unknown writers. As such, they suggest a comparison with the little magazines, *Broom*, *The Little Review* and dozens of others, which flourished and died in the period immediately after the War . . . One difference is significant. The advance guard magazines of the twenties, railing against American civilization from an esthetic point of view, were edited in Rome, Paris, Vienna and half the capitals of Europe. These new arrivals, preaching the international revolution, hail from such plain American addresses as Mount Hope Place, Brooklyn, and Moberly, Missouri.[30]

Jack Conroy, the editor of *Anvil*, was in many ways the midwestern counterpart of Mike Gold. Like Gold, he sought to develop a working-class literature, written by young workers and read by workers; to do so he created networks among the young radicals of Missouri, Chicago, and the Plains. Like Gold, his was a masculinist aesthetic, and all of the contributors and the editorial board of the early *Anvil* were men. Conroy's 1933 novel, *The Disinherited*, was, together with Gold's *Jews without Money* of 1930, the most widely acclaimed novel of the fledgling movement: magazines like *Hub*, *Medallion*, and *Pollen* featured reviews or recommendations of it.[31]

However, like many of the plebeian writers, Conroy was skeptical of and hostile to the literary culture of New York, including that of the New York left. In part, this resulted from his vehement rejection of European modernisms, expressed in the satirical opening of his address to the 1935 American Writers' Congress: "The troubles of a worker who is attempting to mirror the life around him are many and varied. In the first place, very few worker-writers have ever graduated from college, and still fewer of them have been able to spend a year or so in the Paris Latin Quarter where it is possible to learn the writing of proletarian literature in the technical manner of Marcel Proust and James Joyce." Against any "semi-private terminology" created by the "desperate striving for novelty of phrase and imagery," Conroy wanted stories of "clarity" and "simplicity" for the "largest body of readers we can command." Moreover, Conroy distrusted what he called "the ideological tempests raging in the New York coffee pots." For the most part, *Anvil* stayed aloof from the critical and theoretical debates, preferring to publish fiction. When he set up the Anvil League of Writers, with Erskine Caldwell, Nelson Algren, and Meridel Le Sueur as sponsors, he wrote that the league was not meant to compete with the John Reed Clubs, but to support writers of fiction, since the Reed clubs were "not primarily interested in revolutionary short stories."[32]

These tensions between New York and Moberly, and the differences between Gold and Conroy, are more complex than scenes of literary needling and politicking indicate. The proletarian literary movement was deeply inflected by the different ethnic working-class cultures of the US. The reviews each wrote of the other's book are revealing documents of the cultural distance between the two major advocates of American Proletcult. Gold's well-known *Daily Worker* review of *The Disinherited* is a celebration of "a first book ... of a young working class author," a "proletarian shock-trooper whose weapon is literature." "You have given us a picture of a boy's life in a coal-mining town which I have never seen before. I can smell your rubber mill, and have been bored to madness by the work-sodden people in your rooming-houses." But Gold doesn't fully recognize Conroy's drifters and failures, "the floating millions of migratories"; these characters are not "typical" enough, he says, but are "social sports and eccentrics." Moreover, the review turns on a somewhat condescending critique of Conroy's lack of "emotion" and "passion." "You, of the warm tragic Irish blood, had it in you," Gold writes.[33]

Conroy's earlier review of Gold's *Jews without Money* had also pivoted on "passion": "Too many radicals possess intellectuality without passion; Michael Gold has both. Too many radicals are ashamed of emotion; some of the most gripping and forceful passages are ... too exalted in spirit to be called prose." But Conroy's review was dominated by an ethnic reading, as he situates the book against the stock figures of the Jew: "The conventional burlesque Jew, cavorting about the stage and ogling the pulchritudinous chorines, crying 'oi! oi! oi!' The Jews of Israel Zangwill, the familiar Christ-killing Jews, the Russian Jews quailing before a prospective pogrom. We know all these Jews, but it was left to Michael Gold to portray the Jews without money, the tragic proletarian Jews of New York's East Side, the sweat-shop slave, the Yiddish gangster." Despite their common proletarian rhetoric, neither Gold nor Conroy was able to see the other's world and characters as "typical," and these regional and ethnic divides manifest themselves throughout proletarian literature. Despite the fact that Gold is recognized as the most representative polemicist of proletarian literature, few critics have realized that the ghetto or tenement pastoral that Gold helped invent in *Jews without Money* became one of the central forms of proletarian fiction.[34]

Similarly, Gold's sense of Conroy's "lack" of "powerful dramatic form" as the "boy drifts from one industrial hell-hole to another" misses the heart of Conroy's great accomplishment. For Conroy is *not* a novelist but a storyteller, as he assumes the voice of Dos Passos's Vag, the proletarian drifter. The two halves of *The Disinherited* are, as Douglas Wixson has argued, the autobiographical narrative of the mining camp, Monkey Nest, and the industrial lore—jokes, tall tales, and stories of work—that Conroy collected at work and in taverns. All of Conroy's subsequent work builds on this divide: one part of him never escaped Monkey Nest, while the other became a collector of worker narratives, some of which were published in B.A. Botkin's *Treasury of American Folklore* (1944), and folk tales, like the "Uncle Ollie" narratives, published in the Popular Front press and collected as *The Weed King and Other Stories* (1985). There is a clear line from the proletarian narrative of Conroy's *The Disinherited* to the proletarian drifters of Woody Guthrie's *Bound for Glory* or Carlos Bulosan's *America Is in the Heart.*[35]

Conroy's *Anvil* and the New York-based *Blast* became the models for the mushroom mags that appeared in 1933 and 1934. Unlike the Reed club bulletins, these magazines published almost entirely fiction and poetry, broken up by woodcuts and linoleum engravings; they were well produced and, for the most part, avoided political rhetoric and commentary. Some, like *Blast,* came out of the metropolises of the Northeast: New York's *Little Magazine* (1933–34), which published the critical work of Philip Rahv, the stories of the Trinidadian Alfred Mendes and the Filipino José Garcia Villa, as well as a letter attacking the left by Ezra Pound; *Scope—A Magazine of Proletarian Literature* (1934) from Bayonne, New Jersey; *Medallion: An Unbiased Literary Magazine* (1934) from the Bronx; *Dynamo: A Journal of*

Revolutionary Poetry (1934), edited by Sol Funaroff and including what has come to be known as the "*Dynamo* school of poets"—Edwin Rolfe, Kenneth Fearing, Horace Gregory, and Muriel Rukeyser; the elaborately produced, tongue-in-cheek *Latin Quarterly* from Greenwich Village, which featured Art Young cartoons and columns of literary gossip; the Philadelphia-based *Kosmos: Dynamic Stories of Today* (1933–35), which published work by Farrell, Edwin Seaver, and the young Harriette Simpson (later Arnow); and the Boston-based *Challenge* (1934–37), edited by Dorothy West "to bring out the prose and poetry of the newer Negroes."[36]

The marked contrast in style and aesthetics between *Challenge* and the *Saturday Evening Quill* (with which West had been involved earlier) is revealing. Whereas the *Quill* had emulated the Harlem Renaissance journal *Fire!*, with its elegant synthesis of bourgeois refinement and bohemian outrageousness, *Challenge* shared the look and aesthetic of the other proletarian magazines of the spring of 1934. It published the radical black writers Langston Hughes, Arna Bontemps, Claude McKay, William Attaway, and Alfred Mendes, as well as accounts of a Moscow trip by "Mary Christopher," a debate over the meaning and politics of spirituals, and a report on the National Negro Congress. Though it appeared irregularly, *Challenge* outlasted many other magazines of 1934, finding its constituency among the young black writers of the depression: indeed, the Chicago South Side Writers Group, which included Richard Wright, Margaret Walker, and Marian Minus, eventually coedited the 1937 revival of the magazine, *New Challenge*.

That the first issue of *Challenge* should open with Langston Hughes's story "Little Dog" was a sign of Hughes's importance as a model and emblem of proletarian writing. The vernacular blues and jazz poetry of Hughes's *The Weary Blues* and *Fine Clothes to the Jew* had made him one of the best-known young writers of the New Negro Renaissance. He became active on the left in 1931, after a trip to Haiti. "In the second half of 1931," Hughes's biographer writes, "*New Masses* became Hughes's major outlet. In July it published 'A Letter from Haiti'; in August, his poem 'Justice'; in September, another poem, 'Union'; in October, his passionate report on Haiti, 'People without Shoes'; in November, 'Scottsboro Limited,' a Marxist one-act play; and in December, the long, bitterly anti-capitalist verse parody 'Advertisement for the Waldorf-Astoria'." Hughes was deeply involved in the campaign to free the Scottsboro Nine, and spent a year in the Soviet Union in 1932 as part of a project to make a film about black Americans. In the Soviet Union, Hughes read D.H. Lawrence and decided to write short stories in order to make a living as a writer. The stories he wrote in Moscow and in Carmel, California (where he was in the John Reed Club), were collected in *The Ways of White Folks*, one of the key books of 1934's proletarian renaissance.[37]

Though few literary historians have realized it, *The Ways of White Folks* represented a central mode of proletarian writing: at the 1935 American Writers' Congress, it lay at the heart of both James Farrell's talk on the short story and Eugene Clay's address on the Negro in American literature. It was not a topical strike novel, nor a ghetto pastoral, nor a proletarian road narrative: rather, the stories are variations on the theme of racial romance. "Everybody knows can't no good come out o' white and colored love," a woman says in "Mother and Child," which had first appeared in the *New Masses*, and Hughes's tales explore the varieties of "white and colored love": white artists and black models; black artists and white patrons; white fathers and black sons; black mothers with light "passing" sons and daughters; cross-racial adoptions in "Cora" and "Poor Little Black Fellow"; white mothers with "dark" children; masters and servants; mistresses and maids. Hughes's stories play out the possibilities. On the one hand, nothing good does come from "white and colored love." The book begins with forced abortions and death and ends with a father and son effectively killing each other. Lynching stands as a figure of the racial romance, and the book's last line is ominous when read as an allegory of the nation: "The dead man left no heirs." On the other hand, it is clear throughout that there is no stopping "white and colored love," and the stories powerfully evoke the love of Colonel Norwood for his son, the love of Miss Briggs for the janitor who brings meat for the little dog, and the musical union of the pianist Roy and the teacher Miss Reese.[38]

Though the notion that "art would break down color lines, art could save the race and prevent lynchings" is, as the pianist Oceola Jones says, "bunk," Hughes persists. The story of Jack, the young man who ignores his mother in the street because he is passing as white, ends with a plea that is at once self-deception and desperate hope: "I'm glad there's nothing to stop letters from crossing the color line. Even if we can't meet often, we can write, can't we, Ma?" Hughes's letters across the color line continued to appear in the *New Masses* and *Anvil*, as well as *Challenge* and *The Crisis*. He traveled across the country, giving lectures sponsored by local John Reed Clubs and little proletarian magazines, like Chapel Hill's *Contempo*. Though his 1933 collection of radical poems, *Good Morning, Revolution*, had been turned down by his publishers and did not appear until 1938, when *A New Song* was published by a left-wing fraternal order, the IWO, Hughes's blues lyrics and vernacular diction influenced all of the younger radical poets: his work was featured in *Dynamo*. Moreover, Hughes's adoption of the craft of the short story in the early 1930s lay behind his Popular Front creation of the Simple stories, the weekly Chicago *Defender* sketches that lasted from 1943 to 1965. Built around the conversations between a narrator and Simple, Jesse B. Semple, in a Harlem café, these popular vernacular stories became Hughes's "proletarian novel." Hughes's

Simple and Ollie Harrington's cartoon character Bootsie, who appeared in a number of African American newspapers, were two of the most popular imaginative creations of the African American Popular Front.[39]

The magazines of the Middle and Far West united their iconoclastic communisms with a militant regionalism. Taking *Anvil* as a model, they created a "proletarian regionalism." These mushroom mags of the Plains and the Midwest included the mimeographed *Hub* (1934), from Cedar Rapids, Iowa; Karlton Kelm's *Dubuque Dial* (1934–35), which began by publishing Iowan writers and eventually published the major midwestern radical women writers—Josephine Herbst, Meridel Le Sueur, and Josephine Johnson; the "frankly proletarian and revolutionary" *New Quarterly* (1933), from Rock Island, Illinois; J. Niver's *Earth* (1930–32) from Wheaton, Illinois, which took its name from a Whitman poem; Kerker Quinn's *Direction* (1934–35), a more mainstream, less proletarian magazine, not to be confused with the later East Coast *Direction*; B.A Botkin's *Space* (1934–35) from Norman, Oklahoma; *Point* (1934), from Madison, Wisconsin; the *Windsor Quarterly* (1933–35), which began in Vermont but migrated to the Arkansas labor college, Commonwealth College; and Meridel Le Sueur's *Midwest* (1936–37). There was even a brief attempt in early 1934 to create a national forum for the radical regionalists, *The American Scene*, which included Norman MacLeod, Karlton Kelm, and August Derleth as regional editors.

Though *The American Scene* disappeared quickly, its place was taken by *Literary America*, appearing in the spring of 1934 and soon adopting the slogan "devoted to the American scene." *Literary America* serves as an interesting index of the place of the proletarian literary movement in the larger literary culture, for it did not claim to be part of the movement. Nevertheless, it was clearly part of the debate, publishing both critical reviews and sympathetic accounts, serializing Robert Whitcomb's fine proletarian novel, *Talk USA*, and featuring the vernacular stories of the leading writers of the movement, including Langston Hughes, Meridel Le Sueur, and Benjamin Appel.

Both Le Sueur and Appel were central writers in these magazines, yet their forms and aesthetics diverged markedly from those of Gold, Williams, Conroy, and Hughes. Though literary historians of proletarian literature have rarely focused on Meridel Le Sueur (in part because she did not publish a novel and her collection of short stories, *Salute to Spring*, did not appear until 1940), and recent critics have tended to distinguish her from the proletarian aesthetic, any look at the proletarian magazines demonstrates her importance. She was not only a literary organizer—editing *Midwest*, speaking at writers congresses, and running the Midwest Literary League—but her stories regularly appeared in *Anvil*, *New Masses*, *Pagany*,

The Magazine, Dubuque Dial, 1933—A Year, Partisan Review, Windsor Quarterly, and *Literary America,* very often as the magazine's lead story.[40]

Thus, it is more accurate to see Le Sueur as embodying a distinctive and influential proletarian aesthetic in her cultural activities and in her writing. She ran a writers workshop in St Paul, out of which came her manual, *Worker Writers,* and the novel, *The Girl* (unpublished until 1978). *The Girl* was built on the stories told and written by working women in a Workers' Alliance writing group: "there was no tape recorder then so I took their stories down. Some could not write very well, and some wrote them out painfully in longhand while trying to keep warm in bus stations or waiting for food orders at relief offices. They looked upon me as a woman who wrote (like the old letter writers) and who strangely and wonderfully insisted that their lives were not defeated, trashed, defenseless." If Le Sueur's experiments in proletarian culture echo the efforts of Gold and Conroy, her aesthetic differs markedly, combining a radical regionalism, a Lawrentian sexual lyricism, and an explicit feminism.[41]

Le Sueur was one of the crucial figures in the emergence of a left-wing regionalism during the early 1930s, a tendency that can be seen in the writings of Carey McWilliams, Kenneth Rexroth, Norman MacLeod, Constance Rourke, and B.A. Botkin. Much of the writing of the proletarian literary movement was, as Botkin noted, regional writing. The proletarian magazines and the regionalist magazines overlap; regionalist writers like August Derleth were regularly published by the proletarian magazines. The radical regionalists distanced themselves from the primitivism and nostalgia of the local colorists by stressing the social and economic exploitation of sections and invoking regional traditions of dissent. "In the Middle West," Le Sueur writes, "I think we try not to forget the IWW's." For the radical regionalists, the "folk" were working people, proletarians.[42]

For Le Sueur, regionalism was also a link to the vital tradition of midwestern women writers. A common aesthetic can be found in the works of the radical women writers of the Midwest, including Josephine Herbst, Margery Latimer, Josephine Johnson, Edith Summers Kelley, Agnes Smedley, and Tillie Lerner Olsen. All were daughters of Willa Cather, Zona Gale, and Mary Austin, composing narratives that combine a domestic realism in their depiction of women's labor with an intense lyricism regarding the land. Moreover, as the careers of Le Sueur, Herbst, Johnson, Smedley, and Olsen demonstrate, this tradition became one of the important modes of the proletarian movement. Many of Le Sueur's stories are marriage tales of the provincial middle class, evocations of the hunger and discontent of the Mrs Darlings and Mrs Goodwells: "It's difficult to describe Mrs Goodwell. Heaven knows how many such women there are in the Middle West and they are the butt of jokes." However, along with these stories—disciplined in form and language—Le Sueur struggled to create a form in which vernacular working-class voices would speak without the omniscient narrator's "she" and without quotation marks separating narrator and character. The tough telegraphic slang that Le Sueur fashioned—a remarkable synthesis of midwestern women's realism and the masculinist romance of drifters—becomes the vehicle for her classic bank-robbery tale, "O Prairie Girl, Be Lonely," a version of the Bonnie and Clyde story that later became part of *The Girl*.[43]

Benjamin Appel is probably the least known of my half-dozen avatars of proletarian literature. Unlike Gold, Williams, Conroy, Hughes, and Le Sueur, he is now almost entirely forgotten (only one of the literary histories of proletarian literature, classic or revisionary, even mentions him). Yet he was a ubiquitous and prominent figure in the proletarian magazines, often contributing the lead story to *Hub, Literary America, Little Magazine, Anvil, Blast, Medallion, Outlander*, and *New Challenge*. Born in 1907, the son of Polish immigrants, Appel wrote popular gangster novels built out of sketches of working-class kids in New York's Hell's Kitchen: *Brain Guy* (1934) told the story of the gangster Bill Trent; and Trent reappeared in *The Power-House* (1939), a strike novel told from the point of view of a strikebreaker, and *The Dark Stain* (1943), an anti-fascist thriller set in Harlem. Appel was commercially successful, publishing stories in the slick magazines like *Esquire* and *Scribners'*, and was included in the O'Brien and O. Henry prize collections of short fiction. He considered his novels "message" novels. "The message novel, the social forces novel, the propaganda novel, the proletarian novel, the uplift novel (and I am using some of the descriptive phrases that have been knocked around by the critics in the last thirty years) have nearly all ... had one belief in common: to record the bitter meanings of twentieth-century society." Though he didn't think of himself as a "revolutionary writer," he was "appalled by the violence in our country and the inconceivably monstrous violence overseas." He was a Popular Front activist in the League of American Writers, helping European writers escape fascism and teaching at the League's writers school.[44]

Appel's work represents the link between proletarian literature and the popular hard-boiled thrillers of gangsters and detectives, a link that can also be seen in the work of Dashiell Hammett, Horace McCoy, and Chester Himes. As Appel himself noted, "some of the best of the tough guy novels were also among the best of the proletarian novels." Moreover, Appel's work is part of the well-crafted, but non-literary mass that makes up most of popular fiction; as I will suggest below, though the proletarian literary movement was avant-garde, many of its plebeian writers ended up writing works of popular entertainment, not unlike those of Benjamin Appel.[45]

5. The Legacy of Proletarian Literature

The West Coast proletarian magazines—*The Magazine* (1934) from Beverly Hills, *The Outlander* (1933) from Oregon, *Pollen* (1934) from Los Angeles, and *The New Tide* (1934) from Hollywood—shared the look, aesthetics, and contributors of the midwestern magazines. *The New Tide* was published out of Hollywood in the fall of 1934 by a group of young Filipinos that included Carlos Bulosan. The magazine preferred "contributions from the revolutionary and experimental schools"; its "definite aim" was "to interpret the struggles and aspirations of the workers, the fight of sincere intellectuals against fascism and racial oppression in concrete national terms." Its only issue included a poem by Bulosan, a lynching story, a prose poem on leaving the Philippines by Chris Mensalvas, a poem by William Carlos Williams, and a story by the most established Filipino writer in the US, José Garcia Villa.[46]

Carlos Bulosan's account of *The New Tide* is a powerful reminder of the ways the proletarian literary movement transcended the well-worn tales of the New York-based John Reed Clubs, *Partisan Review,* and the American Writers' Congress. Bulosan, who together with Chris Mensalvas had been organizing agricultural workers, tells of distributing a hundred copies of *The New Tide* to the farm workers:

> It did not create a sensation, but we did not expect anything spectacular. It was the first of its kind to be published by Filipinos in the United States, and it was fumbling and immature, but it promised to grow into something important in the history of Filipino social awakening. The magazine was one of several publications that had arisen all over the nation, and had tried to grasp the social realities and to interpret them in terms of the needs of the decade. It sustained our lives, drowned our despair, and gave us hope.

"What awed me, in those early days," Bulosan wrote, "were the sacrifices of its founders. I would ask myself why three starving men were willing to give up their hard-earned money to make an obscure magazine live, denying themselves the simple necessities of food and shelter. They had surrounded the publication as though it were a little life about to die, or dying, or dead—and breathed life into it one after the other, looking desperate and lost when they realized that their efforts were futile." Indeed, most of these little magazines did die after a few issues: when the *Anvil* announced the formation of an Anvil League of Writers in early 1935, it did so in part because so many of the proletarian magazines had not outlasted the strike-torn summer of 1934.[47]

What then was the legacy of these "fumbling and immature" magazines? Most historians have concurred with the observers at the time who maintained that the proletarian literature movement was dead by 1935, the victim of the Communist Party's turn to the Popular Front. The Popular Front, we are told, abandoned both the institutions and the aesthetics of the proletarian avant-garde, seeking instead to enroll literary celebrities and culture-industry hacks. This is deeply mistaken: the coming of the Popular Front did not put an end to left-wing literary magazines and circles, nor to the forms of writing represented by the figures of Gold, Williams, Conroy, Hughes, Le Sueur, and Appel. There were dramatic changes in literary culture generally—paperback books, mass higher education, and the recruitment of writers to the film and radio studios—to which the left-wing writers were not immune. But the writers who were part of the proletarian avant-garde found significant audiences for their work in post-war America and have had a lasting impact on American literature. Thus, the accounts of the "failure" of proletarian literature must be reconsidered.

Most accounts suggest that proletarian literature failed as literature and as politics. "The Old Left effort to transplant Soviet-style proletcult onto American soil was a gross miscalculation," Walter Kalaidjian writes in a recent study. Gold's Proletcult version of *New Masses*, with its worker-correspondents, did collapse in the fall of 1933; it was recreated as a weekly review of politics and culture in early 1934, and its circulation grew from 6,000 to 24,000 by early 1935. It was the 1934 weekly *New Masses* that became the most important left-wing journal of the period, not Gold's earlier experiment. Moreover, most of the proletarian magazines did not last long enough to review the *Proletarian Literature in the United States* anthology when it appeared in the fall of 1935. Finally, the John Reed Clubs did close down when the Communist Party withdrew its support, angering a number of young writers—among them Richard Wright—and, according to Malcolm Cowley, kicking off a "new war between literary generations," as the 1935 American Writers' Congress left out "the kids" and older, more established writers were invited into the new League of American Writers, a Popular Front organization. By the late 1930s, the discussion of proletarian literature had moved to the established literary quarterlies and had a distinctly retrospective air about it.[48]

However, this "autopsy" of proletarian literature, to use Rahv's term, is misleading for a number of reasons. It is true that the "proletarian" and revolutionary rhetoric receded after the upheavals of the summer of 1934. That year's apocalyptic hopes and dreams for a national general strike, a Soviet America, gave way to the everyday struggle of a social movement battling to extend the real accomplishments of the New Deal's relief programs and social security, to organize industrial unions, and to build an alliance against fascism. True, the vogue for proletarian literature among established publishers and book reviews passed quickly. And it is also true that the Popular Front years of the League of American Writers saw, to some degree, the institutionalization of the proletarian avant-garde. If the national conventions of the John Reed Clubs witnessed fiery debates between little-known delegates of the various clubs, the national writers congresses of 1935, 1937, 1939, and 1941, if no less contentious, featured nationally known writers whose speeches were published in a series of books.[49]

Nevertheless, the sense of a radical break with proletarian literature in 1935 is mistaken. A clear continuity exists between the radical avant-garde of the early depression and the cultural politics of the mushrooming Popular Front. Far from being a brief and abortive episode in literary history, the literary formation that emerged under the slogan of "proletarian literature" continued to shape both writers and genres for a generation to come. First of all, despite the melodramatic accounts of the dissolution of the Reed clubs, the people involved in the League of American Writers were in most cases the same people who had been in the Reed clubs. Nelson Algren became the secretary of the Chicago chapter of the League; the western correspondent for the League was Kenneth Rexroth, who sent notes on books as well as labor and anti-fascist activities, and later taught at a LAW school; and Meridel Le Sueur was not only a vice president of the League, but the contact for the Midwest Literary League. Some figures broke with the Communist left, like the early partisans of the New York Reed club, Philip Rahv and William Phillips, but I know of no account in which one of the Reed club "kids" tells of being excluded from the League. Even Wright, who felt betrayed by the decision to abandon the Reed clubs, became a member of the national council of the League, and was an active figure on the cultural left for another decade. Moreover, one of the Reed club "kids," Jerre Mangione, recalled his relief when what he saw as the increasingly sectarian Reed club gave way to the League of American Writers.[50]

The League continued many of the activities of the Reed clubs, organizing the infrastructure of the cultural front. A 1941 New York LAW lecture series was not significantly different from earlier Reed club lectures: Richard Wright read from *Little Sister*, a never-completed novel he was writing about black domestic workers; William Carlos Williams read his poetry; and Ralph Ellison spoke about novels on Harlem and on Arkansas sharecroppers. The League sponsored national tours by writers in exile from fascism, produced radio broadcasts, raised money for medical aid to Spain, and organized writers schools in New York, San Francisco, New Hampshire, and at Commonwealth College in Arkansas. "Some three thousand students attended the League's writing classes," Benjamin Appel recalled, "some hundred and fifty European writers were rescued from the Nazi dragnet." And the League continued to attract young writers: "it was the League of American Writers that gave cohesion to what most of us were deeply concerned with during the Thirties," the poet Ruth Lechlitner later wrote. "Through the League there developed a genuine feeling of fellowship among both established and beginning writers . . . For the young writer especially, the League meetings were a source of hope and encouragement."[51]

Little magazines continued to blossom and die during the next two decades. In 1936, *Hinterland* appeared as the magazine of the Midwest Literary League, explicitly seeking to revive the spirit of radical regionalism. *Challenge*, which had almost expired due to the lack of interest shown at Negro colleges, according to Dorothy West, was revived as *New Challenge* in 1937 by the Chicago South Side Writers Group, a group of black writers including Wright and Margaret Walker (with financial help from the League of American Writers). Jack Conroy revived the *Anvil* as *New Anvil* in 1939 and 1940, publishing stories by Williams, Appel, and Le Sueur, but also featuring new writers like Margaret Walker, Frank Yerby, and Thomas McGrath. In 1939, a California bimonthly, *Black and White*, appeared as the literary magazine of the West Coast Popular Front; two years later, renamed *The Clipper*, it became the journal of the LAW. In those years, it published the writings of John Fante and Toshio Mori, as well as essays on jazz and *Citizen Kane.*[52]

In 1941, Ralph Ellison unsuccessfully attempted to create a League of American Writers journal; a year later he did found *The Negro Quarterly*, together with the African American Communist Angelo Herndon. Though it lasted only four issues, *The Negro Quarterly* published Hughes, Sterling Brown, Richard Wright, and E. Franklin Frazier; its mixture of fiction, poetry, criticism, and political commentary in substantial 96-page issues made it one of the classic intellectual journals of the 1940s, not unlike *Partisan Review.* A similar combination of fiction and essays characterized Louis Adamic's quarterly devoted to the culture and politics of ethnicity, *Common Ground.* Edwin Seaver, a proletarian novelist and critic in the early 1930s, continued to support young writers as an editor and book reviewer for the glossy Popular Front magazine, *Direction*, and then as editor of the annual literary anthology, *Cross-Section* (1943–48), which published the emerging writers of the 1940s, including Ellison, Norman Mailer, Gwendolyn Brooks, and Arthur Miller. Even in the Cold War days of the 1950s, Philip Stevenson, who had been part of the Taos circle of radical artists and writers in the early 1930s, put out the *California Quarterly.*[53]

Several left-wing writers groups brought together young black or ethnic writers from working-class backgrounds in the decades after the demise of the John Reed Clubs, and they had a significant impact on post-war writing. The Futurians were formed in 1938 by radical young science-fiction writers, several of whom were members of the Young Communist League; over the next decade, the group, which included Isaac Asimov, Frederick Pohl, Cy

Kornbluth, Judith Meril, James Blish, and Damon Knight, wrote for and edited the pulp magazines and paperback originals that remade science fiction in the post-war period. A second group met in the back room of Stanley Rose's Los Angeles bookstore in the early 1940s: they included William Saroyan, John Fante, Horace McCoy, Carlos Bulosan, Jo Pagano, and Carey McWilliams. They were loosely connected to the film studios, and occasionally published in the West Coast journal of the League of American Writers, *The Clipper*, as well as in Adamic's *Common Ground*. Finally, in the years after the war, there were several left-wing writers groups in Harlem; the Harlem Writers Club was led by Harold Cruse, and the Harlem Writers Guild, led by John O. Killens, included Paule Marshall, Rosa Guy, and Julian Mayfield.[54]

The publishing institutions of the proletarian literature movement were always fragile. The initial success of the proletarian little magazines depended in large part on the Communist Party's Central Distribution Agency, which assured a sale of three thousand copies. At the 1935 Writers' Congress, Henry Hart spoke about the disappointing sales of the early proletarian novels and hailed the formation of a left-wing book club, the Book Union, as a promising way of supporting left writers. In some ways, the Popular Front years witnessed the expansion of proletarian literature, even as the debates over the term receded. There were a number of attempts to create left literary institutions: the experimental paperback book firm, Modern Age books; George Braziller's Book Find Club; the attempt by Progress Publishing Company to create a prolabor pulp magazine, backed by Adamic, William Carlos Williams, Richard Wright, and the New Jersey CIO; and a network of radical bookstores, including the Communist Party's Workers Bookstores as well as independents like those of Martin Kamin and Stanley Rose.[55]

Moreover, though the claims by anti-communist writers like Eugene Lyons that the communist literati dominated the world of publishing are clearly exaggerated, a number of left-wing critics were influential in publishing houses: Granville Hicks worked as a reader for Macmillan; Bernard Smith became editor-in-chief at Knopf; and Edwin Seaver and Angus Cameron were at Little, Brown. The literary agent Maxim Lieber was also a key figure. "I represented practically the entire left among the writers in America," he later recalled. His first clients were Louis Adamic, Erskine Caldwell, and Albert Halper, and he eventually represented Jack Conroy, Langston Hughes, Josephine Herbst, Albert Maltz, Theodore Dreiser, William Saroyan, and Nathanael West, among others. These editors and agents continued to support the work of the "proletarian" writers long after the initial wave passed. If the best-selling proletarian novel of the first wave was, as Hart claimed, Robert Cantwell's *The Land of Plenty*, which sold only 3,000 copies, by 1939 and 1940 the proletarian novels of Pietro di Donato and Richard Wright were reaching much larger audiences through the Book-of-the-Month Club.[56]

However, in one sense, there was a radical break from the proletarian avant-garde to the cultural front. The "least fortunate" literary generation, as Cowley called them, received an extraordinary, if contradictory, windfall: the New Deal arts programs and the expanding culture industries. If Proletcult died, it was killed by the WPA and Hollywood. The early John Reed Clubs had campaigned for relief for writers and artists; when the Works Progress Administration established that relief, the alumni of the Reed clubs carried their proletarian aesthetics into the guidebooks and folklore collections of the Federal Writers Project. Jack Conroy, Margaret Walker, Chester Himes, Arna Bontemps, Jo Sinclair, Nelson Algren, Kenneth Rexroth, Richard Wright, Meridel Le Sueur, Ralph Ellison, Jerre Mangione: all worked on the project, and Mangione eventually wrote their history in his *The Dream and the Deal*. The other alternative to the depressed literary market was the culture industry studio; many of the plebeian writers who first published in the proletarian magazines ended up writing commercial short stories, radio scripts, and screenplays. These commercial writers made up a large part of the League of American Writers. The contrast between the writers school mounted by the John Reed Club and that run by the League of American Writers a decade later is telling: whereas the former had courses taught by poets and literary critics, the latter had courses in radio scriptwriting, women's pulps and confessions, detective stories and thrillers, writing popular articles, and labor journalism. A League pamphlet, *Writers Teach Writing*, takes an industrial attitude toward writing: it is a job and a craft.

"Looking backward at the careers of the writers of the 1930s," Benjamin Appel wrote in 1951, "a clear design begins to emerge: hack work and easy work, unachieved promise and silence, sensational success that is a little hollow." Like James Farrell, Appel saw the "Temptation" of the "Slicks" and the "Movies" as the tragedy of his generation: "we have all come of literary age at a time when the machine-made cultural product has pushed the 'hand-made' book or play out of the market. Hollywood and the mass circulation magazines, the commercial theatre, the commercialized book publishing industry geared to the 25-cent reprint houses have all placed a premium on literary packaged goods, uniform in workmanship." However, Appel's verdict, though symptomatic of the post-war panic over mass culture, is too easy. For the lasting accomplishments of his generation were often the product of a dialectic between the proletarian avant-garde and the culture industries.[57]

The success of di Donato's *Christ in Concrete* and Wright's *Native Son* reminds us that the Popular Front did not turn its back on working-class writing and the depiction of working-class life after 1935, but it also points to the influence of the Book-of-the-Month Club in distributing these novels. As I have already suggested, Langston Hughes's finest "proletarian" fiction lay in his Simple stories, the "hack" work of a weekly newspaper column. In many ways, the research and interviews conducted for the Writers Project were not unlike the worker-correspondence Gold had called for, not unlike the Reed clubs' call to writers to study a particular industry. As a result, the writings of the plebeian writers who worked on the projects—Algren, Ellison, Himes, Tomasi, Sinclair, Conroy—embodied a dialectic between fictional invention, autobiographical reflection, and urban fieldwork. Appel himself traveled across the United States in 1939, collecting the stories of ordinary workers, which he published as *The People Talk* (1940); though usually cited as one of the New Deal "documentary" books, it is, despite its populist title, as much a product of the worker-writer impulse of the proletarian literature movement as Gold's Proletcult *New Masses* and Le Sueur's *The Girl.*

The forms of proletarian writing—the ghetto pastorals, the tales of unemployed drifters, the racial romances, the gangster stories—were also adapted to the *films noir* and *films gris* of post-war Hollywood: in some cases, the screenwriters were former proletarian writers—Vera Caspary (*Laura*), Daniel Fuchs (*Panic in the Streets*), Alfred Hayes (*Clash by Night*), Ben Maddow (*The Asphalt Jungle*), Albert Maltz (*The Naked City*), Jo Pagano (*Try and Get Me*), Clifford Odets (*Deadline at Dawn*), and Horace McCoy. In other cases, proletarian novels were adapted to the screen: di Donato's *Christ in Concrete* became Dmytryk's *Give Us This Day*; Thomas Bell's *All Brides Are Beautiful* became John Berry's *From This Day Forward*; and Budd Schulberg's *On the Waterfront* became a classic proletarian film directed by Elia Kazan.

Finally, many of the major writings of the proletarian movement— Wright's *Native Son* (1940), Algren's *Never Come Morning* (1942), Bulosan's *America Is in the Heart* (1944), Himes's *Lonely Crusade* (1945), Ellison's *Invisible Man* (1951), Saxton's *The Great Midland* (1948), Arnow's *The Dollmaker* (1954), Pohl and Kornbluth's *The Space Merchants* (1953), Olsen's *Tell Me a Riddle* (1961)—did not appear until well after the proletarian movement was pronounced dead. Moreover, several works—like Henry Roth's *Call It Sleep*—only found readers with the revival of proletarian literature in the 1960s, and others—Wright's *Lawd Today*, Olsen's *Yonnondio*, McGrath's *This Coffin Has No Handles*, Paredes's *George Washington Gomez*, and Le Sueur's *The Girl*—lay unpublished for a generation.

There is no question that, like every literary avant-garde, the proletarian literature movement failed. Few of the plebeian writers who published in the little magazines even made careers as novelists or poets; they were silenced by ordinary labor, by the literary marketplace, by the blacklist, and by exile. Nevertheless, there are many worthy, if half-forgotten, books that new readers may rediscover. There are even more ruins, crumbling emblems of another time, another place. And there are a handful of acknowledged classics that continue to speak to readers. "A Jack London or a Walt Whitman will come out of this new crop of young workers who write in the *New Masses*," Mike Gold promised in 1929, and there was indeed a Richard Wright, a Tillie Olsen. But the meaning of a cultural formation, that union of an artistic form and a social location, is not limited to the books it leaves, the writers who become "classics"; that is why the battles over the "literary canon" are finally so abstract.[58]

The proletarian literary movement was part of a "class war" in literature. As Kenneth Burke recognized, it "represent[ed] a way of life." Burke was right when he suggested that "the 'proletarian' sort of emphases and admonitions can provide a lasting and essential stimulus to the formation of the national 'consciousness'." Proletarian literature enfranchised a generation of writers of ethnic, working-class origins; it allowed them to represent—to speak for and to depict—their families, their neighborhoods, their aspirations, and their nightmares. Even if most of the novels and screenplays are only half-remembered, their cumulative effect transformed American culture, making their ghetto childhoods, their drifters and hobos, their vernacular prose, their gangsters and prostitutes, even their occasional union organizer, part of the mythology of the United States, part of the national-popular imagination. To see this, we need to look more closely at the fundamental forms that emerged out of the proletarian literature movement: the ghetto pastoral and the migrant narrative.[59]

6

"The Tenement Thinking":
Ghetto Pastorals

I was born in a tenement. That tall, sombre mass, holding its freight of
obscure human destinies, is the pattern in which my being has been
cast. It was in a tenement that I first heard the sad music of humanity
rise to the stars ... When I think it is the tenement thinking. When I
hope it is the tenement hoping. I am not an individual; I am all that
the tenement group poured into me during those early years of my
spiritual travail.

   Why should we artists born in tenements go beyond them for our
expression? Can we go beyond them? ... Art is the tenement pouring
out its soul through us, its most sensitive and articulate sons and
daughters.

Michael Gold[1]

The most important genre created by the writers of the proletarian literary
movement was the ghetto pastoral. Ghetto pastorals were tales of growing
up in Little Italy, the Lower East Side, Bronzeville, and Chinatown, written
by plebeian men and women of these ethnic working-class neighborhoods.
They were a new kind of city novel, indebted to but significantly different
from earlier forms. Unlike the nineteenth-century "mysteries of the city,"
they found city streets and neighborhoods ordinary, filled with children,
and they rarely imagined the inner chambers of the city's wealthy elites.
Unlike the muckraking fiction of Upton Sinclair and his heirs, they were
rarely based on the cover stories of class conflict, strikes, and trials: they
were not the novel of Sacco and Vanzetti that Mary French imagined
writing. And unlike the turn-of-the-century "naturalism" to which they were
often assimilated, they were not explorations of how the other half lives.
Rather, they were tales of how *our* half lives. They were the flip side of the
slumming stories that ran from Stephen Crane to Dos Passos himself: not
a proletarian sublime but a proletarian pastoral. These ghetto pastorals

constituted a subaltern modernism and became the central literary form of the Popular Front. They refigured the lineaments of the American tale, inflecting much of twentieth-century fiction, film, and broadcasting.[2]

There had been forerunners: naturalism's "other half" included such works as Abraham Cahan's *Yekl* and Paul Lawrence Dunbar's *The Sport of the Gods*. But these were rare and little known. However, between those early novels and the ghetto pastorals of the depression and after lay the transformation of the modernist metropolis by the children of the migrants from the Black Belt South and the Slavic and Mediterranean East. As a result of the laboring of American culture by those second-generation "ethnics," the tales of "foreign" and "colored" neighborhoods were no longer a species of exotic regionalism but a national tale of daughters of the earth and native sons. By the later decades of the twentieth century, the immigrant saga and the Great Migration had become a central part of American mythology, with the streets of the Lower East Side, Harlem, and Little Italy lovingly recreated in Hollywood films and television miniseries. The emergence of various symbolic ethnicities in popular culture and the ritual invocation of immigrant grandparents by politicians made Ellis Island as sacred as Plymouth Rock. By the time of Francis Coppola's *Godfather* trilogy and Don Bluth's animated epic of the Mousekowitzes, *An American Tale*, the story of the ghetto had become quintessentially American.

However, before the story became popular myth, the plebeian writers who had emerged in and around the proletarian literature movement and the Popular Front attempted to render the world of the ghetto in a series of powerful if contradictory novels. The writers—the "sensitive and articulate sons and daughters," as Gold put it—were aware of being doubly apart, separated not only from the literary culture of the dominant classes but from the culture and language they grew up in. Their little magazines rarely reached the popular audience they addressed, an audience attuned to radio serials and pulp magazines. But the novels they wrote are among the most powerful works in American literature. After examining the sources of the genre and considering the reasons it has rarely been seen as "proletarian literature," I will argue that the ghetto pastoral is a yoking of naturalism and the pastoral, the slum and the shepherd, the gangster and Christ in concrete, Cesspool and Lawd Today. The ghetto pastoral is less a form of social realism than a proletarian tale of terror, an allegorical cityscape composed in a pidgin of American slang and ghetto dialect, with traces of old country tongues.

1. The Emergence of the Genre

Before the emergence of the ghetto pastorals, the ethnic working classes had been represented in American writing by the popular dialect stories that fattened the *Saturday Evening Post* through the first three decades of the century, including Montague Glass's Potash and Perlmutter and Octavus Roy Cohen's Florian Slappey. Montague Glass, Anzia Yezierska later wrote, "turned out his caricatures of Jews like sausage meat for the popular weekly and monthly magazines. Americans reading his Potash and Perlmutter stories thought those clowning cloak and suiters were the Jewish people." "It is the Florian Slappeys that I protest against the most," Richard Wright told a journalist. "Mr. Cohen is a widely read writer in the popular magazines and he sticks to the oldest and most dishonest tricks of the writing trade when he types Negroes." Similarly, Toshio Mori recalled that Peter B. Kyne's humorous tales of a Japanese detective didn't "typify the Japanese community at all"; Mori began writing to "reveal some of the true Japanese lives." Even in the novels of the 1920s American moderns, the "foreigner" had only bit parts. In Hemingway's *in our time*, the "wops" turn up in the interchapters; in Fitzgerald's *The Great Gatsby*, we see the Greek and "negro" witnesses to the accident, Nick's Finnish cleaning woman, a "gray, scrawny Italian child," and of course Meyer Wolfsheim, the gambler who fixed the World Series; in *U.S.A.*, there was only the brief Ben Compton narrative at the end of *Nineteen-Nineteen*. The ghetto pastorals were in large part written against these racial and ethnic types.[3]

The earliest ghetto pastorals were written by figures who had been associated with the Greenwich Village left of the 1910s: Anzia Yezierska, born in 1880, had been close to the Heterodoxy circle of feminists, particularly Henrietta Rodman and Rose Pastor Stokes, in the years when she began writing stories of the Lower East Side; Claude McKay, born in 1889 in Jamaica, had co-edited the *Liberator* with Mike Gold in the early 1920s before writing *Home to Harlem* (1928); and Mike Gold himself, born Itzok Isaac Granich of immigrant parents in New York in 1893, published the first sketches of his "East Side novel" in the *Masses* in 1917.

Though Yezierska's fiction—particularly the 1920 collection of stories, *Hungry Hearts*, and the 1925 novel, *The Bread Givers*—and McKay's Harlem novel were widely read and debated, neither had the impact of Gold's 1930 novel, *Jews without Money*. In part, this was a result of Gold's visibility and work as the editor of the *New Masses*. *Jews without Money* was read (and criticized) as an emblem of the proletarian writing he called for. Moreover, whereas the works of Yezierska and McKay appeared at the height of the American boom and were read as tales of its exotic other side (an influential 1923 review of Yezierska's work was entitled "How the Other Half Lives"), Gold's novel appeared in the midst of the depression: it was published in February of 1930 and had gone through eleven printings by October.

Jews without Money was an exhaustive catalog of the genre's motifs, incidents, and characters, as well as an embodiment of the formal contradictions that came to haunt subsequent ghetto novels. The novel was a fictional memoir of a childhood on the Lower East Side, the adventures of young Mikey between the ages of five and seven. Like Conroy's *The Disinherited, Jews without Money* began as a series of sketches published in the *New Masses* and in Mencken's *American Mercury*. The novel retains an episodic and anecdotal structure, moving from one neighborhood character or incident to another without much direction or chronology, a "newsreel of memory." Two narrative logics structure the book. First, the novel's shape is taken from the seasons, as several years are telescoped in a single movement from memories of spring mornings, to the adventures of hot and glorious summers, to the dreary autumns (it is autumn when his father, a housepainter, is badly injured in a fall and the family begins its descent into poverty), to the winters of despair and destruction, culminating in the death of Mikey's sister, Esther. It is this seasonal structure that makes the final chapter of the book seem so abrupt: though Mikey is only seven in the winter of Esther's death, a few paragraphs take him through the years of adolescence to the soapbox orator's prophecy of a workers revolution and the book's closing words, "O great Beginning."[4]

However, a second, contrary, logic also informs the book. Each of its chapters works by sketching several unrelated motifs that come together in an incident, a crystallized image, a parable: the vision of the Messiah as Buffalo Bill; the pastoral journey to hunt mushrooms in the Bronx; the massacre of the pigeons; and the meeting with the sick Christian boy, among others. The novel as a whole exhibits the same structure, as the chaotic incidents of childhood are crystallized in the final vision of revolution: the narrative logic is embodied in the interrelation of magic, the Messiah, and the revolution. "All poor men believe in such magic," the narrator notes, "and dream of the day when they will stumble on it." The novel's comic glimpses of the Messiah—as coming in a fine automobile, looking like Buffalo Bill, bringing a glass of cream soda—and its recurring lyric apostrophes—"O golden dyspeptic God of America"—culminate in the final invocation of "O workers' Revolution ... You are the true Messiah."[5]

In the wake of Gold's success, a number of younger writers began to publish stories and sketches of ghetto life. Some told the story of a single season in a young person's life: *Young Lonigan* (1932), written between 1929 and 1931 by James T. Farrell (born in 1904), told of one summer— 1916—in the life of fifteen-year-old Studs Lonigan, the son of an Irish painter in Chicago; *Summer in Williamsburg* (1934), a first novel by Daniel

Fuchs (born in 1909), followed twenty-year-old Philip Hayman, caught between his father, a Jewish immigrant news vendor, and his gangster uncle; *Wait Until Spring, Bandini* (1938), by John Fante (born in 1909), is set during the winter of fourteen-year-old Arturo Bandini, the son of an Italian bricklayer. H.T. Tsiang's *And China Has Hands* (1937) narrated a winter and summer in the life of a young Chinatown hand-laundryman. In *Lawd Today*, written in 1934 and 1935 and repeatedly rejected by publishers (finally published in 1963), Richard Wright (born in 1908) compressed the story of Jake Jackson, a black Chicago postal worker, into a single day, a technique also used by Daniel Fuchs in *Homage to Blenholt* (1936), his comic tale of the Williamsburg schlemiel, Max Balkan. Marita Bonner (born in 1899) focuses the stories of her never-completed *The Black Map*, published in *Opportunity* between 1933 and 1941, around a single street, Frye Street, in Chicago.

Others used the same childhood years of Gold's Mikey to capture the ghetto: *Call It Sleep* (1934) by Henry Roth (born in 1906) takes the boy David Schearl from the ages of six to eight in New York's Brownsville; Tillie Olsen's *Yonnondio*, written between 1932 and 1937 but not published until 1974, follows Mazie Holbrook from six to eight as she moves from mining camp to tenant farm to packing-house slum. None of these ghetto pastorals was a great success: those of Wright, Olsen, and Bonner did not find publishers until a generation later; those of Roth and Fuchs were critically acclaimed but sold very few copies; those of Tsiang and Fante were hardly noticed; only Farrell's Lonigan was well known at the time.

Nevertheless, the ghetto pastoral did not die with the proletarian movement that nurtured its writers. On the contrary, the ghetto pastoral became one of the foremost literary forms of the Popular Front. In 1939, *Christ in Concrete* by Pietro di Donato (born in 1911), the story of the twelve-year-old son of an Italian bricklayer, part of which had appeared in the *New Masses*, was chosen as a Book-of-the-Month Club selection; a year later, the Book-of-the-Month Club featured Richard Wright's *Native Son*, the story of Bigger Thomas, set in Chicago's Bronzeville; and in 1941, the club chose *My Name is Aram* by William Saroyan (born in 1908), the stories of an Armenian boy in California's Central Valley. In 1942, Nelson Algren's story of a seventeen-year old Polish boxer, *Never Come Morning*, was widely acclaimed. Though one could hardly imagine more different styles than Saroyan's sentimental comedy and Algren's hard-boiled brutalism, the narrative materials of the ethnic working-class neighborhoods had become central to American fiction.

Throughout the 1940s, Popular Front journals like *Common Ground*, *Direction*, and *PM* reviewed and published a variety of ghetto tales. Among the key works of the 1940s and early 1950s are *Mount Allegro* (1943) by Jerre Mangione (born in 1909); Jo Pagano's *The Golden Wedding* (1943);

Ann Petry's *The Street* (1946); *Wasteland* (1946) by Jo Sinclair (the pen name of Ruth Seid, born in 1913), which was reviewed enthusiastically by Wright in *PM*; Mario Suárez's stories of the Tucson barrio, El Hoyo, published in the *Arizona Quarterly* between 1947 and 1950; the Chinatown stories published in *The Bud* in 1947 and 1948; *Like Lesser Gods* (1949) by Mari Tomasi (born in 1909); *Yokohama, California* (1949) by Toshio Mori (born in 1910), with an introduction by Saroyan; Hisaye Yamamoto's stories of 1949–51 collected in *Seventeen Syllables* (1988); *Maud Martha* (1953) by Gwendolyn Brooks (born in 1917); *The Hit* (1957) by Julian Mayfield (born in 1928); *Brown Girl, Brownstones* (1959) by Paule Marshall (born in 1929); *All I Asking for Is My Body* (1975) by Milton Murayama (born in 1923); and even *Doctor Sax* (1959) by Jack Kerouac (born in 1922).[6]

Curiously, these books have not, for the most part, been seen as proletarian novels for three reasons: their lack of explicit "political" content; their ethnic or racial accents; and the changing nature of the "working-class author." Each of these reasons is worth exploring. First, critics at the time and since have assumed that radical or proletarian novels are characterized either by explicit political didacticism or by events, characters, and situations that would embody a political narrative: narratives of strikes, militant organizers as characters, political debate as part of the texture of the work. Mary French's never-written novel about the Sacco and Vanzetti case is usually taken as the most typical mode of proletarian writing: Dos Passos's character of Mary French was based on the labor journalist Mary Heaton Vorse, who had written one of the five radical novels about the 1929 Gastonia textile strike.

However, the Gastonia novels—Vorse's *Strike!* (1930), Grace Lumpkin's *To Make My Bread* (1932), Fielding Burke's *Call Home the Heart* (1932), Dorothy Myra Page's *Gathering Storm* (1932), and Sherwood Anderson's *Beyond Desire* (1932)—are less products of the proletarian literary movement than descendants of the novels written about the Molly Maguires and the Haymarket anarchists. Even though they were written in the early 1930s, neither the novels nor their authors appear in the little magazines of the proletarian movement. Vorse was an established radical labor journalist; Myra Page had a doctorate in sociology; and Anderson was one of the best-known American novelists of the 1920s. It is not surprising that these works received a good deal of attention in the general press, nor is it surprising that they faded from attention quickly. The novel has traditionally had the role of fictionalizing contemporary events, setting celebrated crimes, disasters, and social conflicts into conventional narratives of family, romance, and community. These novelizations of current events are usually written by professional writers, particularly journalists, and they rarely last beyond the immediate topicality. This is also true of the series of novels written about the Harlan County coal strikes; the lumber strikes in Aberdeen, Washington; the Scottsboro case; and the sit-down strikes of 1937. In most cases, the books were written from the outside, as documentaries, competing with non-fictional accounts of the events. The grand master of this tradition was Upton Sinclair, who covered the great strikes and celebrated trials from his 1906 exposé of the meatpacking industry, *The Jungle,* to his 1928 novel of the Sacco-Vanzetti case, *Boston,* and his 1938 CIO novel, *Little Steel.*

Few of the ghetto pastorals, even those written by Communist or Popular Front writers, had this kind of topical political content. And even though most of the theorists of proletarian fiction explicitly rejected a didactic, propagandist conception of fiction, favoring a conception of realism that would grasp a social totality through the creation of typical characters and situations, few saw the ghetto tales as "political." Both Gold's *Jews without Money* and Henry Roth's *Call It Sleep* were controversial among left-wing critics. *Jews without Money* was "a failure when judged by the standards of proletarian literature," the proletarian writer Melvin Levy wrote in the *New Republic,* because Gold had omitted the Triangle fire and the great garment strikes. In reply, Gold argued that "I could do nothing else honestly and emotionally at the time. I could only describe what I had seen with my own eyes ... I do not believe any good writing can come out of this mechanical application of the spirit of proletarian literature." A similar debate took place in the *New Masses* after a negative review of Roth's *Call It Sleep.* Neither controversy was settled; ironically, years later, when Henry Roth told an interviewer that *Call It Sleep* was *not* a proletarian novel, he added that "probably Mike Gold's *Jews without Money* is a proletarian novel."[7]

In the midst of these debates over definition, Kenneth Burke wrote a letter to the *New Masses* that began to capture the lineaments of the ghetto pastoral with its "pre-political" sense of magic and allegory:

> It seems to me that your reviewer missed the good things in Henry Roth's Call it sleep. I thought that Roth caught, with considerable sympathy and humor, the "pre-political" thinking of childhood, the stage of development wherein we follow much the same patterns of magic as Frazer outlines in the Golden Bough. The great virtue of Roth's book, to my way of thinking, was in the fluent and civilized way in which he found, on our city streets, the new equivalents of the ancient jungle—a parallelism which culminates magnificently when the electric current in the car track takes the place of the lightning that struck down Frazer's sacred oak. Insofar as the propaganda of Communists is an attempt to give people new meanings, I think that Communist critics should show special concern for such a book as Roth's, which deals fluently with the psychological phenomenon of orientation and "rebirth." And insofar as children *are* pre-political savages, living in a world of symbolism and magic, I question whether any realistic philosophy could properly condemn a writer for reviving such a

picture of childhood, particularly when he accomplishes his task with Roth's sound mixture of soberness and fancy. I grant the reviewer's statement that the book would have profited by cutting. Nonetheless, just as it stands, it should be saluted not only for its great promise, but also for its attainments.

Burke's sense of the novel's attainments is a useful guide for literary historians as well. Despite the many visions of a new form of the revolutionary and proletarian novel at the time, the new form that actually emerged was the tale of ghetto childhood that Gold and Roth had written.[8]

Most of the writers of the ghetto pastorals were associated with left cultural initiatives, belonging to radical writers groups and publishing in Popular Front magazines. Some—Wright, Algren, and Mangione—had come to the left through the John Reed Clubs; others, like Olsen and Henry Roth, were members of the Communist Party. Many, including Daniel Fuchs and Pietro di Donato, were members of the League of American Writers. Di Donato told the *Daily Worker* that he had been a "radical" most of his life: "they used to call me Pete the Red." Tsiang and the *Bud* writers were active in New York's Chinese American left with its basis in the Chinese Hand Laundry Alliance. The West Coast writers— Fante, Saroyan, and Bulosan—were part of the circle of left-wing writers who gathered around Carey McWilliams and Louis Adamic at Stanley Rose's bookstore. Mori, Brooks, Sinclair, and Tomasi were all published in Adamic's Popular Front magazine, *Common Ground*. Gwendolyn Brooks was part of the South Side Writers Group around Richard Wright, and Mayfield and Marshall were associated with the left-wing Harlem Writers Guild.[9]

Of course, the political commitments and opinions of these writers varied considerably: some were lifelong people of the left, others had brief affiliations, still others were relatively uninterested in politics and had simply been drawn into the cultural orbit of the left. Moreover, as the genre of the ghetto pastoral grew into a major form of the American novel, it was adopted by writers who were not on the left. Nevertheless, there was an elective affinity between the ghetto pastoral and the cultural figures of the left, which continues to the present, as the postmodern ghetto pastorals of the left-wing novelist E.L. Doctorow, particularly *World's Fair*, testify.

A second reason why the ghetto pastorals were not recognized as the major fiction of the proletarian literary movement was that the ghetto novel, whether by black or ethnic writers, was seen as a minor regional form. Neither of the two major literary histories of the period, Granville Hicks's *The Great Tradition* and Alfred Kazin's *On Native Grounds*, even glimpse the emergence of the ghetto pastoral in these years. Hicks and Kazin, for all their polemical differences, shared the sense that the vital subject of the modern novel was the rise of industrial capitalism. For Hicks, this was manifested in the "literary discovery of the working class," in the history of the "industrial novel." For Kazin, on the other hand, industrial capitalism was figured not by a new working class but by the rule of the businessman and a new "commercialism," which together produced the "greatest central fact about our modern American writing": the "deep and subtle alienation" of writers from American society. Neither Hicks nor Kazin explores the literature of the ethnic and African American communities. Thus, for Hicks, who is sympathetic to the proletarian movement, the key figures of the proletarian movement seem to be Herbst, Farrell, Cantwell, Caldwell, and Conroy; for Kazin, who is extremely critical of the radical writers' "abject surrender to naturalism," the exemplary figures are Farrell and Caldwell. No mention is made of Roth's *Call It Sleep*, a book which Kazin later champions. This absence is particularly striking in Kazin's work because he was to write three classic memoirs of ethnic, working-class New York: *A Walker in the City, Starting Out in the Thirties*, and *New York Jew*. Indeed, in *Starting Out in the Thirties*, Kazin recasts the literary thirties as a time when "the banked-up experience of the plebes, of Jews, Irishman, Negroes, Armenians, Italians, was coming into American books."[10]

Few of the critics of the period were prepared to see the ways in which the proletarian tale would be told in ethnic and racial accents. For the younger writers, a proletarian literature was necessarily an ethnic and racial literature, a reflection on the ethnic complexity of the American working class. "Negro writers must accept the nationalist implications of their lives, not in order to encourage them, but in order to change and transcend them," Richard Wright wrote in the 1937 "Blueprint for Negro Writing," which had been drafted and debated by the South Side Writers Group. "They must accept the concept of nationalism because, in order to transcend it, they must *possess* and *understand* it." The ghetto pastoral became the vehicle for that possession, a means to understand the nationalist implications of working-class lives. Perhaps the first critical survey of the writings of these second-generation ethnic writers was by the young Italian American writer Michael de Capite, in the first issue of Louis Adamic's journal, *Common Ground*. De Capite's essay, "The Story Is Yet to Be Told," is in part a critique of the failures and confusions of second-generation writers, particularly Farrell, di Donato, Fante, and Saroyan, and in part a manifesto, a call to write the story of the "New American."[11]

It is not surprising that the revival of many of the ghetto pastorals and their authors has taken place under the rubric of "ethnic literature." Roth and Fuchs are well known to scholars of Jewish American literature, di Donato and Mangione are part of the canon of Italian American literature, and Tsiang, Mori, and Bulosan are known to scholars of Asian American literature. It is a mistake, however, to see these writers and the ghetto pastoral itself simply as "ethnic," that is, as the national literature of distinct ethnic groups. For one thing, many of them insisted on their common proletarian outlook. For Wright, for Bulosan, and for Tsiang, the slogan "national in form, proletarian in content" was a shorthand for a rich and complex dialectic. The plebeian writers were united by a common historical situation that was not a common ethnicity but a common ethnic formation: the restructuring of the American peoples by the labor migrations of the early twentieth century from Southern and Eastern Europe and the sharecropping South. These peoples were ethnicized and racialized by that social formation.

Ethnicity and race had become the modality through which working-class peoples experienced their lives and mapped their communities. The symbolic structures of ethnicity and race were the products of slavery and migrant labor, segregated labor markets, legal codes of exclusion and restriction, as well as the institutions of community culture and self-defense. Though the forms—the rituals and emblems—of ethnic cultures differed, the content had much in common: it was the content of working-class tenements, sweatshop and factory labor, and cheap mass entertainments. The invention of ethnicity was a central form of class consciousness in the United States.

The third reason that the ghetto pastorals were not seen as proletarian novels was that the image of the working-class writer was changing. Raymond Williams has noted that there have traditionally been two kinds of working-class novelists: the working-class adult who writes a novel, and the writer who comes from a working-class family and community. The former was more common in the late nineteenth and early twentieth centuries, and most of the advocates of working-class writing assumed that the proletarian novelist would be the adult factory worker who wrote. Jack Conroy was such a figure, and is often referred to as the only "authentic" proletarian in the literary movement. However, as Williams observes, it is the second type of working-class writer—the writer who grew up in a working-class family—that has increased in the twentieth century with the expansion of public education and the proletarianization of writing itself in the culture industries.[12]

Few of the writers of the ghetto pastorals were adult workers who wrote a novel; almost all of them had grown up in working-class communities and were trying to become "writers." Several had attended college and worked in white-collar jobs. Yet it would be wrong to see them as middle class: none of them was in the well-paid professions, and none of them came from established families. It is instructive to contrast the backgrounds of these novelists with the backgrounds of the major left critics of the time: none of the novelists had the solid middle-class origins and education of Cowley, Burke, Carey McWilliams, Bernard Smith, or Granville Hicks. A few were schoolteachers: Marita Bonner's father worked as a laborer and machinist; she had gone to Radcliffe and was a high-school teacher. Daniel

Fuchs's parents were immigrants who lived in Williamsburg; he attended City College and was a schoolteacher before heading to Hollywood to write screenplays. Mari Tomasi, the daughter of immigrants, was also a teacher. Di Donato was the son of a bricklayer and had worked as a bricklayer himself since age fourteen; Wright was the child of a sharecropper and a schoolteacher, and had worked as a porter, a busboy, and in the post office. Many returned to working-class jobs after their brief careers as writers: Roth became a machinist; Olsen worked as a "waitress, shaker in a laundry, transcriber in a dairy equipment company, capper of mayonnaise jars, secretary, and 'Kelly Girl'." But it was the memory of a proletarian childhood that lay at the heart of these books and one could say of many of the writers what John Fante wrote of Saroyan: his "childhood was so unhappy it has taken nine books to vindicate that period of his life . . . For he is obsessed with his childhood."[13]

The ghetto pastoral was, then, a curious hybrid: it combined the dream of a new proletarian literature nurtured by the cultural politics of the left, the ethnic and racial modalities through which the relations of class were lived, the recurring obsession with working-class childhood, and the struggle with the most prestigious and lucrative literary form, the novel. The struggle with the novel itself marks all these books: as Raymond Williams once put it, rather than asking how a writer handled the novel, it is better to ask how the novel handled the writer.

The plebeian writers had a deep ambivalence about the novel. Several of the ghetto pastorals even incorporate satiric portraits of the proletarian writer. In Daniel Fuchs's *Summer in Williamsburg*, the protagonist's friend, Cohen, joins the Communists and decides to write a one-act agitprop play. Cohen recounts the plot to Philip: a man loses his job, hits the road, rides the freights, joins the Party in San Francisco, leads a strike, and gets killed. To which Philip quips, "All this goes into a one-act play?" Cohen later abandons the play and the Party, but the satiric portrait of the proletarian writer is an ironic reflection on Fuchs's own attempt to "pick Williamsburg to pieces" in a novel, to make a "dictionary of Williamsburg." "No novel, no matter how seriously intended, was real," the narrator concludes. "The progressive development, the delineated episodes, the artificial climax, the final conclusion, setting the characters at rest and out of the lives of the readers, these were logical devices and they were false. People did not live in dramatic situations."[14]

On the other hand, H.T. Tsiang puts himself—an unnamed proletarian novelist who has written *China Red* and *The Hanging on Union Square*—into *And China Has Hands* in three places. He briefly meets the two main characters, Pearl Chang and Wong Wan-Lee, both of whom are puzzled by him. He tells Pearl "how in spite of the crookedness of those fakers he had succeeded in publishing his works and distributing sixteen thousand copies, and how he, as a proletarian writer, was proud to publish and to sell his own books. Pearl Chang chuckled, for she could not see what was the difference between a man who sold his own books and one who peddled chewing gum and cigarettes in front of a theatre." Similarly, though Wong Wan-Lee invites the fellow to his laundry after seeing him thrown out of a debate, "What Is Proletarian Literature and Who Pays the Printing Bills?", Wong thinks the writer is a bum and only invites him because he "thought the ejection very humiliating to his race." The proletarian writer's third cameo appearance comes at the end, when he joins a picket line of striking cafeteria workers, including Pearl and Wong: "since he had written so much about revolution, he had better do something about it. And picketing is a revolution in a small way." Besides, his new publisher is "hoping the author would get his head clubbed so his picture would appear in the papers." Fuchs's ironic narrator and Tsiang's mocking self-portrait both capture the young radicals' suspicion of the novel as a form.[15]

"What is the sense of bothering with the novel when a novel may not be what we want to write at all?" the humorist Kyle Crichton, who wrote for the *New Masses* under the pseudonym Robert Forsythe, asked in a column entitled "Down with the Novel!" Crichton lamented the young critic, poet, or historian who feels "his life will be incomplete until he has wasted six months manufacturing a set of fictional robots and producing a book which will be read by seven hundred people and have all the artistic significance of a subway advertising poster." After comparing the success of Louis Adamic's memoir, *Laughing in the Jungle,* with the failure of his novel, *Grandsons,* Crichton suggests that left-wing writers should "show their independence of old forms" by attempting "reportage, autobiography, comment, philosophy and even nonsensicality." The non-fictional forms—the proletarian sketch, reportage, autobiography, and documentary—were used by the plebeian writers, continuing a long tradition of working-class writing. "It is a major fact of nineteenth-century cultural history," Raymond Williams has noted, "that the many talented working-class writers did not, with only the occasional exception, include novelists. This has primarily to do with the available *forms* of the novel, centered predominantly on problems of the inheritance of property and of property-tied marriage, and beyond these on relatively exotic adventure and romance ... Where most working-class writers turned, instead, was (apart from essays, pamphlets and journalism, directly related to class causes) to autobiography and memoirs, or to popular verse." In many ways, the same was true of the plebeian writers of the depression; one of the arguments of this book is that the cultural front, the culture of the CIO, was *not* primarily located in novels, even proletarian ones.[16]

Few of the plebeian writers went on to become novelists, in the sense of having a career writing fiction. Several of their novels were aborted or unfinished; only a handful were critical or commercial successes. Many of them eventually adopted non-fiction forms: labor journalism, popular and scholarly history-writing, and professional and technical writing. Moreover, the ghetto pastoral itself hesitates on the line between fiction and autobiography. Gold's *Jews without Money* is often read as an autobiography, and Jack Conroy recast his autobiography as a novel to meet the publisher's desires. "I should prefer not to call the book a novel," Conroy wrote to Granville Hicks, "but I suppose the term fits as well as any. It's really a collection of autobiographical sketches with a cumulative effect." A decade later, Jerre Mangione's tale of growing up Sicilian in Rochester, New York, was published over his protests as fiction, even though it had been contracted as a non-fictional memoir.[17]

Nevertheless, Williams's argument about nineteenth-century working-class writers does not fully apply to twentieth-century writers. Two new forms of novel-writing now provided models for American working-class writers and echoed through the ghetto pastorals: the cheap stories of the popular fiction industry and the experimental fiction of modernism. The plebeian writers had grown up reading dime novels and pulp magazines; the desire to write fiction was instilled by the cheap stories of detectives, working girls, and western outlaws that proliferated in the late nineteenth and early twentieth centuries. "I started to read some of the dime novels, which were popular at that period," Toshio Mori told an interviewer. "For ten cents you were able to read these paper edition books ... by Frank Merriwell, ... Nick Carter detective stories and Horatio Alger stories ... We used to trade the dime novels for a nickel to get a second copy ... That interest started to draw me toward literature at a low level." The Alger stories were "part of the dreams of my youth," Richard Wright recalled in a *PM* review entitled "Alger Revisited, or My Stars! Did We Read that Stuff?" The heroes, plots, and language of pulp fiction haunted the ghetto pastoral: if Michael Gold's Mikey thinks that the Messiah will look like Buffalo Bill in "the gaudy little paper books," James T. Farrell's Studs Lonigan imagines Satan as "just like Deadwood Dick."[18]

The other model was the experimental fiction-writing of Gertrude Stein, William Carlos Williams, and James Joyce, all of whom evaded narrative in their renderings of the everyday life of ordinary workers. Though the lives of servants and patients in the modernist pastorals of Stein, *Three Lives*, and Williams, *The Knife of the Times* and *Life along the Passaic*, are rendered from above, the forms they employed—a vernacular without the condescension of dialect, a patient detailing of ordinary acts with studied objectivity—exercised a profound influence on the plebeian writers. Stein even makes brief appearances in H.T. Tsiang's *And China Has Hands* and Richard Wright's *Lawd Today*. Early in Tsiang's novel, the proletarian novelist complains to Pearl that, after praising his novel as "the first novel with a proletarian theme written in expressionistic technique," the "fakers" changed their minds and condemned him by saying that his "chief literary influence is the decadent Gertrude Stein." The narrator doesn't challenge the influence, only the evaluation. And in the midst of the extraordinary stream of signifying in *Lawd Today*'s post office, one postal worker says:

> "But don't you think all the white folks is smart. Some of 'em's crazy! I saw in the papers the other day where some old white woman over in Paris said a rose is a rose is a rose is a rose . . . She wrote it in a book and when they asked her what it was she wouldn't tell. . . ."
> "Wouldn't tell?"
> "Wouldn't tell, man."
> "Jeeesus, that sounds like old Cab Calloway."

The fusion of Stein and Calloway, of Paris modernism and Harlem jazz, is an emblem of Wright's own project. The example of Joyce was perhaps even more powerful; his works—Irish without Money—were themselves ghetto pastorals, conjuring enchantments—the celebrated "epiphanies"—out of the gutters of Dublin.[19]

For the plebeian writers, modernism meant two things: on the one hand, a way to use a vernacular that was not an "ethnic" dialect, always already a minstrel exercise in misspelling, broken grammar, and comic solecisms; on the other hand, a freedom from plot, a way to avoid the well-crafted intrigues and counterplotting of the novel proper. The most striking aspect of the ghetto pastorals is their lack of unifying narrative, their sketchiness. The writers found it difficult to imagine a narrative, to find a story to tell. In some cases, this led them to adopt the crime stories of the popular thriller, to lay a melodramatic plot over the sketches of everyday life. But for the most part the writers of the ghetto pastorals were left conjuring fiction out of worlds without narrative.

2. "Symphony of Struggle"

The first task of an interpreter of these representations of urban neighbor-hoods is to understand the roots of the form's resistance to narrative. This resistance derives from the nature of the depression itself, from the history and structure of the immigrant communities, and from the imagination of revolution. The depression resisted narrative representation quite power-fully. It was a curious crisis, marked not by upheaval, civil war, or coups d'état, but by an absence: the absence of work. The very term "depression" was a euphemism, coined to avoid the connotations of the earlier "panic." Throughout the years of deepest economic hardship, the paradoxes of overaccumulation were starkly part of popular consciousness: idle factories and unemployed workers, hungry farmworkers and rotting, unpicked crops. Many of the earliest metaphors were ones of inexplicable psychic disorder: "depression," the American "jitters," or the "slump," the baseball term for a good player's unexplained dry spell. These were soon joined by tropes of natural disaster: plagues of locusts, an earthquake, a flood, a dust bowl.[20]

Moreover, the quintessential depression stories were stories of downward mobility, of stockbrokers leaping to their deaths: it was a crash, the comeuppance of the established classes; and its great satiric emblem was the dismembering of Lemuel Pitkin in Nathanael West's inverted Horatio Alger tale, *A Cool Million*. But for working-class black and ethnic Americans, the depression was summed up in the common joke Billie Holiday tells: "By the time Mom and I had got together and found us a place of our own in Harlem the depression was on. At least, so we heard tell. A depression was nothing new to us, we'd always had it." Thus, if the ghetto pastoral came to serve as an allegory of the depression, it did so not by narrating a historical event, a particular crisis in the world economy, but by figuring an imaginative space, a place of poverty and lack, a place where the wish fulfillments of fiction were closely censored, and the economy of desire was regulated by the rule of an absent signifier, the dollar.[21]

But if the ghetto served as an allegorical landscape of poverty and desire, the daily life, social structure, and history of the immigrant ghetto presented several imaginative difficulties for the writer. Were there *stories* in the monotonous routines of work, in the childhoods without futures, in the bleak sweatshops and tenements? Work itself resists representation; and the labor to render the repetitive manual tasks of shop and home can prove as boring as the tasks themselves, not because of the writer's failure but because of the reader's resistance. Stories, after all, come from travels, adventures, romances, holidays, events: interruptions of the daily grind. The strike novel used the interruption of work, a festival of the oppressed, as a solution, but the ghetto pastoral was more often a memorial to daily labor: limning the rituals of a craft or wearying pure toil.

The representation of a craft dominates the novels of stonecutting and bricklaying by Mari Tomasi and Pietro di Donato. "Dabbing mortar on the head of another brick," the narrator of *Christ in Concrete* writes, "he laid it down and pressed it up against the end of the first brick and tapped it down into the soft mortar with the brick-cutting edge of the trowel until it seemed level with the first brick; and then did the same with four more bricks one after the other before the bed of mortar had dried. Bending low and running his left eye along the top outer edge, he tapped the bricks into line. O God you have heard me—*I have laid brick!*" In the course of the novel, work becomes a character, as "Job" is continually invoked, always capitalized and without an article: "This is the fresh stink of Job, this is the eight-houred daily duel, this is the sense of red and gray, and our bodies are no longer meat and bone of our parents, but substance of Job."[22]

Ironing, on the other hand, often signifies relentless, repetitive toil. "Aren't you ever going to finish the ironing, Mother?" the daughter asks in Tillie Olsen's "I Stand Here Ironing." "Whistler painted his mother in a rocker. I'd have to paint mine standing over an ironing board." The same image occurs in Conroy's *The Disinherited*: "Long after Madge and I were abed I could hear the monotonous rhythm of the irons sliding back and forth across the scorched and padded board . . . I stole to the middle door and watched her standing with arm moving as inexorably as a piston." Olsen's story is a monologue of a woman ironing; the same form is found in Marita Bonner's Frye Street stories, one of which opens "Yas'm! I'll jes' iron out these heah damp things and leave the rest 'til tomorrer!" In both cases, stories emerge as the "idle" thoughts of the woman ironing.[23]

If the representation of work presents dilemmas, the representation of the neighborhood is no less difficult: Is it a microcosm of the social totality or is it merely a backwater, apart from "real" life, "real" history? What are its boundaries? What lies beyond its boundaries? What kind of story can link the Lower East Side, Chinatown, or Bronzeville with "America"? What is "America" itself? Daniel Fuchs's *Summer in Williamsburg* begins with an attempt to explain the suicide of Meyer Sussman, the butcher, by making a "dictionary of Williamsburg." By its end, the narrator admits defeat:

> Take Ripple Street with Halper's Stables, Yozowitz's laundry, the Auburn S.C., the life on the roofs, in the cellars, and in lots, Davey and his gang, . . . together with the hundreds of other persons who lived in the tenements on the block; take Ripple Street with the merry-go-rounds in the sunshine, the Italians coming down the street with cheap ice-cream bricks in small carts; take the whole of Ripple Street from morning to night and back again; take it and reproduce it faithfully and you would have a great formless mass of petty incident, the stale product of people who were concerned completely with the tremendous job of making a living so that tomorrow they would be able to make a living another day.

Though some of the books are "a great formless mass of petty incident," all are dictionaries of the ghetto. Some, like Farrell's Studs Lonigan trilogy and Brooks's *Maud Martha*, rely on carefully documented geographical particulars, with the street names of Chicago repeated as if magical charms; others, like di Donato's *Christ in Concrete*, abandon the junk of urban realism for the stark allegory of "Job" and "Tenement":

> Tenement was a twelve-family house. There were two families on each floor with the flats running in box-car fashion from front to rear and with one toilet

between them. Each flat had its distinctive powerful odor. There was the particular individual bouquet that aroused a repulsion followed by sympathetic human kinship; the great organ of Tenement fuguing forth its rhapsody with pounding identification to each sense.

Children are the novels' chorus, watching incidents and accidents, insulting the neighborhood characters, and playing their own games, mock versions of the adult world of work and sex.[24]

The cityscape of the ghetto pastoral is mapped by an intricate geography of ethnicity and race. In a few of them, the main divide lies between the ethnic community and the "Americans," white and Anglo-Saxon. Mari Tomasi's *Like Lesser Gods*, like many of Anzia Yezierska's stories, turns on an ethnic/Anglo romance, ending with a cross-class marriage between the stone cutter's daughter, Petra Dalli, and the quarry owner's son, Denny Douglas. But Petra does not become a Yankee; rather, the quarry owner's son, a sculptor whose hands are crushed in symbolic retribution for the granite dust that kills the stone cutter, becomes a Catholic. In most, however, the "Americans" are absent. There is only one in Gold's *Jews without Money*: "Negroes, Chinese, Gypsies, Turks, Germans, Irish, Jews— and there was even an American on our street. She was Mary Sugar Bum ... an old vagabond woman who sometimes worked as a scrub-woman" but spent most of her days "violently drunk and disorderly." In these books, the neighborhood is a scene of shifting hostilities and alliances among ethnic communities. "Walking along Frye Street," the narrator of Marita Bonner's never-completed *Black Map* tells us,

> you sniff first the rusty tangy odor that comes from a river too near a city; walk aside so that Jewish babies will not trip you up; you pause to flatten your nose against discreet windows of Chinese merchants; marvel at the beauty and tragic old age in the faces of young Italian women; puzzle whether the muscular blond people are Swedes or Danes or both; pronounce odd consonant names in Greek characters on shops; wonder whether Russians are Jews, or Jews, Russians—and finally you will wonder how the Negroes there manage to look like all men of every other race and then have something left over for their own distinctive black-browns.

Gangs of children mark out the ever-changing lines between ethnic communities with skirmishes and curses. However, cross-ethnic tricksters abound: Gold has a Negro Jew and a Jew named Nigger; and Tsiang's Pearl Chang is the southern-born daughter of a Chinese man and an African American woman.[25]

Despite the intricacy of the neighborhood's internal boundaries, few of the ghetto pastorals take their characters out of the neighborhood, except for brief moments of pastoral bliss—the mushroom-hunting trip to Bronx

Park in *Jews without Money*—or sheer terror—the moment when the child in *Call It Sleep*, David Schearl, gets lost following the telegraph poles out of his neighborhood. The only name he has for his own street is his mother's "Boddeh Stritt," which no one understands. The one novel constructed around the crossing of the border is Richard Wright's *Native Son*. For Bigger Thomas, leaving the South Side to take a job as a chauffeur inexorably leads to the killing of Mary Dalton. Bigger flees back into the snow-bound South Side, and follows the house-to-house search for him in the newspaper's "black-and-white" maps: "the shaded area had deepened from both the north and south, leaving a small square of white in the middle of the oblong Black Belt." Ironically, the brutal failure of Bigger Thomas's crossing into the white world made Wright's melodramatic confrontation of the two worlds a "cross-over" success, the most widely read ghetto pastoral. For the most part, there is little crossing in the ghetto pastoral, and they remain "regional" novels.[26]

The geographical boundaries of the community are reinforced by historical boundaries; the ghetto pastoral continually runs up against a historical block. What is the history of these relatively recent communities, formed by migrations, cut off from any past that inhabits the streets, buildings, and even words? The history of the Lower East Side is a "geology," Michael Gold writes, as "each group left its deposits." The back yard of the tenement was once a grave yard: "Some of the old American headstones had been used to pave our Jewish yard. The inscriptions were dated a hundred years ago. But we had read them all, we were tired of weaving romances around these ruins of America." The ghetto pastorals form a sharp counterpoint to Josephine Herbst's Trexler trilogy. Though Herbst shared the Popular Front politics of the young proletarians, writing reportage for the *New Masses*, she did not share their forms and aesthetics: it is no accident that Herbst resisted the label "proletarian writer." Unlike James Farrell's Studs Lonigan trilogy or John Fante's Arturo Bandini trilogy, both of which focus on a single generation, Herbst's trilogy arches across the history of the Lincoln republic, taking the Trexler family from the occupied Confederacy of Reconstruction to the auto plants of the sit-down strikes. Herbst does this by reconstructing the narrative immanent in her own family's papers; her novels directly incorporate the diaries and letters that had been handed down through generations. The ghetto novels, on the other hand, are intense family romances of immigrant parents and American-born children; they rarely have grandparents, except as icons of an unknown old world.[27]

There were exceptions. *Out of This Furnace* (1941) by Thomas Bell (born Adalbert Thomas Belejcak in 1903) is one of the few multi-generational novels of an ethnic working-class community. It begins in 1881 and tells the story of three generations of Slovak steelworkers in Braddock,

Pennsylvania, ending with the victory of the CIO's Steel Workers Organizing Committee in 1937. "As a small boy I could not understand why I
should be ashamed of the fact that I was Slovak," Bell told an interviewer
in 1946. "I made up my mind to write a history of the Braddock Slovaks in
order to tell the world that the Slovaks with their blood and lives helped to
build America." On the other hand, Howard Fast, whose 1937 novella, *The
Children*, was an exemplary ghetto pastoral, turned to "weaving romances
around" the "ruins of America," writing best-selling Popular Front historical novels: *Citizen Tom Paine, Freedom Road*, and *The American*. In the 1970s,
Fast united the two traditions in his multi-generational immigrant saga,
The Immigrants, Second Generation, The Establishment, and *The Legacy*. However, few of the writers of the ghetto pastoral imagined a historical tale;
the past remained another story, a foreign place.[28]

Moreover, if the world beyond the ghetto remained a shadowy land and
the past someone else's history, the future was also an enigma, despite the
revolutionary commitments of the authors. To imagine a transformation
of the ghetto, a magical renewal and refiguration, remained the abiding
quest and failure of these writers. The ghetto pastorals are stories of
children, but they are not, for the most part, stories of growing up. Their
children have no future. Indeed, unlike the radical writers of the late
nineteenth century and the New Left writers of the 1960s, the plebeian
writers of the depression rarely wrote utopian fiction. In part, this was a
result of the powerful prolepsis of the Soviet Revolution: utopian narratives
seemed idle in the face of the actual experiment in social reconstruction
on the Eurasian continent. However, this cut both ways: part of the reason
for the utopian hopes invested in the Soviet Union was the stark reality-
principle of the depression and the inability to imagine a cooperative
commonwealth in Fordist North America.

So the problem of endings haunts all these books. Daniel Fuchs's *Summer
in Williamsburg* seems to conclude with a tenement fire, but it comes to
nothing: "In a book, Philip said, a fire could be an important event, it
could be used to bind together a setting and a story, it offered a neat end.
But actually there was no climax, no end. It went on." At the end of Fuchs's
farcical tale of a gangster's funeral, *Homage to Blenholt*, Colblenz jokes that
Communism is "a new happy ending": the book's actual happy ending is
the result of a racing bet paying off. Some writers did attempt to make
Communism a happy ending, juxtaposing a ghetto childhood and a
communist vocation. This produced the one critical controversy that has
followed proletarian fiction from the beginning: the "problem" of the
"conversion" ending. The scandalous final page of Mike Gold's *Jews without
Money* remains the epitome of this "problem": young Mikey hears a soapbox
orator and makes an entirely unmotivated profession of faith: "O worker's
Revolution, you brought hope to me, a lonely, suicidal boy. You are the

true Messiah. You will destroy the East Side when you come, and build there a garden for the human spirit." If one reads the novel as a work of psychological realism, a novel of education, the conversion of Mikey seems unlikely, a flaw of craft and aesthetic.[29]

But the ghetto pastoral is not a realist genre; or, rather, its realism is the pressure of a reality-principle so unrelenting as to mock the conventions of "realism." Kenneth Burke, who suggested that art forms are *strategies* for dealing with *situations*, defined realism as the successful balancing of strategies and situations: works are unrealistic if they overestimate the power of the strategy and thus make "solace cheap"—as in self-help books, which are a species of simple wish-fulfillment—or if they overestimate the situation, making it so bleak as to evade any strategy—as in the case of naturalism. Burke thought much of proletarian literature erred in both ways, constructing situations so grim that only transparent wish fulfill-ments—the final conversion—could overcome them. However, realism as a social convention *and* as this sense of the appropriate relation between strategy and situation is tied historically to social power: a group must have a sense of agency in order to imagine realistic narratives about itself. The powerless, on the other hand, have characteristically chosen allegory—the world of magic spells and enchanted places. The ghetto pastoral with its magical children in enchanted neighborhoods is thus less a form of realism than a species of allegory.[30]

As I suggested above, this allegorical structure lies at the heart of Gold's *Jews without Money*; its ending is a fulfillment of a promise, not a product of education. A similar logic structures Tillie Olsen's *Yonnondio*, which is, despite its incomplete nature, perhaps the most powerful of these novels. Olsen originally imagined the novel as a realistic narrative in which the children grow up and become writers, jazz musicians, and Communist organizers. But the novel she wrote revolves around the difficulty of reconciling desire and reality: her verbless sentences are a refusal of narrative on the microlevel. No happy ending can be imagined that would remain true to what Olsen called in her journals the "horror of being a working-class child." The redemption in the novel comes not from the logic of realistic narrative but from the allegorical logics of her proletarian grotesque: that of the microcosm and that of the figure. The logic of the microcosm sees the world as the human body writ large: the mine is the "bowels"; Coal, an "artist"; the packing house, a "gigantic heart." If Dos Passos turned his people into machines, Olsen turns her mines and mills into humans. The logic of the figure, on the other hand, unites past, present, and future in a single moment, as when the packing-house heat—"in a dozen dialects, is it hot enough, hot enough, hot enough for you?"—culminates in the explosion of a steam pipe. The scalding fog, an echo of the earlier "mine blowup," is an emblem and a promise of an as-yet unimagined explosion "with the fists of strike, with the pickax of revolution." In the meantime, one only hopes for relief: "I see for it to end tomorrow," Anna says in the final line of the novel, "at least get tolerable."[31]

The repression of any world outside the working-class community, whether in time or space, produces the remarkable sense of claustrophobia in these books; there is no escaping this constricted and impoverished world. But it also produces the characteristic intensification of that world through magical namings and renamings, as the ghetto becomes a landscape of sacred and profane words, places, and rituals. Pietro di Donato's *Christ in Concrete* is largely made up of broken, incomplete sentences: prayers, chants, curses, epithets, conversations between unidentified speakers, people talking past one another. However, his heightened rhetoric, his "g-grand eloquence," sacralizes the "symphony of struggle" that is ordinary life and work, putting "carpenter Christ," "comrade-worker Christ" in concrete.

Thus, the two critical categories most often used in debates over these novels—naturalism and pastoralism—are best seen as the twin temptations of the ghetto tale, the fundamental generic antinomy facing the plebeian writers. Accusations of naturalism emerged at the time from a number of critics, who drew on V.L. Parrington's influential formulation: naturalism was "pessimistic realism, with a philosophy that sets man in a mechanical world and conceives of him as victimized by that world." Though Parrington was a defender of naturalism, critics used his characterization—objectivist, determinist, and amoral—to damn the ghetto novelists for their "brutalism." For Harold Strauss, "the photographic realism of the proletarian novelists is a specialized development of naturalism, its *reductio ad absurdum* ... [T]heir central characters ... are mainly impulsive recipients of sensory impressions; they are creatures of their environment, more acted upon than acting." Alfred Kazin argued that "the basic character" of the new social novels lay in their "abject surrender to naturalism." Kazin's chapter, "The Revival of Naturalism," in *On Native Grounds* (1942) was a sustained attack on the "cheapness" and "vulgarity" of the "fellowship of proletarian naturalism": their "cult of violence," their "calculated brutality," and their "contempt for style"; and his account came to dominate literary interpretation for a generation.[32]

However, at the same time, William Empson suggested that proletarian literature was a version of the pastoral. In the opening chapter of his 1935 *Some Versions of Pastoral*, "Proletarian Literature," Empson argued that "good proletarian art" shared the central "trick of the old pastoral," which "was to make simple people express strong feelings in learned and fashionable language." Echoing Christian storytelling, which put God in the form of a shepherd, the communist writers created a mythical cult-figure, the Worker as sacrificial hero. This "realistic sort of pastoral ...

gives a natural expression for a sense of social injustice." "My own difficulty about proletarian literature," Empson concluded, "is that when it comes off I find that I am taking it as pastoral literature; I read into it, or find that the author has secretly put into it, these more subtle, far-reaching, and I think more permanent ideas." Empson's argument is, like many of the early contributions to the proletarian-literature debates, based more on an imagined literature—"the popular, vague but somehow obvious idea of proletarian literature"—than on the analysis of particular works. Moreover, few American critics even noted Empson's contribution at the time. Nevertheless, Empson's sense of the pastoral element in proletarian writing is an important counterweight to the "naturalist" interpretations of these harrowing yet mythic tales of mining camps and urban slums.[33]

The worlds of adult sexuality, violence, and work hover on the edges of all of these narratives, generating these contrary temptations: the mock-heroic pastoral that replays Tom Sawyer's Hannibal in the ethnic neighbor-hoods of the modern metropolis; and the naturalist brutalism that turns the innocent games of childhood into adolescent gang rapes and street crime. One could, indeed, arrange the ghetto pastorals along a spectrum from pastoralism to naturalism, from the sentimental human comedy of William Saroyan to the visions of hell in Nelson Algren. The schlemiels in Fuchs, Mori's vignettes of the flower shop and Seventh Street, the comic absurdity of the elder Bandini's affair in Fante's *Wait Until Spring, Bandini*, and Tomasi's account of the pastoral duties of the Italian schoolteacher Mr Tiff tend toward the pastoral; the tragic deaths in di Donato, the terror of the mines and cellars in Olsen and Roth, and the rapes and gang rapes in Farrell, Algren, and Wright lean toward the naturalist.

For the ghetto pastoral was neither entirely the "abject surrender to naturalism" that Kazin deplored nor the "covert pastoral" that Empson detected. It was a curious synthesis of the two, as I have tried to suggest with my name for the genre: the yoking of the slum and the shepherd, the gangster and Christ in concrete. Perhaps it is better to say that the ghetto pastoral is the attempt to *avoid* both naturalism and the pastoral, to write out from under the literary lineages that dominated narratives of the "people." For naturalism was a strategy of degradation and debasement, a lowering, a debunking, as Burke put it: as Parrington noted, the naturalist's "low-grade characters" were always in danger of becoming grotesques. Pastoralism, on the other hand, was a strategy of elevating and ennobling the simple. The ghetto pastorals were always caught in this dialectic of degradation and elevation, the grotesque and the simple.

Perhaps the most powerful expression of this dialectic is found in the work of Richard Wright. For Kazin, Wright was an exemplary instance of proletarian brutalism: "If he chose to write the story of Bigger Thomas as a grotesque crime story, it is because his own indignation and the sickness of the age combined to make him dependent on violence and shock, to astonish the reader by torrential scenes of cruelty, hunger, rape, murder and flight and then enlighten him by crude Stalinist homilies." Wright's Chicago novels—*Native Son, Lawd Today,* and *The Outsider*—certainly are, like those of Farrell, Algren, and Himes, acts of literary violence, assaults on their readers. However, it is worth recalling Wright's own account of the violence of *Native Son.* In his "How Bigger Was Born," Wright tells of the reaction to his 1938 collection of stories, *Uncle Tom's Children*: "When the reviews of that book began to appear, I realized that I had made an awfully naïve mistake. I found that I had written a book which even bankers' daughters could read and weep over and feel good about. I swore to myself that if I ever wrote another book, no one would weep over it; that it would be so hard and deep that they would have to face it without the consolation of tears." If *Uncle Tom's Children* had veered toward pastoral elevation with its rural settings, its flood stories, and its innocent Christ-like Big Boys and Johnny-Boys, *Native Son* embraced naturalism's degradation and debasement.[34]

Wright's *Lawd Today*, the story of a day in the life of a young Chicago postal worker, Jake Jackson, embodies this tension. At first glance, it seems to deserve the working title Wright had given it, *Cesspool*: a bleak depiction of a life of violence, ending with the wind "whining and moaning like an idiot in a deep black pit." This is the side the critic Arnold Rampersad has emphasized: the characters are "creatures dominated by lust, avarice, sloth, superstition and a fatal weakness for violence" and have "no potential for redemption." This interpretation is buttressed by Jake's violence against Lil, by the crude sexual economy of the novel's world, and by the pronounced animal imagery associated with the characters—one section is entitled "Squirrel Cage," another "Rats' Alley." In a way, *Lawd Today* is far bleaker than the novels of Nelson Algren because Wright's characters are not skid-row junkies and prostitutes but the rank and file of the working poor. Rampersad even suggests that "the main factor that prevents *Lawd Today* from being thoroughly nihilistic ... is the superior quality of life among whites," though I see little evidence of this.[35]

Nevertheless, the novel's title was not *Cesspool* but *Lawd Today*, a popular expression that Wright's contemporary Margaret Walker translated as "what a mess": an exclamation of wonder, community, agreement, hope, and hopelessness. *Lawd Today* is an exploration of the dreams and yearnings of the migrants to Chicago's Bronzeville, of the unformed sense of a promise never kept, for "Chicago seemed like the Promised Land." Each of the book's three sections begins with an ill-defined sense of hope: "*Now what was I dreaming?* ... [H]e had been thirsting, longing for something"; "Deep in him was a dumb yearning for something else ... All he could see ... was an endless stretch of black postal days"; "Each felt something was lacking, and that lack hungered over and above ordinary hunger." At one point, Jake thinks "*It ain't always going to be this way!*" But "his mind went abruptly blank . . . he did not know where that thought led." *Lawd Today*—this day in the life—is an inventory of the ways that it will be someday: from the parade of the Garveyites to the religious visions of Lil's *Unity* and Father Divine; from the attempts to interpret dreams and win at the numbers to the hopes of Duke, the Red. Jake even daydreams "an imagined epic" of black armies and a black empire. None of these visions works for Jake, whose dreams only foretell frustration—steps and more steps. Jake is even frustrated in his attempts to recapture his dreams of frustration; they haunt him on the edge of consciousness. The only emblem of this unimaginable utopia is music, the music of the Garveyites' parade—"They did not agree with the parade, but they did agree with the music"—and that of the "threepiece jazz band," whose "music caroled its promise of an unattainable satisfaction."[36]

Like other modernists, Wright was fascinated with representing dreams, streams of consciousness, and interior monologues, the various attempts to bend language to the rhythms of the mind. However, compared to his modernist counterparts, it is not Wright's pessimism that is most striking but his promise of community. Whereas many modernists retreated to the private languages of an isolated self, Wright moves from consciousness to conversation in one of the most powerful virtuoso passages in the novel: the stream of signifying in the post office. A twenty-five page conversation between postal workers in which the speakers are unidentified, it combines the call and response of a church service with the dozens of the street in a carefully constructed passage that modulates from sleep to dreams to ghosts and heaven and hell, from blacks and whites to baseball and boxing, from the 1919 race riot to the memory of the first time in the North, from memories of the South and a lynching to stories of sex and women. It is Wright's depiction of common feelings, common knowledge, the "commonplace," a word he uses as the title of the novel's first part.[37]

It is true that the novel's ending drags us back to the here and now, to the violence that, as James Baldwin once said, occupies the place of love in Wright's imagination. In part, this is because Wright was a Gothicist, haunted by ghost stories, horror tales, and sensational murders; in part, it is because Wright wanted to avoid what he called, in a famous *New Masses* review of Zora Neale Hurston's *Their Eyes Were Watching God*, "that safe and narrow orbit in which America likes to see the Negro live between laughter and tears." The novels of Wright and those of his friends and contemporaries, Farrell and Algren, are therefore less clinical studies of the slum—literary equivalents of the Chicago sociology all of them were steeped in—than proletarian tales of terror. All of them used the rise of fascism as an authorial "alibi"; when they addressed the readers of the

Book-of-the-Month Club, they claimed that Bigger Thomas, Studs Lonigan, and Bruno Bicek were figures of an American fascism. The power of these novels, however, derived from the fear they expressed: *not* the fear of a grotesque Other, but the fear of the rages, hungers, and desires of the all-too-familiar self. This is why Farrell protests against the sociological reading of his novels: "Had I written *Studs Lonigan* as a story of the slums, it would then have been easy for the reader falsely to place the motivation and causation of the story directly in immediate economic roots." His desire was, however, "to reveal the concrete effects of spiritual poverty."[38]

3. The Lure of the Gangster

The figure that embodies this spiritual poverty is the gangster, a character that lurks on the edge of virtually all the ghetto pastorals. Although Edward Dahlberg titled his review of Farrell's *The Young Manhood of Studs Lonigan* "Portrait of the Gangster," the ghetto pastorals are not usually gangster stories. The gangster story was the province of the pulps and the movies. The pulp magazines were full of gangster stories; by the early 1930s, there were entire magazines devoted to *Gangster Stories, Racketeer Stories,* and *Gangland Detective Stories.* "In 1929," film historian Robert Sklar notes, "the gangster for the first time surpassed the cowboy as a subject for Hollywood filmmakers." Though the early film gangsters were aristocratic and Anglo-Saxon—polished capitalists organizing the bootlegging industry—the classic gangster emerged with Edward G. Robinson in *Little Caesar* (1931), James Cagney in *The Public Enemy* (1931), and Paul Muni and George Raft in *Scarface* (1932), creating the first "ethnic" hero in American popular culture. The gangster films capitalized on the talkie's ability to capture not only machine guns, screeching brakes, and squealing tires, but ethnic speech and accents. Moreover, the fictions of bootleg liquor proved powerful in American culture because they united Anglo and ethnic communities in a single narrative: the ethnic gangsters distributed the alcohol that was drunk by the smart set, linking Meyer Wolfsheim and Nick Carraway.[39]

The writers of the ghetto pastorals were well aware of the pulp and movie gangsters: the "gangster pictures with Georgie Raft" and James Cagney turn up in Daniel Fuchs's *Summer in Williamsburg.* But their own gangsters were generally off-stage, foils and temptations for the young protagonists. In Tsiang's *And China Has Hands,* the racketeer who tries to shake down Wong Wan-Lee for protection fails because "he could scare plenty of white laundry-men but not Wong Wan-Lee, because he had seldom been in an American movie house." Wong's ignorance of movie gangsters doesn't help, however; the gangster returns to hold up the laundry. In Gold's *Jews without Money,* the leader of Mikey's "gang of little

Yids," Nigger, grows up to be a gangster: "it is America that has taught the sons of tubercular Jewish tailors to kill." However, the novel's only "gangster story" is the tale of Nigger and his gang slaughtering the pigeons of the gangster Louie One Eye, to avenge Louie's attempted rape of Mikey's Aunt Lena and his prostitution of Nigger's sister Lily. Gold avoids directly confronting the gangster—and thereby tends toward the pastoral rather than toward naturalism—by choosing to narrate Mikey's childhood rather than his adolescence. The adolescent Mikey is summed up in a rush on the final page: "Sex began to torture me ... At the age of fifteen I began drinking and whoring with Nigger's crowd ... I don't want to remember it all; the years of my adolescence." His book ends where *Studs Lonigan* begins.[40]

In Fuchs's novels, the protagonists are caught between the examples of their fathers and those of the gangsters: in *Summer in Williamsburg*, Philip's father runs a newspaper concession in a skyscraper but, despite fifty years in the country, he "does not understand America"; Philip's uncle Papravel is a gangster involved in a war between bus companies over the Williamsburg-Catskills route. Papravel understands America, and the novel ends with his ode to America: "America is a wonderful country ... [L]ook how I worked myself up in four short years ... where in the world could a Jew make such a man of himself as right here in America." *Homage to Blenholt* repeats the tale as farce: Max Balkan's father is a Yiddish theater actor reduced to carrying sandwich boards advertising Madame Clara's Scientific Beauty Treatments; and the gangster Blenholt built his reputation as Com- missioner of Sewers. Here, however, the father gets the last word: as he sees his son change from "youth to resigned age, ... it seemed to the old man that this death of youth was among the greatest tragedies in experi- ence and that all the tears in America were not enough to bewail it."[41]

If becoming a gangster was a temptation for the heroes of the ghetto pastoral, the gangster novel or screenplay was a temptation for the writers. Fuchs's third novel, *Low Company*, was a gangster story, but it was not a ghetto pastoral. It takes place not in the tenements of Williamsburg, but in a soda parlor in Neptune Beach. Neptune Beach is a place of amusement and desire, and the novel follows its waitresses, soda jerks, and horse players from cathouses and burlesque shows to movie theaters and race- tracks. There are no children in the novel and no neighborhood. The gangsters are the other side of a world "concentrated wholly on desire and the process of its satisfaction, abject and mean." Its emblem is the gleaming new ice-cream machine that is destroyed by the syndicate as they move in. *Low Company* is a tightly constructed thriller, with beatings and killings: it is more like Horace McCoy's dance-marathon novel, *They Shoot Horses, Don't They?* or Nathanael West's Hollywood novel, *The Day of the Locust*, than *Jews without Money*. Fuchs, McCoy, and West—each of whom became part of the Hollywood Popular Front—were the poet laureates of the culture industry's "extras," and their novels stand as bleak allegories of the great American amusement park, the world of capitalist pleasure.[42]

Indeed, for many writers, the lure of the gangster was the lure of the culture industry itself. After all, several of the early gangster writers, including John Bright, who co-wrote *The Public Enemy*, Francis Faragoh, who co-wrote *Little Caesar* (having worked with Gold and Dos Passos in the New Playwrights' Theatre), and Dashiell Hammett, became active left-wing figures on the cultural front. Though Hammett's work had been written in the decade between 1923 and 1934, it was regularly reprinted and read throughout the Popular Front years; his stories and characters became films and radio serials, and in large part established the hard-boiled aesthetic of the Popular Front. Hammett's *Red Harvest* (1929) was itself a displaced proletarian novel. The Op first appears as a Wobbly, "Henry F. Neill, A.B. seaman, member in good standing of the Industrial Workers of the World." "There wasn't a word of truth in it," he tells us, but the novel's gangster tale has its roots in a strike story: the mine-owner Elihu Willsson defeated the Wobbly strike by bringing in the gangsters who now control "Poisonville," "the ugly city ... set in an ugly notch between two ugly mountains."[43]

The novel that follows begins as a parody of the classic detective story. The murder of Donald Willsson, complete with suspects, clues, and red herrings, is solved a third of the way into the book; but this private act of passion is itself displaced by the gang war the Op provokes. Most of the novel's gangsters are local politicians; the ones with an economic base are Elihu, the legitimate capitalist who owns the mines, the banks, and the newspapers; Reno Starkey, who owns the out-of-town casino; and Pete the Finn, the defiantly ethnic bootlegger whose gang is made up of "swarthy foreign looking men." The book's red harvest is the blood bath that results; but Hammett's obsessive color allegories suggest that the title not only memorializes the defeated Wobblies but promises a Red harvest.

Certainly, the Red writers who followed Hammett saw the gangster tale as a link between the ghetto and the national and international tales of racketeers and fascist thugs. Benjamin Appel inverted the ghetto pastoral by using the Hell's Kitchen in which he had grown up as a background to the story of a respectable, college-educated gangster, Bill Trent, in *Brain Guy*. In subsequent novels, Appel followed Trent from the numbers into strikebreaking—*The Power-House*—and fascism—*The Dark Stain*. More powerful versions of this synthesis of the ghetto and the gangster included Ira Wolfert's *Tucker's People* (1943), a story of the numbers racket in Harlem, which was the basis for Abraham Polonsky's classic film *Force of Evil*, and Thomas McGrath's *This Coffin Has No Handles*, a waterfront novel written in 1947 but not published until 1988. McGrath's novel of a longshoremen's strike combines Joycean experiments in cross-cutting time and consciousness with a Hammett-like tale of fist fights and beatings. The plot eventually dissolves into a world of doubles and mistaken identities: the hired gun Crips kills the young Communist Everson, thinking he's the gangster Blackie, while the goons smash Blackie's knees, mistaking him for Everson. McGrath's novel appropriates the gangster but is hardly a popular thriller.

By the 1940s, a number of writers connected to the proletarian-literature movement had turned to detective and mystery fiction, including Kenneth Fearing, Edwin Rolfe, William Rollins, Bernice Carey, Mike Quin (under the pseudonym Robert Finnegan), Dorothy Hughes, and Rudolf Kagey (under the pseudonym Kurt Steel). And a number of the writers of ghetto pastorals had gone to work in Hollywood, including John Fante, Daniel Fuchs, and Jo Pagano. For others, like James T. Farrell, this turn to the thriller and to Hollywood was a capitulation to what Farrell called "movietone realism," epitomized by the novels of James M. Cain and the Warner Brothers films of Jerry Wald. This "pseudorealistic type of novel and movie" replaced "the pitiless force of circumstance and the equally pitiless drive of human emotions" which cause "the tragic destruction of human beings" in "serious realism" with "the fortuitousness of automobile accidents" and "a melodramatically simplified conception of good girls and bad girls." It was part of the culture of "glamour" and "thrills" that he despised.[44]

Indeed, it is true that only one of the writers, Chester Himes, really succeeded in extending Hammett's proletarian thriller. Himes wrote two powerful thrillers of black workers in Los Angeles's shipyards and aircraft plants, *If He Hollers Let Him Go* (1945) and *Lonely Crusade* (1947), and then embarked on his series of "Harlem domestic novels" featuring two black cops, Coffin Ed Smith and Grave Digger Jones. But the union of the ghetto and the gangster proved to be central to the laboring of American popular culture. One can see this in two classic Hollywood productions—both featuring Marlon Brando—that mark the Popular Front's end and its lasting impact. Both grew out of the congressional hearings that epitomized the powerful reaction against the laboring of American culture and the new visibility of ethnic working-class Americans: the HUAC investigations into Communism, and the Kefauver hearings on organized crime and the Mafia. At the time, in 1954, the Elia Kazan/Budd Schulberg *On the Waterfront* was read as a quintessential "informer" narrative, a justification of Kazan's own "naming names" in front of HUAC. In retrospect, however, its synthesis of the docks, the waterfront neighborhood, and the gangsters marks it as the culmination of the ghetto pastorals and proletarian thrillers, a combination of the proletarian avant-garde of Kazan and the Hollywood Popular Front of Schulberg. Two decades later, Francis Coppola and Mario

Puzo, who had himself written a classic ghetto pastoral, *The Fortunate Pilgrim* (1964), combined the ghetto story with the mythic history of the Mafia that had emerged from the Kefauver hearings, and turned a genre that had always resisted narrative, history, and America into a powerful historical film, *The Godfather* (1972). The ghetto pastoral of the Popular Front had become the American tale.[45]

7

Grapes of Wrath: "The Art and Science of Migratin'"

I looked into the lost and hungry faces of several hundred thousand Oakies, Arkies, Texies, Mexies, Chinees, Japees, Dixies, and even a lot of New Yorkies ... and I got so interested in the art and science of Migratin' that I majored in it—in a school so big you can't even get out of it.

Woody Guthrie[1]

If the ghetto pastorals of the Popular Front have been an influential but underground tradition, the best-known Popular Front genre is probably the "grapes of wrath," the narrative of the migrant agricultural workers in California. Indeed, the "Okie exodus," the tale of southwestern farmers traveling out of the drought-ridden Dust Bowl of Oklahoma, Arkansas, Texas, and Missouri to California remains one of the most striking examples of a Popular Front narrative becoming part of American mass culture. It has always been taken as an emblem of depression-era populism, embodying the "documentary impulse" of representing "the people." The story came to national attention with *The Grapes of Wrath*: John Steinbeck's novel was a national best seller in the spring and summer of 1939 and was made into a film by Twentieth Century Fox, opening in January 1940. The tale of the Joad family making their way across the desert to California in their overloaded Hudson is a powerful, sentimental epic: the film ends with Jane Darwell's Ma Joad saying "We're the people." Although it was an emblem of middlebrow kitsch to New York intellectuals like Robert Warshow, and a "sentimental entertainment (hoked up with heavy-handed symbolism)" to the literary critic Leslie Fiedler, it has nevertheless become an enduring novel and film. However, despite its popular success, *The Grapes of Wrath* is not a true exemplar of the cultural politics and aesthetic ideologies of the Popular Front. It was only one part of the artistic and social formation by which the migrant workers in California's factories in the fields were represented *and* came to represent themselves. To understand this "grapes of wrath" formation, we need to reconsider both the cultural politics of the brief moment in 1939 and 1940 when the "documentary" representations of the "Okie exodus" captured the nation's attention and the enduring and less visible attempt of farmworkers to represent themselves politically and aesthetically, a history that can be glimpsed in the picaresque migrant narratives of Woody Guthrie, Carlos Bulosan, and Ernesto Galarza.[2]

1. The Okie Exodus

The roots of *The Grapes of Wrath* lie in the great 1933 strikes of Mexican, Filipino, Chinese, and Japanese farmworkers, led by the Communist organizers of the Cannery and Agricultural Workers Industrial Union. These crop-wide strikes began with the spring pea harvest and continued throughout the summer, culminating in the cotton fields of the San Joaquin Valley; they were the largest strikes in the history of American agriculture and the great majority succeeded in winning wage increases. Because of the remarkable successes of the strikes, the factory-farm owners together with the railroads and the canning companies organized the Associated Farmers, which used vigilante violence, deportation, and anti-picketing laws to imprison the union's leaders and crush the union.[3]

Like the southern textile battles in the Carolina Piedmont, the struggles of black workers in Alabama, and the Appalachian coal-mining struggles in Harlan County, Kentucky, the agricultural battles of California inspired novels and reportage by radical young writers: Mike Quin, James Rorty, Carey McWilliams, and Ella Winter all wrote articles on the strikes; Langston Hughes and Ella Winter collaborated on a never-completed play based on the San Joaquin Valley cotton strike, *Blood on the Fields*; and Arnold Armstrong's *Parched Earth* (1934), Daniel Mainwaring's *The Doctor Died at Dusk* (1936), and John Steinbeck's *In Dubious Battle* (1936) were proletarian novels inspired by the strikes.[4]

But the winter of 1933–34 also saw the beginning of a remarkable migration of 350,000 southwesterners to the California factories in the fields. In the following year, one of the young radicals who had written about Mexican migrant farmworkers and had been part of the state labor board's investigation of the cotton strike, Berkeley economist Paul Taylor, went to investigate the migrant camps for the state relief administration, bringing with him photographer Dorothea Lange. Lange had been a successful commercial photographer in the 1920s, taking portraits for wealthy families. She had thought of herself as a "tradesman" rather than an artist; but she and her business were hit hard by the depression. In the early 1930s, she had begun to photograph breadlines, May Day marches, and the 1934 San Francisco general strike (Figures 3 and 4). photographs of migrant workers in the camps were published with Tayʟoɪ ɔ report in *Survey Graphic* in July 1935, and they began to draw attention to the migrants. One person who saw them was Pare Lorentz, an established liberal film critic (the Edmund Wilson or Gilbert Seldes of film criticism) who had been hired as the motion picture consultant to the New Deal Resettlement Administration. After seeing the Lange-Taylor report, he decided to make a government documentary on the Dust Bowl; and he hired the radical filmmakers of Nykino, Ralph Steiner, Paul Strand, and Leo Hurwitz. Though Lorentz and the Nykino filmmakers became bitterly divided over the film's scenario, the 1936 release of *The Plow Which Broke the Plains* was immediately seen as a landmark in documentary film.[5]

At the same time, the combination of the "farm fascism" of the Associated Farmers, the Resettlement Administration's efforts to build migrant camps, and the renewed strike activity of independent Mexican and Filipino unions (many of which joined the CIO's new United Cannery, Agricultural, Packing and Allied Workers of America [UCAPAWA] in 1937) made California's agricultural valleys one of the centers of Popular Front social struggle. In 1936, Carey McWilliams wrote a series of articles on farm labor for the Popular Front *Pacific Weekly* and Steinbeck wrote a similar series for the *San Francisco News*; the Steinbeck articles were reprinted with Lange's photographs in a 1938 pamphlet, *Their Blood Is Strong*. Moreover, Steinbeck lent his name to a UCAPAWA union solidarity committee, the Steinbeck Committee to Aid Agricultural Organization, chaired by McWilliams. When Culbert Olsen won the 1938 gubernatorial election with the support of the migrant workers and California's Popular Front social movement, he appointed McWilliams head of the Division of Immigration and Housing.[6]

Thus, the simultaneous appearance of *The Grapes of Wrath* and *Factories in the Field*, a powerful history of California farm labor written by Carey McWilliams, in the spring of 1939 was the culmination of a long campaign by the farmworkers for representation—in unions and state government as well as in the stories and pictures of the cultural apparatus. A major cotton strike in the San Joaquin Valley took place in October 1939, and the actors Will Geer, Frances Farmer, and Waldo Salt led a group of artists supporting the strikers; despite the arrests of picketers and vigilante violence, the strikers won wage gains though not union recognition. In the wake of the cotton strike, the La Follette Senate Civil Liberties Committee went to California and held hearings through December and January on the repression of farm labor. The documentary photobook by Dorothea Lange and Paul Taylor, *American Exodus*, appeared in January 1940, as did the Darryl Zanuck film of *The Grapes of Wrath*, which used Lange's photographs as a model. Despite the national support, the migrant farmworkers were defeated. Though the crisis of the white migrants from the southwest was eased as they were recruited into California's expanding defense industries, the La Follette Committee's oppressive labor practices bill failed in Congress, and the CIO agricultural union, UCAPAWA, was crushed in the fields.

However, if the migrant farmworkers failed in their struggle for union representation, the representation of them in film and photographs, story and song, had an extraordinary resonance in American culture. Why did the story of the "Okie exodus" have this mythic power? What made it the emblem of the populisms of the age? Why did it become the story by which Americans narrated the depression? There were, after all, other possibilities; most of the elements of the "grapes of wrath" cultural offensive can be seen in the earlier battles in the Piedmont textile mills, the mines and mills of Alabama, and the Appalachian mines. In each case, the local Communist organizers formed support committees and delegations led by cultural celebrities. These visits of radical writers and artists were the basis for the reportage of the *New Masses* and the *Labor Defender*, as well as for novels, films, photographs, and documentary books. Local songsters wrote picket-line ballads in vernacular idioms, which were published and spread through the radical movement. None of these struggles, however, achieved mythic status, and they offer illuminating contrasts to the "grapes of wrath" formation.

The first focus of radical attention was the Carolina Piedmont. In 1929, thousands of workers had been involved in textile strikes that were met with savage repression and vigilante violence. Perhaps the most famous strike was the one led by a Communist union, the National Textile Workers Union, at the Loray mill in Gastonia, North Carolina. Here one of the strikeleaders, the balladeer Ella May Wiggins, was shot and killed by company thugs. The story and songs of Ella May Wiggins were recounted by radical folklorist Margaret Larkin, and the textile strikes became the focus of several novels: Mary Heaton Vorse's *Strike!* (1930), Myra Page's *Gathering Storm* (1932), Grace Lumpkin's *To Make My Bread* (1932), Fielding Burke's *Call Home the Heart* (1932), and Sherwood Anderson's *Beyond Desire* (1932).[7]

A second cultural offensive focused on the black South. The arrest of the black communist coal-miner Angelo Herndon for violating a slave insurrection law in 1932, the prosecution of the Scottsboro Nine, and the wave of strikes by black miners, steelworkers, and laundry workers in 1934 brought a number of radical artists to Alabama. Langston Hughes traveled to Alabama in 1932, meeting the Scottsboro defendants; he published a poem about Scottsboro and two plays, *Scottsboro, Limited* (1931) and *Angelo Herndon Jones* (1935). Radical journalist John Spivak covered the Scottsboro trial for the International Labor Defense, and his fictional exposé of southern chain gangs, *Georgia Nigger*, was serialized in the *Daily Worker*. In the *New Masses*, playwright John Howard Lawson wrote about the Alabama terror, novelist Josephine Herbst wrote on Scottsboro, and novelist Erskine Caldwell reported on lynchings in Georgia; the *Labor Defender* published Jack Conroy's account of challenging Alabama's anti-insurrection law. Grace Lumpkin's second proletarian novel, *A Sign for Cain*, focused on a black Communist organizer of sharecroppers. The Workers Film and Photo League shot the now-lost film, *Scottsboro*, and the radical folklorist Lawrence Gellert published a series of articles on Negro songs of protest.[8]

The struggles of coal-miners in Harlan and Bell County, Kentucky, was the third great focus of radical attention in the early years of the depression. The Communist-led National Miners' Union had led a strike in early 1931 that was broken after a pitched battle between deputies and miners. A reign of terror followed, and in the fall of 1931 the novelist Theodore Dreiser led a delegation of writers including John Dos Passos to Harlan County; they held public hearings which were published in the documentary book *Harlan Miners Speak*. The NMU's activists included the singers Aunt Molly Jackson, Sarah Ogan Gunning, and Jim Garland, and their labor ballads became a part not only of the Harlan struggle but of the left-wing movement culture as well, when Aunt Molly Jackson came to New York to win support for the union. A second strike began on 1 January 1932, and another writers committee, which included Malcolm Cowley, Waldo Frank, John Hammond, and Edmund Wilson, was driven out of town; Frank subsequently used his trip to Harlan in his novel *The Death and Life of David Markand*.[9]

The connection between labor struggles and cultural representation that was initiated in Gastonia, Birmingham, and Harlan continued throughout the age of the CIO; it did not disappear with the "end" of the proletarian avant-garde and the beginning of the Popular Front. The CIO struggle in the steel towns inspired Marc Blitzstein's opera *The Cradle Will Rock* and Upton Sinclair's novel *Little Steel*. The Memorial Day massacre at Republic Steel in 1937 was the subject of Meyer Levin's novel *Citizens* and Philip Evergood's painting *American Tragedy*; it served as the climax of Frontier Films's great *Native Land*, which is in part a response to the suppression of the newsreel footage of the massacre. Each of these cultural campaigns sought to inform and engage an audience and to memorialize the events as a mythic narrative. Indeed, what is perhaps finally most interesting about the narratives of such events is not the success or failure of the individual novels, plays, or songs, but the success or failure of the event to become a myth, to create enduring icons in popular culture. By this measure, none of these captured the nation the way the "grapes of wrath" story did: Why?

The easiest answer is simply that none of the other struggles inspired works of art with the power of Steinbeck's novel, Zanuck's film, Lange's photographs, Guthrie's songs, and even McWilliams's vivid social history. But this simply begs the question, for the power of these works derives less from their aesthetic craft than from their mythic character. The difference between the mythic resonance of the "grapes of wrath" and that of the tales of Gastonia, Birmingham, Harlan, and the Memorial Day massacre lies in its story of migration and its forms of populist rhetoric.

Perhaps the central difference lay in what Lange and Taylor called the exodus: unlike the local and regional battles of particular groups of workers, the story of the struggles in California's agricultural valleys was built around a mass migration. The ideological crisis of the depression was in part a crisis of narrative, an inability to imagine what had happened and what would happen next. The apocalyptic dreams of revolution of the young communists and their recurring appeals to the Soviet experiment were dramatic instances of the search for a powerful narrative resolution; the stories of martyrdom and tragic defeat in Gastonia, Scottsboro, and Harlan demanded some way out. The way out was migration, and the representation of mass migration became one of the fundamental forms of the Popular Front. Many of the most powerful works of art of the cultural front are migration stories: the portrayals of the Alabama terror become the first act in the grand narratives of African American migration in Jacob Lawrence's *Migration of the Negro*, Langston Hughes's *One-Way Ticket*, Duke Ellington's *Black, Brown and Beige*, the Chicago novels of Richard Wright, the Chicago blues of Muddy Waters, and Ralph Ellison's *Invisible Man*, which begins with a sharecropping narrative and ends in Harlem.

Indeed, Richard Wright and Edward Rosskam's photobook, *Twelve Million Black Voices*, is the black migration's counterpart to Dorothea Lange and Paul Taylor's *American Exodus*; Arna Bontemps and Jack Conroy's *They Seek a City* was the same kind of popular social history as Carey McWilliams's *Factories in the Field*. Similarly, the stories of the Appalachian mills and mines became epic narrative in Harriette Arnow's *The Dollmaker*, one of the great proletarian novels of the age, though rarely recognized as such. Arnow had first published in the magazines of the proletarian avant-garde, and *The Dollmaker*'s train journey north links a powerful Appalachian pastoral with a Detroit proletarian tragedy. However, California had long seemed a promised land to the nation, and the betrayal of that promise gave the "grapes of wrath" story much of its dramatic power; "California's a Garden of Eden," Woody Guthrie sang in the enduring "Do Re Mi," "a paradise to live in or see / But believe it or not, you won't find it so hot / If you ain't got the do re mi." With its biblical archetype and its historical centrality—the migration of southern whites and blacks to the North and West did reshape the society on the North American continent—the migration as exodus came to be one of the grand narratives, the tall tales, of the mid-century United States.[10]

The story of the Okie exodus also achieved its great popular success because it fused contrary populist rhetorics in a remarkable and unstable amalgam, not unlike the New Deal itself; as the Marxist literary critic Edward Berry Burgum wrote, "Steinbeck met the social crisis . . . within the artistic sphere as successfully as Roosevelt in the political sphere." The success of *The Grapes of Wrath*, Burgum argues, lay in its stylistic blend: "hardly any style practiced today is missing from it," from those of Dos Passos, Joyce, and Hemingway, to those of *Gone with the Wind* and the *Saturday Evening Post.* Creating a kind of stylistic Popular Front, "its appeal was directed to virtually every level of taste in the book-reading public." Thus, the Popular Front laborism embodied in the union organizing of Preacher Casy was only one aspect of the narratives of the Okie exodus; it combined uneasily with a conservative vitalism that saw the depression and class struggle in terms of natural history, with a New Deal technocracy that celebrated the state, and with a racial populism that heroized the "plain people." The tensions between these rhetorics of "the people" are inscribed in the cultural politics of the moment and the aesthetic forms of the works themselves.[11]

A crucial divide between the ideologies of the left and those of the established order lay in the use of metaphors of natural disaster. Metaphors of natural disaster were deeply embedded in popular discourses about the depression. Edmund Wilson had written that "the slump was like a flood or an earthquake," and the terrible Mississippi River floods served both blues singers and novelists as an emblem of economic and social crisis. So even though only a small minority of the migrants came from the Dust Bowl, the desiccated plains and violent dust storms of the Dust Bowl became the foremost natural analogue of the depression and a source of the mythic power of the "grapes of wrath" narrative. This was the heart of the controversy behind the making of *The Plow That Broke the Plains.* For the Nykino cameramen who wrote the first scenario, the story was a political one, that of "capitalism's anarchic rape of the land, and . . . the impoverishment of all the natural resources of America." But for Lorentz, the story lay in the natural disaster of the Dust Bowl: "Our heroine is the grass, our villain the sun and the wind. . . . It is a melodrama of nature— the tragedy of turning grass into dust." A bitter struggle continued throughout the filming; Lorentz complained that the Nykino filmmakers "wanted it to be all about human greed, and how lousy our social system was," and he "couldn't see what this had to do with dust storms." In the end it was Lorentz's film, and Nykino's Paul Strand felt that "the guts had been taken out of it."[12]

Though Popular Front film critics like Otis Ferguson and Irving Lerner hailed the film, they criticized its reduction of politics to nature, of social struggle to "an abstract film on the struggle between Man and Nature." In

Lange and Taylor's book, by contrast, one sees the counterpointing of land and people, landscapes and portraits, as an attempt to evoke the metaphoric fusion of the book's subtitle, a "record of *human erosion*" (my emphasis). Indeed, in a 1941 review of Dorothea Lange's photographs, Lorentz admitted that he had been "more concerned about Texas and the end of the grasslands than I was about people." A similar controversy followed Steinbeck's *Grapes of Wrath*, in which his overwhelming biological metaphors seemed to reduce political struggles to elements of natural history; as Kenneth Burke noted, the novel might be called *Of Land Turtles and Men*. This carried into Zanuck's *Grapes of Wrath* as well: despite the fact that the film's power derives from the confrontation between the migrants and the California mobs and vigilantes, the opening title announces that "This is the story of one farmer's family driven from their fields by natural disasters and economic changes beyond anyone's control."[13]

If the villain's role is often taken by "the sun and the wind," the hero's part is often taken by the New Deal itself. To some extent, this was because the works themselves were sponsored by the agencies within the New Deal state as part of a campaign to win support for state action. The federal camps for migrant farmworkers were in part the result of the investigative work of Lange and Taylor, and Taylor claimed that they were "the first federal public housing in the United States." The chief source for Steinbeck's novel was Tom Collins, the manager of the Farm Security Administration camp in California's Central Valley; he and his camp served as the models for the fictional "Weedpatch," a brief oasis for the Joads. In the Zanuck film of *The Grapes of Wrath*, this New Deal utopia becomes the happy ending. Whereas the novel ends with the killing of Preacher Casy, the defeat of the strikers, and the controversial scene in which Rose of Sharon breast-feeds a starving stranger, the film ends with the episode in the government camp, with its showers, toilets, and Saturday night dances. When the Joads drive off from the camp in the film's final scene, Jane Darwell delivers the famous ending: "We're the people."[14]

At first glance, the film's ending is a ringing endorsement of Roosevelt's New Deal, a long way from the revolutionary rhetoric of the early depression. But the figure of the government camps actually allowed a second, more radical interpretation, which Carey McWilliams expressed in *Factories in the Field*. "In much of the current writing on the problem of farm labor in California," McWilliams wrote, "the migratory camps have been hailed as a solution of the farm-labor problem. But the migratory camps are not a solution: They are merely demonstrations of what might be accomplished." This trope of prefiguration runs throughout Popular Front accounts of New Deal programs from the Federal Theatre to the Tennessee Valley Authority. For the left, the New Deal programs were celebrated not as solutions in themselves but as prefigurations of a future democratic and collective social order. Far from being renunciations of social transformation, they stand as harbingers of it: "the solution of the farm-labor problem," McWilliams writes, "can only be achieved through the organization of farm workers." The popularity of *The Grapes of Wrath* film among Popular Front activists—Joseph Losey said that it was the only Hollywood film to have a real left-wing impact—was a result of this form of allegorical reading.[15]

Finally, the "grapes of wrath" narrative gained much of its popularity because it was told as a story of white Protestant "plain people." The depression years had seen white migrants from the Southwest displacing the Mexican and Filipino farmworkers who were repatriated and deported after the wave of organization and strikes in 1933 and 1934, particularly in the San Joaquin Valley. But the Mexican and Filipino farmworkers had been displaced in fiction earlier. Three-quarters of the workers in the strikes that formed the basis for Steinbeck's *In Dubious Battle* were Mexican; all of the workers in the novel were white. This racial rhetoric runs throughout Steinbeck's political pamphlet, *Their Blood Is Strong*. Though he laments the cruel treatment of "foreign peon labor," he notes that the "future farm workers are to be white and American," and it is their plight that angers him: "They are of the best American stock"; "they are resourceful and intelligent Americans who have gone through the hell of the drought"; they have "strong purposeful faces"; "the names of the new migrants indicate that they are of English, German and Scandinavian descent." In the title of the pamphlet, their *blood* is strong.[16]

Steinbeck's racial populism deeply inflects *The Grapes of Wrath* as well, and this contrasts sharply with Carey McWilliams's *Factories in the Field*. Though the two books have been linked since their appearance and the McWilliams book has often been characterized as the non-fiction *Grapes of Wrath*, they tell remarkably different stories. *Factories in the Field* begins not in the Dust Bowl but in the great agricultural valleys of California, reconstructing their history and the history of the Chinese, Japanese, South Asian, Armenian, Filipino, and Mexican workers who farmed them. The climax of his book is the great strikes of 1933 and 1934 and the farm fascism that emerged in their wake; the story of the Dust Bowl migrants in the final chapter takes its place in the longer history of migrant farm labor. As we shall see, McWilliams became one of the Popular Front's foremost writers on race and ethnicity and an activist in the Sleepy Lagoon case. In the racial populism of Steinbeck, the noble white Americans of *The Grapes of Wrath* are set against the minstrel show Mexican Americans of *Tortilla Flat*.

Thus, the versions of the "Okie exodus" that achieved the greatest success in the state apparatus and the culture industry—the Steinbeck novel and the films of Lorentz and Ford—do reinforce interpretations of

New Deal populism as sentimental and conservative: their biological naturalism lent itself to an account of the depression as a natural disaster and to a racial account of the "people," their "stock," and their "blood." But to take these works as typical of the Popular Front demonstrates the limits of a cultural history that focuses entirely on those moments when cultural-front campaigns succeeded in bringing attention to a particular struggle. There is no doubt that the Popular Front campaign in California's factories in the field was a cultural success; the combined forces of farmworker organizers, Communist militants, left-wing government officials, photographers and filmmakers on the New Deal payrolls, Hollywood actors, and a well-known California novelist made the "grapes of wrath" narrative a national story, and persuaded an innovative, though politically conservative, Hollywood producer to make a major studio film representing the migrant farmworkers.

One should not underestimate the importance of this cultural success; one of the fundamental aspects of the cultural politics of the Popular Front was to bring national attention to organizing campaigns, building solidarity through cultural representations. Thus, if Zanuck's *Grapes of Wrath* was *not* a product of the Popular Front—none of the key figures involved in its production were Popular Front radicals—it was nevertheless enabled by Popular Front cultural politics. And despite the sentimental framing of the film—it opens with a title announcing the Joad's "great journey in search of peace, security and another home" and ends with a vision of peace, security and home—the performances of Henry Fonda, Jane Darwell, and John Carradine (as Preacher Casy) and Greg Toland's cinematography combine to embody the radical social-democratic vision of the Popular Front.

Nevertheless, if one focuses on these campaigns of solidarity, one inevitably sees the culture of the Popular Front as a "documentary" culture, dominated by established intellectuals going to particular sites of intense class conflict and "representing" the "people." But this short-term cultural politics of exposés and solidarity was finally less important than the long-term, less visible struggle for the cultural enfranchisement of working people. This struggle for recognition and self-representation was of course embodied in the unions and associations created by the California farmworkers; but it was also embodied in the Popular Front migrant narratives of Woody Guthrie, Carlos Bulosan, and Ernesto Galarza. Guthrie's work was, as we shall see, closely associated with the "grapes of wrath" narrative that emerged in 1939 and 1940; Carlos Bulosan's *America Is in the Heart* (1946) and Ernesto Galarza's *Barrio Boy* (1971), on the other hand, are rarely connected to the "grapes of wrath" narrative or to Guthrie's *Bound for Glory*. However, all three came out of the communities of California's farmworkers; all three chose picaresque rather than epic forms to tell their

CULTURAL FRONT

Charlie Chaplin's next feature production, "The Dictators," will go before the camera on March 15. Chaplin will speak from the screen for the first time in his career in this story, which, he explains, will present the dictator as an exceptional vehicle for comedy. The subject matter will be such that it will demand production on a scale surpassing any of his previous films. Exhibitors Pictures Corp., at the same time, announces that it has synchronized twelve of Chaplin's best early films and will present them, one by one, in New York, London, Paris and other large cities in the next month or so in honor of Chaplin's fiftieth birthday on April 16.

TAC, (the Theatre Arts Committee, as everybody knows) recently called together an important group of artists who have left their own countries for political reasons, and attempted to crystallize certain reasons for the breakdown of the democratic systems in the countries of their origin, in terms of what can be done to warn and encourage democratic, cultural forces, in the rest of the world. Germany was represented by Klaus and Erika Mann, Kurtner, the actor, Piscator, famous film director; Czecho-Slovakia by Voskovec and Wer'ch, both actors and the originators of the *Liberated Theatre* of Prague. The result is a symposium, published this month in TAC magazine, which will arrest the attention of every lover of the arts.

Cabaret TAC will give gala performances at the Manhattan Center, West 34th Street, on Friday evenings, March 3, 10, and 31, repeating the outstanding numbers of former shows, and introducing new ones. TAC records have now been made of two songs, *Abe Lincoln*, and *Joe Hill*, composed by Alfred Hayes and Earl Robinson, and sung by Michael Loring with the TAC singers. The *Chamberlin Crawl*, and *Picket Line Priscilla* may soon be had on TAC records, obtainable at 132 West 43rd Street, New York.

The League of Composers affiliated with the newly formed American Lyric Theatre, will cooperate this spring in presenting its initial programs for music and stage. The American Lyric Theatre season will open in April, with an opera by Douglas Moore and Stephen Vincent Benet, "The Devil and Daniel Webster," and "Suzanna, Don' You Cry," a musical romance based on Stephen Foster's melodies, by Clarence Loomis with a book by Sarah Newmeyer. Other productions will follow. Leopold Stokowski, Fritz Reiner, Artur Rodzinski and other noted conductors who have been previously associated with stage works presented by the League of Composers, are interested in the development of this new lyric theatre. Robert Edmond Jones will design the scenery and costumes and act as a general advisor in the mounting of productions. Lee Pattison is managing director of the new organization. Further details will be announced soon.

Mischa Elman, renowned violin virtuoso, has given his individual answer to the tragic plight of the refugees from Germany. Mr. Elman is making a three-month tour, the entire proceeds of which are to go equally to the Committee for Catholic Refugees from Germany, the American Jewish Joint Distribution Committee and the American Committee for Christian German Refugees.

The last concert of a series devoted to works by young Americans and arranged by the League of Composers cooperating with the Society of Professional Musicians will take place on Sunday, March 26, at the Town Hall Club. The music for this program has been selected by the Executive Board of the League; the interpreters have been chosen by the Society of Professional Musicians.

Tamiris, Leif Erickson, Vera Zorina and Paula Bass in the Pink Slip Soup Kitchen. See story below

The Pink Slip Soup Kitchen was started when a dancer brought a plan to the Five Arts Council of feeding, at cost, the hundreds of writers, actors, musicians and artists who had just been discharged from WPA because of "reduction in quota." It was no accident that such an idea occurred to a member of the Dance Project, for that division of the Federal Arts Projects was reduced by 70 per cent. With the spontaneous co-operation of many wholesale food dealers and with advice from the Cafeteria Workers Union, a hard working committee of employed and dismissed WPA-ers, headed by this enterprising young dancer, Paula Bass, established the Pink Slip Soup Kitchen. Leif Erickson and Zorina, star of "I Married an Angel," poured the first ladles of soup, and hundreds of people thronged the Garibaldi Club at 41st Street, which was hired for the occasion at a nominal sum. The press was there in full force, but apparently met with a little editorializing, later, from the city desk. So successful was the Soup Kitchen as an organizational center as well as feeding station, that the necessity for a more permanent headquarters became evident. The Garibaldi Club, although warmly hospitable, was not able to hold all the customers and the kitchen moved to 326 West 48th Street. It looks as if they will remain until the emergency situation is negated by further appropriations from Congress.

Figure 1. Cultural Front column from *Direction*, the "lively, entertaining and crusading magazine of the People's Front in the Arts," March 1939.

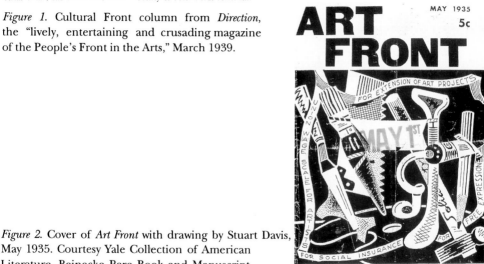

Figure 2. Cover of *Art Front* with drawing by Stuart Davis, May 1935. Courtesy Yale Collection of American Literature, Beinecke Rare Book and Manuscript Library, Yale University.

Figure 3. Dorothea Lange, "San Francisco Waterfront Strike, 1934." Gelatin silver print, 9¹⁄₁₆ x 7¼ (24.3 x 18.4 cm). San Francisco Museum of Modern Art. The Henry Swift Collection. Gift of Florence Alston Swift.

Figure 4. Dorothea Lange, "May Day Listener, San Francisco, 1934." The Oakland Museum.

Figure 5. John Dos Passos arrested for picketing the Massachusetts State House to protest the death sentences of Sacco and Vanzetti in 1927. UPI/Corbis-Bettmann.

Figure 6. Howard da Silva as Larry Foreman (with fist clenched) and Olive Stanton as Moll in the Night Court scene of the 1937 Mercury production of *The Cradle Will Rock.* Lilly Library, Indiana University, Bloomington, Indiana.

Figure 7. Dorothea Lange, "Migrant Mother, Nipomo California, 1936." The
Oakland Museum.

Figure 8. Ruth Rubinstein performing "Chain Store Daisy" in *Pins and Needles.*
Courtesy The Harold Rome Papers, Yale University Music Library. Used by
permission.

Figure 9. Cover of *TAC,* monthly magazine of the Theatre Arts Committee, a Popular Front organization.

Figure 10. Cover of *Photo-History*, a Popular Front photomagazine, July 1937. Street crowds in Aliquippa, Pa., celebrating the CIO victory over Jones & Laughlin Steel Corp in May 1937.

Figure 11. Ben Shahn, *For Full Employment after the War: Register/Vote,* 1944. Lithograph in colors. New Jersey State Museum Collection. Gift of New Jersey Junior and Community College Association, FA1970.64.13.

Figure 12. Cover of special issue of *Ammunition,*
edited by Elizabeth Hawes, August 1944.

Figure 13. Elizabeth Hawes with model.
Reprinted from *American Magazine,* May 1933.

Figure 14. Charles Peterson, "Billie Holiday and Frank Newton recording 'Strange Fruit' at 20 April 1939 Commodore session." Courtesy Don Peterson.

Figure 15. Richard Wright and Orson Welles at the stage production of *Native Son*, 2 April 1941. Courtesy Yale Collection of American Literature, Beinecke Rare Book and Manuscript Library, Yale University.

Figure 16. "Who's Afraid of Big Bad Walt?" drawn by striking Disney cartoonists for the Popular Front magazine *Friday*, 25 July 1941.

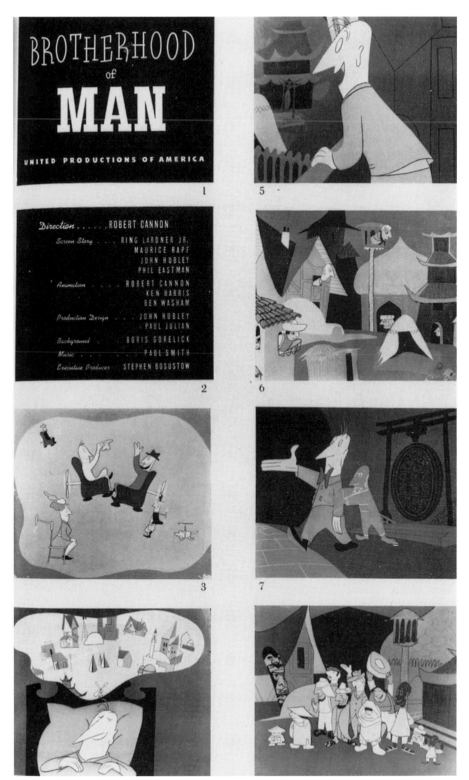

Figure 17. Stills from *The Brotherhood of Man,* a cartoon produced for the United Auto Workers Education Department. Reprinted from *Hollywood Quarterly,* July 1946.

Figure 18. Cover of program for Duke Ellington's *Jump for Joy,* 1941. Department of Special Collections, Stanford University Libraries.

tales of the factories in the fields; and all three were figures of the cultural front.

2. Migrant Narratives

Woody Guthrie, who was born in Oklahoma in 1912, made his way to California in the mid 1930s as an itinerant musician and sign painter. He and his brother Jack landed a radio show on Los Angeles's KFVD in the summer of 1937 as "singing cowboys"; but by the fall Woody had abandoned cowboy songs and joined up with Maxine Crissman in the Woody and Lefty Lou show. Over the next year, Guthrie's mixture of old-time "hillbilly" songs, downhome philosophy, and Dust Bowl ballads became popular among the California migrant workers and thousands of letters poured into the station. He met the young Communists who were organizing the farmworkers, including Will Geer, an actor who had come out of the workers theater movement. Joining Geer's troupe of four, Folksay, Guthrie sang and performed skits at migrant camps and picket lines throughout the San Joaquin Valley. By May 1939, he was writing a column of humor, cartoons, and song lyrics, "Woody Sez," for the *People's World*, and in October 1939 Guthrie and Geer led a group of artists to support the strikers in the Madera County cotton strike.[17]

Thus, Guthrie resembled Gastonia's Ella May Wiggins and Harlan's Aunt Molly Jackson, Jim Garland, and Sarah Ogan Gunning: a local singer radicalized by an organizing campaign and drawn into the Popular Front movement. And just as Wiggins and Jackson were a part of a tradition of textile-mill and coal-mining songsters, so Guthrie stood in a tradition of itinerant southwestern singers, which included Mac McClintock, the Wobbly singer who wrote "Hallelujah I'm a Bum" and "The Big Rock Candy Mountain" and regularly performed on San Francisco's KFRC throughout the 1930s; Jimmie Rodgers, the most popular hillbilly singer of the depression; and the obscure migrants like Flora Robertson and Jack Bryant, who sang for Library of Congress collectors in 1940 and 1941.[18]

Like the Gastonia and Harlan singers, Guthrie went to New York and became part of the movement culture of the Popular Front. On 3 March 1940, he appeared at one of the earliest Popular Front folk-music recitals: the "Grapes of Wrath" benefit for the Steinbeck committee, which featured "American Ballad Singers and Folk Dancers," including Aunt Molly Jackson, Will Geer, Leadbelly, and the Golden Gate Quartet. Guthrie also forged connections with Popular Front figures in the New Deal state and the culture industries. Later in March, he was recorded by the radical folklorist Alan Lomax for the Library of Congress archives. In April, he appeared on Norman Corwin's network radio show, "The Pursuit of Happiness" (which had featured Robeson's "Ballad for Americans"), singing "Do Re Mi." In May 1940, Guthrie recorded the classic *Dust Bowl Ballads,* a song cycle based on the Dust Bowl migration, for RCA Victor.[19]

Singing in the flat, deadpan style that musicologist Wilfrid Mellers has called the "monody of deprivation" and accompanying himself with a relatively unornamented guitar and harmonica, Guthrie used the popular forms and tunes of the "hillbilly" recordings of the 1920s and 1930s— talking blues, ballads, hillbilly blues, hymns, and waltz tunes—to recast the "Okie exodus" as a satirical, picaresque exploration of what he called "the art and science of Migratin'." As a result, *Dust Bowl Ballads* stands as a counterpoint to *The Grapes of Wrath* in several ways. First, Victor agreed to record *Dust Bowl Ballads* to capitalize on the popularity of the film. Moreover, unlike most "hillbilly" and "race" records, which were released as single 78 rpm records with one song on each side, Victor packaged it as a double album: two three-record sets (twelve sides) with a booklet by Guthrie explaining the songs. Steinbeck himself offered a widely quoted endorsement of Guthrie—"He sings the songs of a people and I suspect that he is, in a way, that people"—and Guthrie in turn praised Steinbeck as "a feller that knew us Oakies . . . because early in the deal, he throwed a pack on his back and traipsed around amongst us."[20]

Nevertheless, though Guthrie praised the Zanuck film—it "had more thinkin' in it than 99% of the celluloid that we're tangled up in the moving pictures today"—he was skeptical of the Hollywood version of the "Okie exodus." "I don't know just exactly what all they stirred in with it," Guthrie wrote of Eddie Quillan's rendition of the song "I'm Goin' Down this Road a Feelin' Bad" in the film, "but it was dadgum hard to recognize when it come out." Guthrie's ballad "Tom Joad" offers an illuminating contrast to the novel and the film.[21]

Victor had asked Guthrie to write a song about *The Grapes of Wrath,* and he responded with a long ballad, "Tom Joad." In "Tom Joad," Guthrie turns the epic of a migrant family into an outlaw ballad. Guthrie's series of outlaw ballads about the Dalton Gang, Belle Starr, and Pretty Boy Floyd had been popular with migrant camp audiences, and he used the form to retell Steinbeck's story. The melody of "Tom Joad" was taken from the mountain outlaw ballad "John Hardy," which the Carter Family had made popular; and Guthrie's lyric begins with Tom's parole from prison—"Tom Joad got out of the old McAlester pen"—and culminates in Tom and Preacher Casy's battles with vigilantes and deputy sheriffs. Moreover, Guthrie drops both the novel's ending—Rose of Sharon breast-feeding the stranger—and the film's ending—the Joads leaving the government camp—and uses Tom's parting words to his mother as the basis for the final stanzas: "Wherever little children are hungry and cry / Wherever people ain't free / Wherever men are fightin' for their rights / That's where I'm gonna be, Ma / That's where I'm gonna be." The stanza echoes

Earl Robinson's popular left-wing ballad "Joe Hill," with its lines "Where working men are out on strike / Joe Hill is at their side." The heart of Guthrie's *Grapes of Wrath* is neither the migrant family nor the utopia of the government camp but the itinerant outlaw/organizer, Tom Joad, a figure for the singer himself.[22]

If "Tom Joad" was written specifically for the Victor recording session, the other songs on *Dust Bowl Ballads* were products of Guthrie's performances for the migrants. The trope of dust runs throughout: the liner notes identify Guthrie as the "Dustiest of the Dust Bowlers." But Guthrie refuses the tragic tone that characterizes many of the accounts of the Dust Bowl. His one attempt to turn the storm into a tragic narrative, the unsuccessful ballad "The Great Dust Storm," has the diction of Victorian melodrama—"doom," "death-like black," and "the dust had rung their knell"—without the supernatural terror that usually accompanied its folk uses. Guthrie's successful ballads of the Dust Bowl are instances of his gallows humor, laughing in the face of the dust: the deadpan talking blues, "Talkin' Dust Blues," the upbeat waltz, "Dusty Old Dust" (also known as "So Long, It's Been Good to Know You"), and Guthrie's rare 32-bar popular song, "Do Re Mi."

Guthrie's hillbilly blues also refuse defeat: "I ain't gonna be treated this a way" is the repeated refrain of "I'm Blowin' Down this Old Dusty Road"; and the catalog of disasters in "Dust Cain't Kill Me" is punctuated with the refrain "But it cain't kill me." This trope of refusal also marks Guthrie's homage to the blue yodels of Jimmy Rodgers, "Dust Pneumonia Blues": "There ought to be some yodeling in this song," he sings twice, "But I can't yodel for the rattlin' in my lungs." These hillbilly blues have hardly any narrative and little metaphoric or melodic ornamentation; they are built on musical and lyric drones. Only Guthrie's harmonica, like Rodgers's lonesome falsetto yodels, offers a utopian alternative to the constricted, deadpan vocals.

Perhaps the most powerful song in the cycle is Guthrie's "I Ain't Got No Home in this World Anymore," in which he characteristically turns a lament into an affirmation. Formally, it stands between his prolix story ballads and his laconic hillbilly blues: like many of his best songs, it unites the storytelling impulse of the ballads with the economy of the hillbilly blues. The song is based on a Baptist hymn, "This World Is Not My Home," which had been recorded by popular string bands as well as the Carter Family. Like Joe Hill in his Wobbly hymns and John Handcox in his Southern Tenant Farmers Union gospel songs, Guthrie took this hymn of resignation and other-worldly redemption and turned it inside out. He keeps Maybelle Carter's guitar accompaniment; indeed, his guitar playing was largely based on the Carter Family. And he keeps the hymn's concluding line, "I can't feel at home in this world anymore." But the lyric persona becomes a "wanderin' worker" driven from town to town by the police. Dust storms give way to bankers in this narrative of homelessness: "Rich man took my home and drove me from my door." Indeed, as Guthrie revised and recast his songs, the Dust Bowl narrative of the Okies gave way to this sense of himself as a migrant worker, hounded by vigilantes and the police.[23]

Like many of the migrants, Guthrie had never been comfortable with the word "Okie," which was, after all, used as a slur and an insult. He never uses the word in the songs of *Dust Bowl Ballads*, and his distance from the word can be seen in his chains of substitutions: "Talking about Okie songs, or Arkie songs, or just plain old songs of the Migratious Trail," he writes in *Direction*; "I looked into the lost and hungry faces of several hundred thousand Oakies, Arkies, Texies, Mexies, Chinees, Japees, Dixies, and even a lot of New Yorkies," he quips in the liner notes. He was equally uncomfortable with the name "Dust Bowl refugee": "They say I'm a Dust Bowl refugee," he sings, "and I ain't gonna be treated this a way." Indeed, the song "Dust Bowl Refugee" is torn between its desire to narrate the lives of "we ... ramblers" and its palpable refusal of the identity: "I'm a Dust Bowl refugee / And I wonder will I always / Be a Dust Bowl refugee." In fact, Guthrie rewrites this relatively unsuccessful song into one of his finest lyrics, "Pastures of Plenty," which is explicitly the tale of "us migrants." Thus, the stanza "Yes we wander and we work / In your crops and in your fruit / Like the whirlwind on the desert / That's the Dust Bowl refugees" becomes "I've worked in your orchards of peaches and prunes / Slept on the ground in the light of your moon / On the edge of your city you'll see us and then / We come with the dust and are gone with the wind." Finally, when Guthrie narrates his life in *Bound for Glory* in the early 1940s, he composes a migrant narrative, not a tale of the "Okie exodus" from the Dust Bowl.[24]

Guthrie's *Bound for Glory* bears a striking resemblance to two other migrant narratives that emerged from the Popular Front social movement in California's agricultural valleys: Carlos Bulosan's *America Is in the Heart* (1946) and Ernesto Galarza's *Barrio Boy* (1971). Though the works of Bulosan and Galarza were not visible in 1939 and 1940, they were as much a part of the long struggle of California's migrant farmworkers to represent themselves as were the songs of Guthrie. Bulosan, born in the Philippines in 1913, was a contemporary of Guthrie; he migrated to the United States in 1930, joining his brothers in the migrant world of California's Filipinos. He worked a variety of odd jobs in the farming town of Lompoc and in Los Angeles. After meeting the young Filipino organizer Chris Mensalvas in the early 1930s, Bulosan became part of the movement to organize Filipino farmworkers and the campaign against the attempts to exclude Filipinos from the United States. The movement reached a peak in the summer of 1934, when the Filipino Labor Union led strikes in Salinas, El Centro, and Vacaville; though the union's headquarters was burned by vigilantes and the union leaders were jailed, the strikers won recognition and wage increases. Bulosan and Mensalvas attempted to organize a branch of the union in Lompoc; the Lompoc strike failed disastrously, but it taught Bulosan that he "was definitely a part of the labor movement." Like many young writers and activists across the country, Bulosan and Mensalvas put out a small proletarian literary magazine; *The New Tide* would, they announced, "interpret the struggles and aspirations of the workers, the fight of sincere intellectuals against fascism and racial oppression in concrete national terms."[25]

Mensalvas became a lifetime labor organizer; Bulosan's health failed and he spent two years in a hospital, reading and educating himself. He emerged from the hospital a writer and became part of the left-wing literary circles in Los Angeles, a friend of Sanora Babb, Carey McWilliams, John Fante, and Louis Adamic. Active in the American Committee for the Protection of the Foreign-Born, a Popular Front organization campaigning for US citizenship for Filipinos, he wrote regularly for Filipino newspapers. During the war years, his pastoral stories of the Philippines were published in slick magazines like the *New Yorker, Town & Country* and *Harper's Bazaar*; in 1944, they were collected in *The Laughter of My Father*. Bulosan's success was unexpected and disorienting: "I am mad," he wrote in an essay not unlike Richard Wright's famous "How Bigger Was Born," "because when my book *The Laughter of My Father* was published . . . the critics called me 'the Pure Comic Spirit.' I am not a laughing man. I am an angry man." His anger was embodied in his major work, the 1946 migrant narrative, *America Is in the Heart*.[26]

America Is in the Heart is often taken as a quintessential example of Popular Front Americanism, a prose version of "Ballad for Americans." Its title and its most famous passage—Macario's speech—seem to be the epitome of the sentimental, populist, and humanist nationalism that we are told characterized the wartime Popular Front:

> We are all Americans that have toiled and suffered and known oppression and defeat, from the first Indian that offered peace in Manhattan to the last Filipino pea pickers. . . . America is not merely a land or an institution. America is in the hearts of men that died for freedom; it is also in the eyes of men that are building a new world. America is a prophecy of a new society of men: of a system that knows no sorrow or strife or suffering. . . . America is also the nameless foreigner, the homeless refugee, the hungry boy begging for a job and the black body dangling on a tree. . . . We are all that nameless foreigner, that homeless refugee, that hungry boy, that illiterate immigrant and that lynched black body. All of us, from the first Adams to the last Filipino, native born or alien, educated or illiterate—*We are America!*

In isolation, the inflated rhetoric of this and other "American" passages does appear to be a kind of left-wing Fourth of July oration, the embodiment of the famous slogan that "Communism is twentieth-century Americanism." But in fact the rhetorical excess of these passages is a sign of the narrator's desperate attempt to transcend a United States of violence, "a world of brutality and despair."[27]

One can see this in the contradictory structure of the work. On the one hand, the book is the sentimental education of a writer, with clearly marked turning points. Part one is the story of his childhood in the Philippines, ending with his departure for the US; part two tells of his life as a migrant worker from Alaska to New Mexico, culminating in his discovery of the labor movement and his "intellectual awakening," symbolized by Macario's speech; part three narrates his political education in farmworker strikes, his intellectual education in the hospital, and his eventual decision to become a writer, "to tell the story of our life in America"; and part four covers his life as a writer, culminating in the publication of his first book of poems. But the narrative refuses to obey this structure: every turning point and intellectual awakening is followed by a retreat into despair and aimless movement; every moment of political struggle is juxtaposed with incidents of petty crime and brutal violence. Even the vocation of the writer is less than a triumph: in his travels, the narrator meets two Filipinos who plan to be the "greatest Filipino novelist." The first, Estevan, commits suicide; and the second, Florencio Garcia, is a lonely busboy driven by hate. In one of the narrative's final scenes, Bulosan's book of poems is ripped by a prostitute. The migrant narrative of the "Filipino pea picker" is finally less a sentimental education in Americanism than "one long flight from fear."[28]

That is why *America Is in the Heart* is not really an autobiography. Bulosan's friend John Fante later recalled that Bulosan was "given to telling wildly improbable stories about himself," and both friends and critics have pointed to the "improbabilities" in his written narrative. He was never in Alaska; he did not work in the fields, being too weak; and he had nothing to do with several of the violent incidents he incorporated into the narrative. But like the slave narratives of the mid nineteenth century, the migrant narratives of Bulosan, Guthrie, and Galarza are portraits of a collective condition, in this case, the world of migrant men. The "Carlos" of the narrative works all the jobs, legal and illegal, of that world, witnesses all its shootings, mutilations, and rapes, and assumes all its brutality and pain. The narrative use of this heightened melodrama can be seen in the incorporation of two historical killings that Bulosan was unlikely to have witnessed: the narrator Carlos sees the Filipino farmworker who cracks and kills eight people in a Seattle street; and he later witnesses the assassination of the cannery union president, Dagohoy, by thugs, also in Seattle. The second shooting marks a turning point: "I *knew*—now. This violence had a broad social meaning; the one I had known earlier was a blind rebellion."[29]

However, Bulosan's narrative does not depend entirely upon its picaresque protagonist Carlos. The narrative's character system is organized around a network of migrant brothers. The book opens with Carlos's brother Leon returning from the First World War and it closes with his brothers Macario and Amado going off to the Second World War. The fight between the educated brother Macario and the angry bootlegger brother Amado is a climactic episode, with Carlos forced to strike Amado: "I had no right to strike an older brother. It was a bad omen; I would never be happy again. I had not only transgressed against a family tradition; I had also struck down one of the gods of my childhood." The book's fraternity is not limited to biological brothers; the network of young migrant men from the same region serves not only as a microcosm of the Filipino community, but as a gallery of alternative lives and fates: Luz, who dies in a gambling house; Alonzo, jailed for living with a white woman; José, the union organizer. Many of these figures are thinly disguised versions of Bulosan's friends; but, like Jack Kerouac's similar gallery of male friends, they are less portraits of real people, as one finds in memoir or autobiography, than projections of a collective subject.[30]

The drama of the narrative lies in its attempt to resolve the contradictory nature of this kin structure, which is the source of community and solidarity as well as of strife and violence. On meeting his first migrant "brother" in steerage, Carlos reflects that this "regional friendship" was not only a "bond that bound us together," but, when "developed into tribalism, obstructed all efforts toward Filipino unity in America." This bond runs throughout the narrative. One finds it in Carlos's several traveling companions; in the doubling of the Bulosan brothers with the more political brothers Nick and José (based on Julio and Chris Mensalvas); and in the several migrant collectives: the Los Angeles household of sex and alcohol where he first finds Macario, the Seattle flophouse—a terrifying "building of lost men"; and the San Francisco house where the union organizing campaign is mapped out.[31]

The alliance of brothers provokes a profound ambivalence: if it marks the narrative's moments of utopian solidarity, it is haunted by sexual aggression and anxiety. The gang rape of the young girl on the freight train and Carlos's encounter with the farmworkers' shared prostitute (which is narrated as if the narrator himself were being raped) are only the most striking episodes of the sexual violence of the migrant brothers. The sexual beatings of Carlos and José by vigilantes make explicit the narrative's figurative castrations, particularly José's loss of a leg to the freight train. The anxiety that "regional friendship" might turn to homosexual desire emerges in Carlos's fear of the caresses of the young Mexican and the old man. Moreover, though the narrative presents a gallery of cross-ethnic marriages and liaisons (including Manuel's marriage to an "Okie"), none succeeds, all undermined or destroyed by racial prohibitions and commercial sex. The whipping of Leon and his wife by the Luzon villagers in the opening scene seems to mark the impossibility of weddings; the narrator, like his migrant brothers, "hurled contempt at women" and "flung against them the tides of my hate."[32]

The only exception to the broken marriages and the houses of capitalist pleasure—the houses of gambling, taxi dances, and prostitution—is found in the narrator's relation to the Odell sisters. As sisters, they mirror the world of the brothers and echo the sisters he had left in Luzon. Indeed, the Utah and Iowa of the Odell sisters look much like Luzon: their family, like Carlos's, were poor farmers driven off the land. And just as Carlos and Amado had labored to help send Macario to school, so Alice had helped Eileen through school. They were migrants to California, working as secretaries and at odd jobs. Alice, like Carlos, was a writer of "proletarian short stories"; and Eileen comes to the hospital with books and food for him, emblems of their shared obsessive hunger. "She was," he writes, "undeniably the *America* I had wanted to find in those frantic days of fear and flight, in those acute hours of hunger and loneliness."[33]

The Odell sisters, like the brothers Nick and José, offer a vision of solidarity and hope in a world of brutality and violence. This vision of solidarity manifests itself again and again in the organization of the "Filipino pea pickers." The narrator's life begins again when a placard for striking laundry workers is put in his hands and he is paid to picket: "I could not understand it. I was being paid to walk around a building with a sign." Later, trying to find the house in which his friend Max had killed a white man, he finds—in the dream logic that often controls the narrative—his friend José in the house of the farmworkers' newspaper. This house, presided over by the dying socialist Pascual, brings him into the strikes of Pismo Beach pea pickers and Lompoc lettuce pickers: his life becomes "one long conspiracy ... intensely fired by this dream of a better America."[34]

The subsequent political narrative—the formation of UCAPAWA and the Stockton asparagus strike, the formation of the "Committee for the Protection of Filipino Rights" and the sectarian squabbles within the union, the CPFR, and the Communist Party—is no triumphalist account but a whipsaw of hope and despair. It could share the title Richard Wright imagined for his own account of the Popular Front social movement, "the glory and the horror." The narrator recognizes that he and his brother Macario "belonged to the old world of confusion" and that "in this other world—new, bright, promising—we would be unable to meet its demands." The narrative's political vision is embodied in the figure of the itinerant organizer and the migrant pea picker: "I started a little workers' school and invited the pea pickers . . . I went from town to town, forming workers' classes and working in the fields. I knew that I was also educating myself." In the final scene, the bus taking Carlos to the cannery passes a group of "Filipino pea pickers . . . who stopped working when the bus came into view." He waves, and one of them, "who looked like my brother Amado," takes off his hat. Brother and pea picker, the figure stands at the heart of Bulosan's migrant narrative.[35]

The migrant narrative of Ernesto Galarza, *Barrio Boy*, offers a powerful contrast to Bulosan's *America Is in the Heart*, though it too is an example of Popular Front culture. Though *Barrio Boy* appeared a quarter-century after *America Is in the Heart* and *Bound for Glory*, Galarza was a decade *older* than Bulosan and Guthrie: he was born in 1905 in the mountain pueblo of Jalcocotán, Nayarit, in Mexico. His family migrated to Sacramento, California, when he was a boy and he worked in the barrio and the fields. While studying at Occidental, Stanford, and Columbia (eventually earning a doctorate in economics), he became an important Popular Front labor intellectual, writing on Mexican Americans and working with the labor organizer Luisa Moreno at the Pan-American Union in the mid 1930s. In 1937, he was an editor of *Photo-History*, the left-wing picture magazine that narrated the rise of the CIO. After World War II, Galarza became active in the National Farm Labor Union (later the National Agricultural Workers Union), helping to organize the 1947 strike in the DiGiorgio grape fields and campaigning against the Bracero contract-labor program. By 1950, while Bulosan was working for the cannery workers union, Local 37 of the ILWU, Galarza was director of research and education for the NAWU. In the 1960s and 1970s, Galarza wrote three major works on the Bracero program and the labor struggles in California's factories in the fields: *Merchants of Labor* (1964), *Spiders in the House and Workers in the Field* (1970), and *Farm Workers and Agri-Business in California* (1977). In 1971, he wrote the narrative of his childhood, *Barrio Boy*.[36]

The structure of *Barrio Boy* shares much with Bulosan's *America Is in the Heart*. In both cases sections of the narrative are defined by places: just as Bulosan's narrative opens with a long evocation of the farming village of Binalonan, so Galarza's first part is set in the mountain village of Jalcocotán. Both narratives are accounts of successive geographic displacements: in part two of *Barrio Boy*, the household is displaced by the revolution, moving to Tepic and Mazatlán; the brief third part makes the border crossing to the United States, arriving at Sacramento's Hotel Español; part four is set in the barrio of Sacramento; and the final section takes young Ernesto to the "edge of the barrio" and to the farm labor camps where he makes his "first organizing speech." Both works end with their protagonists leaving the fields—one by bus, one by bicycle—in a gesture that combines solidarity and mobility.

However, these structural similarities throw the dramatic contrasts of the two narratives into relief. *America Is in the Heart* is the angry and often melodramatic work of a young writer (Bulosan was thirty-three when it was published); *Barrio Boy* is a pastoral, often nostalgic, work of an older intellectual and activist (Galarza was sixty-six when it was published). Whereas the childhood of Bulosan's Carlos (called "Allos") is a prelude to the narrative of the migrant brothers, Galarza gives us only the childhood of Little Ernie: we see the world through the eyes of a child as his mother and his uncles go through "the daily match with the job givers, lay-offs, the rent, groceries, and the seasons." Indeed, for all the movement of its household, Galarza's narrative is often written as a *tableau vivant*, with careful physical descriptions of buildings, streets, and markets alternating with accounts of the habitual actions of daily life. The description of the forms and places of work—"I could smell cured tobacco, burning molasses, firecracker powder, rancid tallow, wood shavings, turpentine, leather, and practically everything else the people of Leandro Valle used to earn a living"—dominates the narrative. There are few of the "events" and "incidents" that make up Bulosan's narrative; rather, it is a story of learning to work, of learning what his uncle and mother called "*hacerle la lucha*," to make a living. "Whatever the surprising differences between Mazatlán and the *barrio* in Sacramento," the narrator tells us, "in one thing they were powerfully the same—*trabajo*."[37]

In many ways, *Barrio Boy* resembles the ghetto or tenement pastorals, the forms adopted by plebeian novelists who had grown up in the ethnic neighborhoods of the great industrial cities. Like them, it is a tale of young boys exploring the streets of the ghetto, encountering its characters, and laying claim to its territory in the mock-heroic skirmishes of boys' gangs. The worlds of adult sexuality, violence, and work hover on the edges of *Barrio Boy*, as they do in the ghetto pastorals. If, as I have suggested, the ghetto pastorals tended toward either naturalism or pastoralism, Galarza's *barrio* is surely on the pastoral side. The narrator regards the adventures of Little Ernie with gentle irony: "To the adults on Leandro Valle we were not so much a gang as a *palomilla*, a harmless swarm of young nuisances who had to be swatted now and then." As Renato Rosaldo has argued, Galarza's mock-heroic tone "deflates an overblown masculine ethic" throughout the narrative.[38]

The great formal dilemma of the tenement pastoral lay in turning the anecdotes of the neighborhood into a story, a history. However, for *Barrio Boy*, history arrives with the 1911 Mexican revolution. The revolution appears in the mountain village in the form of the anti-revolutionary police, the *rurales*; in the boy's consciousness, the *rurales* are part of the "troubles," which include a flood, a rabid dog, and Halley's Comet, and which end their life in Jalcocotán. Thereafter, the revolution haunts the narrative, becoming part of the fabric of everyday life and providing many of its memorable events: his mother feeds a passing revolutionary soldier in Acaponeta, and the family lives through the siege of Mazatlán. The revolution and the railroad become intertwined in the narrative, emblems of the upheavals and transformations of Mexican society: the railway stations are centers of the revolution, the train journey to Nogales is interrupted by a dynamited trestle, and, in a wonderful mock-heroic anecdote, Ernie and his uncle become part of the revolution when they are shot at on a railway handcar after his uncle yells "Viva Madero" at a patrol. Even in the Sacramento barrio, the revolution echoes in the stories the miner Duran tells, stories which inspire Ernie to make his first organizing speech in the final scene of the narrative.[39]

The final scene of Ernie's organizing speech takes place in a hop-picking camp in Folsom, and it is the only time the narrative enters California's agricultural factories in the field. Why then consider Galarza's narrative a migrant narrative, a part of the struggle to represent the farmworkers, to tell the story of the "grapes of wrath"? After all, *Barrio Boy* appeared thirty years after the brief popular "discovery" of the "grapes of wrath," and it is neither a narrative of an agricultural strike, like Steinbeck's *In Dubious Battle*, nor a tale of the fields and the labor camps, like *The Grapes of Wrath*. There are, however, several reasons to avoid this literal approach to cultural production and to understand the pastoral narrative of Little Ernie as a product of the struggles in California's fields. First, the fields *are* present in the narrative, though they are rarely depicted. The *barrio* had, the narrator tells us, "two kinds of *trabajo*": the local *chanzas* in the canneries, warehouses, and lumber mills to which you could walk or ride a bicycle, and the "seasonal jobs, some of them a hundred miles or more from Sacramento." The seasonal jobs in the fields are represented in the narrative largely through the periodic absences of his uncles José and Gustavo, for whom the "apartment at 418 L became more of a base than a home." Thus, the *barrio* story is itself the other side of the "grapes of wrath" narrative. It is the world dominated by Ernie's mother. Her divorce had left her with a son, a gold ring (which, if pawned, served as bank and insurance), and an Ajax sewing machine (her carefully guarded means of production). But the Ajax never makes it to the United States, and she is left dependent on the wages of her brothers. Her death in the influenza epidemic is a turning point in the narrative; at that point, Ernie joins the migrant world of his uncles and enters the fields for the first time.[40]

Moreover, it is in those fields that Ernie becomes an organizer and an intellectual. Throughout the narrative, Ernie had emerged as an errand boy, a messenger, and an interpreter, one who could translate the English of the courts, hospitals, and post offices: "when troubles made it necessary for the *barrio* people to deal with the Americans uptown, the *Autoridades*, I went with them to the . . . functionaries who sat, like *patrones*, behind desks, and who demanded licenses, certificates, documents, affidavits, signatures, and witnesses." In the final scene in the Folsom camp, Ernie is "appointed by a camp committee to go to Sacramento to find some *Autoridad* who would send an inspector" to investigate the death of a child. He does so and returns to make his first organizing speech, only to be fired; the narrative closes with Ernie heading to high school, a plebeian intellectual who will deal with the Americans uptown, who will *represent* the farmworkers.[41]

Galarza himself became one of the Popular Front's plebeian intellectuals, spending much of his career representing the *barrio*, organizing farm-workers, and writing the history of the struggles in the fields. Thus, though *Barrio Boy* is not a "documentary" portrait of the "people" of California's agricultural valleys, its concluding pages mark it as a product of the social movement in those fields. Moreover, by juxtaposing *Barrio Boy* with the works of Guthrie and Bulosan, we see that the migrant narrative became one of the forms that "proletarian literature" took in the United States, providing a structure by which plebeian artists, intellectuals, and organizers could represent their world.

The representation of the "grapes of wrath" by the artists and intellectuals of the Popular Front is a complex formation. For the cultural front of California's agricultural valleys included *both* the artists and intellectuals who came to the fields and produced the powerful representations that gripped the nation in 1939 and 1940—figures like Lange, Taylor, Steinbeck, and McWilliams—*and* the artists and intellectuals who emerged from the struggles in those fields—figures like Guthrie, Bulosan, and Galarza. Cultural historians have tended to focus on the first group of figures, precisely because the cultural politics of the movement and of the cultural apparatuses accented their contributions. As a result, the "documentary" stance of these artists and intellectuals has often seemed to characterize the aesthetic ideologies of the cultural front generally. The work of the second group is often overlooked because it rarely coincides with moments of public attention, it rarely attempts to serve as a public document of a social condition, and it depends for its cultural success on the fate of its community.

This is true in the cases of Guthrie, Bulosan, and Galarza. Guthrie had a brief celebrity in 1940 as the Dust Bowl balladeer, appearing on network radio, recorded by Victor; though he never achieved the commercial success of the western swing bands of Bob Wills or Spade Cooley, he was part of the musical culture of the Southwest. Nevertheless, despite the legacy of Oklahoma socialism, Guthrie's Popular Front communism did not take hold among the white migrants from the Southwest; their populism was what James Gregory has called "plain-folk Americanism." With the defeat of the CIO's UCAPAWA, Guthrie left the organizing campaigns of the California fields and found his primary audiences in the movement culture of New York's Popular Front and the CIO unions of the Northeast and Midwest. When Guthrie crossed the country with the Almanac Singers in the summer of 1941, they sang union songs for the Transport Workers in New York, at a labor rally in Philadelphia, at the NMU's convention in Cleveland, for striking furworkers in Cicero, at a Popular Front theater in Chicago and a CIO picnic in Milwaukee, for an International Harvester picket line in Minneapolis, ending with the long-shoremen in San Francisco. Guthrie had reconstructed himself as a CIO singer. But the collapse of the CIO's left-wing movement culture in the face of the anti-Communist purge of the unions coincided with the onset of Guthrie's debilitating illness. It was not until the folk music revival of the New Left that Guthrie was to achieve lasting cultural recognition; the revival of Guthrie's work by Bob Dylan and others in the early 1960s was a crucial part of the New Left's appropriation of depression iconography, occurring at the same time as the revival of Agee and Evans's *Let Us Now Praise Famous Men*, Henry Roth's "lost" *Call It Sleep*, and depression photography in Edward Steichen's exhibition, *The Bitter Years*.[42]

Similarly, Bulosan's work had a brief celebrity in the war years, as he came to represent the "voice of Bataan," where Americans and Filipinos had fought together against the Japanese invasion. In the post-war years, Bulosan was based in Seattle, where the Filipino cannery local of UCA-PAWA had survived after the defeat of UCAPAWA's agricultural locals; Bulosan's old friend Chris Mensalvas was the president of the local and Bulosan was hired to edit the union's yearbook. But it was a difficult time during which the government attempted to deport Mensalvas and other union officials; and Bulosan, increasingly ill and alcoholic, died in 1956. *America Is in the Heart* was not reprinted until 1973, when young Asian American radicals like Epifanio San Juan, Jr and Frank Chin reclaimed Bulosan.[43]

Galarza's *Barrio Boy* perhaps best demonstrates the complex temporality of cultural productions, in part because he outlived Guthrie and Bulosan and was able to participate in the political resurgence of the 1960s. Thus, *Barrio Boy* combines three distinct historical moments and movements: the 1911 Mexican revolution that cast its shadow over his childhood; the Popular Front decades of farmworker organizing, culminating in the 1947 DiGiorgio strike; and the Chicano political and cultural renaissance of the 1960s, in which Galarza was active—he helped organize the Southwest Council of La Raza—and which provided the occasion and the audience for the 1971 *Barrio Boy*.[44]

Guthrie, Bulosan, Galarza: the fate of their work testifies to the lasting, if oblique, consequences of the cultural front. Though they labored in the shadow of *The Grapes of Wrath*, their migrant narratives grow in stature and meaning, and continue the laboring of American culture.

8

Labor on Revue: The Popular Front Musical Theater

The age of the CIO witnessed an extraordinary flowering of American musics: the transition from swing to bop in jazz, with the work of Duke Ellington, Billie Holiday, Charlie Christian, Count Basie, Dizzy Gillespie, and Charlie Parker; the emergence of an American philharmonic music in the compositions of Aaron Copland, Marc Blitzstein, and Virgil Thomson; the influx of émigré composers like Béla Bartók and Hanns Eisler; the new film music of composers like Bernard Herrmann; the experimental musicking of Harry Partch, Henry Cowell, and Conlon Nancarrow; the rise of modern gospel and blues in the work of Thomas A. Dorsey, the Golden Gate Quartet, Josh White, Robert Johnson, and Muddy Waters; the emergence of modern folk, bluegrass, and country music in the work of Woody Guthrie, Pete Seeger, Merle Travis, Bill Monroe, and Hank Williams; and the classic songwriting of Ira and George Gershwin, Harold Arlen, and Yip Harburg. All of these developments were tied to transformations in the music industry, which became less dependent on the sale of sheet music and the circulation of scores than on the recordings of particular performers and performances, and the use of those recordings by broadcasting and film. As a result, the relations between art musics and vernacular musics were refigured. This process produced some of the most rationalized and commodified musics ever invented; the Muzak Corporation is an emblem of the canned recorded musics that provided the soundtrack to daily life. However, this fusion of philharmonic traditions and vernacular musics also created a musical renaissance in the United States that has resonated around the world.[1]

It has long been known that some aspects of this musical renaissance had a Red tinge: the folk music revival was spearheaded by Communists; many of the early jazz critics had ties to the Popular Front; and a number of modern composers passed through the communist Composers Collective in the early years of the depression. But most accounts of Popular

Front music are limited to two formations, both of which have usually been caricatured: on the one hand, a coterie of dissonant modernist composers—including Charles Seeger—who wrote unsingable "mass chants" for workers before turning to patriotic cantatas and ballets based on symphonized folk tunes; and, on the other hand, earnest bands of urban radicals—including Charles Seeger's son Pete—writing protest songs under the guise of "folk" music. Both groups, it is often claimed, disdained the popular musics to which working-class Americans listened and danced.[2]

The Seeger family is without doubt central to Popular Front music and to American music generally. As ethnomusicologists, collectors, singers, and popularizers, they have preserved and passed on a wide range of American folk musics as songs, recordings, performance styles, and instrumental techniques. But they were primarily musical organizers and intellectuals. Charles Seeger's early essays on "proletarian music" in the *Daily Worker* led to a lifelong attempt to reconceptualize musicology by exploring folk musics: he invented the melograph, an electronic transcription device, to facilitate the notation of folk musics. Ruth Crawford Seeger also turned from her experimental proletarian songs, based on H.T. Tsiang's poems, to folk music: she made musical transcriptions for several classic folk-song collections, including Carl Sandburg's *An American Songbag* and John and Alan Lomax's *Our Singing Country*. Pete Seeger's innumerable Folkways recordings of American folk songs and ballads became a comprehensive "song book" establishing folk "standards," and his instructional guides for the banjo and the twelve-string guitar pioneered new forms of education in vernacular instrumental technique. Both Mike and Peggy Seeger became interpreters and preservers of traditional vernacular styles.

Nevertheless, the Seegers were not the most representative musical figures of the cultural front, nor was folk music its central form. Pete Seeger's Kentucky banjo songs led one Communist Party official to tell him that "here in New York hardly anybody knows that kind of music.... If you are going to work with the workers of New York City, you should be in the jazz field." Seeger himself expressed doubts to his fellow Almanac Singers: "I wonder if we really have the right slant on the future of American music—us using so much folk music when jazz is so popular." As we will see in the next chapter, Seeger was right about the *future* of American music; however, he was also right in recognizing that folk music was not the center of the "music front."[3]

Perhaps the most representative emblems of Popular Front music were Olive Stanton's "Nickel under the Foot," Ruth Rubinstein's "Chain Store Daisy," and Ivie Anderson's "I've Got It Bad (And That Ain't Good)." These bluesy working-woman's laments were neither folk songs nor topical protest songs. Rather, they borrowed the forms of Tin Pan Alley and turned them inside out. Each was part of a major Popular Front work of musical theater:

Marc Blitzstein's *The Cradle Will Rock*, Harold Rome's *Pins and Needles*, and Duke Ellington's *Jump for Joy*. "In America," Marc Blitzstein wrote, "the musical theatre is either opera or musical comedy. Opera means only the Met; musical comedy is on its last lap. . . . If you still have the desire to write for the musical theatre, you must find a new form." The works of Blitzstein, Rome, and Ellington attempted to find a new form. They were popular, if controversial, successes, closely linked to the social movements that mobilized their audiences. Their bastard unions of political satire and romantic ballads, art and commerce, folk song and art song, the modern and the middlebrow embodied the Popular Front's fusion of Weimar's *Gebrauchsmusik*—"music for use"—with the vaudeville revue, Tin Pan Alley, and jazz. As a result, *The Cradle Will Rock*, *Pins and Needles*, and *Jump for Joy* came to represent both the vision and the contradictions of the "people's music" of the cultural front.[4]

1.   Epic Theater in Steeltown: Marc Blitzstein

The first performance of *The Cradle Will Rock* is one of the legendary events of the cultural front, often overshadowing the musical itself. Marc Blitzstein's "proletarian opera" about union organizing in "Steeltown, U.S.A." was to be the third production of Orson Welles's Federal Theatre unit, Project 891, scheduled for mid June 1937. However, a few days before the opening, the WPA canceled it as one of the general cuts in the relief projects. Welles defied the order and went ahead on 16 June; when the company found their theater locked, the actors Will Geer and Howard da Silva entertained the audience out front while Welles and Houseman rented a theater and a piano. They then led the audience to the Venice Theatre twenty-one blocks away, and performed *The Cradle Will Rock* without sets, costumes, or pit orchestra. Indeed, since union regulations prevented the actors from appearing on stage, Blitzstein took the stage at the piano, and the actors delivered their lines and sang their songs from the audience. The evening was so successful that they continued staging it in that manner for another nineteen performances at the Venice between 18 June and 1 July.[5]

The march to the Venice Theatre and the impromptu staging that had the spotlight finding the actors in the house made the audience the center of the production. "There had always been the question of how to produce a labor show so that the audience can be brought to feel that it is a part of the performance," Blitzstein wrote at the time. "This technique seems to solve the problem and is exactly the right one for this particular piece." However, the involvement of the audience was not simply a formal trick; rather, since the first performance had been planned as a benefit for the left-wing Downtown Music School, the audience was more a Popular Front crowd than a Broadway one. "I'm more interested in the new theatre audience—that audience which out of ignorance or finances hasn't gone to the theatre or opera until recently," Blitzstein had written before the opera opened. "This group is aware of what is happening in terms of social and economic conflict and is eager to see theatrical presentations dealing with it." "This new audience is at the gates of the theatre, clamoring for something vital," and *The Cradle Will Rock* was its emblem.[6]

In the fall and winter of 1937–38, Orson Welles's new Mercury Theatre presented an "oratorio" version of *The Cradle*: the actors were back on stage, but without scenery; Blitzstein's piano continued to take the place of the pit orchestra. In his review, Virgil Thomson described *The Cradle*'s audience:

> It is roughly the leftist front: that is to say, the right-wing socialists, the communists, some Park Avenue, a good deal of Bronx, and all those intellectual or worker groups that the Federal Theater in general and the Living Newspaper in particular have welded into about the most formidable army of ticket-buyers in the world. Union benefits, leftist-group drives, the German refugees, the Southern share-croppers, aids to China and to democratic Spain, the New York working populace, well-paid, well-dressed, and well-fed, supports them all.

They were also the audience of the seven-record cast-recording of *The Cradle Will Rock* that Musicraft released in April 1938; it was the first full-length Broadway cast album. Blitzstein and Welles were themselves part of this leftist front, and both spoke at a March 1938 symposium on "The Culture of the People's Front."[7]

However, the success of *The Cradle Will Rock* was not simply a product of New York's radical theater; rather, the musical drew on and paralleled the CIO's year-long drive to organize the steel industry. Blitzstein wrote the opera in five weeks in the summer of 1936, just after John L. Lewis had announced the formation of the CIO's Steel Workers Organizing Committee (SWOC). Through the fall and winter of 1936–37, the nation witnessed the sit-down strike of Flint autoworkers and the La Follette congressional hearings on corporate strikebreaking and anti-labor espionage. Just as *The Cradle*'s rehearsals began in March 1937, SWOC reached a stunning agreement with U.S. Steel. The musical's ending, in which the bugles, drums, and fifes of the boilermakers, roughers, and rollers were a sign that "Steel's gettin' together tonight," seemed to be echoed in reality. The struggle against the companies of Little Steel—Jones & Laughlin, Republic, Bethlehem, and others—dominated the spring; after the Supreme Court upheld the National Labor Relations Act in April (in a case involving SWOC and Jones & Laughlin), a huge two-day strike in Aliquippa, Pennsylvania, won a contract from Jones & Laughlin (Figure 10).[8]

The Jones & Laughlin strike was the final success, however; the 26 May strike against the other Little Steel firms met bitter opposition and increased violence. "In the period between the onset of the strike for recognition that began on May 26 and the middle of July," one labor historian has written, "lethal violence, most of it perpetrated by company guards and city police, swept the midwestern steel centers. On Memorial Day 1937, Chicago police killed or wounded dozens of steelworkers and sympathizers. In Cleveland, Youngstown, and Massillon, lawmen also killed steelworkers. All told, the summer of 1937 added 18 dead to the long list of labor's martyrs." Paramount's suppression of its own newsreel footage of the Memorial Day massacre in Chicago was followed a few days later by the federal government's shutdown of *The Cradle*: a WPA production on the struggles in steel was, as Hallie Flanagan, the director of Federal Theatre, recalled, too "dangerous." The Venice Theatre performances coincided with the steel strike and the La Follette Committee's highly publicized investigations of the massacre.[9]

The stripped-down agitprop version of *The Cradle Will Rock* was taken to the steel towns of Pennsylvania and Ohio in the summer of 1937: "an audience of steelworkers represents a new public," Blitzstein told the *Daily Worker*, "wide awake and extremely critical." In the next year, amateur performances were staged by radical theater groups around the country, often with the support of CIO unions: the Chicago Repertory Group's *Cradle* was supported by the United Mine Workers. Scenes from *The Cradle* were used in a Newark CIO fundraising evening, and the Mercury Theatre received a letter of praise from the CIO's national office. With its broad comedy, its allegorical setting and characters—Steeltown, Mr Mister and his Liberty Committee, Joe Worker, and Larry Foreman—and its nursery song warning—"when the wind blows / The cradle will rock"—Blitzstein's labor musical came to embody the hopes spawned by the new industrial unions.[10]

Unlike many of the novels, plays, and artworks that grew out of organizing campaigns—Steinbeck's *The Grapes of Wrath*, Vorse's *Strike!*, or Hughes's *Scottsboro, Limited*—there was little documentary impulse in Blitzstein's work. His sense of the revolutionary promise of industrial unionism probably derived from his reading of William Z. Foster's pamphlets on "Industrial Unionism" and "Organizing Methods in the Steel Industry," not from direct involvement in a union drive. There is no evidence that Blitzstein visited a steel town until after *The Cradle* had opened. The roots of *The Cradle Will Rock* did not lie in a particular steel strike, nor in the accordion-driven Polish and Slavic polkas that dominated the musical culture of the midwestern steel towns. Rather, its roots lay in the American and European musical avant-gardes of the early 1930s.[11]

Blitzstein was part of a circle of young modernists around the League of Composers and the little magazine *Modern Music*. Born in 1905, he had grown up in a well-to-do Jewish banking family and had attended the University of Pennsylvania before going to Europe to study music with Nadia Boulanger and Arnold Schoenberg. In the wake of the 1929 crash and the rise of Hitler, a number of these young modernist composers, including Blitzstein, Henry Cowell, Charles Seeger, Ruth Crawford, Aaron Copland, Lan Adomian, Earl Robinson, Wallingford Riegger, and Elie Siegmeister, joined the left and formed a Composers Collective, "a group of professional musicians whose weekly meetings are devoted to the performance and round-table criticism of each other's current productions in proletarian music." The Collective was loosely connected to New York's Pierre Degeyter Club, a branch of the Communist-affiliated Workers Music League, which was primarily made up of workers choruses and orchestras. The Composers Collective gave concerts, sponsored a competition for a May Day song, which was won by Aaron Copland, and published song books and a magazine, *Music Vanguard*; members also taught at the Downtown Music School.[12]

The Collective had no single notion of "proletarian music." Some, like Copland, were attempting to Americanize European modernisms; others, like Henry Cowell and Wallingford Riegger, were committed to the iconoclastic American experimentalism represented by Charles Ives. A few, like Charles Seeger, Elie Siegmeister, and Earl Robinson, were drawn to rural folk musics. The inaugural issue of *Music Vanguard* illustrates the diversity: it included Lawrence Gellert's "Negro Songs of Protest in America," Aaron Copland's "A Note on Young Composers," Charles Seeger's "Preface to All Linguistic Treatment of Music," and Hanns Eisler's "History of the German Workers' Music Movement." As a result of these competing tendencies, the Collective did not last long; by the time *The Cradle Will Rock* was composed, it had disappeared. Nevertheless, Blitzstein's opera was perhaps the most important product of the Collective; Charles Seeger recalled that "the nearest we ever got to a public hearing was in Marc Blitzstein's *The Cradle Will Rock*, which was a marvelous work."[13]

Curiously, when Blitzstein himself listed the kinds of music the Composers Collective wanted to encourage—mass songs for parades and picket lines, choral music, solo songs, and instrumental music "to carry on the best musical traditions of the past"—he did not include opera or musical theater. Yet the search for a new form of musical theater was at the heart of Blitzstein's work. If the controversies over "proletarian music" in the Composers Collective made him rethink his own work, it was the music of and the aesthetic debates around the *Gebrauchsmusik* movement of Weimar Germany—what he called the "second generation" of "modern music"— that offered a new model for musical theater. Though originally skeptical of this "functional music" or "music for use," Blitzstein was increasingly attracted to the *Songspiel* of Paul Hindemith, Kurt Weill, and Hanns Eisler, all of whom had worked with the playwright Bertolt Brecht. Not only did Brecht and Weill's *Three-Penny Opera* (1928) and Brecht and Eisler's *Measures Taken* (1930) deeply influence Blitzstein, but he met Eisler, Brecht, and Weill when they came to the United States in 1935.[14]

Eisler, like Blitzstein a student of Arnold Schoenberg, arrived for a three-month tour in the spring of 1935, lecturing, meeting Blitzstein and the Composers Collective, and giving concerts with the young left-wing baritone Mordecai Baumann. Eisler returned in the fall to teach at the New School, and Blitzstein joined Eisler on several Timely recordings of Eisler/ Brecht songs. Brecht also came to the US in the fall of 1935 when the Theatre Union decided to produce *Mother*. Though the November 1935 production was a failure, Brecht found sympathetic supporters in set designer Mordecai Gorelik, Living Newspaper director Joseph Losey, and the future Mercury Theatre producer John Houseman, as well as Blitzstein and Blitzstein's wife, Eva Goldbeck. Goldbeck had translated Brecht's songs and poems, and her *New Masses* essay, "Principles of 'Educational' Theatre" was the first American exposition of Brecht's theories. Finally, Kurt Weill arrived in New York in the fall of 1935; Blitzstein seems to have met him the following summer in Connecticut, where Blitzstein was composing *The Cradle* and Weill, *Johnny Johnson*. Blitzstein reviewed the Group Theatre's production of the Weill/Paul Green *Johnny Johnson* and took back the "harsh things" he had written earlier about Weill and his music: "he hasn't changed, I have."[15]

The Cradle Will Rock was dedicated to Bertolt Brecht: "first because I think him the most admirable theatre-writer of our time; secondly because an extended conversation with him was partly responsible for writing the piece." Indeed, the model of the Brechtian *Songspiel* enabled Blitzstein to solve the formal problems he faced. *The Cradle*, he wrote, "was to be a colloquial piece; but it was also to be an opera." To achieve the colloquial, he avoided concert diction by composing vocal parts for singing actors rather than for particular ranges or voice qualities. But he was unwilling to adopt the "'number' form" of musical comedy in which "the alteration of dialogue and music seems over-sprightly and endlessly facetious, a vehicle for girls and gags; useless for any serious purpose." Yet a "continuous music," he argued, tended to shift the drama into the realm of legend and the heroic; though *The Cradle* "had to present a kind of heroism," it also had "to avoid anything like the heroic manner." His solution was what he called a "casual" use of music, a combination of "recitatives, arias, revue-patters, tap-dances, suites, chorals, silly-symphony continuums, incidental commentary music, military music, lullaby music," scored for a revue pit orchestra.[16]

Virtually all of his contemporaries recognized his success in capturing the rhythms of vernacular speech and incorporating the musical materials of American life. "The prosody, which was subtle and complex, neverthe-less had all the naturalness of hard-boiled English as sung in a jazz song," Aaron Copland noted; and Virgil Thomson wrote that "there is a particular musical style to characterize each person or scene; and always that style is aptly chosen, pungently taken off. The work has literary imperfections but musically not one fault of style." The more difficult challenge was finding a narrative that could hold these voices together, and *The Cradle Will Rock* can be seen as a compromise between three different elements: the prostitute's lament, the tale of the middle classes, and the aesthetic of industrial unionism.[17]

The Cradle Will Rock begins with the minor-key evening lament of the prostitute, Moll, played by Olive Stanton, who had had no Broadway experience: "I'm checkin' home now, call it a night." The song's arching melody then modulates into the syncopated encounter with the Gent and the Dick. After she is arrested, she observes and comments on the subsequent action in the night court (Figure 6). Her major song, "Nickel under the Foot," is the backbone of the play: she sings it just before the appearance of the union organizer Larry Foreman in scene 7, and then again as a unison chorus swelling underneath the climactic meeting of Mr Mister and Larry Foreman in scene 10. Moreover, "Nickel under the Foot" was the initial kernel for the show. According to one story, Blitzstein played the song for Brecht, and Brecht jumped up and said, "Why don't you write a piece about all kinds of prostitution—the press, the church, the courts, the arts, the whole system?" Years later, Blitzstein himself pointed to the "theme of literal prostitution, personified by the 'moll,' set against the background of prostitution of another kind—the sellout of one's profes-sion, one's talents, one's dignity and integrity, at the hands of big business or the powers that be."[18]

This story united the otherwise discrete episodes of *The Cradle*, which satirize the members of the Liberty Committee in blackout skits. The night court setting recalls the tribunal in Brecht and Eisler's *Measures Taken*, but it is the preachers, journalists, professors, doctors, painters, and composers who are brought to the bar. Though they have been arrested by mistake and protest their innocence, each has sold out to Mr Mister. "Sister, you should be ashamed," Larry tells Moll, "an amateur like you in the company of all these professionals." "What I really wanted to talk about was the middleclass," Blitzstein wrote. "Where does their allegiance lie? With big business, which is ready to engulf them, buy and sell them out exactly as it does labor, exploit and discard them at will. . . . The play shows various degradations suffered by the middleclass—some of them funny, some of them less funny." It was "*a middle-class allegory for middle-class people.*" It is not surprising that the organizer Larry Foreman is a *foreman* and describes himself as "middle class." As an organizer, "armed to the teeth—with leaflets," he is kin to the journalists, preachers, and artists, part of the play's dialectic of "soliciting." The final conflict between Mr Mister and Larry Foreman is not over union recognition or a contract, but over Mr Mister's unsuccessful attempt to buy off Larry Foreman.[19]

If Blitzstein's Moll owed something to the Jenny of Brecht and Weill's *Threepenny Opera*, his "middle classes" echoed Dos Passos's "writer as technician" and Burke's "complete propagandist." For Blitzstein, as for them, the reflection on the middle classes quickly became a reflection on art. It produced a Veblenite aesthetic, evident both in the relatively crude analysis of patronage and the faith in technique. "Every composer's music reflects in its subject-matter and in its style the source of the money the composer is living on while writing that music," composer Virgil Thomson wrote in his brilliant, satirical portrait of *The State of Music* (1939). "Nothing impresses a man very deeply except what pays him a living wage." This occupational determinism—akin to Kenneth Burke's account of the "occupational psychosis"—coexisted with a sense that the fundamentals of musical technique were as objective as the structural properties of steel in bridge building. *The Cradle* embodied both aspects of this Veblenite aesthetic. On the one hand, its musical caricatures were an anatomy of the corruptions of patronage: the counterpoint of a Bach chorale to Reverend Salvation's war sermons; the use of the college song "Boola Boola" in the satire of higher learning; and Beethoven's *Egmont* motif played by the horn of Mrs Mister's Pierce Arrow. On the other hand, the musical's dissonant harmonizations and shifting meters reflected Blitzstein's commitment to modernist polytonality: "modern music technique is for use," he argued, "the revolutionary composer ... should no more scrap it than a socialist society should scrap a machine because its functioning in a bourgeois system meant abuse or persecution or unemployment.... The technique is ... a kind of musical energy ... an equipment, a way of expressing which belongs to our time and to no other. Behind the mannerisms and stenciled dissonances and hash of styles there are the elements of a musical speech."[20]

However, despite Blitzstein's own assertion that *The Cradle* was a "middle-class allegory"—"unions," he wrote, "... are used as a symbol of something in the way of a solution for the plight of that middleclass"—the musical was always understood as a "proletarian opera," a "labor battle song." This was not a mistake. For the narrative of patronage and prostitution, the story of the classes caught in the "middle," vies with and is finally displaced by a narrative of industrial unionism. It is not that unions are at the center of the play; they remain offstage even at the end, as those in the night court await the outcome of the organizing drive. But Mr Mister's attempt to "prostitute" Larry Foreman is displaced by the bugles, fifes, and drums that signal the victory of the union. The bugles, fifes, and drums join together in the title song "The Cradle Will Rock," promising "a storm that's going to last until / The final wind blows." The song's tonality, Wilfrid Mellers notes, "suggests the uprooting, revolutionary tempest by hovering between a Phrygian E flat minor and E major with chromatic alterations: ending with fortissimo triads of B, A, D and A flat, harmonizing a line rising from D sharp up the scale of E major." This sense of revolutionary anticipation is heightened by the unresolved lullaby. Blitzstein uses only the first half of the nursery rhyme, ending his song, "And when the wind blows . . . The cradle will rock!"[21]

The Cradle's ending, like that of Odets's *Waiting for Lefty* embodied the aesthetic of industrial unionism. Virgil Thomson captured this in his review of the 1947 revival:

> *The Cradle* is a fairy tale, with villains and a hero. Like all fairy tales, it is perfectly true. . . . If the standard Broadway musical plugs what Thurman Arnold called "the folklore of capitalism," this play with (or "in") music recites with passion and piety the mythology of the labor movement. . . . Its power is due in large part to the freshness, in terms of current entertainment repertory, of the morality it expounds. That morality is a prophetic and confident faith in trade unionism as a dignifying force.

This folklore of unionism allows Blitzstein to set an explanation of open and closed shops to music, and reminds us that, as Thomson put it, "union cards can be as touchy a point of honor as marriage certificates." The union narrative recasts the "middle-class allegory." "What do you want us to do, join unions?" the painter Dauber asks Larry Foreman; "A Concert Artists' Union!" echoes Yasha the violinist. "Don't make us laugh!" the Liberty Committee replies, but the play's implicit answer is affirmative. "The composer," Blitzstein wrote at the end of an essay on modern music, takes "a post of an honest workman among workmen." By the time Moll sings "Nickel under the Foot," she no longer embodies the metaphorical space of a prostitute; she is an ordinary working woman.[22]

Nevertheless, if unionism serves as the musical's grand allegory, *The Cradle* remains a divided work, as the *New Masses* reviewer, R.D. Darrell, noted when he suggested that the figure of Larry Foreman upset "the exquisite balance of the work": "The conflict after all is not Mr. Mister and his mercenaries versus Larry Foreman, but the Misters versus the workers and their families for whom Larry is spokesman rather than personification." The steelworkers themselves are absent, indeed dead: the classic love duet of the Polish couple Gus and Sadie is followed by their murder in the bombing of the union headquarters; and the song "Joe Worker" is an elegy for a union worker pushed into a ladle. Though "Joe Worker" has, as Carol Oja has shown, roots in the mass songs of the Composers Collective, it remains a song addressed *to* workers, a Brechtian learning piece: "How many toiling, ailing, dying, piledup bodies, / Brother, does it take to make you wise?" The musical equivalent of the steelworkers' absence was, as Darrell noted, "the failure to make more use of the chorus." Blitzstein himself recognized this, and his second opera, *No for an Answer*, produced in January 1941, solved the formal antinomies of *The Cradle* in a striking manner: he made the working-class chorus the center of the opera.[23]

The working-class amateur chorus was a long tradition in the United States, and in the early years of the depression, radical musicians organized choruses as part of the proletarian avant-garde. When the Workers Music League was formed in 1931, many of its early affiliates were workers choruses. The early choruses were largely foreign-language groups, singing European art songs, traditional ethnic songs, and topical songs and radical anthems composed in those idioms. They were an important part of the radical subculture of a number of nationality groups, offering chorus members and audiences traditional entertainment while reinforcing allegiances to radical movements. Perhaps the largest and most famous of them was the Yiddish singing society, the *Freiheit Gesang Ferein*. One of its founders and leaders, Jacob Schaefer, was also a central figure in the Composers Collective.[24]

Indeed, though the Composers Collective is often caricatured as hopelessly out of touch, attempting to compose radical songs for "ordinary" workers, their actual aim—more modest and more realistic—was to compose songs for the self-selected workers who took part in these radical workers choruses. They were not always successful, and Earl Robinson recalled that Jacob Schaefer "would counsel them to be simpler, because his chorus couldn't sing anything they wrote." However, by the mid 1930s, several members of the Composers Collective were leading new English-language working-class choruses made up of young second-generation workers: Lan Adomian led the New Singers, Elie Siegmeister conducted the Daily Worker Chorus, later called the Manhattan Chorus, and Earl Robinson led the IWO's American People's Chorus. These English-language choruses generally used two kinds of material: the European mass song, developed in large part by Hanns Eisler, who had led workers choruses in Germany, and the traditional American labor hymn. Examples of both were recorded by the small left-wing record company, Timely. In 1935, Timely issued three records by Lan Adomian's New Singers with songs by Eisler and Brecht as well as Maurice Sugar's "Soup Song"; in 1937, they issued three similar records by Siegmeister's Manhattan Chorus, including traditional union songs like "Solidarity Forever," "We Shall Not Be Moved," and "Hold the Fort."[25]

Blitzstein made this working-class chorus the narrative and musical center of *No for an Answer*. The chorus rehearses in the Diogenes Club, a workers social club in the back room of a roadside lunchcounter owned by

Nick Kyriakos. The members are Greek American hotel and restaurant workers of the nearby resort town who are trying to form a union under the leadership of Nick's son, Joe. The conflation of chorus, social club, and union provides a formal unity that escaped *The Cradle*. Moreover, the waiters and chefs of the resort town are service workers in the entertainment industry, not unlike the cabaret singers and piano players in the opera's Pillbox Bar. The divide between workers and artists is not as stark as in "Steeltown, U.S.A."; indeed, Blitzstein based *No for an Answer* on a winter he spent in the resort town of Ventnor, New Jersey.[26]

The opera opens with the chorus rehearsing "The War of the Beasts and the Birds" and "Take the Book," two Brechtian learning pieces. At the end, after the club is burned by the hotel owners' Resort Association, the angry chorus sings "No for an Answer": "Singing is a form of battle too, we say, / When desperate people smile and sing / Beware. Beware . . . / For we will not take no! / No for an answer! No!" These "choral sections were enormously exciting," Aaron Copland wrote, "here the lack of trained voices was least apparent." The choral scenes alternate with passages of musically accompanied speech. In these passages, Copland noted, Blitzstein found his own musical style: "the short, clipped musical sentences, the uneven phrase lengths, the nervous energy, [and] . . . the subtle use of a talky prose rhythm over a musical background." The melodic lines are straightforward, with narrow ranges, but the harmonies are complex, often dissonant.[27]

This "American recitative," as Wilfrid Mellers called it, was able to capture several forms of vernacular speech: that of the hobo, the immigrant worker, and the working girl. Blitzstein's Wobbly hobo Bulge serves as the musical's equivalent of Moll, opening the second act with "Penny Candy," a panhandler's comic "tale of woe," as he solicits a hand-out to satisfy a craving for penny candy: "O lead me to that smell of penny candy! / Although I ain't got any penny handy." Like "Nickel under the Foot," "Penny Candy" is a revision of Yip Harburg's classic depression hit, "Brother, Can You Spare a Dime?" (from the 1932 revue *Americana*). Bulge also sings the birthday song to Joe Kyriakos, "The Purest Kind of a Guy," which Paul Robeson later made famous. Another form of Blitzstein's *Songspiel* is found in the immigrant song of Nick Kyriakos, an ironic tribute to the United States: "One fine day / Me and USA / We get married . . . / The country treats me bad? / I feel good / It's in the family / Invited guests they only treat good, not me and you." Perhaps the epitome of this recitative, however, is the Francie and Joe love scene which opens with Francie's "My hands get all rough from the laundry": on the 1941 recording, the grain of Norma Green's voice is an uncanny double of that of Dorothy Comingore in *Citizen Kane*.[28]

No for an Answer was a richer and more complex representation of working-class life and characters than *The Cradle*, relying less on allegorical types. Most music reviewers found it, as Aaron Copland did, "an advance on the first work in every way." But it was not an allegory of industrial unionism, and it did not succeed in winning over Popular Front audiences. *The Cradle* was, as Virgil Thomson wrote, "prophetic and confident," full of "sweetness, a cutting wit, inexhaustible fancy and faith." It captured the vigorous, self-confident moment of the sit-down strikes; it made the audience the center of the production. *No for an Answer*, on the other hand, was written during a moment of defeat: the defeat of the CIO by Little Steel, the defeat of Republican Spain by Franco, the defeat of the anti-fascist alliance signaled by the Nazi-Soviet Pact. The CIO's second great offensive in the spring and summer of 1941 and the wartime alliance still lay ahead. The opera is characterized by stubborn refusal—No for an answer—and bitterness. In "Make the Heart Be Stone," the chorus sings: "Call, call bitterness out, call, / To the people in all places—bitterness!" It is a long way from the revolutionary lullaby promising that the cradle *will* rock.[29]

2. Needle Trades on Broadway: *Pins and Needles*

We're not George M. Cohans or Noel Cowards
Or Beatrice Lillies or Willie Howards
We've never played in stock or studied at the playhouse. . . .
Dressmakers, cloakmakers, cutters, underwear workers, knit-goods workers, neckwear makers, embroiderers, stampers, checkers, examiners, graders, pressers, trimmers, binders, pinkers
All of us—from the shops!

The same night *The Cradle Will Rock* re-opened at the Mercury Theatre— 27 November 1937—*Pins and Needles* opened in the main auditorium of the International Ladies' Garment Workers Union's (ILGWU) Labor Stage. *Pins and Needles* was a musical revue sponsored by the union and performed by New York garment workers. Written largely by the young songwriter Harold Rome, it ran for three years, drawing working-class audiences to its mixture of political satire and vaudeville song. It became the longest running musical in Broadway history, and the major popular success of the cultural front.[30]

A half century later, *Pins and Needles* lives on in both union and Broadway lore. In the labor movement, it remains an emblem of a time when a union-sponsored theater could be a popular success; on Broadway, it stands as a curious anomaly, its amateur cast and atypical audience peculiar products of the "socially conscious" 1930s. As a leading chronicler of Broadway history writes, "all too many of the sketches and songs gratuitously injected slanted political muckraking into what could have been pleasant apolitical numbers." Unable to fathom the appeal of such a show—"a theatrical historian might well wonder what so much of the hand-clapping was about"—he "suspects that the most receptive playgoers . . . were those who were preconditioned to enjoy it. Fanatics of any ilk will often accept discomforts and tortures more balanced souls would unhesitatingly reject." Other historians attempt to explain the show's success by downplaying its politics: one argues that the revue "did not . . . present ideological solutions or reflect the policies of many of the New York left-wing movements"; another that "the one memorable song from the extremely socially conscious musical *Pins and Needles* is not one of its many realistic and high-minded songs but the romantic 'Sunday in the Park,' which has a lilting melody." Actually, the revue grew directly out of New York's left-wing movements, and, as we shall see, "Sunday in the Park" is one of the few "realistic and high-minded" songs in the revue.[31]

It is tempting to see *Pins and Needles* as simply a colorful bit of depression glass, a happy accident, unconnected to the main currents of American cultural history; but this would be a mistake. For the remarkable success of *Pins and Needles* lay in the way the garment workers' performances of Harold Rome's songs brought together traditions of the vaudeville stage and the radical theater, of workers choruses and Tin Pan Alley. As a result, *Pins and Needles* was not only a Popular Front political satire, but a powerful song cycle of working-class romance. The bluesy laments of Ruth Rubinstein, Millie Weitz, and Nettie Harary became the folk songs of women garment workers, and *Pins and Needles* proved to be one of the music front's lasting achievements.

i. "All of Odets in six minutes"

Pins and Needles began as a controversial marriage of vaudeville revue and radical theater. The ILGWU had organized a drama division of its Educational and Recreational Department in 1934, and, together with other needle trades unions, created Labor Stage, Inc. at the 1935 AFL convention, hoping to found a labor-based professional theater. When support from the other unions dried up, Labor Stage became an amateur theater of the ILGWU, and the ILGWU Players performed several proletarian plays, including John Wexley's *Steel.* However, Louis Schaffer, the head of the ILGWU's drama division, wanted to produce a musical revue: workers, he argued, went to the theater to be entertained, not "just because it is a labor theater." When Joseph Losey introduced him to Harold Rome, a young songwriter who had been working in an Adirondack resort, the collaboration that produced *Pins and Needles* began. Initially, they met resistance from the young workers active in the Labor Stage, most of whom saw themselves as part of the proletarian avant-garde symbolized by Clifford Odets's *Waiting for Lefty*. However, after staging a run-through of their musical show with a cast of unemployed actors on 14 June 1936, the union was impressed and went ahead with the production, hiring Rome as a rehearsal pianist and Charles Friedman as director.[32]

Charles Friedman shared the cast's connection to the proletarian theater: he had been part of the Shock Troupe, a group of young worker-actors, including Nicholas Ray and Earl Robinson, who lived communally and were the core of the Workers Laboratory Theatre. But Friedman had moved the Workers Laboratory Theatre toward more professional productions; he was a co-author of their first major production, *The Young Go First* (under the WLT's new name, the Theatre of Action). He had also worked as a director at the Theatre Union, the most professional of the radical theaters.[33]

In many ways, Friedman was responsible for *Pins and Needles*'s unique fusion of proletarian drama and vaudeville revue. On the one hand, he fully adopted the revue form: "I directed in the music hall tradition where you sing directly to the people in the audience," Friedman recalled later. "I did not direct it as an illusionistic play. I broke down the fourth wall for them." He encouraged a burlesque humor that the cast was often reluctant to adopt. One member of the original cast, Ruth Rubinstein, remembered that "Charlie Friedman had some trouble with our prudish nature. We were naive kids from the shops and it was difficult for us to act uninhibited, especially when we had to do burlesque-type humor. Poor Mr Friedman had a lot to put up with—temperamental Stanislavsky garment workers, prudish leading ladies, and a whole crew of inexperienced actors." At the same time, the revue built on the earlier radical theater. Its cheap and cartoon-like sets were the work of Sointu Syrjala, who had designed sets for the Theatre Union's production of *Stevedore*. *Pins and Needles*'s satirical sketches were comic versions of the agitprop street drama of the WLT and the theatrical newsreels of the Federal Theatre Project's Living Newspaper: several were even written by the head playwright of the Living Newspaper, Arthur Arent. Finally, like Blitzstein, Harold Rome drew on the radical German theater music: "a writer for the theater," he once noted, "composes what Hindemith called 'gebrauchs' music—music for use."[34]

For a year and half, Friedman and Rome rehearsed the cast at the Labor Stage, the ILGWU's arts center in the old Princess Theater on 39th Street. *Pins and Needles* opened in November 1937 with nineteen numbers performed by a cast of forty-four; the musical accompaniment was provided by two pianos, one played by Rome himself. The cast was made up of cutters, pressers, operators, and finishers who worked in the Seventh Avenue needle trades. "While at work, I would keep peeping into my machine drawer where I kept the lines of the new skit or song," Ruth

Rubinstein later recalled, "memorizing as the brassieres flowed out of the machine." At first, the revue played only on weekends since the cast continued to work during the week. Later, they were given leave from the shops, and by 1938 the cast joined the Actors' and Chorus Equity unions. Over the years, the numbers and cast changed: a second edition, *Pins and Needles 1939*, opened on 21 April 1939 and moved to the larger Windsor Theater on 26 June 1939; and a third edition, *New Pins and Needles*, opened on 20 November 1939. Only a handful of numbers lasted the entire run: "Sing Me a Song with Social Significance" (originally called "Why Sing of Skies Above!"); "Sunday in the Park"; "Dear Beatrice Fairfax," which included the song "Nobody Makes a Pass at Me"; and "Four Little Angels of Peace" (though the number of angels varied from three to five). Audiences returned to see the new numbers, contributed not only by Rome, but also by screenwriter Joseph Shrank and lyricist John LaTouche: by 1940, between forty and fifty different numbers had been part of the show.[35]

For the most part, critics and historians have paid closest attention to the topical sketches, of which there were three main kinds: satires of the radical theater, satires of wealth and reaction in the United States, and anti-fascist satires. From its beginings, *Pins and Needles* repaid its debts to the proletarian theater in satire, lampooning Brechtian epic theater in Emmanuel Eisenberg's "The Little Red Schoolhouse," attacking censorship in the Federal Theatre Project in Marc Blitzstein's "FTP Plowed Under," and presenting "all of Odets in six minutes" in Joseph Shrank's hilarious "Paradise Mislaid." Eventually, the revue made fun of itself; in Harold Rome's "Give Me the Good Old Days," a member of the *Pins and Needles* cast sings of the simple days back in the shop, without the problems of the stage—"two songs a night, and diction worries."

The second type of satirical sketch went after American reactionaries: these included "Slumming Party," with its dance tune, "Doing the Reactionary," a parody of "Putting on the Ritz"; "Lesson in Etiquette," in which a wealthy woman sings "it's not cricket to picket"; and the "Red Mikado," which built on the popular parodies of the Mikado—there was a "Swing Mikado" and a "Hot Mikado"—to lampoon the right-wing Daughters of the American Revolution and the German American Bund.[36]

However, the anti-fascist numbers were probably the best-known of the topical sketches. They got their bite from particular events: few lasted throughout the show's run. They included the early satires of Mussolini, "Mussolini Handicap" and "Public Enemy Number One"; an attack on British appeasement, "Britannia Waives the Rules"; a sketch on the Nazi suppression of the work of Heinrich Heine, "Lorelei on the Rocks"; and an allegorical account of the Biblical tyrant Belshazzar, "Mene, Mene, Tekel." One 1939 sketch, "Stay Out Sammy," opposed US intervention in the European war; a later one from the road show, "History Eight to the Bar," supported intervention. Since the show's writers, cast, and audience included both Popular Front Communists and anti-Communist social democrats, the revue was caught in the fallout of the Nazi-Soviet Pact of September 1939. The most celebrated anti-fascist song, "Four Little Angels of Peace," began by caricaturing Eden, Hitler, Hirohito, and Mussolini; at a later point Chamberlain replaced Eden; then Chamberlain was dropped and the angels reduced to three; and, finally, after the Pact, Chamberlain was returned and Stalin added as a fifth angel. At one point, Rome replaced the "Angels" number with a sketch called "International Situation," "a long announcement explaining that the rapid changes in the international situation had driven the author insane," reducing him to writing nursery rhymes.[37]

But Friedman's synthesis of *Waiting for Lefty* and the *Ziegfeld Follies* was not entirely unique. A year earlier, in May 1935, the radical authors of *Stevedore*, Paul Peters and George Sklar, collaborated with Jerome Moross on a left-wing musical revue, *Parade*. Its twenty-eight numbers included blackout sketches and songs not unlike those of *Pins and Needles*: satires of radio demagogues like Huey Long and Father Coughlin, of society matrons who call out the militia (written by Marc Blitzstein), of a Hearst reporter photographing a hungry American family to illustrate a story of Russian famine, of tabloid accounts of bomb-throwing Reds, and of a college girl trying to get a job at a department store. However, the production was not a great success, closing after forty performances. Why did *Pins and Needles* succeed where *Parade* failed? In retrospect, critics and historians have concluded that *Pins and Needles* was simply the better show; as Morgan Himelstein writes of *Parade*, "the lyrics lacked the sparkle of Harold Rome's lines, and the sketches lacked both the precise bite and the good humor of the Labor Stage revue." But the crucial difference lay not simply in the sparkle of Rome's lyrics and the bite and good humor of the sketches. After all, Rome's subsequent political revue, *Sing Out the News*, failed to repeat the success of *Pins and Needles*. The latter's success was not primarily the result of its satires of current political events: that is why the show successfully navigated the crisis on the left created by the Nazi-Soviet Pact. Despite the attention given these topical sketches by reviewers and historians, at no point did they comprise more than half of the show's numbers. The real difference between *Parade* (and Rome's later show) and *Pins and Needles* lay in the latter's working-girl songs.[38]

ii. "What good is love?"

Pins and Needles was fundamentally a song cycle about working-class romance, a gentle parody of "moon songs and June songs" and their place

in working-class life. It uniquely combined the ethnic traditions of radical
workers choruses with the forms and cadences of Tin Pan Alley. The *Pins
and Needles* singers stood clearly in the tradition of working-class choruses:
some, like Olive Pearlman, had sung in the ILGWU's choral group before
joining *Pins and Needles*, and many were the products of the ILGWU's
cultural programs, which included the chorus, drama classes, a modern
dance group, and a mandolin orchestra. Like the English-language choruses led by Adomian, Siegmeister, and Robinson, the *Pins and Needles* cast
were young, second-generation Jews and Italians. However, their songs
were not the mass chants of Hanns Eisler, but the Tin Pan Alley tunes of
Harold Rome.

Tin Pan Alley, the New York-based industry of popular song publishing,
had developed at the turn of the century together with the rise of vaudeville
theater and the beginnings of a recording industry. By the 1920s, a group
of young, largely Jewish, songwriters, including Jerome Kern (born in
1885), Ira and George Gershwin (born in 1896 and 1898), and Harold
Arlen (born in 1905), had begun to transform American popular music.
Though most came from middle-class backgrounds and had formal educations, they had grown up in the multi-ethnic and multi-racial modern
metropolis and served apprenticeships as song pluggers and rehearsal
pianists. They combined a street sophistication with a knowledge of urban
vernacular music, particularly African American jazz and the tenement
songs of Jewish and Italian workers. Their songs, sung by Fanny Brice,
Sophie Tucker, Al Jolson, and Eddie Cantor, became the soundtrack of
the lives of the young second-generation workers who were to build the
CIO. A number of them shared the Popular Front politics of their
audiences, most notably Jay Gorney, Ira Gershwin, and Yip Harburg:
Harburg's immigrant parents had been garmentworkers on New York's
Lower East Side. The major precedent for Rome's *Pins and Needles* songs
was probably Harburg and Gorney's hit song of 1932, "Brother, Can You
Spare a Dime?," written for the satirical Broadway revue *Americana* and
recorded by Bing Crosby and Al Jolson.[39]

The songs of Tin Pan Alley were remarkable in several respects. Their
32-bar *a a b a* form was an exception in the history of American popular
song. Both nineteenth-century songs and the country-and-western and
rhythm-and-blues songs that emerged after World War II were largely
based on either the traditional ballad form, a series of narrative verses
answered by a short 8- or 16-bar refrain, or the 12-bar blues form. The Tin
Pan Alley song was marked by the attenuation of the ballad's verse, and
the expansion of the refrain or chorus to 32 bars. As the verse was reduced
to a recitative introduction, the song became a tighter, more compact,
whole. As with many small forms, the 32-bar song gave shelter both to
hacks manufacturing repetitive and die-cast formulas and to tunesmiths

crafting elegant and eloquent miniatures. Whereas the verses of earlier popular ballads told stories, the 32-bar song was a vehicle for the evocation of a mood or a feeling. Thus, as most historians of popular song have noted, the Tin Pan Alley song focused on romantic love to a far greater degree than popular song before and after. The great formal problem of Tin Pan Alley was, as Philip Furia noted, that posed by a Harburg/Arlen song of 1932: "What can you say in a love song that hasn't been said before?"[40]

Though Harold Rome was an unknown songwriter when he wrote *Pins and Needles*, he shared much with the more established songwriters. Born in 1908 in Hartford, he was also Jewish and had come from a business-class background, graduating from Yale. For him, the work on *Pins and Needles* was first of all a job; he later recalled being less excited at having his songs sung than at having regular employment as a rehearsal pianist. But his songs proved to be a powerful vehicle for the young garment workers, resonating with their urban working-class audiences; though their forms were taken from Tin Pan Alley, they became as much the "folk songs" of New York's garment workers as were the southern mill songs of Gastonia's Ella May Wiggins or the mining ballads of Harlan County's Aunt Molly Jackson and Sarah Ogan Gunning.

In many respects, the success of *Pins and Needles* lies in the fact that the eight songs at the heart of the show make up a witty, satirical, and realistic conversation about love songs, romance, and working-class life. The centrality of these songs may be gauged in several ways. Of the four songs that were kept throughout the show's run, three are in this category: "Sing Me a Song with Social Significance," "Nobody Makes a Pass at Me," and "Sunday in the Park" (the fourth was "Four Little Angels of Peace"). Of the seven songs from the original show published as sheet music, six are in this category: the three above as well as "Chain Store Daisy," "What Good Is Love?", and "One Big Union for Two" (the other song published was "Doing the Reactionary"). The two Decca 78 recordings featured these songs: one included Millie Weitz of the original cast singing "Nobody Makes a Pass at Me" together with the popular duo Kay Weber and Sonny Schuyler singing "One Big Union for Two"; the other had Ruth Rubinstein of the cast singing "Chain Store Daisy" and Kay Weber and Sonny Schuyler singing "Sing Me a Song with Social Significance."[41]

The show begins with a song about songs, a refusal of the love song: "I'm tired of moon songs of star and of June songs." What follows is a clever exhortation to "Sing Me a Song with Social Significance," a self-conscious justification of the topical song: "Sing me of wars and sing me of breadlines," the bridge elaborates, "Sing me of strikes and last minute headlines." But this is done without the agitprop seriousness and marching rhythms of the Eisler mass songs. The square march-like rhythms of the bridge—"Tell me of mills and mines"—resolve to the witty reminder to "dress your observation in syncopation." The syncopated sibilants of the title phrase remind us that the song mocks itself, accenting its very ordinariness: "I want a song that's satirical, / And putting the mere into miracle." For though it calls for songs "packed with social fact," it remains a love song, both in form—the standard 32-bar *a a b a* structure—and in each of its perfect cadences, which sing "or I won't love you."[42]

"What Good Is Love?," originally sung by Nettie Harary, a felling-machine operator, also begins as a rejection of the love song. The only torch song in the show, it is a 16-bar slow blues. Like "Sing Me a Song," it opens with a recitative invocation of moon songs and June songs:

> Everywhere I go I hear sweet songs about the moon
> Songs about the stars above and songs of love in June
> Songs of hearts that beat as one to some sweet lovers tune
> But they're not songs that sing for me

However, in this case the singer rejects not only the songs of romance, but romance itself: "What good is love / If you have to face / Cold hungry days and sighing? . . . What good is love / If you haven't got / All that makes life worth living?" In its brief rhetorical questions, the song evokes the daily deprivations of the garment worker's culture of necessity. Despite the plaintive despair of "Where is my chance / For the call of romance," the song avoids self-pity in the singer's final bluesy defiance, "You can keep your little songs . . . What good is love to me?" In different ways, both songs represent the garment workers, not by depicting them, but by singing for them.

Set against these rejections of love and its "sweet songs" are several tunes that "re-function"—to use Brecht's term—the love song and reclaim romance for workers. Two are humorous union love songs sung by the ensemble: "One Big Union for Two," from the original show, and the song that replaced it in *New Pins and Needles*, "It's Better with a Union Man." "One Big Union for Two" is a clever, if relatively straightforward, play with the tropes of labor relations:

> I'm on a campaign to make you mine
> I'll picket you until you sign
> In one big union for two.
>
> No court's injunction can make me stop
> Until your love is all closed shop
> In one big union for two.

Nevertheless, this song, with its rousing "Fifty million union members can't be wrong," was too dangerous for network radio and was banned by NBC until the recorded lyrics were modified to "Fifty million happy couples can't be wrong."[43]

"It's Better with a Union Man" was part of an elaborate sketch entitled "Bertha, the Sewing Machine Girl," set in the 1890s as a parody of the period's popular working-girl melodramas. A waltz-time ballad, the song tells of the seduction of Bertha, "a winsome, and class conscious lass," by a non-union villain with "six wives on the sly." Lured by his "black caviar and champagne," she forgets her "true union lover / Waiting at Local 16 all in vain." Like the sentimental songs of the turn of the century, the ballad's storytelling is punctuated by an uptempo refrain, "It's better with a union man."

"I've Got the Nerve to Be in Love," originally sung by Al Levy and Ruth Elbaum in *Pins and Needles 1939*, is a witty duet in the style of Gershwin's "Let's Call the Whole Thing Off" or Cole Porter's "Let's Do It (Let's Fall in Love)." After denying that "love is a luxury," "good enough for Woolworth heirs / Debutants and millionaires," the singers trade phrases of the 32-bar song: though "I buy my things at Woolworth's, no charge account at Sak's / . . . why should I deny myself a try at love." Whereas "What Good Is Love?" simply hints at the "things" the singer did not have, "I've Got the Nerve to Be in Love" catalogues the stocks, charge accounts, penthouses, limousines, and yachts that the lovers lack in long multi-syllabic lines. The song's bridge sets the world of the shop against the resorts of the wealthy: "I prefer to keep away / From Newport and the gay / Society affairs / Sewing underwear all day / Don't give much time to play / With millionaires." Alluding to the Federal Theatre Project's Living Newspaper on tenement housing, *One-Third of a Nation*, the song concludes: "Our economic standing / Won't need investigation / We know that we're included / In one-third of the nation / It's very plain to see / But still I've got the nerve to be / In love with you." The song not only asserts the garment worker's right to be in love, it also stakes a proletarian claim on the witty and sophisticated lyrics of a Cole Porter.

This dialectic of romance and its promises runs through the show's two most successful satirical songs, Millie Weitz's "Nobody Makes a Pass at Me" and Ruth Rubinstein's "Chain Store Daisy." The working-girl laments were the only songs from the original show recorded by cast members. Weitz, a felling-machine operator, had performed in several ILGWU proletarian plays including *So It Didn't Work*, a comedy set in a garment shop, and *Who Is Getting Excited*, the story of a dress shop strike. Rubinstein had spent three years as a brassiere operator after quitting Brooklyn College, and was taking dance classes at the Labor Stage when she joined *Pins and Needles*. Unlike the songs that were recorded by professionals, these songs capture the accents and knowing humor of the garment workers; their satire seems to require the amateur voices of Weitz and Rubinstein.[44]

The success of "Nobody Makes a Pass at Me" and "Chain Store Daisy" derived in part from the way Millie Weitz and Ruth Rubinstein sang out of an urban ethnic tradition: they adapted the brassy style of Jewish popular singers like Fanny Brice and Sophie Tucker. Brice, born Fannie Borach in 1891, rose from obscurity through the vaudeville stage to star in Ziegfeld's *Follies* from 1910 to 1923. She sang sophisticated French cabaret songs as well as comic songs and sketches done in a Yiddish accent. "Second Hand Rose," "Rose of Washington Square," and "Mrs Cohen at the Beach" were ethnic self-caricatures, not unlike African American minstrel perform- ances. Sophie Tucker, born Sonia Kalish in Russia, began performing in blackface and became one of vaudeville's greatest stars; her Decca record- ing of "My Yiddishe Momme," which had an English version on one side of the 78 and a Yiddish version on the other, not only invoked the "humble East Side tenement," but, as Mark Slobin has suggested, drew on the musical culture of the immigrant ghetto. This mixture of sentiment and caricature made Brice and Tucker vital, if contradictory, voices of New York's Jewish workers; and it was their legacy that Millie Weitz and Ruth Rubinstein invoked in their comic songs.[45]

However, the *Pins and Needles* songs did not take the ethnic neighbor- hood as an object of sentiment or caricature. Both "Nobody Makes a Pass at Me" and "Chain Store Daisy" were satires of the consumer culture in which the young second-generation workers were saturated, the world of advertising and department stores. Unlike much of the period's radical satire of advertising—including *Pins and Needles*'s own "Song of the Ads" and "Cream of Mush Song"—these are not simple denunciations of advertising's mindlessness and manipulation. Rather, they recognized the power of advertising's promise, a promise not unlike that of the love song itself, a promise betrayed.

"Nobody Makes a Pass at Me" is the lament of a woman betrayed by advertising's sexual sell:

> I wash my clothes with Lux,
> My etiquette's the best,
> I spend my hard earned bucks,
> On just what the ads suggest.
> O dear what can the matter be?
> Nobody makes a pass at me.

If we don't believe the sincerity and effort of the singer, the song breaks into double time with a torrent of rhyming brand names:

> I use Coca Cola and Marmola,
> Crisco, Lesco, and Mazola,

> Exlax and Vapex,
> So why ain't I got sex?
>
> I use Albolene and Maybellene,
> Alka Seltzer, Bromo Seltzer,
> Odorono and Sensation,
> So why ain't I got fascination?
>
> I use Pond's on my skin,
> With Rye-Crisp I have thinned,
> I get my culture in,
> I began *Gone with the Wind.*
> O dear what can the matter be?
> Nobody makes a pass at me.

The song ends with a recognition of the discrepancy between the singer's knowing desire, with its slang, its double entendres, and its burlesque evasions—"I want attention / And things I can't mention"—and the cleanliness and purity promised by the ads which continually make a pass at her. As the singer laments, the ads work all too well: "Like Ivory Soap I'm ninety-nine and forty-four one-hundredths percent pure."

If "Nobody Makes at Pass a Me" is the lament of the unsatisfied shopper, "Chain Store Daisy" is the saleswoman's lament (Figure 8). The song works on a double conceit: the complaint of a college graduate working in a department store, and the employee's satire of the department store's well-to-do shoppers. The first tale is told in the recitative verse: "They told me my fine education / Would help improve my stituation / So then I crammed and crammed til I was almost in a coma / And thesised and examed until I got me a diploma / Aha they said now comes admission / Into a very high position / Out I went and looked around / And Macy's is the place I found." Much of the song's chorus plays on the gap between the singer's aspirations, figured by the sorority daisy chain, and the realities of the shop:

> Once I wrote poems, put folks in tears
> Now I write checks for ladies brassieres
> I used to be on the daisy chain
> Now I'm a chain store daisy.

But the song is rescued from self-pity by its satire of the department store's own promises of satisfaction: "I'm selling things to fit the figure / Make the big things small and the small things bigger." The bridge turns into a fawning address to a customer: "Oh yes madame / Oh no madame / I guess madame / That's so madame / Of course madame / That's the very best / Exactly the kind that's worn by Mae West."

The success of *Pins and Needles* lay in its union of class, ethnic, and feminist energies, in the way it sang for young Jewish and Italian working-class women of the garment trades. Though women were only a quarter of the wage-labor force in 1940, they were a large majority of the needle trades. And though the women of the ILGWU were unable to achieve representation in the union's leadership in these years—Rose Pesotta was the lone woman vice-president in the decade between 1934 and 1944—they did achieve representation in *Pins and Needles*. Unlike most proletarian drama, it was largely a woman's show. This was not the intention of the men who wrote and directed the show: the archives and the oral histories suggest that the "political" sketches were the subject of more attention and controversy than the women's songs. Moreover, other ILGWU cultural events did not share the labor feminism of *Pins and Needles*. The huge pageant staged by Louis Schaffer at the 1940 ILGWU convention, *I Hear America Singing*, a cavalcade of American history based on a Whitman poem, was a memorable extravaganza with its cast of a thousand, but it had none of the feminist resonance of *Pins and Needles*; and the usual ILGWU "women's" events were the union fashion shows and beauty contests that Pesotta herself recalls with affection.[46]

Pins and Needles was neither a pageant of labor Americanism nor a beauty pageant, though it had elements of both. Its major songs were sung by women, and many of its satiric sketches set women at the center: "Not Cricket to Picket" is a satire of notions of "unladylike" behavior, and the two anti-fascist satires of Mussolini were aimed at the gender politics of fascism, lampooning fascist policies to increase the birth rate. The feminism of *Pins and Needles* was in part a result of the fact that, unlike the proletarian dramas and pageants, it was not a play, scripted in advance and then performed. The songs and sketches of the revue were interchangeable, and they were written and rewritten, added and dropped, throughout the year and a half of rehearsals and the three years of performances. As a result, cast members like Rubinstein, Weitz, and Harary shaped and interpreted their songs and skits; as the satires of international politics came and went, the labor feminism of the working women's songs became the backbone of the show.

The show was not without conflicts, however. Since the revue itself lacked an overall narrative, the history of the show has been the subject of most accounts of *Pins and Needles*. Three conflicts stand out: the political conflicts, the ethnic conflicts, and the professional conflicts. Several historians interpret the show as firmly opposed to the Communists: Himelstein even argues that *Pins and Needles* was the major alternative to the Communist-oriented radical theater, a product of the "non-Communist left." The show was buffeted by two major crises on the left: the civil war between the AFL and the CIO, and the Nazi-Soviet Pact. The first was intensified when the ILGWU's leader, David Dubinsky, a founder of the CIO, took the ILGWU out of the CIO and back into the AFL in late 1938; the division between the two federations was the subject of a humorous sketch, "Papa Lewis, Mama Green." The crisis of the Nazi-Soviet Pact led, as I noted earlier, to a number of changes in the revue, which were criticized by the *Daily Worker* in late 1939. Moreover, the show's impresario, Louis Schaffer, was bitterly anti-Communist and led the attack on the Popular Front Theatre Arts Committee in 1939. Several cast members later claimed that if Schaffer learned someone was a Communist, he would fire them; both the first director, Charles Friedman, and one of the stars, Millie Weitz, were pushed out for their Communist politics.[47]

Nonetheless, the revue's cast and writers were further to the left than Schaffer and the ILGWU administrators. Both of the directors who replaced Friedman, Robert Gordon and Howard da Silva, were Popular Front radicals: Gordon had directed sketches in Cabaret TAC and da Silva had played Larry Foreman in *The Cradle Will Rock.* "Everyone was socially conscious," Dorothy Tucker recalled of the cast, "there were a few socialists and few Communists among us"; another cast member, Joe Alfasa, remembered that "there were a lot of left-wing kids there." Harold Rome himself was a quintessential figure of the Popular Front, working in the Wallace campaign in 1948; he was later listed in the blacklister's handbook, *Red Channels.* Thus, *Pins and Needles* was neither a "Communist" nor a "non-Communist" show; it embodied the alliances and tensions of the Popular Front social movement.[48]

Popular Front tensions were hardly restricted to the divisions between Communists and social democrats (not to mention the ex-Communists associated with Jay Lovestone, who were influential in the ILGWU's Local 22). Though *Pins and Needles* did not stress the ethnic origins of its Jewish and Italian cast, and few of its songs or sketches made any explicit reference to ethnicity, the ethnic tensions within New York's working classes scarred the production. "Ethnic lines were drawn even in the locals," Jean Nicita, who played Rubinstein's part in the second company, recalled. The ILGWU's Local 89 was largely Italian, and Local 22 was largely Jewish. Moreover, Louis Schaffer was as wary of the casts' accents as of their radical politics: "eventually Schaffer weeded out those people with thick Jewish accents," cast member Al Levy recalled. Hyman Goldstein was asked to change his name by the show's public relations man, and he became Hy Gardner; and Schaffer tried to persuade both Rubinstein and Harary to get nose jobs. These backstage struggles and controversies are themselves evidence of the way the show's energy derived from its attempts to resolve the contradictions faced by the second-generation ethnic workers who used the products of American commercial culture—like the Tin Pan Alley song—to create a culture that was distinct from the enclave culture of their immigrant parents and yet was marked by its own class and ethnic accents.[49]

Finally, *Pins and Needles* never escaped the labor relations of the culture industry itself. "I was a shop-worker and getting into *Pins and Needles* was like being freed from slavery," Joe Alfasa recalled. But the world of Broadway was itself a workplace, and there were conflicts between the Labor Stage and Actors' Equity over the status of these "amateur" performers. Indeed, in one satiric sketch, Millie Weitz sits in front of a makeup mirror, reflecting on the work of acting, and singing "Give Me the Good Old Days" in the dress shop. The first company were all amateurs; subsequent companies included more and more semiprofessionals from the radical stage, Katherine Dunham's dance troupe, cellar clubs, and Catskill entertainment. A few cast members went on to work in the entertainment industry; most went back to the shops. "Two weeks after I left the show," Nettie Harary recalled, "I was back in the shops at the felling machines." She didn't stay there, however: "one of the more positive things about *Pins and Needles* was that I was politically active, and I was aware of the world around me." Harary later sang in Blitzstein's *No for an Answer.*[50]

Despite the conflicts over politics and ethnicity, and the compromises made in the transition from the Labor Stage to Broadway, *Pins and Needles* managed to combine the aesthetic and folklore of industrial unionism, which it shared with Blitzstein's *The Cradle Will Rock*, with a casual but telling representation of working-class daily life. "Sunday in the Park" was the show's most successful song; it was a popular hit for the Hudson-DeLange Orchestra, spending five weeks on the charts in the spring of 1938. Many critics and historians have argued that it succeeded because it was an apolitical romantic song. This misunderstanding stems from the fact that Harold Rome claimed it was not a political song in order to get it past the NBC radio ban. However, if "Sunday in the Park" is not a topical protest song, neither is it an apolitical romance. Part of the show's song cycle on working-class life, it represents a laboring of popular song. Despite its lilting C major melody, the song begins in the shop—"All week long I work in the shop, I work and work and never stop"—and the tenement— "our hot and stuffy flat"—and longs for "the only day that you might say is mine." That day of rest is Sunday, and the place of rest is the park, the "summer home" and "fashionable resort" of workers. The biting irony of the bridge—"Rich folks go away to the country you know / When the days get hot / But we all decided that we wouldn't go / We prefer this quiet spot"—is tempered by the quiet affection for the park, the ordinary "play and sport" that it represents. If the satirical songs of *Pins and Needles* debunk the stars and moons of June songs, replacing them with love lyrics of pickets and closed shops, "Sunday in the Park" elevates the working-class urban park with its simple "trees and grass and flowers everywhere" to a grand country resort. In a way, "Sunday in the Park" stands as an allegory of the entire show, the reclaiming of leisure and entertainment from the leisured classes, and the celebration of the common pleasures and ordinary songs of working-class life.[51]

3. "Fare Thee Well, Land of Cotton": Duke Ellington

> I think a statement of social protest in the theatre should be made without saying it, and this calls for the real craftsman.
>
> Duke Ellington, on *Jump for Joy*

Soon after the *Pins and Needles* road show closed in Los Angeles in May 1941, Duke Ellington's revue *Jump for Joy* opened there, running through the summer of 1941. By fall, Ivie Anderson's recording of the show's "I've Got It Bad (And That Ain't Good)" was a hit. Though largely forgotten by both jazz critics and historians of the Popular Front, *Jump for Joy* was a major Popular Front revue, a direct descendant of *Pins and Needles* (Figure 18). When Ellington was asked in 1952 to list the highlights of his 25-year career, one was *Jump for Joy*; and when he "interviewed" himself in the epilogue to his 1973 memoir, he wrote: "Q. Is there any achievement, outside the realm of music, that you are proud of and happy about? A. The first social significance show, *Jump for Joy*, and its various successors continually since." *Jump for Joy* "left enough of an impression," one critic wrote in 1946, "so that most of those who saw it and are concerned with a vigorous and honest Negro theater continually refer to it as *the* Negro musical."[52]

The two decades between the first major "Negro" musical, 1921's *Shuffle Along*, and 1941's *Jump for Joy* had witnessed an uneven development in African American musical theater. The rise of jazz and black dance had made the shows and revues of Eubie Blake, Fats Waller, and James P. Johnson musically exciting and innovative; playing in theaters and clubs both in Harlem and on Broadway, *Chocolate Dandies*, *Keep Shufflin'*, *Hot Chocolates*, and Lew Leslie's series of *Blackbirds* revues featured major African American artists, including Florence Mills, Josephine Baker, Bill "Bojangles" Robinson, and Louis Armstrong. But the sketches and stories in these revues were a continual recycling of plantation scenes, jungle skits, comic rent parties, and caricatured camp meetings: as one historian notes, though "Lew Leslie's *Blackbirds of 1928* ... represented what many still regard as the pinnacle of black musical achievement on Broadway in the Twenties," it was also "a culmination ... for an insidious stereotyping of the black musical on Broadway, a hardening of perceptions, even a segregating of the form by white critics into a circumscribed theatrical ghetto narrowly defined by a few largely racist formulas derived primarily from *Shuffle Along* and *Shuffle Along*'s minstrel precursors." Even these productions had virtually ceased by the early years of the depression.[53]

The idea of a radical black musical like *Jump for Joy* first emerged in 1936 when Ellington and Langston Hughes planned to collaborate on *Cock o' the World* as a vehicle for Paul Robeson. "It was," Hughes later said, "about a wandering Negro minstrel type who went all around the world, and he was a seaman and a roustabout, . . . and there were various scenes laid in New Orleans." Ellington wrote some music for it, but nothing came of it. Nevertheless, both Hughes and Ellington remained interested in musical theater, and their paths crossed again in *Jump for Joy*.[54]

Hughes was active in the various attempts to create a left-wing Negro theater, which had been triggered in part by the success of the Theatre Union's 1934 production of *Stevedore*. A proletarian play about New Orleans dockworkers, *Stevedore* starred Rex Ingram and Leigh Whipper and broke the unwritten segregation of New York's orchestra seats. Within a year, Rose McClendon had founded the Negro People's Theatre at Harlem's Lafayette Theatre, performing an adaptation of *Waiting for Lefty*. In July 1935, Hughes wrote an account of the struggle against Washington's segregated theater by the black angels in *Green Pastures* for the July 1935 issue of the left-wing *New Theatre* on black theater arts; the issue also included Paul Robeson's "I Breathe Freely," and Eugene Gordon's history "From *Uncle Tom's Cabin* to *Stevedore*." In the fall of 1935, Hughes not only won a *New Theatre* prize for his one-act play, *Angelo Herndon Jones*, but his play *Mulatto* was produced on Broadway with Rose McClendon starring in the role of the mother, Cora. That same fall McClendon met with Hallie Flanagan and John Houseman to plan the Lafayette unit of the Federal Theatre Project: the Negro Theatre's first productions in the spring of 1936 were Frank Wilson's *Walk Together, Chillun* and Orson Welles's adaptation of *Macbeth*.[55]

Ellington also had links to the left in these years, though they were more casual. He played at a Harlem Communist dance in early 1930 and at Scottsboro benefits in 1932 and 1935. In 1935, Ellington criticized Gershwin's *Porgy and Bess* in an interview with the left-wing *New Theatre*: after arguing that *Porgy and Bess* did "not use the Negro musical idiom," Ellington pointed to his own short film, *Symphony in Black*, as an example of a socially critical musical play: "I put into the dirge all the misery, sorrow and undertones of the conditions that went with the baby's death. It was true to and of the life of the people it depicted. The same thing cannot be said for *Porgy and Bess*." Ellington's comments about *Porgy and Bess* and *Symphony in Black* lay behind *Jump for Joy*: throughout the late 1930s, there were reports that "the dream of Duke Ellington is a musical with an entire Negro cast."[56]

The success of *The Cradle Will Rock* and *Pins and Needles* in late 1937 also generated a new enthusiasm for radical musical theater with black music and performers. In 1938, the ILGWU's Labor Stage commissioned Langston Hughes and James P. Johnson to compose a musical, *The Organizer*; though it was a success at the ILGWU convention in 1939, it closed after a brief run, and a radio version was rejected by CBS as "too controversial." Hughes's newly formed Harlem Suitcase Theatre also presented his *Don't You Want to Be Free?*, a montage of poems, blues, and spirituals presented on a stage with little more than a slave block, a rope noose, and a tree stump, and *Limitations of Life*, a series of skits satirizing *Uncle Tom's Cabin* and the film *Imitation of Life*. Hughes was also part of the Negro Cultural Committee, which presented a musical revue, "The Bourbons Got the Blues," on "the great upsurge of the Negro people against oppression and discrimination" in May 1938; it included sketches of Denmark Vesey (played by Frank Wilson) and Frederick Douglass (played by Rex Ingram) as well as a satire of the congressional filibuster of the anti-lynching bill.[57]

The original cast of *Pins and Needles* had only one black member, Olive Pearlman; but later casts drew on the dance company of Katherine Dunham, who taught at the Labor Stage. Archie Savage, who danced with Dunham and joined the *Pins and Needles* cast, had performed in the Negro Theatre's *Macbeth* and the Mercury Theatre's *Doctor Faustus*. But a black performer wasn't featured until the show's third edition, *New Pins and Needles*, in November 1939, when Dorothy Harrison sang two of the new numbers, "Mene, Mene, Tekel," and "Stay Out, Sammy." One black cast member, Dorothy Tucker, recalled that Robert Gordon, the show's second director, "really tried to get a number for a black person into the show. We talked about it many times and he was disappointed that it didn't happen sooner than it did. He had worked with black performers in the Café Society in Greenwich Village. I thought it was surprisingly hard to get a black number in, in view of the fact that the show was a platform for liberalism and unions." Even when "Mene, Mene, Tekel" was added, done in the style of Cab Calloway, there was a fight over having Dorothy Harrison dress as a "Mammy." In the meantime, however, the most popular sketch in Harold Rome's second revue, *Sing Out the News*, a musical "living newspaper" directed by Charles Friedman which opened on Broadway in September 1938, was the Harlem block party celebrating the birth of FDR Jones. "FDR Jones," which featured Rex Ingram singing and the young Hazel Scott on piano, proved one of Rome's most successful compositions, as hit versions were recorded by Ella Fitzgerald and Cab Calloway.[58]

The success of these Popular Front revues in New York led to the formation of the Hollywood Theatre Alliance, a group of left-wing Hollywood writers including Dashiell Hammett, Lillian Hellman, Langston Hughes, and Ira Gershwin, in the spring of 1939. Their first production was *Meet the People*, a satirical labor revue written by Henry Myers, Edward Eliscu, and songwriter Jay Gorney. It opened in Los Angeles in December 1939 and played in San Francisco, Chicago, and New York. One sketch featured the young black actor, Dorothy Dandridge; and its satire of Jim Crow, "It's the Same Old South," was recorded by Count Basie in December 1940. In the song's final eight bars, Jimmy Rushing sings, "Oh, honey, shut my mouth / Where the bloodhounds that once chased Liza / Chase a poor CIO organizer / It's the same old South."[59]

In 1940, the Hollywood Theatre Alliance decided to produce a "Negro Revue" with the company of Langston Hughes's New Negro Theatre, the West Coast successor to the Harlem Suitcase Theatre. Hughes began working on the revue with Donald Ogden Stewart, a left-wing writer known for his witty and sophisticated screenplays. Though Hughes wrote a few songs, including "America's Young Black Joe," a Joe Louis song that parodied Stephen Foster's "Old Black Joe," the collaboration did not work. Hughes left in December 1940 and resigned from the Hollywood Theatre Alliance. Just as Hughes was leaving, however, the Hollywood Theatre Alliance began talking to Ellington about producing a musical revue, and Hughes's sketch, "Mad Scene from Woolworth's," ended up as part of *Jump for Joy*.[60]

Ellington and his backers formed the American Revue Theatre for *Jump for Joy*; the production was supervised by the Hollywood radical Henry Blankfort, who had been the stage manager for *Meet the People*. The show was written in the spring of 1941 and opened at Los Angeles's Mayan Theatre on 10 July; the music was written largely by Ellington, the lyrics by Paul Webster and Sid Kuller. "*Jump for Joy* provided quite a few problems," Ellington told John Pittman of the *People's World*. "There was the first and greatest problem of trying to give an American audience entertainment without compromising the dignity of the Negro people. Needless to say, this is the problem every Negro artist faces. He runs afoul of offensive stereotypes, instilled in the American mind by whole centuries of ridicule and derogation. The American audience has been taught to expect a Negro on the stage to clown and 'Uncle Tom,' that is, to enact the role of a servile, yet lovable, inferior." Ellington solved the problem by combining elements of both the Cotton Club and *Pins and Needles* with his ambition to compose a musical history of black America.[61]

The structure of *Jump for Joy* was borrowed from the Cotton Club revues of a decade earlier. Ellington's band had taken shape and become famous during their extended stay at Harlem's Cotton Club in the late 1920s and early 1930s. It was during these years at the Cotton Club, Gunther Schuller argued, that Ellington developed his "decided leaning toward 'show music'"; moreover, "the need for new background music for continually changing acts at the Cotton Club in a sense *required* Ellington to investigate composition (rather than arranging) as a medium of expression." The famous 1933 *Cotton Club Parade*, written by the songwriting team of Harold Arlen and Ted Koehler, was a classic example of the genre: after an overture by the Ellington orchestra, its first act had eighteen scenes, the second, fourteen. With a cast of fifty and a chorus line of eighteen, the revue alternated blackout skits like "Harlem Hospital" with the comedian Dusty Fletcher, dance numbers by the Nicholas Brothers, and songs like "Calico Days" and "Happy as the Day Is Long." The highlight of the show was the scene "Cabin in the Cotton Club," in which Ethel Waters sang "Stormy Weather" in front of a log-cabin backdrop. Spectacular costumes, lighting, dancing, and music took the place of drama or narrative.[62]

At first glance, *Jump for Joy* was very similar. There were two acts of seventeen and fourteen scenes, respectively; songs and sketches were added and cut throughout the run. The young comedian Wonderful Smith (who later joined the "Amos 'n' Andy" television cast) was featured in a number of skits, as were Pot, Pan, and Skillet, one of the leading comedy teams on the black vaudeville circuit. Dancers Al Guster and Garbo had numbers, and there were romantic songs by Ivie Anderson, Herb Jeffries, and Marie Bryant. Each of the main types of pieces developed by Ellington and his orchestra in the Cotton Club years—dance numbers, the "jungle"-style productions, the "indigo" tone poems, and the 32-bar ballads of Jimmy McHugh-Dorothy Fields and Harold Arlen-Ted Koehler—were found in *Jump for Joy*: Al Guster's dance to "Stomp Caprice"; the stylized instrumental Africanisms of "Chocolate Shake"; the "Flame Indigo" of the "Garbo and Hepburn" sketch; and Ivie Anderson's classic rendition of Ellington's own popular ballad, "I Got It Bad (And That Ain't Good)."[63]

However, *Jump for Joy* diverged from the style of the Cotton Club revues when Ellington and his collaborators borrowed the political satire of *Pins and Needles* and *Meet the People* in order, in Ellington's words, to "take Uncle Tom out of the theatre" and "eliminate the stereotyped image that had been exploited by Hollywood and Broadway." They did this both on and off stage. On stage, the show opened with Ellington's spoken introduction, "Sun-Tanned Tenth of the Nation," the title itself a play on the Living Newspaper's exposé of tenement conditions, *One-Third of a Nation*. Rather than focusing on social conditions, however, Ellington commented on the representations of black Americans, in words not unlike his critique of *Porgy and Bess*:

> Now, every Broadway colored show,
> According to tradition,
> Must be a carbon copy
> Of the previous edition.
> With the truth discreetly muted,

> And the accent on the brasses.
> The punch that should be present
> In a colored show, alas, is
> Disinfected with magnolia
> And dripping with molasses.
> In other words,
> We're shown to you
> Through Stephen Foster's glasses.

The revue was punctuated by a series of satirical songs pronouncing the death of Stephen Foster and Uncle Tom: "no crying, no moaning," Ellington wrote, "but entertaining, and with social demands as a potent spice." "I've Got a Passport from Georgia (And I'm Going to the U.S.A.)" was, like *Meet the People*'s "It's the Same Old South," an answer to sentimental ballads like "Dear Old Southland" and "Georgia on My Mind": "I'm gone with the wind, and I'm glad to be going," Paul White sang, "far from the South of Octavus Roy Cohen . . . I've got a passport from Georgia / And I'm goin' up . . . Where you wear no Dixie necktie, / Where the signs read, 'Out to Lunch,' not 'Out to Lynch'." "Passport from Georgia" drew protests from right-wing whites and death threats against the singer, Paul White; it was eventually withdrawn from the show. The first act ended with a plantation cabin mutating into a Los Angeles restaurant: "Jemimah doesn't work no more for RKO / She's slinging hash for Uncle Tom and coinin' dough. / Just turn on your headlights, and she'll take a bow, / Cause Uncle Tom's Cabin is a drive-in now!"[64]

The second act opened with the revue's title song, a joyous celebration of the break with Jim Crow:

> Fare thee well, land of cotton,
> Cotton lisle is out of style, honey chile,
> Jump for joy.
>
> Don't you grieve, little Eve,
> All the hounds, I do believe,
> Have been killed, ain't you thrilled,
> Jump for joy.

The song's release takes a jab at Hollywood—"Have you seen pastures, groovy? / Oh, *Green Pastures* was just a technicolor movie." By the end of the show, the plantation cabins have been routed, and they are replaced by an evocation of popular urban dress, notably the new "zoot suit," in the finale's Easter promenade: "Easter Sunday is the one day / When the sun-tanned tenth of the nation / Celebratin', start creatin' / A sartorial sensation."[65]

If the sketches offered an implicit narrative on stage, the offstage revisions to the Cotton Club revue were no less important. Whereas the Cotton Club had admitted only whites as customers, *Jump for Joy*'s audience was, as Ellington recalled, "of unusual composition, for it included the most celebrated Hollywoodians, middle-class ofays, the sweet-and-low scuffling-type Negroes, and dicty Negroes as well (doctors, lawyers, etc.). The Negroes always left proudly, with their chests sticking out." *Variety* noted that half of the audience came from the "colored colony." Moreover, Ellington stopped all the comedians from using cork on their faces, and the actors refused to speak the dialect lines that one of the writers had written for them. *Jump for Joy* captured "a new mood in the theatre," the black journalist Almena Davis wrote, and the West Coast's African American newspapers, the *Los Angeles Tribune* and the *California Eagle*, followed the show's progress. Both on and offstage, *Jump for Joy* spoke as much for Los Angeles's black community as *Pins and Needles* had for New York's garment workers.[66]

The third aspect of *Jump for Joy* derived neither from the Cotton Club nor from *Pins and Needles*: it was Ellington's project to compose a musical history of black Americans. The project was clearly on Ellington's mind as he was writing *Jump for Joy*: he told John Pittman of his "own special job," an opera that would trace the history of the Negro people from chattel slavery to the present. "Hear that chord," he said to Pittman. "That's us. Dissonance is our way of life in America. We are something apart, yet an integral part." Ellington's project echoed the Spirituals to Swing concerts that John Hammond had organized at Carnegie Hall, sponsored in 1938 by the *New Masses* and in 1939 by the Theatre Arts Committee (TAC). Hammond had constructed a powerful genealogy of black American music by bringing together musicians playing spirituals, gospel, country blues, boogie-woogie piano, traditional New Orleans jazz, and contemporary swing; the concerts were a striking contrast to the slumming narratives of Lew Leslie's *Blackbirds* revues.[67]

Jump for Joy is the first of Ellington's "Spirituals to Swing" compositions; when he later wrote about *Jump for Joy*, he saw it as a precursor to *Black, Brown and Beige*—the 1943 "tone parallel to the history of the American Negro"—and to the subsequent concert pieces of the mid 1940s, *New World a-Comin'* and *The Deep South Suite*. *Black, Brown and Beige* began with the "Work Song" and "Come Sunday" themes and ended with "Beige," which "depicts the contemporary Negro." Ironically, a number of jazz critics, including Hammond himself, criticized the experiment: "by becoming more complex," Hammond wrote, "he has robbed jazz of most of its basic virtue." Ellington, however, was less interested in the confines of "jazz": he had told Almena Davis that his band didn't "make any attempt at playing jazz or swing," but played "unadulterated American Negro music."[68]

Though *Jump for Joy* is not organized as a musical history, elements of Ellington's historical project appear in the revue. Ellington felt the initial show had neglected the blues, so he signed up Joe Turner to sing "Rocks in My Bed," as well as other numbers; after that, he wrote, "we really had great blues in the show." The song "Jump for Joy" had the form of a commercial ballad, but its music carried a gospel sensibility. Finally, the Ben Webster solo from "Concerto for Klinkers" was used in the "Blues" section of *Black, Brown and Beige*. For Ellington, part of the "social significance" of *Jump for Joy* lay in its use of the "Negro musical idiom."[69]

Jump for Joy's success in the summer of 1941 was not only a product of Ellington's music and the desire of Ellington and his collaborators to "take Uncle Tom out of the theatre." For 1941 had also witnessed an upsurge of African American militancy in what were later recognized as the beginnings of the modern civil rights movement. Just as Marc Blitzstein's *Cradle Will Rock* was made possible by the union struggles of steelworkers, so *Jump for Joy* was made possible by the new activism of African Americans. In January 1941, A. Philip Randolph, the most respected black labor leader in the country, called for a March on Washington by ten thousand black Americans to protest employment discrimination in the defense industries: the march was planned for 1 July 1941. At the same time, Ellington assumed a new public voice, marked dramatically by the radio broadcast and newspaper publication of his 1941 Lincoln Day speech, "We, Too, Sing 'America'." "Music is my business, my profession, my life," he said, "but [...] I often feel that I'd like to say something [...] on some of the burning issues confronting us, in another language . . . in words of mouth." Basing his remarks on Langston Hughes's poem, he contended that "the Negro is the creative voice of America. . . . [W]e fought America's wars, provided her labor, gave her music, kept alive her flickering conscience, prodded her on toward the yet unachieved goal, democracy." Clearly influenced by the Popular Front rhetoric of Hughes and Robeson, Ellington's speech occurred just as he was conceiving *Jump for Joy*.[70]

Throughout the winter and spring of 1941, March on Washington committees mobilized around the country. "Both the NAACP and the National Negro Congress supported the march actively," Roi Ottley wrote, ". . . and those efficient couriers—the Pullman porters—carried the word to Negro communities throughout the country." Meanwhile, in March 1941, Orson Welles's Mercury Theatre production of Richard Wright's *Native Son*, starring Canada Lee, opened in New York; in May 1941, Paul Robeson, the leading voice of the National Negro Congress, made a dramatic appearance in Detroit to support the United Auto Workers' organizing drive on the eve of the successful NLRB election at Ford's River Rouge. In the weeks before the March on Washington, Randolph and other march leaders met with President Roosevelt. When Roosevelt issued Executive Order 8802 banning discrimination in defense industries on 25 June, the march was called off. In early July, just as *Jump for Joy* opened in Los Angeles, the first Fair Employment Practices Commission (FEPC) was formed. Though many of the rank-and-file members of the March on Washington Movement were disappointed at the march's cancellation, Roosevelt's Executive Order and the FEPC were recognized as major victories. The March on Washington Movement continued to organize rallies and meetings, as the first FEPC hearings were held in Los Angeles in the fall of 1941.[71]

During the summer and fall of 1941, as *Jump for Joy* was playing, Ellington renewed his ties to the Popular Front, appearing at a fundraiser for the Hollywood chapter of the Veterans of the Lincoln Brigade and a dinner to aid anti-fascist refugees; he also lent his name to the cultural front's Hollywood Democratic Committee and, later, to the Independent Citizens Committee of the Arts, Sciences and Professions. In September, Ellington, Ivie Anderson, and Herb Jeffries performed parts of *Jump for Joy* on an NBC "Salute to Labor" broadcast, hosted by the actor Melvyn Douglas, a leading Popular Front activist.[72]

African American activism grew throughout the war years. The African American Popular Front was an unstable mixture of alliances and rivalries between leaders like Randolph, Adam Clayton Powell, Jr, and Benjamin Davis, and organizations like the March on Washington Movement, the National Negro Congress, Harlem's Negro Labor Victory Committee, the NAACP, and the newly formed Congress of Racial Equality (CORE). Ellington, like many other black musicians, artists, and writers, was drawn into this wartime front. When he returned for extended stays at New York's Hurricane in 1943 and 1944, he regularly appeared at rallies and concerts with Paul Robeson, Josh White, and Teddy Wilson. As he later wrote, "the annual Carnegie Hall concerts were," like *Jump for Joy*, "really a series of social-significance thrusts." *Black, Brown and Beige*, which premiered at Carnegie Hall on 23 January 1943, was the second in a series of left-wing benefits for Russian War Relief: the first had been a program called "Music at Work," directed by *Pins and Needles*'s Robert Gordon, and including segments by Marc Blitzstein, Harold Rome, and jazz pianist Teddy Wilson.[73]

Nevertheless, Ellington was "not a crusader," but "an entertainer," as he told the young activist James Farmer in 1946. When faced in 1950 with an incident not unlike the ones that had led to the persecution of Paul Robeson and W.E.B. Du Bois the previous summer—he was said to have signed the Stockholm Peace Petition while in Europe—he quickly published a statement in the anti-Communist social democratic weekly, the *New Leader*, disavowing the Peace Petition and the American Communists, asserting that "movements of a political nature . . . any kind but orchestral

movements—have never been part of my life." The ironies of Ellington's
disavowal no doubt escaped the blacklisters. The article is framed around
an account of his European collaboration with Orson Welles, an unrepen-
tant Popular Front figure: "I never sign petitions. . . . I don't have to possess
the genius of a Welles to know that were I to sign something like the
Stockholm petition it would be like Faust signing up with Mephistopheles."
"The only 'communism' I know of," Ellington wrote slyly, "is that of Jesus
Christ."[74]

Ellington was not primarily a signer of petitions. He was less interested
in the politics of affiliations than the politics of form. For Ellington,
political and orchestral movements were inextricably connected; throughout his career he composed varieties of "program" music. *Jump for Joy* is
perhaps best seen as Ellington's answer to Gershwin's *Porgy and Bess*, the
musical completion of his 1935 comments to *New Theatre*. "Grand music
and a swell play," he said of *Porgy and Bess*, "but the two don't go together
. . . the music did not hitch with the mood and spirit of the story . . . it does
not use the Negro musical idiom." Moreover, he continued, "if you hadn't
been around the band and if you did not know the backgrounds of the
musicians you couldn't interpret them or use their idioms." By the time of
Jump for Joy, Ellington had not only assembled what is generally regarded
as his finest band, but he had made the orchestra his instrument, writing
for the particular idioms, timbres, and voices of his players. As one
biographer has noted, *Jump for Joy* was his most successful musical because
it was the only one for which his own band played; trumpeter Rex Stewart
recalled that "we all liked the show and enjoyed doing it." Moreover, in
Jump for Joy, his music did "hitch with the mood and spirit of the story."
Thus, perhaps, the most "political" number in the show was not one of the
satirical sketches about Uncle Tom, but Ivie Anderson's interpretation of
the Paul Webster/Duke Ellington ballad, "I Got It Bad (And That Ain't
Good)": the recorded version, Gunther Schuller wrote, is "one of the truly
magical moments in all jazz vocal literature."[75]

"I Got It Bad" is a characteristic Ellingtonian combination of a blues
melody—it opens on a blue fifth—with the harmonies and form of the
popular ballad. Though ostensibly a simple lament of a woman done
wrong—"Never treats me sweet and gentle, the way he should"—it had
wider resonances. The descending phrase at the start of the bridge—
"when the fish are jumpin'"—quotes Gershwin's "Summertime," and the
ballad can be seen as an answer to Gershwin's lullaby of easy living and
high cotton, where nothing can harm you. In the context of *Jump for Joy*,
Ivie Anderson's song becomes not only an individual complaint, but a
blues allegory of a people: "I got it bad," a statement of "the misery, sorrow,
and undertones of the conditions . . . of the people it depicted," to quote
Ellington's earlier comment; "And that ain't good," a statement of moral

and political refusal. Did any of those who bought and listened to the hit recording in the fall of 1941 hear this song as a song of Negro protest? Perhaps not; it is the song's political unconscious. But then, as Ellington himself said, "a statement of social protest ... should be made without saying it, and this calls for a real craftsman."[76]

4. Jazz/Opera: The Antinomies of Popular Front Musical Theater

Despite the aesthetic and political successes of *The Cradle Will Rock*, *Pins and Needles*, and *Jump for Joy* at the time, the works of Popular Front musical theater did not succeed in creating a vibrant and lasting model for American music or for socialist cultural politics. The failures of several post-war experiments in political musical theater are revealing emblems of both the political collapse of the Popular Front and the transformations in vernacular music that left radical musical theater behind. In December 1946, Ellington and John LaTouche, the TAC cabaret lyricist who had written "Ballad for Americans" and a number of *Pins and Needles* sketches, collaborated on a musical version of Gay's *Beggar's Opera*, entitled *Beggar's Holiday*. Directed at first by John Houseman and Nicholas Ray, it opened in December 1946, and was, Ellington wrote, "a long time before its time so far as social significance was concerned." A month later, both the tenement opera *Street Scene*, by the team of Kurt Weill, Langston Hughes, and Elmer Rice, and the pioneering book musical *Finian's Rainbow*, by Yip Harburg and Burton Lane, opened. In November 1947, a month after the Hollywood Ten hearings, the young Leonard Bernstein mounted a revival of *The Cradle Will Rock*, and Virgil Thomson hailed it, writing that "in a year when the Left in general, and the labor movement in particular, is under attack, it is important that the Left should put its best foot forward." But none of these were great popular or political successes.[77]

   In part, the political repression throughout the culture industry prevented the full development of these experiments in musical theater. However, the main reason for the failure of Popular Front musical theater was its inability to resolve formally and musically its central antinomy: the relation between African American musics, particularly jazz, and the operatic tradition. The attempt to unite opera and African American music ran throughout the cultural front: not only did Ellington long plan an opera, *Boola*, but John Houseman's first theatrical venture had been the famous production of Virgil Thomson and Gertrude Stein's *Four Saints in Three Acts* with black singers in 1934. Langston Hughes worked on a number of opera libretti over his career: indeed, his biographer found Hughes's "continued link to the world of opera ... something of a puzzle, since he was no passionate lover of the form." Orson Welles used the dialectic of opera and jazz as one of the informing structures of *Citizen Kane*.[78]

Perhaps the clearest elaboration of this desire to connect jazz and opera lies in the curious final chapter of Sidney Finkelstein's *Jazz: A People's Music* (1948). The first six chapters of Finkelstein's study are a powerful history and analysis of jazz from its origins to bebop; they have influenced many subsequent accounts, notably those of LeRoi Jones and Eric Hobsbawm, and constitute jazz orthodoxy. The final chapter, "The Future of Jazz," is, on the other hand, a curious period piece that illuminates the aesthetic ideology of Popular Front musical theater. In it, Finkelstein turns away from the virtuoso improvisations of Parker and Gillespie that proved to be "the future of jazz" and looks instead at the possibilities of extended jazz compositions: "most important of all, because it takes in so many of the other musical forms, is opera . . . a drama with music." He sees Ellington and Blitzstein as complementary paths beyond Gershwin: the weakness of *The Cradle Will Rock* is that it "does not go deeply into jazz," drawing on "a torch-song imitation of the blues." Nevertheless, "the very fact that Blitzstein did so much with so small a range of musical idiom shows what can be done with jazz in the larger musical forms." The union of Ellington and Blitzstein represents, for Finkelstein, the future of jazz and American music generally.[79]

In retrospect, this Popular Front vision of a "people's music"—reflected also in Wilfrid Meller's pioneering history of American music, *Music in the New Found Land*—that would unite the philharmonic and the vernacular in a new musical theater was utopian. This is evident in two quite different post-war productions: the 1947 film *New Orleans* and Marc Blitzstein's full-scale opera of 1949, *Regina*. For jazz critics and historians, *New Orleans* is an example of a Hollywood travesty of jazz. Not only did the studio put Billie Holiday in a maid's role, but each rewrite made Holiday and Louis Armstrong less important. The film's history of jazz is full of anachronisms, and the entire jazz story is overshadowed by the romance between the white characters. Nevertheless, the story of the making of *New Orleans* is revealing. The film, made by an independent producer, Jules Levey, for United Artists, was an indirect descendant of one of the Popular Front's most interesting uncompleted projects: Orson Welles's film of the history of jazz, starring Louis Armstrong, for which Ellington was to compose the music and Hazel Scott was to play Lil Hardin Armstrong. Welles's project died when RKO fired him; however, his screenwriter, Elliot Paul, who had written on jazz in Popular Front magazines, together with the Communist screenwriter Herbert Biberman, wrote the story, "Conspiracy in Jazz," that became *New Orleans*. Thus, though the film that was released was the result of studio rewrites and compromises, the original project was a product of the Hollywood left. Indeed, according to the bassist Red Callender, who appeared in it, the film was a victim of the Red scare: "It was gradual the way McCarthyism seeped in. . . . Eventually things became more and more uptight. The picture was brought to a hasty finish. . . . In the original script Louis's band was slated to appear on the same bill as Woody Herman's at the big stage concert. We . . . filmed it, but thanks to McCarthyism it was never shown." By the fall of 1947, the film's assistant producer, Herbert Biberman, had been called before HUAC as one of the Hollywood Ten.[80]

Bowdlerized though it was, the film was never really a jazz story; rather, it was a sentimental version of the Popular Front marriage of jazz and opera. The film's scenes cut back and forth between the jazz singing of Billie Holiday and the operatic singing of Dorothy Patrick, between Armstrong's band and a chamber ensemble, between the Storyville funeral march and a philharmonic recital. Through it all, the true musicians respect each other and play for and with each other: the world of white "Society" keeps them apart. That is why the film loses not only its nerve but its coherence when Dorothy Patrick appears with Woody Herman's Band at the end: Herman has had no place in the story, and the proper Hollywood ending would have Armstrong, Holiday, Patrick, and the musical society's conductor (who has played with Armstrong) on stage together.

In the end, *New Orleans* became a routine low-budget film, rescued only by the musical performances of Holiday, Armstrong, and the band of New Orleans musicians. However, its narrative conceit was echoed in Marc Blitzstein's ambitious 1949 opera *Regina*, based on Lillian Hellman's play *The Little Foxes*. To Hellman's narrative of the struggle in the Hubbard family between the planter aristocracy and the New South's capitalists, Blitzstein added a traditional New Orleans jazz band, in order to stage a confrontation between the two musics and the two worlds. The jazz band's opening number, "Naught's a Naught," forms the basis of the opera's prologue; they vie with a chamber trio in the ball at the end of act two; and they return at the end to drown out the family and proclaim "a new day a-coming." Nevertheless, the relation between the two musics remains caught in the narrative of mistress and maid. In *New Orleans*, the black domestic, played by Billie Holiday, takes her employer's daughter, the opera singer Dorothy Patrick, to the jazz club against the wishes of her (Dorothy's) mother; similarly, in *Regina*, it is the daughter Alexandra who is drawn to the jazz band of the servants against the objections of her mother. In both instances, the imagined musical union proves to be another version of the racial romance of domestic labor.[81]

The drama of music and race was not to be played out in the musical theater, however. The Popular Front musical theater, with its ties to Broadway, the Cotton Club, and Tin Pan Alley, was displaced musically and politically by a new vernacular music, based on the recently invented electric guitar: country and western and rhythm and blues. Blitzstein's *Regina* came to stand, along with Ellington's suites, Leonard Bernstein's *West Side Story*, and Langston Hughes's musicals of the late 1950s, *Simply Heavenly* and *Tambourines to Glory*, as the culmination and the end of the music front's long and often contradictory attempts to create a new musical theater.

9

Cabaret Blues

"Even the better swing orchestras subscribe to the rule that requires a singer to be their downright concession to publisher and manager," wrote the *Daily Worker*'s music critic, Martin McCall (the pseudonym of Max Margulis, a former editor of the Composers Collective journal, *Music Vanguard*), in the summer of 1939.

> Ordinarily the singer—usually a woman—smiles and smiles, and affectedly simpers, in something like a Southern accent, the bare melody and lyric of a Tin Pan Alley tune. There are a few singers who are exceptions, and notable among them is Billie Holiday. The young Negro singer has the directness, intensity and expressiveness common to an older generation of blues-singing artists. She was born too late to become part of the blues-singing tradition which produced the late Bessie Smith, but she fortunately has an insight of the dignity, austerity and significance of the blues. . . . The Commodore Music Shop of New York has recently made some outstanding records of Billie Holiday at her best. Assisting her is Frank Newton's Orchestra which is heard nightly with the singer at Café Society. A traditional blues, here entitled "Fine and Mellow," with trumpet obligato by Newton, is easily one of the finest vocal records since Bessie Smith's last records in 1934. It is backed by a modern song which Billie Holiday has made widely famous, "Strange Fruit," a dramatic and bitterly restrained cry against lynching.[1]

If Olive Stanton's performance of "Nickel under the Foot" in *The Cradle Will Rock* and Ruth Rubinstein's rendition of "Chain Story Daisy" in *Pins and Needles* marked the emergence of a distinctive left-wing musical theater in 1937, Billie Holiday's singing of "Strange Fruit" at Café Society in the spring of 1939 marked the emergence of a Popular Front cabaret blues, a fusion of jazz and political cabaret, of Louis Armstrong and Bertolt Brecht, of Bessie Smith and Lotte Lenya. Moreover, the cabaret blues of Café Society was the product of a complex alliance between jazz and the Popular

Front that had its political origins in the campaign to free the Scottsboro Nine and its social origins in the working-class musical culture of hot jazz and swing. This alliance between jazz and the Popular Front social movement permanently altered the shape of American music.

It is perhaps not surprising, however, that both Holiday's "Strange Fruit" and Café Society have been widely criticized. For many critics and historians, "Strange Fruit" represents a corruption of Holiday's work, a piece of agitprop that is, according to jazz critic Martin Williams, "moving propaganda perhaps, but not poetry and not art." Even some who sympathized with the song's politics have lamented its effect on Holiday. John Hammond, who produced most of her early recording sessions, later wrote that "artistically the worst thing that ever happened to her was the overwhelming success of . . . 'Strange Fruit'." For Hammond, "Strange Fruit" represented a growing stylization in Holiday's work: "the more conscious she was of her style, the more mannered she became."[2]

But if Hammond saw "Strange Fruit" as the result of Holiday's perception of herself as an artist, others have blamed the people and institutions represented by Hammond and Café Society, her "supper club following." "As she performed it, night after night, before an enthralled audience of young white intellectuals," Michael Brooks writes, "subliminally she began to feel that she had to be the spokesperson for those who were in the Lower Depths and her repertoire and arrangements began to reflect a mordant bent." "Her tragedy," he concludes, "was that she didn't let her natural instincts take charge and just sing. . . . Instead she began to interpret."[3]

In part, these assessments reflect the antipathy of one tradition of jazz criticism to the self-conscious aesthetic ambitions of jazz musicians, and the assumption that the best jazz is the result of "natural instincts." But they also represent a widespread sense that Café Society, with its "Park Avenue liberals" and "Greenwich Village intellectuals and bohemians," was the most frivolous of political gestures, a bizarre union of celebrity culture and political posturing. Indeed, for Irving Howe and Lewis Coser, the "social-minded night club" stands as a "perfect symbol" of Popular Front culture, a place where politics for "the middle-class fellow travelers and the middle-brow progressives" is "a thrill over cocktails." For most critics and historians, the story of jazz and the left has been a curious dance of black musicians with "natural instincts" and slumming white leftists.[4]

However, these accounts misunderstand the cultural politics and aesthetic ideologies that came together in the formation of Café Society. For Café Society represented a remarkable synthesis of the radical political cabarets of Berlin and Paris with the African American jazz clubs and revues of Harlem. This synthesis is at the heart not only of Holiday's agitprop song "Strange Fruit," but of the cabaret repertoire of the radical singers and musicians of Café Society, including Frank Newton, Teddy Wilson, Lena Horne, and Josh White: Holiday's "Fine and Mellow" was later adopted by Horne and "Strange Fruit" by White. These figures are often dismissed as mere "nightclub" performers, outside the main traditions of jazz and blues, but their work grew out of the African American radicalism of Harlem and the Carolina Piedmont. A reconsideration of the Americanization of the cabaret and the connections between jazz and the Popular Front allows us to understand the cabaret blues of Billie Holiday and Josh White.

1. Weimar on the Hudson: The Popular Front Political Cabaret

Café Society began as an attempt to transplant the tradition of the political cabaret to the United States. The cabarets of Paris, Zurich, Vienna, and Berlin had been a modernist invention, and their small impromptu stages alternated avant-garde theatrical experiments with satirical songs and monologues. The cabaret performer played directly to the audience; as one historian notes, in "an ambience of talk and smoke, . . . the relationship between performer and spectator is one at once of intimacy and hostility." In the decade after World War I, the Weimar *Kabarett* became the center of a political, musical, and literary counterculture whose emblems included the satires of Kurt Tucholsky, the *chansons* of Walter Mehring, Erich Kästner, and Friedrich Hollaender, the revues of Erwin Piscator, and the plays of Brecht and Weill, as well as singers like Lotte Lenya and Rosa Valetti (who appears in von Sternberg's film *The Blue Angel*). "I had been to Europe in the early thirties," Café Society's founder Barney Josephson later recalled, "and had visited the political cabarets, where there was very pointed satire. . . . I conceived the idea of presenting some sort of satire and alternating it with jazz music."[5]

Josephson, who had grown up in Trenton, the child of Latvian immigrant garment workers, was a young shoe salesman with close connections to the left: his brother Leon was a well-known lawyer for the International Labor Defense and had worked in the anti-Nazi underground in Europe. With the help of the left-wing jazz critic and producer John Hammond, Josephson raised the money for what was the first integrated nightclub outside Harlem. "It was the time of the labor organizers and the Ladies Garment Workers' show called *Pins and Needles* and the W.P.A. Art Movement and *The Cradle Will Rock*," Josephson recalled in 1971. "I wanted a club where blacks and whites worked together behind the footlights and sat together out front." Josephson turned to the talents of the Popular Front arts community for the Greenwich Village club: he brought in a group of WPA artists including William Gropper and Adolf Dehn to paint a mural satirizing "café society"; he hired the director of *Pins and Needles*, Robert Gordon, to orchestrate the nightclub's floor show; and he turned to John Hammond to organize the music. "Café Society, a night club to take the *stuffing out of stuffed shirts*, has opened in the Village," the Popular Front arts magazine, *Direction*, noted. "Entertainment is artistically tops."[6]

However, Café Society was not the first attempt to create an American political cabaret: there were at least two earlier experiments whose history illuminates the success of Café Society. The first was Le Ruban Bleu, which was opened in December 1937 by Harold Jacoby. Jacoby was part of the political and artistic counterculture of the European cabaret: he had come to New York from Paris, where he had been an editor of Leon Blum's Popular Front newspaper, and the press agent for "Le Boeuf sur le toit," the foremost Parisian cabaret. In part, Le Ruban Bleu drew on the exiles from fascism: Lotte Lenya made her first US appearance there in April 1938, singing songs by Kurt Weill and Marc Blitzstein. But though Jacoby's clubs, Le Ruban Bleu and, later, the Blue Angel, were successful—his one-time partner Max Gordon recalled that Jacoby "had more to do than anyone else with establishing the supper club over here"—they remained tied to European culture. His bookings, Gordon recalled, "tended to follow a delicate, almost esoteric line. . . . Jacoby doted on French acts, and there were nights at the Blue Angel when I never heard a word of English." When Billie Holiday sang at Le Ruban Bleu in 1944, in the wake of her Café Society success, she hated it.[7]

The second experiment in political cabaret was organized by the Theatre Arts Committee (TAC), a Popular Front alliance of film, theater, and radio entertainers, "anyone who draws his bread and butter, or his champagne and caviar, from the amusement industries." TAC had grown out of the Theatre Committee to Aid Spanish Democracy, formed in the spring of 1937 by members of the Theatre Union's production of John Howard Lawson's *Marching Song*. By the spring and summer of 1938, TAC was publishing a monthly magazine, issuing recordings, broadcasting radio shows, and producing a weekly cabaret. Cabaret TAC made its debut on 5 May 1938 and continued for almost two years with a series of shows— "Radio Show," "Hollywood Show," "Chinese Cabaret"—made up of skits, dances, and topical songs. They featured exiled cabaret artists like the mime Lotte Goslar; radical dancers like Si-Lan Chen; satires of the federal theater ("One Third of a Mitten"), Hollywood film ("Gone with the Movie Rights"), and Tin Pan Alley (Marc Blitzstein's "What's Left?"); and topical songs including Harold Rome's "One Big Union for Two" (which ended up in *Pins and Needles*), Earl Robinson's "Joe Hill," and Lewis Allan's "Strange Fruit." "Many anti-Nazi dramatizations were written and per-formed there by people like Howard da Silva, Martin Gabel—even Kate Smith," Joseph Losey recalled. "I don't think it ever came near the German political cabaret of the late 1920s because we didn't have that kind of sophistication or experience. But it was a tremendously vital thing."[8]

What Cabaret TAC lacked, however, was not European sophistication, but African American music. "The many expert hot jazz musicians now playing in New York could ... contribute much toward Cabaret TAC," John Hammond wrote in the monthly *TAC*, after sketching a quick history of "hot jazz." "The Theatre Arts Committee has a great opportunity to make the cause of this indigenous art its own." Though there were a few attempts to incorporate jazz into the TAC alliance—Ellington wrote an article for *TAC*, there was a Cabaret TAC "Negro Show," and TAC sponsored the second Spirituals to Swing concert at Carnegie Hall in December 1939 (staged by Joseph Losey)—for the most part Cabaret TAC drew its talent from the Broadway theater, where there were few figures like Ellington, Basie or Holiday.[9]

Café Society, on the other hand, opened as a jazz cabaret, combining political satire with jazz. Left-wing comedians like Jack Gilford, Jimmy Savo, Carol Channing, and Zero Mostel alternated with singers like Billie Holiday, Lena Horne, and Hazel Scott, boogie-woogie pianists like Albert Ammons, Pete Johnson, and Meade Lux Lewis, and the small-group "chamber jazz" of Teddy Wilson, Frankie Newton, and Eddie Heywood. "Strange Fruit," though not typical of Café Society entertainment, was nonetheless representative. A minor key dirge about a southern lynching written by a left-wing schoolteacher, Lewis Allan (a pseudonym for Abel Meeropol), it had been performed at Cabaret TAC and other Popular Front gatherings for about a year before Allan brought it to Barney Josephson and Robert Gordon. They in turn gave the song to Billie Holiday. Though Holiday was apparently at first reluctant to sing the song and "was scared people would hate it," it was a great success. It was staged as a theatrical performance; "I was doing agitprop," Josephson later recalled, "to me it was a piece of propaganda." "I insisted she closed every show with it every night. Lights out, just one small spinlight, and all service stopped.... There were no encores after it. My instruction was walk off, period. People had to remember 'Strange Fruit,' get their insides burned with it."[10]

Over the next two decades, "Strange Fruit" became one of Holiday's signature songs; she made it her own, both artistically and personally, associating it with the death of her father, jazz guitarist Clarence Holiday. She often implied that she had written the song. When her record company, Columbia's Brunswick label, refused to issue the song, she recorded it for Milt Gabler's small label, Commodore Records. Moreover, Holiday's nine-month stay at Café Society proved to be the most rewarding of her career. In 1941, she told Teddy Wilson that "she'd really found herself as a singer—whereas everyone else felt that she had found herself before. But a person doesn't always hear herself as others do. She was singing very much to her personal satisfaction in 1941. She was beginning to hear herself." As Robert O'Meally, the finest of Holiday critics, has argued, "Strange Fruit" marked the beginning of "the second Holiday," the period dominated not by the jump tunes of her early recordings, but by her torch songs in "a new key of dramatically enacted sadness."[11]

Nevertheless, any suggestion that Holiday was a political artist has usually been greeted with scorn. In large part, this is because, unlike many political artists, she was not an intellectual. Holiday was a reader of comic books; and Lewis Allan noted that when she first heard "Strange Fruit," she did not know what the word "pastoral" meant. But this should not disqualify her as a political artist: most of the people who made up the Popular Front social movement were not intellectuals, and their political convictions and activities grew out of the political formations in their neighborhoods and workplaces. To understand Billie Holiday's politics, we must reconsider the connections between the Popular Front and the world of jazz.[12]

2. "Hot Jazz and the CIO"

It is surely true that there were substantial differences between the jazz left and other parts of the cultural left. Perhaps the most important ones were due to the fact that jazz bands were never organized by the young radicals of the proletarian culture movement. The John Reed Clubs and their offspring had organized poets, novelists, painters, sculptors, actors, photographers, filmmakers, ballet dancers, labor balladeers, and classical musicians and composers, but not jazz musicians. So, unlike Richard Wright and Tillie Olsen in the John Reed Clubs, Elie Siegmeister and Marc Blitzstein in the Composers Collective, Elia Kazan and Nicholas Ray in the Workers Laboratory Theatre, Ruby Dee and Sidney Poitier in the American Negro Theater, and Jacob Lawrence at the American Artists School, there are almost no cases of jazz musicians finding their artistic as well as political voice in the communist movement. The closest ties were to the radical theater, as is illustrated by the career of Howard "Stretch" Johnson, a key activist in the Harlem cultural left. Johnson had been a dancer at the Cotton Club when he joined the Negro People's Theater, and their production of *Waiting for Lefty* brought him into contact with the Communist Party.[13]

Moreover, given the presence of the powerful and conservative AFL musicians union, the American Federation of Musicians, jazz musicians did not find their way to the left through struggles for unionization, as was the case in the Hollywood studios and the Newspaper Guild. Rather, the jazz left was the product of three forces: first, the emergence of jazz and swing as the dominant popular music of the young workers who built the CIO;

second, the development of a powerful Harlem Popular Front in the campaigns to free the Scottsboro Nine and Angelo Herndon; and third, the struggle by radicals in the jazz world against racism and Jim Crow in the music industry.

The latter-day success of the folk music revival—of the music of Woody Guthrie, Huddie Ledbetter, and Pete Seeger—has often led historians and cultural critics to assume that folk music was the soundtrack of the Popular Front. This is not true: the music of the young factory and office workers who made up the social movement was overwhelmingly jazz. The emergence of jazz as a mass commercial success—the "beginning" of the "swing era" conventionally dates from Benny Goodman's triumphant appearance at Los Angeles's Palomar Ballroom on 21 August 1935—not only coincides with the beginning of the Popular Front, but it was in large part a sign of the cultural enfranchisement of the second-generation children of migrants from the Black Belt South and from Jewish, Italian, and Slavic Europe.

Though most of the arrangers and composers who fashioned the music of the big bands—figures like Duke Ellington, Don Redman, Fletcher Henderson, Benny Carter, and Sy Oliver—came from families of the established black middle class and often had had college or conservatory training, the majority of the musicians and band leaders came from working-class families. This was true not only of the black musicians who had grown up in the nation's Bronzevilles—the black neighborhoods of New York, Chicago, New Orleans, Pittsburgh, and Kansas City that were the cradles of jazz—but of the young Italian and Jewish musicians who were drawn to the jazz cabarets and clubs. It is often argued that the majority of white musicians attracted to jazz were middle class, Anglo midwesterners like the famous Austin High gang of the late 1920s and early 1930s. Despite the lack of definitive research on the social origins of jazz musicians, however, my own reading of jazz memoirs and biographical dictionaries suggests that most of the white jazz musicians who came of age in the 1930s and 1940s were from plebeian backgrounds: the typical white jazz musician was a figure like Flip Phillips, born Joseph Filipelli in New York in 1915, a solid clarinet and tenor saxophone player with Frankie Newton's small groups as well as the big bands of Benny Goodman and Woody Herman, or Ziggy Elman, born Harry Finkelman in Philadelphia in 1914, whose trumpet solos with the Goodman band incorporated Yiddish "fralich" elements.[14]

Often, jazz musicians came from families who earned a living in music or vaudeville entertainment, the local band leaders and music teachers who maintained the musical subcultures of working-class communities: Lester Young's father was a blacksmith who had become a traveling carnival musician; Charlie Christian grew up in an Oklahoma City tenement, the son of a blind guitarist; and though Billie Holiday grew up with her mother, who was a domestic worker, her father was a guitarist who went on to play with Fletcher Henderson's big band.

Moreover, many of the band leaders who became heroes to the swing audiences of the depression were working-class stars. Count Basie (born in 1904) was the son of black service workers—his father was a groundskeeper and his mother a laundress—who had migrated from Virginia to New Jersey. Both Benny Goodman (born in 1909) and Artie Shaw (born Arthur Arshawsky in 1910) were children of immigrant Jewish garment workers: Goodman grew up in the tenements of Chicago's Maxwell Street ghetto and got his early musical training in a synagogue band and the Hull House band; Shaw was born on New York's Lower East Side and grew up in New Haven. Jimmy and Tommy Dorsey (born in 1904 and 1905) were the sons of a Pennsylvania coal-miner who had become a local band leader and music teacher. And Chick Webb (born in 1909), whose band ruled Harlem's Savoy Ballroom in the 1930s, grew up poor in black Baltimore; like his Baltimore contemporary Billie Holiday, he began working as a musician in New York in his teens.

This is not to say that swing was a "proletarian" culture in the way that radical theater was; on the contrary, swing, like Tin Pan Alley, Hollywood film, and broadcast radio, was a mass commercial culture that forged an "American" style out of the city styles of the black and ethnic working classes. The contradictions of the process were not lost on its practitioners. As Artie Shaw later wrote, "it was a zigzag path indeed, the various interacting processes that brought about the curious metamorphosis of a shy, introspective little Jewish kid named Arthur Arshawsky into a sort of weird, jazz-band-leading, clarinet-tooting, jitterbug-surrounded Symbol of American Youth." "It would be simple enough," he wrote, "to tell the facts that led to the creation of a publicized symbol called Artie Shaw . . . which, as I've indicated, is nothing but a label for a commodity." And it would be simple enough for the cultural historian to see this commodity, "swing," as simply part of middle-class American culture, the dance music played at Ivy League colleges and metropolitan hotels, with little or no connection to the social movement that gave birth to the CIO unions. Nonetheless, for the young second-generation ethnics and northern blacks who listened to the radio broadcasts and crowded the Savoy Ballroom and the Paramount Theater as well as dance halls across the country, there was a connection between, as the composer and music critic Virgil Thomson put it, "hot jazz and the CIO."[15]

Swing was recognizably their own music: "Across the yard a radio goes full blast with Benny Goodman's band," the narrator writes in the final scene of Toshio Mori's fictional portrait of "Lil' Yokohama." Unlike the traditional musics of the "race" records and the foreign-language ethnic records (what the recording industry in the 1920s called "folk music"), swing did not carry the "unsophisticated" marks of the South or the Old Country: it was as urban and "American" as baseball. At the same time, the traditional musics retained a presence in swing: this can be seen in the remarkable "crossover" successes in 1938 and 1939 of the Yiddish song, "Bei Mir Bist Du Schoen," the Czech polka, "Beer Barrel Polka," and the barrelhouse piano blues, "Boogie Woogie." Though the popular swing versions of these and similar tunes by Benny Goodman, Eddie DeLange, Tommy Dorsey, and others are usually seen as "novelty" hits, part of passing "crazes" for Yiddish songs, polkas, and boogie-woogie, they are better understood as trickster tunes, mediating the social and musical contradictions between the "national" and apparently "American" music, swing, and the still vibrant but "regional" musics of ethnic and racial communities.[16]

It is notoriously difficult to capture the sensibilities of popular audiences, to assess the meanings popular music carried for the vast numbers of people who heard it. One is forced to draw inferences not only from social history—the recognition that there is probably a link between the fact that swing was primarily an urban popular music and the fact that, by 1930, two-thirds of the population of the major cities were immigrants or the children of immigrants—but also from the testimonies of figures who, though perhaps not typical, may prove representative of the Popular Front jazz audience. Two such figures are the novelist Ralph Ellison and the record producer Jerry Wexler, both of whom came of age in the depression (Ellison was born in 1914, Wexler in 1917), and both of whom have written memoirs of their involvement with the world of jazz and the world of the Popular Front.

Ellison was the child of black migrants to Oklahoma City—"of the city," he says of himself, with "none of the agricultural experiences of my mother." He was early attracted to music and "jazz was inescapable." He knew Charlie Christian when they were both children, and he "hung around the old Blue Devils Orchestra out of which the famous Basie band was formed." When he came to New York from Tuskegee at the age of twenty-two he wanted to be a musician and composer, and studied composition with Wallingford Riegger, a left-wing modernist who had been part of the Composers Collective. In New York, Ellison was quickly drawn into the world of the Popular Front left and became a writer: he later recalled hanging around the Harlem bureau of the *Daily Worker* with his older friend Richard Wright, and remembered that "through one of those odd instances which occur to young provincials in New York, I was to hear Malraux make an appeal for the Spanish Loyalists at the same party where I first heard the folk singer Leadbelly perform." The young Ellison worked on the Federal Writers Project in New York, regularly wrote reviews for the *New Masses* and *Direction* in 1940 and 1941, and became the managing editor of the left-wing *Negro Quarterly* in 1942. He covered the National Negro Congress for the *New Masses*, writing to Richard Wright that "my experience of the Congress was almost mystical in its intensity." However, like most of the young people drawn to the world of the cultural front, Ellison was not primarily a political activist, and for Ellison these years also belonged to the young musicians of the swing bands who were creating the new music that came to be known as bop. When Ellison wrote about jazz in his celebrated essays for the *Saturday Review* and *Esquire* of the late 1950s, he returned to the music of his early New York years, to Charlie Christian, Charlie Parker, and Jimmy Rushing, and to the "continuing symposium of jazz" at Minton's in the early 1940s, "where it was possible to hear its resources of technique, ideas, harmonic structure, melodic phrasing and rhythmical possibilities explored more thoroughly than was ever possible before."[17]

To juxtapose the record producer Jerry Wexler to the novelist Ralph Ellison is incongruous, yet they shared the "jazz-shaped" world of the Popular Front. Jerry Wexler's father was a Polish Jewish immigrant window-washer; his mother was "one of those working-class self-taught Jewish New Yorkers" who would "congregate in cafeterias like the Automat or Bick-ford's to drink endless cups of coffee and argue over Lenin and Trotsky." "It's a pretty good bet she was a card-carrying member of the Party," he writes, while his brother was a Trotskyist who "could analyze the complexities of Trotsky's splinter groups—the Cannonites versus the Shachtmanites—with absolute precision." Wexler's passion was not politics but music, but he was, as he says, "a product ... of all those ingredients that melded into swing." He became an avid record collector, part of the circle who congregated at Milt Gabler's Commodore Record Shop; his role models were the jazz producer John Hammond, "with his brush haircut, Brooks Brothers tweed, button-down Oxford shirt, and intellectual-radical periodicals—*New Masses, Masses and Mainstream, The Worker*—tucked under his arm," and "a Brooklyn bartender ... a jazz scholar with an Irish dock worker's accent who, when drunk, wept for the brave Spanish rebels while swearing vengeance on the head of Franco."[18]

Ellison and Wexler mark the elective affinities between the world of swing and the world of the Spanish Civil War. It is not surprising, therefore, that many of the big band leaders supported the political struggles of the Popular Front. Any number of musicians and band leaders—including Duke Ellington, Count Basie, Benny Carter, Benny Goodman, Artie Shaw, Fletcher Henderson, Cab Calloway, Billie Holiday, Sidney Bechet, Dizzy Gillespie, Miles Davis, and Charlie Parker—played at Popular Front events: benefits for the Scottsboro Nine; Harlem political rallies; fundraisers for the Spanish Republicans, the anti-fascist exiles, and Russian War Relief; concerts sponsored by the *New Masses*, as well as dances at left-wing conventions and summer camps. Nevertheless, most historians of jazz have seen these events as irrelevant, simply another gig.[19]

It is true that few of these musicians became activists in Popular Front organizations, and few thought of themselves as "political" artists. As virtually all the memoirs and interviews make clear, the jazz musicians were primarily interested in their craft, and their "political" statements usually deal with the injustices faced by musicians, the day-to-day exploitation, petty tyrannies, and color line of the music industry. However, they recognized the social crises of the depression and fascism, and were attracted to the hopes and energies of the Popular Front social movement. As stars, representatives of their communities, they supported the political campaigns that were mobilizing their popular audiences. The benefit concerts and the letterheads of the various ad hoc musicians committees are not simply the ephemera of cultural history, but the traces of the intangible relationship between a popular star, the star's audience, and a political movement.

One can see this link most clearly in the campaigns to free Angelo Herndon and the Scottsboro Nine. Angelo Herndon was a young black Communist organizer arrested in Atlanta in 1932 for organizing a relief demonstration and convicted under a slave insurrection statute; the Scottsboro Nine were young African American men accused and convicted of raping two white women in the spring of 1931. Both cases were taken up by the International Labor Defense (ILD), the Communist Party's legal defense organization, and achieved national attention through the efforts of two black Communist lawyers, William Patterson and Benjamin Davis. As the legal proceedings continued for the next several years—Herndon's conviction was overturned by the Supreme Court and four of the Scottsboro Nine were released in 1937—the rallies and campaigns to free the defendants mobilized black communities across the country, as well as black artists, including jazz musicians.

In addition to marches and rallies, the ILD organized benefit concerts for the Scottsboro Nine: on 15 May 1932, a Rockland Palace benefit featured speeches by Louise Thompson and writer Eugene Gordon as well as a performance by Cab Calloway's orchestra. By the end of the year, John Hammond was recruited to organize larger benefits: in the winter of 1932–33, Benny Carter's orchestra played a Rockland Palace benefit, with Duke Ellington at the piano. Hammond himself went to Decatur, Alabama, to cover the second Scottsboro trial for the *Nation*. Subsequent Scottsboro benefits in early 1934 featured the big bands of Benny Carter and Fletcher Henderson.[20]

A key figure in organizing these events was Louise Thompson, a social worker who had taught at an Arkansas black college and the Hampton Institute before coming to New York as an Urban League fellow. Thompson became a close friend of the ILD lawyer and organizer, William Patterson (whom she later married), and of Langston Hughes; and her Convent Avenue apartment became a meeting place of the left-wing black intelligentsia. In 1932, she helped organize a tour of the Soviet Union by black artists; by 1934, she had helped form a cultural group, the Vanguard, which sponsored dance and theater groups, a summer musical program, political forums, and a Marxist study group.[21]

This black cultural front forged an alliance between the worlds of jazz and the Harlem left that was to continue for two decades. There were Carnegie Hall concerts sponsored by the Musicians' Committee for Spanish Democracy in 1937 and 1938, featuring Cab Calloway, Count Basie, W.C. Handy, Fats Waller, and Jimmie Lunceford. Benny Goodman played benefits for the Spanish Republicans in 1937, and his support was visible enough to provoke right-wing pickets at his famous Carnegie Hall concert. Count Basie was part of a *New Masses* evening, Hitting a New High, in January 1938, which included performances of Marc Blitzstein's radio musical, "I've Got the Tune," and Aaron Copland's school opera, "The Second Hurricane." Chick Webb's band with Ella Fitzgerald played at events sponsored by the *Daily Worker*'s Harlem bureau; and Billie Holiday sang at the May Day celebrations in 1941. Artie Shaw supported various left-wing peace groups and was active in the campaign for civil rights in employment (particularly for the FEPC, the Fair Employment Practices Commission). A self-described activist in the crucial organization of the Hollywood Popular Front, HICCASP (the Hollywood Independent Citizens Committee of the Arts, Sciences and Professions), Shaw was called before the House Committee on Un-American Activities in 1953. Finally, the young Italian American singer from working-class Hoboken who sang with the big bands of Harry James and Tommy Dorsey, Frank Sinatra, was also aligned with the Popular Front HICCASP in the mid 1940s: a friend recalled that "both Frank and I were fairly close to the Communist Party line at that time. Neither of us was a card-carrying member, of course, but we were both very close to people like Albert Maltz who were, and we shared their beliefs for the most part."[22]

Perhaps the apex of the jazz Popular Front came in the campaign to elect Benjamin Davis to the New York City Council in 1943. The pianist Teddy Wilson chaired an artists committee for Davis which enlisted the support of Lena Horne, Duke Ellington, Count Basie, Mary Lou Williams, Coleman Hawkins, Billie Holiday, Jimmie Lunceford, Art Tatum, Josh White, and Ella Fitzgerald, among others. Wilson organized a Davis Victory rally two weeks before the election at which Hawkins, Hazel Scott, Holiday, Fitzgerald, and Williams apppeared. A 1944 Davis rally at the Golden Gate featured Basie, Williams, Holiday, and White. A 1945 re-election fundraiser featured Ellington, Holiday, and Roy Eldridge.[23]

The anti-Communist purge took its toll on the jazz left. In 1948, Benjamin Davis, along with eleven other leaders of the Communist Party, was arrested for teaching and advocating the overthrow of the government; after a nine-month trial, he was convicted in October 1949. He lost the 1949 election, was ousted from the city council, and jailed. At the same time, the most powerful agents, including Moe Gale, Joe Glaser, and the William Morris Agency, threatened to cancel the contracts of figures like Erskine Hawkins, Basie, Holiday, and Goodman unless they cut their ties to the left. Even so, some musicians continued to support Davis: Charlie Parker played at a Free Ben Davis birthday ball at Rockland Palace in September 1952. Parker "was very much interested in the social order," Dizzy Gillespie later wrote, "and we'd have these long conversations about it, and music. We discussed local politics too, people like Vito Marcantonio, and what he'd tried to do for the little man in New York. We liked Marcantonio's ideas because as musicians we weren't paid at all well for what we created." Both Hazel Scott and Lena Horne were blacklisted for their connections to the left.[24]

For the most part, the political allegiances and affiliations of the band leaders and musicians did not appear in their music. As Dizzy Gillespie put it, "artists are always in the vanguard of social change, but we didn't go out and make speeches or say, 'Let's play eight bars of protest.' We just played our music and let it go at that. The music proclaimed our identity; it made every statement we truly wanted to make." The exceptions were generally unsuccessful. Count Basie recorded a song about Jim Crow from the left-wing revue *Meet the People*, "It's the Same Old South," in 1940; in 1941, he recorded "King Joe," a topical blues about Joe Louis, written by Richard Wright and sung by Paul Robeson. Frank Sinatra attracted much attention for his role in the ten-minute short film on racial tolerance, *The House I Live In*, written by the left-wing screenwriter Albert Maltz. Sinatra sang, and later recorded, the title song, a Popular Front anthem written by Earl Robinson and Lewis Allan. But these were rare occasions: the only jazz musician to attempt large-scale works incorporating Popular Front politics was, as we have seen, Duke Ellington. Nevertheless, Holiday's "Strange Fruit" needs to seen in the context of these two decades of political appearances and affiliations.[25]

The third link between jazz musicians and the left was the Popular Front jazz subculture, a network of aficionados, critics, promoters, and collectors, who organized concerts, nightclubs, record stores, magazines, and recording companies, and fought for an end to the color line in the music industry and the recognition of African American musics. In part, this grew out of the movement culture of the Popular Front. A number of jazz musicians played at dances sponsored by left-wing groups and at the left-wing summer camp, Camp Unity. "We used to play for all the communist dances," Dizzy Gillespie recalled. "The communists held a lot of them, in Brooklyn, the Bronx, and Manhattan. At those communist dances, they were always trying to convert you. As a matter of fact, I signed one of those cards; I never went to a meeting, but I was a card-carrying communist because it was directly associated with my work, the dances, Camp Unity and all that kinda stuff." As late as 1951, Miles Davis, Sonny Rollins, and J.J. Johnson were playing for a Labor Youth League dance.[26]

Sidney Bechet, whose US career had been rekindled by the revival of traditional jazz, spent the summers of 1941 and 1942 working at Camp Unity, and recruited a variety of musicians, including trumpeters Frankie Newton and Bill Coleman and pianist Willie "the Lion" Smith. Virtually all the memoirs of the camp have stressed its interracial sexuality: Willie "the Lion" Smith, who "couldn't see anything in that Communism stuff," recalled that it was "the most mixed-up camp I ever saw or heard about— the races, the sexes, and the religions were all mixed." "The people there were all talking racial equality," drummer Roy Porter recalled, "and I must admit I didn't hear one derogatory remark or see any incidents while I was there. Still I think all 'racial equality' boiled down to there was that the black musicians had to be with white women since there were no black women in camp." Similarly Dizzy Gillespie remembered that "white-black relationships were very close among the communists. . . . I thought it was pretty funny myself, being from the South. I found it strange that every couple, almost, was a mixed couple one way or the other. That was the age of unity."[27]

But if the interracial unity of Camp Unity seemed the artificial product of a summer in the country, the campaign against the color line in the music industry was a central part of the cultural politics of the jazz left. "Radio staff and studio orchestras were closed to us," Benny Carter recalled. "What was holding us back was not just the individual differences but a whole system of discrimination and segregation involving musicians, audiences, bookings, productions and so on." The integration of recording sessions, of white swing bands, of radio network and studio orchestras, and of nightclubs and concert halls was a continual struggle through the 1930s and 1940s, and Popular Front producers and promoters like John Hammond and Norman Granz played an important role. Hammond regularly campaigned against segregation and exploitation in the music industry: in 1937 he attacked record company practices in a series of articles under the pseudonym Henry Johnson in the *New Masses*; and in 1940 he founded a magazine, *Music and Rhythm*, that "editorialized against discrimination in the recording companies, radio networks and musicians' unions."[28]

Though there had been a few interracial recording sessions in the 1920s, the sessions in 1933 in which John Hammond brought together white musicians like Benny Goodman and Jack Teagarden and black musicians like Frank Newton and Shirley Clay to back Bessie Smith and Billie Holiday marked the beginning of integrated jazz recording. Hammond also persuaded Goodman to make Teddy Wilson a permanent member of his band in 1936, and afterwards the Goodman band became one of the few mixed bands, featuring Charlie Christian and Lionel Hampton. Billie Holiday's eight-month stay with Artie Shaw's orchestra in 1938 and Lena Horne's four-month appearance with Charlie Barnet's orchestra in 1941 were among the few instances of black singers appearing with white bands; both tenures were marked by racist incidents despite the commitment of Shaw and Barnet to integration. On the West Coast, a young film editor, Norman Granz, organized integrated jam sessions, which led to the successful series of Jazz at the Philharmonic concerts: the first was a 1943 benefit for the Mexican American defendants in the Sleepy Lagoon case. Though Jazz at the Philharmonic "wasn't much musically," Dizzy Gillespie later wrote, "it was the original 'first class' treatment for jazz musicians. . . . You traveled 'first class,' stayed in 'first class' hotels, and [Granz] demanded no segregation in seating." Granz's Jazz at the Philharmonic was, along with Hammond's Spirituals to Swing and Ellington's Carnegie Hall concerts, part of the development of the jazz "concert" between 1935 and 1945. These attempts to bring vernacular music into the concert hall were often the work of left-wing producers.[29]

The Popular Front jazz subculture also created a network of critics, collectors, record shops, and independent labels. Though there were heated debates over jazz in the left press and some left-wing music critics criticized contemporary jazz, virtually all of the major jazz critics of the period were on the left. The revival and recovery of traditional New Orleans jazz was largely the work of Charles Edward Smith and Frederic Ramsey, Jr, who together edited the pioneering collection *Jazzmen* and produced records by Bechet and Bunk Johnson. Alan Lomax recorded Jelly Roll Morton's music and memories for the Library of Congress in 1939: he later used the recordings in writing Morton's "autobiography," *Mister Jelly Roll* (1950). Charles Edward Smith reviewed jazz for the *Daily Worker*, B.H. Haggin wrote for the *Nation*, and Otis Ferguson wrote for the *New Republic*; a number of the leading European critics, including Eric Hobsbawm (who wrote under the name Francis Newton), André Hodier, and Joachim Berendt (who debated with Adorno over jazz), were also Popular Front figures. Indeed, James Lincoln Collier has even claimed that the early Popular Front critics so dominated jazz criticism that their "falsifications" invented the "myth" of American indifference to jazz and the "myth" that jazz was a music of the ghetto. However, when he tried to find a serious critic of jazz who was not on the left and "not involved in the politicizing of jazz," he could only come up with R.D. Darrell: Collier seems unaware that Darrell too was a Popular Front figure, a music critic for the *New Masses*.[30]

Milt Gabler's Commodore Music Shop was regularly advertised in the Popular Front press; he distributed the releases of the left-wing record company Timely, and his Commodore Records issued Holiday's "Strange Fruit." Eric Bernay, the business manager of the *New Masses*, also had a record store, The Music Room, and founded Keynote Records in 1940. Keynote specialized in jazz and folk music and issued a variety of Popular Front recordings, including the Almanac Singers, Harold Rome's versions of *Pins and Needles* songs, Marc Blitzstein's *No for an Answer*, and Josh White's *Chain Gang* and *Southern Exposure*. Under its jazz A&R (artists and repertory) man, Harry Lim, Keynote drew on the Café Society bands for a series of small-group sessions, "nearly a third of which," Whitney Balliett has argued, "are among the best of all jazz recordings." Eventually, John Hammond became the president of Keynote and in 1947 it merged into Mercury Records.[31]

So Café Society was not merely a "socially-minded night club," in Irving Howe's condescending phrase; it, like *Music and Rhythm*, Jazz at the Philharmonic, Keynote Records, and Commodore Records, was a Popular Front jazz institution. However, Café Society was more than an integrated nightclub: the group of Popular Front jazz, blues, and gospel musicians who worked there developed a distinctive music, a cabaret blues, epitomized by the work of Billie Holiday and Josh White.

3. Jazz at the Cabaret: Billie Holiday's "Love" Songs

Most critics and historians have seen Café Society as a marriage of convenience between radical white entrepreneurs like Josephson and Hammond and apolitical black musicians. This picture became part of the public record when two of the musicians, Hazel Scott and Josh White, testified before the House Committee on Un-American Activities in the early 1950s. Challenging the *Red Channels* account of her political affiliations, Scott maintained that she had been instructed by her employer, Barney Josephson, to appear at the rally for the Communist candidate, Benjamin Davis. Similarly, Josh White maintained that "artists are not often smart about politics" and were thus "easy prey for anyone who appeals to our sense of justice and decency." Both found it necessary to repudiate the Communist Party and Paul Robeson. However, historians should be wary of taking these testimonies at face value; the sense that the Café Society musicians were political innocents manipulated by their employers is not sustained by the historical record. On the contrary, the group of musicians around Billie Holiday were remarkably self-conscious about their politics and art, and Holiday herself, Josh White recalled, "was more race-conscious than people thought."[32]

Lena Horne, who began singing at Café Society in early 1941 at the age of twenty-three, later wrote that "Josh White ... introduced [me] to another kind of music—protest songs and sin songs. More important, he reinforced the notion ... that singing could be an art." Hazel Scott, who "had the fiercest sort of racial pride," was also "an influence" on Horne, "despite the frequent clash of ... temperaments." Moreover, when Dizzy Gillespie later recalled the radical musicians of the period, he cited Café Society band leaders. "There were a bunch of musicians more socially minded," he wrote, "who were closely connected with the Communist Party. Those guys stayed busy anywhere labor was concerned.... A few enlightened musicians recognized the importance of Paul Robeson, amongst them Teddy Wilson, Frankie Newton, and Pete Seeger—all of them very outspoken politically." Seeger, of course, was a young folk singer, but Wilson and Newton were both band leaders at Café Society.[33]

Teddy Wilson, remembered by one contemporary as the "Marxist Mozart," was a key figure in Café Society circles, both musically and politically. By the time Café Society opened, he was already the Jackie Robinson of swing, the first black musician in a white big band, appearing with Benny Goodman. Born in 1912, Wilson came from an educated family; his father was an English professor and his mother chief librarian at the Tuskegee Institute. He came to New York to play with Benny Carter and joined Goodman in 1936 after Carter's band broke up. Beginning in 1935, Wilson made a series of classic recordings with Billie Holiday, and he briefly led his own big band before leading a sextet at Café Society between 1940 and 1944 (first at the Downtown club, and then at the second Uptown club). Wilson taught jazz at the left-wing Metropolitan Music School, appeared at *New Masses* benefits, took part in the Russian War Relief benefit organized by Marc Blitzstein, Music at Work, in May 1942, and chaired the artists committee for Benjamin Davis.[34]

Frankie Newton was a highly respected trumpet player, born in Virginia in 1906 and active in a number of bands in the 1930s; he was part of the interracial band that John Hammond assembled in 1933 to accompany Bessie Smith. In 1938, he formed the band that opened at Café Society, and accompanied Billie Holiday on her 1939 Commodore recordings that included "Strange Fruit." "At Café Society," one musician recalled, "Frankie Newton, who could be a very serious guy, would get some listeners round him, and he'd talk about pretty deep subjects like 'the economics of Marcus Garvey's return to Africa scheme,' or 'The Soviet Five Year Plan.'" Though Newton's career was interrupted by illness and he died in 1954, he and Wilson were both musical and political leaders at Café Society.[35]

Moreover, for the musicians, the key political influences were less

Josephson and Hammond than the group of black artists and intellectuals who frequented the cabaret. These included Sterling Brown (who had introduced the 1939 Spirituals to Swing concert), Walter White, E. Franklin Frazier, Romare Bearden, Duke Ellington, Canada Lee, Joe Louis, Richard Wright, Langston Hughes, and Paul Robeson. Hughes was not only a regular, but wrote songs and skits for Café Society performers, joined Arna Bontemps in introducing Hazel Scott, and worked on a Café Society revue that was to star Scott and dancer Pearl Primus. Robeson had returned from almost a decade abroad in October 1939 and he quickly became a leading figure in the US Popular Front and the circle around Café Society. Several Café Society performers, including Lena Horne, Pearl Primus, and Sarah Vaughan, recalled Robeson's encouragement. Robeson, Lena Horne remembered, "did everything he could to reinforce my weakened, mostly dormant sense of racial identity. . . . Thanks to Paul and Josh White and to the whole atmosphere around Barney's clubs, . . . I began to interest myself in matters like Civil Rights and equal opportunities for everyone." Both Hughes and Robeson stood as important political examples for the Café Society musicians.[36]

The cabaret blues of Café Society was actually three distinct musics: boogie-woogie piano, the small-group swing bands fronted by women singers, notably Billie Holiday, and the Piedmont blues and gospel of Josh White and the Golden Gate Quartet. Each had a powerful impact on American music. The boogie-woogie pianists received the greatest public acclaim in the early years of Café Society but were perhaps least influenced by the political-musical milieu. Boogie-woogie was a blues piano music that had emerged in the South and the Southwest at the time of the First World War; the brief revival of boogie-woogie was ignited by the appearance of Albert Ammons, Pete Johnson, and Meade Lux Lewis at the first Spirituals to Swing concert, and continued through their stay at Café Society, where they accompanied the blues singer Joe Turner.

If the boogie-woogie pianists played a hard, driving blues dominated by the ostinato basses of the left hand, Café Society's small groups—Frankie Newton's septet and Teddy Wilson's sextet, as well as subsequent bands led by Eddie Heywood, Joe Sullivan, Edmond Hall, and Mary Lou Williams—played a chamber jazz, with the piano's melodic improvisations alternating with the riffs and short solos of the horns. These small groups were also a marked contrast to the dominant sound of the large orchestras. As Gunther Schuller has noted, "when the big swing bands roamed the land, small groups were quite rare . . . 'combo jazz,' as it became known in the 1940s, . . . was . . . the exception rather than the rule." The origin of these small groups was the Billie Holiday/Teddy Wilson recording sessions that began in 1935. Jukeboxes had become a major outlet for records by the mid 1930s, and John Hammond persuaded ARC's Brunswick label to produce black covers of white popular songs for the juke joints in black neighbor-hoods. Between 1935 and 1942, Holiday and Wilson played more than two dozen sessions together, recording tunes that had been hits for singers like Bing Crosby and Fred Astaire. The sessions were informal, drawing on musicians from the Basie, Ellington, and Goodman bands. Wilson and Holiday would go over the tunes the day before, and would "pass out solos so everybody would get sixteen or eight bars." The records sold well for Brunswick, regularly making the charts. However, the Wilson/Holiday small groups were for the most part confined to the recording studio: Holiday herself went on the road with the big bands of Count Basie and Artie Shaw.[37]

When Café Society opened in December 1938, it became a major venue for small jazz combos. "The various groups which Teddy Wilson, Billie Holiday and Frankie Newton gathered," Sidney Finkelstein wrote, "... served as the experimental laboratories" of jazz: "the job they tackled was the exploration of the full tonal possibilities of the instrument, and the absorption of the popular ballad." Frankie Newton's septet backed Holiday during her first nine-month stay at Café Society in 1939. Teddy Wilson's band followed in July 1940, and Hazel Scott replaced Holiday; after Wilson and Scott moved to Josephson's new Café Society Uptown, which opened in October 1940, Holiday returned for a second stint at Café Society Downtown, accompanied by Joe Sullivan's band and later by Art Tatum. In 1941, Lena Horne took over, followed by the Basie singer, Helen Humes, and, toward the end of the war, Sarah Vaughan. During the war years, Café Society hosted Eddie Heywood's sextet (who accompanied Holiday on her 1944 Commodore recordings), Edmond Hall's sextet, and Mary Lou Williams's trios and sextets.[38]

Billie Holiday's singing and influence dominated Café Society's combo jazz. Wilson, Newton, and Heywood are now best remembered for their recordings with Holiday, and the singers Scott, Horne, and Humes never escaped her shadow. Moreover, much of Holiday's best work was a product of the Café Society years, and the Popular Front musicians, audiences, and promoters at Café Society had a profound impact on Holiday. Holiday was only twenty-three when she began at Café Society, but she had been performing for almost a decade. Born in 1915, she had grown up as Eleanora Fagan in working-class black Baltimore. Her mother worked as a domestic, a waitress, and a machine operator in a shirt factory. Her father, who never lived with them, was a banjo and guitar player in jazz bands; one stepfather was a longshoreman, another was a porter. In 1929, Holiday and her mother moved to Harlem, and she began singing in speakeasies and nightclubs, developing her art in after-hours jam sessions. John Hammond heard her at Monette's in 1933 and set up a recording session with Benny Goodman; she made her debut at the Apollo Theater in 1934 and appeared in Ellington's short film, *Symphony in Black*, in 1935. By the time she began at Café Society, her recordings had been jukebox hits and she was a successful big band singer.[39]

It is hard to reconstruct her Café Society performances: neither the memoirs of Café Society nor the biographies of Holiday give a full sense of her cabaret repertoire other than "Strange Fruit." However, her recordings of 1939, 1940, and 1941 reveal the continuities and changes in Holiday's work. On the one hand, Holiday continued to sing the "jump" tunes and Tin Pan Alley songs she had recorded for the jukebox; her only live recording from Café Society—a radio aircheck—was a version of her 1938 hit "I'm Gonna Lock My Heart (And Throw Away the Key)." She recorded two classic uptempo swing tunes—"Them There Eyes," a song she had been singing since her early speakeasy days, and "Swing Brother Swing"— with the Café Society band (without Frankie Newton) a month after the recording of "Strange Fruit." Throughout the Café Society years, she continued to record standards: her brilliant rendition of Gershwin's "The Man I Love" had a classic tenor solo by Lester Young; she recorded Harold Arlen's "I Gotta Right to Sing the Blues" and Jerome Kern's "Yesterdays" at the "Strange Fruit" session (the minor key nostalgia of "Yesterdays" has eerie echoes of "Strange Fruit"); and turned to Cole Porter's "Night and Day" and Johnny Green's "Body and Soul" in the winter of 1939–40.[40]

In this respect, she inherited Louis Armstrong's enduring synthesis of blues-based hot jazz and the popular ballad, symbolically initiated by his 1929 hit, "Ain't Misbehavin'": as Dan Morganstern has written, "Armstrong was the one who turned many Tin Pan Alley tunes into jazz evergreens." Holiday later said that she "copied [her] style from Louis Armstrong"; it was "not that she imitated Armstrong," one critic notes, "but she took over in principle Armstrong's concept of improvisatory liberty and the notion of phrasing like a horn." She often returned to the songs he had recorded in the early 1930s, including "Them There Eyes," "I Gotta Right to Sing the Blues," "All of Me," and "Georgia on My Mind."[41]

However, Holiday also added new kinds of songs at Café Society: European cabaret tunes, the ballads of Irene Kitchings, and her own compositions. Many of these were in slower tempos and grew out of the theatrical nature of the Café Society. The European cabaret songs included "Gloomy Sunday," a Hungarian dirge that Paul Robeson had recorded, and "Falling in Love Again," written by Friedrich Hollaender, Weimar's leading cabaret songwriter, and sung by Marlene Dietrich in *The Blue Angel*. Neither of these songs are particularly important in themselves; however, they illuminate Holiday's engagement with the cabaret tradition and highlight the particular accomplishment and limits of "Strange Fruit" itself. For the paradox of "Strange Fruit" was that it was neither in the African American tradition—it was not a blues or a spiritual—nor in the

Tin Pan Alley tradition that jazz musicians, including Holiday, had made their own. This is why jazz critics from John Hammond on have never fully accepted it. "Strange Fruit" was closer to the cabaret songs of Marc Blitzstein, perhaps not surprisingly since Lewis Allan had worked on the TAC Cabaret.

Holiday experimented with Popular Front cabaret songs on several occasions. While she was at Café Society, Marc Blitzstein and Emmanuel Eisenberg wrote "Jobless Blues" for her, but she did not like it. A year after the success of "Strange Fruit," she sang Harold Rome's "The Yanks Aren't Coming" during her stay at Kelly's Stables. It is likely that she got the song from Hazel Scott, who was singing at Café Society that summer and had recorded it for the Theatre Arts Committee, along with "Mene, Mene, Tekel" from *Pins and Needles*. In any case, Holiday's rendition drew attention: "F.B.I. agents got wind of it," the *Amsterdam News* reported, "and had the management restrain Miss Holiday from singing this type of song. . . . Just why, it's hard to say, except possibly that they felt that it was very un-American for a Negro to sing a pacifist song. So [. . .] swing habitues of Kelly's Stables will have to be content to hear Miss Holiday sing such standbys as 'Fine and Mellow' and 'Them There Eyes' because there's no obvious propaganda connected with them." The suggestion that the FBI would miss all but the most obvious propaganda reminds us that Holiday was seen as a voice of the social movement. This was not only due to "Strange Fruit" and her association with Café Society; of the Popular Front's three favorite bands, she had performed with two—those of Basie and Shaw—and was closely associated with Teddy Wilson, who had broken swing's color line with the third—that of Goodman. So it is not surprising that Holiday was part of Harlem's Popular Front during these years, singing "Strange Fruit" at a May Day rally in 1941 and appearing at Golden Gate Ballroom rallies for Ben Davis in the fall of 1943 and the spring of 1944.[42]

With the exception of "Strange Fruit," however, the European-style cabaret song never became part of Holiday's repertoire. For all her theatricality, she was never drawn to the satire at the heart of political cabaret; moreover, the cabaret song, unlike the "bluish" songs of Gershwin and Arlen, had little connection to African American traditions. The stylized theatrical quality of the cabaret did, however, leave its mark on her performances of a host of original songs, some written by her friend Irene Armstrong Kitchings, and some by herself. Holiday recorded four of Kitchings's songs in 1939 and 1940—"Some Other Spring," "Ghost of Yesterday," "What Is This Going to Get Us," and "I'm Pulling Through"— and they became a distinctive part of her repertoire. Kitchings had been a piano player and band leader in Chicago in the late 1920s before marrying Teddy Wilson and giving up performing. Her songs were written after breaking up with Wilson. "Lady and I were very close," she later recalled.

"She started coming up to the house . . . to rehearse for the records [with Wilson]. She often stayed with me, especially later when the break with Ted was not far off." If Holiday's collaboration with Teddy Wilson recorded in the Brunswick sessions has always been recognized as central, her collaboration with Irene Kitchings was probably no less important.[43]

For not only did Holiday adopt the work of her friend—the mutual debt is acknowledged when Holiday sings "thanks for this song" in Kitchings's "I'm Pulling Through"—she too began to compose songs. These women's laments, including "Everything Happens for the Best," "Long Gone Blues," "Fine and Mellow," "Our Love Is Different," and "Tell Me More and More and Then Some," all recorded in 1939 and 1940, marked a new form of expression for Holiday, one which resulted in such classics as "God Bless the Child" (1941) and "Don't Explain" (1944). They are Holiday's cabaret blues. Like Kitchings's songs, they are dramas of desire, tales of resignation and assertion. "I've been told that nobody sings the word 'hunger' like I do," Holiday says in *Lady Sings the Blues*, "Or the word 'love'." Even the most technical musical analysis of Holiday's work, that of Gunther Schuller, agrees: after analyzing her vowels and consonants, he concludes that "no one ever sang the word 'love' as she could." The "love" songs of Holiday and Kitchings are as much a product of the Popular Front cabaret as "Strange Fruit"; they are not unlike the torch songs of the Popular Front musical theater—*The Cradle*'s "Nickel under the Foot," *Pins and Needles*'s "What Good Is Love?," and *Jump for Joy*'s "I Got It Bad (And That Ain't Good)."[44]

As many critics have noted, Holiday's "love" songs share the slow tempo and melancholy manner of "Strange Fruit." They are not dance tunes for jukeboxes but torch songs for the intimacy of the cabaret. They also seem to share the violence and gloom of "Strange Fruit." Love too is a pastoral scene that yields a bitter crop, and Holiday's songs have often been seen as tales of women who love the men who beat and mistreat them. There are, indeed, many examples of this, beginning with the early "Billie's Blues" of 1936: "I love my man, tell the world I do / I love my man, tell the world I do, / But when he mistreats me, I feel so blue." However, the 1939–40 love songs of Holiday and Kitchings have a richer palette: "our love is different," Holiday sings. The word "hope" is crucial to her finest recording of a Kitchings song, "I'm Pulling Through," in which she is echoed by Lester Young's solo. Moreover, the 1939 "Long Gone Blues" includes a vengeful couplet that she will add to "Billie's Blues" in a 1944 recording: "I've been your slave ever since I been your babe, / I've been your slave ever since I been your babe, / But before I'd be your dog, I'd see you in your grave." The FBI may have missed this blues allegory of slavery, but it is unlikely that audiences did.

These songs are also closer to the blues than anything else in Holiday's repertoire. It has often been remarked that Holiday was not a blues singer and did not think of herself as one. She did not sing blues while traveling with either Count Basie or Artie Shaw, and the 1936 "Billie's Blues" was her only recorded 12-bar blues before beginning at Café Society. However, in the spring of 1939 she recorded both "Long Gone Blues," with Tab Smith on soprano sax and Hot Lips Page on trumpet (though it was not released until 1947), and the classic "Fine and Mellow," which was, Milt Gabler recalled, "the first modern blues session, really." "I had the saxophones play a riff behind her that Tab Smith sketched out, and rambling piano and Frankie Newton's muted trumpet, like Joe Smith would play behind Bessie Smith." "Fine and Mellow" was released together with "Strange Fruit"; it was not only an immediate hit, but remained one of Holiday's signature numbers (Figure 14).[45]

To listen to "Fine and Mellow" and "Long Gone Blues" alongside Holiday's other recordings of the period illuminates her relation to the blues. If the blues are understood simply as a particular commercial song form, Holiday was not a blues singer. She rarely adopted the conventional blues *form*, with its call and response couplets. The popular ballad, with its lyric contrast between chorus and bridge, served as the vehicle for most of her dramatic miniatures. Even the exception proves this: at first glance, "Fine and Mellow" is a twelve-bar blues with five verses. However, Holiday sings the fourth verse as if it were a bridge, with a contrasting melodic and rhythmic line. As a result, unlike the simpler "Long Gone Blues," "Fine and Mellow" becomes a miniature drama, as its conventional opening— "My man don't love me, treats me oh so mean"—is resolved in the final vernacular conceit—"Love is just like a faucet, it turns off and on, / Love is just like a faucet, it turns off and on, / Sometimes when you think it's on baby, it has turned off and gone." Like "St Louis Blues," which it echoes, "Fine and Mellow" is a fusion of the 12-bar form and the popular song.

However, blues harmony and song form—the standard 12-bar sequence of chords—are not really the heart of the blues. As musicologist Christopher Small has written, "the interest of blues lies elsewhere than in the harmony; for the musician who is playing and singing blues, harmony is only a kind of underpinning for what really interests him, which is the melodic and rhythmic invention, as well as the inflection of vocal and instrumental styles." Blues melody—with its non-diatonic "blue" intervals, syncopated rhythms, and rich vocabulary of slurs, scoops, and dips—lay at the heart of Holiday's singing: "in Billie's case," Sidney Finkelstein wrote, "this style is made up of an entrancing tone color, a subtle slurring of pitch, a suspenseful delayed attack and a partial transformation of the melodic line into a blues line." When Holiday said, "I don't think I'm singing. I feel like I am playing a horn. I try to improvise like Les Young, like Louis Armstrong," she was referring to this ability to turn Tin Pan Alley melodies and rhythms into blues phrases.[46]

Thus, most of Holiday's art involved revising and reshaping ready-made narratives, whether "The Man I Love," "Strange Fruit," or Kitchings's "Some Other Spring." Turning blues phrases into songs was an art that she rarely practiced: indeed, songwriter Arthur Herzog, who received co-credits on several of the songs by Holiday and Irene Kitchings, later said that Holiday never wrote "a line of words or music." However, Herzog's own account of the origins of two of Holiday's compositions, "Tell Me More and More and Then Some" and "God Bless the Child," are revealing. Holiday began by playing with phrases, either musical (an echo of "St James Infirmary") or verbal (the expression "God bless the child"); Herzog then put them into song form with her; and Holiday remade them in her singing.[47]

If Holiday was not a tunesmith, nevertheless these phrases—vernacular commonplaces—were the heart of her own songs. One of the earliest songs with which she is credited is built around a folk saying: "Since the world began / The old folks say / Everything happens for the best." The song "Don't Explain" grew out of a fight with her husband: "the words 'don't explain, don't explain,' kept going through my damned head," and the song is little more than the phrase repeated and elaborated. Similarly, the wonderful "Tell Me More and More and Then Some" doesn't tell us more; it is little more than the playful repetition of the phrase.[48]

The most powerful of these commonplace songs was not a "love" song, but is perhaps her most "political" song: "God Bless the Child." In *Lady Sings the Blues*, which Robert O'Meally rightly calls her "dream book," she tells of writing the song after a fight over money with her mother. Herzog also recalls the incident and says he asked her what her expression "God bless the child" meant. "You know," she replied, "That's what we used to say—your mother's got money, your father's got money, your sister's got money, your cousin's got money, but if you haven't got it yourself, God bless the child that's got its own." The commonplace folk expression takes memorable form in Holiday's recitative, her jazz *Songspiel*:

> Them that's got shall get
> Them that's not shall lose
> So the Bible says
> And it still is news
> Mama may have
> Papa may have
> But God bless the child that's got his own
> That's got his own.

Both the opening echo of Holiday's signature phrase, "them there eyes," and the unorthodox ten-bar A sections suggest that the song followed Holiday's own phrasing rather than ordinary song form: it was the only lyric included in *Lady Sings the Blues*. "God Bless the Child" combines the working-class realism of the bridge—"Money, you got lots of friends, Crowding round your door/ But when it's done and spending ends, They don't come no more"—with a utopian assertion not far from Richard Wright's "Lawd today": "God bless the child that's got his own." Holiday's songs of love and hunger appeared at the same time as Wright's *Native Son*: they were both young migrants to New York, dedicated to their art, and sustained by the audiences and institutions of the Popular Front.[49]

Holiday's cabaret blues set a powerful example for her successors at Café Society, Hazel Scott and Lena Horne. Scott and Horne were only a few years younger than Holiday, and both began performing at an early age; nevertheless, they both use the same term—"protective"—to characterize her attitude toward them. Both had grown up in New York's black middle class, and they were more active politically than Holiday, the result of their family and social ties. Scott, born in Trinidad in 1920, was a musical prodigy, playing in her mother's all-women band, the American Creolians, before studying at Julliard. By 1938, she was fronting her own band and was appearing in Harold Rome's revue *Sing Out the News*. She took over from Holiday at Café Society in November 1939, and played at the Downtown and Uptown clubs until 1945, when she married Harlem's left-wing congressman, Adam Clayton Powell, Jr. She was known not only as a jazz singer, but for "swinging the classics" on the piano. Scott was active in the Harlem left throughout the war years. She also appeared in a few Hollywood films, and was the first black woman to host a television show, "The Hazel Scott Show," in 1950. However, she lost the program after being blacklisted by *Red Channels* and called before HUAC.[50]

Lena Horne, born in Brooklyn in 1917, also ended up blacklisted. She grew up in a black bourgeois family, "a stranger in the white world . . . but also a stranger in the world which most Negroes inhabit." At sixteen, in 1933, she auditioned at the Cotton Club and became a dancer; she went on to sing with Noble Sissle's "sweet" orchestra and Charlie Barnet's big band. Horne opened at Café Society in early 1941 and quickly became a favorite of Popular Front audiences, featured in *PM* and *Friday*. Though she was more a band singer than a jazz or blues artist, she adopted many of Holiday's songs, recording "The Man I Love," "Fine and Mellow," and "I Gotta Right to Sing the Blues." She went to Hollywood in late 1941—arriving in time to see *Jump for Joy*—and became the first black performer to sign a long-term studio contract, appearing in *Cabin in the Sky* and *Stormy Weather*. She was active on the Hollywood left, particularly in the post-war Civil Rights Congress, and was blacklisted by *Red Channels* in 1950.[51]

Neither Scott nor Horne escaped Holiday's shadow as singers; moreover, though both had more success than Holiday in Hollywood, the studio's color line and blacklist limited their film and television careers. Holiday was not officially blacklisted by *Red Channels*; her career had already been broken in 1947, just after her first Hollywood film role, when she was arrested by federal authorities and imprisoned for a year on a narcotics charge. None of her biographers has been able to figure out the politics of the case: one concludes that "the conduct of Billie Holiday's case was by any standards extraordinary." As a result, Holiday lost her cabaret card and was unable to work in New York's nightclubs. Café Society also fell victim to the Red scare in 1947: after Barney Josephson's brother Leon was found guilty of contempt by HUAC, the gossip columnists of the Hearst press attacked Café Society: "His Cafes Society have been hangouts for Communists and their fellow travellers for years," Westbrook Pegler wrote. Business dropped by 45 percent in three weeks, and within a year Josephson had sold the clubs.[52]

Although Lena Horne and Hazel Scott seem to be more typical Popular Front artists—signing petitions, speaking out on civil rights, traveling in the political and social circles of Robeson, Hughes, and Powell—their political stances were in large part the result of their association with Billie Holiday, a working-class singer who found her voice in the formation of musicians and activists around Café Society. "Her whole life, the way she sang, made everything very plain," Lena Horne later wrote. "Hazel Scott and I ... we'd go to hear Billie together, and that's one time we would settle down and not fight. Because here was this voice speaking for the people."[53]

4. Blues from the Piedmont: Josh White's Jim Crow Blues

Billie Holiday was not the only singer to perform "Strange Fruit" at Café Society. In 1946, the blues songster Josh White adopted the song. "I loved her interpretation of the song, but I wanted to do 'Strange Fruit' my way," he recalled. "For a time, she wanted to cut my throat. . . . One night she called by the Café to bawl me out. We talked and finally came downstairs peaceably together. . . . We became the best of friends." White, who had been one of the most important musicians at Café Society since his first appearance in 1940, was also one of the most interesting and neglected blues singers of his generation. Unlike his contemporaries Robert Johnson, T-Bone Walker, and Muddy Waters, he is not part of the blues canon; unlike Woody Guthrie and Huddie Ledbetter, he is rarely revived or revered by the folk music tradition. Moreover, White occupies the limbo of those Popular Front leftists who renounced their left-wing affiliations in front of HUAC: suspected by the right and left alike, White's career never recovered and he did not benefit from the blues and folk revivals of the 1960s.[54]

For blues scholars, White is too "sophisticated," a crossover to "folk" music: a recent historian calls him a "mannered pseudo-bluesman." "It was not the cry of an impoverished southern black that one was to hear," another writes, "for Josh White opened at the Café Society Downtown in Manhattan ... at $100 a week and by 1947 was earning $750 a week there." For the postmodern purists of the folk revival, White was a cabaret singer who abandoned folk performance styles: he is hardly mentioned in Robert Cantwell's history of the folk revival. Nevertheless, Josh White was in many ways the quintessential vernacular musician of the Popular Front, more accomplished and more important than Leadbelly, Guthrie, or the Almanac Singers. White's cabaret blues at Café Society combined the musical and political traditions of the Carolina Piedmont with Harlem's cultural front, and his three classic song cycles of 1940 and 1941, *Harlem Blues*, *Chain Gang*, and *Southern Exposure*, are among the lasting achievements of the cultural front.[55]

White was born in 1914 in Greenville, South Carolina, the son of a Baptist minister. His father had been jailed, beaten, and committed to an asylum after defying a bill collector; he died in the asylum. In the early 1920s, the young White became a guide for blind blues singers, leading Blind Man Arnold, Joe Walker, and Joe Taggart, among others, through the cities and towns of the Piedmont and the Black Belt. He learned the fingerpicking guitar style of the Piedmont, and by 1928 was accompanying Joe Taggart in a Paramount recording session. In April 1932, he recorded more than a dozen blues songs for ARC's "race" labels: Banner, Oriole, Perfect, and Romeo. They were a success, and in August 1933 he returned to the studio. Over the next three years, he recorded dozens of songs for ARC, releasing blues as "Pinewood Tom" and sacred songs as "Joshua White (The Singing Christian)." He was one of the most successful blues and gospel singers on race records; in contrast, Leadbelly's two ARC race records of early 1935 failed to find an audience and the majority of his recordings were never even released. White's sacred style was drawn from that of Blind Willie Johnson, whose Columbia recordings of 1927–30 had been a landmark in black sacred music. On his blues recordings, White often played with pianist Walter Roland, adopting the piano-guitar duo form of Leroy Carr and Scrapper Blackwell, the most popular urban blues singers of the 1930s. White also occasionally accompanied Carr and Blackwell, and once recorded with them as "Pinewood Tom and His Blues Hounds."[56]

In these years, White developed the style that was the heart of his cabaret blues: the clear, light, and rounded vocals, answered by an almost delicate guitar line embellished with choking slides and bends. His guitar playing combined the Piedmont's ragtime-based fingerpicking with the jazz-inflected single-note lines of urban bluesmen like Lonnie Johnson and Scrapper Blackwell. His style was far from the drumlike guitars and moaning vocals of the Delta blues. White settled in New York in 1934, occasionally performing with blues pianist Clarence Williams and his Southernaires on WEAF's "Harlem Fantasy Show." Unable to perform after injuring his hand, he worked as a janitor, elevator operator, and longshoreman; his last ARC session was in February 1936. In 1938, however, he met Leonard de Paur, who was working in the WPA's Negro Theatre, conducting the chorus in their production of *Androcles and the Lion*: de Paur had also conducted the chorus in Welles's black *Macbeth* and composed the score for *Haiti*. De Paur cast White for the part of the bluesman Blind Lemon in the 1940 musical *John Henry*, which was Paul Robeson's first New York role since returning from a decade in Britain. Though *John Henry* closed after only seven performances, it not only brought White into the circle of black radicals around Robeson but revived his recording career. In March 1940, White recorded a Blue Note single with jazz clarinetist Sidney Bechet and a three-disk album, *Harlem Blues*, for Musicraft. De Paur also helped him form a quintet with members of the *John Henry* chorus, including the young Bayard Rustin; in the summer of 1940, White and his Carolinians recorded a four-disk album, *Chain Gang*, for Columbia records. Soon after, White and the Carolinians appeared at Café Society.

A year later, White recorded a third three-disk song cycle, *Southern Exposure: An Album of Jim Crow Blues*, with liner notes by Richard Wright. From 1940 to 1947, White performed regularly at Café Society and the Village Vanguard and became a major Popular Front artist, bridging Harlem and Greenwich Village. He was part of the circle of jazz artists who appeared at Benjamin Davis's large Harlem rallies; and he made jazz recordings for Decca with Mary Lou Williams, trumpeter Bill Coleman, and Edmond Hall's Café Society band. He was also part of the left-wing folk music circle around Woody Guthrie, Pete Seeger, and his fellow Piedmont bluesmen, Sonny Terry and Brownie McGhee. He joined the Almanac Singers on their 1941 Keynote recordings, *Songs for John Doe* and *Talking Union*. As the impromptu Union Boys, he, together with McGhee, Terry, Seeger, Burl Ives, and Tom Glazer, recorded *Songs for Victory: Music for Political Action* in 1944; a few months later, he joined Glazer in *Songs of Citizen CIO*. In 1944, he was featured several times on Roi Ottley's pioneering black radio program, "New World A-Coming": White starred in an episode on black music, joined actor Leigh Whipper in a tribute to W.C. Handy, and enacted Langston Hughes's story "White Folks Do Some Funny Things" along with the actor Canada Lee.

Meanwhile, his series of albums of blues, ballads, and sacred songs for

Keynote, Asch, and Decca made him the best-known black songster in the country. His first national concert tour in 1946 capitalized on the post-war boom in folk music, and by the late 1940s he was appearing in Broadway plays and Hollywood films: one, *The Crimson Canary*, was a 1946 B-thriller about the murder of a jazz musician written by Henry Blankfort, the producer of *Jump for Joy*. After a successful European tour in 1950, however, he was blacklisted by *Red Channels*; in September he was called to testify before HUAC. "They've got me in a vise," he told Paul Robeson, and Robeson advised him to do what he had to do while avoiding naming names. Even though White did publicly distance himself from Robeson and the left—his *Negro Digest* article, "I Was a Sucker for the Communists," was not unlike Ellington's *New Leader* piece—his American career collapsed. He moved to Great Britain, where his BBC radio series, "The Glory Road," was very successful. In the late 1950s, the folk revival created a new audience for White, and one of the new folk music labels, Elektra, issued a series of long-playing albums by White between 1955 and 1962. Nevertheless, White was overshadowed by the "rediscovery" of a group of country blues singers, most of whom were a generation older than him—Bukka White, Skip James, Mississippi John Hurt, and Son House—by young blues aficionados and promoters in the wake of Samuel Charter's influential *The Country Blues* (1959).[57]

Most folk and blues critics and historians have seen White's Popular Front song cycles as the product of his involvement with the New York left, a lamentable departure from his "purer" and ostensibly non-political race records of the early depression. The leading scholar of Carolina blues argues that White's *Chain Gang* "had nothing to do with grassroots secular music" and that *Southern Exposure* is marked by "the conscious hand of intellectual liberalism." In fact, both albums derive directly from the forms and concerns of his "race" records. Moreover, White's radical politics derives less from New York's folk music scene than from the radical traditions of the Carolina Piedmont. It is striking that many of the black blues and gospel musicians who affiliated with the Popular Front were from the Carolinas: White, Sonny Terry and Brownie McGhee, and the Golden Gate Quartet. This is in marked contrast to the blues singers from the Mississippi Delta. Though some Delta singers like McKinley Morganfield (Muddy Waters) and Son House were also recorded by Popular Front collectors like Alan Lomax, they rarely became involved in the cultural front.[58]

It is not that the musicians of the Delta were less critical of Jim Crow than those of the Carolinas: Alan Lomax's 1946 interview with the Chicago blues musicians Big Bill Broonzy, Memphis Slim, and Sonny Boy Williamson revealed a powerful and self-conscious critique of the Delta regime of sharecropping, lynching, and segregation. However, after the interview, the musicians insisted on anonymity, worried that their remarks would endanger their southern relatives. The Delta's racial terror forced black resistance underground, as the autobiographies of black radicals like Nate Shaw and Hosea Hudson later demonstrated. "Farm worker organizers," one historian concludes, "from the Imperial Valley in California to the Black Belt of Alabama and the Delta of Arkansas, all suffered tremendous repression." As a result, there were few links between organizers and artists, and little public space for a "cultural front."[59]

The Piedmont musicians, on the other hand, were inheritors of a more open tradition of black labor activism and political radicalism in the Carolinas and Virginia. Lying between the coastal plain and the mountains, the Piedmont belt stretches from Richmond in the north to Atlanta in the south. Its textile mills and tobacco factories were not only a center of southern industry but also of southern labor radicalism. The 1929 Gastonia textile strike, led by a small Communist union, had drawn national attention; a few years later, in 1934, the organization of the predominantly white United Textile Workers culminated in an extraordinary, if unsuccessful, general strike. This wave of labor militancy, sparked by the National Industrial Recovery Act, also revived the Tobacco Workers International Union (TWIU) in the tobacco factories of Durham and Richmond; and Durham's black and white TWIU locals supported the textile workers general strike in 1934. As a result, Durham was one of the best-organized towns in the Piedmont by World War II.[60]

Black workers made up three-quarters of the workforce in the tobacco processing plants of North Carolina; two-thirds of them were women. Though there were active black locals of the TWIU in Durham and Reidsville throughout the 1930s, for the most part the TWIU concentrated on organizing white workers until they were challenged in 1937 by the Southern Negro Youth Congress (SNYC) and the CIO's United Cannery, Agricultural, Packing and Allied Workers Union of America (UCAPAWA). The Southern Negro Youth Congress had been formed at a Richmond conference in February 1937 by the young black radicals who had worked in the campaigns to free Angelo Herndon and the Scottsboro Nine. Led by the young Richmond Communist James E. Jackson Jr, the SNYC organized five thousand Richmond tobacco workers in the independent Tobacco Stemmers and Laborers International Union, and conducted a successful sit-down strike. The SNYC also created a left-wing culture of community drama and recreational groups, including a People's Theatre, founded by the young actor Thomas Richardson in Richmond.[61]

"We organized the tobacco industry in Virginia," Jackson recalled. "That set off a kind of chain reaction for struggles in the Carolinas." When the CIO's UCAPAWA was formed in July 1937, the SNYC activists joined the CIO organizers; as Jackson remembered, "workers on their own initiative wrote out on paper their names and so on and the words CIO." While "the TWIU organizers were spending most of their time servicing the white locals," one historian writes, ". . . the CIO was holding large meetings at black churches and winning [the NLRB] election." The success of UCA-PAWA revitalized the TWIU. Between 1937 and 1943, UCAPAWA locals across North Carolina and Virginia, as well as the TWIU's black locals in Durham and Reidsville, won recognition, culminating in the 1943 strike and victory of UCAPAWA's Local 22 at the R.J. Reynolds factory in Winston-Salem. With ten thousand workers, two-thirds of whom were black, the Reynolds factory had the South's largest concentration of black workers; and Local 22 became "the most significant black-led civil rights union in the South."[62]

The tobacco towns of Durham, Richmond, and Winston-Salem that were the home of this black working-class left also nurtured the Piedmont's blues and gospel culture. As blues historian Bruce Bastin succinctly noted, "where blacks worked, black musicians earned." The ragtime-flavored Piedmont blues was almost entirely a working-class music, played by semi-professional musicians in barbershops and cafés as well as on street corners and at house parties. Though Josh White left the Piedmont "glory road" for New York in 1934, he had learned his craft in the tobacco towns of the Carolinas, as did the other radical Piedmont musicians. In 1938, the guitarist Walter Brown "Brownie" McGhee—born in 1915, a year younger than Josh White and the SNYC's James E. Jackson—traveled through the tobacco towns, including Winston-Salem: he "found plenty of work there, planning his own factory circuit to play for operatives when they came off shift." McGhee's future partner, the blues harmonica player Sonny Terry, born Saunders Terrell in Greensboro in 1911, regularly played for Durham's tobacco workers.[63]

The industrial towns of the Southeast were also the home of working-class black gospel quartets, sponsored by unions, companies, schools, and churches. In Birmingham, Alabama, the center of the southern steel industry, jubilee gospel quartets were an important part of black working-class culture, and two quartets—the Bessemer Big Four and the Sterling Jubilee/CIO Singers—were active in CIO organizing drives. The most famous of these jubilee quartets was the Norfolk-based Golden Gate Quartet, who began broadcasting from a Columbia, South Carolina, radio station in 1936 and recording for Bluebird in 1937. They were, as one gospel historian remarks, "*the* model for innumerable quartets in the Carolinas, Virginia, Maryland, and the urban corridor between Washington, D.C., and New York City." Josh White's Carolinians were based on them. Like White, the Golden Gates performed at Café Society and became active in the cultural front, singing Popular Front spirituals like "No Segregation in Heaven" as well as topical songs of anti-fascism like the wartime "Stalin Wasn't Stallin'." Through the 1940s, White and the Golden Gates often did concerts together.[64]

The Piedmont musicians first came to national attention at the Spirituals to Swing concert that featured the Golden Gate Quartet, Sonny Terry, and Mitchell's Christian Singers, a popular gospel quartet. This was in large part due to the fact that the Piedmont was linked to the national race record industry through a local chain store manager and ARC talent scout, J.B. Long, who had been inspired to enter the race record business by hearing Josh White's "Low Cotton." Mitchell's Christian Singers had won one of Long's talent contests. When John Hammond, who had not only covered the Scottsboro trials in 1933, but, as chair of the Trade Union Service, whose People's Press published a host of union newspapers, was well aware of the labor struggles of 1937 and 1938, was recruiting musicians for the 1938 Carnegie Hall concert, he went to J.B. Long, forging a lasting link between the Piedmont's blues and gospel culture and the New York cultural front.[65]

But Hammond was not the only link between the New York left and the Piedmont left. The Negro Theatre's Leonard de Paur was looking for Josh White for the 1939 production of *John Henry* because he knew White's powerful "Pinewood Tom" records of the mid 1930s: "Low Cotton," "Bad Depression Blues," "Welfare Blues," "Silicosis Is Killing Me," and "No More Ball and Chain." Moreover, in the summer of 1939, a radical young actor from the SNYC's People's Theater in Richmond, Thomas Richardson, had come to New York to work in the Harlem Suitcase Theatre; he also appeared with Robeson in a summer stock revival of *The Emperor Jones*. Richardson's trajectory was not only typical of young radicals of the cultural front, but offers an instructive parallel to Josh White: after working as a labor and cultural organizer for SNYC and the Tobacco Workers Organizing Committee, and then as an actor and director in the Harlem Suitcase Theatre, he returned to Washington where, as a federal employee, he eventually became vice-president of the CIO's United Federal Workers.[66]

The overlap between tobacco unionism and Piedmont blues in the black working-class cultures of Durham, Winston-Salem, and the other tobacco towns explains why the Piedmont blues were more explicitly political than other blues traditions and why Piedmont musicians like White, Terry, and McGhee became active in the cultural front. It also offers a way of understanding the long debate over the politics of the blues, memorably summed up in Ralph Ellison's comment about LeRoi Jones's *Blues People*: "The tremendous burden of sociology which Jones would place upon this body of music is enough to give even the blues the blues." "For the blues are not primarily concerned with civil rights or obvious political protest," Ellison argues; "they are an art form and thus a transcendence of those conditions created within the Negro community by the denial of social justice." This divide between "protest" and "art" continues to bedevil the blues: if the burden of sociology haunts analyses of blues lyrics as well as ethnographies of blues communities, the equally weighty burden of art possesses Albert Murray's Ellisonian *Stomping the Blues*, with its invocations of Shakespeare and Beethoven. In a way, both sides are right: since the blues were performed by a wide range of amateur, semiprofessional, and professional musicians, they can be seen as a form of "vernacular musicking," expressing the desires and resentments of a community in an anonymous body of lyric and melodic fragments, and as the highly self-conscious art of accomplished musicians.[67]

The Piedmont example illuminates the politics of both sides of this dialectic. On the one hand, the tobacco city blues were, like urban blues generally, a highly skilled, competitive, and commercial art form; they were not simply the amateur musicking of tobacco workers. On the other hand, the songsters knew their audiences. Like the authors of the ghetto pastorals, they rarely told of strikes or topical events; their songs were more often allegories of "mistreatment." "Mistreatment," a common word in the blues of the period, could be addressed to a variety of figures: usually a lover, whether woman or man, often a bossman, a captain, or a relief office. The prison or chain gang was the ultimate emblem of "mistreatment," not least because chain gangs of convicts were a visible spectacle, building and maintaining state roads. Virtually every singer had a version of a prison or chain gang blues.

Josh White's Popular Front works of the early 1940s, particularly *Chain Gang* and *Southern Exposure*, are a powerful and self-conscious synthesis of the blues of "mistreatment" and the sacred songs of the jubilee quartets. *Chain Gang* is, along with Woody Guthrie's *Dust Bowl Ballads* and Leadbelly's *The Midnight Special and Other Prison Songs* (with the Golden Gate Quartet), a landmark in American vernacular music. All three were recorded in May and June 1940 by major labels: White by John Hammond at Columbia, Guthrie and Leadbelly by RCA Victor at the urging of Alan Lomax. In all three cases, the singers were packaged thematically: Guthrie's Dust Bowl songs were intended to capitalize on the success of *The Grapes of Wrath*, and the albums of White and Leadbelly were issued to capitalize on the popular exposés of the South's oppressive convict labor system, which had come to national attention through John Spivak's muckraking journalism and the Paul Muni film, *I Am a Fugitive from a Chain Gang*. As a result, the three albums were somewhat artificial. Nevertheless, each was a powerful work of art, and their appearance on major labels marked a unique moment in American popular culture. Neither Guthrie nor Leadbelly ever recorded on a major label again, and White didn't have another major label album until his post-war Decca releases.[68]

White's *Chain Gang* appeared in the wake of Lawrence Gellert's 1939 collection of chain gang songs, *"Me and My Captain" (Chain Gang)*. Gellert, the son of Hungarian immigrants and the brother of Communist illustrator Hugo Gellert, lived in North Carolina with a black woman, and he published the songs he collected about work and politics—including ones about the Scottsboro Nine and Angelo Herndon cases—in left-wing journals like the *New Masses* and *Music Vanguard*: his musical arrangements were made by radical composers Elie Siegmeister and Lan Adomian. Since Gellert protected the anonymity of the singers, his collections were controversial, and folklorists who had never heard such frankly political songs accused him of fabricating them. It was not until the 1980s that Gellert's recordings and field notes became available, vindicating his extraordinary work.[69]

Apparently, Gellert thought that White had used his songbook without acknowledgement; White insisted that he had known the songs for many years. In retrospect, one is inclined to agree with White. Though five of the seven songs on White's *Chain Gang* do overlap with songs in Gellert's collection, they are hardly identical: in some cases, only a single verse is shared, and White's versions generally have a stronger narrative. Moreover, the unaccompanied hollers, work songs, and guitar blues that made up *Negro Songs of Protest* (1936) and *"Me and My Captain" (Chain Gang)* (1939) had been recorded in the same years—1924–32—and the same places—Georgia and the Carolinas—that White had learned his art: a number of songs came from the county jail of White's home town, Greenville, South Carolina.[70]

White's *Chain Gang* drew on the same musical culture as Gellert's collection, but it was certainly not a field recording. White and the Carolinians borrowed the form of the jubilee quartet—not unlike RCA Victor's later use of the Golden Gate Quartet to accompany Leadbelly—and the black choral director Leonard de Paur arranged and conducted the session. They did not attempt to reproduce or "document" the sound of the chain gang; nor was it a theatrical performance, with the singers playing the roles of convict laborers. Rather, as in many earlier prison and chain gang blues, including White's own "Prison Bound," the chain gang became a spiritual and social allegory of trouble, mistreatment, and danger: "Chains 'round my shoulders; my feet is bracelet boun'." All of the songs are first-person laments, tales of arrest, trial, conviction, work, and abuse. However, they are not the blues of an individual. The choral singing and the subdued and economical guitar lines make them secular spirituals. "Forty years on the hard-rock pile" is an exile into slavery, a descent into hell: "Sleep on a pallet in a dirty cell / Sho' could sleep better if I was dead in hell." The chain gang narrative is also one of the major instances in African American song where the white world is directly invoked: "Well, I always been in trouble, cause I'm a black-skinned man / Oh, I hit a white man, they locked me in the can." The emblematic characters of the chain gang songs—the captain, the judge, the buddy—recur in a dance of danger and death: "I hear danger singin', I hear danger moan" is the refrain of the powerful "Cryin' Who? Cryin' You."[71]

Chain Gang's journey through the "world of trouble" finds several forms of release, redemption, and revolt. "Goin' Home Boys" is a simple farewell song: "My time is up. Throw these chains away." "Trouble" ends with the promise of escape: "Trouble, trouble, jail break due some day." "Told My Cap'n," a work song in which White inserts the tale of the murder of his buddy by the captain, ends with a verse that Gellert had also collected: "Buzzard circlin' 'round the sky, / Knows that Cap'n sure is boun' to die." The song cycle ends with the death of the captain in "Jerry," one of White's enduring songs. A work song with a rhythmic guitar accompaniment, Jerry is an "Arkansas mule" hauling timber, who rebels, ducks a bullet, and stomps the boss to death. Like Guthrie's Dust Bowl, White's chain gang was a self-conscious artifact of a particular political and commercial moment, and neither singer completely escaped the persona he had created. Just as Guthrie remained the Dust Bowl balladeer, White continued to sing and record chain gang songs throughout his career; they were his secular spirituals, powerful allegories of imprisonment, exploitation, and Jim Crow.

Except for Hammond, the Columbia producers were not enthusiastic about *Chain Gang*: they were afraid that it couldn't be sold in the South, a major obstacle since the audience for jubilee quartets was largely southern. In August 1940, Columbia recorded White and the Carolinians singing sacred songs, hoping they might repeat RCA Victor's success with the Golden Gate Quartet. But only a couple of sides were released, and White returned to solo performances. If *Chain Gang* represented the continuation of "Joshua White, the Singing Christian," *Southern Exposure: An Album of Jim Crow Blues*, recorded in 1941, was a direct descendant of his "Pinewood Tom" blues recordings. *Southern Exposure* was recorded by Eric Bernay's left-wing independent label, Keynote, and the three-disk set was accompanied by Richard Wright's "Notes on Jim Crow Blues":

The blues, contrary to popular conception, are not always concerned with love, razors, dice, and death; they are concerned with every item of experience that disturbs and moves the imagination of the Negro folk. Hitherto, the best known blues songs have had love as their main theme, and, as a result, the public has gotten a rather one-sided impression of their real scope and function in Negro life. With the issuance of this album, SOUTHERN EXPOSURE, Keynote presents the "other side" of the blues, the side that criticizes the environment, the side that has been long considered "non-commercial" because of its social militancy.

Southern Exposure was a collaboration between Josh White and the poet Waring Cuney, and it remains a fascinating if contradictory experiment.[72]

The White/Cuney collaboration had some of the awkwardness of the other Popular Front collaborations: Lewis Allan and Billie Holiday producing "Strange Fruit"; Richard Wright, Paul Robeson, and Count Basie coming up with "King Joe"; Earl Robinson and Yip Harburg writing "Free and Easy Blues." These hybrids of jazz, blues, poetry, and Tin Pan Alley didn't fit the well-worked genres, and their promise of a new form—the "other side" of blues, jazz, and poetry—was rarely completely convincing. The White/Cuney songs are, however, remarkably successful. Waring Cuney was a leading radical poet: he had published in proletarian literary magazines like *Challenge*, was a member of Langston Hughes's Harlem Suitcase Theatre, and had become, according to historian Robin Kelley, the "most prolific and popular literary figure" of the Southern Negro Youth Congress. His blues poems—including "Uncle Sam Says" from *Southern Exposure*—were published in the SNYC's magazine, *Cavalcade*, as well as the left-wing *Negro Quarterly*. White not only set Cuney's poems in a variety of blues forms, but he performed them with an idiomatic assurance. White's vocals and stinging guitar lines make them stand out among his finest work.[73]

"Southern Exposure" is a reworking of "Careless Love," a song White had recorded several times; "Bad Housing Blues" is a reworking of White's "Welfare Blues" of 1934; and "Defense Factory Blues," like White's earlier "Blood Red River," is part of what has been called the "Crow Jane" family of tunes. "Jim Crow Train" is a virtuoso display of train effects on the guitar. However, it would be wrong to see the songs as simply marriages of vernacular music and political lyrics. The most powerful songs on *Southern Exposure* are based on the political vernacular of the blues. For the commercial blues that shaped White—the urban songs of Carr and Blackwell, Peetie Wheatstraw, Big Bill Broonzy, and White's sometime partner Walter Roland—regularly sang of relief, rent men, and, occasionally, Jim Crow itself. "More than any other period before or since," blues scholar Paul Oliver writes, "the thirties witnessed the devising of blues on themes of social relevance by recorded singers." Cow Cow Davenport's "Jim Crow Blues"—"gonna leave this Jim Crow town"—had been recorded in 1929, and in the next decade there were many versions of welfare blues and WPA blues. White and Cuney's "Bad Housing Blues" echoes these: "Lord, it ain't no reason, I shouldn't live this way / I done lost my job, can't even get on the W.P.A."[74]

Two topical songs on *Southern Exposure* grew out of the 1941 March on Washington Movement: "Uncle Sam Says" and "Defense Factory Blues" are satiric commentaries on racial segregation in the army and the defense industries, and both try to get "democracy" and "liberty" into the blues: "If you ask me I think democracy is fine / I mean democracy without the color line." Here Cuney's blues diction seems strained. Nevertheless, the White/Cuney collaboration marked an important aspect of White's subsequent work. He would continue as a songster, recording a variety of blues, ballads, children's songs, and chain gang songs, but, like the Piedmont team of Sonny Terry and Brownie McGhee, he would also record topical songs in the African American vernacular. Some of the most successful include his "Jim Crow," recorded with the Union Boys; "No More Blues" and Langston Hughes's "Freedom Road" on *Songs of Citizen CIO*; the songs recorded in support of the 1946 steel strike, "I'm the Guy" and "Little Man Sittin' on the Fence"; and, of course, his famous recording of "Strange Fruit."[75]

Josh White and his Piedmont colleagues, McGhee and Terry, have been overshadowed by Guthrie, Leadbelly, and Pete Seeger in most accounts of the cultural front's folk music movement. This is not only an injustice to White, Terry, and McGhee, the most accomplished musicians of the movement, it has also distorted the history of the left-wing "folk revival." There was no single "folk revival." The resurgence of American vernacular musics in the cultural front was the product of several distinct musical traditions: the Harlan County singers of the National Miners' Union, including Aunt Molly Jackson, Jim Garland, and Sarah Ogan Gunning; the Piedmont blues and gospel singers; the singers of the Highlander Folk School and Commonwealth College, notably Claude Williams, John Handcox, and Lee Hays; traditional New Orleans jazz figures like Sidney Bechet and Bunk Johnson; and the southwestern country musician Woody Guthrie. Many of these figures did work together as a result of the efforts of the remarkable group of promoters and collectors of vernacular musics, including Lawrence Gellert, John Hammond, the Seegers, Alan Lomax, Margaret Larkin (who publicized the songs of Gastonia balladeer Ella May Wiggins in the *Nation* and *New Masses*), and the NYU professor Mary Barnicle (who recorded mining songs in Kentucky and was a key intermediary between Leadbelly and the Harlan County singers). Curiously, however, the folk music collectors themselves and the short-lived folk-singing groups and organizations that emerged out of this world—the Almanac Singers, People's Songs, and the Weavers—have often received more attention than the vernacular musicians they labored to promote.

The Piedmont singers, like Billie Holiday, remind us that the radical musics of the Popular Front had their roots in African American culture. The work of Holiday and White was a volatile mixture of popular race records, black unionism and political activism, and the Harlem literary and intellectual elite. The cultural front not only crossed the lines of Jim Crow, creating new and often uneasy collaborations between black and white artists—Welles and Wright, Guthrie and Leadbelly, Benny Goodman and

Teddy Wilson—it also crossed class lines in the black community, bringing together working-class artists with little formal education like Wright, Holiday, and White, with black intellectuals like Hughes, Robeson, and Waring Cuney.

The careers of Brownie McGhee and Sonny Terry illustrate this. Both were musicians by necessity: McGhee's polio and Terry's blindness had pushed them to the uncertain edges of the laboring world. In the late 1930s and early 1940s, they sang on street corners and earned a little recording for J.B. Long's ARC. Though Terry had performed at the Spirituals to Swing concert, neither left the South until they played together in a Washington concert with Paul Robeson in early 1942. They came to New York in the summer of 1942 to perform at a series of Popular Front concerts, including "Folk Songs on the Firing Line," a program sponsored by Earl Robinson and Richard Wright, and a salute to Spain in which they appeared along with Josh White and Marc Blitzstein. They began recording for Moses Asch's folk music label—together with Guthrie, White, and Leadbelly—as well as for Herman Lubinsky's Savoy label, the first of the new rhythm and blues labels that would dominate post-war vernacular music. Throughout the 1940s, McGhee and Terry were active on the cultural front, appearing at Harlem rallies for Benjamin Davis and singing union songs with the Union Boys.[76]

The Piedmont musicians remind us that the lines separating folk, gospel, blues, jazz, rhythm and blues, and Broadway musicals were not as absolute for the musicians of the cultural front as they have become for critics and historians. Josh White, like the Café Society where he played, crossed all of these lines. If he is not a "real" blues, folk, jazz, gospel, or cabaret singer, it is because he combined all of these: he recorded with jazz clarinetist Sidney Bechet and pianist Mary Lou Williams, with urban blues singers like Scrapper Blackwell and Leroy Carr, with country singers like Woody Guthrie, and with popular torch singers like Libby Holman. His "second" career began on Broadway, with the Robeson musical *John Henry*. Terry and McGhee were also drawn into the Popular Front musical theater: Sonny Terry's harmonica was featured in *Finian's Rainbow*, Yip Harburg's left-wing musical of 1947 about the Jim Crow South; both Terry and McGhee appeared in Elia Kazan's 1955 production of *Cat on a Hot Tin Roof*; and McGhee was in Langston Hughes's 1957 musical, *Simply Heavenly*.

The worlds of Popular Front music—the big bands, the radical musical theater, the folk stylings of Guthrie and Leadbelly, the cabaret blues of Holiday and White—were all caught in the extraordinary upheaval in vernacular musics in the 1940s. On the one hand, the battle between the radio broadcasters and both songwriters (represented by ASCAP) and musicians (represented by the musicians union) over royalties not only led to the highly publicized boycotts and recording bans of the early 1940s but to a dramatic restructuring of the music industry. The song pluggers of Broadway and Tin Pan Alley gradually gave way to the record pluggers of the mushrooming independent labels.

At the same time, the extraordinary wartime migration from South to North re-made the working classes racially, ethnically, culturally, and musically. Southern and southwestern musics—the honky-tonk country of Hank Williams, the jump blues of Louis Jordan, the rockabilly of Elvis Presley, and the electric guitar-based blues of Muddy Waters and Howling Wolf in Chicago, B.B. King in Memphis, and T-Bone Walker in Los Angeles—reconfigured American vernacular musics. Though Josh White was a contemporary of Muddy Waters and T-Bone Walker, he never adopted post-war rhythm and blues; though he cut one Savoy single, he never traded his acoustic guitar for an electric one. Brownie McGhee and Sonny Terry, themselves wartime migrants, did record for a variety of small R & B labels, including Shad and Sittin' In. McGhee was probably the only Popular Front musician to play an electric guitar until Bob Dylan, a child of the Popular Front folk revival, plugged in at the Newport Folk Festival.

The demise of Café Society in the anti-Communist cultural war also crushed the dream of a cabaret blues, an interracial union of Brechtian political theater and African American music. Billie Holiday was imprisoned and denied a cabaret card; Benjamin Davis was hounded from the New York City Council to prison; Paul Robeson was persecuted; and a host of musicians—Ellington, White, Lena Horne, and Hazel Scott, among them—were publicly humiliated, forced to distance themselves from Davis and Robeson. By 1955, all that remained was Louis Armstrong's hit version of "Mack the Knife," the Brecht-Weill song that Marc Blitzstein had adapted, and even that was occasionally banned and boycotted because of Blitzstein's Communist affiliations. Nevertheless, out of the ruins of Café Society, the cabaret blues of Billie Holiday and Josh White continue to disrupt the pastoral scene of the American Century.

10

The Politics of Magic:
Orson Welles's Allegories
of Anti-Fascism

The people's front can get along without the theatre and get along—if
Mr Blitzstein will forgive me—without music, but we cannot get along
without the people's front.... When our art has some temporary
connection, some valid and live relationship with such things as
reported in this evening's newspapers (Hitler's invasion of Austria),
then it is worth making plays and writing songs for them and acting in
these plays, and designing productions for them. The minute we lose
sight of this, we are necromancers, spellbinders; and, as spellbinders
always find out, the amount of magic we can dispense in a single town
is always limited and we discover ourselves beating it across the county
line before the moon is full again.

Orson Welles, "Theatre and the People's Front"[1]

Orson Welles was the American Brecht, the single most important Popular
Front artist in theater, radio, and film, both politically and aesthetically.
He was, as Irving Howe later said, "one of the cultural monuments of the
Popular Front era." "Welles was a quick draught of the lightning we went
to the theater for," Alfred Kazin wrote in his memoir, *Starting Out in the
Thirties.*

My friend Herschel ... could never believe that Orson Welles was just our age,
for Welles in his Federal Theater production of *Doctor Faustus* and of *Julius Caesar*
at the Mercury Theater was so masterful that his face swelled and brooded over
the empty stage like an inflated goblin's. Herschel and I spent a lot of time
studying Welles, for he was more the actor than anyone else we had ever
seen.... His productions usually had no scenery but himself. The hulking,
bullying insistence of his presence was disturbing, fitted in too well with the
"revolutionary" rhythms with which the crowd stormed up and down in his
production of *Julius Caesar*.... In the routine "social dramas" of the time, every
effort was made to shake the audience up, to unnerve it—before sending new

hope and determination through it. But Welles was naturally unnerving. . . . We went to anything he did just to see what he would bring off next.

Having conquered the stage, Welles invaded radio and became the greatest innovator in radio drama, though the panic created by his broadcast of "The War of the Worlds" has often obscured his accomplishments. His first film, *Citizen Kane*, is one of the most celebrated of the twentieth century. If our Elizabethan age is called Rooseveltian, and classic Hollywood, for better or worse, is our theater, then Welles is our Shakespeare, the Mercury, our Globe. And if that comparison is made with tongue in cheek, it is nevertheless the comparison that Welles demanded; his vision of a "people's theater" imagined a radical democratic revival of the Elizabethan popular audience.[2]

Moreover, from his first appearance in New York in 1935 to his departure for Europe in 1947, Welles was active in the Popular Front social movement, lending his name, voice, and work to the New Theatre League, the League of American Writers, the Sleepy Lagoon Defense Committee, the California Labor School, the Hollywood Independent Citizens Committee of the Arts, Sciences and Professions (HICCASP), and the Progressive Citizens of America. Curiously, Welles is often overlooked in accounts of Popular Front culture, which usually suggest that Clifford Odets and the Group Theatre were the heart of the radical stage, and that the Communist screenwriters—the Hollywood Ten—were the center of the film industry left. However, none of the other Popular Front theater or film artists, either in New York or Hollywood, produced a body of work comparable to that of Welles: neither writers like John Howard Lawson, Ring Lardner, Jr, Clifford Odets, or Dalton Trumbo, nor directors like Elia Kazan, Abraham Polonsky, or Joseph Losey. Eugene O'Neill and Charles Chaplin are perhaps Welles's only equals, and they are both products of an earlier modernist moment.[3]

Welles, of course, had far more control over his work than almost any other Popular Front artist in theater, radio, or film. Though his conflicts with the federal government, the Hollywood studios, and the advertising agencies that controlled radio programming left a trail of canceled or mutilated productions—the original *Cradle Will Rock*, the original *Magnificent Ambersons*, and the unfinished and discarded *It's All True*—his aesthetic and political triumphs took advantage of the brief moments when he had the resources of the Federal Theatre, CBS radio, and RKO studios at his disposal. The left-wing screenwriters never had that kind of control, and they often argued amongst themselves about whether they could hope to affect the form or content of Hollywood's product. The politics of the radical screenwriters and studio workers took the form of culture industry unionism, as in the Disney strike I will discuss in the next chapter. Welles, on the other hand, was largely outside the world of the Hollywood unions. If John Howard Lawson organized writers as workers, Welles organized a repertory theater inside the studio system. As a result, Welles was not blacklisted in the same way as the studio employees: his productions were simply no longer financed. At the same time as the Hollywood Ten were subpoenaed by HUAC, Welles left the country for Italy. Two years later, the FBI, which had been tracking Welles since 1941, canceled his Security Index Card, noting that "in the event that the subject again becomes active in CP matters upon his return to the United States, consideration should be given by you [the Director] to reactivate his Security Index card."[4]

Many of those who celebrate *Citizen Kane* as a film masterpiece distance Welles from the culture of the Popular Front. Formalist and auteurist critics have generally ignored Welles's political aesthetic. Film critic Pauline Kael goes further, suggesting that *Citizen Kane* avoided the "show-business-Stalinism" of the Popular Front; the talkies were destroyed, she tells us, not by McCarthyism and the blacklist, but by the "politics of Stalinist 'anti-fascism'." Similarly, the intellectual historian Richard Pells writes that "insofar as [Welles] shared the attitudes of the Left, he seemed more attuned to the questioning spirit of the early 1930s than to the pious certitudes of the Popular Front." These judgements mistake the nature of the cultural front and of Welles's work. The FBI agent who wrote that "*Citizen Kane* is nothing more than an extension of the Communist Party's campaign to smear one of its most effective and consistent opponents in the United States," that is, William Randolph Hearst, may have had too crude a notion of the relation between politics and culture, but he was not entirely wrong in suggesting that "Orson Welles' film, *Citizen Kane*, was inspired by his close associations with communists over a period of years.... [I]n fact, 'inspired' is much too mild to express the source of Welles' idea for the production of the picture." Not only was Welles's Mercury Theatre born out of and enabled by the cultural front and the audiences it mobilized, but the Mercury productions testify to the over-looked richness and vitality of Popular Front culture.[5]

Nevertheless, Welles's Mercury Theatre was an unstable formation, always caught between a people's theater and RKO's radio pictures, between the Sleepy Lagoon Defense Committee and Nelson Rockefeller's Office on Inter-American Affairs, between the life and times of the depression and the *Time* and *Life* of Henry Luce. This contradiction was both institutional and ideological. Institutionally, Welles's success depended on the patronage of *both* the cultural apparatuses of the federal government, Hollywood studios, and the radio networks *and* the audiences mobilized by the Popular Front. The collapse of Welles's US career was not, as most biographers have insisted, simply the fruit of his extravagances. "We can not get along without the people's front," he said in 1938, and he was right: the political and cultural energies of the Popular Front social movement provided the stage for the Harlem *Macbeth* and *Julius Caesar*, for *Citizen Kane* and *Native Son*, for the never-completed collaborations with Duke Ellington and Bertolt Brecht.

But an aesthetic and ideological struggle also lay at the heart of Welles's work: the political ambiguity of magic, hypnosis, and spellbinding. "It is now possible to bewilder and hypnotize an audience to an extent that they believe they are in the most high-priced bedroom ever seen, or that they are listening to the most high-priced foreign actresses available to Mr. Goldwyn," Welles warned. "This kind of hypnosis is dangerous, not only politically, but esthetically and culturally." But Welles himself was a hypnotist: "I always felt, when I saw that too, too expressive face on the stage," Alfred Kazin recalled, "that he was trying to impress his own will on the audience, to lead it on a string, to hypnotize it." Though Welles was famous for his magic shows, he always associated necromancy with evil. This is why fascism dominated Welles's political *and* aesthetic vision. "Fascism, we know, sells itself by making its appeal to the emotions rather than to reason," he wrote, "to the senses rather than to the mind. Showmanship is fundamental to the fascist strategy, and the chief fascist argument is the parade." Against the fascist threat of a hypnotized mass public, Welles held out the democratic promise of a people's theater, and the left-wing theaters of the depression provided the context for the work of Welles and the Mercury Theatre. Welles was fascinated by fascism, and his great works—*Julius Caesar*, "The War of the Worlds," *Citizen Kane*, *Native Son*, the Isaac Woodward broadcasts, and *Touch of Evil*—are allegories of fascism.[6]

1. Toward a People's Theatre: New Theatre and Film

"When the Mercury Theatre opens its doors early in November, we believe another step will have been taken towards a real People's Theatre in America. We enter the field of the popular-priced theatre not underestimating the work done by Eva LaGallienne, the Group Theatre, the Theatre Union, the Theatre of Action and other socially-conscious groups, but to carry on where they left off, to widen the cultural and social base of the People's Theatre." With these words, John Houseman and Orson Welles introduced the Mercury Theatre to the readers of the *Daily Worker* in September 1937. From the start, Welles and the Mercury Theatre were part of the left-wing theatrical renaissance of the depression. Houseman and Welles had first worked together in the 1935 production of Archibald MacLeish's peculiar combination of mass chant and verse drama, *Panic*, a few weeks after the electrifying success of Clifford Odets's *Waiting for Lefty*.

To understand Welles and the Mercury Theatre, one must understand the "People's Theatre."[7]

"The left theater" was "in many ways the real cultural center of the radical movement during the Depression," Annette Rubinstein, a New York Communist activist, recalled. "The theater was the center for a very large segment of radical social life. Ordinarily your plans would be to go to the theater with somebody and if you were having dinner you would go before or after the theater." The radical theater was regularly reviewed in the *Daily Worker* and the *New Masses*, and it generated its own little magazines, including *New Theatre* (which became *New Theatre and Film*) and *TAC*, the Theatre Arts Committee monthly (Figure 9). "The crowds that filled the houses on *New Theatre* nights and made *Lefty* and *Bury the Dead* and *Stevedore* the thrilling theatrical events they became" were, Houseman later recalled, part of "that new left-wing audience that had sprung up with the Depression." "Fifty percent of our public came from organized theatre parties, mostly of the Left—prejudiced and semieducated but young and generous and eager to participate in the excitement which the stage alone seemed to offer them." The theater also became the model for collective activity on the part of artists. Radical photographers, composers, novelists, poets, folk singers, and fashion designers all gravitated to the theater.[8]

The theater was also the privileged form of radical culture for most left-wing critics of the time. Theatrical metaphors were as ubiquitous in the cultural front as mapping metaphors are in postmodern cultural discourse. It was a commonplace that Marxism was a dramatic theory of history, and this informed Kenneth Burke's grand theory of "dramatism" as well as Harold Rosenberg's use of the categories of drama in his modernist rewriting of Marxism. Even the contradictions of the cultural front seemed starkest in the theater. In his critique of the cultural front, *The Crisis of the Negro Intellectual*, Harold Cruse argued that "the theater—a collective art— is the cultural form that most signally reflects *all* the collective and critical liabilities of Negro creative intellectuals as a class."[9]

The importance of the theater made Mordecai Gorelik's *New Theatres for Old* one of the major cultural studies of the period, at once a manifesto for the new theater and a history of its genesis. Gorelik, who had designed the sets for the Theater Union's production of Brecht's *Mother*, the Group Theatre's production of Odets's *Golden Boy*, and the Theatre Guild's production of Lawson's *Processional*, was the most influential left-wing designer of the period. His work united Brecht's epic theater with the "new stagecraft" of Provincetown's Robert Edmond Jones. "Gorelik is the most contemporary of our scene designers, and . . . the most intelligent," Orson Welles wrote in one of the few book reviews of his career. "When a better book about the theatre is written," Welles added with characteristic bravado, "an actor will write it." *New Theatres for Old* was "a study of the theatre from the . . . standpoint of *production* rather than of the playscript"; it viewed "stage history not as a succession of scripts, . . . but as a long-continued search for theatrical truths . . . revealed on a stage platform with the help of actors, dramatist, designer, settings, lights, sound effects and all the rest of the personnel and apparatus of the stage." Gorelik recounted the history of modern theater since the 1880s, analyzing the production techniques of Max Reinhardt, Vsevolod Meyerhold, and Erwin Piscator; he also offered a sympathetic if critical survey of the radical stage in the United States: "the cradle of a possible new American theatre is being rocked in an arc between propagandist drama and the learning-play."[10]

Though small labor theaters affiliated with the New Theatre League sprang up in Popular Front cities and towns across the country, there were four major formations of the "People's Theatre" that left an enduring imprint on American theater and film: the circle that originated in the Group Theatre and went on to the productions of Elia Kazan and Arthur Miller; the circle that came together around Joseph Losey and Nicholas Ray in the Living Newspaper and continued in their Hollywood productions; the various attempts by actors and writers around Langston Hughes to create an independent black theater in Harlem; and the Mercury group. These circles overlapped in particular individuals and productions, but they mark distinctive tendencies in the radical stage and film.

The Group Theatre emerged in the early 1930s out of the union between the established modernists around the director Harold Clurman and his "Group idea"—his close friends included the composer Aaron Copland, the playwright John Howard Lawson, and the photographer Paul Strand—and the hungry young radicals of the agitprop Workers Laboratory Theatre, including set designer Max Gorelik and the actor Elia Kazan. The Group kept one foot on Broadway and one foot in the agitprop theater, and, through Lee Strasberg, they adopted the theories of psychological realism in acting, the "method" of Stanislavsky's Moscow Art Theatre. They recruited a number of young working-class talents: the actor and would-be playwright Clifford Odets who had never finished high school; Julius Garfinkle, who was born in 1913 on the Lower East Side and was to become one of the Popular Front's leading stars as John Garfield; and Stella Adler, a child star of the Yiddish stage. Between 1931 and 1940, the Group staged a range of new works written by contemporary playwrights, including John Howard Lawson—*Success Story* and *Gentlewoman*—and Clifford Odets—*Waiting for Lefty, Awake and Sing!, Paradise Lost*, and *Golden Boy*.

Though the Group Theatre has often been remembered as *the* left-wing theater, this was partly the result of Kazan's HUAC testimony, in which he named the Communist Party members in the Group and claimed that they manipulated and dominated the Group. Actually, the Communists were never more than a quarter of the company, which, before the success of *Waiting for Lefty*, was seen primarily as an "art" theater: as late as 1937 the Group turned down Lawson's *Marching Song*, a play about the autoworkers sit-down strike. "The essential cause of the agonizing personal and professional discontents tearing the Group apart," historian Wendy Smith concluded, "was the inherent difficulty of running a theatre with uncommercial ideals—artistic or political—in a commercial system. They couldn't change Broadway, and they were unwilling to be relegated to the fringe of the American theatre by working elsewhere." This same contradiction dogged the Group veterans who went to Hollywood: Clurman, Lawson, Odets, Kazan, Garfield, and Frances Farmer. Lawson had a few successes, notably the screenplays for Hollywood's only film on the Spanish Civil War, *Blockade*, and for the World War II trilogy, *Action in the North Atlantic*, *Sahara*, and *Counter-Attack*; and Garfield's incarnations as the tough city kid, culminating in *Body and Soul* and *Force of Evil*, made him a Popular Front star. However, the Group's legacy was most evident in the method actors trained by Lee Strasberg's post-war Actors Studio, many of whom were part of the company assembled by Elia Kazan for his theater productions of Arthur Miller's *All My Sons* (1947) and *Death of a Salesman* (1949) and his classic films of the 1950s, including *On the Waterfront* and *Face in the Crowd*.[11]

The left-wing theater was torn, as Gorelik put it, between "the school of Naturalism as exemplified by Stanislavsky and that of Theatricalism led by Meyerhold." If the Group was the American incarnation of Stanislavsky, a second theatrical formation around Joseph Losey and Nicholas Ray in the Federal Theatre Project's Living Newspaper was drawn to the work of Meyerhold, the Soviet director whose theatrical spectacles broke down the naturalist illusions of the proscenium stage and brought the theater directly into the audience. Losey and Ray, like Welles, were products of the midwestern "business class," to use the term with which the Lynds characterized the provincial bourgeoisie of Muncie, Indiana. Losey later said that he would have liked to have directed *The Magnificent Ambersons*; it depicted the world he, Ray, and Welles had all grown up in. Like Welles, they were drawn less to the psychological realism of the Group than to the magic and machinery of the theater itself. Losey, along with Gorelik and the Mercury's Marc Blitzstein, was one of the few Americans interested in Brecht's epic theater: Losey introduced Brecht to John Houseman, and Losey and Houseman were both involved (as director and producer) in Brecht's American production of *Galileo* in 1947.[12]

Losey became the director of the Living Newspaper's *Triple A Plowed Under* (1936) and *Injunction Granted* (1936) (for which he hired Ray as stage manager). In *Injunction Granted*, they used horns, bells, loudspeakers, masks, characters in the audience, and projected film clips and photographs to create an extraordinary stage newsreel: a history of the repression of labor unions by court injunctions, culminating in a vision of the CIO's industrial unionism. "Will the courts help you?" a worker asked the steelworkers at the end. "No!" they answer. "Then the answer is in ourselves," the first worker replied. "In you . . . in me. All workers must be brought into unions." Groups of workers with union banners marched up the ramps, runways, and steps of Losey's stage. *Injunction Granted* was one of the most controversial Federal Theatre productions: the Federal Theatre's director, Hallie Flanagan, thought that it was "bad journalism and hysterical theatre." When it was shut down, despite its successful three-month run in the summer of 1936, Losey resigned from the Federal Theatre.[13]

Losey and Ray continued to work, separately and together, directing Popular Front cabarets and staging left-wing musical events: Losey, a friend of John Hammond, directed the second Spirituals to Swing evening, and Ray worked with Alan Lomax in "Back Where I Come From," the radio program that featured the music of Guthrie, Leadbelly, Josh White, and the Golden Gate Quartet. Both Ray and Losey went to Hollywood in the 1940s and directed several expressionistic B-thrillers of the post-war era, including Ray's *They Live By Night* and *Knock on Any Door* and Losey's *The Lawless*. Ray managed to avoid the anti-Communist purge and was neither blacklisted nor forced to name names; he made several classics of the 1950s, including *Johnny Guitar* and *Rebel without a Cause*. Losey, on the other hand, who had joined the Communist Party in Hollywood, went into exile in Britain; he, not unlike Welles, became a "European" director with a series of classic collaborations with Harold Pinter.

The third theatrical formation was the radical Harlem theater, which, as I noted earlier, first took shape in Rose McClendon's Negro People's Theatre in the summer of 1935. McClendon then helped form the Negro Theatre unit of the Federal Theatre, which put on thirty productions between 1935 and 1939, including Welles's *Macbeth* with Jack Carter, Edna Thomas, and Canada Lee, *Haiti* with Rex Ingram, and Augustus Smith's agitprop *Turpentine*. The success of the Negro Theatre led Langston Hughes and others to create a series of independent black theaters. The Harlem Suitcase Theatre produced a number of Hughes's short sketches in 1938 and 1939, including *Don't You Want to Be Free?*, which had, as Hughes recalled, "the longest run of any dramatic show in Harlem so far, 135 performances, weekends over a period of almost two years." In 1940, the short-lived Negro Playwrights Company was formed; it produced Theodore Ward's *Big White Fog*.[14]

The most successful black theater, however, was the American Negro Theatre, founded in 1940 by Abram Hill and Frederick O'Neal. Hill, the son of a railroad fireman, had gone to City College and Lincoln University

370 *The Cultural Front*

before joining the Federal Theatre. Together with John Silvera he wrote the unproduced Living Newspaper, *Liberty Deferred*, a history of African Americans from slavery to the anti-lynching campaign of 1937 that ended with A. Philip Randolph addressing the National Negro Congress. After briefly joining the Negro Playwrights Company, Hill formed the American Negro Theatre, which included Ruby Dee, Alice Childress, and cartoonist Ollie Harrington. For five years, they produced new plays, including Hill's own *On Striver's Row*, and ran a studio that trained Sidney Poitier and Harry Belafonte. Their greatest success, *Anna Lucasta* (1944), launched the career of Ruby Dee, a young Harlem actor, born in 1923, the daughter of a railway porter and a schoolteacher. After the collapse of the ANT, Dee and her husband, Ossie Davis, together with Belafonte, Poitier and Childress, became central figures in the Harlem cultural left, represented in part by the Committee for the Negro in the Arts (CNA).[15]

Hollywood's color line prevented the Harlem theater artists from having a major impact on Hollywood in the 1930s and 1940s: Langston Hughes's Hollywood sojourns were unsuccessful and even Paul Robeson was unable to get serious parts. Rex Ingram starred in the all-black productions of *Green Pastures* and *Cabin in the Sky*, and had a few supporting roles, including one in Lawson's World War II film *Sahara*. Canada Lee, who had starred in *Macbeth*, *Haiti*, *Big White Fog*, and Welles's production of *Native Son*, appeared in a few films, including Polonsky's *Body and Soul*, before being blacklisted. Ruby Dee, Ossie Davis, and Sidney Poitier all made their film debuts in Darryl Zanuck's 1950 racial melodrama, *No Way Out*. Poitier became the first major black movie star in the late 1950s, and he and Dee appeared together in two classic "late" Popular Front productions: Martin Ritt's waterfront film, *Edge of the City* (1957), and the stage and film versions of Lorraine Hansberry's *A Raisin in the Sun* (1959, 1961).[16]

The Mercury Theatre was the fourth major theatrical formation. As a theater company, the Mercury lasted only two seasons: 1937–38 and 1938–39. But as a loose group of theater, radio, and film professionals who worked with Orson Welles in New York and Hollywood, it lasted from 1935 to 1947. Welles, born in 1915 to an established if declining midwestern family, had been a prodigy of the prep school stage and had appeared in Dublin's Gate Theatre and Katharine Cornell's Broadway company while still in his teens. Houseman, born Jacques Haussmann in Romania in 1902, had been educated in private schools in Paris and England before gaining and losing a fair amount of money in the 1920s and early 1930s; he then turned from business to theater. They first worked together in the 1935 production of *Panic*, and then in the Negro Theatre. Together they created a repertory company, Project 891, inside the Federal Theatre. After the cancellation of *The Cradle Will Rock*, they left the Federal Theatre and formed a theatrical corporation, the Mercury Theatre, with its own theater and payroll.

The Mercury began by publishing a manifesto in the *Daily Worker* that outlined their vision of a people's theater. This was less an ideological theater than one marked by a new and wider audience. The WPA theater, they wrote, had changed the theater-going habits of the American people, adding "a great and hitherto untapped audience of moderate means." This was not simply a matter of the WPA's cheap ticket prices: "aesthetically, this new fresh public, entering the theater as on a voyage of rediscovery, succeeded in reestablishing the audience as an organic part of the theater. And again, as in all the great theatrical periods, the audience is becoming a live, participating force to be taken into account by playwright, actor and director. The Mercury Theatre will present at popular prices great plays of all periods with a special view to their contemporary significance."[17]

The Mercury's vision of a people's theater emphasized the revival of the classics. "A lasting and healthy People's Theatre cannot exist unless it is founded on a solid base of the great plays of the past," the Mercury manifesto asserted. "We hope to develop a company of actors who will be prepared to revitalize the classics and be able to turn from them, more keenly atuned and aware, to handling great plays of the contemporary social scene." The Mercury's revival of Elizabethan drama was one of many examples of Popular Front classicism, which included Lukács's defense of critical realism, Malraux's vision of a museum without walls, Gramsci's reclamation of Dante, and F. O. Matthiessen's recovery of the writers of the American Renaissance. Welles, like other Popular Front popularizers, wanted to use the new mass media to democratize elite culture, expropriating the cultural wealth of the past for the working classes. He not only revived Shakespeare on stage, but published adaptations for school staging under the title *Everybody's Shakespeare*, produced radio broadcasts and popular recordings of the plays, and filmed *Othello, Macbeth*, and *Falstaff*. Welles was without doubt the major twentieth-century inheritor of the popular Shakespeare in the United States, linking the nineteenth-century tradition, whose history Lawrence Levine has recounted, with Joseph Papp's Public Theater productions of Shakespeare in the Park in the second half of the twentieth century.[18]

Though Welles and Houseman were the founding partners and ran the Mercury until they split, their success depended on the artists and craftspeople they assembled: actors like Will Geer, Hiram Sherman, Canada Lee, Ray Collins, Mady Christians, Agnes Moorehead, Joseph Cotten, and Dorothy Comingore; composers like Virgil Thomson, Marc Blitzstein, and Bernard Herrmann; writers like Howard Koch, Herman Mankiewicz, Robert Meltzer, and John Fante; and theater and film professionals like lighting director Jean Rosenthal, set designer Sam Leve, cinematographer Gregg Toland, and art director Perry Ferguson. The heterogeneity of the Mercury's personnel was a result of its changing institutional status. From a stage company, they became a production unit subcontracted to radio networks and advertising agencies—the Mercury Theatre on the Air and later the Campbell Playhouse—and to RKO studios—Mercury Productions (in film credits, they appear as the Mercury Players). The Mercury brought together anonymous radio actors that Welles had met doing "The March of Time," "The Shadow," and "Cavalcade of America" with veterans of the radical stage who had migrated to the Federal Theatre.

The Mercury shared aspects of the other three radical theater groups. Like the Group, they combined elements of Broadway, Hollywood, Provincetown, and Union Square; and the tension between the dream of a "People's Theatre" and the realities of commercial success—particularly Welles's emergence as a star—led to battles within the company. The Mercury's aesthetic, however, was closer to that of Losey and Ray; like them, Welles drew on the new stagecraft of Meyerhold, and Blitzstein's *The Cradle Will Rock* was, as I noted earlier, an American translation of Brecht's epic theater. Finally, the Mercury had closer ties to the black theater than any other white theater group. This was a legacy of Welles and Houseman's early work with the Negro Theatre and led to the Mercury stage production of Richard Wright's *Native Son* in 1941.

The politics of Welles and the Mercury Theatre have often been discounted. The Mercury Theatre was "sensational but not controversial," Harold Clurman, the director of the Group, later wrote. "It had the rebel air of a 'hep' and hearty youth that suited the rejuvenated epoch of the late thirties. The Mercury was safe. It treaded on no toes, but rather kicked the seat of plays and traditions for which our reverence is more advertised than real." It had, he concluded, a "fundamental lack of seriousness." Though Houseman disagreed with Clurman's assessment of the Mercury's theater work—"in the theater," he wrote, "it was we who were the radicals, they who were conservative and conventional. The Group's productions were consistently and obstinately naturalistic: almost without exception they worked inside the proscenium arch in the obsolescent tradition of realistic scenery and the fourth wall"—he conceded the political point: "personally and collectively the Group was more 'social-minded' and held far more radical social views than ours—which were virtually non-existent." However, Houseman's account both overestimates the radicalism of the Group Theatre, and underplays the politics of Welles and the Mercury.[19]

It is true that Welles was politically unformed when he first encountered the radical theater at the age of nineteen, but this was equally true of figures like Clurman or Hughes, relatively apolitical modernists who had turned to the left, or Losey, a product of the Ivy League theater. For

Welles, the collaboration with Marc Blitzstein on *The Cradle Will Rock* and *Julius Caesar* was the turning point; though Welles never shared Blitzstein's communism, Blitzstein brought him into the Popular Front social movement. By the winter and spring of 1938, Welles was a regular part of Popular Front events: in February, he introduced a *New Masses* concert; in March, he and Blitzstein appeared at a Workers Bookstore symposium on the "Culture of the People's Front"; in April, he appeared at the American Student Union's Peace Ball.

Welles had several similar moments of political visibility over the next decade, usually following moments of intense work. In 1941, having completed *Citizen Kane* and *Native Son*, he once again emerged as a Popular Front activist. In April, he, along with John Hammond and F.O. Matthiessen, led a committee to protest the deportation of the radical ILWU leader Harry Bridges; endorsed the call for the American Writers' Congress; and produced a controversial episode of the Popular Front radio series, "The Free Company," entitled "His Honor, the Mayor." This flurry of activity, together with the controversy over *Citizen Kane*'s portrayal of newspaper publisher William Randolph Hearst and the collaboration with the black Communist Richard Wright, led the Hearst press to attack him as a Communist and the FBI to begin tracking his activities and associations.

Between 1943 and 1946, Welles was almost continually active in politics, regularly speaking across the country on racism and fascism. In 1943, he contributed a foreword to a pamphlet defending the Mexican American defendants in the Sleepy Lagoon case; from the fall of 1943 to the fall of 1945, he was active in the anti-fascist Free World Congress and published his speeches in its magazine, *Free World*; in 1944, he campaigned vigorously for Roosevelt; and in 1945 he began working as a political commentator, with a *New York Post* newspaper column and an ABC radio show, "Orson Welles Commentaries." His most powerful and important political work—the radio campaign around the blinding of black veteran Isaac Woodward—took place in the summer of 1946, after which ABC canceled his show.

Welles's political activities had three sources: his associates, his audience, and his anti-fascism. Much of Welles's early activism was provoked by his collaborators: Blitzstein had joined the Communist Party in the spring of 1938 while working with the Mercury, and he may have recruited others. Both Houseman and Blitzstein were active in the Theatre Arts Committee, and one of the Mercury's major actors, Hiram Sherman, was a key figure in Cabaret TAC. Sherman was a close friend of Welles, the star of *The Shoemaker's Holiday* and the associate director of *Caesar*: at one point, he was to be the Mercury's second director. He was also, according to Houseman, the "conscience of the company," the leader of a "voluble minority of the company" who were passionately committed to the Mercury's vision of a people's theater.[20]

After moving to Hollywood, Welles continued to work with Communists. The FBI concluded that "although Welles had never been identified as a Communist Party member, many of his associates and assistants were identified as such." Welles's main advisor during the Brazil film project was the Communist writer Robert Meltzer, who had been Chaplin's assistant on *The Great Dictator*: Richard Wilson wrote that he was the "best writer Welles ever had (according to Welles)." Meltzer, who had a cameo in *Journey into Fear*, recruited Welles to the Harry Bridges defense committee; he was later drafted and killed in action. By the late 1940s and early 1950s, a number of writers and actors who had been associated with the Mercury Theatre were blacklisted, including Will Geer, Howard da Silva, Canada Lee, Martin Gabel, Norman Lloyd, Mady Christians, Howard Koch, Paul Stewart, Jack Berry, and Dorothy Comingore.[21]

If Welles's political stances were sometimes influenced by his radical associates, at other times they were influenced by his audience. His 1938 appearances for the *New Masses* and the Workers Bookstore followed the success of *The Cradle Will Rock* and *Julius Caesar* with Popular Front audiences, and can be seen as efforts to strengthen their allegiance to the Mercury Theatre. Similarly, Welles's political statements of early 1941 were part of the publicity campaign for *Citizen Kane* and *Native Son*. *Citizen Kane*'s critique of Hearst had been celebrated in both the *New Masses* and the more popular left photomagazine, *Friday*. The *Friday* article, "Orson Delivers," was so explicit that Welles himself published a humorous disclaimer—"*Citizen Kane* Is Not about Louella Parson's Boss." *Friday* later published a feature on Dorothy Comingore, "Mrs Citizen Kane." For some, this smacked of Welles's opportunism, portraying himself as more radical than he was; for others, it seemed self-destructive, positioning himself with left-wing critics of Hearst and Hollywood and jeopardizing his film career in the process. Actually, Welles's symbolic affiliations were a recognition of his core Popular Front audience.[22]

One aspect of Welles's politics transcended the world of letterheads and publicity: his abiding anti-fascism. The struggle against fascism gripped Welles's imagination as no other political conflict did: for him, the Popular Front was the anti-fascist alliance. Despite his support for Harry Bridges, Welles was not, for the most part, drawn to tales of labor; his one "proletarian" production, *The Cradle Will Rock*, was more Blitzstein's work than his. The ghetto pastoral only once emerged in Welles's work, when John Fante's tale of Italian immigrants, "Love Story," was briefly considered for a segment of *It's All True*. Fascism, on the other hand, is everywhere in Welles. It shaped the politics of his allegiances. Most of his Popular Front affiliations are with anti-fascist organizations: the Stars for Spain benefit, a benefit for the Exiled Writers Committee, the Friends of the Abraham Lincoln Brigade, Russian War Relief, and Yugoslav Relief. But it also shaped the form and content of virtually all of his productions. If the Mercury was a "People's Theatre," it was dominated by an aesthetic of anti-fascism.

2. The Aesthetics of Anti-Fascism

The rhetoric of fascism and anti-fascism runs throughout Welles's career. "Our *Julius Caesar* gives a picture of the same kind of hysteria that exists in certain dictator-ruled countries of today," a Mercury press release asserted of the 1937 modern-dress production. The most famous scene in the Mercury *Julius Caesar* was the killing of Cinna the poet (played by Norman Lloyd) by the mob. One critic wrote that it was "a scene which for pure power and sinister meaning has never been surpassed in the American theatre"; "not even the Group Theater in all their frenzy against dictators," another wrote, "ever devised a more thrilling scene than that in which the poet, Cinna, is swallowed up by an angry mob." "It's the same mob," Welles told the *New York Times*, "that hangs and burns Negroes in the South, the same mob that maltreats the Jews in Germany. It's the Nazi mob anywhere." When Welles went to Hollywood two years later, his first project, the unfinished film of *Heart of Darkness*, was, in his own words, "a parable of fascism": "the picture," he told his assistant Herbert Drake, "is, frankly, an attack on the Nazi system." Three decades later, Welles told Peter Bogdanovich that *Touch of Evil* (1958) was "if anything *too clearly* antifascist." But, Welles continued, "the French are convinced it's the absolute proof that I'm a fascist."[23]

It is not surprising to discover that during Welles's brief career as a political commentator his great theme was fascism. Touring the United States in 1944 and 1945, he lectured on "The Survival of Fascism" and "The Nature of the Enemy." These lectures do not reveal Welles to be a profound or original political theorist; rather, they should be interpreted as a compendium of political narratives and metaphors by which Welles and his Popular Front audiences understood fascism. Thus, they offer a way of understanding the lineaments of the anti-Fascist aesthetic that informs Welles's plays, broadcasts, and films. Fascism, for Welles and for the Popular Front, was a matter of politics *and* aesthetics.

Welles elaborated several tangled and contradictory accounts of fascism. The first, which might be called the gangster theory of fascism, had long been part of Popular Front common sense: a classic instance was, as I suggested earlier, Dashiell Hammett's *Red Harvest*. As Welles tells the story: "A group of industrialists finance a group of gangsters to break trade-unionism, to check the threat of Socialism, the menace of communism or the possibility of democracy. . . . When the gangsters succeed at what they were paid to do, they turn on the men who paid them. . . . [T]he puppet masters find their creatures taking on a terrible life of their own." This story reminds us that anti-fascism was not simply an *international* politics for the Popular Front. Welles, like many of his contemporaries, saw a contin- uum between European fascism and domestic fascism, between Hitler and Hearst, the Brown Shirts and the Black Legion. When Welles became a political commentator in 1945 and 1946, he regularly wrote and spoke about the dangers of American fascism, warning that "even the uncondi- tional surrender of the Axis will not automatically destroy the fascist principle."[24]

However, Welles's fictions rarely drew directly on this account of industrialists hiring gangsters. Rather, Welles was more apt to draw on a second definition: "What is Fascism? . . . In essence it is nothing more than the original sin of civilization, the celebration of power for its own sake." The confrontation with power for power's sake—the touch of evil in Welles's moral universe—was the core of *Heart of Darkness*, Welles's "parable of fascism" (which, though never filmed, was twice produced by Welles as a radio play). Welles's scenario not only moved the story to Latin America, but translated the imperialist boundary between civilization and the jungle to a boundary between civilization and fascism. This fascination with the face of power also informed both of Welles's characteristic—and apparently contrary—genres: the revived classics and the pulp thriller, each of which is central to Popular Front anti-fascism.[25]

Welles's revival of the classics was not only an act of preservation in the face of fascism, a defense of civilization against barbarism. For Welles, the Elizabethan tragedies and histories of Shakespeare and Marlowe offered a critique of fascism's worship of power, and their giant protagonists paralleled the "great dictators" of modern times. *Julius Caesar*, the Mercury manifesto asserted, "might well be subtitled 'Death of a Dictator'. . . . In our production the stress will be on the social implications inherent in the history of Caesar and on the atmosphere of personal greed, fear and hysteria that surround a dictatorial regime." "Welles played Brutus," Alfred Kazin recalled, "and Brutus was a liberal intellectual in a shabby overcoat plotting against Caesar, who was a Fascist dictator in a garish Middle European military uniform; Brutus was the nervous thread of the action, he was the conspirator, the assassin, the general, the suicide, whose movements incarnated the disturbance of our time."[26]

The tale of the "great dictator" haunted the Popular Front imagination, informing Chaplin's *The Great Dictator* (1940) and Peter Blume's surrealist history painting *The Eternal City* (1937), with its grotesque portrait of Mussolini growing out of a classical landscape. These narratives drew not only on the fascist dictators Hitler, Franco, and Mussolini, but on the flamboyance and popular notoriety of the "robber barons" like J.P. Morgan, the Du Pont's Liberty League, and William Randolph Hearst; the fear and loathing of radio demagogues like Father Charles Coughlin and Huey Long; and the fascination with the giant protagonists of the Soviet Revolution and its aftermath—Lenin, Stalin, and Trotsky. Though Welles played the dictator's foil in *Julius Caesar*—he was Brutus to Joseph Holland's Mussolini-like Caesar—he more often played the giant figure himself: he was, as he told BBC interviewer Leslie Megahey, a "king actor," one who had to play authoritative roles. Welles's roles combine a political demonology with overtones of Shakespearean tragedy, Gothic supermen, and, with his heavy makeup, horror movie monsters.[27]

Welles's gigantic hero-villains were both fascinating and repulsive, tricksters that disobeyed any straightforward political logic. As a result, they were the subject of continual political controversy. Welles himself told a reporter that "Caesar was a great man. Why present him otherwise just because the play is anti-Caesar? That is. . . . the error of left-wing melodrama, wherein the villains are cardboard Simon Legrees." Two years earlier, Welles had played a ruined capitalist driven to suicide by the 1932 bank failures in Archibald MacLeish's *Panic*. One performance of *Panic* was followed by a debate, sponsored by the radical New Theater League and the *New Masses*, over the political significance of the play's focus on the individual tragedy of the capitalist, McGafferty. A similar controversy erupted before the 1938 Mercury production of *Danton's Death*, as the Mercury company argued about the parallels between the conflict of Robespierre and Danton and that of Stalin and Trotsky: as a result of Marc Blitzstein's objections, the script was eventually revised.[28]

Welles's great dictators turned up not only in his classical revivals but in his pulp thrillers, the series of *film noir* melodramas that included *Journey into Fear* (1943), *The Stranger* (1946), *Lady from Shanghai* (1948), the film and radio versions of *The Third Man* (1949, 1951), *Mr Arkadin* (1955), and *Touch of Evil* (1958). "More or less voluntarily, you know," Welles later remarked, "I've played a lot of unsavory types. I detest Harry Lime, that little black market hustler, all of these horrible men I've interpreted. . . . Quinlan [in *Touch of Evil*] is the incarnation of everything I struggle against, politically and morally speaking." But Welles's performances always had an element of sympathy with the devil: "in melodrama, one's sympathy is drawn forcibly to the villain." He was, he admitted, "more than the devil's advocate": "in becoming these characters, I transfigure them by giving them the best I have. But I detest what they are." The fascination and repulsion evoked by Hearst, Morgan, Hitler, Mussolini, Stalin, Trotsky, and Roosevelt gave Welles's tycoons and dictators their political edge for Popular Front audiences.[29]

Welles's thrillers were not only the core of his film work but were also part of a distinctive genre of Popular Front anti-fascism. Beginning with the spy novels of Eric Ambler and Graham Greene, the espionage thriller with its international intrigues proved particularly amenable to the anti-fascist aesthetic. Anti-fascist politics were often international, mobilizing support for the Spanish Loyalists as well as anti-fascist exiles and resistance movements, and the spy thriller—once an imperial genre—was one of the few popular forms that narrated international plots. Eric Ambler's villains, Alfred Hitchcock wrote in 1943, "are big business men and bankers; the cheap scum of the low cafés of the ancient Continental city; the pro-fessional, suave, well-heeled gangsters whom we have learned to recognize as the incipient chiefs of Gestapos and fascist conspiracies. In brief, they are not only real people, they are actually the kind of people who have generated violence and evil in the Europe of our time." Eric Ambler himself later remarked that he had taken the "right wing" and often "outright fascist" thriller and turned it "upside down," making "the heroes left wing and Popular Front figures."[30]

The espionage genre was quickly adopted by Popular Front directors and screenwriters as a way to combine Hollywood formulas and anti-fascist politics. The only Hollywood film made about the Spanish Civil War, *Blockade* (1938), was a spy story. Written by Communist screenwriter John Howard Lawson and directed by left-wing émigré William Dieterle for liberal producer Walter Wanger, *Blockade* attempted to combine, as Lawson later noted, "the story of the woman trapped into spying for the fascists" with mass crowd scenes influenced by Soviet cinema. Espionage melo-drama also dominated Hollywood's only pre-war anti-Nazi film, Warner Brothers' semi-documentary *Confessions of a Nazi Spy* (1939) (written by John Wexley and starring Edward G. Robinson), as well as the left-wing wartime thrillers like Lillian Hellman's *Watch on the Rhine* (1943), in which an anti-Fascist refugee is pursued by Nazi agents in Washington; *Hangmen Also Die* (1943), Fritz Lang's film about the killing of Heyrich (written by Wexley from a story by Brecht); and *The Fallen Sparrow* (1943), in which John Garfield played a Spanish Civil War veteran hounded by Nazis in New York (based on Dorothy Hughes's popular thriller). The most enduring of these thrillers was of course *Casablanca* (1942) (written in part by Mercury scriptwriter Howard Koch), in which Humphrey Bogart played the cynical and reluctant American—who had fought for the Spanish Loyalists—drawn into the anti-fascist war.[31]

When Welles arrived in Hollywood in 1939, he was immediately drawn to the anti-fascist thriller; after all, he was a veteran of pulp radio, having played Lamont Cranston, the millionaire playboy who is secretly the mysterious foe of evil, the Shadow. Welles's earliest Hollywood projects included two adaptations of Popular Front spy novels: *The Smiler with the Knife* by Nicholas Blake (the pseudonym of poet C. Day Lewis) and *The*

Way to Santiago by Arthur Calder-Marshall. Day Lewis had edited and Calder-Marshall had contributed to an influential British anthology, *The Mind in Chains: Socialism and the Cultural Revolution*. Welles's screenplay of *The Smiler with the Knife* transplanted Day Lewis's story of British fascists to the United States, depicting an American S.S. (Stars and Stripes) led by "rich people with too much time on their hands." Welles's screenplay of *The Way to Santiago* was the tale of a man who awakes with amnesia and finds himself among Nazi spies in Mexico.[32]

Neither of these projects was filmed, but one of the earliest Mercury films was an adaptation of an Eric Ambler thriller, *Journey into Fear*, produced and designed by Welles. The first and best of several Hollywood adaptations of Ambler, it was a version of his distinctive plot: the innocent abroad who gets entangled against his will in a sordid web of espionage. Joseph Cotten plays the engineer—"a ballistics expert who has never fired a gun"—who finds himself the target of Nazi assassins; he is initiated into the world of international intrigue by the Turkish secret policeman, Colonel Haki, played by Welles. A fast-paced, low-budget film, *Journey into Fear* is one of the earliest *films noir*; its pervasive paranoia is heightened by night-time settings, low-key lighting, expressionistic camera angles, and the scratchy 78 that becomes the assassin's signature. The film ends with a virtuoso struggle on a hotel balcony, the first of Welles's increasingly baroque endings.

The tension and interplay between Joseph Cotten's naive engineer and Welles's powerful and threatening secret policeman was to serve as the narrative fulcrum for many of Welles's productions: Cotten's Leyland and Welles's Kane in *Citizen Kane*; Edward G. Robinson's Nazi-hunter and Welles's Nazi in *The Stranger*; Cotten's pulp writer and Welles's criminal black marketeer in Carol Reed's *The Third Man*; Robert Arden's young con man and Welles's shadowy tycoon in *Mr Arkadin*; and Charlton Heston's narcotics detective and Welles's corrupt policeman in *Touch of Evil*. The narrative of *The Stranger*, in which Edward G. Robinson finds the escaped Nazi, played by Welles, teaching at a Connecticut boarding school, was not only part of the genre of *post-war* anti-fascist thrillers—like Hitchcock's *Notorious* (1946) and John Wexley and Edward Dmytryk's *Cornered* (1946)— but also drew directly on Welles's post-war political writings against resurgent fascism: "the phony fear of Communism is smoke-screening the real menace of renascent Fascism," he wrote in his *New York Post* column.[33]

Like Graham Greene, who called his thrillers "entertainments" to distinguish them from his serious "novels," Welles did not approach his thrillers with the aesthetic ambitions of *Citizen Kane* or *The Magnificent Ambersons*. As a result, *Journey into Fear*, *The Stranger* (1946), and Welles's extraordinary performance as Harry Lime in the film of Greene's "entertainment" *The Third Man* have often been discounted by critics (and by

Welles himself) as simply studio products. However, just as Greene was to discover that the line between "novel" and "entertainment" blurred, so Welles was to become increasingly ambitious in his thrillers: *Lady from Shanghai* (1948)—in which Welles adopts the guise of Bogart and Garfield's Popular Front proletarian, complete with service in the Spanish Civil War—*Mr Arkadin* (1955), and *Touch of Evil* (1958) all join pulp plots to virtuoso filmmaking.

In these films, the political "content" seems overshadowed by the formal showmanship. Critics who have discounted Welles's politics have generally suggested that this showmanship is more important than his politics or his plots. "The great directors all had great personal stories to tell," Norman Lloyd, a Mercury Theater actor, once noted, "but not so with Welles." For Lloyd, *Julius Caesar* was the definitive Mercury production because of its "supreme theatricality." There is no doubt that the originality of Welles and the Mercury lay in their combination of the resources of theater, film, and radio to develop a repertoire of expressionistic devices and special effects. Among these are compositions in depth (not only in the cinematography of *Citizen Kane* and *The Magnificent Ambersons*, but in the distorted extensions of the stage apron in *Dr Faustus* and the tilting of the stage away from the audience in *Julius Caesar*); the bare, non-naturalistic sets; the use of radio sound effects in both film and theater, including the adaptation of radio's cross-fade into the famous "lightning mix," where a temporal and scenic shift is glued by continuity of sound; the elaborate lighting effects; the fondness for the omniscient voice-over and first person narration (the Mercury radio program was originally called "First Person Singular"); filmic montage editing on the stage; and the play on the conventions of news reporting.[34]

However, one cannot so easily separate Welles's showmanship from his politics. The magic of theater, film, and radio was not, for Welles, merely a formal device. Since Welles understood fascism as itself a form of showmanship, his exploration of that showmanship became a reflection on fascism, the other side of his anti-fascist aesthetic. "Showmanship is fundamental to the fascist strategy," Welles argued, "and the chief fascist argument is the parade":

> Inspiration for the showmanship of fascism comes from the military, the old dumb-show of monarchy and mostly from the theater. In Germany, the decor, the spectacular use of great masses of people—the central myth itself was borrowed from grand opera. In Italy, the public show, the lavish props, the picturesque processions were taken from the movies. Even the famous salute, the stiff arm up-raised, comes not from history, but from Hollywood. Surely one of the most amusing footnotes in all the chronicles of recorded time is that Hitler and Mussolini stole their showmanship from Richard Wagner and Cecil B. DeMille!

Welles in turn stole *his* showmanship from the Nazis. "Orson dictated clearly and exactly the look he wanted," the pioneering Mercury lighting designer Jean Rosenthal recalled of the spectacular lighting of *Julius Caesar*: it was "a very simple look based on the Nazi rallies at Nuremberg. . . . The up light was taken entirely from the effect the Nazis achieved."[35]

Welles was not alone in his fascination with the rhetoric of fascism; the German Marxist Walter Benjamin had argued in 1936 that "the logical result of Fascism is the introduction of aesthetics into political life," to which "Communism responds by politicizing art." In the United States, Benjamin's counterpart was the Popular Front cultural critic Kenneth Burke, whose writings on the "great dictators" included a 1935 analysis of the "Great Demagogue" in Shakespeare's *Julius Caesar*, a detailed reading of Peter Blume's *The Eternal City* in 1937, and a famous address to the 1939 American Writers' Congress on "The Rhetoric of Hitler's *Battle*." "This book is the well of Nazi magic," Burke wrote, "crude magic, but effective. A people trained in pragmatism should want to inspect this magic." Welles and the Mercury Theatre attempted to turn the magic of the Nazis against them.[36]

Just as Welles's portrayals of his grotesque hero-villains were always ambiguous, so too was his deployment of the magic and showmanship of the mass media, not least in the celebrated panic caused by the radio broadcast of "The War of the Worlds" on 30 October 1938. "The War of the Worlds" is a particularly interesting example of Welles's anti-fascist aesthetic, because it was entirely a "formal" triumph; it has no "political" content or plot. Institutionally, the Mercury Theatre's radio program was an example of the contradictory compromises between Popular Front struggles and the culture industry. A campaign in the early years of the New Deal to nullify broadcasting licenses and reallot frequencies with a quarter of them going to "educational, religious, agricultural, labor, cooperative, and similar non-profit associations" had been defeated by the broadcasting industry, but the networks agreed to create their own "public service" programs, using unsponsored air time to lend an image of prestige and cultural uplift to the radio. CBS's "Columbia Workshop" was the first of these "sustaining" programs, and it sparked a brief renaissance of radio drama, where experiment and innovation were subsidized, and poets and playwrights addressed a mass audience. In the summer of 1938, CBS brought "an entire theatrical institution to the air": the Mercury Theatre on the Air. Welles and the Mercury arrived at CBS, as they would later arrive at RKO studios, as a prestige property, with a license to innovate.[37]

Welles and his collaborators took the forms of radio drama seriously; "radio," Welles said, "is a popular, democratic machine for disseminating information and entertainment." They began by adapting popular classics into first-person radio narratives: "Dracula" and "Treasure Island" were their first two programs. "The War of the Worlds" broadcast was at first glance nothing special, though it departed from the usual format by prefacing the long first person narrative of the survivor, Professor Pierson, with the mock news broadcast of the Martian invasion. Its structure resembles the later *Citizen Kane*, but unlike *Kane* the persuasiveness of the newsreel overwhelmed the pedestrian narrative that followed, triggering a panic. According to sociologist Hadley Cantril's analysis of public opinion polls about the panic, six million people heard part of the broadcast, and over a million of them believed it was a real news broadcast and were frightened by it. The panic came to figure, for writers, politicians, and journalists, the power and dangers of the still relatively new mass culture of broadcasting. For some, Welles was as irresponsible as the right-wing radio demagogues; for others, the program was a salutary warning. For Welles and the Mercury Theatre, the panic represented not only national notoriety, but the other side of the people's theater, of this "popular, democratic machine": the lure and danger of hypnotizing an audience.[38]

Cantril's study, a landmark work in mass communications research, offered several explanations of the panic. Some were formal, stressing the program's effective illusion of real time duration by the extended cuts to the music of Ramon Raquello and his orchestra between news bulletins; others appealed to the peculiarities of radio, whether to the common experience of tuning in late and missing the frame, or to the authority the conventions of special on-the-spot bulletins had acquired in the recent war crisis of the early fall of 1938. However, the central explanation pointed to the audience, arguing that "it was the people who were closest to the borderline of economic disaster who were most apt to take the program as news." For Cantril, working-class people, particularly those with religious beliefs, had little "critical ability."[39]

However, listeners like Sylvia Holmes, a black woman from Newark who assumed that the invasion by Martians that the radio reported was actually an invasion by the Nazis with a terrifying new weapon, were not misreading the broadcast. For not only does the actual broadcast play down the Martian identity of the invaders—a "critical" listener like Sylvia Holmes could easily dismiss the Martian stuff as the mistake of the clearly distressed radio announcer—but the drama was based on the conventions of the anti-fascist radio dramas to which Welles himself had contributed. "The War of the Worlds" did not have to be an explicit "parable of fascism" because its very form was part of the anti-fascist aesthetic.[40]

The central device of "The War of the Worlds", the use of the radio announcer as a character, had been created in the experimental radio dramas depicting fascist invasions and air raids. As one critic has noted, unlike the radio serial—"The Shadow," for example—where "everything that happens, happens in front of the mike as a result of the dialogue, thus evoking the illusion that the characters are in control of the plot," the new radio dramas foregrounded the announcer. There was little dialogue and the action took place off-mike, beyond the control of the announcer/ reporter. Welles's first major radio appearance had been as one of these fictional announcers in the April 1937 "Columbia Workshop" production of Archibald MacLeish's thirty-minute verse drama, "The Fall of the City." Produced in an armory with a cast of two hundred drama students for the crowd, "The Fall of the City" was a critical and popular success, inaugurating the Popular Front genre of serious radio drama and making Welles one of its representative voices. Welles's announcer witnesses the fall of an unnamed city to a conqueror, and his climatic narration of the arrival of "the conqueror" foreshadows the description of the Martians: "We can't see for the glare of it ... Yes! ... Yes! ... / He's there in the end of the street in the shadow. We see him! / He looks huge—a head taller than anyone / [...] They cover their faces with fingers. They cower before him. / They fall." When his visor opens, there is no face: "The helmet is hollow! / The metal is empty! [...] I tell you / There's no one at all there: there's only the metal." But the people respond to his raised arm, the fascist salute: "The people invent their oppressors: they wish to believe in them," the announcer concludes. "The city is fallen."[41]

Welles also used this form for the Mercury radio broadcast of *Julius Caesar* in September 1938: deprived of the Nuremberg lights and his stark stage design, Welles recruited the radio news commentator H.V. Kaltenborn to "report" the play, using passages from Plutarch's history. Moreover, just three days before "The War of the Worlds" broadcast, Welles listened to another of these anti-fascist dramas, the "Columbia Workshop" production of MacLeish's *Air Raid*. *Air Raid*'s announcer, played by Mercury actor Ray Collins, reported the attack on a fictional European border town: "You are twenty-eight miles from the eastern border: / You are up on top of a town on a kind of a tenement," the announcer said over continuous static and a background of women's voices. The program ends with the roar of planes and machine guns: "We hear them: we can't see them. / We hear the shearing metal: / We hear the tearing air." Again, the broadcast was a critical and popular success, featured in *Time* magazine. In the spring of 1939, Norman Corwin's "They Fly through the Air" continued the Popular Front "air raid" genre. A CBS broadcaster noted in 1939 that "we have been flooded with scripts about bombing planes—not entirely, we believe, because of the success of MacLeish's 'Air Raid' or Corwin's 'They Fly through the Air,' but because of the fact that people are conscious of bombing planes these days." The technological terror of fascist air raids in Spain as well as Hitler's March 1938 invasion of Austria was the subtext for these pervasive invasion and air raid narratives: the most famous was not a radio show but Picasso's huge mural, *Guernica*, painted for the 1937 Paris

World's Fair in the wake of the 28 April 1937 Fascist bombing of the city of Guernica.[42]

The Martian broadcast is thus best understood as one of these anti-fascist "air raid" stories. It may seem ironic that a tale of Martian invasion should cause a panic, rather than the more "realistic" dramatizations of air raids. In fact, the persuasiveness of the Martian broadcast lay not simply in the Mercury's technical mastery of the conventions of news broadcasting but also in their depiction of the failure of radio. If the panic demonstrated radio's power, "The War of the Worlds" narrative emphasized the limits of mass communication. Though Cantril argued that the susceptibility of listeners was demonstrated by their uncritical faith in the authority of scientists, radio announcers, and military officers, in fact the broadcast repeatedly shows the inability of any of these authorities to comprehend the invasion, whether the radio reporter Carl Phillips who "can't find words" or the scientist Pierson whose wordy explanations explain nothing. Moreover, the Martians "avoid destruction of cities and countryside," attacking the means of communication and transportation. This "fall of the city" takes place not with the crowd prostrate in front of the conqueror's salute but on top of Broadcasting Building. "This may be the last broadcast," the announcer says, and the mock broadcast ends with the radio operator's haunting "2X2L calling CQ. . . . Isn't there anyone on the air?" It is precisely radio's inability to generate a mass resistance to the Martians that is the heart of the broadcast.

The Martian panic generated the "live, participating audience" the Mercury manifesto had promised, but not in the way they intended. The magic and showmanship of "The War of the Worlds" seemed closer to the fascist demagogues and to Hearst's propaganda than to the "popular, democratic machine" the Mercury imagined. It captured the contradictions of anti-fascist culture: at once trying to create a "people's culture" with the new means of communication, while fearing that the "people" constituted by the apparatuses of mass culture were less a participating audience than a dispersed series of panicked individuals. This dialectic between the people and the apparatus became the heart of the Mercury's masterpiece, *Citizen Kane*.

3. *Citizen Kane*'s Anti-Fascist Newsreels

Citizen Kane combined the two fundamental elements of Welles's anti-fascist aesthetic: the portrait of the great dictator and the reflection on showmanship and propaganda. The wit and tragedy of the story of the yellow journalist Kane are produced by the jokes, fulminations, drunken diatribes, and soapbox rhetoric about the mass media. The first line that Kane speaks (after the deathbed "Rosebud") is an allusion to the Martian panic: "Don't believe everything you hear on the radio." Lest our gullibility persist, Leland says of Rosebud, "I saw that in *The Inquirer*. Well, I've never believed anything I saw in *The Inquirer*." Unlike the other of Hollywood's now forgotten tycoon "biopics," Kane's story becomes a hall of mirrors in which the cultural apparatus sees itself.

This gives Welles's portrait of Charles Foster Kane its rich and contradictory character. On the one hand, Kane certainly was an attack on William Randolph Hearst. Welles's "sympathies were," as a *New Masses* writer noted, "with the opponents of either alien or native fascism," and for Welles and the Popular Front left, Hearst was an emblem of American fascism, a powerful capitalist who was also a visible demagogue. His public statements supporting Hitler and Mussolini were notorious, and his newspapers were rabidly anti-labor. He had led the attack on the 1934 San Francisco general strike and continued to hound the ILWU leader Harry Bridges. His papers were the major antagonist of the left-wing Newspaper Guild. As a result, the Popular Front press regularly attacked Hearst: there were "Anti-Hearst" rallies and a National People's Committee Against Hearst.[43]

This picture of Hearst was by no means limited to Communist militants. "Out of the westcoast haze comes now and then an old man's querulous voice," Dos Passos wrote in *U.S.A.*'s portrait of Hearst, "hissing dirty names at the defenders of civil liberties for the workingman; / jail the reds, / praising the comforts of Baden-Baden under the blood and bludgeon rule of Handsome Adolph." The Wisconsin sociologist Edward A. Ross wrote that "Hearst, with his twenty-seven newspapers, his thirteen magazines, his broadcasting stations and his film studios is a greater menace to the lovers of American institutions than any other man in the country. In the last three years it has become evident that he has an understanding with European Fascist leaders and is using his vast publicity apparatus to harry and discredit those who stand up for American democracy." *Citizen Kane*'s depiction of Hearst was deeply indebted to this anti-Hearst sentiment, and particularly to Ferdinand Lundberg's muckraking biography, *Imperial Hearst* (1936). When Hearst tried to suppress *Citizen Kane*, the Popular Front rallied to Welles's defense, with the League of American Writers campaigning for the film's release. "If you've never seen a picture before and never see another, if you have to picket your neighborhood theater until they show it to you in desperation (because although this week it was shown to the press its release is not yet assured) see *Citizen Kane*," Molly Castle wrote in the left-wing newsweekly, *US Week*.[44]

However, Welles's Kane, like his other great dictators, elicited sympathy for the devil. For some Popular Front critics, this was the film's strength. "Welles does not merely show us one aspect of the man and pound on it," Cedric Belfrage argued in *The Clipper*. "He comes not to praise nor to indict Kane, but to reveal him.... The result is that a profound pity is stirred up in the audience, and the indictment is not of a man but of environments and social and economic factors which make him what he becomes ... the might and majesty and profits of dark yellow journalism— exposed by *Kane* so effectively, because so humanly and with such inspired craftsmanship." Others were more wary: "Citizen Welles becomes so fascinated by the lonely vortex of sad violence and failure of the flesh into which he hurls his main character, that Citizen Kane is lost," Muriel Draper wrote in *Direction*. "The life and death connection between the man as editor of a paper that affects the daily lives of millions of people who read it, is volatilized in the cocoon of personal conflict and frustration he spins about himself." Writing decades later, John Howard Lawson maintained that even though "*Citizen Kane* inherits the class consciousness of the thirties in its portrait of a millionaire who is a prototype of American fascism, ... the film treats Kane with ironic sympathy, ignoring the implications of his conduct. It recognizes the dark forces in American society but avoids a direct challenge to these forces."[45]

Welles himself articulated this ambivalence. "Kane is a detestable man," Welles told the *Cahiers du Cinéma* interviewers in 1958, "but I have a great deal of sympathy for him so far as he's a human being." On other occasions, Welles's sympathy seemed to outweigh his horror: he once suggested that his disagreement with screenwriter Herman Mankiewicz over the character "probably gave the film a certain tension: that one of the authors hated Kane and one of them loved him." For Mankiewicz, Kane was simply Hearst: "in his hatred of Hearst," Welles remarked, he had the "point of view of a newspaperman writing about a newspaper boss he despised." But for Welles, who had never worked in newspapers, Kane was always more than Hearst. Welles had far closer connections to Henry Luce, the publisher of *Time, Life,* and *Fortune,* and Luce is, I will suggest, as important to *Citizen Kane* as the aged Hearst. Indeed, *Citizen Kane* might best be seen as a combination of two different films: what we might call "Citizen Hearst" and "Citizen Luce."[46]

"Citizen Hearst" is the historical film inside *Kane*, Welles's rendition of the decline and fall of the Lincoln republic, an American version of the Shakespearean history plays that haunted him. Like the trilogies of Dos Passos and Josephine Herbst, *Citizen Kane* returns to the 1870s (it opens in 1871) to show the rise and fall of a boy brought up by a bank. The scene in which Mrs Kane, played by Agnes Moorehead, gives up her son to the banker Thatcher remains one of the most powerful in the film. Its elements—the echo of the dying Kane's snowy glass globe, the boy yelling "The Union forever," the fairy tale of the boarder who leaves the "worthless stock" that founds the copper-mine fortune, the unexplained estrangement of Kane's parents, and the sled that will be Rosebud—condense the story of Kane's lost childhood into that of the republic itself. The tremendous visual and narrative energy in the scenes of the 1890s and the Spanish-American War underline the ironic legacy that Kane's, and America's, fortune proved to be. The arc of Kane's career follows that of the United States: "News on the March" superimposes "1929" over factory closings, intoning "for Kane, in four short years, collapse."

The story of the Lincoln republic also informed Welles's second film, *The Magnificent Ambersons*, the tale of a family torn between the genteel tradition and the world of the automobile—Fordism. "The magnificence of the Ambersons began in 1873," Welles's voice-over tells us. "Their splendor lasted all the years that saw their Midland town spread and darken into a city." "The whole point," Welles later said, "was to show the automobile wrecking it—not only the family but the town." Welles's vision of the decline and fall of the Ambersons was as bleak as Dos Passos's *Big Money*, and its ending was too harsh for RKO. The eight-minute final reel, with Joseph Cotten's visit to Agnes Moorehead in a cheap boarding house and Welles's concluding voice-over—"Ladies and gentlemen, that's the end of the story"—was cut. "Everything is over," Welles recalled in an interview, "her feelings and her world and his world." Welles's "U.S.A." trilogy comes to an end with *The Stranger*, in which the Lincoln republic is figured as a New England town, complete with folksy general store, white church, and prep school. The town unwittingly adopts an escaped Nazi as teacher and son-in-law (he marries the daughter of a Supreme Court justice): he is, metaphorically, one of them. Despite its macabre evocation of Americana, however, it has little historical resonance, and becomes one of the pulp thrillers that came to supplant Welles's "history plays."[47]

Neither *The Magnificent Ambersons* nor *The Stranger* succeeds in uniting social content with formal experiment. In *The Magnificent Ambersons*, the narrative of the automobile inventor (played by Joseph Cotten) remains relatively peripheral, with the striking exception of the virtuoso scene cross-cutting between the sleigh and the automobile in the snow. As a result, the confrontation between the inventor and the Ambersons is locked in a static, if sometimes frenzied, family romance. In *The Stranger*, the only magic the Welles character exercises is his repair of the town's medieval clock, and that is little more than an excuse for one of Welles's characteristically baroque endings. In *Kane*, however, the film's magic is a reflection on Kane's magic.[48]

In this respect, Kane is no longer Hearst, for Welles was not particularly interested in the magic of newspapers. "Not one glimpse of the actual content of his newspapers is afforded us," the *New Masses* critic complained in an exaggerated but not inaccurate comment. It was the radio newsreel, "The March of Time," that taught Welles and his Mercury colleagues the craft of radio drama. "I'd been years on *The March of Time* radio program," he told Peter Bogdanovich. "Every day. It was a marvelous show to do.

Great fun, because, half an hour after something happened, we'd be acting it out with music and sound effects and actors. . . . One day they did as a news item . . . the opening of my production of the black *Macbeth*, and I played myself on it. And that to me was the apotheosis of my career—that I was on *March of Time* acting *and* as a news item." *Citizen Kane*'s real subject is the *newsreel*, whose magic it mocks and mimics.[49]

If "Citizen Hearst" is the historical film inside *Kane*, "Citizen Luce" is *Kane* as newsreel. The first account of Kane's career is given by an imitation newsreel, "News on the March," which was edited by RKO's newsreel editors to approximate the real thing. Welles's model was Henry Luce's film newsreel (also called *The March of Time*), which had been widely praised, on the left as well as in the mainstream press, for its innovative showmanship and politics. When Welles argued in *Friday* that the film was *not* about Hearst, he emphasized its connection to *The March of Time*: "*Citizen Kane* is the story of a search by a man named Thompson, the editor of a news digest (similar to *The March of Time*) for the meaning of Kane's dying words." In *Kane*'s projection room scene, the Luce figure, Rawlston, is lit as a conductor.[50]

Unlike "The War of the Worlds," however, in which the formal trick of imitating a news broadcast was far more interesting than the narrative that followed, *Citizen Kane* trumped its mock newsreel with its own magic, its own showmanship. The film is not an homage to the newsreel but a critique of it; it implicitly offers a richer and truer way of seeing Kane and his world than that of the newsreel. *Kane*'s response to the newsreel and its ideology takes three forms: the virtuoso newsreel, composition in depth, and the moving camera. The first, the virtuoso newsreel, is embodied in the several scenes, usually lit in high contrast, with a highly foregrounded montage, that narrate the triumphs of young Kane. These scenes use the staple of the newsreel, flashing newspaper headlines, to remarkable effect, as in the sequence where the increasingly irritated Thatcher reads the headlines condemning the Traction Trust. The newsreel's use of still photographs is then elaborated in the cut from the still of the reporters to the photographing of the same reporters six years later. Many of these sequences are narrated by Bernard Herrmann's music, which uses popular dance forms to create, as he wrote, "a kind of ballet suite in miniature." This part of the film is less a critique of the newsreel than a virtuoso riff on its forms.

The second filmic response to the newsreel is the composition in depth, the use of deep-focus cinematography, wide-angle lenses, deep sets with ceilings, in-camera matte shots, a careful attention to sound effects, and the avoidance of shot reverse-shot cutting and conventional close-ups to create a sense of an elongated space in which actors revolve in an elaborate dance, moving from light to shadow and occasionally into a ballooned foreground presence but never out of focus. This composition marks moments of crisis that the commercial newsreel is unable to narrate: the boarding house scene; the confrontation between Kane, Gettys, Emily, and Susan; the two scenes with the drunken Jedediah Leland. Depth of field becomes the correlative of a historical and psychological depth that escapes the shallow, foreshortened newsreel.

The third response to the newsreel is perhaps the most ambiguous, calling attention to itself while masking its supposed agent. This is the invasive camera that displaces the supposed representative of the viewer, the journalist Thompson. As Peter Wollen has noted, "the decision to use sequence-shots in the framing story is clearly a decision not to use classical field reverse-field cutting, and thus to de-emphasize the role of Thompson, the narratee. Thompson only appears as a shadowy figure with his back to the camera." The obscured narrator combined with the moving camera produce the visual equivalent of a Mercury trademark, the Wellesian voice-over. Unlike the relatively static camera of the newsreel, the film's camera ignores "No Trespassing" signs, dissolves through skylights into nightclubs, through steel doors into the sanctum of the Thatcher Library, and into the flames to reveal Rosebud. The magic of *Citizen Kane*'s "newsreels" is, therefore, not simply showmanship and formal experiment, but, like the radical newsreels of the Film and Photo League and the staged Living Newspapers of Losey and Ray, an attempt to transform and refunction the newsreel.[51]

"Citizen Luce," however, haunts more than *Kane*'s newsreels. *Life*'s still photography was, as Robert Carringer has noted, one of the models for Gregg Toland's cinematography, and *Fortune*'s feature on San Simeon lay behind the design of Kane's Xanadu. Moreover, Welles had come into contact with Luce through the poet Archibald MacLeish, and *Citizen Kane* draws on the relationship between Luce and MacLeish for its portrait of Kane and Leland. Luce and MacLeish were both Yale graduates: Luce was the innovative young editor, MacLeish the slightly older modernist poet. In 1929, Luce persuaded MacLeish to join the staff of *Fortune*, and MacLeish became a major contributor of social commentary. His *Fortune* essays, though never collected, are as much classics of depression reportage as Edmund Wilson's *American Jitters*. At the same time, MacLeish moved to the left. His 1935 play, *Panic*, which starred the nineteen-year-old Welles, brought MacLeish into the radical theater: "the New Theatre-New Masses gang turned up Saturday night," he wrote to Dos Passos, "it was superb. A better audience I have never seen & the symposium afterwards, with Lawson & Burnshaw & V.J. Jerome & myself (with the grippe), was exciting as hell. I have never had such a sense of *audience* before." MacLeish began writing for *New Theatre* and became active in Popular Front organizations.[52]

Welles's performance in *Panic* led MacLeish to suggest him for the part of the announcer in his 1937 radio drama, "The Fall of the City." A few months later, MacLeish took part in the unsuccessful negotiations with the Federal Theatre Project over *The Cradle Will Rock.* When they failed, MacLeish joined Welles on stage at *The Cradle*'s historic opening, delivering an impromptu speech after the production. When the Mercury Theatre was established in the fall of 1937, Welles and Houseman appealed to MacLeish for money, and he arranged a meeting with the Luces: Luce contributed $2,500 to the Mercury, a figure that echoes the one with which Kane tries to pay off Jed Leland. Soon after, in May 1938, Welles was featured on the cover of *Time* magazine.[53]

By 1938, however, MacLeish had grown increasingly critical of *Time*'s coverage of the Spanish Civil War, and he resigned from *Fortune.* In a long and anguished letter of July 1938, he accused Luce of betraying his journalistic ideals:

> I don't know you very well these days. . . . I wish some things had gone differently with you. . . . Maybe what I mean is that I wish you hadn't been so successful. Because it's very hard to be as successful as you have been and still keep your belief in the desperate necessity for fundamental change. I think what you have done amazing and I give you all credit and all honor for it. It would have been very easy for you to forget everything you believed true when you were twenty. . . . But I don't know—you were meant to be a progressive. . . . You were meant to make common cause with the people—all the people. . . . You would have been very happy inside yourself as one of the leaders in a democratic revolution in this country. . . . Maybe I'm wrong. It's presumptuous to guess about another man's happiness but I think you would have been. I think you hate being rich. . . . I think you would have liked to write *The People Yes.*

We don't know if Welles ever saw this letter, but he may well have talked to MacLeish about Luce. For MacLeish's ambivalent disillusionment with Luce seems to inform *Citizen Kane* as much as Mankiewicz's hatred for Hearst. Certainly MacLeish's account of the conflict between Luce's wealth and his populism is echoed throughout the film, and particularly in the conflict between Leland and Kane.[54]

"You talk about the people as though you owned them," the drunken Leland tells Kane. "As though they belong to you. As long as I can remember, you've talked about giving the people their rights as if you could make them a present of liberty, as a reward for services rendered. . . . You used to write an awful lot about the workingman." Kane's tragedy, of course, is not simply that he sold out his declaration of principles; from the beginning he had told Thatcher that there were two Kanes: the crusading publisher defending the "decent, hard-working people" and the owner of Metropolitan Transfer stock who knows exactly the extent of his holdings. Rather, the tragedy is the loss of his magic, his inability to tell the people what to think, the taking of "the love of the people of this state away from" him. It is the shift from the self-confidence of the exchange with Emily—"Really, Charles, people will think. . . . What I tell them to think"—to the frustration of his response to Susan's music teacher—"The people will think. . . . People will think. You're concerned with what people will think, Signor Matisti? I may be able to enlighten you a bit. I'm something of an authority about what people will think. The newspapers, for example." "Such men as Kane," Welles once said, "always tend toward the newspaper and entertainment world. They combine a morbid preoccupation with the public with a devastatingly low opinion of the public mentality and moral character."[55]

Ironically, this dialectic—morbid preoccupation with the public together with a low opinion of the crowd—ran throughout the Mercury's own productions. As "The War of the Worlds" broadcast demonstrated, the other side of Welles's fascination with propaganda and media manipulation was an inability to imagine a popular resistance to it. Even the anti-fascist *Julius Caesar* had, as the *New York Times* critic noted, "the somewhat ambiguous effect . . . of implying that there is no use rebelling against a fascist state." The *Daily Worker* had criticized its "slanderous" picture of the masses swayed by a demagogue. Welles's crowds were more often lynch mobs than strikers.[56]

Citizen Kane has few crowd scenes: Welles avoided both the crowd scene and the close-up, which had been, as Walter Benjamin suggested, film's great perceptual advances. Traces of the crowd may be seen: the sight gag of the stagehand holding his nose at Susan's performance, and the street cleaner sweeping up the debris of the election campaign. Moreover, the existence of the crowd is suggested by a variety of technical tricks. These tricks include the elaborate use of lights, sound, and painted sets to produce the effect of crowds without hiring large numbers of extras. Robert Carringer has emphasized the technical success of these tricks: shooting into the lights in the opera scene to suggest but not show a large audience; and carefully rerecording the soundtrack of the Madison Square Garden rally to suggest the noise if not the presence of the crowd. These techniques were in part the result of budgetary constraints. The Mercury productions had always lacked money for extras, and the painted hall and audience in *Kane*'s Madison Square Garden scene had its origins in the cyclorama of skulls in *Danton's Death*, where the revolutionary mob was suggested by five thousand Halloween masks glued to canvas. But these magical, disembodied crowds take on an ideological meaning as well; the illusions of the political rally and the opera house yield a curiously hollow phantasmagoria where the people are an effect of the apparatus.[57]

Luce also became an important ally in the struggle over *Kane*. According to Welles, he was "one of the first people to see the movie—in New York.

He and Clare Luce loved it and roared with laughter at the digest.... They saw it as a parody and enjoyed it very much as such—I have to hand it to them. He saw it as a joke—or *she* saw it as a joke and he had to because she did." Luce "ordered his staff to unleash their guns to get the film released," *Variety* reported. *Time* published a laudatory article on the film, and *Life* did a feature spread, using photographs taken by Toland to illustrate the technical accomplishments of the film, including its "pan focus."[58]

Welles's connections to Luce and MacLeish were, for the New York intellectuals around *Partisan Review, Politics,* and *Dissent,* symptoms of the Popular Front's middlebrow character. For them, Welles's appearances in *Time* and *Life* were of a piece with his anti-fascist politics, his dramatizations of thickly plotted bestsellers by Booth Tarkington, his revivals of Victorian classics like *Treasure Island* and *Dracula* on "highbrow" radio, and his modernizations of Shakespeare. "Mr. Welles, to judge from his interpretations of *Macbeth, Dr. Faustus,* and *Caesar,* has the idea an Elizabethan play is a liability which only by the most strenuous showmanship, by cutting, doctoring, and modernizing, can be converted into an asset," Mary McCarthy wrote in *Partisan Review.* "Mr. Welles's method is to find a modern formula into which a classic can somehow be squeezed. In the case of *Macbeth,* the formula was *The Emperor Jones*; for *Dr Faustus* it was a Punch and Judy show; for *Caesar* it was the proletarian play." For McCarthy and the *Partisan* critics, the Mercury Theatre, far from being a genuine experiment in radical or avant-garde art, was, like the cultural front generally, a political disguise for kitsch, a middlebrow travesty of the aesthetic experience.[59]

There is no doubt that the Mercury Theatre was always on the edge of the new "middlebrow" culture which, as Joan Shelley Rubin has suggested, modernized the genteel tradition for the world of mass communications and consumption. The entrepreneurs of middlebrow culture abandoned the genteel tradition's traditional hostility to the lively and disreputable arts in order to regulate and "improve" them. The Mercury shared the strategies and techniques of such middlebrow institutions as the Book-of-the-Month Club, NBC's radio symphonies, and radio's cultural commentators like Yale English professor William Lyon "Billy" Phelps. The Mercury recordings of Shakespeare were, like Penguin's paperback classics and the "great books" of Robert Hutchins and Mortimer Adler, an attempt to popularize and to market high culture.[60]

However, the anatomists of "midcult" like Mary McCarthy and Dwight Macdonald missed the social contradictions at the heart of middlebrow culture. For the middlebrow was not only a form of cultural "uplift"; it was also a form of plebeian self-improvement, and could carry radical democratic energies. Perhaps the most powerful and persuasive defense of the autonomy, legitimacy, and, one might even say, greatness of middlebrow taste has been mounted by Pierre Bourdieu, the sociologist of culture. Middlebrow culture, Bourdieu argues, is the culture of the autodidact. The autodidact is one who takes the game of culture too seriously and is thus liable to know too much or too little, condemned to amassing cultural information which is to legitimate culture "as his stamp collection is to an art collection, a miniature culture." The culture of the middlebrow is always a culture of pretension, "divided between the tastes they incline to and the tastes they aspire to." The middlebrow consumer buys the cut-rate cultural product because it is "cheaper and creates the same effect." So middlebrow culture consists of "accessible versions of avant-garde experiments or accessible works which pass for avant-garde experiments, [and] film adaptations of classic drama and literature." By this definition, the Mercury productions are clearly middlebrow.[61]

However, for Bourdieu, these tastes are not "bad" taste, but are rather the signs and weapons of class conflict, an embattled attempt at distinction by people with little cultural capital. The middlebrow is a tragic hero, able neither to live by culture nor to live without it. It is not surprising that the aesthetics of the Popular Front should have a middlebrow accent. The Popular Front alliance was made up of classes and peoples in transition: second-generation workers caught between the immigrant cultures of their parents and the Americanist culture of high school, radio, and the movies; children of working-class families finding white-collar employment in the expanding industries of leisure and entertainment; women entering the wage-labor world of the wartime industries and the expanding service sector. For these young workers, culture itself was a labor, an act of self-enrichment and self-development. The very terms and values of cultural capital were in flux in the age of the CIO, and this created the space for both high culture popularizers, plebeian avant-gardes, and the arts that were not quite "legitimate"—jazz, cinema, photography, science fiction, detective stories, folk music—all of which thrived in the cultural front.

Citizen Kane was not only an emblem of the culture of the Popular Front; its working-class heroine, Dorothy Comingore's Susan Alexander, spoke in its middlebrow accent. The girl Kane finds in the gutter is shrill, not "high-class," a seller of sheet music misplaced as a diva, a Stella Dallas lost in Xanadu. "You know what Charlie called her," Leland tells the reporter. "He said she was a cross-section of the American public." Despite the rhetoric of the workingman that Leland invokes, Kane always thought of "the people" as female. The older editor objects to Kane's newspaper on the grounds that it will print "the gossip of housewives," and the key scene of Kane winning the love of the people establishes them as women: his dance with the chorus line who sing the Charlie Kane song, a scene that includes one of the few kisses in the film. *Citizen Kane* recodes politics in sexual terms, as Kane's public life is displaced by his private life.[62]

Moreover, in spite of the cruel jokes—the line called out at the end, "Twenty five thousand bucks. That's a lot of money to pay for a dame without a head," is surely some kind of filmic parapraxis—Susan triumphs: "everything was his idea, except my leaving him," something that not even Leland can claim. When scored with a jazz band rather than an operatic orchestra, she can break with Kane and tell her story to Thompson. "The last ten years have been tough on a lot of people," Thompson tells her. "Aw, they haven't been tough on me. I just lost all my money." Popular Front audiences recognized Comingore's Susan Alexander as one of their own: Comingore was featured in the Popular Front picture weekly, *Friday*, and the *New Masses* critic wrote that she was "the most astonishing young actress since Garbo was a pup." An active member of the Sleepy Lagoon Defense Committee in 1943, Comingore married Communist screenwriter Richard Collins. After their marriage ended, Collins became an informer, and Comingore was blacklisted for refusing to name names in 1951.[63]

The destruction of Comingore's career paralleled the collapse of the Mercury Theatre's unstable mixture of the Lucepapers and the people's theater, as the brief alliance of Luce and Welles ended. On 17 February 1941, a few weeks before *Citizen Kane* was released, Luce's own manifesto, "The American Century," appeared in *Life*. It was a statement of war aims and a vision of an imperial United States exporting capitalism and the American way of life to the post-war world. If "Mr Luce's prediction of the American century will come true," Welles later wrote, "God help us all. We'll make Germany's bid for world supremacy look like amateur night, and the inevitable retribution will be on a comparable scale." By 1944, Welles was speaking out against Clare Luce, who had become a right-wing, anti-New Deal congresswoman from Connecticut; she in turn attacked Welles as part of "the whole Broadway-Browder axis." Having gone from theatrical angel to Red-baiter, she was no longer laughing at *Citizen Kane*.[64]

4. Black Jacobins, Native Sons, and the Mexican Border: Race, Nation, and Fascism

In the early 1940s, Welles became increasingly active in promulgating an internationalist vision. His speeches on "Moral Indebtedness" and "The Survival of Fascism" were, like Henry Wallace's "The Century of the Common Man," an answer to the nationalism of Henry Luce's American Century. "Harry Luce isn't a Fascist," he said in a speech attacking *Time*'s friendly coverage of Latin American fascists, "but Luce and men like him ... are, in fact, preparing the way for the survival of fascism." "If I must sum up the meaning of Fascism," he concluded, "I think the best way I can put it is that whatever form it takes, no matter how it may adapt itself to local conditions, to regional myths and prejudice, it will always be some form of nationalism gone crazy." Moreover, since "we are entering upon a new era in the history of man," Welles writes, "nationalism would have to go crazy to assert itself now. The only sanity for any sort of citizen today is the beautiful sanity of Wilkie's 'One World'."[65]

This account of fascism as nationalism gone crazy lay behind Welles's passionate embrace of various "one-worldisms." His most enduring political connection was to Louis Dolivet's International Free World Association and the magazine *Free World*, a forum for anti-fascist émigrés and resistance movements. Dolivet took Houseman's place as a mentor to Welles. Like Houseman, Dolivet was a European émigré who had connections to wealthy social circles—he had married into the Whitney family—and to the left—his involvement in the anti-fascist underground led the FBI to assume that he was a Comintern agent, and he was eventually denied reentry into the United States in 1949. The Free World group—which included Popular Front liberals like Max Lerner, Archibald MacLeish, and *Nation* editor Freda Kirchwey—was deeply committed to the United Nations; Welles did a series of ABC broadcasts from the UN's founding San Francisco conference in 1945.[66]

The "one-worldism" of Welles's anti-fascism produced the often windy and abstract quality of his speeches, which wander from platitudes of pro-Soviet internationalism to platitudes of the State Department's Good Neighbor policy. What distinguished Welles from Dolivet and his Free World associates was his linking of fascism and racism. For Welles, racists were fascists:

> We still hear it said that race prejudice has always existed in the world, that it flourished before Fascism, that to call a man a Fascist because he discriminates against another man on account of race is an improper use of the term. I agree that Fascism is a strong word ... but I think that history itself has widened the meaning of the word. I think that long after the last governments that dare to call themselves Fascist have been swept off the face of civilization, the word "fascism" will live in our language as a word for race hate.

Though the one-world idealism of Wilkie and Wallace had little impact on Welles's art, narratives of race and racism were central to his anti-fascist aesthetic. From the Harlem *Macbeth* to the Isaac Woodward radio broadcasts, from his preface to the Sleepy Lagoon defense pamphlet to *Touch of Evil*, Welles not only took part in the politics of racial justice but created a number of the Popular Front's most powerful racial stories.[67]

The first was the Harlem *Macbeth* of 1936. When Welles turned the Scotland of Shakespeare's *Macbeth* into the Haiti of the years following the Haitian Revolution, casting Macbeth as the black Haitian emperor Henri

Christophe, it was not, as virtually all white theater critics wrote, simply Shakespeare done as *The Emperor Jones*. The Negro Theatre production with its huge amateur cast—there were only four experienced professionals out of more than one hundred actors—was an overwhelming success—"by all odds the great success in my life," Welles later recalled—because it embodied the black radicalism that took the Haitian revolution as an allegory of African American uprising. The Negro Theatre itself had been created in the wake of the Harlem Riot of March 1935. That battle between police and Harlem residents had led to a year of public hearings on housing, health, employment, and relief. The Harlem Communist Party presented detailed analyses of discrimination at the hearings and organized community protests, emerging as an important political force in Harlem. By February 1936, they had joined with leading Harlem radicals like A. Philip Randolph, Adam Clayton Powell, Jr, and Roi Ottley of the *Amsterdam News* in forming the National Negro Congress. This political organizing was accompanied by the formation of the Negro People's Theatre, composed of the casts of *Stevedore* and *Green Pastures*, in the summer of 1935; this became the core of the Federal Theatre's Lafayette unit. So the standing-room-only crowds that greeted the "magnificent and spectacular production of a Haitian *Macbeth*," as Roi Ottley called it in the *Amsterdam News*, were an expression of the political and cultural ferment in Harlem.[68]

Moreover, the narrative of Haiti's "black Jacobins" ran throughout Popular Front culture. C.L.R. James wrote not only his classic history, *Black Jacobins*, but a play, *Toussaint L'Ouverture*, which was produced in London with Paul Robeson; after the Haitian *Macbeth*, the Federal Theatre's black companies produced *Haiti* (in New York) and *Black Empire* (in Los Angeles); Langston Hughes reworked his Haitian play, *Emperor of Haiti*, in several forms, including the opera *Troubled Island*, composed by William Grant Still; Jacob Lawrence painted a sequence of history paintings on Toussaint L'Ouverture; and Arna Bontemps's *Drums at Dusk* and Guy Endore's *Babouk* were proletarian historical novels about the Haitian revolution. These representations had several sources. Toussaint L'Ouverture and the Haitian revolution had long been a part of African American culture: Leonard de Paur, the musical director of the Negro Theatre's *Haiti*, recalled a school debate over whether Toussaint L'Ouverture was a greater leader than George Washington. The end of the American military occupation of Haiti in 1934, the resurgence of anti-colonial struggles in the Caribbean, and the popular protests against Mussolini's invasion of Ethiopia all made the Haitian narrative an allegory of anti-colonialism. Moreover, at a time when Du Bois's *Black Reconstruction* was hardly recognized by the historical profession and the Communist historian Herbert Aptheker was just beginning his pioneering study of slave revolts, the story of Haiti's black Jacobins was one of the few narratives in American popular culture that allowed the representation of black insurrection.[69]

In the years after *Macbeth*, Welles remained active in Popular Front civil rights struggles. The majority of his FBI file tracks his involvement with black organizations like the Negro Cultural Committee. In 1941, Welles collaborated with two major African American artists, Duke Ellington and Richard Wright. The Ellington project grew out of Welles's interest in jazz. He had become friendly with Ellington and Billie Holiday in Los Angeles, and featured boogie-woogie pianist Meade Lux Lewis on the first radio broadcast of his "Orson Welles Show." During the run of Ellington's *Jump for Joy* in the summer of 1941, Welles and Ellington began collaborating on a film history of jazz, based around the life of Louis Armstrong. Ellington was to write the music, Armstrong was to play himself, and Hazel Scott of Café Society was signed to play Lil Hardin Armstrong. The project received much attention in the jazz press, since Hollywood had never made a serious film about jazz. However, the film was delayed by Welles's trip to Brazil and then canceled when RKO fired Welles. Had it been completed, it would have been a remarkable complement to Welles's "history plays": the history of Louis Armstrong would have taken its place next to the histories of Charles Foster Kane and the Amberson family.[70]

Welles continued to explore African American music during his 1942 trip to Brazil, where he was making a wartime "Good Neighbor Policy" documentary, *It's All True*, financed by RKO and sponsored by the federal Office of the Coordinator of Inter-American Affairs (headed by Nelson Rockefeller). *It's All True*, which began as a depiction of Rio's carnival, became a story of samba, "an illustrated musical constructed of Brazilian popular tunes." Welles recruited a number of major Brazilian performers, including the black comic actor Grande Otelo and black samba musician Pixinguinha. Welles and his assistant, Robert Meltzer, carefully researched Brazil's samba, and the project paralleled the "jazz story" project: "Samba, we learned, comes from the hills, so our picture had to be oriented to the hills." They began filming in the samba clubs of the *favelas*, to the outrage of RKO. "We are shooting the same stuff—carnival—recording the same songs—carnival sambas—and a large percentage of it is as black as a storm cloud," RKO's publicity man Tom Pettey wrote back to the studio. "We have a closed set, a studio full of jigiboos [sic] and a little set depicting a hut in the hills.... God, if I see another torso shot of a nigger wench waving her hips I'm going to shoot that French still man." Before Welles returned to the US in August 1942, RKO had terminated the Mercury contract.[71]

The footage that remains of *It's All True* is a remarkable contrast to Welles's US work; both the story of samba and carnival and the related political documentary about the protest of Brazilian fishermen, "Jangadeiros," are documentary depictions of working people. Welles's footage alternates between extraordinary crowd scenes and portraitlike close-ups. Shots of carnival are counterpointed to a slow funeral march. Episodes of dancing are mixed with long takes of work: building boats, trimming sails, lacemaking, women sewing on looms. The story of the fishermen from Fortaleza, reenacted by non-actors, is close in narrative and style to Paul Strand's left-wing documentary about Mexican fishermen, *The Wave (Redes)* (1937), and to Luchino Visconti's neo-realist tale of Sicilian fishermen, *La Terra Trema* (1948).[72]

Welles's collaboration with Richard Wright on the stage production of *Native Son* in 1941 was a major success (Figure 15). "We have already enough plays and movies showing Negroes in . . . traditional roles," Wright had written to Welles and Houseman. "Can such a book be done in a light that presents Bigger Thomas as a *human being?* . . . Bigger Thomas is not presented in 'Native Son' as a victim of American conditions or environment; neither is he presented as a boy destined to a bad end by fate. . . . [H]ere is a human being trying to express some of the deepest impulses in all of us through the cramped limits of his life." By all accounts (except the Hearst paper which complained that the play's "propaganda . . . seems nearer to Moscow than Harlem"), Welles's production captured both Bigger as a human being and the "cramped limits of his life." Led by "Canada Lee's great performance of Bigger," the cast brought together the white actors of the Mercury company with the black actors of the Negro Theatre (Lee had played Banquo in *Macbeth*). Lee, like John Garfield, with whom he appeared in the 1947 boxing melodrama *Body and Soul*, was a classic Popular Front proletarian star; an ex-boxer, he brought Bigger Thomas to life, in the words of one critic, "as a major dramatic character, thwarted, rebellious, tormented by the alternating rhythms of fear and hate and pride."[73]

The "cramped limits" of Bigger's life were captured in Welles's design: "the idea of framing each set within walls of dingy yellow brick was his," Wright told an interviewer. The curtain of yellow brick "held the various scenes together," the Popular Front's leading theater critic, John Gassner, wrote. "This design appears at the beginning when Bigger's home is thus framed, and is carried out to the very last scene, in which the brickwork of the condemned Negro's death-cell is continued straight through the lofty section of the prison revealed by the set. . . . [I]t was the wall of social circumstance or racial disadvantage that hems him in." Ironically, Gassner's only complaint about the play was that it failed to make Bigger "a victim of society": in this Welles had fulfilled Wright's intention.[74]

Native Son was the first of Welles's productions about trials, police, and the law. Welles framed the story of Bigger with trial scenes that took place on an apron stage in front of the proscenium arch, a form that Gassner likened "to the analytical 'epic' style that was previously exemplified by the work of Piscator and Brecht." The lawyer Paul Max, played by Ray Collins, stood at a railing on the apron and directly addressed the audience, as if they were the jury. Part of the power of *Native Son* was the way it resonated with left-wing defense campaigns from Sacco and Vanzetti and the Scottsboro Nine to the Harry Bridges and Sleepy Lagoon cases, in which Welles himself would become involved.[75]

The Sleepy Lagoon case began when seventeen young Chicanos were arrested in August 1942 for the murder of José Díaz. Two of the defendants were severely beaten by the police, and their trial took place in a lynch-mob atmosphere whipped up by Hearst headlines about a Mexican American "crime wave." Welles chaired a forum to raise money for the defense in November 1942, but the seventeen youths were convicted in January 1943. A Citizen's Committee for the Defense of Mexican-American Youth (which later became the Sleepy Lagoon Defense Committee) was organized by Chicana activist Josefina Fierro de Bright and was chaired by Carey McWilliams. Welles was a leading spokesman for the defense committee, and he was joined by several of his Mercury colleagues, including Joseph Cotten, Rita Hayworth, Dorothy Comingore, and Canada Lee. In June 1943, Welles contributed a foreword to the committee's pamphlet about the case. The committee drew on anti-Fascist rhetoric to attack the "Nazi logic" of the Los Angeles Sheriff's Office as well as "Falangists and Sinarchists" of the Mexican right. In October 1944, the appeals court overturned the convictions.[76]

Welles was also active in getting CBS to carry radio broadcasts in response to the race riots that had broken out across the United States in the summer of 1943. At a meeting of the left-wing Hollywood Writers' Mobilization, where it was agreed that a broadcast about the race riots should "show the Fascist nature of these outbreaks," Welles proposed "a melodramatic presentation of a spy story along the lines of 'Five Graves to Cairo,' 'Background to Danger.' . . . [W]hile the material must be well written, expertly produced, etc., . . . it should nevertheless be a popular exciting mystery story." One of the programs that resulted—William Robson's "Open Letter on Race Hatred"—was less a mystery than a newsreel about the Detroit riots, but Welles himself persuaded CBS to produce Howard Koch's radio drama "Snowball," the story of a black man framed for murder in a race riot.[77]

Perhaps Welles's most important radio production was his series of broadcasts about Isaac Woodward, a black veteran beaten and blinded by a South Carolina policeman in the summer of 1946. Welles used his radio show, "Orson Welles Commentaries," to bring the case to national attention. "I got in touch with Orson Welles through his agent," the NAACP's public relations director, radical cartoonist Oliver Harrington, later wrote, "and we corresponded by telephone every Saturday and he would make a broadcast every Sunday evening. It was a fantastically dramatic and interesting program in which he took the role of somebody out hunting down these men who had committed that crime. As a result, they actually discovered the two policemen who had done this." Welles's political drama began with a reading of Woodward's own affidavit, followed by a direct address to the policeman that the blinded veteran had been unable to identify, the "policeman ... who brought the justice of Dachau and Oswiekem to Aiken, South Carolina," "Officer X." Welles's narrative combined Shakespearean bombast with echoes of the Shadow:

> Wash your hands, Officer X. Wash them well. . . . You won't blot out the blood
> of a blinded war veteran, nor yet the color of your skin. . . . You'll never wash
> away that leperous lack of pigment . . . the guilty pallor of the white man. . . .
> What does it cost to be a Negro? In Aiken, South Carolina, it cost a man his eyes.
> What does it cost to wear over your skeleton the pinkish tint officially described
> as "white?" In Aiken, South Carolina, it cost a man his soul. . . . Who am I? A
> masked avenger from the comic books? No, sir. Merely an inquisitive citizen of
> America.

Welles made the search for Officer X a continuing and successful political drama; eventually, an eyewitness was found and it was discovered that Woodward had been taken off the Greyhound bus in Batesburg, a few miles from Aiken. Welles apologized to the town of Aiken, but the controversy led ABC to cancel his show.[78]

The Woodward case marked the end of Welles's US political career. By 1947, the anti-Communist purge had come to Hollywood, and one of the earliest victims was the Mercury radiowriter, Howard Koch. Welles, like Richard Wright, chose exile in Europe in the summer of 1947; he did not return until the fall of 1955 (except for a brief 1953 television appearance in *King Lear*). In December 1956, Welles began work on *Touch of Evil* (1958), his greatest pulp thriller, the story of the attempt to frame a young Chicano. It was Welles's most powerful portrait of domestic fascism, because it combined the crime melodrama of his Popular Front thrillers with the racial narratives of *Native Son* and the Isaac Woodward case. Welles's previous thrillers had never completely worked: *Mr Arkadin*'s shadowy tycoon was a pastiche of *Citizen Kane* without *Kane*'s historical ambitions; and neither the escaped Nazi of *The Stranger* nor the evil lawyers of *The Lady from Shanghai* had the mixture of power, evil, and charisma that Welles needed. But *Touch of Evil*'s corrupt policeman, Quinlan, embodied "Officer X": "the most personal thing I've put in this film," Welles told an interviewer, "is my hatred of the abuse of police power."[79]

Moreover, Welles's earlier thrillers had never succeeded in locating themselves in North America. *Journey into Fear* was essentially a European thriller, surpassed by Welles's own performance in Carol Reed's *The Third Man*, set in occupied Vienna; *The Stranger*'s escaped Nazi in Connecticut was not really convincing; and *The Lady from Shanghai* was set on an allegorical ship. *Touch of Evil*, however, rooted Quinlan in a social location, the Mexican border. Mexico had long been Hollywood's other, and several Popular Front filmmakers had directed border tales. William Dieterle's *Juarez* (1939) with Paul Muni was one of the Popular Front's favorite films, its story serialized in the *Daily Worker* and its shooting script published in *TAC*. John Huston's *The Treasure of the Sierra Madre* (1948) with Humphrey Bogart adapted B. Traven's popular proletarian novel; Joseph Losey's *The Lawless* (1950) depicted a California lynch mob pursuing a young Mexican American; Elia Kazan and John Steinbeck collaborated on the controversial story of the Mexican revolution, *Viva Zapata* (1952); and the blacklisted Paul Jarrico and Herbert Biberman made the classic strike film about Chicano zinc-miners in New Mexico, *Salt of the Earth* (1954). Welles himself added the border story to Paul Monash's screenplay of the hard-boiled thriller, *Badge of Evil*: he moved the story from a Southern California city to the border town of Los Robles, and made the hero a Mexican narcotics detective and the defendant a Mexicano. Moreover, Quinlan's racial slurs against Mexicans are a far more convincing index to an American fascism than *The Stranger*'s curious superman rhetoric or even Harry Lime's parable of the cuckoo clock.[80]

The Sleepy Lagoon case lies behind *Touch of Evil* just as the Harry Bridges case lies behind *The Lady from Shanghai*. Obviously, there is no literal connection between the cases and the films. However, *The Lady from Shanghai*'s Black Irish Mike—a radical sailor who fought in Spain, is described as a "notorious waterfront agitator," and is framed for murder in San Francisco—is a kind of funhouse metamorphosis of Harry Bridges, the radical Australian sailor and San Francisco waterfront leader whom the government spent a decade trying to deport. And the framing of young Manolo Sanchez by the corrupt policeman Quinlan in *Touch of Evil* is a similar metamorphosis of the Sleepy Lagoon case. In both cases, Welles mashes the overt political story into a pulp brew of race, sex, and power.

Touch of Evil is also the culmination of Welles's showmanship, a virtuoso display of filmmaking. The most famous example is the four-minute opening crane shot of Vargas (Charlton Heston) and his new wife (Janet Leigh) crossing the border only to be interrupted by the bombing of an American contractor. However, Welles himself tended to downplay that shot as "one of those shots that *shows* the director making 'a great shot'." "I think great shots should conceal themselves," Welles went on, and pointed to the "much more difficult crane shot in *Touch of Evil* which nobody ever recognizes as such; it runs almost a reel, and it's in the Mexican boy's apartment—it's in three rooms—where the dynamite is found in the bathroom.... It's much more a shot than the famous opening." Indeed, like the other great sequence shot that conceals itself— Quinlan's first interrogation of Sanchez, the young man he will frame— this shot contains the film's core narrative, the confrontation of Quinlan, Vargas, and Sanchez: the shot ends with Vargas shouting "You framed that boy. Framed him!" Welles drew attention to this shot because it united the film's form and content, its showmanship and politics.[81]

Those who live by magic die by magic, however, and *Touch of Evil* ends with one of Welles's most remarkable allegories of the apparatus: Vargas's use of the "listening apparatus," as Welles called it, to trap Quinlan into admitting his guilt. The feedback of the listening apparatus turns it into an audio house of mirrors in which the final shoot-out takes place. The anti-fascist Vargas uses the machine against the fascist Quinlan, but, as Welles remarked, the "job doesn't suit him.... He becomes the crude type who deliberately eavesdrops.... I tried to make it seem that the listening apparatus is guiding him, that he's the victim of the apparatus.... He doesn't know very well how to use his recording machine; he's able only to follow and obey it because this device doesn't really belong to him. He isn't a spy, he isn't even a cop." The devices of the mass media never really belonged to Welles; though he knew how to use his "recording machine," he too was as much a victim of the apparatus as its master, crafting his anti-fascist allegories that were, more often than not, recut and reedited by the studios he worked for.[82]

Many of Welles's projects—including *Touch of Evil* itself—exist only as ruins, incomplete fragments. Elia Kazan wrote that Welles, "the most talented and inventive theatre man of my day," was like "a great beached whale, driven onshore by a storm," one of those "whom the waves of thought and art in the forties, when they retreated, left stranded." Welles was not alone: Kazan realizes that he himself was a beached whale, his great Popular Front productions scarred by his HUAC testimony, his naming of names. But Welles's ambitions, accomplishments, and failures remain the most fitting emblem of the unfinished labors of the cultural front itself.[83]

11

"Who's Afraid of Big Bad Walt?" Disney's Radical Cartoonists

(with Holly Allen)

Legend has it that the clowns who sing the song "We're Gonna Hit the Big Boss for a Raise" in Walt Disney's 1941 feature *Dumbo* were "malicious caricatures of striking Disney Studio cartoonists" done by the strikebreakers. Whether or not the Disney strike of 1941 was immortalized in film, it has become part of Hollywood legend, a central event and turning point for Disney Studios, the studio labor unions, the Hollywood Red scare, and animated film generally. The 1941 strike marked the end of Disney's classic period, its golden age; out of the strike emerged two of the key actors in the post-war Hollywood battles: Herb Sorrell's progressive labor alliance, the Conference of Studio Unions, and the anti-labor, Red-baiting producers group initiated in part by Walt Disney, the Motion Picture Alliance for the Preservation of American Ideals. The strike also helped provoke the July 1941 hearings of California's "little HUAC," the Tenney Committee, which foreshadowed the post-war Un-American Activities Committee investigations and the blacklist. The radical animators who came together in the strike subsequently created a new language for animation at UPA (United Productions of America), the most acclaimed post-war animation studio.[1]

In 1941, Disney was at the peak of his success. The popularity of Mickey Mouse and the Silly Symphonies in the early 1930s had encouraged Disney to attempt a full-length animated feature film. *Snow White and the Seven Dwarfs*, which premiered in December 1937, met with extraordinary critical and popular acclaim. As Robert Feild wrote in 1942, "With the advent of *Snow White*, something so challenging happened that we could no longer merely sit back and condescend. We became aware that the days of the animated cartoon, as we had known it, were over." In the wake of *Snow White*, the Disney Studio expanded: the 200 employees of 1935 had grown to 1100 by 1940, and a state-of-the-art studio had been built in Burbank. Work had begun on three new features: *Pinocchio*, *Fantasia*, and *Bambi*. In

1940, both *Pinocchio* and *Fantasia* were released, and Disney was recognized by American and European intellectuals as one of the great innovators of American culture, held in the same regard as Chaplin. "If I were asked to list the most important movie activity of 1937 ten years from now, I should have only one item to report," Pare Lorentz wrote after *Snow White.* "Walt Disney made a full length movie. . . . Disney is as unique today as Chaplin." In 1942, the first book-length scholarly study of Disney, Harvard art historian Robert Feild's *The Art of Walt Disney*, celebrated Disney's union of "the Arts and Sciences" and carefully analyzed the aesthetics of animation.[2]

But the spring of 1941 found contradictions within Disney's world. The outbreak of war in Europe had substantially cut into film revenues; neither *Pinocchio* nor *Fantasia* recovered the monies invested in them; and the Disney Corporation was forced to seek outside capital through a public sale of stock in 1940. The expansion and relocation of the studio changed the working conditions for the animators, ending the moment when the studio was an intimate and informal, if paternalistic, community.

Meanwhile, the film industry, like the mass-production industries of automobiles, steel, rubber, and textiles, faced an insurgent industrial union movement. The long jurisdictional battles between the AFL craft unions and IATSE (International Alliance of Theatrical Stage Employees) had apparently been resolved by the Studio Basic Agreement in 1926, but unhappiness with the corrupt and racketeering IATSE spurred several groups of insurgents—dissidents in IA, Herb Sorrell's Painters (who had been forced out of the Studio Basic Agreement), and CIO organizers backed by Harry Bridges—to create a series of alternative alliances to IATSE: the Federated Motion-Picture Crafts (which lost a strike in 1937); the United Studio Technicians Guild (which lost an election in 1939); and, most successfully, the Conference of Studio Unions (which emerged in the wake of the Disney strike in 1941).

After the defeats of the CIO at Ford and Little Steel in the spring of 1937, and in the recession that followed, the national industrial union drive had waned considerably. It was not until 1940 that an economic boom, kicked off by war mobilization, cut unemployment and raised prices, igniting a new wave of labor militancy. In the spring of 1941, the losses of 1937 were reversed, as Ford signed a union contract with the United Auto Workers (UAW) and the Little Steel corporations reached agreements with the Steel Workers Organizing Committee (SWOC). Across the nation, but particularly in California, the CIO industrial unions moved to organize the new defense plants: the success of the November 1940 UAW strike at Vultee Aircraft in Los Angeles was followed by one of the largest strike years on record. As one labor historian has noted, "one out of every twelve workers took part in a strike at some point in [1941]." In June 1941, federal troops were used to break the UAW strike at North

American Aviation in Los Angeles. In the midst of this insurgent spring, the confrontation between Disney and the Screen Cartoonists Guild erupted in a walkout on 29 May 1941, initiating a strike that would last throughout the spring and summer and whose repercussions were felt for a decade to come.[3]

"Who's afraid of big bad Walt?" the strikers asked in the comic strip they published in *Friday* (Figure 16). Though Walt Disney's anti-union, anti-Communist account of the strike has dominated most histories, the 1941 Disney strike stands as a powerful emblem of the culture industry unionism that formed the base of the cultural front. The striking cartoonists and the union organizers wished not only to redress their immediate grievances but to restructure work and politics throughout the motion picture industry. Moreover, the radical animators who came together in the strike went on to reshape animated film, creating a Popular Front vision of cartoons "beyond pigs and bunnies."

1. The Sorcerer's Apprentices: Cartoonists on Strike

The cartoonists strike at the Disney Studio began on 29 May 1941, following an organizing drive by the Screen Cartoonists Guild. Cartoonists in the film industry had begun to organize in the mid 1930s, but with little success. The independent Screen Cartoonists Guild had been founded by animators in the Hollywood studios in 1936; and, in the first labor conflict in the animation industry, the Commercial Artists and Designers Union (AFL) had won a bitter strike in 1937, after organizing cartoonists at the New York-based Fleischer studio. In 1940, the cartoonists had turned for help to Herb Sorrell, the business agent of the Painters, and the Screen Cartoonists Guild was chartered as a local of the International Brotherhood of Painters, Decorators and Paperhangers (AFL). The Screen Cartoonists Guild was divided into three units, representing the major animation studios: MGM, Schlesinger (of Warner Brothers), and Disney. By May 1941, animators at MGM and Schlesinger were "a hundred percent organized," according to Sorrell; the SCG had won contracts with MGM and, after a six-day lock-out that coincided with the opening days of the Disney strike, with Schlesinger.[4]

Disney animators were more difficult to organize. As cartoonist Shamus Culhane recalls, many of the animators at Disney considered themselves a caste apart, because of the commercial and artistic preeminence of Disney animations and the superior training that Disney animators received at the studio's internal art school. As the leading firm in the business, Disney could afford to accommodate its animators' artistic integrity, making its employees the envy of others in the business. From the outside, being an animator at Disney meant having ample time and optimal resources to do animated productions well. Thus, establishing the Screen Cartoonists Guild at the Disney Studio meant that the gifted Disney animators would be included in a craft community with animators at other studios, promising a new level of creative achievement and craft equality in the industry.[5]

But to say that Disney animators were considered the best and most privileged in the industry is not to suggest that their working conditions were ideal. The cartoonists had long been subject to Disney's paternalism, which took the form of poor wages and arbitrary wage scales, long hours without pay for overtime, and total submission to Disney's executive authority in studio operations. Neither salaries nor working conditions were systematized under Disney's regime. "I felt that the union was necessary because there was no rhyme or reason as to the way the guys were paid," animator Willis Pyle recalled. "You might be sitting next to a guy doing the same thing as you and you might be getting $20 a week more or less than him." Since Disney felt that men and women should not work together, the "girls" who worked in the lowest ranks as inkers and painters were in a separate building and often received less than subsistence wages. Animators in training at the Disney art school sometimes were paid as little as six dollars a week on the pretense that they were students, not workers, even though they did many hours of tedious tracing work. When these "students" reached the end of their education, they were often dismissed and replaced with fresh novices. Throughout the ranks of the animators, increases in wages and benefits were unevenly distributed and depended on one's standing with Disney himself.[6]

Moreover, cartoonists at Disney did not receive professional screen credits for their work, despite the fact that, unlike the other unionized workers at the studio, they were viewed as "artists" rather than "technicians." Indeed, for the art historian Robert Feild, who studied the Burbank studio during 1939 and 1940, "one of Walt's great accomplishments" was "to recover that great workshop tradition . . . in which the artist as worker is dedicated to the fulfillment of a purpose and is satisfied to remain anonymous." However, cartoonists became increasingly unhappy with anonymity, and with Disney's policy of crediting himself for work that was completed by a variety of artists. This disgruntlement reached a high point once the studio began to produce feature-length animated films, for Disney did grant participating animators screen credits on *Snow White*, thus giving the animators new stature in the professional community. The precedent of screen credits for features created a ground swell of agitation for screen credit for all Disney animations, and this sentiment contributed to the strike.[7]

Not only were animators denied screen credits, but all of their work, even that done away from the studio on non-Disney characters, belonged to Disney. "That was the principal fight," SCG business agent Bill Pomerance recalled. "He had them tied up to individual contracts that we did away with ... he claimed that everything they drew belonged to him." Disney's paternalism had always been pronounced at the studio, but it reached a crisis point in 1940 and 1941 with the growth and relocation of the company. The onset of war disrupted the celebrated move from Hyperion Avenue to vastly expanded company quarters in Burbank, a move accomplished on credit in anticipation of continuing financial success. Not only did this move leave Disney 4.5 million dollars in debt in 1940, it also radically changed the work atmosphere for studio cartoonists. Accustomed to working in closer contact with Disney himself and with each other, cartoonists now found themselves part of a much larger and more clearly demarcated workforce, in which the strategy of paternalism lost much of its effectiveness.[8]

Yet Disney's paternalism persisted, as exemplified by the conditions surrounding the public sale of Disney stock. In 1940, Disney first attempted to gain leverage with his employees by convincing them that the studio was facing severe financial difficulties. He proposed wage cuts and temporary lay-offs, after having failed to come through with bonuses promised in lieu of overtime for work completed earlier on *Snow White*. Then he astonished many of the animators by turning around and more than recouping his losses through the public sale of company stock. He even gave some company stock to employees in the hope that it would keep more of the stock closer to company hands, but the stock was distributed on a typically arbitrary and unequal basis, increasing dissatisfaction.[9]

The groundwork for a strike was laid early in the fall of 1940, when the Screen Cartoonists Guild began its organizing drive at Disney. Throughout early 1941, the SCG appealed to the National Labor Relations Board to recognize the Disney unit and to censure Disney for unfair labor practices for fostering a company union. These pleas were still pending in late May, when Disney's refusal to recognize the SCG and his decision to lay off union activists precipitated the strike. The lay-off of twenty-four cartoonists, including top animator Art Babbitt and other members of the SCG, was intended as a purge of SCG activists and was accompanied by rumors of a lock-out. Despite Sorrell's efforts to discourage a strike because the SCG organizing drive was not complete, the Disney cartoonists voted to begin a walkout on 29 May until SCG demands for recognition and a settlement were reached.

The walkout split the studio, with approximately half of the one thousand cartoonists going out. Only a small number of the women inkers and painters struck. "Those of us who went on strike," Mary Eastman recalled, "were really scared." Large picket lines were maintained outside company gates, yet many cartoonists drove through. All accounts attest to the increasing bitterness between strikers and nonstrikers as the weeks went by. "Cries of 'fink,' 'scab,' and other epithets were hurled against the non-strikers, who retaliated by calling strikers 'commies'," Jack Kinney recalled. The hostilities were aggravated by the cartoonists' inexperience in labor actions: "I was very naive as far as the labor movement was concerned but most of my friends were planning to go on strike," Willis Pyle recalled. "I really hated going out on strike, but I couldn't have stayed in because of the people I would have passed on the picket line." From the other side, Jack Kinney remembered that "those of us who crossed the picket line were in shock. We were naive, having never been exposed to the workings of capital and labor."[10]

The cartoonists strike took place at a time of increased government involvement in labor struggles; only a week after it began, the United States Labor Conciliation Service stepped in to mediate the conflict. However, the government mediators had a difficult task in front of them, because Disney proved to be recalcitrant in the face of the strikers' demands. According to several accounts, his behavior was juvenile and ill-advised, and his primary tactic was to intimidate the strikers. Animation director Jack Kinney recalled that on the first day of the strike Disney had enlarged photographs of the picket lines made and placed on the walls of his office. He then made it known to all nonstrikers that he could identify picketers individually, thus instilling fear into anyone who might consider joining the strike. He would also later note the presence on the picket lines of people whom he could not identify personally, a claim he used to reinforce his argument that the strikers were not actually his own employ-ees but were outsiders brought in by Sorrell.[11]

Disney's account of the strike depicted it as a simple jurisdictional dispute between the loyal employees who belonged to the company union and the disloyal members of the SCG, whom he would characterize as Communist agitators or dupes. Without acknowledging the lay-off of SCG activists, Disney later insisted that he refused to comply with Sorrell's demand for SCG recognition because his employees were already repre-sented by a company union. He claimed to have told Sorrell that the union could only be unseated by a National Labor Relations Board election, whereupon Sorrell called the strike then and there, in order to preempt an election that might have favored the company union.[12]

According to Sorrell, Disney's effort to cast the SCG strike at his studio as a jurisdictional dispute provoked by outside Communist influences was a bald attempt to prevent meaningful union representation for what he (Disney) considered to be a privileged segment of his workforce. The company union at Disney was just that: it reinforced the interests of the company and was not effective in ensuring satisfactory working conditions for cartoonists at the studio. Some of its officers, like Art Babbitt, switched over to the Screen Cartoonists Guild once the organizing drive was undertaken at the studio. In the midst of the strike, Disney's company union was cited by the National Labor Relations Board as an unfair labor practice; however, as Sorrell would later observe, Disney responded to the NLRB citation simply by changing the company union's name and resuming its activities.[13]

In some ways, the strike *was* a jurisdictional battle, for not only did the SCG vie with the company-sponsored union at Disney, but it also challenged the powerful jurisdictional authority of the International Alliance of Theatrical Stage Employees. Throughout the late 1930s, the IATSE in Hollywood was dominated by racketeers; despite the fact that its leaders were facing charges of extortion in the spring of 1941, they managed to interfere in the SCG strike. The IATSE had long been hostile to Sorrell and opposed the Painters' intervention. Since both the IATSE and the Painters were members of the AFL, the dispute over who should organize the cartoonists had consequences for AFL internal politics. Meanwhile, the emerging Congress of Industrial Unions was seeking to gain entry into the studio system; CIO organizers waited eagerly in the wings throughout the SCG strike in the hopes that the IATSE and the Painters would reach an impasse that would give them an opening in the industry.[14]

In this context, the vision of a cartoonists union that represented its own members and allied them with other members of their craft and with other workers in the industry was a radical and contested notion. Sorrell was accused of being "CIO-minded" and a "Communist" during the strike. When the Disney strike led California State Senator Jack Tenney to begin his hearings on un-American activities in July 1941, Sorrell was the first witness called. The subsequent success of the SCG drive at Disney, followed by Sorrell's creation of the Conference of Studio Unions (CSU), represented sufficiently radical challenges to the labor status quo in Hollywood to make Sorrell and the organizations he sponsored frequent targets of the vitriolic anti-labor politics of the years to come.

The strike lasted nine weeks. As befits a cartoonists strike, it had its lighter moments. The Disney strikers were renowned for the humor and originality of their picket signs, and they were aided in their anti-Disney gags by their fellow craftsmen at Warner Brothers. A veteran of many strikes, Sorrell recalled that

> it was particularly picturesque because these artists insisted on depicting everything in their picket lines . . . it was their duty when off the picket line to make gags and signs. . . . The kids hung an effigy of Gunther Lessing [Disney's attorney], with the red hair, in front of the gate upon a pole. Disney had made a picture . . . the *Reluctant Dragon*. One day the picket line assumed a dragon three or four blocks long, the head weaving, with Disney's face as the dragon's face. . . . There were all kinds of things like this. . . . Then, lo and behold, about

five o'clock would come along the Schlesinger group in automobiles decorated all about Disney. The fact of the matter is, Mr. Schlesinger's artists, I think, spent all their time making up gags about Disney, so that when work was out they picketed him with them.

The Disney strikers also published comic strip accounts of the strike in both *PM* and *Friday*.[15]

Throughout the strike, the cartoonists received considerable support from other unions and consumer groups. The Society of Motion Picture Film Editors voted to support the strike, and the processing of Disney films at the Technicolor, Williams, and Pathe labs ceased, at least for a time. Disney products were placed on the unfair lists of both the AFL and the CIO. In addition, Disney strikers supported union locals in other labor disputes in Los Angeles; UAW leader Richard Frankensteen told of seeing picket signs drawn by Disney cartoonists at the North American Aviation strike, which was broken by federal troops in June.

Pickets went up in Los Angeles and elsewhere at theaters where Disney shorts and features were being shown; such actions received the support of Popular Front organizations like the League of Women Shoppers and Film Audiences for Democracy. In the middle of the strike, the League of Women Shoppers sent Disney a letter, telling him that they had "recently asked the Hollywood League of Women Shoppers to investigate the strike taking place at your studio.... The League ... is a consumers' organization where thousands of members believe in using their buying power in such a way as to help workers attain decent living standards and working conditions. We never, in a labor dispute, support either the workers or the management without a full and impartial investigation by one of our League investigating committees." The letter notified Disney that upon completion of its investigation "[t]he committee voted to support the striking employees" and "is sending a full report of the investigation to all branch Leagues, with the recommendation that they notify their members and all sympathetic organizations of the facts and of our decision."[16]

The negative publicity affected Disney deeply. Throughout his 1947 testimony before HUAC, Disney tied his charges of Communist influence in the strike to the strikers' ability to mobilize a wide-reaching network of publicity in order to "smear" him and his movies. Sorrell was a Communist, he said, because "[w]hen he pulled the strike the first people to smear me and put me on the unfair list were all of the Commie front organizations. I can't remember them all, they change so often, but one that is clear in my mind is the League of Women Voters [Disney would later amend this from "Voters" to "Shoppers"], the *People's World*, the *Daily Worker*, and the *PM Magazine* in New York. They smeared me. Nobody came near to find out what the true facts of the thing were."[17]

"I even went through the same smear in South America," he told investigators, "and generally throughout the world all of the Commie groups began smear campaigns against me and my pictures." In fact, the South American story testified to the inventiveness of the strike's organizers and their effective use of bluffs to bring about a favorable settlement. At the time of the strike, the Roosevelt government was attempting to reinforce its wartime geopolitical interests in South America by pursuing what it termed a "Good Neighbor Policy." Under this policy, which included cultural exchange, the Rockefeller Commission for the Development of Cultural Relations with South America made Disney a "Goodwill Ambassador," and a tour was planned to several South American cities. Disney's departure was temporarily delayed by the strike at his studio, until finally he was convinced to leave the country and let the government settle the strike in early August. His departure came as a relief to government conciliators, who subsequently were able to reach a settlement favorable to the strikers on 6 August. However, when the company threatened another lay-off of 207 strikers (as compared to only 47 nonstrikers) on 15 August, it provoked another two-week shutdown at the plant, and SCG business agent Bill Pomerance helped to settle things once and for all.[18]

"Disney made one mistake," Bill Pomerance recalled. "He accepted the government's proposal that he go on a goodwill trip to South America. . . . Whereupon I got in touch with Blackie Myers [the leader of the National Maritime Union], and he gave me the names of the heads of the unions in South America in the cities where Disney was going to visit . . . so I wrote all these people about Disney and asked if they would do something when I gave the signal. I didn't propose what; they had enough trouble of their own. I wired the State Department and the Labor Department who had handled the case, promising that I was going to have Disney picketed in South America." "Labor organizations in South America are being contacted and arrangements are being made to picket the Disney tour and his pictures," Pomerance's telegram to the State Department read. "It is not our desire to do a thing to embarrass the Administration in South America, but we must insist that the company immediately comply with all terms of the government's award and make immediate adjustments of the monies due employees. The State Department should insist that the Disney company comply with American standards of fair treatment of labor . . . before permitting Disney to represent the United States as a goodwill ambassador in South America."[19]

The SCG telegram led the Labor Conciliation Service to invite representatives of both sides to come to Washington, D.C., and the strike was settled. The settlement reached was very favorable to the strikers: it included nondiscriminatory reemployment of all those on the payroll as of 15 May 1941; permanent reinstatement of the twenty-four employees discharged before the strike; equalization of pay; establishment of a system of salaries and classifications; severance pay; a draft clause providing six weeks' payment for draftees; and a grievance clause. All this established the SCG as the collective bargaining representative for the Disney cartoonists. The settlement left Disney a bitter man. As a founding member (and first vice president) of the Motion Picture Alliance for the Preservation of American Ideals and as a "friendly" witness before HUAC, Disney used his anger over the strike and his growing hostility to the radical labor movement to fuel the Red-baiting reaction of the post-war years.[20]

Disney's lurid accusations—in the midst of the strike, he published an open letter in *Variety* claiming that "communistic agitation, leadership, and activities have brought about this strike"—were discounted by the striking animators themselves. One said that "there weren't more than three or four leftists in the whole studio," and another recalled that "later, I heard that there may have been some communists involved in that [the union]. Well, this was news to me; I had no idea that there were any communists involved in that strike." Six years later, when Disney was asked by the House Committee on Un-American Activities who the Communists were, he named "one artist in my plant," David Hilberman: "he came in about 1938, and he sort of stayed in the background, he wasn't too active, but he was the real brains of this and I believe he is a Communist." Hilberman was indeed a key organizer in the strike and a central figure in the emerging group of radical cartoonists. And, in 1953, Charlotte Darling Adams, a secretary of the SCG, did testify before HUAC, naming the names of her fellow Communists among the cartoonists and maintaining that the small group of Communists in the Guild worked "mainly in support of the organization."[21]

The division between strikers and nonstrikers was less one of communism, as Disney would later ask HUAC investigators to believe, and more one of generation and work experience. Animators who had been with Disney since the early days at Hyperion Avenue and who owed their entire art education to the studio fell on one side of the picket line, while the younger, more artistically innovative cartoonists who occupied the lower rungs of the job ladder at the factorylike Burbank studio fell on the other.

But not all of the strikers were of this younger generation; two of its central figures were among Disney's most established and prominent animators: Art Babbitt and Bill Tytla. Babbitt, the renowned creator of Goofy, the mushroom dance in *Fantasia*, the wicked stepmother in *Snow White*, and Geppetto in *Pinocchio*, had been an executive of the company union and had agitated for a militant stance before the SCG arrived at Disney. He then switched allegiance to the SCG out of disgust with the company union's lack of autonomy from management. An advocate of fair wages and work conditions, Babbitt was fired for insisting that his assistant receive a salary closer to his own. Well respected among the younger generation of animators, his dismissal triggered the strike.

Also on the outside with the strikers, Bill Tytla was widely believed to be one of Disney's best animators; the "Michelangelo of animation," he was responsible not only for Dumbo but for many of the great Disney villains, including *Pinnochio*'s Stromboli and *Fantasia*'s Yen Sid. For both Tytla and Babbitt, participation in the strike was less a matter of personal grievance than of principle: "I went on strike because my friends were on strike," Tytla explained. "I was sympathetic with their views, but I never wanted to do anything against Walt." Both Babbitt and Tytla served as exemplars to the younger strikers artistically and politically. "People like Art and Bill had everything to lose and nothing to gain by going out on strike," said Bill Melendez, one of the strikers. "They weren't underpaid, but they felt honor-bound to do something for the lower echelons." Tytla's disillusionment with Disney and his return to New York after the strike was one of Disney's greatest losses. While Babbitt defied Disney's vow that he would never be rehired by staying on at the studio for a year after the strike, many of the younger strikers like John Hubley and Zachary Schwartz followed Tytla's lead by leaving the Disney studio altogether, taking both their considerable talent and their political vision with them.[22]

Animators at Disney still refer to the strike of 1941 as "The Strike"; they view it as a central event that closed the door on Disney's golden age. While Disney himself would claim that the strike was a blessing in disguise, enabling him to oust politically radical malcontents, its legacy for the studio was more ambiguous. Certainly, as Disney admitted to HUAC investigators, staffing and production at the studio were reduced by more than half in the wake of the strike. Animator Shamus Culhane commented that "the esprit de corps that made possible all the brilliant films of the 1930s was as dead as a dodo."[23]

For the strikers, the strike was at least temporarily successful in challenging the established practices of company paternalism and IATSE racketeering. The strike victory enabled Herb Sorrell to form the Conference of Studio Unions, an industrial union for the film industry. For the animators, it affirmed their vision of themselves as both artists and workers, and as members of a broader social movement. The radicalism of this sentiment was reflected in the Red-baiting backlash that it provoked, and in the exodus of many strikers from the studio. For them, the politics of the strike would transform the politics of animation.

2. Animation Learns a New Language

The 1941 strike marked more than a turning point in Hollywood labor relations, more than a transformation in the Disney Studio: it also marked the emergence of a group of radical animators whose craft had been nurtured in the Disney Studios, but whose politics had been formed in the Popular Front. Though the strike's most visible figures were Art Babbitt and Bill Tytla, two of Disney's most important animators, the heart of the strike lay in a group of younger artists—including David Hilberman, John Hubley, Phil Eastman, Zachary Schwartz, Steve Bosustow, Phil Klein, Eugene Fleury, Bill Hurtz, Willis Pyle, Ade Woolery, Leo Salkin, and Bill Melendez—whose work over the next two decades would help reshape animated film.

Not only were the radical animators of the Disney strike militant unionists, they also sought to create a new language for animation, to combine the extraordinary technical advances they had made in creating the Disney features with a radical social and political content and meaning. This Popular Front vision of animation underlay the formation of UPA, the animation studio that was to break from the Disney model and chart new directions in animation in the years after the Second World War.

The young cartoonists were, for the most part, of the depression generation, in their late twenties and early thirties at the time of the strike. Some had come out of Southern California art schools, particularly Chouinard Art Institute. As Chuck Jones, the great Warner Brothers animator, recalled, "those of us who had gone to Chouinard Art School in Los Angeles, where could we work? We could go into commercial art or we could go into animation." For those who went into animation, Disney's studio was the most exciting and innovative; it seemed, in John Hubley's words, "like a marvelous big Renaissance craft hall." However, as Bill Hurtz later said, "the younger people were also sufficiently independent and didn't have stars in their eyes about Walt, so that when the strike came at Disney's they were the leaders. They had knocked about during the depression, and they had some kind of social consciousness." That social consciousness was developed in the political climate of the California left in the late 1930s.[24]

Some of the animators became members of the Communist Party; others were part of the broad California labor left, whose political face was the Democratic Federation for Political Unity, formed in 1938 to support the successful gubernatorial campaign of Culbert Olsen. The voice of the California left was the *People's World*, which featured popular columns by Woody Guthrie and Mike Quin. Harry Bridges, the radical leader of the longshoremen and the Pacific Coast CIO director, was the left's emblem of militant labor, and they rallied to his defense when the federal government tried to deport him. A variety of cultural and political journals emerged in the midst of Popular Front politics, among them *Equality*, *Black and White*, and *Films for Democracy*.

Several of the radical animators had come together in the late 1930s in a small Communist Party cartoonists group. Half a dozen in number, they included David Hilberman, a layout artist at Disney who had studied at the Leningrad State Theater in 1932, Libby Hilberman, Phil Klein, and Charlotte Darling Adams, an inker and background artist at Leon Schlesinger Productions. Adams's story is a common one: one of the many low-paid "girls" who traced the drawings onto the "cels" in ink and painted on the colors, she came to the Communist Party through a combination of union and cultural activities. While working at Schlesinger Productions and beginning to organize a union, she was also taking classes on the social history of theater and helping out at the left-wing Contemporary Theatre in Los Angeles. As in the case of many Communists, her union activity preceded her Party activity: "my reason for joining the party," she later told the HUAC investigators, "was to organize the union." Adams served as the secretary of the Screen Cartoonists Guild in 1936–37 and was the guild's delegate to the Studio Unemployment Conference, which Herb Sorrell convened in 1939.[25]

The strike moved a number of animators to the left, leading them to form professional and political alliances with the radicals. After the strike, some of the Disney strikers, including Phil Klein, David Hilberman, John Hubley, and Zachary Schwartz, were hired by Frank Tashlin at Columbia for a brief moment of experiment: as Hubley said, "Under Tashlin, we tried some very experimental things; none of them quite got off the ground, but there was a lot of ground broken. We were doing crazy things that were anti the classic Disney approach." Others, including Phil Eastman and Eugene Fleury, moved to Schlesinger/Warner Brothers; Fleury, an instructor in Disney's training school, joined Bernyce Polifka and John McGrew as layout artists experimenting on highly stylized backgrounds with Chuck Jones, one of animation's great innovators.[26]

In March 1942, *The Animator*, a magazine edited by Hubley, Eastman, and Fleury, expressed the emerging if still somewhat abstract vision of the radical animators: "a progressive, intelligent approach to animation, and realization that it is an expressive and not a mechanical medium, is imperative if we want to keep animated cartoons from stagnating. Development and growth of animation is dependent upon varied, significant subject matter presented in an organized form, evolved from elements inherent in the medium." The next four years would see the beginnings of a fulfillment of these hopes.[27]

One avenue that brought "significant subject matter" to animated films was the US entry into the war. While the studios enlisted Bugs Bunny and Donald Duck in propaganda films for the general public, the former Disney animators were making humorous training cartoons for servicemen that broke with many Hollywood conventions: Eastman was writing the Private Snafu cartoons at Warners; Hubley, Bill Hurtz, and Willis Pyle joined the animators in the army's First Motion Picture Unit making the Trigger Joe cartoons. The anti-Fascist war also reinvigorated the California Popular Front, giving new life to left organizations that had been embattled by the Red scare of 1940 and 1941. The war years were stimulating, Edwina Hammond Pomerance recalled, "the activity there was vigorous and always hopeful ... wherever I'd go, people were enthusiastic about what was happening in California." The Communist Party achieved its widest appeal and largest membership during these years, dissolving itself as a party in May 1944 and becoming a part of the larger labor-left alliance as the Communist Political Association.[28]

A number of animators, painters, and sculptors in Hollywood came together in the war years in a Communist motion picture group. The group included cartoonists like John Hubley, Phil Eastman, Cecil Beard, Maurice Howard, Charlotte Darling Adams, Alice Provenson, John McGrew, and Zachary Schwartz, and artists like Edward Biberman, Kate Lawson, Eugene Fleury, Bernyce Polifka Fleury, and Edwina Hammond Pomerance, as well as the business agent of the Screen Cartoonists Guild, Bill Pomerance. Active in a variety of Popular Front and labor politics, they often provided posters for rallies and events.

Like other Popular Front artists groups, the Communist cartoonists were drawn together by their position as artists within the culture industry, as they tried to reconcile their personal aesthetics, the collective, highly rationalized work demanded by the studios, and their anti-fascist socialist politics. They met informally in each other's homes to discuss contemporary politics as well as the artist's place in society. A lecture by Edward Biberman, a painter and WPA muralist, on Marxism and art generated a memorable discussion over the responsibilities of artists, with vehement disagreements over Biberman's advocacy of social realism. Edwina Hammond Pomerance, an artist in the group, recalled that "we did think art was terribly important and I think there were members particularly in the hierarchy who thought realistic art was most important. That's easily understood, most people think that.... The social realists were in New York, for the most part, and they were older, by ten or more years.... We were more influenced by Klee and Miro and the Surrealists." Edward Biberman, she recalled, was "a realist. He didn't like the kind of thing we were doing, I don't think. He was a dear, sweet man. He encouraged us anyway."[29]

The animators too were reaching beyond social realism—they associated realism with Disney's aesthetic. "Whenever you talked with John Hubley or Phil Eastman," Edwina Hammond Pomerance recalled, "you talked about pictures, about art and politics ... there was constant talk about technique in cartoon-making." Like the painters, the animators were developing a visual style out of European and Soviet modernism: John Hubley recalled that "in the early days it was Picasso, Dufy, Matisse that influenced the drive to a direct, childlike, flat, simplified design rather than a Disney eighteenth-century watercolor." The Soviet modernisms that had so influenced the radical theater and film collectives of the depression years were crucial for the animators as well: David Hilberman had studied at the Leningrad State Theater in the early thirties, and John Hubley recalled that "a Russian cartoon showed up on the Disney lot one day, brought by Frank Lloyd Wright. It was very modern, with flat backgrounds, highly stylized characters, modern music. It was very exciting and had a big influence on me."[30]

In the fall of 1943, the radical animators outlined their political and aesthetic project at the UCLA Writers' Congress, which was organized by the Hollywood Writers' Mobilization, the key left cultural organization in Hollywood in the war years. Sponsored by the screen guilds, including the cartoonists, it began as a clearing house for wartime activities ranging from speechwriting and troop entertainment to producing radio plays and documentary films; as the war went on, it became an important cultural alliance on the left, increasingly concerning itself with the shape of the post-war world. At the October 1943 Writers' Congress, the committee of animators was chaired by Zachary Schwartz, and both Hubley and Eastman spoke on cartoons.

Hubley's talk, "The Writer and the Cartoon," is one of the clearest statements of the vision of the radical cartoonists. The central problem of the art of cartooning, Hubley argued, lies in the relation between narrative and image, "the medium of storytelling and the medium of graphics." Historically, this mixture of story and caricature had made the cartoon a popular social form; cartoons had always been "a comment on the times and problems of the people." However, the twentieth-century comic strip and animated cartoon "drifted away from the cartoon's original role as a commentary on the contemporary scene," substituting technical perfection and a focus on "gags." The emergence of Disney marked a "great period of formal and technical development," but even the Disney films that reflected contemporary social forces did so inadvertently: "story men avoided anything labeled 'social' in writing for what they considered a 'pure' medium." Storytelling was reduced to "a single action situation," particularly struggles between characters and natural forces or between characters and mechanical props: "Pluto stuck in flypaper, Pluto swallowing a flashlight, Pluto swallowing a magnet, the Duck caught in a washing machine. . . ." For Hubley, "'Fantasia,' became the ultimate example of the entire creative skill of animation artists devoted to serving the form."[31]

Against this formalism, Hubley proposed the example of Chaplin, who "utilized essentially the same abstract symbolism that cartoons have continually used," but whose "stories have been written in terms of human behavior and broad social caricature." Disney's name had long been linked with Chaplin's as the two great innovators of American film, but the Popular Front animators increasingly used Chaplin as a model against Disney, setting the political and social ambitions of *Modern Times* and *The Great Dictator* against Disney's *Snow White* and *Fantasia*.[32]

While Hubley criticized the "limited conception of the function of the story in the cartoon ('The gag's the thing,' and 'As long as it gets laughs')," Phil Eastman criticized the technical limitations of the animation industry: "why are we so graphically out of date?" In themes that would continue to inform the work of the radical animators, Eastman called for "more extensive use of satire" and "the wider use of human caricature" ("beyond pigs and bunnies," as Hubley was to put it in a 1975 essay). Both Hubley and Eastman cited Chuck Jones's satiric "The Dover Boys," which lampooned the Frank Merriwell-type college boy story, as an example of the directions animation should be taking.[33]

The ideas of the radical animators began to take visual shape in several independent political cartoons sponsored by the Hollywood Writers' Mobilization and the United Auto Workers. In 1943, John Hubley did the animated sections of a Mobilization-sponsored documentary about the American electoral process, *Tuesday in November*. In 1944, a number of the cartoonists came together to produce an animated film for the labor movement's political campaign. The CIO's Political Action Committee (CIO-PAC) had been founded in the summer of 1943 to provide an organizational base for labor political action and support for Roosevelt's reelection campaign in 1944. CIO-PAC also developed a "People's Platform of 1944," a wide-ranging plan for social welfare, Keynsian planning, and an Economic Bill of Rights. As part of this labor political initiative, the left-led Education Department of the United Automobile Workers approached Bill Pomerance about producing an animated campaign film. The UAW's Education Department had been actively trying to develop a film production program to accompany their summer schools, correspondence courses, pamphlets, and radio programs. Pomerance contacted Hubley, then stationed with the Army's First Motion Picture Unit, and Hubley, together with Eastman and Bill Hurtz, prepared the storyboard for *Hell-bent for Election*. The UAW Education Department then brought the film to David Hilberman and Zachary Schwartz, who had rented studio space; together with another former Disney striker, Steve Bosustow, they formed Industrial Films and Poster Service to produce the film in time for the August 1944 Democratic convention.[34]

With a small budget, the work was done largely at night by freelancers and volunteers; Chuck Jones directed the film, and Earl Robinson and "Yip" Harburg wrote the song "Gotta Get Out and Vote" for it. "It was one of the most exciting and fulfilling experiences of my life," Schwartz, the production designer, said, "and I could probably say the same for everyone else who knocked himself out to deliver that picture on time." The film was a success, shown non-theatrically to approximately four million people. One UAW local education director reported that the film was "very powerful . . . in organizing and effectively working toward the re-election of President Roosevelt." The fifteen-minute color cartoon caricatures Roosevelt and Dewey as two trains on parallel tracks, the Win the War Special and the Defeatist Limited, with Joe Worker at the switch. When a Senator Blow lulls Joe to sleep with champagne and cigars, Joe dreams that the Defeatist Limited gets through with its anti-labor boxcars. Joe awakens in time, throwing the switch that derails the Defeatist Limited and sends the Win the War Special on to victory.[35]

The film's success led Industrial Films and Poster Service, which changed its name to United Productions of America (UPA) in 1945, to produce more films and filmstrips for the army, navy, and defense contractors: the highly regarded *Flat Hatting*, directed by Hubley, was part of the "Flight Safety" series done for the navy. But UPA continued its ties to the labor movement: Steve Bosustow spoke at the UAW's 1945 Education Conference, commending the union's "stand to produce its own films . . . using the professional people who for years have studied to produce the type of information that you want told on screen."[36]

The second UAW project was an animated film on race, intended to help in Operation Dixie, the post-war organizing drive in the South. *The Brotherhood of Man*, based on a 1943 pamphlet, *The Races of Mankind*, by Columbia anthropologists Ruth Benedict and Gene Weltfish, was scripted by Hubley, Eastman, Maurice Rapf, and Ring Lardner, Jr (who in 1947 was to become one of the Hollywood Ten and was later imprisoned), and directed by Robert Cannon. An eleven-minute color film, it uses animation to dissolve skin colors and physical features into one another, while its narrative depicts the overcoming of a little green man, suspicious and hostile, within each of the characters, ending with a multi-racial group in working clothes. It was shown throughout the country by unions and religious groups in February 1947 (Figure 17).[37]

The film was the political high point of the Popular Front UPA, and a stylistic turning point. Hubley later remarked that "we went for very flat stylized characters, instead of the global three-dimensional Disney characters. It was very influenced by Saul Steinberg and that sharp-nosed character he was doing at the time. . . . Paul Julian did all the backgrounds very flat; he used areas of color that would be elided from the line. Very advanced graphics for that period." A *New York Post* reviewer said of these early UPA films that "not since the first Disney cartoons established new standards of humor, art and animation for the movie cartooning industry has anything as startling as these pictures and their makers come along."[38]

The script and a number of stills of *The Brotherhood of Man* were published in an early issue of *Hollywood Quarterly*, the post-war left-wing film journal that had grown out of the Hollywood Writers' Mobilization and the 1943 Writers' Congress. The same issue featured a manifesto by Hubley and Schwartz, "Animation Learns a New Language." The brief essay summarized the wartime reevaluation by animators and argued for the unique possibilities inherent in the medium, particularly its ability to "visualize areas of life and thought which photography was incapable of showing." They concluded by declaring: "we have found that the medium of animation has become a new language. It is no longer the vaudeville world of pigs and bunnies. Nor is it the mechanical diagram, the photographed charts of the old 'training film.' It has encompassed the whole field of visual images. . . . We have found that line, shape, color and symbol in movement can represent the essence of an idea, can express it humorously, with force, with clarity."[39]

The Brotherhood of Man was the high point of the left cartoonists' vision of a stylistically innovative and political animated film, and its moment was short-lived. Hilberman and Schwartz sold out their interest in UPA to Bosustow in 1946, in part because of tensions between the partners, and in part because of Hilberman's interest in helping to establish animation studios in the post-war Soviet Union. The 1946 purge of the left-wing in the UAW's Education Department ended the connection between the union and UPA. In the fall of 1947 the left screenwriters and directors were subpoenaed, and the hopes for a post-war Popular Front died in the midst of the Cold War and the anti-Communist purges.[40]

The blacklist hit the radical animators hard, particularly after HUAC's 1951–53 series of hearings about Hollywood. A few of the cartoonists— Bernyce Polifka Fleury, Eugene Fleury, Charlotte Darling Adams, and Zachary Schwartz—testified as "friendly" witnesses before the House Committee on Un-American Activities, informing on their former comrades. Phil Eastman, Bill Pomerance, and John Hubley were called in front of the committee and refused to cooperate. Right-wing blacklisting newsletters like *Counterattack* and *Alert* picked up the testimony and targeted producers and advertisers. In the wake of the hearings, John Hubley, Phil Eastman, and Bill Scott resigned from UPA; Bill Hurtz recalled that "we were all on the lists of sympathizers or otherwise from the Disney strike on. We were all busy in labor activities, making labor films. . . . Columbia [the distributor of UPA films] sent us a list of people who had to go or they'd yank the release. . . . People volunteered to leave, rather than sink the studio— because it was that bald: either these guys left or the studio went under. Those of us who were labeled 'com-symps' stayed."[41]

After selling their share of UPA, Hilberman and Schwartz had joined Bill Pomerance in setting up Tempo, which had become one of the three largest New York animation studios producing television commercials. In 1952 and 1953, *Counterattack* targeted Tempo, going after the advertising agencies, and Walter Winchell attacked them in his column: "we were cut by all the agencies that we did business with," Pomerance recalled, "and I was forced to sell the business."[42]

Nevertheless, the years of the Red scare, what Dalton Trumbo called the "time of the toad," saw some of the best work of the radical animators, and of left filmmakers generally. In a fine essay on the left in Hollywood, Thom Anderson suggested that the best work of left directors and screenwriters in Hollywood came not at the height of the Popular Front, but in the years between 1947 and 1951, in a genre of films he calls *film gris*, which "may be distinguished from the earlier *film noir* by its greater psychological and social realism": it includes Robert Rossen's *Body and Soul*, Abraham Polonsky's *Force of Evil*, and Nicholas Ray's *They Live by Night*. "The filmmakers who created *film gris* were Browderite Communists and left-liberals," Anderson argues. "During the war they had enthusiastically made patriotic films, and at the beginning of 1945 they had shared Browder's optimism about the postwar world. Anything seemed possible if the energies harnessed to win the war could be utilized to build a better society." But as Joseph Losey, one of the left *film gris* directors, said, "after Hiroshima, after the death of Roosevelt, after the investigations, only then did one begin to understand the complete unreality of the American dream."[43]

If *film gris* depicted that unreality in bleak black and white, a similar political tone is captured in the post-war UPA cartoons. There were no further UAW films made at UPA after *The Brotherhood of Man*; though the stylistic innovations of *Hell-bent for Election* and *The Brotherhood of Man* were continued, the optimism of those labor cartoons gave way to a bleaker satiric vision in the critically acclaimed UPA cartoons of Mr Magoo and Gerald McBoing Boing. These owed much to Hubley's vision of getting beyond pigs and bunnies; as Bill Melendez said, recalling Hubley's crucial role at UPA: "Hub could draw like nobody else—very expressive drawings that would capture the essence of almost anything, in a style that was completely opposite of what was at Disney and the rest of the industry. I always felt that it was Hub that started us in the direction of cari-caturing humans, rather than animals." The UPA cartoons were flat, two-dimensional: "animation with no unnecessary drawings," Melendez called it. UPA artists sought to avoid both "Disney cute" and "Warner Brothers humor." The stubborn, near-sighted Mr Magoo, created largely by Hubley, seems to be an elaboration of the suspicious little green man inside each of the characters in *The Brotherhood of Man*. The world of the crotchety Magoo and of the boy rejected by his parents and schoolmates for his inability to talk—he goes boing-boing—is far from the triumph of the Win the War Special and the multi-racial call for brotherhood. In the collapse of the Popular Front and the vision of a post-war "Century of the Common Man," the radical animators created a new language for animation and a powerful caricature of the unrealities of the American dream.[44]

12

American Culture and
Socialist Theory

One of the earliest manifestations of the cultural front was, as I have said, the 1932 publication of the pamphlet *Culture and the Crisis* by a group of intellectuals who came together as the League of Professional Groups for Foster and Ford. "The struggle for the emancipation of society from the blight of capitalism is not only an economic question," they wrote, "it is a cultural question as well. Both in theory and practice, capitalism is hostile to the genuine culture of the past and present and bitterly opposed to the new cultural tendencies which have grown out of the epic of working class struggle for a new society." They spoke out on "behalf of a new cultural renaissance." I have explored the cultural renaissance that grew out of the Popular Front movement, as artists—Dos Passos, Olsen, Wright, Guthrie, Blitzstein, Ellington, Holiday, Welles, among others—represented the struggles of the age of the CIO. However, this laboring of American literature, music, and film was accompanied by a laboring of American thought, as socialist thinkers challenged dominant intellectual traditions, particularly in the study of culture.[1]

This socialist intellectual tradition has often been ignored and suppressed, as three influential accounts of the "thirties" came to serve as screen memories, versions of the events told as part of the formation of post-war disciplines and professions. The emerging profession of literary criticism focused its attention on the left-wing *literary* debates of the 1930s, carving a myth of origin out of the history of *Partisan Review*. In this story, the Popular Front intellectuals—usually referred to as fellow travelers—were not "intellectuals" at all, but were anti-modernist philistines, celebrating middlebrow kitsch; the New York intellectuals, epitomized by Lionel Trilling, took their stand against the Popular Front in formulating their own practice of literary and art criticism as cultural critique. The emerging American Studies movement was more indebted to the Popular Front, but the euphemism and caution of the Cold War years obscured its political roots and ended up turning the totemic figure of F.O. Matthiessen into the founder of a new nationalist canon. Moreover, the culture concept, which had, by mid century, become "one of the key notions of contemporary American thought," seemed to be synonymous with conservative notions of organicism and consensus. Though "the idea of culture was anything but new in the 1930s," Warren Susman has written, there was a "general and even popular 'discovery' of the concept of culture ... [I]t is not too extreme to propose that it was during the Thirties that the idea of culture was domesticated." "The discovery of the idea of culture," Susman concluded, "... could and did have results far more conservative than radical, no matter what the intentions of those who originally championed some of the ideas and efforts."[2]

For the cultural critics of the New Left, like Susman himself, the Popular Front was a discredited kind of corporate liberalism, a sentimental and nationalist populism epitomized by the films of John Ford and Frank Capra. "It is true that socialists in America have never been able to sustain a mass movement," Susman wrote in 1974, "but ... why have we produced no Luxemburg, no Gramsci, no Lukács, no Gorz, no Althusser—no theoretical contributions to the great discussion Marx began well over a century ago? why have we produced no school of social analysis equal to the work of the Frankfurt School to help us come to an understanding of the nature of our industrial society? why no school of historical scholars in the tradition of the English *Past and Present* group, for example, to make it possible for us to understand our past and present?" Few have challenged Susman's account of the poverty of American Marxism.[3]

In fact, the 1932 pamphlet *Culture and the Crisis*, the *Port Huron Statement* of its generation, written by what might now be thought of as an "interdisciplinary" group—a Marxist economist, a literary critic, a historian, a philosopher, and a poet who had worked in advertising agencies—was part of a rich and often forgotten American Marxism. Though the ambitions of the League of Professionals were not realized—they did hold a lecture series on "Capitalism and Culture," but the plans for a magazine and for a book to survey the state of American culture never materialized— the league stands as an emblem of the emergence of a generation of radical intellectuals who developed a tradition of socialist cultural studies in the United States.[4]

This is not to suggest that there was a "cultural studies" movement in the middle decades of the twentieth century, nor that there was an "American" parentage for the cultural studies that has largely been imported from Great Britain. Rather, the revival of a radical conception of culture in the "cultural studies" that has emerged in the decades since Susman rendered his judgement (his influential essay first appeared in 1970) allows us to challenge the configurations we have inherited from the historians, critics, and memoirists of the last half century, and to reconsider the intellectual work of the Popular Front in new ways. The Cold War anti-Communist purge of the culture industries and state cultural apparatuses left a deep cultural amnesia, as radical intellectuals were jailed, lost jobs, were deported or went into exile, were unable to publish, reedited their earlier work and downplayed their earlier affiliations, or, in some cases, killed themselves.

For the Western Marxists Susman invoked were not part of a visible "tradition": Lukács, Gramsci, and the Frankfurt School were exiles and prisoners, hardly read or known in their own time. They were reclaimed by a New Left: "Western Marxism" was invented in the process of reconstructing it. The work of the radical intellectuals of the Popular Front must also be reconstructed and reclaimed: their theoretical contributions and social and cultural analysis are often obscured by the legacy of sectarian conflict, self-censorship, and intellectual repression. Sidney Hook, Kenneth Burke, Louis Adamic, Carey McWilliams, Oliver C. Cox, Elizabeth Hawes, Sidney Finkelstein, and C.L.R. James: they, among others, are the American "Western Marxists." Their attempts to "Americanize" Marxism by fusing it with pragmatism; their exploration of culture as both the means of communication and the ways of life of communities and peoples; and their engagement with the popular or vernacular arts: all remain powerful contributions to any emancipatory cultural studies.

1. The Americanization of Marx

One of the authors of *Culture and the Crisis* was a young New York University philosopher, Sidney Hook. Born in 1902 in Brooklyn's Williamsburg, the child of working-class Jewish immigrants, Hook had been formed by the socialist milieu of City College, where he studied with Morris Cohen. After writing a dissertation directed by John Dewey, Hook traveled to Europe, attending the lectures of the Marxist theorist Karl Korsch in Berlin in 1928 and doing research in Moscow's Marx-Engels Institute in the summer of 1929. By the early 1930s, he was one of the most accomplished American Marxist theorists. His first book, *Towards the Understanding of Karl Marx* (1933), drew on Lukács's *History and Class Consciousness* and Korsch's *Marxism and Philosophy*—both had appeared in 1923 but neither was available in English—for an eloquent exposition of Marx's theory and method. Like Lukács and Korsch, Hook criticized the mechanical Marxisms of the Second International and recovered the Hegelian roots of Marxism. He emphasized "the role of activity in Marxism, as contrasted with the mechanical and fatalistic conceptions of the social processes which prevail in orthodox circles," and the notion of totality—"every society for Marx is a structurally interrelated cultural whole"—over any notions of economic determinism. In addition, he adopted Lukács's pathbreaking analysis of reification, the process by which "the social relations between human beings are 'thingified' into impersonal, automatic laws."[5]

Hook's work bears striking resemblances to that of the other Western Marxists. Like Hook, many of the Western Marxists were professors of philosophy and cast their discussions in philosophical terms. Their work was largely a discourse of commentary and exegesis—works "on Marxism, rather than in Marxism," as Perry Anderson puts it—and they were preoccupied with questions of method, and questions of the "superstructure"—that is, culture, aesthetics, and ideology—rather than questions of the "base"—that is, political economy or imperialism. Hook, like his contemporaries, reconsidered Marx's Hegelian legacy, and thoroughly rejected Engels's natural philosophy and his attempt to build a complete *Weltanschauung* of dialectical materialism.[6]

But Hook was not simply a translation of Lukács and Korsch; he also shared what Perry Anderson has called "the most striking single trait of Western Marxism as a common tradition": "the constant presence and influence on it of successive types of European idealism." If Western Marxism is best defined as the encounter between national philosophical traditions and Marxism—the engagement of Lukács with Weber and Simmel, of Gramsci with Croce, of Adorno and Marcuse with Freud, of Sartre with Heidegger and existentialism, of Althusser with the structuralisms of Levi-Strauss and Lacan—then Hook's engagement with Dewey's pragmatism made it a distinctive form of US Western Marxism. Trained in the pragmatist tradition, Hook recast Marxism in the philosophical vernacular of the United States; his book remains one of the most powerful "Americanizations" of Marx.[7]

Hook's attempt to unite Marxism and pragmatism was not unprecedented. Virtually all the attempts to "Americanize" Marxism adopted the idiom of pragmatism. US Marxism had developed largely among German American socialists in the late nineteenth and early twentieth centuries, and its major works—like Louis Boudin's *The Theoretical System of Karl Marx* (1907)—addressed the debates within German social democracy. In the face of this, a leading Socialist Party theorist, William English Walling, tried to unite Marxism and pragmatism in the 1910s, but his work had little lasting impact. The first major "American" revision of Marx was Max Eastman's *Marx, Lenin and the Science of Revolution* (published in the United States in 1928). Eastman, like Hook, had been a student of Dewey, and Hook's hostile review of Eastman's book in V.F. Calverton's *Modern Quarterly* provoked a debate over the relation between Marxism, pragmatism, and the United States that lasted almost two decades and shaped the most influential American book about Marxism for a generation, Edmund Wilson's *To the Finland Station* (1939).

Eastman was, in the late 1920s, one of the foremost American leftists. The child of Yankee Congregationalist ministers, he was teaching aesthetics at Columbia in 1912 when he became a Socialist and the editor of the *Masses*. A flamboyant figure in Greenwich Village's bohemia, he helped found the Communist Party and spent two years in the Soviet Union, where he became close to the left opposition around Trotsky. Eastman began with the issue of American exceptionalism—why Marxist theories and programs had not taken root in the United States—and concluded that the barrier was the German metaphysics Marx inherited from Hegel. He wanted, he told Trotsky, "to clear out of this revolutionary science the last vestiges of the influence of Marx's bourgeois philosophy teacher. It is the only form in which Marxism will ever take root in the Anglo-Saxon intelligence." Fortunately, he argued, Lenin and the Bolsheviks had demonstrated the efficiency of the core of Marx's thought, "the science of revolutionary engineering." Though the Bolsheviks persisted in a "theological" worship of dialectical materialism, Eastman would complete their revision by, in John Diggins's apt word, exorcising Hegel.[8]

For Eastman, the whole problem with Marxism was Hegel. Marx never broke with his idealist, theological self: the Hegelian journey of Mind through History was merely turned upside down in the theological worldview of dialectical materialism, in which History, now conceived of as material production, advances by negation and contradiction to the "inevitable" socialist society. That this acceptance of a disguised Hegelianism became part of the fatalistic German Marxism of the Second International and, despite the assertion of will by the Bolsheviks, of the orthodox dialectical materialism of the Soviet Union, Hook did not deny. The attack on this "Hegel" was part of most Western Marxisms (usually couched in terms of rejecting the "dialectic of nature," the notion that nature itself obeys dialectical laws) from Lukács to Althusser. It involved a critique of orthodox Marxism's notion of history as an unfolding series of predetermined stages, gradually moving toward fulfillment in communism, and of its notion of the social whole as entirely determined by the forces of production, the so-called economic determinism.

However, Eastman and Hook embodied the two different responses that followed from this critique of Second International Marxism. Eastman, like the Western Marxists who were in contact with anti-Hegelian philosophies and non-positivist conceptions of science, denounced all of Hegel as ideological, animistic, and unscientific. Indeed, he dismissed all philosophies as animisms and held out a pragmatic and technical notion of science as purposive engineering. Marx and Marxism, he repeated endlessly, was merely a form of "animism," the essentially religious attempt "to transfer your own wishes into the external world, and so get them realized." The dialectic is a form of mysticism, the projection into history and nature of a wished-for movement toward an "inevitable" revolution. However, for Eastman, no complete rejection of Marxism was warranted, since the "rejection of illusions—religious, moralistic, legal, political, aesthetic—is the immortal essence of Marx's contribution to the science of history, and to history itself." Thus, the point was to "take the revolutionary motive back out of 'history,' where Marx and Engels surreptitiously projected it, and locate it in the human breast where it belongs."[9]

Eastman's variation on the Enlightenment debunking of religion was largely derived from the work of Thorstein Veblen, as is indicated in the crucial term "animism." However, without Veblen's self-corroding ironies, Eastman's debunking often took on the anti-intellectual character of the tough, practical man "who is not accustomed to taking holidays in libraries." Eastman is the only Marxist theorist who sometimes reads like Dashiell Hammett. He adopted a functionalist conception of thought, as an instrument for adjusting the dynamic organism to its complex environment. To the Marxist critique of "vulgar," that is, mechanical, materialism, Eastman replied that vulgar meant profane; hence, his vulgar materialism was the more anti-theological conception. Moreover, though he recognized the affinities between his "affirmative scientific skepticism" and the pragmatism of William James and John Dewey, he rejected James as an animistic thinker and criticized Dewey for not giving up philosophy after having shown the unreality of its potential problems. "Why not suggest," Eastman asked, "that 'philosophers' devote themselves, say, to the more fruitful and more needed task of clearing up the defects in Ford motors?" The ambiguity in Eastman's formulation—should they clear up the technical defects in Ford's motors or the social defects in Ford's company—runs throughout his work. Eastman's Marxism was a thorough-going pragmatic instrumentalism.[10]

The other half of Eastman's revision of Marxism was summed up in his view of Lenin, "the first purely scientific engineer of revolution." Lenin "converted Marxism, albeit unconsciously, from an antiquated Hegelian philosophy into a modern engineering science." Here too echoes of Veblen, with his "soviet of technicians," can be heard. But Eastman's position was based on a much closer interpretation of the events in the Soviet Union. Like the young Gramsci, who called the Bolshevik Revolution a "revolution against *Capital*," Eastman saw the Soviet Revolution as an act of will, not of historical necessity; the fact that Russia was not an advanced capitalist nation disproved the Marxist theories of the necessary stages and preconditions to socialist revolution. Lenin led a revolution in a country where it was "*philosophically* not to be permitted." The distinctive innovations of Lenin, including his continual changes in program and slogans—the "policy of the sharp turns"—were evidence of his engineering flexibility.[11]

It was not the soviets, those prototypes of workers democracy, to which Eastman was drawn, but the Leninist party, "the creation of an organization of purposive revolutionists capable of standing above and outside all specific forms and formulations, using them and discarding them according to their transitory relation to a more general social purpose." The party combined "certain essential features of a political party, a professional association, a consecrated order, an army, a scientific society." For all his enthusiasm for the Bolshevik engineers, Eastman was not uncritical of them, and it was precisely their institutionalization of dialectical materialism that he refused. The Bolsheviks were as reactionary in theory as they were progressive in practice. Moreover, he saw that the end of private property did not entail the "necessary" liberation of women or the withering away of the state, and he called on the Bolsheviks for further acts of revolutionary engineering.[12]

Hook, like the Western Marxists who had been shaped by the post-Hegelian philosophies reacting against nineteenth-century positivism, reclaimed Marx's Hegelian legacy by stressing Hegel's method over his system. Marxism was not a science but a critical theory. "Whereas Marx projected it [the materialistic conception of history] as a *method* of understanding and making history," Hook argued, "his disciples have tried to convert it into a *system* of sociology." Though Hook's background in pragmatism made him less wary of the word "science" than, for example, the Frankfurt School theorists, his conception of Marxism is that of critical theory. Thus, Hook attacked both of Eastman's major arguments, defending the Marxist dialectic against the charge of "animism" and challenging Eastman's "engineering conception of Marxism."[13]

Against Eastman's accusation of animism, Hook maintained that there is nothing a priori about Marxism: it was historical, naturalistic, and empirical. For Hook as for Lukács, Marxism was fundamentally a method, "criticism based on the observable tendencies of social development." The dialectical method was, Hook argued, built around "Marx's startling anticipation of the pragmatic theory of knowledge and truth": the activity of mind in perception and knowledge; and the test of practice as the verification of knowledge. Drawing from Marx's *Theses on Feuerbach* (1845), Hook argued that Marx, unlike Engels, Lenin, and the "orthodox" Marxists, rejected a "spectator" theory of knowledge. Ideas were not "copies" or "reflections" of reality, as in mechanical and contemplative materialisms. Rather, "the starting point of perception is ... an *interacting process*," embodied in practical activity. Human thought is functional because it comes from "the standpoint of the doer not the spectator." Thus, the verification of thought lies not in a supposed correspondence of idea to reality, but in practice, in the changing of the world. "Marxism therefore appears in the main as a huge judgment on practice, in Dewey's sense of the phrase, and its truth or falsity (instrument adequacy) is an experimental matter. Believing it and acting upon it helps make it true or false."[14]

This did not, however, justify Eastman's assertion that Marxism was "the science of revolutionary engineering." "No more eloquent commentary upon the 'Marxism' of the parties of the left in this country can be found than their helplessness before the 'bluff common sense approach' of the American engineer," Hook wrote. First, historical materialism was a theory of the limits set upon practice by economic and social structures: "In order to show that the sentimentality of the Utopians and the mere criticism of the left Hegelians, no matter how well intentioned, were instrumentally useless, Marx pointed to the economic structure of society which controlled and set the limits of effective action." Second, Eastman's technocratic celebration of the engineer created a cult of leadership at odds with communist ideals, separating the "scientists" of revolution from the working class and turning a dictatorship *of* the proletariat into a dictatorship *over* the proletariat. Unlike Eastman, who celebrated the role of the Party, Hook outlined an alternative conception of workers councils and workers democracy.[15]

Eastman attacked Hook's position as "dialectical pragmatism," Marxism as "if Marx had studied under Dewey," and the debate continued until the editor of *Modern Quarterly* (which had become *Modern Monthly*), V.F. Calverton, called it quits in September 1933; by then it had declined into ad hominem attacks and charges of plagiarism, incompetent scholarship and distorted interpretation. Before it was over, however, Dewey himself, as well as Louis Boudin, Waldo Frank, Reinhold Niebuhr, and Bertrand Russell, had contributed to the controversy. This controversy over the "Americanization" of Marx was not merely theoretical. Both Eastman and Hook were opposed to the Communist Party's uncritical stance toward the Soviet Union and Soviet Marxism, and their theoretical arguments were intended to develop an American communism that would be independent of Soviet politics and that would address the particularities of the United States. This became the basis for an important, if short-lived, formation of dissident communist intellectuals around V.F. Calverton's *Modern Quarterly*, who became involved in one of the radical parties that emerged in the militant upheavals of 1933 and 1934, the American Workers Party.[16]

Calverton's *Modern Quarterly* was an important radical journal in the early years of the left-wing cultural front, bringing together radical intellectuals of a variety of tendencies. In its heyday, between 1927 and 1931, it was the voice of the modernist turn to the left, conducting a debate with the apolitical literary experimentalism of Eugene Jolas and *transition*, publishing a series of pathbreaking articles and anthologies on "sex radicalism," as well as running the Hook-Eastman debate. Calverton's New York salon brought together figures like Eastman, Hook, Louis Adamic,

Mike Gold, and Matthew Josephson. In the early 1930s, *Modern Quarterly* was caught in the splintering of the Communist Party, as both the "left opposition," those sympathetic to Trotsky, led by James Cannon and Max Shachtman, and the "right opposition," led by Jay Lovestone and Bertram Wolfe, had been expelled and formed new parties in 1928 and 1929. A number of these dissident communists became associated with Calverton's magazine, and in 1933 and 1934 *Modern Monthly* began to call for an Americanized Marxism and an American labor party. These themes were echoed in pamphlets by Calverton—*For Revolution* (1932)—and Bertram Wolfe—*Marx and America* (1934)—as well as in Leon Samson's *Toward a United Front: A Philosophy for American Workers* (1933).

Samson's book was an idiosyncratic but symptomatic exploration of American exceptionalism: "If now American society is ripe for socialism and the American working class for revolution, the question once more arises: Why, then, is the socialist revolution so remote from the American scene?" Samson, a *Modern Monthly* contributor, dismissed the classic explanations—prosperity, the frontier, ethnic and racial heterogeneity— and argued that "Americanism is to the American not a tradition or a territory, ... but a doctrine—what socialism is to a socialist ... a solemn assent to a handful of final notions—democracy, liberty, opportunity, to all of which the American adheres rationalistically much as a socialist adheres to his socialism—because it does him good, because it gives him work, because, so he thinks, it guarantees him happiness. Americanism has thus served as a substitute for socialism. Every concept in socialism has its substitutive counter-concept in Americanism, and that is why the socialist argument falls so fruitlessly on the American ear." Samson analyzed this Americanism—its utopianism, its theatricalism, and its pragmatism—in a sweeping interpretation of American culture and history, and then returned to "the idea of Americanizing socialism [which] is as old as the movement . . . Instead of finding for Marxism an American mask, discover in Americanism the kernel of a Marxist meaning." Samson's book, which concludes with a call for an American labor party, was neither a scholarly study nor a political treatise. Rather, it stands with Emerson's *The American Scholar* and Van Wyck Brooks's *America's Coming-of-Age* as a speculative exploration of the "national character" and as such is a remarkable document of the ferment of the early depression.[17]

In late 1933, several of the dissident communist intellectuals including Calverton, Hook, and James Rorty took up the call for an American labor party and joined the radical labor leader A.J. Muste and his Conference for Progressive Labor Action in founding the American Workers Party (AWP). The American Workers Party was an important part of the militant labor upsurge in 1934, organizing Unemployed Leagues as well as the Toledo Auto-Lite strike, which triggered a general strike. The *Modern*

Monthly became the unofficial organ of the AWP, and Max Eastman and Edmund Wilson joined its editorial board. However, in late 1934 the AWP merged with the Trotskyist party and lost its identity in the more orthodox Leninism of the new Workers Party, led by Cannon and Shachtman. Muste and most of the AWP intellectuals, including Calverton, Hook, and Rorty, left the new party.

Ironically, when the Communist Party itself adopted the "Americanizing" strategies and rhetoric of the American Workers Party and became supporters of the broad-based Popular Front social movement, the veterans of the AWP attacked not only the Communist Party but also the larger social movement. Hook, who had been an eloquent critic of the Communist attack on social democrats as "social fascists" in the early 1930s, adopted a similar rhetoric against the Popular Front: "A Socialist who calls for the formation of a Popular Front cannot do so without in effect surrendering his socialism," Hook wrote, "no matter what he says in his heart ... A Socialist who supports a Popular Front government may find that as a result of its program of defense of capitalism, it may open the gates to the Fascists." However, other figures who had been influenced by Calverton and *Modern Monthly*, like Kenneth Burke and Louis Adamic, developed a Popular Front engagement with American culture that paralleled the earlier work of the dissident communists.[18]

The last, and most interesting, gasp of the dissident communists was their founding of an independent Marxist theoretical journal, *Marxist Quarterly*, in 1937: Lewis Corey was its managing editor. Though it lasted only three issues, it explored American history and culture, publishing Louis Hacker's studies of American economic history, Meyer Shapiro's work on abstract art, Hook's "Dialectic and Nature," as well as reconsiderations of the work of Dewey and Veblen. By the early 1940s, however, their attempt to develop an independent American Marxist theory had gone the way of their independent Marxist politics. Calverton died at the age of forty in 1940, an increasingly isolated figure. Eastman and Wilson had both abandoned the editorial board of *Modern Monthly* in 1935. In 1940, Eastman revised and expanded his *Marx, Lenin and the Science of Revolution* into a thorough repudiation of Marxism, *Marxism: Is It Science?*, which included his critique of Hook, now entitled "The Americanization of Marx." By 1940, Hook had also concluded that "Marxism as a movement is dying," though he remained indebted to Marx's thought: in his autobiography he claimed that "the thesis" of his first book, *Towards the Understanding of Karl Marx*, "still ... has much to be said for it historically." Anti-communism dominated the work and thought of Hook and Eastman in the years after World War II: "I no longer believe that the central problem of our time is the choice between capitalism and socialism but the defense and enrichment of a free and open society against totalitarianism," Hook wrote. Both enlisted in the cultural Cold War, supporting the post-war purge of Communists and Popular Front leftists, and both became intellectual activists in the New Right.[19]

Nevertheless, the Eastman-Hook debate had two enduring legacies for the understanding of Marxism in American intellectual life. First, the most influential American study of Marx and Marxism in the age of the CIO, Edmund Wilson's classic narrative *To the Finland Station*, was deeply indebted to the Eastman-Hook debate. Unfortunately, Wilson had been persuaded by Eastman's caricature of Marx's dialectical method: he concluded that "the Dialectic ... is a religious myth, disencumbered of divine personality and tied up with the history of mankind ... From the moment that they [Marx and Engels] had admitted the Dialectic into their semi-materialistic system, they had admitted an element of mysticism." Hook's careful refutations of Eastman and his own powerful exposition of Marx's thought were largely forgotten in American culture, as Wilson's redaction of Eastman's Marx became the common sense of American intellectuals for a generation. It was not until 1971 that the philosophical richness of the Marxist tradition was recovered by a second generation of works by US Western Marxists, particularly Bertell Ollman's *Alienation* and Fredric Jameson's *Marxism and Form*.[20]

Second, the uneasy synthesis of Marxism and pragmatism that Eastman and Hook represented did not end with their turn to the political right. C. Wright Mills, whose work brought together many of the unfinished debates of the cultural front, represented a powerful if incomplete synthesis of the pragmatism that was the subject of his dissertation—posthumously published as *Sociology and Pragmatism*—and the Marxist tradition he surveyed in his last work, "a primer on marxisms," *The Marxists* (1962). The relation between pragmatism and Marxism remains central to US socialist thought, since pragmatism is not simply a philosophical school but is an organic part of popular ideology.

Pragmatism developed together with the cultural institutions of modern American capitalism: the schools, universities, and Progressive intellectual journals whose history Mills examined; as a result, it has always served both ideological and utopian ends in American culture, at once the philosophical expression of what Mills called "crackpot realism" and the source of a continuing tradition of democratic thought. Pragmatism is an idiom, a vernacular, that inflects a wide range of American social, educational, aesthetic, and political thought, not only, in Hook's words, "the bluff 'common sense' of the American engineer," but the Deweyan common sense of American teachers and the folklore of American liberalism and "progressivism." Thus, the antinomies of pragmatism—whether expressed in the everyday distinction between the "pragmatic" and the "ideological" or in the contradictions of Dewey's democratic theory—are not simply ideological phantoms or errors; they are the sedimented accumulations of American culture and history. Any Marxism that would seek to interpret, and to change, that history, must be tempered in its pragmatism. Though the pragmatic Marxism of the young Sidney Hook is one of the ruins of the cultural front, a victim of Eastman's (and Wilson's) "pragmatic" dismissal of any dialectical theory and of Hook's own obsessive anti-communism, it remains an emblem of an American Marxism.[21]

2.   Means of Communication: Kenneth Burke's Symbolic Acts

Virtually all of the major studies of left-wing cultural criticism in the age of the CIO have focused on *literary* criticism. In part, this is because literary criticism enjoyed a moment of excitement and prestige, suspended between the literary manifestos and "cultural" reflections of the modernists, like T.S. Eliot's "Tradition and the Individual Talent," and the professionalizing zeal of the new teachers of literature, like F.R. Leavis and the New Critics. The teaching of American literature, which had hardly existed at the turn of the century, was a new discipline, and left-wing literary writers of several tendencies—literary historians like Granville Hicks, William Charvat, and Alfred Kazin, reviewers and essayists like Malcolm Cowley, Edmund Wilson, Irving Howe, and Lionel Trilling, and historical critics like F.O. Matthiessen—became central figures in the formation of post-war literary scholarship. This was a product of retreat; as the Cold War constricted the wide-ranging political, social, and cultural debates of the 1930s and 1940s, literary intellectuals turned increasingly inward, adopting the rarefied, technical modes of literary analysis developed by the conservative Southern Agrarians, who had become the "New Critics" (even though the term had originally been applied to the modernist rhetorical criticism associated with I.A. Richards, R.P. Blackmur, William Empson, and Kenneth Burke).

A few of these "literary" critics, notably Wilson and Howe, objected to this narrowing of intellectual focus: Howe later told an interviewer that "while ... literary criticism is *very* difficult ...., I also think that it is not enough by itself to absorb the energies of a serious person." However, for the most part, the "close reading" of authorized texts became the dominant mode, and the socialist and Marxist literary journalism of the 1930s was explicitly and repeatedly exorcised. Moreover, in a somewhat astonishing manner, the history of the radical culture of the 1930s was reduced to literary history: the *New Masses* and *Partisan Review* were seen as "literary" magazines, and Michael Gold, the lively, popular, and always controversial Communist newspaper columnist, became the emblem of the Marxist "literary critic." By the 1970s, even the resurgent Marxism of the New Left was developing its own forms of literary criticism.[22]

The waning prestige of literary criticism and the rise of cultural studies offer a new perspective not only on the Popular Front arts but also on Popular Front cultural criticism. Cultural studies as an intellectual project developed from two senses of the term "culture": the means of communication and the ways of life of communities and peoples. The first of these takes the means of communication as its central object of understanding: both the institutions that control modern communication—the mass media and culture industries—and the forms and codes through which communication takes place. The former explores the political economy of mass communications; the latter investigates the figures and tropes, the signs and signifiers, that organize culture. The ancient sciences of rhetoric and hermeneutics were dusted off because the new cultural studies was founded on the idea that films, musical works, even subcultures could be "read" as if they were "texts."

Both of these forms of analysis were pioneered by writers of the cultural front. One of the first critical studies of a modern culture industry was James Rorty's *Our Master's Voice: Advertising* (1934). Rorty, an author of *Culture and the Crisis* and a former advertising copywriter, depicted the "American apparatus of advertising" as "a grotesque, smirking gargoyle set at the very top of America's sky-scraping adventure in acquisition . . . The gargoyle's mouth is a loud speaker, powered by the vested interest of a two-billion-dollar industry." "That two-billion-dollar advertising budget," Rorty argued, "is . . . the tax which business levies on the consumer to support the machinery of its super-government—the daily and periodical press, the radio." Rorty explored the political economy of radio, the movies, and the popular magazines; the popular fiction of magazines like *True Story* and the *Saturday Evening Post*; and the writings of advertising ideologues like Elbert Hubbard and Bruce Barton. In the debates over the 1934 Communications Act Rorty became a leading critic of the broadcasting industry.[23]

The complement to Rorty's political economy of mass communications was Kenneth Burke's exploration of the rhetoric of communication: the original title of his *Permanence and Change* was "Treatise on Communication." Kenneth Burke remains a starting point for reconstructing the cultural theory of the Popular Front. During most of the post-war period, Burke was considered a kind of eccentric New Critic, the inventor of a vast symbolic system based on a metaphor of drama. He was referred to with reverence, had a few disciples who explicated his system, and was generally ignored. With the emergence of literary theory in the late 1970s, Burke underwent a slight revival, but it is only in the last few years that we have begun to see his project as a major cultural theory, and to see its political contexts. Burke, who was born in 1897, began as an experimental fiction writer and music critic in the 1920s; his first work of critical theory, *Counter-Statement* (1931), was a major study of modernist aesthetics. However, like a number of the American moderns, Burke was radicalized in the early years of the depression, and, in what he later called his "Thirtyminded" essays, he emerged as the most important communist cultural theorist in the United States. "So far as I can see," he wrote in *Permanence and Change* (1935), "the only coherent and organized movement making for the subjection of the technological genius to humane ends is that of Communism, by whatever name it may finally prevail." His writing of the Popular Front years was a remarkable mixture of occasional pieces on the political culture of the time—reviews of proletarian novels, the radical theater, and political theory in left magazines—and dense essays outlining a theory of symbolic action and its consequences for thinking about political transformation.[24]

For the most part, critics have generally discounted Burke's symbolic acts of the 1930s, portraying him as the quintessential fellow traveler. Both his topical agitprop essays—the "Revolutionary Symbolism in America" lecture, the "My Approach to Communism" manifesto, the occasional pieces on politics in *Direction*—and his "fellow-traveling" loan of his name to various Popular Front organizations are usually seen as incidental to the major theoretical projects of his books—the analysis of symbolic action and the theory of dramatism.

Moreover, the prevailing view of Burke's work suggests that the early provisional essays and books culminate in the theory of dramatism, elaborated in the great unfinished trilogy of the 1940s and 1950s—*A Grammar of Motives, A Rhetoric of Motives,* and the incomplete *A Symbolic of Motives.* There is then a break, and the later Burke emerges primarily as the expounder of "logology," building an ontology of language around the resemblance between theology—words about God—and logology, words about words. The principal expounders of Burke as a theorist of "man the symbol-using animal" have ignored his political affiliations: this is true both of literary critics like William Rueckert and Greig Henderson and of social scientists like Hugh D. Duncan and Joseph Gusfield. The few critics who consider Burke's politics have concluded that he was a New Deal liberal. Fredric Jameson writes that Burke, "in the thick of a New Deal and Deweyan rhetoric of liberal democracy and pluralism," made a "desperate and ambitious attempt, in the *Grammar* and *Rhetoric of Motives*, to endow the American capitalism of the thirties and early forties with its appropriate cultural and political ideology." Similarly, though Frank Lentricchia suggests that Burke is part of the genealogy of Western Marxism—"one of the chapters of a full-scale history of Marxist thought will have to be on Kenneth Burke"—he argues that Burke's "comedic vision," translated into "an anthropological generalization about 'all people'," is an "affirmation of bourgeois class values as universal, the mark of horizontal or democratic political desire." Both of these views miss the radical nature of Burke's project and his accomplishments, in part because of Burke's own self-censorship in the face of the anti-Communist inquisition.[25]

The editions of *Permanence and Change* and *Attitudes toward History* that we have had since the 1950s eliminated their Communist conclusions: as Burke coyly put it in his 1953 essay of intellectual autobiography, "Unfortunately for the standing of this book [*Permanence and Change*] in these uneasy times, the family of key words that includes 'communication,' 'communicant,' 'community,' and 'communion' also has a well-known relative now locally in great disgrace—and the experimental author, then contritely eager to think of himself as part of an over-all partnership, had plumped grandly for that word, too." Burke was not the only left critic to emend his books in the 1950s: the endings of Malcolm Cowley's *Exile's Return* and Edmund Wilson's *The American Jitters* (retitled *The American Earthquake*) were revised in the midst of the Cold War.[26]

When Burke explained his editing of *Permanence and Change* (in an April 1953 prologue) and *Attitudes toward History* (in an August 1955 introduction), he implied that the changes were minor, simply "five or six pages speculating on the form that such material cooperation should take." He went on to say that "since, under present conditions, the pages could not possibly be read in the tentative spirit in which they were originally written, the omissions help avoid troublesome issues not necessary to the book as such. There is even a sense in which the omissions could be called a kind of 'restoration,' since they bring the text back closer to its original nature." The line I quoted earlier will not be found in later editions of *Permanence and Change*.[27]

However, the changes are more significant than Burke lets on. *Permanence and Change* consists of three parts. Each part concluded with a section arguing that communism was the social equivalent of his theory of communication. Thus, Burke's argument that "the conclusion we should draw from our thesis is a belief that the ultimate metaphor for discussing the universe and man's relations to it must be the poetic or dramatic metaphor" is significantly modified—in the first edition—by the arguments that "Communism is a cooperative rationalization, or perspective, which fulfills the requirements suggested by the poetic metaphor" and "once the Communistic way of life [was] firmly established in human institutions, I believe that the poetic metaphor would be the best guide (indeed the only conceivable guide) in shaping new pieties of living."[28]

Among the many cuts in *Attitudes toward History*, two involved direct statements of position. In the section defining one of Burke's key terms, "Perspective by Incongruity," Burke wrote that "we hold that a multiplicity of perspectives becomes purely gratuitous, even anarchistic, unless it is organized about a specific point of reference . . . And we would suggest that in the field of human relations this point of reference is provided by the social criteria of Marxism." A more striking cut occurred in the important section on "Symbols of Authority," in which Burke laid out "our own program, as literary critic," arguing that "since the whole purpose of a 'revolutionary' critic is to contribute to a change in allegiance to the symbols of authority, we maintain our role as 'propagandist' by keeping this subject forever uppermost in our concerns. This approach, incidentally, gives one an 'organic' view of literature, sparing him the discomforts of discussing the 'social' and the 'technical' as though they were on two different levels." This passage was the clearest statement of Burke's critical stance in the 1930s and 1940s.[29]

What difference do these changes make? First, the original editions of *Permanence and Change* and *Attitudes toward History* are more coherent than the later ones. Burke did not write new conclusions to the three parts of *Permanence and Change*; he simply excised the existing ones. Second, the original editions demonstrate a closer connection between the politics of Burke's affiliations and the politics of his theory than most critics have allowed: as Burke himself never tired of arguing, "often you cannot take a sentence at face value (you do not 'understand its meaning' until you know the biographical or historic context subsumed by the speaker when he spoke it)." The original editions of Burke's "Thirtyminded" work are not only major contributions to cultural theory, but must be understood against the "biographical or historic context" that Burke subsumed.[30]

The heart of Burke's work lies in the theory of symbolic action elaborated in *Permanence and Change* (1935), *Attitudes toward History* (1937), and *The Philosophy of Literary Form* (1941) which is more accurately described by its subtitle, *Studies in Symbolic Action*. In these works, Burke combined technical and social criticism to develop a notion of symbolic action, to construct a theory of society and history around the concept of allegiance to the symbols of authority, and to explore the nature of the symbolic alignments of artists and thinkers. The *Motives* trilogy that followed is best seen as a narrowing of focus, a magnification of specific aspects of the theory of symbolic action, and, to some degree, a turning away from the Marxist and modernist stance of the earlier books. The flexible strategy/situation model of the early books is replaced by the more rigid act/scene/agent/agency/purpose model of "dramatism." He began by "treating the terms 'dramatic' and 'dialectical' as synonymous." However, as his "dialectical criticism" hardened into a system (a "bureaucratization of the imaginative" to use one of Burke's own concepts), "dramatism" became a cautious marker of Burke's move from his idiosyncratic communist politics to a politics of "Neo-Stoic resignation" in the face of the Cold War.[31]

The theory of symbolic action is perhaps best outlined in the short essay, "Literature as an Equipment for Living," first published in the Popular Front magazine *Direction* (for which he was fiction editor): cultural texts, from proverbs to works of literature, are strategies for dealing with situations, "strategies for selecting enemies and allies, for socializing losses, for warding off evil eye, for . . . consolation and vengeance, admonition and exhortation, implicit commands or instructions of one sort or another. Art forms like 'tragedy' or 'comedy' or 'satire' would be treated as *equipments for living*, that size up situations in various ways and in keeping with correspondingly various attitudes." "Every document bequeathed to us by history," he writes in another place, "must be treated as a *strategy for encompassing a situation*." Having thus defined culture as a kind of "word magic" or "secular prayer," he developed a distinctive theory of ideology: for typical situations, he argued, we develop typical strategies, what he called "attitudes," "frames of acceptance," or "orientations." Individual symbolic acts could be seen as the dancing of an attitude. In *Permanence and Change*, Burke combined Veblen's notion of "trained incapacity," the situation in which one's abilities serve as a blindness, with Dewey's notion of an "occupational pyschosis," the habits of mind developed from a way of making a living, to develop a remarkable account of the way ideologies work and change. This served as the basis for both the book's discussion of the crisis of the capitalist orientation and his call for a new communist orientation.[32]

Burke invented his own terms for ideology for two reasons. First, as he noted in a 1932 letter to Malcolm Cowley, "I am, in the deepest sense a translator. I go on translating, even if I must but translate English into English . . . I can only welcome Communism by converting it into my own vocabulary . . . My book [*Permanence and Change*] will have the communist objectives, and the communist tenor, but the approach will be the approach that seems significant to me. Those who cannot recognize a concept, even [if] it is their concept, unless this concept is stated in exactly the words they use to state it, will think my book something else." The excitement and difficulty of Burke's work lies in the subtleties and nuances of his translations, his dancing of a communist attitude. Second, Burke was more a communist—one of the hard c words he so liked—than a Marxist. For Burke, Marxism was the orthodox tradition—represented by John Strachey's influential works—that stressed the primacy of productive forces. He saw Marx's theory of ideology as a version of debunking, part of the tradition of Bentham and Veblen. For the debunkers, Burke maintained, ideology was always pejorative; since Burke wished to stress the necessity of symbolic action, of word magic, he "translated" ideology into more neutral terms, like "attitude" and "orientation."[33]

In *Attitudes toward History*, Burke developed the argument of the earlier book into a powerful theory of cultural change, a theory based on the notion of allegiance to symbols of authority.

> Our own program ... is to integrate technical criticism with social criticism (propaganda, the didactic) by taking the allegiance to the symbol of authority as our subject. We take this as our starting point, and "radiate" from it. Since the symbols of authority are radically linked with property relationships, this point of departure automatically involves us in socio-economic criticism. Since works of art, as "equipments for living," are formed with authoritative structures as their basis of reference, we also move automatically into the field of technical criticism (the "tactics" of writers). And since the whole purpose of a "revolution-ary" critic is to contribute to a change in allegiance to the symbols of authority, we maintain our role as propagandists by keeping this subject forever uppermost in our concerns.

In a short but brilliant essay, "Twelve Propositions on the Relation between Economics and Psychology," written for the new Marxist journal *Science and Society* (of which he was a contributing editor), Burke argued that "the basic concept for uniting economics and psychology ('Marx' and 'Freud') is that of the 'symbols of authority'."[34]

Burke's notion of the allegiance to symbols of authority plays a similar role to the concept of hegemony in his communist contemporary, Antonio Gramsci. For Gramsci, hegemony is the process by which a social group, a historical bloc, exercises power and leadership in society by winning consent, establishing patterns of loyalty and allegiance. For Burke, symbols of authority are the crucial mechanisms by which social orders win allegiance; they are a society's equipments for living. Allegiance to symbols of authority, Burke maintained, is natural and wholesome, for cultures are built around symbols of authority; indeed, Burke suggested that "one 'owns' his social structure insofar as one can subscribe to it by wholeheart-edly feeling the reasonableness of its arrangements."[35]

However, "insofar as such allegiance is frustrated," Burke continued, "both the materially and the spiritually dispossessed must suffer... even the dispossessed tends to feel that he 'has a stake in' the authoritative structure that dispossesses him; for the influence exerted upon the policies of education by the authoritative structure encourages the dispossessed to feel that his only hope of repossession lies in his allegiance to this structure that has dispossessed him." Moments of crisis occur when these allegiances to the symbols of authority break down; these are times of what Burke calls "impiety," when there is a struggle over new symbols. A revolutionary period, he argued in the famous American Writers' Congress speech,

"Revolutionary Symbolism in America," is one when people drop their allegiance to one symbol of authority or myth and shift to another.[36]

As social theory, Burke's account is somewhat thin; though he argued that "periods of social crisis occur when an authoritative class, whose purpose and ideals had been generally considered as *representative* of the total society's purposes and ideals, becomes considered as antagonistic," he did not attempt to analyze the social bases of such a crisis. And as a theory of history, it remains sketchy: Burke's "curve of history" constructs a homology between modes of production and their corresponding "'collective poems,' the total frames of thought and action, roughly classifiable under the heads of primitive evangelism (in the midst of Hellenistic decay), mediaeval theocracy, Protestantism, capitalism, and socialism." As cultural theory, however, Burke's attention to the symbols of authority not only mediates between property relations and psychology, political domination and works of art, but offers a powerful way of looking at both the *means* and the *agents* of cultural struggle. Burke's notorious vocabulary of idiosyncratic concepts—the stealing back and forth of symbols, secular prayer, discounting, the socialization of losses, symbolic merger, perspective by incongruity, and the rest of his "dictionary of pivotal terms"—is a catalogue of the formal devices and mechanisms by which cultural conflicts and symbolic struggles take place.[37]

The *means* of cultural struggle was, for Burke, metaphor itself. The core of any social or political discourse lay in its metaphors: even the "mixed dead metaphors of abstract thought are metaphors nonetheless." Burke's work combined a theory of metaphor as a form of word magic or secular prayer with an analysis of the ways metaphors and symbols were stolen, reclassified, and rearticulated in works of political and social thought. If his controversial address to the 1935 American Writers' Congress, "Revolutionary Symbolism in America," was a programmatic proposal to the left to adopt the "myth" and "word magic" of "the people," his equally celebrated address to the 1939 American Writers' Congress, "The Rhetoric of Hitler's 'Battle'," was an anti-fascist examination of the "word magic" of fascism. The making of new "attitudes," new "orientations," required not only the stealing of revered symbols, but the creation of new metaphors. Burke's core concept was "perspective by incongruity," which was, he said, a "'methodology of invention' in the conceptual sphere." "Perspective by incongruity" was the juxtaposition of incongruous words, the grotesque violation of received categories and classifications, the impious rebellion against proper orders and rightful places. For Burke, this strategy characterized both modernism and Marxism—the "grotesque tends to be revolutionary"—and it was the justification for his own theoretical gargoyles.[38]

Burke's theory also emphasized the *agents* of cultural conflicts, the intellectuals whom he called the "spiritual bankers," the specialists in secular prayer. In general, "those in possession of the authoritative symbols tend to drive the opposition into a corner, by owning the priests (publicists, educators) who will rebuke the opposition for its disobedience to the reigning symbols." However, the shape of the future, he argued, "is really disclosed by finding out what people can sing about. What values can enlist the most vigorous and original craftsmen? And what values, on the other hand, can merely enlist the public relations counsel?" His understanding of the relation between intellectuals and social movements is captured in this metaphor of enlistment and affiliation. On considering a work in its historical contexts, he suggested, "we might well find that the given philosopher, by manipulating the possibilities of emphasis in one way rather than another, was able symbolically to enroll himself in one social alliance, with its peculiar set of expectancies, rather than another. Here we should see what participation in a Cause caused his work, by what Movement it was motivated, on what sub-stance it made its stand."[39]

Burke's own symbolic enrollments—the communist tenor of *Permanence and Change* and *Attitudes toward History*; his contributions to the *New Masses*; his involvement in the left-wing League of American Writers over a number of years; his stance as a contributing editor of *Science and Society*, a leading journal of Marxist thought, and an advisory editor of *Direction*, the cultural front's glossy arts magazine—have often been summed up in the legendary anecdote about his address to the 1935 American Writers' Congress. It was recounted by Burke himself, remembered in print by his friends Matthew Josephson and Malcolm Cowley, fictionalized by James T. Farrell in *Yet Other Waters*, and retold as the opening of Frank Lentricchia's influential critical study of Burke. Though it is an appealing story of the outcast ironically triumphant, the heretic justified, it is generally misinterpreted. However, since the story of the American Writers' Congress is an example of the way Burke symbolically enrolled himself in a "social alliance," it provokes us into asking "what participation in a Cause caused his work, by what Movement [was it] motivated, on what substance [did] it [make] its stand?"

The Writers' Congress was part of the militant cultural resurgence during the spring of 1935. A call had been issued in January with a long and distinguished list of signatories, and it appeared to be the culmination of the left avant-garde renaissance, the burgeoning of the proletarian literature movement with its little magazines, its John Reed Clubs, and its theater groups. It was the first national gathering of writers in US history, and it led to the formation of the League of American Writers. Burke, in his late thirties, was a relatively well-known modernist writer—author of a novel, short stories, poems, and a pathbreaking study of modernist aesthetics, *Counter-Statement*—who had moved closer to the left in 1934. In his address to the congress, "Revolutionary Symbolism in America," he suggested that the symbol of the "people" would provide a more powerful basis for propaganda than the symbol of the "worker"; and the talk was taken as a critique of the left's rhetoric of class and the notion of a "proletarian" literature. Burke remembered that "the incident" had "a certain literary quality, or sociological quality."[40]

As Burke told the story, he was worried about the response to the talk from the start: he even showed it to a Communist friend to see if it would be considered wrong. He had, he said, a "terrific desire to belong" and a great fear of audiences. The initial applause from the audience reassured him, then the attack from the Party's literary heavies began. "Joe Freeman gets up, throbbing like a locomotive, and shouts, 'We have a snob among us!' . . . Then Mike Gold followed, and put the steamroller on me . . . Then a German émigré, Friedrich Wolf . . . pointed out the similarity between this usage and Hitler's harangues to the *Volk*. And so on, and so on—until I was slain, slaughtered. The whole situation was reversed now. I felt wretched. I remember, when leaving the hall, I was walking behind two girls. One said to the other, as though discussing a criminal, 'Yet, he *seemed* so honest!' "[41]

Burke's anguish continued: he dreamed his name had become "a kind of charge against me—a dirty word," and fantasized that "excrement was dripping from my tongue." The next day he was referred to as Mr—not Comrade—Burke in a meeting. Nevertheless, before the congress was over Freeman came up to Burke, all smiles and apologies: "all was forgiven," Burke remembered, "I often think of that story when I think about politicians."[42]

The story became a representative anecdote because of the larger dramatic reversal: before the year was out, Burke's "populist" heresy, his call for a politics around the symbol of the "people," became orthodoxy, as the Communist left adopted the strategy of the Popular Front. The Burke incident became, in retrospect, a focal point of the congress because, as Cowley noted, Burke "was pointing toward the future and most of the Congress was pointing toward the past." "Poor Burke was overborne by so much censure," Matthew Josephson recalled, "but he held his ground, smiling . . . In truth he had worked better than he knew." Ironically, Burke became, as Cowley later put it, "a premature adherent of the People's Front."[43]

What does this twice-told tale tell us about the left and Kenneth Burke? The apparent lessons are, first, that Burke was lured to the left through a "terrific desire to belong"; second, that he was always the heretic, never fully accepted by the orthodox, that he had, in Frank Lentricchia's phrase, "tough times with American Marxists in the 1930s"; and third, that he was, nevertheless, more perceptive and profound than the orthodox, that he "refused," to quote Lentricchia again, "the self-congratulating poses of literary and social radicalism in the 1920s and 1930s." The story of Kenneth Burke and the left, it would seem, is that of Kenneth Burke against the left.[44]

This is profoundly misleading: the story of Burke at the American Writers' Congress is not one of Burke against the left, but one of a controversy within the left. Burke had "tough times with American Marxists in the 1930s" because he was a leading American Marxist of the 1930s. Not only did he *not* "refuse the self-congratulating poses" of the radicalism of the 1930s, but he struck those "poses," took those "stands," symbolically enrolled himself in that alliance. There is no doubt that Burke was anguished at the response to his paper: Farrell's fictional account has a "chunky little man, with an esoteric critical reputation ... monotonously reading" to an audience that was "restless" until Jake [the Joseph Freeman character] rushes up, shouts and bangs his fist. But it did not lead him to abandon the congress or its organizers.[45]

Two weeks later, Burke hailed the congress as "an extremely impressive matter" in the *Nation*: "to those of us who had been taught to think of a literary renaissance as six men assembled in the back room of a saloon to discuss the need of a new magazine, it was a revolution in itself to behold four thousand people packing the pit, balcony, gallery, and stage of Mecca Temple to consider the problems of literature." Burke was elected to the Council of the League of American Writers and returned to address both the 1937 and 1939 American Writers' Congresses. The Burke story also illustrates the fact that the Popular Front had emerged as a social movement from the upheavals of 1933 and 1934, before the Communist Party itself adopted the position. Despite the quarrel with Freeman and Gold, Burke was not really prophetic; he was simply articulating a common position on the left, one that he had developed both from the New York John Reed Club school, where he had taught, and from Calverton's *Modern Monthly*.[46]

Burke's symbolic enrollments came back to haunt him when he was denied a teaching position in the early 1950s at the University of Washington. Though Burke covered his tracks, reediting his books, he refused to give in to the anti-Communist hysteria. "God knows, I was sluggish about making the change from aestheticism to the social emphasis," he wrote to Cowley. "I never did make it completely. At the beginning of it all, I used to say that I'd never join the Communist Party because, so long as I didn't, they'd never throw me out—and now, at the end of the decade, I might rephrase it by saying that, through never having been hunkydory with the Party, I now find no occasion to welch. I am grateful for the Party for this much: that at a time when I was in pieces, they upheld a program that enabled me to put myself together again."[47]

Nevertheless, the story of the heretic outraging the orthodox, of the independent mind bringing down the wrath of the party-liners, remains the legend. Indeed, similar tales are told about many of the figures who are central to the cultural front, including Langston Hughes, Orson Welles, and Richard Wright. The same characters often appear in different roles; in versions more sympathetic to Freeman and Gold, one discovers that they too, being literary figures, were always suspected and never quite trusted by the Party's political leaders. On the other hand, Burke himself appears in the role of the orthodox hatchet-man in stories told from the point of view of James Farrell (Burke wrote one of the negative reviews of his controversial *A Note on Literary Criticism*) or of Sidney Hook: the vitriolic exchange between them in *Partisan Review* carried the titles "Is Mr. Hook a Socialist?" and "Is Mr. Burke Serious?"[48]

These melodramas of orthodoxy and heresy are finally less interesting than the larger drama of the symbolic alliance itself, the Movement and Cause (to use Burke's terms) that enabled the work. Burke was the major cultural theorist of the Popular Front. His symbolic acts—the theoretical work of his major books, his critical interventions as a reviewer of contemporary music, poetry, theater, fiction, painting, and theory in the weekly and monthly magazines of the left, and his affiliations with Popular Front organizations—were not only his "dancing of an attitude," strategies for naming the crisis of capitalist culture and the rise of fascism, they were also part of the Popular Front's equipment for living.

3. Common Ground: Louis Adamic, Carey McWilliams, Oliver C. Cox, and the "Racial-Cultural Situation"

If one side of cultural studies has taken its project from the notion of culture as communication, as language and media, the other is rooted in the notion of culture as "community" and has explored the ways of life and of struggle of "peoples" and the ways those peoples have been formed as ethnicities, races, and nations. The concepts that produce a people— "nation," "race," "ethnicity," "colony," "margin," "color" (as in the older "colored" or the newer "people of color"), "minority," "region," "diaspora," "migrant," "post-colonial"—and the national and imperial discourses that underlie these fantasies of racial and ethnic identity inform much of contemporary cultural studies. This concern for what they called "the racial-cultural situation" was also at the center of Popular Front social and cultural theory, though the pioneering work on race and ethnicity by figures like Louis Adamic, Carey McWilliams, and Oliver C. Cox has rarely been recognized.

In part, this is because it was overshadowed by the explosion of studies of the *national* culture and "character" of the United States. By the early 1950s, a new field of "American Studies" had taken shape in the rapidly expanding universities. It was a divided field from the start. On the one hand, American Studies served as the embodiment and explicator of the American Way, the "genius of American politics." Its interdisciplinary ambitions and "pluralist" ideology made it the quintessential alternative to Marxism itself, which was understood simply as Soviet ideology. American Studies in its imperial guise was based on the uniqueness and exceptionalism of American experience, and this Cold War vision of America attracted corporate funding and moved overseas as an intellectual arm of US foreign policy. The work of Daniel Boorstin stands as the epitome of this American Studies: both his testimony before the House Un-American Activities Committee, naming names, affirming that "a member of the Communist Party should not be employed by a university," and placing his own work in the service of the anti-Communist crusade; and his three-volume *The Americans* (1958, 1965, 1974), the finest cultural history of the United States from the point of view of capitalism.[49]

On the other hand, American Studies was also, for many of the young intellectuals it attracted, a "movement," the practice of American cultural history as a form of radical cultural critique. This American Studies inherited its search for a "usable past" from the union of the "Young America" critics of *Seven Arts*—figures like Van Wyck Brooks, Lewis Mumford, and Waldo Frank—and the Popular Front. Brooks, Mumford, and Frank were established intellectuals by the time of the depression, and all lent their names and time to Popular Front organizations. The Popular Front generation was epitomized by F.O. Matthiessen, whose *American Renaissance* (1941), a study of Emerson, Thoreau, Hawthorne, Melville, and Whitman, became the basis for the reconstruction of American literary history.

Nevertheless, even this critical American Studies of the post-war years was scarred by the intellectual repression of the Cold War, and in many ways it represented a retreat from the cultural history that had been pioneered by Popular Front scholars. It shared the post-war consecration of literary criticism, even as it dissented from the formalism of the New Critics. Though Matthiessen described himself as a "cultural historian," he argued that "an artist's use of language is the most sensitive index to cultural history." Though this proved an enabling dictum for *American Renaissance* itself, it turned American Studies away from other forms of symbolic action. The overestimation of literature as the key to American cultural history led to the relative eclipse of one of the most significant bodies of Popular Front cultural history, the remarkable work produced by Carolyn Ware, Constance Rourke, and Alice Felt Tyler. Ware's community study of work and culture, *Greenwich Village, 1920–1930* (1935); Rourke's readings of the American national-popular through forms of popular art and theater in *American Humor* (1931) and *The Roots of American*

Culture (1942); and Tyler's *Freedom's Ferment* (1944), the still unsurpassed synthesis of the "other" American Renaissance, the antebellum cultural revolution that, as Matthiessen himself noted, might be called the Age of Fourier or the Age of Swedenborg: all were important contributions to what Ware called in 1940 "the cultural approach to history."[50]

Moreover, the American Studies founded on *American Renaissance* was captured by the discourse of national character and American exceptionalism. As Jonathan Arac has argued, "Matthiessen's Popular Front figure of 'America' suffered a sobering fate." It "became a postwar myth of empire. A mobilization intended as oppositional became incorporated hegemonically; American studies gained power by nationalistically appropriating Matthiessen." As a result, many historians have projected this nationalism backwards, arguing that the Popular Front itself celebrated a sentimental nationalism and ignored or downplayed the racial and ethnic formations in the United States. In fact, the Popular Front's engagement with the "national" question led to a remarkable rethinking of the "peoples" of the United States, particularly in the work of a group of California leftists including Louis Adamic and Carey McWilliams around the journal *Common Ground*, and in the work of Popular Front sociologist Oliver C. Cox.[51]

Common Ground was a journal founded by Louis Adamic and M. Margaret Anderson in 1940 to explore "the racial-cultural situation" in the US. Looked at a half-century later, it seems the very embodiment of the cautious, semi-official "cultural pluralism" of the time. It was sponsored by a mainstream liberal organization, the Common Council for American Unity, funded initially by the Carnegie Foundation, aimed at schools and public libraries, and featuring many of the icons of the middlebrow New Deal, including Eleanor Roosevelt, Archibald MacLeish, Van Wyck Brooks, and Pearl Buck. But it was also a crucial magazine for younger black and ethnic writers: Langston Hughes, a member of the editorial board, published more in *Common Ground* than in any other journal in the 1940s, and the magazine sponsored his 1944 tour of high schools. In its ten years, *Common Ground* published such black writers as Arna Bontemps, Melvin Tolson, Margaret Walker, Zora Neale Hurston, Ralph Ellison, Gwendolyn Brooks, and Chester Himes; the Asian-American writers Toshio Mori, Mary Oyama, Younghill Kang, Carlos Bulosan, and Jade Snow Wong; and the Chicano scholar George Sanchez. In a number of cases, this was the writer's first national publication. The magazine's illustrators included Miné Okubo, Jacob Lawrence, and Ollie Harrington.[52]

The magazine was the brainchild of Adamic, a key figure in the history of US ethnicity. A Slovene immigrant of the modernist generation who arrived in the United States in 1913, he emerged in the California literary bohemia of the 1920s as an iconoclastic devotee of Nietzsche and Mencken, and the chronicler of Los Angeles. Like other US moderns, he turned to the left during the depression, traveling across the US and writing one of the finest accounts of the emerging labor movement. He also became deeply involved in understanding the backbone of that labor movement, the second-generation children of Southern and Eastern European immigrants; he called them the "new Americans." Beginning with a widely read magazine article, "Thirty Million New Americans" (1934), and an oft-given lecture, "Ellis Island and Plymouth Rock," he wrote widely on what were coming to be called "ethnic groups." For the most part, his writing was not theoretical or sociological; at its best, he narrated the life stories of ordinary people he had met. His books—*My America* (1938) and *From Many Lands* (1940)—were unwieldy but fascinating compendiums of these narratives, the lectures he gave, autobiographical sketches, the letters he received from the "new Americans," and his manifestos for educational and political organizations and projects. Though always skeptical of the Communist Party, Adamic became a key figure in the Popular Front; he was the leader of the United Committee of South Slavic Americans (which helped to sway US public opinion toward support of Tito), a vice-chair of Progressive Citizens of America, and, subsequently, a victim of the post-war Red scare.

The success of the "ethnic renaissance" in the United States since the 1940s often leads to an underestimation of the depth of American nativism and the importance of Adamic's project to create a "new conception of America." Until the Second World War, the dominant culture of the United States saw itself as Anglo-Saxon and Protestant, descended from the founding fathers, and besieged by, in the title of a popular race tract of the 1920s, the "rising tide of color." Adamic's vision was one of uplift and education: his "nation of nations" project was a series of books on different ethnic and racial groups, a vast counterencyclopedia of America. *Common Ground* was invented as the voice of this "diversity," this "multicultural America," to use terms to which Adamic himself appealed. It became a forum for left-liberal investigations into racial and ethnic issues, a clearing house that surveyed and reviewed materials about the "nation of nations," and, most substantially, a forum for young plebeian writers telling tales of life in racial and ethnic neighborhoods, a Popular Front equivalent of the John Reed Club magazines of the previous decade.

Common Ground was one of the first journals to use the term "ethnicity." "The term 'ethnic'," the authors of a 1943 essay proposing an "institute of ethnic democracy" wrote, "... is more colorless, less weighted with emotion, than 'racial,' 'minority,' or 'colonial'." Despite this desire for a "colorless" term, ethnicity became less a substitute for race than a way of distinguishing between ethnics of European origins and other racial and ethnic groups. Though *Common Ground* refused to make this separation, and featured an increasing number of articles about African Americans,

Asian Americans, and Mexican Americans, this met resistance from read-ers. Langston Hughes's satirical 1944 article, "White Folks Do the Funniest Things," which appeared together with Chester Himes's essay on the previous summer's race riots and Larry Tajiri's essay on the internment camps, drew more reaction than any other article the journal had published. Letters from readers complained that the magazine was paying too much attention to black Americans and that Langston Hughes was "offensive," "truculent," and a "smart-aleck." "Even with readers who go the whole way with us on the foreign-language groups, there is apparently very real emotional or intellectual withdrawal when we touch too frankly or too vigorously on matters of color," the journal's editor, Margaret Anderson (who had taken over when Adamic went on to other projects), wrote in response to these letters.[53]

"The problems of the foreign-born in assimilation in the American scene, while still concrete, have not appreciably worsened in this moment of world crisis," she argued. "But the racial tensions mount; they lie like dynamite ready to explode into a series of disastrous Detroits." *Common Ground* continued to be a forum for Popular Front writers on race and ethnicity, and over the next several years its guiding spirit shifted from Adamic, whose attention was always primarily focused on the "new Ameri-cans," to Carey McWilliams, one of the leading voices of Popular Front anti-racism.[54]

McWilliams was a California lawyer and writer who was greatly influ-enced by his friend Adamic, about whom he wrote a short book. Beginning as a literary critic and a voice of western regionalism, McWilliams turned to political life, becoming famous for his book *Factories in the Fields* (1939), which, together with Steinbeck's *The Grapes of Wrath*, drew national attention to the struggles of migrant farmworkers. As a result, he became the head of California's Division of Immigration and Housing under the Popular Front governor Culbert Olsen and subsequently wrote four major books on racism and the peoples of the US during the 1940s: *Brothers under the Skin* (1943), *Prejudice: Japanese-Americans* (1944), *A Mask for Privilege: Anti-Semitism in America* (1948), and *North from Mexico: The Spanish-Speaking People of the United States* (1950). McWilliams was also a key figure in bringing together a group of young West Coast ethnic writers, which included John Fante, William Saroyan, and Carlos Bulosan.

Though McWilliams always insisted on his debts to Adamic in thinking about the nation of nations, his angle of vision was from the start markedly different. Three major threads guided McWilliams's work. First, he insisted that the central issue was not the drama of "old-stock American" and European "new-immigrant"; rather, it was the color lines between white Americans and various peoples of color. His pathbreaking book *Brothers under the Skin* was organized by essays on American Indians, Chinese

Americans, Chicanos, Japanese Americans, the colonies of Hawaii, Puerto Rico, and the Philippines, and black Americans, an organization remarkably different from either Adamic's *Nation of Nations* (which was predominantly focused on European immigrant groups) or the "caste" theories of American black/white relations that dominated the liberal social science of the 1940s. In this sense McWilliams was one of the earliest US figures to see race through Californian eyes, arguing in 1943 that the US was "in the process of being orientated toward Central and South America" and the Pacific.[55]

Second, McWilliams suggested a new periodization in the history of US racial and ethnic formations, noting that "the year 1876 seems to have marked a turning point in our dealings with all colored minorities, for about that time we decided to exclude the Chinese, place the Indians on reservations, and surrender the Negro to the South." McWilliams's arguments about the relation between the end of the slave trade and the emergence of Chinese migrant labor suggest that the birth of modern racial systems with their legal codes of segregation, exclusion, reservations, and anti-miscegenation in the mid nineteenth century was a consequence of the ending of the forced labor systems of slavery, Czarist serfdom, and transportation. Because of his attention to the colonial histories of the Philippines, Hawaii, and Puerto Rico, McWilliams's history of US peoples of color does not have the feeling of multi-cultural juxtaposition that one gets in Adamic's work—a chapter on the French, a chapter on the Irish, a chapter on the Chinese—but rather offers a synthetic account of the history of the modern color line.[56]

Third, McWilliams's experience in California state government combined with his social democratic sensibilities generated an underlying argument for state intervention in racial matters. He continually attacked "laissez faire" approaches to racism, arguing for federal intervention, particularly in the Jim Crow South, and emphasizing the need to legislate group rights. "There is nothing undemocratic or invidious," he argued, "about regarding minorities, for administrative purposes, as special groups." This call for state intervention also produced some of the least persuasive parts of the book: McWilliams's qualified endorsements of the New Deal actions of the Bureau of Indian Affairs and the internment and relocation of Japanese Americans. To his credit, however, McWilliams quickly reversed these opinions and became one of the few white critics of the camps. For three years, he visited the camps and campaigned against them in print and on national radio.[57]

McWilliams's work and its wide dissemination in the world of the CIO unions and the Popular Front political groups marked a major advance not just for the American left, but for US culture generally. The meaning of this intellectual shift—marked by such works of liberal social thought as

Gunnar Myrdal's *An American Dilemma* (1944), Ashley Montagu's *Man's Most Dangerous Myth: The Fallacy of Race* (1942), and Ruth Benedict's *The Races of Mankind* (1943)—has too often been understood as simply an intellectual affair, provoked by the needs of wartime nationalism. Thus, Gary Gerstle has argued that this wartime "cultural pluralism" was largely an intellectual ideal aimed at mobilizing a unified nation for war; it eventually turned energies and attention away from the issues of class, the "labor" question: "the liberal fascination with the cultural pluralist ideal that the war had spawned diminished the stature that the labor question had long occupied in the minds of American reformers." But this account—which founds an increasingly dominant interpretation of the "rise and fall of the New Deal Order," in which the Americanism that held the New Deal coalition and the Popular Front together was destroyed by a turn to race—misses the social transformations behind the emergence of this discourse on race, peoples, and cultural pluralism.[58]

As McWilliams later noted in his autobiography, the irony of his four books of the 1940s on racial matters was that they were not planned; he did not intend to spend the decade writing on race and the peoples of the US. Rather, they emerged as a response to what he calls the "racial revolution" of the 1940s. "The fact is," McWilliams writes, "—and it deserves emphasis—that the civil-rights movement of a later period is to be understood only in terms of what happened from 1941 to 1945 ... [C]atastrophe initiates social change; it was the war that set the racial revolution in motion." The emergence of the *Common Ground* thinkers was a product of the racial and ethnic transformations at the time. The racial and ethnic formation constructed in the 1870s and 1880s, based on racialized legal codes and the importation of proletarian labor from Southern and Eastern Europe, was beginning to unravel in the face of the anti-fascist war, the migrations of black Americans out of the apartheid, sharecropping South, and the emergence of civil rights movements.[59]

In retrospect, 1942 was as much a turning point in the US racial formation as 1876 had been: the war with Japan began thirty-five years of war in Asia—in the Philippines, Korea, Indonesia, Vietnam, and Cambodia; the 1942 evacuation and internment of Japanese Americans was a watershed in Asian American political consciousness; 1942 marked the beginning of the Bracero program, which organized the importation of Mexican contract labor for agribusiness; and 1942 marked the beginning of the largest migration of black Americans out of the South to the war-industry cities of the North and the West. The first stirrings of the black civil-rights movement can be seen in the 1941 March on Washington movement as well as in the extraordinary success of Richard Wright's *Native Son*. Nineteen forty-three was a year of exceptional racial conflict: a group of young Chicanos were framed for murder in the Sleepy Lagoon case; a few months later, white servicemen attacked Chicano youths across Los Angeles in the week-long zoot-suit riots. A summer of race riots followed in San Diego, Philadelphia, Chicago, Evansville, and Beaumont, culminating in the major riots in Harlem and Detroit.

This was the context for Oliver C. Cox's theoretical work on race and ethnicity. Cox was a Trinidadian contemporary of Adamic and McWilliams who migrated to Chicago for his education. After being partially disabled by polio, he gave up plans to practice law in Trinidad and became a scholar, earning his doctorate in the University of Chicago's sociology department in 1938, and then teaching through the 1940s at black colleges, Wiley College and the Tuskegee Institute. *Caste, Class and Race* (1948) brought together his essays of the 1940s, and it has been usually treated as a distinguished but idiosyncratic work, often cited but rarely engaged. Outside the political battles of Harlem, and, in contrast to his contemporary C.L.R. James, uninvolved in the internal polemics of left-wing parties, Cox has rarely been seen for what he is: the most important Popular Front theorist of "the racial-cultural situation."[60]

Cox's Popular Front political stance is evident throughout the book: in his hopes for the organization of black workers in the South in the CIO's post-war Operation Dixie; in the section on "Negro leadership," which concludes by pointing to the election of a black Communist, Benjamin Davis, to the New York City Council; and in his interpretation of the racist meaning of the Cold War anti-Communist campaign. However, just as his Wiley College colleague, the poet Melvin Tolson, stayed aloof from the metropolitan literary skirmishes over "proletarian literature" and the "writer's responsibility" in order to develop an independent Marxist poetics, so Cox devoted his main energies to theoretical clarification, developing an account of the ways a capitalist world system not only proletarianizes the masses but racializes them as well.

Caste, Class and Race began with Cox's critique of the attempts to use the concept of "caste" to analyze race relations: caste theories dominated the work of white and black sociologists of the period as they tried to explain the racial formation of the segregated, sharecropping South. Against these works, Cox maintained the historical originality of capitalist race relations, which were based on the "commoditizing" of human labor in the New World. If McWilliams pointed to 1876 as a *turning* point in the forms of capitalist racism, Cox added a *starting* point: "if we had to put our finger upon the year which marked the beginning of modern race relations," he wrote, "we should select 1493–94. This was the time when total disregard for the human rights and physical power of the non-Christian peoples of the world, the colored peoples, was officially assumed by the first two great colonizing European nations." Without capitalism, Cox argued, there would be no racism.[61]

Cox's essays attempted to work out the theoretical consequences of this stance. On the one hand, he developed and defined a variety of abstract concepts that would characterize the relations between peoples, refusing the conflation of racism, ethnocentrism, and intolerance just as he refuses the conflation of race and caste. If "ethnic" becomes the generic term for the social relations between peoples who think of each other as distinct, ethnic relations become racialized or nationalized only in particular historical circumstances. Thus, the other side of Cox's project is the account of how racialized social relations are formed not as a "natural, immemorial feeling of mutual antipathy," but as an "instrument of . . . economic exploitation." "Our hypothesis," Cox wrote, "is that racial exploitation and race prejudice developed among Europeans with the rise of capitalism and nationalism, and that because of the world-wide ramifications of capitalism, all racial antagonisms can be traced to the policies and attitudes of the leading capitalist people, the white people of Europe and North America." Unlike those thinkers for whom racism is an irrationality within capitalism, a survival of earlier modes of exploitation, Cox offered an account of capitalism as a world system in which racialization is a fundamental economic and political process.[62]

This attention to the world system also avoided reducing race to "the American dilemma." Cox did not see US race relations as exclusively a question of blacks and whites, and offered a provocative analysis of the racialization of Asian Americans, based in part, one should add, on the historical work of Carey McWilliams. He also refused the redemptive rhetoric of "Americanism" that one finds in many Popular Front figures, including McWilliams, Adamic, Hughes, and even Cox's friend Melvin Tolson, whose poem "Rendezvous with America," first published in *Common Ground*, stands with Robeson's "Ballad for Americans" as one of the great counter-anthems of the Popular Front. Finally, Cox rejected the exceptionalism of the "American dilemma": "the dilemma is not peculiarly American; it is world-wide, confronting even the white masses of every capitalist nation." Cox went on to chart a pioneering "world-systems" theory of capitalism in a series of books between 1959 and 1964.[63]

Caste, Class and Race remains a fundamental work both for its rigorous interrogation of the concepts used in theorizing "peoples" and for its attention to the specific forms of capitalist racialization. It also deeply influenced the group of Popular Front Marxist economists and social theorists around *Monthly Review*, a magazine that had been founded in 1948 by Paul Sweezy, Leo Huberman, and Otto Nathan, with the financial help of F.O. Matthiessen. "On race relations," Sweezy later wrote, "I am quite simply his pupil. Before *Caste, Class and Race*, I had never really thought about the theoretical issues involved." Monthly Review Press reprinted *Caste, Class and Race* in 1959, and it, along with Paul Baran's *The*

Political Economy of Growth (1957), formed the basis for the distinctive *Monthly Review* analysis of imperialism and underdevelopment that had wide ranging influence on the New Left throughout the Americas.[64]

The work of the Popular Front theorists of race and ethnicity—Adamic, McWilliams, and Cox—is a central, if largely forgotten, legacy of the cultural front. The racial revolution of the 1940s that Adamic, McWilliams, and Cox witnessed and tried to make sense of created the racial and ethnic formation that continues to structure the United States. It is the true meaning of the supposed "turn to race" that the political commentators lament; it is the subtext behind the controversies over the very terms "race" and "ethnicity"; it was the basis for the "liberation politics" of the 1950s and 1960s and the "identity politics" of the 1980s and 1990s. The complexity of that formation unites the zoot-suit riots of 1943 with the Los Angeles riots of 1992. If the tropes of reconciliation we inherit from the writers of the 1940s—"a nation of nations," "common ground," "multi-culturalism,"—seem so many failures, so many pious wishes, it is because the racial revolution they heralded remains unfinished.

4. The Popular Arts

The cultural front began as an iconoclastic and experimental avant-garde, a vanguard of young proletarian writers and artists seeking to revolutionize American culture as well as society. Like many such avant-gardes, it was hostile to the mass-produced products of the culture industries. To the self-taught proletarian intellectuals of the movement, the *Saturday Evening Post* seemed the epitome of middle America's stultifying synthesis of advertising and gentility. However, as the Popular Front grew into a powerful social movement, encompassing working-class communities across the continent, the avant-garde's passionate rejection of capitalist culture was displaced by a complex engagement with the popular and vernacular arts. Hollywood movies, popular music, radio serials, pulp magazines, sports, and fashion were the subjects of debate, parody, and imitation in the institutions and forums of the Popular Front. It is easy to reduce this left-wing discourse about popular culture to a clear-cut stance for or against. In their post-war critique of "mass culture," the New York intellectuals repeatedly assailed the writers and intellectuals of the Popular Front for their "surrender" to mass culture and "kitsch." Postmodern defenders of popular culture, on the other hand, have not found it difficult to find condemnations of Hollywood and jazz in the *Daily Worker* or the *New Masses*, and have often concluded that the Popular Front was as hostile to the popular arts as was Dwight Macdonald.[65]

In fact, the engagement with movies, radio, and popular music is more telling than the particular positions taken. The popular or vernacular arts were controversial because they brought together the two different senses of culture: popular entertainments are produced by the industries and rhetorics that make up the means of communication; they are also part of the "equipment for living" of particular peoples and communities. The popular arts were an emblem of the new working-class culture built at the crossroads of the culture industries and the symbolic forms of subaltern daily life. As a result, debates over the popular arts often became either debates over the power and influence of the means of communication, "mass culture," or debates over the culture and politics of working-class communities, "popular culture." The stances taken in the controversies that periodically broke out in the left press are less significant than the fact that Popular Front cultural critics wrote the first serious studies of the popular arts in the United States. For example, though left-wing critics continually attacked Hollywood's dream factory, they were the first to develop a lasting film criticism and history in journals like *Experimental Cinema, Filmfront,* and *Hollywood Quarterly,* and in the work of figures like Harry Potamkin, the young proletarian critic who died at the age of thirty-three in 1933, Lewis Jacobs, whose *The Rise of American Film* (1939) was the first major history of film, and Jay Leyda, the translator and editor of Eisenstein's writings on film.

Three writers on the popular arts, all of whom stand outside the post-war moral panic over "mass culture," developed particularly powerful reflections on the vernacular cultures of the CIO working classes: Elizabeth Hawes, Sidney Finkelstein, and C.L.R. James. For all three, the analysis of popular aesthetics and vernacular culture was informed by an understanding of work and the labor process. The dialectic between the analysis of the labor process and the analysis of mass culture—an attention to the laboring of culture—is one of the enduring legacies of Popular Front cultural criticism.

Elizabeth Hawes represents an important and almost entirely unrecognized type of intellectual who was central to the Popular Front as a social movement: the labor union intellectual. The organization of the mass industrial unions of the CIO not only attracted the sympathies and allegiances of traditional intellectuals, like Kenneth Burke, it also created its own organic intellectuals, including organizers, economists, lawyers, writers, journalists, historians, musicians, theater workers, and cartoonists. They worked in the education departments of the unions and in the labor press, including the Federated Press, the important left-wing labor news agency. Hawes was one of these union intellectuals, working for the education department of the United Automobile Workers, writing a weekly column in the *Detroit Free Press* (the first of which called for public nurseries and a thirty-hour work week), editing pamphlets and a special issue of the UAW's magazine, *Ammunition,* and traveling the country visiting UAW locals. She eventually left the UAW as the anti-Communist purge was beginning; though she was not a Communist Party member, the education department had been a stronghold of the left-wing of the union. One of the major consequences of the anti-Communist purge of the unions after the war was that these radical intellectuals were driven out of the unions, destroying the cultural initiatives of the labor movement and widening the gap between radical intellectuals and the labor movement.

However, Hawes's road to the UAW was equally striking: she had been one of the leading fashion designers in the United States. Like Kenneth Burke, Hawes was one of the moderns, born in 1903 to a bourgeois family: her father was an assistant manager of a steamship line, her mother a Vassar-educated daughter of a railroad vice-president. She graduated from Vassar in 1925 and went to Paris to learn dress design, working in an illegal copy house and writing fashion reports for the newly launched *New Yorker*. On the fringes of the expatriate artist community in Paris, she, like many other "exiles," returned to the US in the late 1920s, and opened a successful fashion business. By the mid 1930s, Lord and Taylor had taken her up as part of a campaign to promote American designers, and she was well known in the elite New York arts world. As parts of that world moved left, so too did Hawes, and she worked with the left-wing director Joseph Losey, who she later married, in the WPA theater, designing the costumes for the famous Living Newspaper production *Triple A Plowed Under*.

The books Hawes wrote in these years were not only widely read in the Popular Front social movement, but also stand as pioneering reflections on work and culture, mediated through a fundamental form of vernacular culture, clothing. Her first book, the best-selling *Fashion Is Spinach* of 1938, was, in the words of her biographer Bettina Berch, a "fashion declaration of independence," criticizing Paris fashion and calling for the democratization of style; and *Men Can Take It* (1939) was a radical and satirical account of clothing for men (she had staged what may have been the first all-male fashion show in 1937). She also wrote two pioneering accounts of the transformations in women's work brought on by their large-scale entry into Fordist mass-production: *Why Women Cry* (1943), which was in part a war-plant diary of her time at Wright Aeronautics, and *Hurry Up Please Its Time* (1946), an account of her work for the UAW.[66]

Perhaps her finest book, however, is *Why Is a Dress?* (1942). Despite its informal style, it is a theoretical work. Its form—advice to the aspiring dress designer—allowed her to raise fundamental questions: why clothes are worn, how clothes are made, what makes clothes beautiful. *Why Is a Dress?* begins as a critique of her own earlier work: "the day of made-to-order clothes is over," she wrote, ". . . our most important problem is to perfect the mass production of clothes." For Hawes, this task derived from the increasing economic independence of women. "I posed a specific clothing problem at the beginning of this book," she wrote. "There are in the United States thousands of secretaries . . . who must dress every day for work. What are they to wear?"[67]

Her answer, embodied in the book and in her own designs, was a kind of feminist functionalism. The abstract, geometrical designs of the modernist Schiaparelli were, she argued, beautiful designs but not beautiful clothes; they only looked good on a hanger. The sense of line in clothing must derive from the body in motion. By cutting on the bias and building yokes and belts into the dress, Hawes designed clothes that would be comfortable and attractive while working. In a striking anecdote in *Fashion Is Spinach*, she tells of seeing the architect Frank Lloyd Wright speaking in a tuxedo: "Every time he said 'modern' his stiff shirt cracked. Every time he said 'functional,' the shirt rose a little more out of the vest." Afterward, Hawes asked Wright if he was comfortable in his clothes. "Of course," he answered. "Really, I thought your collar was cutting into your neck," she said. "It's an old collar and it's rough on the edge," he explained. Then he added belligerently, "There is *nothing wrong* with these clothes." Hawes aimed to do for clothing what Wright and others were doing in architecture (Figure 13).[68]

However, Hawes's functionalism was not abstract. Dressing was a form of acting, she argued, and the designer had to be a psychologist of public taste. She needed to know what working women were talking about, the movies they were watching, the books they read. Moreover, the wholesale designer had to know every step of the production process, and Hawes's book is a guide to the garment industry, describing its contractors, its skilled craftworkers, and its low-paid machine operators. For Hawes, clothes were "the most accurate artistic index of life." "Clothes are an expression of the social life of the time," she wrote, and "clothes designing is the expression of the social life of the time in terms of finished garments."[69]

Hawes never succeeded in uniting innovative design and mass production in her own work: caught between her training in custom-made dressmaking and her experiences in the garment industry's form of wholesale design, she admitted that she had "not found a satisfactory way of plying [her] original trade." French design was supported by an alliance between the government and the fabric manufacturers; to create the equivalent support for designers in the United States, she argued, they would need to form a union. Nevertheless, she was unwilling to abandon the hope that one could bring together mass-production and good design, that there could be a genuine democratization of style, and she became deeply involved in the politics of women's work and women's consumption. Discussing her reasons for going to work for the UAW, she wrote, in a passage that echoes *Culture and the Crisis*, that "no one is more hampered in his or her work today than the artist, no matter what his field. When that artist is as closely bound to commerce as is the dress designer, the hampering of her work is obviously traceable to the same things which prevent a third of the nation from being adequately clothed, housed and fed."[70]

In the years after the war, Hawes became increasingly critical of the subordination of style and design to fashion, to the logic of the consumer market. Her last major work, *Anything But Love* (1948), was a critique of the mass media's continual hard sell to women, surveying women's magazines, radio soap operas, screen magazines, and advice books, with their post-war messages of the Happy Housewife and Consumption as the Answer to Everything. A contemporary of de Beauvoir's *The Second Sex*, it is an early left feminist account of what would come to be called "the feminine mystique."

If Elizabeth Hawes's writings on dress design and women's work offered a rich reflection on a vernacular culture torn between the fashion industry and the symbolic forms and needs of daily life, the often-overlooked writings of left-wing critics on jazz stand as a powerful analysis of a vernacular art form. As I suggested earlier, the cultural left is usually depicted as being hostile to jazz, and Soviet writings, as well as those of non-Communist Marxists like Adorno, are regularly invoked. However, historians of jazz have long recognized that many of the major figures in jazz criticism were associated with the Popular Front, including Ralph Ellison, John Hammond, Otis Ferguson, Charles Edward Smith, Fredric Ramsey, and R.D. Darrell, not to mention such key European leftists as André Hodeir, Joachim Berendt (who debated with Adorno), and Eric Hobsbawm. Indeed, the most important early study of jazz, *Jazz: A People's Music* (1948), was written by a Popular Front critic, Sidney Finkelstein.

Finkelstein, who was born in 1909 in Brooklyn's Williamsburg and had graduated from City College, was one of the Popular Front's public intellectuals, writing his first book, *Art and Society* (1947), while working at the Brooklyn Post Office. Since Finkelstein's first books were published as the Cold War began, they received—and continue to receive—far less attention than the Marxist works of the 1930s, despite the fact that Finkelstein is a far more interesting Marxist critic than Gold, Freeman, Hicks, or Calverton. *Jazz* was his most influential work, largely because its musical analysis informed both Francis Newton's (a.k.a. Eric Hobsbawm) *The Jazz Scene* (1959) and Leroi Jones's *Blues People* (1963). Though the book's subtitle, *A People's Music*, makes it seem all too familiar—another version of left populism—it was not a work of folk sentimentality or romantic authenticity. Finkelstein began by placing jazz in world music and by refusing the high/low culture distinction, an artificial construct of the commodity status of music. Moreover, he criticized the nostalgia and primitivism of jazz critics who demanded that musicians limit themselves to "folk" practices. "Commercialism," Finkelstein wrote, "should not be applied ... to the desire of the musician to be paid for his work," nor to "the desire of the jazz musician to use the prevailing musical language of his period and audience"; "commercialism should be restricted, as a term, to what is really destructive in culture: the taking over of an art by business."[71]

Finkelstein rejected the notion of "purity" in music, seeing a dialectic of folk and non-folk practices in jazz: "the mixture, absorption and highly conscious interplay of many musical languages" characterized New Orleans jazz as well as bebop. He argued that "bebop and modern jazz ... raise the contradictions inherent in jazz from its beginnings, to their highest level. These contradictions in the music are directly a product of the contradictions in our social life, predominantly rising out of the place of the Negro people in American life." Finkelstein's work is an exploration of the ways social contradictions are expressed as formal problems, which are faced and resolved by jazz artists.[72]

Thus, just as the social history of jazz derived from the interplay and contradictions between the cultures of the black metropolises of the United States and the cultures of the urban "new Americans," so its formal history derived from the interplay and contradictions between the blues and the popular ballad. This dialectic grounded Finkelstein's brilliant formal interpretations of the different ways Coleman Hawkins, Lester Young, and Charlie Parker solved the "problem" of the popular ballad, and of the way Duke Ellington solved "the problem of form and content for the large band":

> He made the large band ... capable of the most delicate shades of tone and the most blasting power. This was an achievement not of mechanical instrumental knowledge, but a knowledge of harmony, and mastery of the musical problem of the relation of harmony to instrumental timbre ... Ellington built his chords on the understanding that when two or three instruments perform together, their overtones also combine, along with the notes directly played, and either strengthen or muddy the resulting harmony ... Ellington created not only a new sound for the large band, but also a new idiom for it; an idiom drawn partly out of the blues, partly out of the popular ballad ... Ellington preserved the harmonic character of the blues, but developed them melodically ... With the popular ballad idiom ... he dropped the melodic line ... and developed the diatonic and chromatic harmonies that had entered jazz with the popular ballad.

Finkelstein's attention to instrumental timbre ran throughout the work. He argued that "it has always been a new instrument that made a new music possible, and this is the basis of jazz instrumentation." The saxophone choir came to serve the jazz band as violins had served the orchestra, and the invention of the jazz rhythm section created "one of the most extraordinary and beautiful achievements of jazz sound": a "harmonized percussion," a "tuned rhythm."[73]

In some ways, Finkelstein's work remained tied to the traditions of philharmonic music in which he was trained. This orientation allowed him to see Ellington in the same terms as Ives and Bartók, moderns who explored the new harmonic implications of folk melody and created new instrumental timbres with folk instrumentation. For Finkelstein, as for Popular Front music theorists like Charles Seeger and Elie Siegmeister, the development of music was a dialectic of learned and folk traditions. It also led him to see the future of jazz in terms of what we might now call the Lincoln Center model: large forms—operas and symphonies—and large bands—he called for each American city to sponsor a permanent large jazz band. Though he wrote perceptively about the innovators of bebop, he did not imagine that their small-group forms would dominate jazz for the next generation. Nor did he completely register the impact that recording technologies would have on the dialectic of composition and improvisation.

Nevertheless, Finkelstein's ability to combine social and aesthetic criticism derived from a fundamental aspect of Popular Front cultural theory: its labor theory of culture. Though Popular Front musical theory is often described as "nationalist" because of its interest in folk traditions, all of the major Popular Front music theorists—Finkelstein, Elie Siegmeister, Alan Lomax, and Charles Seeger—rejected national and racial myths of musical purity in favor of what Finkelstein called "the basic truth that beauty is a product of labor."[74]

Hawes's writing on dress design and Finkelstein's book on jazz stand as two examples of the attempt to read the beauty of the new vernacular cultures of the mid twentieth century as a product of labor. This dialectic of art and labor also informs the outstanding synthesis of the period, C.L.R. James's legendary manuscript on American civilization, written in 1950 but only published after his death. James was yet another kind of intellectual in the cultural front: the party intellectual. After coming to the United States in 1938, his American writings were composed largely for the magazines and mimeographs of the small Trotskyist groups to which he belonged. *American Civilization* was written in a period of defeat: the anti-Communist purge was on, and James himself—though a bitter critic of the Communists—was unsuccessfully fighting a deportation order issued in 1948. He embarked on his account of American civilization as a kind of modern Tocqueville; it was written at the time when a number of studies of the American "national character" were being written, including David Potter's paean to abundance, *People of Plenty*, and Max Lerner's encyclopedic *America as a Civilization*. None of them can match the power and insight of James's account.[75]

The heart of James's discussion of American civilization was his understanding of mass production. For James, as for many modern social thinkers, Americanism was Fordism, and Fordism signified *both* the assembly line and the family car, the creation of a new labor process and a new form of mass-produced culture. The two central chapters of James's study are the ones on the labor process and the popular arts, and the dialectic between labor and culture runs throughout James's work. Though he was aware that the logic of mass production was to colonize leisure and trivialize work, he also maintained that "*mass production* has created a vast populace, literate, technically trained, conscious of itself and of its inherent right to enjoy all the possibilities of the society." Unlike the critics of mass culture, James did not reject Fordism but sought the seeds of the future in the utopian promise of mass production.[76]

The central question was that of popular desire. The manuscript returned again and again to the question: "What is it that the people want?" The answer, he suggested, is the fulfillment of the promises of mass production in both the popular arts and the labor process. His account of the popular arts remained sketchy, surveying the serial narratives of comic strips, Hollywood films, and radio soap operas. As was the case for many intellectuals of his generation, Chaplin stood above all, holding out the promise of a new democratic art. But James argued that the American popular arts since 1929 were haunted by the sense of crisis: "the blight (and the turn to murder and violence) which has descended upon the American people since 1929 expresses the fact that the bottom has fallen out of the civilization, men have no confidence in it any longer and are brought sharply up against the contradiction between the theories, principles, ideas etc., by which they live and the realities which they actually face." At the end, he returned to ancient Greek theater as an emblem of the possibilities of popular art.[77]

James united this account of the popular arts with a version of the radical industrial unionism that characterized the social movement of the time. American workers, he argued, "want to manage and arrange the work they are doing without any interference or supervision." This is the meaning of the CIO. Against the illusion that the CIO was formed as an instrument of collective bargaining or a means to negotiate about wages, James argued persuasively that "it was the first attempt of a section of the American workers to change the system as they saw it into something which would solve what they considered to be their rights, their interests and their human needs." For James, the call for workers control was the other side of a democratic popular culture. Both entailed the reuniting of work and culture, manual and mental labor: "The division between manual mechanistic labor and scientific intellectual labor was never so great as now."[78]

James captured the true meaning of the CIO, the reason the period needs to be remembered as the age of the CIO. The failure of the social movement represented by the CIO, the social movement I have called the Popular Front, resulted in the settlement we have come to call post-Fordism, postmodernism, the passive revolution of the American Century. James himself was deported in 1953, but his work was kept alive by a small group of Detroit radicals and reappeared in New Left magazines like *Radical America, Cultural Correspondence,* and *Urgent Tasks.* Our own "cultural studies" emerged out of that transition from modernism to postmodernism, Fordism to post-Fordism. By the late 1950s, a New Left was emerging from the ruins of the Popular Front. C. Wright Mills's influential "Letter to the New Left," which appeared in the British *New Left Review* in 1960 and the American *Studies on the Left* in 1961, was best known for its rejection of what he called the "labor metaphysic," the sense of "'the working class' of the advanced capitalist societies as *the* historic agency" of social change. However, what Mills saw as a failure of theory was actually the defeat of a movement. The "labor metaphysic" of the Popular Front was deeper and richer than Mills allowed. It was not simply the relatively abstract and theoretical "belief" in the historical role of the industrial working class. Rather, it was a laboring of culture itself: the assertion of the dignity and beauty of working-class arts and entertainment; the alliance between unions of industrial workers and unions of artists; the defense of arts and crafts in the face of commercial exploitation; and the profound sense that the dialectic between work and art, labor and beauty, was fundamental to human culture.[79]

Conclusion

The Old Left:
Eleven Outlined Epitaphs

In times behind, I too
wished I'd lived
in the hungry thirties
an' blew in like Woody
t' New York City
an' sang for dimes
on subway trains
satisfied at a nickel fare
an' passin' the hat
an' hitting the bars
on eighth avenue
an' makin' the rounds
t' the union halls
but when I came in
the fares were higher
up t' fifteen cents an' climbin'
an' those bars that Woody's guitar
rattled . . . they've changed
they've been remodeled
an' those union halls
like the cio
an' the nmu
come now! can you see 'em
needin' me
for a song
or two

ah where are those forces of yesteryear?
why didn't they meet me here
an' greet me here?

Bob Dylan, "11 Outlined Epitaphs," 1964[1]

> The productive use of earlier radicalisms ... lies not in their trium-
> phant reassemblage as a radical precursor tradition but in their tragic
> failure to constitute such a tradition in the first place. History pro-
> gresses by failure rather than by success, as Benjamin never tired of
> insisting; and it would be better to think of Lenin or Brecht (to pick a
> few illustrious names at random) as failures—that is, as actors and
> agents constrained by their own ideological limits and those of their
> moment of history—than as triumphant examples and models in some
> hagiographic or celebratory sense.
>
>   Fredric Jameson[2]

When the generation of the Popular Front looked back at the history they
had inherited, they often told a story of the decline and fall of the Lincoln
republic. When we at the end of the twentieth century look back to the
history we inherit, we write stories of the "rise and fall of the New Deal
order," the "American Century." The social, political, and cultural settlement that emerged out of the crises of the depression and World War II—
the Cold War, the US version of the warfare-welfare state, the Democratic
Party coalition built by Roosevelt, the cultural apparatus of classic Hollywood, network broadcasting, and mass higher education—dominated the
rest of the century. It was the Establishment against which both the New
Left *and* the New Right of "1968" mobilized.

This book has been a tale of that "New Deal order," though I have not,
for the most part, looked at the dominant political and economic forces,
the "corporate" or "multi-national" liberalism of Roosevelt's historical bloc,
that won the struggles of "1934." Rather, I have looked at the social
movement, the Popular Front, that emerged in the midst of the upheavals
of the depression, became one of the social forces that shaped the New
Deal order, and was defeated in the shakedown of 1947–48. One part—
the Communists and their "fellow travelers"—was repressed and expelled
from public culture; it became a beleaguered subculture whose emblems
were the Weavers, the Rosenbergs, and Paul Robeson. Another part—the
social democrats that made up the purged CIO as well as the Cold War
cultural fronts like the Congress for Cultural Freedom—was incorporated
as a chastened junior partner in the post-war order, pledging allegiance to
the anti-Communist crusade in the unions and universities of the United
States as well as in the cities and jungles of Vietnam.

However, as Stuart Hall has reminded us, the "social forces which lose
out in any particular historical period do not thereby disappear from the
terrain of struggle." Just as the radical republicans, black reconstructionists,
Knights of Labor, and populists embodied the democratic promise of the
Lincoln republic, so the CIO, the Popular Front social movement, and the
artists and intellectuals of the cultural front embodied the democratic

promise of the New Deal era, the "People's Century" within the "American Century." If history progresses by failure rather than success, the failure of the Popular Front remains part of the dialectic of American history. To conclude, I want to consider several endings of the cultural front, reflections on failure and defeat.[3]

"The basic failure of the Left in America," the narrator of Clancy Sigal's novel *Going Away* said, was "that it failed to prepare us for defeat." *Going Away: A Report, A Memoir* (1961) is the first of my endings. Sigal, born in 1927, was part of the youngest generation of the Popular Front. "The thirties had been my time," his autobiographical narrator writes, "and I had been fourteen in 1940." The narrator, a combination of Dos Passos's Vag and Kerouac's Sal Paradise, is a "second-generation immigrant" whose life mimics the trajectory of the plebeian radicals who moved into the cultural apparatus: "How could I tell him what it does to be brought up to organize socialist trade unions and find yourself a Hollywood agent at the age of twenty-nine?" The novel's long rambling road story—there are no chapter breaks—is a return trip: he leaves Hollywood in 1956 and drives cross-country to New York. Stopping in virtually all the Popular Front cities and factory towns, he revisits former comrades and rekindles old arguments; like Kerouac, Sigal gives his friends and associates thinly disguised names, and it is not hard to uncover figures like Nelson Algren and Elizabeth Hawes among his portraits of proletarian novelists, Communist screenwriters, union organizers, and Party militants. Throughout the journey, the radio broadcasts of the Hungarian uprising and the subsequent Soviet invasion serve as a counterpoint to the flashback tales of the narrator's own political past: the "League of Anti-Fascist Youth," a Durham textile strike, the factional struggle in the "Amalgamated Vehicle Builders-CIO" (the United Auto Workers), and the organization of a tiny union of 16-mm film cleaners.[4]

"I really wanted, while I was on the road, to look at America and try to figure out why it wasn't my country anymore," Sigal's narrator writes. When he blames it on "party mistakes," he is rebuked by the retired labor organizer Logan Moore: "Son, don't shoot your mouth off if you don't know what you're talking about. America changed, and the Reds were trapped in that change. They weren't born for our time." Throughout the novel, the characters rehearse all the arguments and explanations of that change: television and the mass media, the post-war prosperity of cars and suburbs, racial conflicts (Chicago feels like it is "waiting for a race riot"). In his search for America, the narrator even considers taking a Ph.D. in American Studies.[5]

A generation later, the debate over the change continues. The post-war settlement marked the failure not of socialist revolution—revolutions usually take place in defeated nations and American capitalism had emerged from World War II victorious and largely unchallenged—but of a laborist social democracy. For some, the defeat was caused by the Red scare and the repression of the left. Indeed, there is probably a larger historical literature on the Red scare, the blacklists, and McCarthyism than on the Popular Front itself. However, the repression of labor and the left, even the witch-hunts and the un-American activities committees, shadowed the Popular Front from its beginnings; it is its greater *success* in the late 1940s and 1950s that must be explained. Others continue to look to the left itself to account for the defeat, citing the Communist Party's undying fidelity to the Soviet Union, magnified by the onset of the Cold War. However, since the Popular Front was always much broader than the Communist Party, this does not explain why the militancy of the post-war strike wave did not become a social democratic force in American politics, why Henry Wallace's Progressive Party failed to create a new historical bloc, why even the anti-Communist social democracy of the UAW's Walter Reuther stalled.

Perhaps the most influential recent interpretation of the "rise and fall of the New Deal order" points to the eclipse of the "labor question" in American politics, "the substitution of race for class as the great unsolved problem in American life." In this account, pioneered by conservative populists and adopted by a number of contemporary liberal Democrats, the populist and patriotic Roosevelt coalition, built on the votes of white ethnic workers, was destroyed by the racial politics created by an alliance between the rhetorically aggressive black leaders of a welfare underclass and the anti-American "limousine liberals," including the student radicals of the New Left. The implicit and sometimes explicit counsel in these accounts is that liberals and the left should turn away from the politics of racial justice to lure back the "Reagan Democrats" with a politics of white populism. This advice is often combined with a cultural attack on the "identity politics" of the supposedly "politically correct" adversary culture in the arts, culture industries, and universities.[6]

There are two difficulties with this interpretation. First, though Roosevelt's Democratic Party itself tolerated the apartheid regime of segregation and sharecropping in the South, and interned Japanese Americans during the war, the Popular Front social movement was, as I have tried to show, as committed to the politics of racial justice as it was to the politics of industrial unionism. Though racial and ethnic hostilities and conflicts were evident in the movement, one does not find a "class" politics yielding to a "race" politics. The "labor question" was intimately connected with the "national question," and the "peoples" of the United States were recognized in the rhetoric, images, theories, and organizations of the Popular Front.

Second, the accounts of the eclipse of class and the "labor" question often lack any class analysis. Whereas the earlier party systems invoked by Fraser and Gerstle were brought to an end by a crisis—the crisis over slavery that led to a civil war, the economic crisis of the 1890s, and the crash of 1929—the New Deal order seems to evaporate because of a rhetorical shift, a curious forgetting about class, a preoccupation with "cultural pluralism," combined with the New Left's alleged contempt for white workers and its refusal to adopt the language of Americanism and populism. However, the racialization of American politics that *did* take place after World War II was *not* the result of a rhetorical shift on the part of the left, but of a dramatic transformation in class relations. Perhaps the most striking of these changes was the extraordinary wartime migration of black and white southerners to the defense plants of the North and West. The largest internal migration in US history, it remade the American working class.

The inheritance of the Jim Crow South moved north, and southern political leaders from Martin Luther King, Jr to George Wallace became national figures. After 1960, the only Democrats to win the presidency were white southerners: Johnson, Carter, and Clinton. American culture acquired a southern accent. Southern religions—the black and white Baptist, Pentecostal, and Holiness churches—grew rapidly: Jimmy Carter became the first Southern Baptist to be elected president. Southern musics—"race" and "hillbilly"—were renamed rhythm and blues and country and western and dominated post-war vernacular music. The second-generation immigrant working class that had built the CIO and the Popular Front was displaced by a new working class, and the shape of working-class politics and culture was changed irrevocably.

The last and perhaps greatest proletarian novel of the age of the CIO was an epic of this migration, and it stands as a second ending for my story: Harriette Arnow's *The Dollmaker* (1954). Arnow, born in Kentucky in 1908, was a typical plebeian writer of the depression. She had moved to Cincinnati in 1934 to be a writer, and supported herself as a waitress and as a sales clerk. Her first story was published in one of the proletarian little magazines, *Kosmos*, in 1935; she later worked on the Federal Writers Project guide to Ohio. In 1943, she and her husband moved to Detroit, living in a housing project for wartime workers: out of this experience came *The Dollmaker*, the story of a Kentucky hill family that migrates to Detroit. The novel takes place in the last year of the war, from the fall of 1944 to the fall of 1945. Like the ghetto pastorals, the novel places the political events—the war, V-E day in the spring of 1945, the atom bomb in August 1945, the factional struggles in the UAW, and the fall 1945 General Motors strike—in the background. The novel's foreground is the daily domestic struggle of Gertie Nevels in the alley where "all the new Detroit words—adjustment, down payment, . . . eviction and communism—would get into her head and swim round for days until she got them fastened down just right so that they lay there, handy to her thinking." This is the site of the larger historical drama, the tragedy of "adjustment" to the work, clocks, money, and commodities of industrial capitalism, figured in the "Icy Heart" icebox.[7]

Unlike *Going Away*, *The Dollmaker* was not a reflection on the defeat of the left, but it is a story of the civil war that led to it. Sigal's narrative of the battles in the UAW—"the rivalry of Victor Hauser [Walter Reuther] and K.T. Tolliver [R.J. Thomas] for presidency of the union was the expressed essence of all the conflicting drives in the American working class immediately after the war"—focused on the union staff and militants. Arnow's novel depicts the battle in the housing project neighborhood: the echoes of the race riots and hate strikes; Gertie's worries about lay-offs and wildcat strikes; the mysterious beatings of Clovis and his fellow unionists; the daily ethnic and racial bickering in the alley—"hillbilly," spat out at Gertie as if it "shaped a vile thing to be spewed out quickly" and "the words she didn't know, like 'wop' and 'kike' and 'shine'."[8]

But *The Dollmaker* is also a narrative of a larger defeat. Two of Gertie's children refuse to adjust to Detroit: Reuben returns to Kentucky and the dream of a farm; Cassie dies in the novel's most intense and moving passage. Gertie's long, laborious and losing battle with Detroit is charted through her whittling. In Kentucky, she whittles handles for use, "hoe handles, saw handles, ax handles . . . it takes a heap of handles"; dolls for her daughter, what she calls "whittlen foolishness"; and an unfinished head of Christ in a piece of cherry wood. In Detroit, she reluctantly begins to sell her "whittlen foolishness." At first, it is an extension of her craft: a teacher buys a doll as folk art; and her neighbors commission her to carve crucifixes and religious icons. Eventually, her husband and children persuade her to turn their kitchen into a home factory, turning out cheap, machine-cut, painted dolls: "the work of creating ugliness." Throughout it, however, she continues to work on the head of Christ, searching for his face in Detroit. The novel ends against the backdrop of the 1945 General Motors strike: with Clovis on strike, she sacrifices the head of Christ in order to make more painted dolls. Gertie is defeated by the world of Fordist capitalism.[9]

The Dollmaker was a powerful imaginative rendering of the wartime migration. But it never had the cultural success of the earlier Popular Front migration epic, *The Grapes of Wrath*. Though it finished second to Faulkner's *A Fable* for the National Book Award, it was not filmed until 1984. Few American writers or artists recognized the significance of the migration. Again, Clancy Sigal's novel is symptomatic: his cross-country driver picks up a hitchhiker with "long Elvis sideburns" who is on his way "back to Kentucky after two years in California working in an aircraft plant near Oakland." But the Kentucky hitchhiker is not the America Sigal's narrator is looking for; he doesn't want his company and lies to avoid taking him as far he can. But the hitchhiker haunts the book; as the narrator tries to get the news from Hungary on the radio, he hears Elvis Presley singing "Love Me Tender" and "Heartbreak Hotel." Like many on the cultural front, Sigal did not fully register the meaning of Elvis or his Kentucky hitchhiker.[10]

The Popular Front uncertainty about Elvis Presley can be seen in the fascinating and contradictory film made by Elia Kazan and Budd Schulberg, *Face in the Crowd* (1957), a third ending to this story. Though Kazan and Schulberg had renounced their Popular Front politics, they continued to share its aesthetic: their *On the Waterfront* (1954) was the culmination of the Group Theatre's proletarian drama. Even *People's World* saw the irony of *Face in the Crowd*, noting that "two stool pigeon witnesses before the Un-American Committee" have produced "one of the finest progressive films we have seen in years." However, *Face in the Crowd* is a divided film. On the one hand, it is a straightforward Popular Front satire on the mass media. An innocent young entertainer, played by Andy Griffith, is taken up and corrupted by television advertisers, becoming a mouthpiece for a right-wing senator and his cronies. The classic depression concerns with radio demagogues and native fascists fuse with the Cold War panic over mass culture. As Kazan noted years later, the film "anticipated Ronald Reagan."[11]

On the other hand, the film is also a story of a "hillbilly" guitarist and singer who becomes a star. Andy Griffith's Lonesome Rhodes, an Arkansas hobo whose bluesy rockabilly songs are first recorded in jail, combined elements of Woody Guthrie and Elvis Presley. But Kazan and Schulberg did not do justice to the music of Lonesome Rhodes. Though the film's score (composed by Tom Glazer, a Popular Front folk singer who had recorded *Songs of Citizen C.I.O.* with Josh White) incorporates folk and country music, and Griffith's early jailhouse songs are powerful, the advertising story takes over the film. Rhodes's music recedes in importance, and the film viewer can hardly identify with Rhodes's screaming fans. The film sees his stardom as a fraud, a scam. This is a remarkable contrast to *Jailhouse Rock* (1957), in which Elvis Presley himself plays the role of the country boy who learns his music in prison and goes on to stardom. Here, however, Presley's memorable performances of the classic Lieber and Stoller songs convince us that the film's protagonist is a star. *Face in the Crowd* uses the narrative of the rise of country music and the new "hillbilly" working class, but it is unable to take it seriously, reducing the culture of Elvis Presley to an advertisers' plot.

The missed connection between the cultural front and the southern migrants deeply affected the course of post-war American culture. The left never had the impact on the new working-class musics—country and western, rhythm and blues, and rockabilly—that it had had on the musical cultures of swing and jazz. Benny Goodman, Count Basie, and Frank Sinatra lent their names to Popular Front benefits and alliances; Muddy Waters, Hank Williams, and Elvis Presley never did. Decades later, the inheritors of Popular Front musical culture were still arguing whether "[Pete] Seeger should have put away his banjo and apprenticed himself to Elvis Presley."[12]

The figure who apprenticed himself to Elvis Presley as well as to Woody Guthrie, Bob Dylan, also stands at the end of this story. Dylan's homage to Guthrie in 1962—not only his "Song to Woody" but his appropriation of Guthrie's political and musical persona—was one of several by which New Left artists and intellectuals used the legacy of the thirties to create a new cultural renaissance. In 1962 also, the young cabaret singer Barbra Streisand revived the Popular Front musical theater tradition, singing on the twenty-fifth anniversary recording of *Pins and Needles.* The civil rights movement in the South spurred several young jazz musicians to reinvent Ellington's experiments in political jazz composition: in 1959, Charles Mingus's classic, *Mingus Ah Um,* included his "Open Letter to Duke," as well as the satiric "Fables of Faubus" (though Columbia suppressed his lyrics attacking Orville Faubus, the racist governor of Arkansas). Both Sonny Rollins's *The Freedom Suite* (1958) and Max Roach's *We Insist! Freedom Now Suite* (1960) inherited the ambitions of *Black, Brown and Beige.*

In the early 1960s, a lasting image of the "thirties" was created by postmodern revivals of folk music, documentary photography, depression literature, and Hollywood film. By 1962, Pete Seeger had become the link between the now legendary Guthrie and Leadbelly and the young topical folk singers like Dylan, Joan Baez, and Bernice Johnson of the Freedom Singers. Edward Steichen's 1962 Museum of Modern Art exhibition, The Bitter Years, brought new attention to Popular Front photography; and Walker Evans and James Agee's *Let Us Now Praise Famous Men* (1941) became a New Left classic after its 1960 republication. Daniel Aaron's *Writers on the Left* (1961) was the first and most influential history of the "literary class war" of the 1930s. Henry Roth's ghetto pastoral *Call It Sleep* (1934), which had originally sold only a few hundred copies and was not mentioned by Aaron, was reprinted as an Avon paperback in 1964 and acclaimed as a forgotten classic by critics like Irving Howe, Alfred Kazin, and Leslie Fiedler. The legacy of the Old Left haunted the novels of E.L. Doctorow, who became, as Fredric Jameson noted, "the epic poet of the disappearance of the American radical past."[13]

There was a similar revival of the Popular Front in Hollywood during the 1960s and 1970s, though it was overshadowed by the European New Waves of the late 1950s and early 1960s and the resurgence of an aesthetically and politically experimental filmmaking in the late 1960s. But if Godard's *Weekend* and the great Newsreel documentaries of the late 1960s remain the films *of* the New Left, they were nevertheless accompanied by the films of Hollywood's New Left auteurs, actors like Jane Fonda, Donald Sutherland, and Jack Nicholson, and directors like Robert Altman, Sidney Lumet, and Francis Coppola. In many cases, Hollywood's second golden age depended not only on the reappropriation of Orson Welles—Peter Bogdanovich organized the first US Welles retrospective at the Museum of Modern Art in 1961—but on the filming of depression stories: *Bonnie and Clyde, The Day of the Locust, They Shoot Horses, Don't They?*, and Robert Altman's *Thieves Like Us*, a remake of Nicholas Ray's *They Live By Night*. Though Warren Beatty's *Reds*, with its parade of Old Left witnesses, returned to the 1910s, it was also the culmination of the Popular Front's infatuation with the figure of John Reed and the story of the Bolshevik Revolution.

These films often drew on the talents of the Popular Front veterans of the blacklist: Ring Lardner Jr, one of the Hollywood Ten, was the screenwriter for Altman's *M.A.S.H.* (which starred Donald Sutherland); Waldo Salt wrote *The Day of the Locust, Midnight Cowboy, Serpico,* and *Coming Home* (with Jane Fonda); and Martin Ritt directed several of Hollywood's finest "proletarian" films, *Sounder, Norma Rae* and *The Molly Maguires*. *Sounder* stands in a tradition of narratives of black sharecroppers that reaches back to the Scottsboro case and the early proletarian stories of Richard Wright; *Norma Rae* builds on the saga of southern textile organizing, with its roots in the half-dozen radical novels written about the Communist-led Gastonia strike of 1928; and the story of *The Molly Maguires* had long been a part of Popular Front culture: one of the first historical studies of the Mollies was written by the young Communist Anthony Bimba in 1932. Ritt also directed *The Front* (1976), which was the first Hollywood feature about the blacklist as well as Woody Allen's homage to Popular Front comedian Zero Mostel, whose final role is as a victim of the blacklist.

In 1974, Tillie Olsen's "lost" novel, *Yonnondio: From the Thirties,* was published. "Reader, it was not to have ended here," she wrote, "but it is nearly forty years since this book had to be set aside, never to come to completion." *Yonnondio* proved to be the Popular Front's lyric masterpiece, a fragmentary lament for the cultural front's incomplete laboring of American culture, a tribute to the "human dumpheap where the nameless FrankLloydWrights of the proletariat have wrought their wondrous futuristic structures of flat battered tin cans, fruit boxes and gunny sacks, cardboard and mother earth." The symbolic acts of the cultural front are a similar dumpheap of half-remembered songs, forgotten novels, and legendary performances. "I think the New Playwrights' Theatre failed," John Dos Passos concluded in one of the cultural front's earliest reflections on failure, a 1929 epitaph for the theater that Dos Passos, along with four other radical playwrights, including John Howard Lawson and Michael Gold, had directed for three seasons. Nevertheless, Dos Passos continued, "the fact that it existed makes the next attempt in the same direction that much easier." He went on to reflect on the political consequences of cultural insurgencies. "I think we can cross out political results," he wrote. "The American mind of all classes and denominations is too accustomed to keeping art or ideas in separate watertight compartments. Their influence on action is infinitesimal and only to be measured in generations and major emotional movements." Though the young radicals of the proletarian avant-garde promised a new culture overnight, some of the most important works of the cultural front did not appear until a generation later. Others remained ruins, unfinished fragments and failed projects. In this book, I have tried to measure those ruins, the symbolic acts of the cultural front, in generations and movements. The failure of their laboring of American culture remains our starting point.[14]

Notes

Notes to Introduction

1. Tillie Lerner, "The Strike," *Partisan Review* 1.4 September–October 1934, reprinted in Jack Salzman, ed., *Years of Protest: A Collection of American Writings of the 1930s* (New York: Pegasus, 1967), pp. 138, 144.

2. Lerner, "The Strike," p. 140. Robert Cantwell, "The Literary Life in California,"*New Republic*, 22 August 1934, p. 49. Tillie Lerner, "Thousand-Dollar Vagrant," *New Republic*, 29 August 1934, pp. 67–9. Tillie Olsen, *Yonnondio: From the Thirties* (1974; rpt New York: Delta, 1989), p. 21.

3. Meridel Le Sueur, "I Was Marching," *New Masses*, 18 September 1934, reprinted in Meridel Le Sueur, *Ripening: Selected Work, 1927–1980* (Old Westbury, N.Y.: The Feminist Press, 1982), pp. 158, 165. Carlos Bulosan, *America Is in the Heart: A Personal History* (1946; rpt Seattle: University of Washington Press, 1973), pp. 199, 205.

4. Wendy Smith, *Real Life Drama: The Group Theatre and America, 1931–1940* (New York: Alfred A. Knopf, 1990), p. 200.

5. Malcolm Cowley, *Exile's Return: A Narrative of Ideas* (New York: W.W. Norton, 1934), p. 300. Kenneth Burke, *Permanence and Change: An Anatomy of Purpose* (New York: New Republic, 1935), p. 93. League of Professional Groups for Foster and Ford, *Culture and the Crisis: An Open Letter to the Writers, Artists, Teachers, Physicians, Engineers, Scientists and Other Professional Workers of America* (New York: Workers Library Publishers, 1932), p. 30.

6. Sean Wilentz, "Red Herrings Revisited: Theodore Draper Blows His Cool," *Voice Literary Supplement*, June 1985, p. 6.

7. Mumford quoted in Judy Kutulas, *The Long War: The Intellectual People's Front and Anti-Stalinism, 1930–1940* (Durham, N.C.: Duke University Press, 1995), p. 33. Commonwealth College letter quoted in Douglas Wixson, *Worker-Writer in America: Jack Conroy and the Tradition of Midwestern Literary Radicalism, 1898–1990* (Urbana: University of Illinois Press, 1994), pp. 277–8. Paul Jay, ed., *The Selected Correspondence of Kenneth Burke and Malcolm Cowley* (New York: Viking, 1988), p. 202.

8. On Farrell, see Alan Wald, *Writing from the Left* (London: Verso, 1994), p. 51 n. 19.

9. I am indebted here to Alan Trachtenberg's distinction between the "politics of affiliation and allegiance" and the "politics of aesthetics" in his essay on a major Popular Front photographer, Paul Strand. Trachtenberg suggests that "in the narrow sense of affiliation and allegiance, Strand's politics bear an uncertain relation to his art, and seeking out connection between them is probably fruitless. . . . What we want most to understand about Strand's work and career is the politics of his aesthetics." This seems to me too much a concession to a formalism; as uncertain as the relation between the political consciousness of the artist and the political unconscious of the work may be, it is that connection which demands exploration,

particularly in the case of the figures who made up the cultural front, that is to say those for whom particular affiliations and allegiances were considered choices. It is not clear that the two politics will necessarily coincide, which is why Trachtenberg's working distinction between the politics of affiliation and the politics of aesthetics, which I translate as the distinction between "cultural politics" and "aesthetic ideologies", is so useful. Trachtenberg, "Introduction," to Maren Stange, ed. *Paul Strand,* (New York: Aperture, 1990), p. 4.

10. For the notion of the political unconscious, I am indebted to Frederic Jameson, *The Political Unconscious* (Ithaca, N.Y.: Cornell University Press, 1981). The phrase "socially-conscious" or "socially-significant" runs throughout the cultural front.

11. Raymond Williams, "The Uses of Cultural Theory," in his *The Politics of Modernism: Against the New Conformists* (London: Verso, 1989), pp. 174–5.

Notes to 1

1. Lionel Trilling, "A Novel of the Thirties," in his *The Last Decade* (New York: Harcourt Brace Jovanovich, 1979), p. 15.

2. "The Fortune Survey," *Fortune* 26.1, July 1942, p. 12.

3. David Roediger, "Foreword," to Jessie Lloyd O'Connor, Harvey O'Connor,and Susan Bowler, *Harvey and Jessie: A Couple of Radicals* (Philadelphia: Temple University Press, 1988), p. x.

4. On the double meaning of the historical bloc and its relation to representation and hegemony, note the following passages from the *Prison Notebooks*: "An appropriate political initiative is always necessary to liberate the economic thrust from the dead weight of traditional policies—i.e. to change the political direction of certain forces which have to be absorbed if a new, homogeneous politico-economic historical bloc ... is to be successfully formed." "If the relationship between intellectuals and people-nation, between the leaders and the led, the rulers and the ruled, is provided by an organic cohesion in which feeling-passion becomes understanding and thence knowledge ... then and only then is the relationship one of representation. Only then can there take place an exchange of individual elements between the rulers and ruled, leaders and led, and can the shared life be realised which alone is a social force—with the creation of the 'historical bloc'." Croce's thought "has forcefully drawn attention ... to the moment of hegemony and consent as the necessary form of the concrete historical bloc." Antonio Gramsci, *Selections from the Prison Notebooks* (London: Lawrence and Wishart, 1971), pp. 168, 418, 195.

5. On the analysis of historical blocs, note the following passages from the *Prison Notebooks*: "Structures and superstructures form a 'historical bloc.' That is to say the complex, contradictory and discordant ensemble of the superstructures is the reflection of the ensemble of the social relations of production." "The conception of *historical bloc* in which precisely material forces are the content and ideologies are the form, though this distinction between form and content has purely didactic value, since the material forces would be inconceivable historically without form and the ideologies would be individual fancies without the material forces." Gramsci, *Prison Notebooks*, pp. 366, 377.

6. Robert H. Zieger, *The CIO 1935–1955* (Chapel Hill: University of North Carolina Press, 1995), p. 1. In the year after the NIRA, the AFL grew by 500,000 (from 2 to 2.5 million) and the Communist-led affiliates of the Trade Union Unity League grew by 100,000: Howard Kimeldorf, *Reds or Rackets: The Making of Radical and Conservative Unions on the Waterfront* (Berkeley: University of California Press, 1988), p. 85.

7. Len De Caux, *Labor Radical* (Boston: Beacon, 1970), p. 242. De Caux had been the publicity director of the CIO and the editor of the *CIO News.* For the international migration of laborers, see David Montgomery, *The Fall of the House of Labor* (Cambridge: Cambridge University Press, 1987), particularly pp. 68–74, 171–9, and 457–64. Marcus Klein, *Foreigners: The Making of American Literature, 1900–1940* (Chicago: University of Chicago Press, 1981), pp. 13–14. For two fine synoptic accounts of the CIO working class, see Mike Davis, "The Barren Marriage of American Labor and the Democratic Party," in his *Prisoners of the American Dream* (London: Verso, 1986), and Steve Fraser, "The 'Labor Question'," in Steve Fraser and

Gary Gerstle, *The Rise and Fall of the New Deal Order, 1930–1980* (Princeton, N.J.: Princeton University Press, 1989).

8. In 1950, C.L.R. James pointed to the wider meaning of the CIO: "the first and most fundamental illusion to be shattered," he argued, "is that the C.I.O. was formed as an instrument of 'collective bargaining,' to negotiate about wages, to protect the 'interests' of workers, to ensure higher wages in order to prevent the economy from collapsing, to help in the redistribution of income, etc . . . the C.I.O. was not originally what so many people seem to think it is today. It was no instrument of collective bargaining and getting out the vote for the Democratic Party. It was the first attempt of a section of the American workers to change the system as they saw it into something which would solve what they considered to be their rights, their interests, and their human needs." C.L.R. James, *American Civilization* (Cambridge: Blackwell, 1993), pp. 172–3. More recently, the historian Thomas Göbel has argued that the CIO was "not just . . . a union movement trying to increase the wages of workers but [w]as something of a civil crusade, a movement that promised a sense of dignity and power to a great number of people previously excluded from full participation in American life." Thomas Göbel, "Becoming American: Ethnic Workers and the Rise of the CIO," *Labor History* 29.2, Spring 1988, pp. 196–7.

9. Gary Gerstle, *Working-Class Americanism: The Politics of Labor in a Textile City 1914–1960* (Cambridge: Cambridge University Press, 1989), p. 13. See also Gerstle's discussion of rank-and-file militancy, pp. 125–6. Lizabeth Cohen, *Making a New Deal: Industrial Workers in Chicago, 1919–1939* (Cambridge: Cambridge University Press, 1990), p. 8.

10. Labor historians have suggested a number of terms to capture the mixture of radicalism and conservatism that characterizes this moment: for "working-class Americanism," see Gerstle, *Working-Class Americanism*; for "worker statism," see Cohen, *Making a New Deal*, p. 283; for "social unionism," see Kim Moody, *An Injury to All: The Decline of American Unionism* (London: Verso, 1988), pp. 58–60; for corporatism, see Nelson Lichtenstein, "From Corporatism to Collective Bargaining: Organized Labor and the Eclipse of Social Democracy in the Postwar Era," in Fraser and Gerstle, *The Rise and Fall of the New Deal Order*; for "moral economics," see Robert S. McElvaine, *The Great Depression* (New York: Times Books, 1984), pp. 221–3. In general this attempt by labor historians to find terms to characterize working-class ideologies owes much to similar work on nineteenth-century artisan or labor republicanism. For a fine discussion of the relation between popular initiatives and government decision-makers, see David Montgomery, "Labor and the Political Leadership of the New Deal," *International Review of Social History* 39, 1994, pp. 335–60. For a synoptic portrait of the industrial working class in 1941, see Zieger, *The CIO*, pp. 111–21.

11. Reeve Vanneman and Lynn Weber Cannon, *The American Perception of Class* (Philadelphia: Temple University Press, 1987), pp. 134, 140. On the rhetoric and iconography of class, see Elizabeth Faue, *Community of Suffering and Struggle: Women, Men and the Labor Movement in Minneapolis, 1915–1945* (Chapel Hill: University of North Carolina Press, 1991), particularly chapter 3; Gerstle, *Working-Class Americanism*, particularly chapter 5; and Cohen, *Making a New Deal*, pp. 286–7.

12. McElvaine, *The Great Depression*, p. 223. On Catholic corporatism, see Gerstle *Working-Class Americanism*, pp. 215, 247ff. On syndicalism, see Edward P. Johanningsmeier's excellent *Forging American Communism: The Life of William Z. Foster* (Princeton, N.J.: Princeton University Press, 1994), pp. 56, 159, 164. On industrial democracy, see Steven Fraser, *Labor Will Rule: Sidney Hillman and the Rise of American Labor* (New York: Free Press, 1991).

13. Davis, *Prisoners of the American Dream*, p. 89; Göbel, "Becoming American," p. 195; Gerstle, *Working-Class Americanism*; Fraser, "The 'Labor Question'," p. 73.

14. Zieger, *The CIO*, p. 154.

15. It is this continuing impasse that draws contemporary political historians and writers back to the Popular Front; for contemporary socialists in and around the Democratic Socialists of America (DSA), for example, there is a curious parallelism between "Browderism," the Popular Front politics of the CP under Earl Browder, and "Shachtmanism," the realignment strategy of the small band of Trotskyists led by Max Shachtman. Here, Theodore Draper's complaint that the revisionist history of the Popular Front is simply an academic "radicalism of nostalgia" is wrongheaded. He himself suggests that "if the Popular Front had been permitted to run its course, it might well have turned out to be the forerunner of a

nonsocialist reform movement somewhat to the left of the Democratic Party or even a left wing of the Democratic Party." Precisely this political legacy attracts socialist writers like Maurice Isserman to the Popular Front experience; and it united a former "Browderite" like Dorothy Healey and a former "Shachtmanite" like Irving Howe in the DSA. Draper, "Afterword," to his *American Communism and Soviet Russia* (New York: Vintage, 1986), pp. 480, 469–70. Irving Howe's later thoughts on Popular Front politics are more interesting in this regard: see "The Brilliant Masquerade: A Note on 'Browderism'," in his *Socialism and America* (San Diego, Calif.: Harcourt Brace Jovanovich, 1985).

16. John Gunther, *Inside U.S.A.* (New York: Harper & Brothers, 1947), pp. 98–9.

17. The "liberalism" of the Popular Front runs through many of the left-wing critiques. But even Harvey Klehr argues that "the keynote of the Democratic Front was that the Communists went over to the New Deal; the New Deal did not go over to the Communists." Klehr, *The Heyday of American Communism* (New York: Basic Books, 1984), p. 414. Ira Katznelson, "Was the Great Society a Lost Opportunity?," in Fraser and Gerstle, *The Rise and Fall of the New Deal Order*, p. 190. "By social democracy," Katznelson adds, "I mean the attempts by labor and socialist movements in Western capitalist democracies to work through their electoral and representational political systems to achieve two principal goals: first, to effect interventions in markets that in the short run mitigate unequal distributional patterns, in the medium run promote more basic public controls over markets, and in the long run bring about a shift in social organization from capitalism to socialism; and, second, to secure the solidarity of their working-class base while reaching out for the allies they need to achieve majorities in elections and legislatures," p. 186. See also Joseph Gaer, *The First Round: The Story of the CIO Political Action Committee* (New York: Duell, Sloan and Pearce, 1944), which reprints many of the CIO-PAC pamphlets.

18. See Larry Ceplair's *Under the Shadow of War: Fascism, Anti Fascism, and Marxists 1918–1939* (New York: Columbia University Press, 1987); Peter N. Carroll, *The Odyssey of the Abraham Lincoln Brigade: Americans in the Spanish Civil War* (Stanford, Calif.: Stanford University Press, 1994); and Paul Buhle's excellent "Anti-Fascism," in Mari Jo Buhle, Paul Buhle, and Dan Georgakas, *Encyclopedia of the American Left* (New York: Garland, 1990), pp. 46–8. Buhle argues that there were three key limitations to the politics of anti-fascism: the erosion of antiwar sentiments; the shift away from anti-imperialist politics in order to defend the western democracies; and the disappearance of the rhetoric of socialist transformation in the common front against fascism.

19. See William L. O'Neill, *A Better World: The Great Schism: Stalinism and the American Intellectuals* (New York: Simon and Schuster, 1982); for a discussion of the meaning of "Stalinism" for literary intellectuals, see Jonathan Arac, *Critical Genealogies* (New York: Columbia University Press, 1989), pp. 309–11. Perhaps the finest reflection on the contradictions of solidarity politics that emerged from the Popular Front is Al Richmond's "An Old Problem of American Radicalism," in his *A Long View from the Left* (New York: Delta, 1972). For a powerful account of the way the narrative of the Indian war structured the global imagination of Americans, see Richard Slotkin, *Gunfighter Nation: The Myth of the Frontier in Twentieth-Century America* (New York: Atheneum, 1992). Michael Harrington offers a powerful account of the internationalist "vision of the Popular Front" in *The Vast Majority* (New York: Simon and Schuster, 1977), p. 175: "In it, one joined Spanish antifascism and the CIO and the black struggles and the New Deal and the Warsaw Ghetto and, for many, the Soviet Union, in a gigantic confraternity of the overwhelming majority of mankind which, if only given its head, if only freed from the plutocrats and fascists and colonialists, would rapidly and instinctively inaugurate a reign of human niceness, of fraternity (they would have said) and sorority (we would add). There were many, many things wrong with that vision, and it was sometimes manipulated to rationalize cruelty rather than to promote kindness. And yet, for all of its confusions and evasions and contradictions, if it was a corruption, it was a corruption of something good that always remained in it: of an internationalism that is still the only hope of mankind. I had read and internalized my Orwell; I knew the crimes committed by the GPU in the name of antifascism in Spain; and yet, I never cease to thrill at the songs of the International Brigade."

20. See Robin D.G. Kelley, *Hammer and Hoe: Alabama Communists during the Great Depression* (Chapel Hill: University of North Carolina Press, 1990); Charles H. Martin, "International

Labor Defense," in Buhle, Buhle, and Georgakas, *Encyclopedia*; Marlene Park, "Lynching and Antilynching: Art and Politics in the 1930s," *Prospects* 18, 1993.

21. On the IUCs, see Zieger, *The CIO*, pp. 148, 272.

22. See Fraser, *Labor Will Rule*; Rose Pesotta, *Bread upon the Waters* (1944, rpt Ithaca, N.Y.: ILR Press, 1987); Kenneth Waltzer, "The Party and the Polling Place: American Communism and an American Labor Party in the 1930s," *Radical History Review* 23 1980, pp. 104–29; Gerald Meyer, *Vito Marcantonio: Radical Politician 1902–1954* (Albany: State University of New York Press, 1989); and Joshua B. Freeman, *In Transit: The Transport Workers Union in New York City, 1933–1966* (New York: Oxford University Press, 1989).

23. On Broun and the Newspaper Guild, see Bruce Minton and John Stuart, *Men Who Lead Labor* (New York: Modern Age, 1937), pp. 115–42 (Minton and Stuart were editors of the *New Masses*, so this gives a good sense of Broun's meaning to the left); Walter M. Brasch, ed., *With Just Cause: Unionization of the American Journalist* (Lanham: University Press of America, 1991); and Heywood Hale Broun, ed., *Collected Edition of Heywood Broun* (New York: Harcourt Brace, 1941). Sharon Hartman Strom, "'We're No Kitty Foyles': Organizing Office Workers for the Congress of Industrial Organizations, 1937–1950," in Ruth Milkman, ed., *Women, Work, and Protest* (Boston: Routledge & Kegan Paul, 1985), pp. 217–8. See also the autobiography of Bella Visono Dodd, the Italian American Communist and teachers union activist: Dodd, *School of Darkness* (New York: P.J. Kennedy & Sons, 1954).

24. "My memory and knowledge," the Communist Party organizer Howard "Stretch" Johnson later told a historian, "is that 75% of black cultural figures had Party membership or maintained a regular meaningful contact with the Party." Quoted in Mark Naison, *Communists in Harlem during the Depression* (Urbana: University of Illinois Press, 1983), p. 193. See also Charles V. Hamilton, *Adam Clayton Powell, Jr* (New York: Atheneum, 1991); Gerald Horne, *Black Liberation/Red Scare: Ben Davis and the Communist Party* (Newark: University of Delaware Press, 1994); Jervis Anderson, *A. Philip Randolph* (New York: Harcourt Brace Jovanovich, 1973); and Earl Ofari Hutchinson, *Blacks and Reds: Race and Class in Conflict 1919–1990* (East Lansing: Michigan State University Press, 1995). Minton and Stuart, *Men Who Lead Labor* also has a contemporary profile, "A. Philip Randolph: Negro Labor's Champion."

25. Robert Cohen, *When the Old Left Was Young: Student Radicals and America's First Mass Student Movement, 1929–1941* (New York: Oxford University Press, 1993). For a memoir of the "alcoves," see Paul Jacobs, *Is Curly Jewish? A Political Self-Portrait Illuminating Three Turbulent Decades of Social Revolt 1935–1965* (New York: Atheneum, 1965), pp. 17–18.

26. Paul Buhle, "Daily Worker," in Buhle, Buhle, and Georgakas, *Encyclopedia*. New York's Popular Front also faced a local version of HUAC, the Rapp-Coudert hearings in 1940–42: see Stephen Leberstein, "Purging the Profs: The Rapp Coudert Committee in New York, 1940–1942," in Michael E. Brown and others, *New Studies in the Politics and Culture of U.S. Communism* (New York: Monthly Review Press, 1993).

27. Charles P. Larrowe, *Harry Bridges: The Rise and Fall of Radical Labor in the U.S.* (New York: Lawrence Hill, 1972), p. 72. Bridges is quoted in Kimeldorf, *Reds or Rackets*, p. 6. See also Bruce Nelson, *Workers on the Waterfront: Seamen, Longshoremen, and Unionism in the 1930s* (Urbana: University of Illinois Press, 1988).

28. Zieger, *The CIO*, p. 72. Guthrie's "Ballad of Harry Bridges" and "Song of Bridges" are reprinted in Larrowe, *Harry Bridges*, pp. 177, 233–4. See John Hammond, "That Man Bridges," *US Week* 1.20, 26 July 1941, pp. 12–13; Theodore Dreiser's interview with Bridges in *Friday*, 4 October 1940, p. 8; and F.O. Matthiessen's comments on Bridges in his *From the Heart of Europe* (New York: Oxford University Press, 1948), pp. 85–7.

29. Dorothy Bintang Fujita Rony, *"You Got to Move Like Hell": Transpacific Colonialism and Filipina/o Seattle, 1919–1941*, Ph.D. diss., Yale University, 1996; Chris Friday, *Organizing Asian American Labor: The Pacific Coast Canned-Salmon Industry, 1870–1942* (Philadelphia: Temple University Press, 1994), chapters 7–8; Karl G. Yoneda, *Ganbatte: Sixty-Year Struggle of a Kibei Worker* (Los Angeles: UCLA Asian American Studies Center, 1983); Vicki L. Ruiz, *Cannery Women, Cannery Lives: Mexican Women, Unionization, and the California Food Processing Industry, 1930–1950* (Albuquerque: University of New Mexico Press, 1987); Mario T. García, "The Popular Front: Josefina Fierro de Bright and the Spanish-Speaking Congress," in his *Mexican Americans* (New Haven, Conn.: Yale University Press, 1989); Mario T. García, ed., *Memories of Chicano History: The Life and Narrative of Bert Corona* (Berkeley: University of California Press,

1994); David G. Gutiérrez, *Walls and Mirrors: Mexican Americans, Mexican Immigrants, and the Politics of Ethnicity* (Berkeley: University of California Press, 1995), p. 111.

30. On the California Popular Front in these years, see García, *Memories*, pp. 67–154; Richmond, *A Long View From the Left*, pp. 264–94; Steve Nelson, James R. Barrett, and Rob Ruck, *Steve Nelson: American Radical* (Pittsburgh Pa.: University of Pittsburgh Press, 1981), pp. 240–76; and Carey McWilliams, *The Education of Carey McWilliams* (New York: Simon and Schuster, 1979), pp. 63–142. The columns of Guthrie and Quin have been collected: Woody Guthrie, *Woody Sez* (New York: Grosset & Dunlap, 1975); and Harry Carlisle, ed., *On the Drumhead: A Selection from the Writing of Mike Quin* (San Francisco: Pacific Publishing, 1948).

31. Larry Ceplair and Steven Englund, *The Inquisition in Hollywood: Politics in the Film Community, 1930–1960* (Berkeley: University of California Press, 1983); Nancy Lynn Schwartz, *The Hollywood Writers' Wars* (New York: Alfred Knopf, 1982); Bernard Dick, *Radical Innocence: A Critical Study of the Hollywood Ten* (Lexington: University Press of Kentucky, 1989); Mike Davis, *City of Quartz: Excavating the Future in Los Angeles* (London: Verso, 1990), p. 18.

32. Zieger, *The CIO*, p. 128. Edward L. Barrett, Jr, *The Tenney Committee* (Ithaca, N.Y.: Cornell University Press, 1951).

33. The argument about "community-based unionism" is from Faue, *Community of Suffering and Struggle*, pp. 4, 12. For the CIO's "culture of unity," see Cohen, *Making a New Deal*, p. 333. Many of the new studies of the CIO era are community studies: see Faue (on Minneapolis, Minn.); Cohen (on Chicago); Gerstle, *Working-Class Americanism* (on Woonsocket, R.I.); Peter Friedlander, *The Emergence of a UAW Local 1936–1939: A Study in Class and Culture* (Pittsburgh, Pa.: University of Pittsburgh Press, 1975) (on Detroit); Kelley, *Hammer and Hoe* (on Birmingham, Ala.); Ronald Edsforth, *Class Conflict and Cultural Consensus: The Making of a Mass Consumer Society in Flint, Michigan* (New Brunswick, N.J.: Rutgers University Press, 1987) (on Flint, Mich.); Michael K. Honey, *Southern Labor and Black Civil Rights: Organizing Memphis Workers* (Urbana: University of Illinois Press, 1993) (on Memphis, Tenn.); García, "Border Proletariats," in *Mexican Americans* (on El Paso, Tex.); Amy Kesselman, *Fleeting Opportunities: Women Shipyard Workers in Portland and Vancouver during World War II and Reconversion* (Albany: State University of New York Press, 1990) (on Portland and Vancouver); Daniel Nelson, *American Rubber Workers and Organized Labor 1900–1941* (Princeton, N.J.: Princeton University Press, 1988) (on Akron). See also Ronald W. Schatz, *The Electrical Workers: A History of Labor at General Electric and Westinghouse* (Urbana: University of Illinois Press, 1983).

34. Thomas J. E. Walker, *Pluralistic Fraternity: The History of the International Workers Order* (New York: Garland, 1991). I am indebted to a number of fine entries in Buhle, Buhle and Georgakas, *Encyclopedia*, including George Pirinsky, "Bulgarian Americans"; Matjaz Klemencic, "Slovenian Americans"; Peter Rachleff, "Croatian Americans"; Mary Cygan, "American Slav Congress," "Polish Americans"; and Gerald Markowitz, "Hungarian Americans." See also Nelson, Barrett, and Ruck, *Steve Nelson*; Margaret Collingwood Nowak, *Two Who Were There* (Detroit, Mich.: Wayne State University Press, 1990); and Zoltán Deák, *This Noble Flame: Portrait of a Hungarian Newspaper in the USA* (New York: Heritage Press, 1982).

35. The great journalistic narratives of the midwestern struggles include Mary Heaton Vorse, *Labor's New Millions* (New York: Modern Age, 1938); Louis Adamic, *My America* (New York: Harper and Brothers, 1938); Ruth McKenney, *Industrial Valley* (New York: Harcourt Brace, 1939); Pesotta, *Bread upon the Waters*; and Elizabeth Hawes, *Hurry Up Please Its Time* (New York: Reynal & Hitchcock, 1946). On Malden, see Peter D. Bubresko, "American-Serbian Literature," in Wolodymyr T. Zyla and Wendell M. Aycock, eds, *Ethnic Literatures since 1776*, Proceedings of the Comparative Literature Symposium, Texas Tech University, vol. IX, 1978, part 2, p. 543 n. 3. David Caute, *The Great Fear: The Anti-Communist Purge under Truman and Eisenhower* (New York: Simon and Schuster, 1978), p. 216. See also Nelson, Barrett, and Ruck, *Steve Nelson*, pp. 298–340.

36. It is also worth mentioning the Washington, D.C. Popular Front, which was less a social movement than the muted presence of left-wing radicals in the New Deal agencies. There seem to have been three crucial and overlapping clusters: the radicals in Rexford Tugwell's AAA (the so-called Ware group, who became the focus of the Hiss case); the radicals who worked on the staff of the La Follette Committee and the National Labor Relations Board; and the radical folklore and folk music collectors like Alan Lomax, Charles Seeger, and Nicholas Ray, who worked in the Library of Congress and the Resettlement Administration.

37. For Ira Levine, "the 1934–35 season was the apex of left-wing theatrical activity . . . the vitality of the left-wing drama . . . ebbed after mid-decade . . ., its energy and purpose redirected by the Popular Front"; for Barbara Foley, "literary proletarianism failed to move ahead and develop because the priorities of the left-wing movement . . . altered dramatically with the Popular Front." Ira Levine, *Left-Wing Dramatic Theory in the American Theatre* (Ann Arbor: UMI Research Press, 1985), pp. 131, 177; Barbara Foley, *Radical Representations: Politics and Form in U.S. Proletarian Fiction, 1929–1941* (Durham N.C.: Duke University Press, 1993), p. 127. Malcolm Cowley, *The Dream of the Golden Mountains: Remembering the 1930s* (New York: Viking, 1980); Daniel Aaron, *Writers on the Left: Episodes in American Literary Communism* (New York: Harcourt, Brace & World, 1961). Many of the works on literature and independent film focus on the early years and are skeptical of the Popular Front: see Paula Rabinowitz, *Labor and Desire: Women's Revolutionary Fiction in Depression America* (Chapel Hill: University of North Carolina Press, 1991); William Alexander, *Film on the Left: American Documentary Film from 1931 to 1942* (Princeton, N.J.: Princeton University Press, 1981); Russell Campbell, *Cinema Strikes Back: Radical Filmmaking in the United States, 1930–1942* (Ann Arbor: UMI Research Press, 1982).

38. Most of the books on Hollywood follow the story through the blacklist, including Ceplair and Englund, *The Inquisition in Hollywood*, and Schwartz, *The Hollywood Writers' Wars.* See also Robbie Lieberman, *"My Song Is My Weapon": People's Songs, American Communism, and the Politics of Culture 1930–1950* (Urbana: University of Illinois Press, 1989); and Frances K. Pohl, *Ben Shahn: New Deal Artist in a Cold War Climate, 1947–1954* (Austin: University of Texas Press, 1989).

39. Gramsci, *Prison Notebooks*, p. 178.

40. Gramsci, *Prison Notebooks*, p. 210. For a rich elaboration of Gramsci's notions of conjuncture and crisis, see Stuart Hall, *The Hard Road to Renewal* (London: Verso, 1988).

41. My chronology of the Popular Front social movement implicitly suggests that the best way to understand its development is to track the fortunes of the labor movement. Virtually all previous scholarship has taken its chronology from international events: beginning with the Comintern's announcement of the Popular Front strategy, moving on to Franco's uprising against the Spanish Republic, the Moscow purge trials, the Nazi-Soviet Pact, the Nazi invasion of the USSR, the dissolution of the Comintern and the Duclos letter. I do not underestimate the importance of these events for the period or for the Communist Party itself. However, this chronology has led many historians to track the history of the Popular Front social movement by way of Moscow's instructions. The fortunes of the Popular Front—notably its remarkable and often unremarked resurgence in early 1941—requires a different periodization.

42. James J. Matles and James Higgins, *Them and Us: Struggles of a Rank-and-File Union* (Boston: Beacon Press, 1974), pp. 128, 130. Godfrey Hodgson, *America in Our Time* (New York: Vintage, 1978), p. 77. For the view that "the Nazi-Soviet Pact halted the forward momentum of progressives and intellectual Communists" and that 1940 and 1941 were dismal years, see Judy Kutulas, *The Long War: The Intellectual People's Front and Anti-Stalinism, 1930–1940* (Durham, N.C.: Duke University Press, 1995), p. 184.

43. Zieger, *The CIO*, p. 223. On the 1945 strike wave and the post-war general strikes, see George Lipsitz, *Rainbow at Midnight: Labor and Culture in the 1940s* (Urbana: University of Illinois Press, 1994), pp. 99–154. On the post-war "settlement," see Lichtenstein, "From Corporatism to Collective Bargaining," p. 122. Gallup Poll quoted in Hodgson, *America in Our Time*, p. 77.

44. Richard Hofstadter, *The American Political Tradition and the Men Who Made It* (1948, rpt. New York: Vintage, 1974), p. xxvii.

45. Paul Jacobs, *Is Curly Jewish?*, pp. 34–5.

46. Raymond Williams, *The Long Revolution* (New York: Harper and Row, 1966), pp. 48–9.

47. Two historians who have been particularly good at stressing the longer legacy of the Popular Front are Alan Wald, *Writing from the Left* (London: Verso, 1994) and Paul Buhle, "The Hollywood Left: Aesthetics and Politics," *New Left Review* 212 July–August 1995, pp. 101–19.

48. Fredric Jameson, *Postmodernism, or, The Cultural Logic of Late Capitalism* (Durham, N.C.: Duke University Press, 1991), p. xiv.

49. Hobsbawm quoted in David Gordon, Richard Edwards, and Michael Reich, *Segmented Work, Divided Workers: The Historical Transformation of Labor in the United States* (Cambridge: Cambridge University Press, 1982), p. 103.

50. Malcolm Cowley, *Exile's Return: A Literary Odyssey of the 1920s* (1934, rpt. New York: Penguin, 1976), p. 64. On the relation between modernism and Fordism, see Peter Wollen, *Raiding the Icebox: Reflections on Twentieth-Century Culture* (Bloomington: Indiana University Press, 1993), pp. 1–71. On the origins of the term "feminism," see Nancy Cott, *The Grounding of Modern Feminism* (New Haven: Yale University Press, 1987), pp. 13–16. Sandra M. Gilbert and Susan Gubar, *No Man's Land: The Place of the Woman Writer in the Twentieth Century. Volume 1: The War of the Words* (New Haven, Conn.: Yale University Press, 1988), p. vii.

51. Between 1940 and 1945, the number of women working for wages jumped by 50 percent from 12 million to 19 million; three-quarters of the new workers were married; one-third of women workers were in manufacturing in 1944, and they were one-third of all factory workers. Susan Hartmann, *The Home Front and Beyond: American Women in the 1940s* (Boston: Twayne, 1982), pp. 21, 86. Maureen Honey summarizes the debate over the effects of World War II: Honey, *Creating Rosie the Riveter: Class, Gender and Propaganda during World War II* (Amherst: University of Massachusetts Press, 1984), p. 2.

52. Sandra M. Gilbert and Susan Gubar, *No Man's Land: The Place of the Woman Writer in the Twentieth Century. Volume 2: Sexchanges* (New Haven, Conn.: Yale University Press, 1989), p. xi.

53. Lois W. Banner, *American Beauty* (New York: Alfred Knopf, 1983). For the exploration of the gender crisis of the depression, I am particularly indebted to the dissertations in progress of Holly Allen, "Fallen Women and Forgotten Men: Gendered Concepts of Community, Home and Nation, 1932–1945," and Margaret McFadden, "'Anything Goes': Gender and Knowledge in the Comic Popular Culture of the 1930s." On the decline in the birthrate, see Alice Kessler-Harris, *Out to Work: A History of Wage-Earning Women in the United States* (New York: Oxford University Press, 1982), p. 257. In 1942, Philip Wylie's bestselling *Generation of Vipers* coined the term "momism" to attack "overprotective" and "overindulgent mothers"; in 1946, a military psychiatrist blamed mothers for the emotional disorders that led men to be rejected or discharged from the military in a book entitled *Their Mother's Sons*. James Thurber's well-known 1943 series of *New Yorker* cartoons, "The War between Men and Women," stands as an example of the heightened rhetoric of the mid century "war between the sexes."

54. Kessler-Harris, *Out to Work*, pp. 258–9. Claudia Goldin, *Understanding the Gender Gap: An Economic History of American Women* (New York: Oxford University Press, 1990), p. 26. Goldin argues that the increase in labor-force participation by married women is the single most important change in the twentieth century. Married women's labor-force participation essentially doubles between 1930 and 1950, going from 11.7 percent to 21.6 percent and to 30.6 percent by 1960. Single women's participation hardly changes, going from 50.5 percent in 1930 to 50.6 percent in 1950 (47.5 percent in 1960): p. 17. The change in married women's participation is more striking for white than for nonwhite women; white married women's participation goes from 9.8 percent in 1930 to 20.7 percent in 1950, whereas non-white women's participation, already substantially higher, does not grow until the 1950s: 33.2 percent in 1930 to 31.8 percent in 1950 and 40.5 percent in 1960. Goldin argues that the demand for women's labor in 1940–60 was the key factor in the increase in married women's labor force participation; see pp. 160–79 on the marriage bar. On the continuation of job segregation by sex, see Ruth Milkman, *Gender at Work: The Dynamics of Job Segregation by Sex during World War II* (Urbana: University of Illinois, 1987).

55. In 1940, 2 million women worked as servants, one out of five women workers, half of whom were black or Hispanic. Kessler-Harris, *Out to Work*, p. 270. Goldin notes that in 1930, domestic servants made up 20.3 percent of white women workers and 62.6 percent of non-white women workers. Goldin, *Understanding the Gender Gap*. By 1950, the proportion of employed women in domestic service was less than 10 percent; and though black women were a higher percentage of all domestic workers, the proportion of employed black women who were domestic workers had dropped to 40 percent. Hartmann, *The Home Front and Beyond*, p. 94.

56. Dorothy Cobble, *Dishing It Out: Waitresses and their Unions in the Twentieth Century* (Urbana: University of Illinois Press, 1991).

57. On "progressive maternalism," see Molly Ladd-Taylor, *Mother-Work: Women, Child Welfare, and the State, 1890–1930* (Urbana: University of Illinois Press, 1994); the fiction ranges from Anzia Yezierska's stories of the 1920s to Tillie Olsen's famous story, "I Stand Here Ironing," of the 1950s. See also Rabinowitz, *Labor and Desire*, p. 35. Geraldine Youcha, *Minding the Children: Child Care in America from Colonial Times to the Present* (New York: Scribner, 1995), p. 309.

58. Steven Mintz and Susan Kellogg, *Domestic Revolutions: A Social History of American Family Life* (New York: Free Press, 1988), p. 115. John D'Emilio, *Sexual Politics, Sexual Communities: The Making of a Homosexual Minority in the United States, 1940–1970* (Chicago: University of Chicago Press, 1983).

59. Faue, *Community of Suffering and Struggle*, p. 12; Annelise Orleck, *Common Sense and a Little Fire: Women and Working-Class Politics in the United States, 1900–1965* (Chapel Hill: University of North Carolina Press, 1995). On women workers in wartime industries, see Milkman, *Gender at Work*; Kesselman, *Fleeting Opportunities*; Nancy Gabin, *Feminism in the Labor Movement: Women and the United Auto Workers, 1935–1975* (Ithaca, N.Y.: Cornell University Press, 1990); and Dorothy Sue Cobble, "Recapturing Working-Class Feminism: Union Women in the Postwar Era," in Joanne Meyerowitz, ed., *Not June Cleaver: Women and Gender in Postwar America, 1945–1960* (Philadelphia: Temple University Press, 1994).

60. On clerical organizing, see Strom, "'We're No Kitty Foyles'," and Sharon Hartman Strom, "Challenging 'Woman's Place': Feminism, the Left, and Industrial Unionism in the 1930s," *Feminist Studies* 9.2, Summer 1983, pp. 359–86. Cobble, "Recapturing Working-Class Feminism"; Harriet Hyman Alonso, "Mayhem and Moderation: Women Peace Activists during the McCarthy Era," in Meyerowitz, ed., *Not June Cleaver*; Amy Swerdlow, "The Congress of American Women: Left-Feminist Peace Politics in the Cold War," in Linda K. Kerber, Alice Kessler-Harris, and Kathryn Kish Sklar, eds., *U.S. History as Women's History* (Chapel Hill: University of North Carolina Press, 1995); D'Emilio, *Sexual Politics, Sexual Communities*, pp. 57–74; Stuart Timmons, *The Trouble with Harry Hay: Founder of the Modern Gay Movement* (Boston: Alyson Publications, 1990).

61. This argument owes much to Carey McWilliams, one of the leading Popular Front theorists of race and ethnicity, whose work I discuss below. See his *Brothers under the Skin* (Boston: Little Brown, 1945), p. 317.

62. On the housing conflicts, see Margaret Crawford, "Daily Life on the Home Front: Women, Blacks and the Struggle for Public Housing," in Donald Albrecht, ed., *World War II and the American Dream* (Cambridge, Mass.: MIT Press, 1995). On the "hate strikes," see Zieger, *The CIO*, pp. 154–5; on the Philadelphia transit hate strike, see Freeman, *In Transit*, pp. 252–9. On the zoot-suit riots, see Mauricio Mazón, *The Zoot-Suit Riots: The Psychology of Symbolic Annihilation* (Austin: University of Texas Press, 1984).

63. Ronald Takaki, *Strangers from a Different Shore: A History of Asian Americans* (Boston: Little, Brown and Company, 1989), pp. 357–405.

64. Herbert Garfinkel, *When Negroes March: The March on Washington Movement in the Organizational Politics for FEPC* (New York: Free Press, 1959). Manning Marable, *Black American Politics: From the Washington Marches to Jesse Jackson* (London: Verso, 1985), pp. 79–87; James Farmer, *Lay Bare the Heart: An Autobiography of the Civil Rights Movement* (New York: Arbor House, 1985) pp. 67–168.

65. Sanford Zalburg, *A Spark is Struck! Jack Hall and the ILWU in Hawaii* (Honolulu: University of Hawaii Press, 1979). Several histories of the Communist Party suggest that the struggle for African American economic justice and civil rights was subordinated to the war effort during the war years, but this is not the case with the Popular Front generally, in which racial struggles take on increased prominence in part due to the electoral success of Powell and Davis, and in part due to the cultural prominence of figures like Robeson, Hughes, and Wright.

66. Hodgson, *America in Our Time*, p. 62. Reynolds Farley and Walter R. Allen, *The Color Line and the Quality of Life in America* (New York: Oxford University Press, 1989), pp. 113–14.

67. Caldwell had been a radical novelist of the 1930s, part of the proletarian literary avant-garde, writing works intended as exposes of the sharecropping system but which became sensational stories of the degraded lives of white tenant farmers. He became a mass success with the paperback revolution of the early 1940s; in 1946, a Penguin edition of *God's Little Acre* sold 3 million copies with a famous peephole cover by the pulp illustrator Robert Jonas.

The voyeurism of the cover was not only a hook for the sexual content of the books but for the sense that the South and its secrets opened up to the reader through the peephole. It is not an accident that the one Faulkner novel that was a commercial success was *Sanctuary*: though critics have long debated Faulkner's characterization of it as a potboiler written to make money, it is true that its success lies in its curious ventriloquism. Its real title might well be *Under Northern Eyes*. Like Stowe, Melville, Twain, and Elvis Presley, Faulkner may be deemed a racist, but unlike Hemingway, Fitzgerald, Cather, and James, they did not evade the matter. Faulkner's early novels have only minstrel roles for blacks; it was not really until *Light in August*, with its violent rewriting of the conventional tale of the tragic mulatto, that race became central; he once called *Go Down Moses* "the race-relations book."

68. "Whereas before 1940 no racial or ethnic group in American history had ever experienced an isolation index above 60%, by 1970 this level was normal for blacks in large American cities." In 1940, only two of the twenty largest cities—New Orleans and Washington—were a quarter or more black; by 1980, five had black majorities and seven were more than a quarter black. Douglas S. Massey and Nancy A. Denton, *American Apartheid: Segregation and the Making of the Underclass* (Cambridge, Mass.: Harvard University Press, 1993), pp. 33, 57.

69. One exception was the radical Arkansas preacher, Claude Williams, who directed Commonwealth Labor College in the 1930s, went to Detroit in the war years to defuse tensions in the defense plants, and returned to Birmingham, Alabama after the war to work in the CIO's Operation Dixie. See Mark Naison, "Claude Williams," in Buhle, Buhle, and Georgakas, *Encyclopedia*. See Kelley, *Hammer and Hoe*, pp. 107–8, 114–15, 196 on religion and Alabama Communists. On the tensions between southwestern socialism, the Klan, and the holiness and pentecostal movement, see James N. Gregory, *American Exodus: The Dust Bowl Migration and Okie Culture in California* (New York: Oxford University Press, 1989), pp. 158–62, 191–221.

70. See Michael Goldfield, "The Failure of Operation Dixie: A Critical Turning Point in American Political Development?" in Gary M. Fink and Merl E. Reed, *Race, Class, and Community in Southern Labor History* (Tuscaloosa: University of Alabama Press, 1994); and, for the South's political effect on the social democratic alliance, see Ira Katznelson, Kim Geiger, and Daniel Kryder, "Limiting Liberalism: The Southern Veto in Congress, 1933–1950," *Political Science Quarterly* 108.2, 1993, pp. 283–306.

71. Robert Hill, "Afterword" to C.L.R. James, *American Civilization*, p. 337; David Noble, *Forces of Production: A Social History of Industrial Automation* (New York: Alfred Knopf, 1984); Daniel Bell, *The Coming of Post-Industrial Society* (1973, rpt. New York: Penguin, 1976), pp. 130, 134; David Harvey, *The Condition of Post-Modernity* (Oxford: Basil Blackwell, 1989), p. 157.

72. Stuart Hall, "Gramsci's Relevance for the Study of Race and Ethnicity," in David Morley and Kuan-Hsing Chen, eds, *Stuart Hall: Critical Dialogues in Cultural Studies* (London: Routledge, 1996), p. 423.

73. Irving Howe and Lewis Coser, *The American Communist Party* (New York: Frederick Praeger, 1963), pp. 363, 366.

74. C. Wright Mills, "The Cultural Apparatus," in Irving Louis Horowitz, ed., *Power, Politics and People: The Collected Essays of C. Wright Mills* (New York: Ballantine, 1963), p. 406. The classic accounts of modern Taylorism and the rise of corporate research are Harry Braverman, *Labor and Monopoly Capital* (New York: Monthly Review Press, 1974) and David F. Noble, *America by Design* (New York: Alfred Knopf, 1977).

75. Michael Denning, *Mechanic Accents: Dime Novels and Working-Class Culture in America* (London: Verso, 1987).

76. Douglas Gomery, *The Hollywood Studio System* (London: Macmillan, 1986), pp. 6–7.

77. The phrase "music becomes a thing" is from Evan Eisenberg, *The Recording Angel: Music, Records and Culture from Aristotle to Zappa* (London: Picador, 1987). See also Michael Chanan, *Repeated Takes: A Short History of Recording and Its Effects on Music* (London: Verso, 1995).

78. Andre Millard, *America on Record: A History of Recorded Sound* (Cambridge: Cambridge University Press, 1995), p. 174. Chanan, *Repeated Takes*, p. 83; Susan Smulyan, *Selling Radio: The Commercialization of American Broadcasting, 1920–1934* (Washington, D.C.: Smithsonian Institution Press, 1994).

79. Barton quoted in Erika Doss, *Benton, Pollock, and the Politics of Modernism: From Regionalism*

to *Abstract Expressionism* (Chicago: University of Chicago Press, 1991), p. 152. On the new styles in advertising and the "invention of a corporate aesthetic," pp. 151–6; Henry R. Luce, *The American Century* (New York: Farrar & Rinehart, 1941), p. 33. See also James Sloan Allen, *The Romance of Commerce and Culture: Capitalism, Modernism and the Chicago-Aspen Crusade for Cultural Reform* (Chicago: University of Chicago Press, 1983).

80. Thomas Ferguson, *Golden Rule: The Investment Theory of Party Competition and the Logic of Money-Driven Political Systems* (Chicago: University of Chicago Press, 1995), p. 136, 220–221; he cites *Newsweek*, owned by Vincent Astor and Averill Harriman, in particular. Nick Roddick, *A New Deal in Entertainment: Warner Brothers in the 1930s* (London: British Film Institute, 1983).

81. "Unemployed Arts," *Fortune*, May 1937, p. 111. The major administrative history remains William F. McDonald, *Federal Relief Administration and the Arts* (n.p.: Ohio State University Press, 1969).

82. Roosevelt quoted in Steven C. Dubin, *Bureaucratizing the Muse: Public Funds and the Cultural Worker* (Chicago: University of Chicago Press, 1987), p. 159.

83. Armand Mattelart, *Mapping World Communication: War, Progress, Culture* (Minneapolis: University of Minnesota Press, 1994), pp. 83, 86. Scott Donaldson, *Archibald MacLeish: An American Life* (Boston: Houghton Mifflin, 1992), pp. 348–50. Gary O. Larson, *The Reluctant Patron: The United States Government and the Arts, 1943–1965* (Philadelphia: University of Pennsylvania, 1983), p. 23. Paul Jay, ed., *The Selected Correspondence of Kenneth Burke and Malcolm Cowley* (New York: Viking, 1988), p. 248. See Larson for an excellent account of government patronage of the arts in the interregnum between the 1943 end of the WPA programs and the 1965 establishment of the NEA and NEH.

84. Davis, *Prisoners of the American Dream*, pp. 191–2; Bell, *The Coming of Post-Industrial Society*, p. 250.

85. Max Horkheimer and Theodor Adorno, *Dialectic of Enlightenment* (1944; rpt. New York: Seabury, 1972), p. 142; C.L.R. James, *American Civilization*, pp. 122–3. "The question remains," James writes, "why, at this particular time, this particular method of distraction should have arisen and met with such continuous success" (p. 122); "The modern popular film, the modern newspaper (the *Daily News, not* the *Times*), the comic strip, the evolution of jazz, a popular periodical like *Life*, these mirror from year to year the deep social responses and evolution of the American people" (pp. 118–119). For another classic formulation of the dialectic of distraction, see Walter Benjamin, "The Work of Art in the Age of Mechanical Reproduction," in *Illuminations* (1936; rpt. New York: Shocken, 1969), pp. 239–40. Benjamin maintains that "distraction" is itself a mode of aesthetic appropriation: "Reception in a state of distraction, which is increasingly noticeable in all fields of art and is symptomatic of profound changes in apperception, finds in the film its true means of exercise."

86. David Nasaw, *Going Out: The Rise and Fall of Public Amusements* (New York: Basic, 1993).

87. Cohen, *Making a New Deal*, pp. 147, 357. For a contrary view of the effects of consumer culture, see Edsforth, *Class Conflict and Cultural Consensus*.

88. See Dick Netzer, *The Subsidized Muse: Public Support for the Arts in the United States* (Cambridge: Cambridge University Press, 1978), pp. 55–6 for representative figures of arts projects productions: "Federal One employed 45,000 in June 1936; 37,250 in May 1937; 28,000 in June 1938, and 39,000 in February 1939." Harold Rosenberg, "Literature without Money," *American Stuff*, a special issue of *Direction* 1.3, 1938, p. 10. See also Rosenberg, "The Profession of Art: The WPA Art Project," in his *Art on the Edge* (New York: Macmillan, 1975), pp. 195–6.

89. Edward Lindeman, "Farewell to Bohemia," *Survey Graphic* 26, 1937, p. 207. Bell distinguishes the "cultural mass" from the "creators of culture." The cultural mass are "*transmitters*: those working in higher education, publishing, magazines, broadcast media, theater and museums, who process and influence the reception of serious cultural products. It is itself large enough to be a *market* for culture, purchasing books, prints, and serious music recordings. And it is also the group which, as writers, magazine editors, movie-makers, musicians, and so forth, produces the popular materials for the mass cultural audience." Daniel Bell, *The Cultural Contradictions of Capitalism* (New York: Basic Books, 1976), p. 20.

90. Calculated from Bureau of the Census, *Historical Statistics of the United States Colonial Times to 1957* "Detailed Occupations of the Economically Active Population: 1900–1950",

Series D 123–572. I have not included the other large categories of "professional, technical, and kindred workers," the engineers and the health care professionals.

91. C. Wright Mills, "The Cultural Apparatus," pp. 418–19.The United Office and Professional Workers of America was a pioneering white-collar union in the CIO; its strength lay mainly among insurance agents.

Notes to 2

1. Virgil Thomson, *The State of Music* (New York: William Morrow, 1939), pp. 18–19.

2. Davis quoted in Garnett McCoy, "The Rise and Fall of the American Artists' Congress," *Prospects* 13, 1988, p. 328; Lange quoted in Milton Meltzer, *Dorothea Lange: A Photographer's Life* (New York: Farrar Straus Giroux, 1978), p. 77. By the summer and fall of 1934, Lange's documentary photographs had their first exhibition, and the first important critical essay about her work had been published, pp. 81, 84.

3. Malcolm Cowley, *The Dream of the Golden Mountains: Remembering the 1930s* (New York: Viking, 1980), p. 187; Conroy quoted in Douglas Wixson, *Worker-Writer in America: Jack Conroy and the Tradition of Midwestern Literary Radicalism* (Urbana: University of Illinois Press, 1994), p. 394.

4. Mary McCarthy, *Intellectual Memoirs: New York 1936–1938* (San Diego, Calif.: Harcourt Brace, 1992), pp. 1–3. Richard Wright, *American Hunger* (New York: Perennial, 1979), pp. 130–35. It is worth noting that this incident did not lead to Wright's estrangement from the cultural front: he remained an active and visible part of the cultural front for another decade.

5. "Thirty Years Later: Memories of the First American Writers' Congress," *American Scholar* 35.3, Summer 1966, p. 501.

6. Kenneth Burke, *Attitudes toward History* (New York: New Republic, 1937), vol. 2, pp. 244–5. Kenneth Burke, "Revolutionary Symbolism in America," in Henry Hart, ed., *American Writers' Congress* (New York: International Publishers, 1935), pp. 87–94. I discuss Burke's speech below: as this speech has often been taken to indicate Burke's distance from the labor movement since he calls for substituting the symbol of the "people" for the symbol of the "worker," it is worth recalling that Burke explicitly addressed it to "propagandists," noting that "the needs of the propagandist are not wholly identical with the needs of the organizer," p. 88.

7. Kenneth Burke, *The Philosophy of Literary Form* (1941; rpt. Berkeley: University of California Press, 1973), p. xix.

8. The term "commitment" structured one of the memorable intellectual exchanges of the period: Jean-Paul Sartre's influential essay, *What is Literature?* (1947; rpt. New York: Harper and Row, 1965), and Theodor Adorno's trenchant reply, "Commitment," reprinted in Ernst Bloch, Georg Lukács, Bertolt Brecht, Walter Benjamin, and Theodor Adorno, *Aesthetics and Politics* (London: NLB, 1977). Warren Susman's powerful essays on the culture of the "thirties" are built around an extension of the political notion of "commitment" to a more general existential sense of commitment: the entire age becomes an age of "commitment." See Susman, *Culture as History* (New York: Pantheon, 1984). The finest brief history and critique of the notion of commitment remains Raymond Williams's "The Writer: Commitment and Alignment" in his *Resources of Hope* (London: Verso, 1989). See also David Caute, "On Commitment," in his *The Illusion* (New York: Harper and Row, 1971).

9. Arnold Rampersad, *The Life of Langston Hughes. Volume II: 1941–1967. I Dream a World* (New York: Oxford University Press, 1988), p. 96.

10. Paul Jay, ed., *The Selected Correspondence of Kenneth Burke and Malcolm Cowley, 1915–1981* (New York: Viking, 1988), p. 232.

11. Williams, *Resources of Hope*, pp. 86–7.

12. The subsequent conversion of a few Communist activists to forms of religious anti-Communism gave rise to a "religious" reading of political activity and of Communism as, in the title of one famous book, "the god that failed." The key "apostates" included Whittaker Chambers, Bella Dodd, and Louis Budenz; Malcolm Cowley's oft-quoted memoirs also offered a religious explanation of Communism's attractions.

13. See Malcolm Cowley, *Exile's Return: A Literary Odyssey of the 1920s* (1934; rpt. New York: Penguin, 1976), pp. 61–4, 207–17. Granville Hicks, *The Great Tradition* (New York: International, 1935), pp. 257–62, is good on the general situation of the Ivy League aesthetes who made up the flowering of the 1920s. See also Marcus Klein, *Foreigners: The Making of American Literature, 1900–1940* (Chicago: University of Chicago Press, 1981): "To a remarkable extent, the modernism made by Americans had a Harvard education," p. 8.

14. Josephine Herbst, "A Year of Disgrace," in her *The Starched Blue Sky of Spain* (New York: HarperCollins, 1991), p. 98.

15. See Franklin Folsom, *Days of Anger, Days of Hope: A Memoir of the League of American Writers, 1937–1942* (Niwot: University Press of Colorado, 1994), pp. 41–59; Anthony Heilbut, *Exiled in Paradise: German Refugee Artists and Intellectuals in America from the 1930s to the Present* (New York: Viking, 1983); James K. Lyon, *Bertolt Brecht in America* (Princeton, N.J.: Princeton University Press, 1980); Salka Viertel, *The Kindness of Strangers* (New York: Holt, Rinehart and Winston, 1969).

16. In 1890, less than 4 percent of the nation's 14–17 year olds were in high schools; by 1920, the proportion had risen to 32 percent, by 1930 to 51 percent, and by 1940 to 73 percent. David Nasaw, *Schooled to Order: A Social History of Public Schooling in America* (New York: Oxford University Press, 1979), pp. 163, 239.

17. McCarthy, *Intellectual Memoirs*, p. 68. On Rahv, see McCarthy, pp. 65–8, 78–82; Alan Wald, *The New York Intellectuals* (Chapel Hill: University of North Carolina Press, 1987), pp. 76–7; and Alexander Bloom, *Prodigal Sons: The New York Intellectuals and Their World* (New York: Oxford University Press, 1986), pp. 311–12. Wright, *American Hunger*, pp. 93, 63–4.

18. Robert Sklar, "Welles before *Kane*: The Discourse on a 'Boy Genius'," *Persistence of Vision* 7, 1989, pp. 63–72. See also, Cowley, *Exile's Return*, pp. 311–16; and Malcolm Cowley, "And Jesse Begat" in his—*And I Worked at the Writer's Trade: Chapters of Literary History, 1918–1978* (New York: Penguin, 1979).

19. See Alfred Kazin, *Starting out in the Thirties* (Boston: Little, Brown, 1965), pp. 15–19, 67, 138, 145–6; Irving Howe, *A Margin of Hope* (San Diego, Calif.: Harcourt Brace Jovanovich, 1982), pp. 141–3. Olsen quoted in Constance Coiner, *Better Red: The Writing and Resistance of Tillie Olsen and Meridel Le Sueur* (New York: Oxford University Press, 1995), p. 148. On the MacLeish and Dreiser controversies, see Daniel Aaron, *Writers on the Left: Episodes in American Literary Communism* (New York: Harcourt, Brace and World, Inc., 1961), pp. 264–7, 276–9. Edmund Wilson, *The Thirties: From Notebooks and Diaries of the Period* (New York: Farrar Straus & Giroux, 1980), p. 379; See also John Dos Passos, *The Fourteenth Chronicle: Letters and Diaries* (Boston: Gambit, 1973), pp. 446–8. However, I am not persuaded by Judy Kutulas's generational argument that identifies the Popular Front with the older Anglo modernists and anti-Stalinism with the younger ethnics: the Stalinist/anti-Stalinist fault line clearly runs across both the moderns and the plebeians. Kutulas, *The Long War: The Intellectual People's Front and Anti-Stalinism, 1930–1940* (Durham, N.C.: Duke University Press, 1995), pp. 3–4.

20. Eugene Lyons, *The Red Decade: The Stalinist Penetration of America* (Indianapolis, Ind.: Bobbs-Merrill Company, 1941), p. 166; Irving Howe, "The Brilliant Masquerade: A Note on 'Browderism'," in his *Socialism and America* (San Diego, Calif.: Harcourt Brace Jovanovich, 1985). The Communist Party itself used the metaphor of the "transmission belt" for the front groups, invoking a factory image of the social movement and seeing the party as its motor. See Arthur J. Sabin, *Red Scare in Court: New York versus the International Workers Order* (Philadelphia: University of Pennsylvania Press, 1993), pp. 47, 55, 57, 118.

21. It is worth recalling that Gramsci's prison notes were written in the context of the international debates among Communists and Socialists over the strategy of united fronts. I discuss the relevance of Gramsci's concepts to cultural studies in Michael Denning, "The End of Mass Culture," *International Labor and Working-Class History* 37, 1990, pp. 4–18. See also Stuart Hall, "Gramsci's Relevance for the Study of Race and Ethnicity," in David Morley and Kuan-Hsing Chen, eds, *Stuart Hall: Critical Dialogues in Cultural Studies* (London: Routledge, 1996).

22. See Mike Budd, Robert Entman, and Clay Steinman, "The Affirmative Character of U.S. Cultural Studies," *Critical Studies in Mass Communication* 7, 1990, for an important critique of the "optimism and affirmative tone about audiences" which characterizes "the new discourse of U.S. cultural studies."

23. The "Shock Troupe" was the name of the permanent collective of the Workers Laboratory Theatre living on 13th Street in New York: it included Nicholas Ray, Earl Robinson, and Al Saxe. It served as a model for other proletarian collectives. See Jay Williams, *Stage Left* (New York: Charles Scribner's Sons, 1974), pp. 79–99; and Bernard Eisenschitz, *Nicholas Ray: An American Journey* (London: Faber and Faber, 1993), pp. 22–32.

24. Anita Brenner, "Revolution in Art," *The Nation*, 8 March 1933, pp. 267–9, reprinted along with other reviews in David Shapiro, ed., *Social Realism: Art as a Weapon* (New York: Frederick Ungar, 1973). On Vanguard, see Mark Naison, *Communists in Harlem during the Depression* (Urbana: University of Illinois Press, 1983), p. 100. On the JPAL, see Karl G. Yoneda, *Ganbatte: Sixty-Year Struggle of a Kibei Worker* (Los Angeles: UCLA Asian American Studies Center, 1983), pp. 37–60.

25. For the Film and Photo League, see William Alexander, *Film on the Left: American Documentary Film from 1931 to 1942* (Princeton, N.J.: Princeton University Press, 1981); Russell Campbell, *Cinema Strikes Back: Radical Filmmaking in the United States, 1930–1942* (Ann Arbor: UMI Research Press, 1982); Louis Stettner, "Cezanne's Apples and the Photo League: A Memoir," *Aperture* 112, Fall 1988, pp. 14–35.

26. See Karen Malpede Taylor, *People's Theater in Amerika* (New York: Drama Book Specialists, 1972), pp. 30–60; Williams, *Stage Left*, pp. 33–50; Elizabeth Fones-Wolf, "Industrial Unionism and Labor Movement Culture in Depression-Era Philadelphia," *Pennsylvania Magazine of History and Biography* 109, January 1985, p. 17; Eisenschitz, *Nicholas Ray*, pp. 22–32; Joel Saxe, "Workers Laboratory Theatre," in Mari Jo Buhle, Paul Buhle, and Dan Georgakas, *Encyclopedia of the American Left* (New York: Garland, 1990), pp. 850–52.

27. Stacey Prickett, "From Workers' Dance to New Dance," *Dance Research* 7.1, Spring 1989, pp. 47–64; Prickett, "Dance and the Workers' Struggle," *Dance Research* 8.1, Spring 1990, p. 47–61; Prickett, "'The People': Issues of Identity with the Revolutionary Dance," *Studies in Dance History* 5.1, Spring 1994, pp. 14–22; and Prickett, "Reviewing on the Left: The Dance Criticism of Edna Ocko," *Studies in Dance History* 5.1, Spring 1994, pp. 65–103. Franklin Rosemont, "Modern Dance," in Buhle, Buhle, and Georgakas *Encyclopedia*.

28. David King Dunaway, "Unsung Songs of Protest: The Composers Collective of New York," *New York Folklore* 5.1, Summer 1979, pp. 1–19. Barbara Tischler, *An American Music* (New York: Oxford University Press, 1986), pp. 109–20. Aaron Copland and Vivian Perlis, *Copland: 1900 through 1942* (New York: St Martin's, 1984), pp. 222–30. Eric A. Gordon, *Mark the Music: The Life and Work of Marc Blitzstein* (New York: St Martin's, 1989), pp. 96–122. Carol J. Oja, "Composer with a Conscience: Elie Siegmeister in Profile," *American Music* 6.2, Summer 1988, pp. 159–80. Richard A. Reuss, "The Roots of American Left-Wing Interest in Folksong," *Labor History* 12, Spring 1971, pp. 259–79.

29. Helen Harrison, "John Reed Club Artists and the New Deal: Radical Responses to Roosevelt's 'Peaceful Revolution'," *Prospects* 5, 1980, p. 247; McCoy, "Rise and Fall of the American Artists' Congress," p. 326; Jerre Mangione, *The Dream and the Deal: The Federal Writers Project, 1935–1943* (New York: Avon, 1972), pp. 34, 36.

30. On the ILD and the theory of labor defense, see Charles Martin, "International Labor Defense," and Ellen Schrecker, "American Committee for Protection of Foreign Born," both in Buhle, Buhle, and Georgakas, *Encyclopedia*. Yoneda, *Ganbatte*, gives a good sense of the importance of the ILD.

31. Robinson quoted in Eisenschitz, *Nicholas Ray*, p. 27.

32. Walter Kalaidjian's *American Culture between the Wars* (New York: Columbia University Press, 1993) is particularly good on this "proletarian subculture," noting both its satire of conventional American stereotypes and its stylized use of proletarian icons like hammers, sickles, wrenches, and raised fists. See pp. 47–51 and 59–63.

33. The notion of a "movement culture" was elaborated by Lawrence Goodwyn in his classic history of the populists. See Goodwyn, *The Populist Moment* (New York: Oxford University Press, 1978), pp. 19, 32–5.

34. Louis Adamic, "Notes on the Difficult Task Facing the CIO," in his *My America* (New York: Harper & Brothers, 1938), p. 443; Joshua B. Freeman, *In Transit: The Transport Workers Union in New York City, 1933–1966* (New York: Oxford University Press, 1989), p. 121; Annelise Orleck, *Common Sense and a Little Fire: Women and Working-Class Politics in the United States,*

1900–1965 (Chapel Hill: University of North Carolina Press, 1995), pp. 175–9; Labor Stage, Program for *Pins and Needles*, 1938.

35. Perhaps the best discussion of labor-movement culture is Elizabeth Fones-Wolf, "Industrial Unionism and Labor Movement Culture in Depression-Era Philadelphia," in which she makes the argument about the influence of welfare capitalism. Many of the studies of CIO-era unions have discussions of union education and recreation programs. On the Transport Workers Union, see Freeman, *In Transit*, pp. 122–3. On Minneapolis, see Elizabeth Faue, *Community of Suffering and Struggle: Women, Men and the Labor Movement in Minneapolis, 1915–1945* (Chapel Hill: University of North Carolina Press, 1991) , pp. 110, 116, 226 n.23. The Independent Textile Union of Woonsocket, R.I. built on French Canadian culture, sponsoring festivals of quadrille dancing and French-Canadian folk songs, as well as a drama group that produced *Waiting for Lefty*. Gary Gerstle, *Working-Class Americanism: The Politics of Labor in a Textile City, 1914–1960* (Cambridge: Cambridge University Press, 1989), pp. 197–201. The PWOC and SWOC in Chicago sponsored dances, bowling, and a CIO softball league. Lizabeth Cohen, *Making a New Deal: Industrial Workers in Chicago, 1919–1939* (Cambridge: Cambridge University Press, 1990), pp. 340–41.

36. Richard Flacks, *Making History: The American Left and the American Mind* (New York: Columbia University Press, 1988), pp. 130–31. Steve Nelson, James R. Barrett, and Rob Ruck, *Steve Nelson, American Radical* (Pittsburgh, Pa.: University of Pittsburgh Press, 1981), p. 55. "Only years later," Nelson added, "could I see some of the shortcomings of the school: it was rather narrow in subject matter with not enough attention given to American history and political life. It was geared toward convincing us of the meaningfulness of communism or socialism and demonstrating that the 1917 Revolution was the great historical event of our times. Yet I cherished the chance to attend." On labor education, see Jon Bloom, "Workers' Education," in Buhle, Buhle, and Georgakas, *Encyclopedia*, and Joseph Kett, *The Pursuit of Knowledge under Difficulties: From Self-Improvement to Adult Education in America, 1750–1990* (Stanford, Calif.: Stanford University Press, 1994), pp. 352–67. The summer schools were usually held in conjunction with a university or a labor college: in the early 1940s, UAW summer schools were held at the University of Michigan, the University of Wisconsin, the Highlander Folk School, and the Hudson Shore Labor School: see Thomas E. Linton, *An Historical Examination of the Purposes and Practices of the Education Program of the United Automobile Workers, 1936–1959* (Ann Arbor: University of Michigan School of Education, 1965), p. 113.

37. Joyce L. Kornbluh, *A New Deal for Workers' Education: The Workers' Service Program, 1933–1942* (Urbana: University of Illinois Press, 1987), pp. 48, 98, 58. Fones-Wolf, "Industrial Unionism and Labor Movement Culture," p. 16; Faue, *Community of Suffering and Struggle*, p. 226 n. 23.

38. Norman Eiger, *Toward a National Commitment to Workers' Education: The Rise and Fall of the Campaign to Establish a Labor Extension Service, 1942–1950* (New Brunswick, N.J.: Rutgers University, 1975). Most of these schools had roots in the Communist Party network of "workers schools"; but whereas the Party schools served largely to train members, these reached out to the workers who had been organized by the CIO unions and who had used the WPA night-classes. Marshall Field was an important financial supporter of a couple of these schools. Isobel Cherney, "California Labor School," in Ann Fagan Ginger and David Christiano, *The Cold War against Labor* (Berkeley, Calif.: Meiklejohn Civil Liberties Institute, 1987); Charles Wolfe and Kip Lornell, *The Life and Legend of Leadbelly* (New York: Harper-Collins, 1992), p. 233. Williams quoted in Howard Kimeldorf, *Reds or Rackets? The Making of Radical and Conservative Unions on the Waterfront* (Berkeley: University of California Press, 1988), p. 147.

39. Marvin Gettleman, "Jefferson School of Social Science," in Buhle, Buhle, and Georgakas, *Encyclopedia*, p. 389. Diane Johnson, *Dashiell Hammett: A Life* (New York: Fawcett Columbine, 1985), pp. 212–14; David King Dunaway, *How Can I Keep from Singing: Pete Seeger* (New York: McGraw-Hill, 1981), p. 123. On attending the Jefferson School, see Stanley Aronowitz, *Roll over Beethoven: The Return of Cultural Strife* (Hanover: Wesleyan University Press, 1993), p. 147–8. On Gwendolyn Bennett, see Gerald Horne, *Black Liberation/Red Scare: Ben Davis and the Communist Party* (Newark: University of Delaware Press, 1994), pp. 93–4, 113. Douglas Wixson, *Worker-Writer in America: Jack Conroy and the Tradition of Midwestern Literary Radicalism, 1898–1990* (Urbana: University of Illinois Press, 1994), pp. 453–4.

40. See Edward L. Barrett, Jr, *The Tenney Committee* (Ithaca, N.Y.: Cornell University Press, 1951), pp. 105–21; Stuart Timmons, *The Trouble with Harry Hay: Founder of the Modern Gay Movement* (Boston: Alyson Publications, 1990), pp. 120, 127. Paul Sweezy, "Labor and Political Activities," *Monthly Review* 2.6, October 1950, p. 242. See also Marvin Gettleman, "The New York Workers School," in Michael E. Brown, Randy Martin, Frank Rosengarten, and George Snedeker, *New Studies in the Politics and Culture of US Communism* (New York: Monthly Review Press, 1993). For a sense of the place of these Popular Front labor schools in the labor movement, see Caroline Ware, *Labor Education in Universities* (New York: American Labor Education Service, 1946), pp. 81–2; and International Union, United Automobile, Aircraft and Agricultural Implement Workers of America, *Proceedings of the First Annual Education Conference*, 1944, p. 61.

41. Hilda Worthington Smith, *Women Workers at the Bryn Mawr Summer School* (New York: Affiliated Summer Schools, n.d.); Florence Hemley Schneider, *Patterns of Workers' Education: The Story of the Bryn Mawr Summer School* (Washington, D.C.: American Council on Public Affairs, 1941). Muste's labor radicalism lost Brookwood its AFL support; a battle over Muste's leadership of the Conference for Progressive Labor Action (which was to become the American Workers' Party) led to his resignation in 1933. Joann Ooiman Robinson, *Abraham Went Out: A Biography of A.J. Muste* (Philadelphia: Temple University Press, 1981), pp. 32–48; Archie Green, *Only a Miner: Studies in Recorded Coal-Mining Songs* (Urbana: University of Illinois Press, 1972), pp. 253–8. Eisenschitz, *Nicholas Ray:* pp. 37–8. Steve Fraser calls Brookwood the "cadre school" of the "embryonic CIO": Fraser, *Labor Will Rule: Sidney Hillman and the Rise of American Labor* (New York: Free Press, 1991), p. 332. One of the best first-hand accounts of Brookwood is that of Len De Caux, who became the CIO's publicity director: De Caux, *Labor Radical* (Boston: Beacon Press, 1970), pp. 94–107.

42. For a memoir of Commonwealth College, see Raymond and Charlotte Koch, *Educational Commune: The Story of Commonwealth College* (New York: Schocken, 1972). Wixson, *Worker-Writer in America*, pp. 407–8; Doris Willens, *Lonesome Traveler: The Life of Lee Hays* (New York: Norton, 1988), pp. 37–47 on Highlander and pp. 50–59 on Commonwealth College. On Highlander, see Kett, *The Pursuit of Knowledge under Difficulties*, pp. 365–6; Adamic, *My America*, pp. 448–9, and Pete Seeger and Bob Reiser, *Everybody Says Freedom* (New York: Norton, 1989), p. 8.

43. Fraser, *Labor Will Rule*, pp. 402–3. Barrett, *The Tenney Committee*, p. 114. Frances K. Pohl, *Ben Shahn: New Deal Artist in a Cold War Climate 1947–1954* (Austin: University of Texas Press, 1989), pp. 9–25. On the UAW's film work, see Linton, *Historical Examination*, p. 153; I discuss the UAW cartoons in chapter 11.

44. On "Labor for Victory", see Erik Barnouw, ed., *Radio Drama in Action: Twenty-Five Plays of a Changing World* (New York: Rinehart, 1945), pp. 32–3, 80–81. On Quin, see Nelson, Barrett, and Ruck, *Steve Nelson*, 258; and Harry Carlisle, ed., *On the Drumhead: A Selection from the Writing of Mike Quin* (San Francisco: Pacific Publishing, 1948), p. xxxiii. By 1946, ten CIO unions had educational departments: Mark Starr, *Labor Looks at Education* (Cambridge: Harvard University Press, 1946), p. 23.

45. On Cohn, see Orleck, *Common Sense and a Little Fire*. Zieger, *The CIO*, p. 87. Jessie Lloyd O'Connor, Harvey O'Connor, and Susan Bowler, *Harvey and Jessie: A Couple of Radicals* (Philadelphia: Temple University Press, 1988). There are two studies of labor-union intellectuals in this period: Harold L. Wilensky, *Intellectuals in Labor Unions* (New York: Free Press, 1956); and the final chapter of C. Wright Mills, *The New Men of Power: America's Labor Leaders* (New York: Harcourt, Brace, 1948).

46. *Time* quoted in *Leo Huberman* (New York: Monthly Review Press, 1968), p. 8. Huberman's *We, the People* and *The Labor Spy Racket* were best sellers at the UAW bookstore. *Ammunition*, March 1944, back cover. In 1949, Huberman and Paul Sweezy founded *Monthly Review*. On the Seaman's Bookstore, see Nelson, Barrett, and Ruck, *Steve Nelson*, p. 259.

47. Robbie Lieberman, *"My Song Is My Weapon": People's Songs, American Communism, and the Politics of Culture, 1930–1950* (Urbana: University of Illinois Press, 1989), p. 92; Dunaway, *How Can I Keep from Singing*, p. 121.

48. The best accounts of the IWO are Thomas J.E. Walker, *Pluralistic Fraternity: The History of the International Workers' Order* (New York: Garland, 1991), and Sabin, *Red Scare in Court*. The best accounts of the left-wing Jewish culture are Arthur Liebman, *Jews and the Left* (New York: John Wiley, 1979) and Paul Buhle, "Jews and American Communism," *Radical History Review*

23, Spring 1980. Camp Unity in Wingdale, New York, was another important left-wing adult summer camp with a well-known cultural program, including leading jazz musicians like Sidney Bechet, Dizzy Gillespie, and Frank Newton. See Linn Shapiro, "Summer Camps" in Buhle, Buhle, and Georgakas, *Encyclopedia.* The coops were exceptional but not unique. New York also had a socialist housing cooperative, sponsored by the ACWA, and a Labor Zionist coop, the Farband Houses; Philadelphia had the Mackley Houses, sponsored by the American Federation of Full Fashioned Hosiery Workers. Fones-Wolf, "Industrial Unionism and Labor Movement Culture," pp. 17–18.

49. The IWO grew more slowly in the 1940s, reaching 185,000 in 1947, just before the federal and state governments began to attack it. Walker, *Pluralistic Fraternity,* pp. x, 15, 20. On the depression decline of ethnic benefit associations, see Cohen, *Making a New Deal,* pp. 227–30; and David Montgomery, "Labor and the Political Leadership of New Deal America," *International Review of Social History* 39, 1994, pp. 345–7.

50. See Walker, *Pluralistic Fraternity,* pp. 36–7 for the political struggles within the IWO and pp. 71–81 for the history of the Lincoln-Douglass Society.

51. Roger Keeran, "The International Workers Order and the Origins of the CIO," *Labor History,* Fall 1989. Paul Buhle, "Interview with Ernie Reymer on the I.W.O.," *Cultural Correspondence* 6–7, Spring 1978, pp. 98–101.

52. Martin Duberman, *Paul Robeson* (New York: Alfred A. Knopf, 1988), p. 250. Arnold Rampersad, *The Life of Langston Hughes. Volume I : 1902–1941. I, Too, Sing America* (New York: Oxford University Press, 1986), pp. 356–60.

53. Nicolás Kanellos, *A History of Hispanic Theatre in the United States: Origins to 1940* (Austin: University of Texas Press, 1990), pp. 117–21. Jesus Colon, *A Puerto Rican in New York and Other Sketches* (1961, rpt. New York: International Publishers, 1982), p. 140. For an account of women dressmakers in a Yiddish IWO study-circle in Los Angeles, see Norma Fain Pratt, "Culture and Radical Politics: Yiddish Women Writers in America, 1890–1940," in Lois Scharf and Joan M. Jensen, *Decades of Discontent* (Boston: Northeastern University Press, 1987). Vicki L. Ruiz, *Cannery Women, Cannery Lives: Mexican Women, Unionization, and the California Food Processing Industry, 1930–1950* (Albuquerque: University of New Mexico Press, 1987), p. 6. Mario T. García, *Memories of Chicano History: The Life and Narrative of Bert Corona* (Berkeley: University of California Press, 1994), pp. 75–6.

54. Sabin, *Red Scare in Court,* p. 351.

55. Williams, *Stage Left,* p. 231.

56. On Conroy and the FWP, see Wixson, *Worker-Writer in America,* pp. 420–49.

57. For a general account of the Treasury Department's PWAP and Bureau of Fine Arts and the Federal Art Project, see Richard D. McKinzie, *The New Deal for Artists* (Princeton, N.J.: Princeton University Press, 1973) and Francis V. O'Connor, ed., *Art for the Millions: Essays from the 1930s by Artists and Administrators of the WPA Federal Art Project* (Greenwich, N.J.: New York Graphic Society, 1973). William Alexander, *Film on the Left: American Documentary Film from 1931 to 1942* (Princeton, N.J.: Princeton University Press, 1981), pp. 60–61.

58. On the Composers' Forum-Laboratory, see *Direction* 1.4, April 1938, p. 31; on folk music, see William F. McDonald, *Federal Relief Administration and the Arts: The Origins and Administrative History of the Arts Projects of the Works Progress Administration* (Columbus: Ohio State University Press, 1969), pp. 636–41.

59. McKinzie, *The New Deal for Artists,* p. 57; Tischler, *An American Music,* p. 141. See John O'Connor and Lorraine Brown, *Free, Adult, Uncensored: The Living History of the Federal Theater Project* (Washington, D.C.: New Republic, 1978), pp. 28–9 on censorship battles in the Federal Theatre, and McKinzie, *The New Deal for Artists* pp. 110–11 on local battles over murals. On Pollock, see Peter Wollen, *Raiding the Icebox: Reflections on Twentieth-Century Culture* (Bloomington: Indiana University Press, 1993), p. 87.

60. See O'Connor and Brown, *Free, Adult, Uncensored;* Karal Ann Marling, *Wall to Wall America: A Cultural History of Post Office Murals in the Great Depression* (Minneapolis: University of Minnesota Press, 1982); Barbara Melosh, *Engendering Culture: Manhood and Womanhood in New Deal Public Art and Theater* (Washington, D.C.: Smithsonian Institution Press, 1991); Carla Cappetti, "Writers in a Strange Land: The Federal Writers' Project", Unpublished essay, 1981; Carla Cappetti, "Folklore of the New Deal: The Federal Writers' Project", Unpublished essay, 1981.

61. There is a large literature on FSA photography: see Carl Fleischhauer and Beverly W. Brannan, *Documenting America, 1935–1943* (Berkeley: University of California Press, 1988); and James Curtis, *Mind's Eye, Mind's Truth: FSA Photography Reconsidered* (Philadelphia: Temple University Press, 1989). On the RA music program, see Charles Seeger and Margaret Valiant, "Journal of a Field Representative," *Ethnomusicology* 24, May 1980, pp. 169–210; and Benjamin Filene, "Romancing the Folk: Public Memory and American Vernacular Music in the Twentieth Century," Ph.D. diss., Yale University, 1995, pp. 220–22. On the Shahn mural, see Harrison, "John Reed Club Artists and the New Deal," p. 254; Eisenschitz, *Nicholas Ray*, pp. 39–45: Thomas quoted on p. 41.

62. John Houseman, *Front and Center* (New York: Simon and Schuster, 1979), pp. 19–104. Yoneda, *Ganbatte*, 155. See also Daniel Belgrad, "The Social Meanings of Spontaneity in American Arts and Literature, 1940–1960," Ph.D. diss., Yale University, 1994, vol. 1, pp. 47–58.

63. See Holly Cowan Shulman, *The Voice of America: Propaganda and Democracy, 1941–1945* (Madison: University of Wisconsin Press, 1990), p. 38. On the Office of Facts and Figures and the Cowley incident, see Scott Donaldson, *Archibald MacLeish: An American Life* (Boston: Houghton Mifflin, 1992), pp. 348–65. On the Almanac Singers, see Lieberman, *"My Song Is My Weapon"*, p. 55.

64. I borrow the useful phrase "aesthetics of social significance" from Paula Rabinowitz, *Labor and Desire: Women's Revolutionary Fiction in Depression America* (Chapel Hill: University of North Carolina Press, 1991), p. 60.

65. W.A. Swanberg, *Luce and His Empire* (New York: Charles Scribner's Sons, 1972), pp. 81–4. Thomas Ferguson, *Golden Rule: The Investment Theory of Party Competition and the Logic of Money-Driven Political Systems* (Chicago: University of Chicago Press, 1995). Dwight Macdonald, *Politics Past* (New York: Viking, 1970), pp. 8–9.

66. Michael Wreszin, *A Rebel in Defense of Tradition: The Life and Politics of Dwight Macdonald* (New York: Basic, 1994), pp. 21–53. Laurence Bergreen, *James Agee: A Life* (New York: E.P. Dutton, 1984), pp. 178–80. Roy Hoopes, *Ralph Ingersoll: A Biography* (New York: Atheneum, 1985), pp. 155–86.

67. The commission and subsequent destruction of Diego Rivera's Rockefeller Center mural in 1933 is a classic story of the relation between left-wing artists and corporate liberalism. See Laurance P. Hurlburt, *The Mexican Muralists in the United States* (Albuquerque: University of New Mexico Press, 1989), pp. 159–74. The story of the relations between the foundations and the Popular Front left is yet to be told, though Harvey Klehr summarizes the debate over the connections between a few foundations and the Communist Party: Klehr, *The Heyday of American Communism: The Depression Decade* (New York: Basic Books, 1984), p. 477 n. 25.

68. Whittaker Chambers, *Witness* (1952, rpt. South Bend, Ind.: Regnery/Gateway, 1979), p. 475. Robert T. Elson, *Time Inc.: The Intimate History of a Publishing Enterprise, 1923–1941* (New York: Atheneum, 1968), pp. 388–90. Swanberg, *Luce*, pp. 161–4.

69. Kazin, *Starting out in the Thirties*, pp. 103–4, 113.

70. Cole quoted in Larry Ceplair and Stephen Englund, *The Inquisition in Hollywood: Politics in the Film Community, 1930–1960* (Berkeley: University of California Press, 1983), p. 303; see also p. 324. For a pathbreaking account of the film genres influenced by the left, see Paul Buhle, "The Hollywood Left: Aesthetics and Politics," *New Left Review* 212, July–August 1995, pp. 101–19; for a reading of the films of the Hollywood left in relation to earlier scripts and treatments, see Brian Neve, *Film and Politics in America: A Social Tradition* (London: Routledge, 1992); see also Bernard F. Dick, *Radical Innocence: A Critical Study of the Hollywood Ten* (Lexington: University Press of Kentucky, 1989). If the influence of the Hollywood radicals is hard to measure, it is even more difficult to judge the impact of Chicago radicals like Jack Conroy, who made a living in that city's encyclopedia industry: see Harry T. Moore's recollection in David Madden, ed., *Proletarian Writers of the Thirties* (Carbondale: Southern Illinois University Press, 1968), p. vi; and Wixson, *Worker-Writer in America*, pp. 452, 460. Perhaps my only quarrel with Douglas Wixson's great biography of Jack Conroy is that he doesn't do full justice to Conroy's twenty-three years as a worker-writer in the encyclopedia industry. Mike Davis, *City of Quartz: Excavating the Future in Los Angeles* (London: Verso, 1990), pp. 38, 37.

71. Joseph R. Starobin, *American Communism in Crisis, 1943–1957* (Berkeley: University of California Press, 1972), p. 31 stresses the importance of culture-industry organizing. For surveys of particular unions, I am indebted to Gary Fink, ed., *Labor Unions* (Westport, Conn.: Greenwood Press, 1977).

72. Very little has been written on the Writers' Union. See Mangione, *The Dream and the Deal*, pp. 34–8, 164–9, 248–52 (on the New York Writers' Union), pp. 194–200 (on the St Louis Writers Union). McDonald, *Federal Relief Administration and the Arts*, pp. 653–7. Folsom, *Days of Anger, Days of Hope:* p. 6. The local Writers' Unions seem to have been affiliated with the Workers' Alliance, a national federation of unemployed councils and organizations which, by 1937, had 1600 locals in 43 states. Nelson, Barrett, and Ruck, *Steve Nelson*, p. 436 n 5. On the Artists' Union, see O'Connor, *Art for the Millions*, pp. 237–47; and Robert C. Vitz, "Clubs, Congresses, and Unions: American Artists Confront the Thirties," *New York History* 54.4, October 1973, pp. 425–47.

73. Bruce Minton and John Stuart, *Men Who Lead Labor* (New York: Modern Age, 1937), p. 131. See also Isidor Schneider's article on the Macaulay strike in *Literary America*, October 1934; Schneider was a proletarian novelist who wrote regularly on the economic situation of writers and publishing in the *New Masses* at this time.

74. The Broun column is reprinted in Walter M. Brasch, *With Just Cause: Unionization of the American Journalist* (Lanham, Md.: University Press of America, 1991).

75. On radio unions, see Fink, *Labor Unions*; Richard Fine, *James M. Cain and the American Authors' Authority* (Austin: University of Texas Press, 1992), pp. 75–7; and Gregory Schubert and James Lynch, "Broadcasting Unions: Structure and Impact," in Allen E. Koenig, ed., *Broadcasting and Bargaining: Labor Relations in Radio and Television* (Madison: University of Wisconsin Press, 1970), pp. 41–66.

76. Murray Ross, *Stars and Strikes* (1941, rpt. New York: AMS Press, 1967). Ceplair and Englund, *The Inquisition in Hollywood*. Nancy Lynn Schwartz, *The Hollywood Writers' Wars* (New York: Alfred A. Knopf, 1982). Lary May, "Movie Star Politics: The Screen Actors' Guild, Cultural Conversion, and the Hollywood Red Scare," in Lary May, ed., *Recasting America: Culture and Politics in the Age of the Cold War* (Chicago: University of Chicago Press, 1989). The Screen Writers' Guild also supported a major initiative to reorganize the economy of writing, a proposal for a licencing authority not unlike the songwriter's ASCAP. See Fine, *James M. Cain*.

77. Robert D. Leiter, *The Musicians and Petrillo* (1953; rpt. New York: Octagon, 1974).

78. Bella V. Dodd, *School of Darkness* (1954, rpt. New York: Devin-Adair Company, 1963), p. 102; Jerome Davis, *A Life Adventure for Peace: An Autobiography* (New York: Citadel Press, 1967), p. 97ff. On teachers' unions, see Marjorie Murphy, *Blackboard Unions: The AFT and the NEA, 1900–1980* (Ithaca, N.Y.: Cornell University Press, 1990); Stephen Leberstein, "Purging the Profs: The Rapp-Coudert Committee in New York" in Brown, Martin, Rosengarten, and Snedeker, *New Studies in the Politics and Culture of US Communism*, pp. 91–122. On the Newspaper Guild, see Robert G. Picard, "Anticommunism in the New York Newspaper Guild," in Brasch, *With Just Cause*, pp. 277–92; on AFTRA, see Gary Gumpert, "Blacklisting," in Koenig, *Broadcasting and Bargaining*, pp. 229–55. Local 802 of the Musicians was never led by the left, but its Communist minority was investigated by HUAC in 1957.

79. See The Free Company, *The Free Company Presents . . . A Collection of Plays about the Meaning of America* (New York: Dodd, Mead, 1941), p. 143. Arch Oboler and Stephen Longstreet, eds, *Free World Theatre* (New York: Random House, 1944). Left-wing radio writers of some importance include Morton Wischengrad, Norman Rosten, Arthur Miller, and Roi Ottley. All are represented in the best collections of Popular Front radio drama: Eric Barnoux, ed., *Radio Drama in Action* (New York: Rinehart, 1945); and Joseph Liss, ed., *Radio's Best Plays* (New York: Greenberg, 1947).

80. Lomax quoted in Eisenschitz, *Nicholas Ray*, p. 52; on the Lomax radio programs, see pp. 52–3, 56–60; Filene, "Romancing the Folk", pp. 234–42; Joe Klein, *Woody Guthrie: A Life* (New York: Alfred A. Knopf, 1980), pp. 155–6, 165ff; and Wolfe and Lornell, *The Life and Legend of Leadbelly*, pp. 218–9. Earl Robinson and Will Geer produced another early radio program on American song for NBC's *Cavalcade of America*.

81. See Neve, *Film and Politics in America*, pp. 14–27, 68–74, 84–144. On *film gris*, see Thom Andersen, "Red Hollywood," in Suzanne Ferguson and Barbara Groseclose, eds, *Literature and*

the Visual Arts in Contemporary Society (Columbus: Ohio State University Press, 1985), pp. 141–96; George Lipsitz, *A Rainbow at Midnight: Labor and Culture in the 1940s* (Urbana: University of Illinois Press, 1994), pp. 279–302; and Buhle, "The Hollywood Left" pp. 101–19. On Chaplin and the Popular Front, see Charles Maland, *Chaplin and American Culture: The Evolution of a Star Image* (Princeton, N.J.: Princeton University Press, 1989).

82. Vitz, "Clubs, Congresses, and Unions," pp.432–4; Shapiro, ed., *Social Realism*, pp. 32 n. 33, 35 n. 75. I will discuss the Mercury Theatre and Café Society at greater length in chapters 9 and 10.

83. There is virtually nothing written about *Direction*. Like many such magazines it was not always a monthly: at times it cut back to bimonthly and quarterly publication. The major shift in the magazine took place in 1940 when it incorporated Jay Leyda's quarterly, *Films*; Tjader Harris briefly joined forces with Martin Kamin, the publisher of *Films* and director of a New York gallery. During the war, the journal contracted and the editor Edwin Seaver worked with Tjader Harris. Most of *Direction*'s advertisers were publishers and galleries. I am indebted to Lawrence E. Hussman for his assistance and for showing me sections of Marguerite Tjader Harris's unpublished memoir that call *Direction* a "shoestring affair." See also Lawrence E. Hussman, "Marguerite Tjader Harris: A Remembrance," *Dreiser Newsletter* 17, Fall 1986, pp. 21–2.

84. On *Ken*, see Arnold Gingrich, *Nothing But People: The Early Days at Esquire. A Personal History, 1928–1958* (New York: Crown, 1971), pp. 131–40, 145–9; George Seldes, *Witness to a Century* (New York: Ballantine, 1987), pp. 328–32; Jessie Lloyd O'Connor, Harvey O'Connor, and Susan Bowler, *Harvey and Jessie: A Couple of Radicals* (Philadelphia: Temple University Press, 1988); and Judy Kutulas, *The Long War: The Intellectual People's Front and Anti-Stalinism, 1930–1940* (Durham: Duke University Press, 1995), p. 137.

85. *Friday* 1.1, 15 March 1940, p. 20. There are few secondary accounts of *Friday*: see Benjamin Stolberg, "Muddled Millions: Capitalist Angels of Left-Wing Propaganda," *Saturday Evening Post* 213.33, 15 February 1941, pp. 9–10, 89–92.

86. On *PM*, see Hoopes, *Ralph Ingersoll*; Stolberg, "Muddled Millions"; Dan Georgakas, "*PM*," in Buhle, Buhle, and Georgakas, *Encyclopedia*; and James A. Wechsler, *The Age of Suspicion* (1953, rpt. New York: Donald I. Fine, 1985).

87. On Frontier Films, see Alexander, *Film on the Left*; on American Labor Films, see Alexander, p. 125. On the Motion Picture Guild, see Ceplair and Englund, *The Inquisition in Hollywood*, p. 116. Xanadu Films was a project of Ring Lardner Jr., Dalton Trumbo, and Hugo Black, modeled on the Playwrights Theatre. Lardner wrote a screenplay of Christina Stead's *The Man Who Loved Children*. Interview with Ring Lardner, Jr, by Paul Buhle and Michael Denning, 23 August 1990.

88. See John Hammond, *John Hammond on Record: An Autobiography* (New York: Summit Books, 1977), pp. 213–19; Whitney Balliett, *Goodbyes and Other Messages: A Journal of Jazz, 1981–1990* (New York: Oxford University Press, 1991), pp. 189–92; Klein, *Woody Guthrie*, pp. 191–2; Eric A. Gordon, *Mark the Music: The Life and Work of Marc Blitzstein* (New York: St Martin's Press, 1989), p. 204; Arnold Shaw, *Honkers and Shouters: The Golden Years of Rhythm and Blues* (New York: Macmillan, 1978), pp. 329–31.

89. Eagleton quoted in Arnold Krupat, *The Voice in the Margin* (Berkeley: University of California Press, 1989), p. xi.

90. Paul Buhle, *Marxism in the United States: Remapping the History of the American Left* (London: Verso, 1991), p. 100. The emergence of "Fosterism," Communist syndicalism, is well argued in Edward P. Johanningsmeier, *Forging American Communism: The Life of William Z. Foster* (Princeton: Princeton University Press, 1994), pp. 5, 36, 56, 157–64. He notes that Bertram Wolfe suggested that "Foster's belief that the unions were the most important focus of revolutionary activity in America was 'the first expression' of American exceptionalism in the Communist party" (p. 5). The other theoretical contribution of the Communist movement was its notion of a working-class federation of nationalities, a kind of ethnic internationalism that I will discuss in the next chapter.

91. James F. Murphy, *The Proletarian Moment: The Controversy over Leftism in Literature* (Urbana: University of Illinois Press, 1991) offers the best account of the US controversy over aesthetic "leftism," situating it in the context of the German and Soviet debates.

92. Perry Anderson, *Considerations on Western Marxism* (1976, rpt. London: Verso, 1979), pp. 75–6.

93. League of Professional Groups for Foster and Ford, *Culture and the Crisis: An Open Letter to the Writers, Artists, Teachers, Physicians, Engineers, Scientists and Other Professional Workers of America* (New York: Workers Library Publishers, 1932), pp. 28, 11.

94. League, *Culture and the Crisis*, pp. 29, 18. On the conference, see McDonald, *Federal Relief Administration and the Arts*, pp. 655–7; and Mangione, *The Dream and the Deal*, p. 38.

95. See Paul Buhle, *A Dreamer's Paradise Lost: Louis C. Fraina/Lewis Corey (1892–1953) and the Decline of Radicalism in the United States* (New Jersey: Humanities Press, 1995); and Giuseppe Fiori, *Antonio Gramsci: Life of a Revolutionary* (New York: Shocken, 1973).

96. Antonio Gramsci, *Selections from Cultural Writings* (Cambridge, Mass.: Harvard University Press, 1985), p. 106. Lewis Corey, *The Decline of American Capitalism* (New York: Covici Friede Publishers, 1934), p. 508. There are also remarkable parallels between Gramsci and Corey in their use of Jacobinism and Caesarism in their analysis of fascism.

97. Lewis Corey, *The Crisis of the Middle Class* (New York: Covici Friede Publishers, 1935), pp. 24, 249, 259, 344–5, 355.

98. *Modern Monthly* 7.1, February 1933, p. 6. The freewheeling atmosphere of Calverton's salon is recalled in memoirs by Adamic, *My America*, pp. 87–95; Granville Hicks, *Part of the Truth: An Autobiography* (New York: Harcourt, Brace and World, Inc., 1965), pp. 95–6; Kazin, *Starting out in the Thirties*, pp. 61–76; and Sidney Hook, *Out of Step: An Unquiet Life in the Twentieth Century* (New York: Harper and Row, 1987), pp. 144–6. See also Leonard Wilcox, *V.F. Calverton: Radical in the American Grain* (Philadelphia: Temple University Press, 1992), pp. 161–3.

99. Both Judy Kutulas and Leonard Wilcox note that the dissident communists were "premature united fronters," to use Kutulas's phrase: Kutulas, *The Long War*, p. 67. However, since both studies focus on the figures who attacked (and were attacked by) the Communist Party, they miss the significance of those intellectuals like Burke and Adamic who became important Popular Front figures. See Wilcox, *V.F. Calverton*, p. 148 for Calverton's influence on Burke.

100. Burke's characterization of *Permanence and Change* is in Jay, *The Selected Correspondence of Kenneth Burke and Malcolm Cowley*, p. 210.

101. Kenneth Burke, "Revolutionary Symbolism in America," in Hart, ed., *American Writers' Congress*, pp. 93, 90–91.

102. Walter Benjamin, "The Author as Producer," in *Understanding Brecht* (London: NLB, 1977), pp. 89, 93–4, 102.

103. Gramsci, *Selections from Cultural Writings*, pp. 99–102. The relation between "The Author as Producer" and Becher's notion of proletarian literature is noted in Walter Benjamin, "Conversations with Brecht," *Understanding Brecht*, pp. 106–7. Despite Gramsci's early enthusiasm for the Proletkult, the association between Gramsci's *Prison Notebooks* and a Popular Front conception of culture is surely uncontroversial. The connection between Walter Benjamin and Popular Front culture is more controversial. Jonathan Arac sets Benjamin against the Popular Front by opposing him to Andre Malraux, focusing on Benjamin's critique of the "cultural treasures" notion of culture. Jonathan Arac, *Critical Genealogies: Historical Situations for Postmodern Literary Studies* (New York: Columbia University Press, 1987), pp. 173–4; and Jonathan Arac, "The Struggle for the Cultural Heritage: Christina Stead Refunctions Charles Dickens and Mark Twain," in H. Aram Veeser, ed., *The New Historicism* (New York: Routledge, 1989), pp. 116–17. For Benjamin, however, the "cultural treasures" position is the legacy not of the Popular Front but of German social democracy, as is clear from his essay on Fuchs. Moreover, Arac oversimplifies Malraux's essay which shares much with Benjamin, as is indicated by their mutual citations. For a more complex account of Benjamin's relation to the French Popular Front, see Phillipe Ivornel, "Paris, Capital of the Popular Front," *New German Critique* 39, 1986, pp. 61–84 and Chryssoula Kambas, "*Politische Aktualität*: Walter Benjamin's Concept of History and the Failure of the French Popular Front," *New German Critique* 39, 1986, pp. 87–98. Both attempt to separate Benjamin from the Popular Front by offering a relatively simple view of Popular Front culture; the letters they cite, however, suggest how much Benjamin saw himself as part of the Popular Front social movement. His criticisms of particular figures—like Aragon and the

magazine *Vendredi*—are clearly in the context of a larger "respect [for] the 'populism' of the Popular Front," as Ivornel puts it (pp. 77–8). Benjamin's disagreements with particular Communist Party cultural figures are not unlike the arguments that Burke and Corey had with figures like Joseph Freeman: they should not overshadow the substance of their political and intellectual positions. As for Benjamin's own place in the "production process," he remained a favored contributor to *Das Wort*, which David Caute called "the most orthodox of all Popular Front periodicals." David Caute, *The Fellow-Travellers: A Postscript to Enlightenment* (New York: Macmillan, 1973), p. 153.

104. See Michael Denning, *Cover Stories: Narrative and Ideology in the British Spy Thriller* (London: Routledge & Kegan Paul, 1987) for an analysis of Ambler's Popular Front thrillers. Leo Huberman's *The Labor Spy Racket* was a popular paperback account of the La Follette hearings. See also Jerold S. Auerbach, *Labor and Liberty: The La Follette Committee and the New Deal* (Indianapolis, Ind.: The Bobbs-Merrill Company, Inc., 1966), pp. 164–6. One of the few accomplishments of Harvey Klehr, John Earl Haynes, and Fridrikh Igorevich Firsov, *The Secret World of American Communism* (New Haven, Conn.: Yale University Press, 1995) is its inadvertent demonstration of the pervasive US government espionage against the Communist Party and corporate espionage against the CIO.

105. Leslie A. Fiedler's *An End to Innocence: Essays on Culture and Politics* (Boston: Beacon Press, 1955) opened with three essays that took Hiss, the Rosenbergs, and, to a lesser degree, Fuchs as emblems of the Popular Front.

106. Loyd D. Easton and Kurt H. Guddat, eds, *Writings of the Young Marx on Philosophy and Society* (Garden City, N.J.: Anchor Books, 1967), pp. 185–6. Chambers, *Witness*, p. 269. A left-wing version of the same conceit can be found in Raymond Williams's fine thriller *The Volunteers*, in which a group of radicals decides to infiltrate the state and the mass media.

107. Stephen Koch, *Double Lives: Spies and Writers in the Secret Soviet War of Ideas against the West* (New York: Free Press, 1994), p. 220. On the OSS use of Popular Front networks, see Peter N. Carroll, *The Odyssey of the Abraham Lincoln Brigade: Americans in the Spanish Civil War* (Stanford, Calif.: Stanford University Press, 1994), pp. 254–60, 269–78.

108. Koch, *Double Lives*, pp. 15, 12.

109. Chambers, *Witness*, p. 86.

110. James T. Farrell, "The End of a Literary Decade," *American Mercury* 48, 1939, reprinted in Ralph Bogardus and Fred Hobson, eds, *Literature at the Barricades: The American Writer in the 1930s* (University: University of Alabama Press, 1982), p. 207. Farrell's list was echoed in Irving Howe and Lewis Coser's contemptuous catalog of the Popular Front's "horde of second-rank intellectuals, Hollywood scripters, radio hacks, popular novelists, English professors, actors, dancers, newspapermen and publicity agents." Howe and Coser, *The American Communist Party: A Critical History* (1957; rpt. New York: Frederick A. Praeger, 1962), p. 314. James T. Farrell, *The League of Frightened Philistines and Other Papers* (New York: Vanguard Press, 1945), pp. 182–3.

111. See Farrell's "The Language of Hollywood" and "More on Hollywood," collected in *The League of Frightened Philistines*. See also Harold Leonard, "Recent American Film Writing," *Sight and Sound* 16.62, Summer 1947, pp. 73–5. Max Horkheimer and Theodor W. Adorno, *Dialectic of Enlightenment* (1944; rpt. New York: Seabury Press, 1972), pp. 129, 149. The other early essay of this sort was Clement Greenberg, "Avant-Garde and Kitsch," *Partisan Review* 6.5, Fall 1939.

112. C.L.R. James, *American Civilization* (Cambridge: Blackwell, 1993), pp. 255, 258. It is worth noting that Lewis Corey adopted much of this analysis of a new class of "power intellectuals" in his work of the 1940s, using it to critique not only the Communists but the new Cold War liberalism of Arthur Schlesinger, Jr. See Buhle, *A Dreamer's Paradise Lost*, p. 164.

113. Robert Warshow, *The Immediate Experience: Movies, Comics, Theatre and Other Aspects of Popular Culture* (New York: Atheneum, 1971), pp. 38, 37. See Andrew Ross, *No Respect: Intellectuals and Popular Culture* (New York: Routledge, 1989), for a fine account of the Cold War intellectuals' attack on Popular Front culture.

114. Michael Denning, "New York Intellectuals," *Socialist Review* 88/1, January–March 1988, pp. 136–47.

115. There are several essays that seem to make up Mills's *Cultural Apparatus* project: the 1955 "Knowledge and Power," a reflection on intellectuals, published in *Dissent*; the 1958

"Man in the Middle: The Designer" which first introduces the term "cultural apparatus"; the three BBC lectures of 1958–59 published in *The Listener*, "Culture and Politics," "The Cultural Apparatus," and "The Decline of the Left"; and the famous 1960 "Letter to the New Left." All are collected in C. Wright Mills, *Power, Politics, and People: The Collected Essays* (New York: Ballantine, 1963).

116. Mills, *Power, Politics, and People*, pp. 236, 238, 241.

117. Mills, *Power, Politics, and People*, pp. 405–6, 412, 411.

118. Mills, *Power, Politics, and People*, p. 418.

119. Mills, *Power, Politics, and People*, p. 419.

120. Mills, *Power, Politics, and People*, pp. 232, 256–7.

121. Mills, *Power, Politics, and People*, pp. 408, 383, 233, 232.

122. Daniel Bell, "The Mood of Three Generations," in his *The End of Ideology: On the Exhaustion of Political Ideas in the Fifties* (New York: The Free Press, 1962), p. 313; Raymond Williams, *The Long Revolution* (New York: Chatto & Windus, 1961); Leo Marx, "Notes on the Culture of the New Capitalism," *Monthly Review* 11, July–August 1959, pp. 111–16. The British Popular Front predecessor to Williams was Cecil Day-Lewis, ed., *The Mind in Chains: Socialism and the Cultural Revolution* (London: Frederick Muller, 1937), with its essays on education, the film industry, the press and the radio.

123. Harold Cruse, *The Crisis of the Negro Intellectual* (New York: William Morrow, 1967), pp. 541–2, 87, 81, 188. The discussion of C. Wright Mills can be found on pp. 65–7 and 459–75.

Notes to 3

1. See John O'Connor and Lorraine Brown, *Free, Adult, Uncensored: The Living History of the Federal Theater Project* (Washington: New Republic, 1978), pp. 184–93; and Ned Lehac, "The Story of *Sing for Your Supper*," in Glenn Loney, ed., *Musical Theatre in America* (Westport, Conn.: Greenwood, 1984). For a brief account of radio's "ballad opera" form, see Erik Barnouw, ed., *Radio Drama in Action: Twenty-Five Plays of a Changing World* (New York: Rinehart, 1945), pp. 240–41. Martin Duberman, *Paul Robeson* (New York: Alfred A. Knopf, 1988), pp. 236–8. "Radio: Bravos," *Time* 34.21, 20 November 1939, pp. 58–9. Earl Robinson, "On 'Ballad For Americans'," Liner notes for *Paul Robeson Sings 'Ballad for Americans'*, Vanguard VSD 79193. The Victor record was Victor 26516 & 26517.

2. Robert Warshow, "The Legacy of the Thirties," in his *The Immediate Experience* (New York: Atheneum, 1971), pp. 36, 34, 33. The letter by Ethel Rosenberg can be found in Michael Meeropol, ed., *The Rosenberg Letters: A Complete Edition of the Prison Correspondence of Julius and Ethel Rosenberg* (New York: Garland Publishing, 1994), p. 157. See Andrew Ross's fine discussion of how the letters of the Rosenbergs came to stand "as an expressive document of the disparate range of cultural references that had organized meaning for a lower middle-class Popular Front family." Ross, "Reading the Rosenberg Letters," in his *No Respect: Intellectuals and Popular Culture* (New York: Routledge, 1989), p. 24. For examples of the New York Intellectuals' attack on the Popular Front, see Lionel Trilling, "A Novel of the Thirties," in his *The Last Decade: Essays and Reviews, 1965–1975* (New York: Harcourt Brace Jovanovich, 1979); Leslie Fiedler, "The Two Memories," in his *Unfinished Business* (New York: Stein and Day, 1972); Irving Howe and Lewis Coser, "The Popular Front: Success and Respectability," in their *The American Communist Party: A Critical History* (1957; rpt. New York: Frederick A. Praeger, 1962); Dwight Macdonald, *Politics Past* (New York: Viking, 1970); James Farrell, "The Literary Popular Front," and "Note on a New Literary Controversy," in his *Literature and Morality* (New York: Vanguard Press, 1947); and Irving Howe, "The Thirties in Retrospect," in Ralph Bogardus and Fred Hobson, eds, *Literature at the Barricades: The American Writer in the 1930s* (University: University of Alabama Press, 1982).

3. Stanley Aronowitz, *The Crisis in Historical Materialism: Class, Politics and Culture in Marxist Theory* (New York: Praeger, 1981), p. 236. I quote the Aronowitz passage for its value as a symptom of New Left thinking. Aronowitz wrote the 1976 essay "Culture and Politics" as "a militant defender of modernism," reacting against his own childhood formation in the Popular Front ("Postscript to Culture and Politics," p. 270). I am greatly indebted to many conversations with Stanley about the Popular Front, and to his recent essay, "Cultural Politics

of the Popular Front," in *Roll over Beethoven* (Middletown, Conn.: Wesleyan University Press, 1993). Christopher Lasch, "Introduction," to Richard Hofstadter, *The American Political Tradition and the Men Who Made It* (New York: Vintage, 1974), p. x. Warren I. Susman, *Culture as History: The Transformation of American Society in the Twentieth Century* (New York: Pantheon Books, 1984), pp. 80, 205.

4. Sidney Blumenthal, *The Rise of the Counter-Establishment* (New York: Times Books, 1986), p. 284. Blumenthal's paragraph is a good example of the received wisdom, since it is a pastiche of earlier writers. The phrase "democratic schwarmerei" echoes Howe and Coser, *The American Communist Party*, p. 314; and his misquotation of "Ballad for Americans" is identical to Warren Susman's misquotation that I discuss below. I owe the phrase "folk idiom and documentary expression" to Maurice Isserman's reply to Jesse Lemisch's attack on the persistence of Popular Front aesthetics in the left culture of the 1980s. Maurice Isserman, "Letter," *The Nation*, 13 December 1986, p. 658. Lemisch's "I Dreamed I Saw MTV Last Night," *The Nation*, 18 October 1986, pp. 373–6, provoked a number of heated responses. A striking aspect of the debate was that no one challenged Lemisch's sense that Popular Front culture was bounded by the folk idiom and the documentary aesthetic.

5. Maurice Isserman, *Which Side Were You On? The American Communist Party during the Second World War* (Middletown, Conn.: Wesleyan University Press, 1982), p. 22. Joe Klein, *Woody Guthrie: A Life* (New York: Alfred A. Knopf, 1980), p. 147.

6. Fredric Jameson, *Postmodernism, or, The Cultural Logic of Late Capitalism* (Durham, N.C.: Duke University Press, 1991), p. 209.

7. Tom Wolfe, *The Painted Word* (New York: Farrar, Straus & Giroux, 1975), pp. 40–41.

8. Alfred Kazin, *On Native Grounds: An Interpretation of Modern American Prose Literature* (New York: Reynal & Hitchcock, 1942), p. 495.

9. Stott's "Afterword" to the 1986 edition of his book is useful in situating it in the culture of the 1960s. There are a number of recent studies of documentary in this period including David P. Peeler, *Hope Among Us Yet: Social Criticism and Social Solace in Depression America* (Athens: University of Georgia Press, 1987); Michael E. Staub, *Voices of Persuasion: Politics of Representation in 1930s America* (Cambridge: Cambridge University Press, 1994); Carl Fleischhauer and Beverly W. Brannan, *Documenting America, 1935–1943* (Berkeley: University of California Press, 1988). Paula Rabinowitz, *They Must Be Represented: The Politics of Documentary* (London: Verso, 1994) takes the story of documentary beyond the "thirties" and into the postmodern.

10. Staub, *Voices of Persuasion*, p. 20. Leo Hurwitz, "One Man's Voyage: Ideas and Films in the 1930s," in David Platt, ed., *Celluloid Power* (Metuchen, N.J.: Scarecrow Press, 1992). I am indebted to Joseph Entin for calling my attention to this essay.

11. Wolfe, *The Painted Word*, pp. 40–41. Jameson, *Postmodernism*, p. 305. See Aronowitz's "Culture and Politics" in his *The Crisis of Historical Materialism* for a powerful example of this argument. James Murphy persuasively demonstrates that, though there were left-wing debates over formal experimentation and specific modernist artists, there was no campaign against formalism or modernism in US left cultural journals. Murphy, *The Proletarian Moment: The Controversy over Leftism in Literature* (Urbana: University of Illinois Press, 1991), p. 139.

12. Malcolm Cowley, *Exile's Return: A Narrative of Ideas* (New York: W.W. Norton, 1934), pp. 69–73. Andreas Huyssen, *After the Great Divide: Modernism, Mass Culture, Postmodernism* (Bloomington: Indiana University Press, 1986). See also Walter Kalaidjian's critique of Huyssen in Kalaidjian, *American Culture between the Wars: Revisionary Modernism and Postmodern Critique* (New York: Columbia University Press, 1993), pp. 5–8.

13. On Leger and Davis, see Peter Wollen, *Raiding the Icebox: Reflections on Twentieth-Century Culture* (Bloomington: Indiana University Press, 1993), p. 83. On Strand, see Mike Weaver, "Dynamic Realism," in Maren Stange, ed., *Paul Strand: Essays on His Life and Work* (New York: Aperture, 1990). Note also Basil Davidson's memory of the term "neo-realism" in his essay "Working with Strand" in the same collection. Dorothy C. Miller and Alfred H. Barr, Jr, eds, *American Realists and Magic Realists* (New York: Museum of Modern Art, 1943), p. 5. Oliver Larkin, *Art and Life in America* (New York: Rinehart, 1949), pp. 453–4, 471. Larkin's book is the major work of art history to come out of the Popular Front, a complement to the literary histories of Hicks, Kazin, and Matthiessen and the theater history of Gorelik. "Proletarian

Surrealism," *Direction* 1.4, April 1938, pp. 3, 5, 6, 7. On the importance of surrealism to the Popular Front left, see Wollen, *Raiding the Icebox*, pp. 87–92.

14. Both Cécile Whiting, *Antifascism in American Art* (New Haven, Conn.: Yale University Press, 1989) and Erika Doss, *Benton, Pollock, and the Politics of Modernism: From Regionalism to Abstract Expressionism* (Chicago: University of Chicago Press, 1991) tend to stress a social realist, documentary account of Popular Front art; Whiting dates the end of left-wing modernism in 1928 (p. 25). I am more persuaded by the arguments of Peter Wollen, "The Triumph of American Painting" in *Raiding the Icebox* (in part a rejoinder to Doss) and of Patricia Hills, *Social Concern and Urban Realism: American Painting of the 1930s* (Boston: Boston University Art Gallery, 1983). Hills is good on the limits of the "social realism" designation, and points to Grace Clement's 1936 *Art Front* essay, which claims montage, surrealism, and cubism for radical art.

15. Kenneth Burke, *Permanence and Change: An Anatomy of Purpose* (New York: New Republic, Inc., 1935), pp. 147, 148. For Burke's discussions of the grotesque, see *Permanence and Change*, pp. 146–56; Burke, *Attitudes toward History* (New York: New Republic, 1937), vol. 1, pp. 73–90; and Burke, *The Philosophy of Literary Form: Studies in Symbolic Action* (1941; rpt. Berkeley: University of California Press, 1973), pp. 350–60. Tillie Olsen, *Yonnondio: From the Thirties* (New York: Delta/Seymour Lawrence, 1974), p. 20.

16. Kenneth Burke, "Revolutionary Symbolism in America," in Henry Hart, ed., *American Writers' Congress* (New York: International Publishers, 1935), p. 89.

17. Sillen quoted in Lawrence H. Schwartz, *Marxism and Culture: The CPUSA and Aesthetics in the 1930s* (Port Washington, N.Y.: Kennikat Press, 1980), p. 90. Susman, *Culture as History* p. 212.

18. Leslie Fiedler, *Waiting for the End: The Crisis in American Culture and a Portrait of Twentieth Century American Literature* (New York: Stein and Day, 1964), p. 61.

19. The classic studies of populism include Lawrence Goodwyn, *The Populist Moment: A Short History of the Agrarian Revolt in America* (Oxford: Oxford University Press, 1978); Michael Kazin, *The Populist Persuasion: An American History* (New York: Basic Books, 1995); Carl Boggs, *Social Movements and Political Power: Emerging Forms of Radicalism in the West* (Philadelphia: Temple University Press, 1986), pp. 129–69; and Harry Boyte and Sara Evans, *Free Spaces: The Sources of Democratic Change in America* (New York: Harper and Row, 1986). However, my account of populism as the politics of rent, credit, and taxes draws more on James Green, "Populism, Socialism, and the Promise of Democracy," *Radical History Review* 24, Fall 1980, pp. 7–40.

20. Kalaidjian, *American Culture between the Wars*, p. 138.

21. Antonio Gramsci, *Selections from the Prison Notebooks* (London: Lawrence and Wishart, 1971), p. 210. Susman, *Culture as History*, p. 212.

22. Michael Mann, "Sources of Variation in Working-Class Movements in Twentieth-Century Europe," *New Left Review* 212, July–August 1995, p. 34. Nancy MacLean, *Beyond the Mask of Chivalry: The Making of the Second Ku Klux Klan* (New York: Oxford University Press, 1994), p. xi.

23. George Wolfskill, *The Revolt of the Conservatives: A History of the American Liberty League, 1934–1940* (Boston: Houghton Mifflin Company, 1962).

24. Alan Brinkley, *Voices of Protest: Huey Long, Father Coughlin, and the Great Depression* (New York: Vintage Books, 1982) attempts to distinguish Long and Coughlin from fascism, downplaying Coughlin's post-1938 rhetoric. See John Gunther, *Inside U.S.A.* (New York: Harper and Brothers, 1947), pp. 382, 518, 787, 810, on the presence of American fascism in the post-war US.

25. This official populism is the subject of the pathbreaking essays of Warren Susman and Lawrence Levine; however, they both tend to see the oppositional populisms of the left and right merely as variants of this mainstream consensus. I would suggest that the official populism was a short-lived attempt to appropriate the energies of the social movements; it gave way to patriotic populisms with distinct enemies—the wartime mobilization against the external enemy and the post-war crusade against Communism. Susman, *Culture as History*, pp. 150–229; Lawrence W. Levine, *The Unpredictable Past: Explorations in American Cultural History* (New York: Oxford University Press, 1993), pp. 206–319.

26. Susman, *Culture as History*, p. 205. Paul Robeson, "Ballad for Americans," 1940 on his *Ballad for Americans and Carnegie Hall Concert*, vol. 2, Vanguard VSD–79193, 1965.

27. Jonathan Arac, *Critical Genealogies: Historical Situations for Postmodern Literary Studies* (New York: Columbia University Press, 1987), p. 163. For a good summary of the general argument, see Gary Gerstle, "The Politics of Patriotism: Americanization and the Formation of the CIO," *Dissent* 33.1, Winter 1986. For the most powerful account of the turn to race interpretation, see Steve Fraser and Gary Gerstle, eds, *The Rise and Fall of the New Deal Order, 1930–1980* (Princeton, N.J.: Princeton University Press, 1989). Gary Gerstle, *Working-Class Americanism: The Politics of Labor in a Textile City, 1914–1960* (Cambridge: Cambridge University Press, 1989) is a defense of this politics of patriotism; see in particular the concluding remarks (pp. 333–6) in which he argues that black nationalists and the New Left "refused to speak the language of Americanism." On the other hand, Jonathan Arac's essay on F.O. Matthiessen, in *Critical Genealogies*, is a good example of the radical critique of Popular Front Americanism: "Matthiessen's national awakening obliterated class and ethnic divisions... Matthiessen's Popular Front figure of 'America' suffered a sobering fate. The war ... reconstellated American politics, and the figure of 'America' that began as a Depression tactic of harmony became a postwar myth of empire" (p. 167).

28. Gerstle, "The Politics of Patriotism," p. 85.

29. "What is Americanism?," *Partisan Review & Anvil* 3.3, April 1936, pp. 3–16; the Josephson quotation is on p. 8. On the Marxist symposia, see Daniel Aaron, *Writers on the Left: Episodes in American Literary Communism* (New York: Harcourt, Brace and World, Inc., 1961), pp. 243–7; Harvey Klehr, *The Heyday of American Communism: The Depression Decade* (New York: Basic Books, 1984), pp. 79–80; Granville Hicks, *Part of the Truth: An Autobiography* (New York: Harcourt, Brace and World, Inc., 1965), pp. 97–8, 107; Leah Levenson and Jerry Natterstad, *Granville Hicks: The Intellectual in Mass Society* (Philadelphia: Temple University Press, 1993), p. 51; Leonard Wilcox, *V.F. Calverton: Radical in the American Grain* (Philadelphia: Temple University Press, 1992), pp. 127–9; and Bernard Smith, *A World Remembered, 1925–1950* (New Jersey: Humanities Press, 1994), p. 2. Though most accounts see these Marxist symposia on American culture as failures, victims of sectarian battles, the subsequent work of the proposed contributors did constitute a Marxist symposium on American culture. The proposed table of contents included: Sidney Hook's "A Preface to Marxism" (his *Towards an Understanding of Karl Marx* appeared in 1933); Lewis Corey's "The Social and Economic Scene" (his *Decline of American Capitalism* appeared in 1934); Bernard Smith's "Criticism" (his *Forces in American Criticism* appeared in 1939); James Rorty on radio (his *Our Master's Voice: Advertising* appeared in 1934); Newton Arvin on poetry (his *Whitman* appeared in 1938); Granville Hicks on magazines (his literary history, *The Great Tradition*, appeared in 1933); Harry Potamkin on movies (Potamkin died in 1933 but the posthumous collection of his writings established him as one of the foremost film critics of the period); Meyer Shapiro on the fine arts (he went on to become the leading art historian of his generation); and Merle Curti on historiography (his *The Growth of American Thought* appeared in 1943).

30. "What is Americanism?," p. 9.

31. "What is Americanism?," p. 14. Despite being condemned by the Communist Party, Freeman's 1936 autobiography, *An American Testament*, was one of the classics of the Popular Front. Joseph Starobin notes that it "made a great impression on the youth of the thirties, and was one of the few American radical memoirs to echo abroad, where Victor Gollancz's *Left Book Club* reprinted it." Starobin, *American Communism in Crisis, 1943–1957* (Berkeley: University of California Press, 1972), p. 253 n. 32. Joshua Freeman notes that "until the 1930s the accepted image of the United States was still as the land of the founding fathers, a white, Protestant, middle class nation. By the end of World War II the dominant image had become 'A House for All People,' as immortalized in scores of movies and books in which the metaphor for the nation was the platoon consisting of soldiers from every class, regional, and ethnic background." Freeman, *In Transit: The Transport Workers Union in New York City, 1933–1966* (New York: Oxford University Press, 1989) p. v.

32. Gerstle, "The Politics of Patriotism," emphasizes this aspect of Popular Front Americanism in his brief sketches of Vito Marcantonio and the Reuther brothers; he misses, I think, the contrary impulses I discuss below. On Howard Fast, see Alan Wald, "The Legacy of Howard Fast," in his *The Responsibility of Intellectuals: Selected Essays on Marxist Traditions in*

Cultural Commitment (New Jersey: Humanities Press, 1992); and Priscilla Murolo, "History in the Fast Lane," *Radical History Review* 31, December 1984, pp. 22–31. The remarkable resurgence of interest in John Brown which can be seen in W.E.B. Du Bois's 1935 biography, Mike Gold's *Battle Hymn*, and Jacob Lawrence's series of history paintings, is a rarely noticed part of Popular Front culture: see James D. Bloom, *Left Letters: The Culture Wars of Mike Gold and Joseph Freeman* (New York: Columbia University Press, 1992), pp. 45–7. Since Earl Browder was from Kansas, the Communist Party often linked Browder to John Brown and the spirit of Ossatowanmie. The banners at the Communist Party's Popular Front convention of 1936 were of John Brown and Frederick Douglass: Earl Ofari Hutchinson, *Blacks and Reds: Race and Class in Conflict, 1919–1990* (East Lansing: Michigan State University Press, 1995), p. 97. The Lincoln story was more a part of mainstream New Deal populism, as in John Ford's film *Young Mr. Lincoln*; Howard Koch's Federal Theater Play which starred a young John Huston; Aaron Copland's *Lincoln Portrait*; and the work of the poets and playwrights who have been called Roosevelt's image brokers, Carl Sandburg, Robert Sherwood, and Stephen Vincent Benet.

33. Richard Wright, "Blueprint for Negro Writing," *New Challenge* 2.2, Spring 1937, p. 58. On the divide between trade union and nationality work, see Steve Nelson, James R. Barrett, and Rob Ruck, *Steve Nelson, American Radical* (Pittsburgh, Pa.: University of Pittsburgh Press, 1981), p. 67.

34. Thomas Göbel, "Becoming American: Ethnic Workers and the Rise of the CIO," *Labor History* 29.2, Summer 1988, pp. 173–98. Werner Sollors, *Beyond Ethnicity: Consent and Descent in American Literature* (New York: Oxford University Press, 1986), p. 215. Wright, "Blueprint," p. 58. Wenquan, "Chinatown Literature during the Last Ten Years (1939–1949)," *Amerasia* 9.1, 1982, pp. 89–90. See David Montgomery, "Labor and the Political Leadership of New Deal America," *International Review of Social History* 39, 1994, pp. 346–7, on the pan-ethnic appeal to younger people and the split between right and left in ethnic communities.

35. Wenquan, "Chinatown Literature," p. 90; Kent quoted in Arthur J. Sabin, *Red Scare in Court: New York versus the International Workers Order* (Philadelphia: University of Pennsylvania Press, 1993), p. 252. Olsen, *Yonnondio*, p. 50 (the ellipses in brackets are mine; the others are part of the text).

36. On regionalism, see Benjamin A. Botkin, "The Folk in Literature: An Introduction to the New Regionalism," *Folk-Say*, 1929; Carey McWilliams, *The New Regionalism in American Literature* (Seattle: University of Washington Book Store, 1930); Babb quoted in Douglas Wixson, *Worker-Writer in America: Jack Conroy and the Tradition of Midwestern Literary Radicalism, 1898–1990* (Urbana: University of Illinois Press, 1994), p. 377; Constance Rourke, "The Significance of Sections," *New Republic*, 20 September 1933, pp. 148, 149.

37. Benjamin A. Botkin, "Regionalism and Culture," in Henry Hart, ed., *The Writer in a Changing World* (n.p.: Equinox Cooperative Press, 1937), pp. 141, 150. Meridel Le Sueur, "Proletarian Literature and the Middle West," in Henry Hart, ed., *American Writers' Congress* (New York: International Publishers, 1935), pp. 135, 138. On Botkin's career, see Bruce Jackson, ed., *Folklore and Society* (Hatboro: Folklore Associates, 1966); on Rourke's career, see Joan Shelley Rubin, *Constance Rourke and American Culture* (Chapel Hill: University of North Carolina Press, 1980).

38. Gramsci's definitions of the "people" are worth recalling: "the people (the sum total of the instrumental and subaltern classes of every form of society that has so far existed)"; "the people themselves are not a homogeneous cultural collectivity but present numerous and variously combined cultural stratifications which, in their pure form, cannot always be identified within specific historical popular collectivities." Antonio Gramsci, *An Antonio Gramsci Reader*, by David Forgacs, ed. (New York: Schocken, 1988), p. 360; Antonio Gramsci, *Selections from Cultural Writings* (Cambridge, Mass.: Harvard University Press, 1985), p. 195. See also David Forgacs, "National-Popular: Genealogy of a Concept," in *Formations of Nation and People* (London: Routledge and Kegan Paul, 1984), pp. 83–98.

39. Gramsci, *Selections from Cultural Writings*, p. 102. Rourke, "The Significance of Sections," p. 149.

40. Gramsci, *Selections from Cultural Writings*, p. 98. Constance Rourke, *American Humor: A Study of National Character* (1931; rpt. Tallahasse: Florida State University Press, 1986). Rourke, *The Roots of American Culture and Other Essays* (New York: Harcourt Brace and Company, 1942).

41. Gramsci, *Selections from the Prison Notebooks* p. 130. Susman, *Culture as History*, p. 80. Michael Denning, "'The Special American Conditions': Marxism and American Studies," *American Quarterly* 38.3, 1986, pp. 356–80.

42. Ellen C. Dubois uses the term "left feminist" to characterize Popular Front women like Eleanor Flexner: Dubois, "Eleanor Flexner and the History of American Feminism," *Gender and History* 3.1, Spring 1991, p. 84. Dorothy Sue Cobble, "Recapturing Working-Class Feminism: Union Women in the Postwar Era," in Joanne Meyerowitz, ed., *Not June Cleaver: Women and Gender in Postwar America, 1945–1960* (Philadelphia: Temple University Press, 1994). On the organizing of housewives, see Annelise Orleck, "'We Are that Mythical Thing Called the Public': Militant Housewives during the Depression," *Feminist Studies* 19.1, Spring 1993, pp. 147–72. On the teachers union, see Marjorie Murphy, *Blackboard Unions: The AFT and the NEA, 1900–1980* (Ithaca, N.Y.: Cornell University Press, 1990); and Bella V. Dodd, *School of Darkness* (1954; rpt. New York: Devin-Adair Company, 1963). Communists of the early depression were overwhelmingly men (fewer than 10 percent were women in 1930); women began to join the Party in large numbers during the Popular Front years of the late 1930s, and by 1943 women made up more than half of the Young Communist League and almost half of the Communist Party. Isserman, *Which Side Were You On?* p. 148; see also Klehr, *The Heyday of American Communism* p. 163. On women in the metalworking trades, see Ruth Milkman, *Gender at Work: The Dynamics of Job Segregation by Sex during World War II* (Urbana: University of Illinois Press, 1987); Nancy F. Gabin, *Feminism in the Labor Movement: Women and the United Auto Workers, 1935–1975* (Ithaca, N.Y.: Cornell University Press, 1990). Amy Swerdlow, "The Congress of American Women: Left-Feminist Politics in the Cold War," in Linda K. Kerber, Alice Kessler-Harris, and Kathryn Kish Sklar, *U.S. History as Women's History: New Feminist Essays* (Chapel Hill: University of North Carolina Press, 1995).

43. Paula Rabinowitz, *Labor and Desire: Women's Revolutionary Fiction in Depression America* (Chapel Hill: University of North Carolina Press, 1991), p. 8; Elizabeth Faue, *Community of Suffering and Struggle: Women, Men, and the Labor Movement in Minneapolis, 1915–1945* (Chapel Hill: University of North Carolina Press, 1991), p. 20; Wendy Kozol, "Madonnas of the Fields: Photography, Gender and 1930s Farm Relief," *Genders* 2, Summer 1988, p. 15.

44. Faue, *Community of Suffering and Struggle*, pp. 71, 83. I am particularly indebted to Rachel Rubin's discussion of left-wing modernism and masculinity: Rubin, "Reading, Writing and the Rackets: Jewish Gangsters in Interwar Russian and American Narrative, Ph.D. diss., Yale University, 1995. See also Rabinowitz, *Labor and Desire*; Barbara Melosh, *Engendering Culture: Manhood and Womanhood in New Deal Public Art and Theater* (Washington, D.C.: Smithsonian Institution Press, 1991); and Kalaidjian, *American Culture between the Wars*. On the masculinism of modernism, see Sandra M. Gilbert and Susan Gubar, *No Man's Land: The Place of the Woman Writer in the Twentieth Century. Volume 1: The War of the Words* (New Haven, Conn.: Yale University Press, 1988); and Andreas Huyssen, "Mass Culture as Woman," in his *After the Great Divide*. Several critics, particularly Kalaidjian, seem to see this as distinctive to the Communist left; see, however, Mary McCarthy's memoir of the masculinism and heterosexism of the anti-Stalinist "second" *Partisan Review*. McCarthy, *Intellectual Memoirs: New York, 1936–1938* (San Diego, Calif.: Harcourt, Brace and Company, 1993), p. 80.

45. Faue, *Community of Suffering and Struggle*, p. 83. Rabinowitz, *Labor and Desire*, pp. 55, 137, 136; note particularly pp. 55–8 and 97–136 for the overall argument.

46. Discussions of Lange's photo include Kozol, "Madonnas of the Fields"; Lawrence Levine, "The Historian and Icon," and Alan Trachtenberg, "From Image to Story: Reading the File," both in Fleischhauer and Brannan, eds, *Documenting America*; and James Curtis, *Mind's Eye, Mind's Truth: FSA Photography Reconsidered* (Philadelphia: Temple University Press, 1989), pp. 45–67. Kozol suggests that "'Madonnas of the Fields' were of critical importance in the RA/FSA's narrative of poverty and need, for they constructed and reasserted dominant societal views on women and the family," p. 13.

47. Robert H. Zieger, *The CIO, 1935–1955* (Chapel Hill: University of North Carolina Press, 1995), p. 86. Ann Schofield, "Introduction," to Rose Pesotta, *Bread upon the Waters* (1944; rpt. Ithaca, N.Y.: ILR Press, 1987), p. xi.

48. Steven Fraser, *Labor Will Rule: Sidney Hillman and the Rise of American Labor* (New York: Free Press, 1991), p. 224; Pesotta, *Bread upon the Waters*, p. 395; Faue, *Community of Suffering and Struggle*, pp. 95–7.

49. Lois W. Banner, *American Beauty* (New York: Alfred Knopf, 1983), pp. 16, 271–91. Fannia Cohn, "Can We Organize the Flapper?" *Labor Age*, December 1927. For a superb discussion of the generation of 1909, see Annelise Orleck, *Common Sense and a Little Fire: Women and Working-Class Politics in the United States, 1900–1965* (Chapel Hill: University of North Carolina Press, 1995): on "industrial feminism," see pp. 6, 54, 173.

50. Pesotta, *Bread upon the Waters*, pp. 40, 333–4, 359–60.

51. Dorothy Sue Cobble, *Dishing It Out: Waitresses and their Unions in the Twentieth Century* (Urbana: University of Illinois Press, 1991), pp. 127–8; Vicki L. Ruiz, *Cannery Women, Cannery Lives: Mexican Women, Unionization, and the California Food Processing Industry, 1930–1950* (Albuquerque: University of New Mexico Press, 1987), p. 34. *Friday*: Law in 22 March 1940; Crane in 3 January 1941; Dunham in 19 April 1940, p. 7; Hayworth in 31 May 1940, p. 19; Comingore and Horne in 13 June 1941, pp. 38–9.

52. On Olsen, see Constance Coiner, *Better Red: The Writing and Resistance of Tillie Olsen and Meridel Le Sueur* (New York: Oxford University Press, 1995); and Kay Hoyle Nelson and Nancy Huse, eds, *The Critical Response to Tillie Olsen* (Westport, Conn.: Greenwood Press, 1994). For the account of "worker correspondence" poetry, see Cary Nelson, *Repression and Recovery: Modern American Poetry and the Politics of Cultural Memory, 1910–1945* (Madison: University of Wisconsin Press, 1989), pp. 104–6. On *Working Woman*, see Rabinowitz, *Labour and Desire*, pp. 24–9; Barbara Foley, *Radical Representations: Politics and Form in U.S. Proletarian Fiction, 1929–1941* (Durham: Duke University Press, 1993), pp. 228–31, 389; Laura Hapke, *Daughters of the Great Depression: Women, Work, and Fiction in the American 1930s* (Athens: University of Georgia Press, 1995), pp. 71–9, 109–16; and Sherna Berger Gluck, "Socialist Feminism between the Two World Wars: Insights from Oral History," in Lois Scharf and Joan M. Jensen, *Decades of Discontent: The Women's Movement, 1920–1940* (Boston: Northeastern University Press, 1987).

53. Tillie Olsen, "I Want You Women up North to Know," *The Partisan*, March 1934, reprinted in Selma Burkom and Margaret Williams, "De-Riddling Tillie Olsen's Writings," in Nelson and Huse, *Critical Response to Tillie Olsen*, pp. 35–7.

54. Olsen, *Yonnondio*, pp. 109, 107, 51–2.

55. Hope Hale Davis, *Great Day Coming: A Memoir of the 1930s* (South Royalton, Vt.: Steerforth Press, 1994), p. 1.

56. Hale's speech is reprinted in Donald Ogden Stewart, ed., *Fighting Words* (New York: Harcourt, Brace and Company, 1940), pp. 43–7. *True Story* was far and away the magazine most read by young working-class women: see Hazel Grant Ormsbee, *The Young Employed Girl* (New York: Woman's Press, 1927), p. 80; and William Frank Rasche, *The Reading Interests of Young Workers* (Chicago: University of Chicago Libraries, 1937).

57. Davis, *Great Day Coming*, pp. 326–7, 333.

58. Ruth McKenney, *Love Story* (New York: Harcourt, Brace and Company, 1950), p. 118.

59. McKenney, *Love Story*, pp. 66, 121–2, 10.

60. Christina Stead, *I'm Dying Laughing* (New York: Henry Holt, 1986), pp. 43, 118–19. McKenney quoted in Hapke, *Daughters of the Great Depression*, p. 126.

61. Vera Caspary, *The Secrets of Grown-Ups* (New York: McGraw-Hill, 1979), p. 192

62. Caspary, *The Secrets of Grown-Ups*, pp. 170–71. Vera Caspary, *Laura* (Garden City, N.J.: Sun Dial Press, 1944), p. 41.

63. Caspary, *The Secrets of Grown-Ups*, p. 180.

64. Inman's *In Woman's Defense* ran in *People's World* from 19 October 1939 to 20 March 1940: see Gluck, "Socialist Feminism Between the Two World Wars," pp. 291–5. See *Direction* 3.2, February 1940, inside back cover, for the promotion of *Restless Wave*. The prospectus for *PM* is in Roy Hoopes, *Ralph Ingersoll: A Biography* (New York: Atheneum, 1985), p. 407.

65. Most of the biographical information is from Haru Matsui, *Restless Wave* (New York: Modern Age, 1940) and from Karl G. Yoneda, *Ganbatte: Sixty-Year Struggle of a Kibei Worker* (Los Angeles: Asian American Studies Center, UCLA, 1983), pp. 23, 58, 63, 102, 155. See also Janice and Stephen MacKinnon, *Agnes Smedley* (Berkeley: University of California Press, 1988), pp. 295, 337, 339, 341.

66. Matsui, *Restless Wave*, pp. 4, 5, 115.

67. Matsui, *Restless Wave*, pp. 115, 230.

68. See Bettina Berch, *Radical by Design: The Life and Style of Elizabeth Hawes* (New York: E.P.

Dutton, 1988); David Caute, *Joseph Losey: A Revenge on Life* (London: Faber and Faber, 1994); Michael Ciment, *Conversations with Losey* (London: Methuen, 1985); Elizabeth Hawes, *Fashion Is Spinach* (New York: Random House, 1938), pp. 267–73, 291–4.

69. Hoopes, *Ralph Ingersoll,* p. 408; Elizabeth Hawes, *Why Is a Dress?* (New York: Viking, 1942), pp. 26, 73. On the child-care committee, see Berch, *Radical by Design,* pp. 95–6; Elizabeth Hawes, *Why Women Cry, or Wenches with Wrenches* (Cornwall: Reynal & Hitchcock, 1943), pp. xvii, 55, 189–92; and Dodd, *School of Darkness,* pp. 135–7.

70. Hawes, *Why Women Cry,* p. 57.

71. Hawes, *Why Women Cry,* pp. xiv–xv, 42.

72. Hawes, *Why Women Cry,* p. 162. See Dolores Hayden, *The Grand Domestic Revolution: A History of Feminist Designs for American Homes, Neighborhoods, and Cities* (Cambridge, Mass.: MIT Press, 1981), for an account of this tradition in the early years of the twentieth century; Paul Buhle, *Marxism in the United States: Remapping the History of the American Left* (London: Verso, 1991), also writes of this aspect of the American left, but sees it as largely absent from the Popular Front.

73. Elizabeth Hawes, *Hurry Up Please Its Time* (New York: Reynal & Hitchcock, 1946), p. 26. The epic CIO narratives include Ruth McKenney, *Industrial Valley* (1939; rpt. Ithaca, N.Y.: ILR Press, 1992); Edward Levinson, *Labor on the March* (1938; rpt. New York: University Books, 1956); Mary Heaton Vorse, *Labor's New Millions* (New York: Modern Age Books, 1938).

74. Hawes, *Hurry Up Please Its Time,* pp. 86–7, 215; Hawes, *Why Women Cry,* p. 151.

75. Hawes, *Why Women Cry,* p. 41; Elizabeth Hawes, *Anything but Love* (New York: Rinehart, 1948), pp. 7–8.

76. Pesotta, *Bread upon the Waters,* pp. 352–6.

77. On the production of *Mildred Pierce,* see Albert J. LaValley, "Introduction: A Troublesome Property to Script," in Ranald MacDougall, *Mildred Pierce* (Madison: University of Wisconsin Press, 1980). Billie Holiday, *Lady Sings the Blues* (1956; rpt. New York: Avon, 1976), pp. 88–91. Tillie Olsen, *Tell Me a Riddle* (New York: Dell, 1976), p. 21.

78. Susman, *Culture as History,* p. 192.

79. Susman, *Culture as History,* pp. 192, 81.

80. The phrase "nameless FrankLloydWrights of the proletariat" is from Olsen, *Yonnondio,* p. 48; Olsen's author's note in *Partisan Review* is quoted in Coiner, *Better Red,* p. 172.

81. Ciment, *Conversations with Losey,* p. 70.

82. Artie Shaw, *The Trouble with Cinderella: An Outline of Identity* (1952; rpt. New York: Da Capo, 1979), p. 37.

83. C.L.R. James, *American Civilization* (Cambridge: Blackwell, 1993), pp. 142, 144. Eric Hobsbawm, *The Jazz Scene* (New York: Pantheon, 1993), pp. 170, 172.

84. Paul Buhle, "The Hollywood Left: Aesthetics and Politics," *New Left Review* 212, July–August 1995, p. 112. Charles Maland, *Chaplin and American Culture: The Evolution of a Star Image* (Princeton, N.J.: Princeton University Press, 1989), pp. 234, 197.

85. On the notion of a "star image," see Richard Dyer, *Stars* (London: British Film Institute, 1979); Maland, *Chaplin and American Culture;* and Danae Clark, *Negotiating Hollywood: The Cultural Politics of Actors' Labor* (Minneapolis: University of Minnesota Press, 1995). On Garfield, see Robert Sklar, *City Boys: Cagney, Bogart, Garfield* (Princeton, N.J.: Princeton University Press, 1992); on Lee, see Glenda E. Gill, "Canada Lee: Black Actor in Non-Traditional Roles," *Journal of Popular Culture* 25.3, Winter 1991, pp. 79–89.

86. Barbara Leaming, *If This Was Happiness: A Biography of Rita Hayworth* (New York: Ballantine, 1989), p. 105. See Lary May, "Movie Star Politics: The Screen Actors' Guild, Cultural Conversion, and the Hollywood Red Scare," in Lary May, ed., *Recasting America: Culture and Politics in the Age of the Cold War* (Chicago: University of Chicago Press, 1989); and David W. Stowe, *Swing Changes: Big Band Jazz in New Deal America* (Cambridge, Mass.: Harvard University Press, 1994), pp. 50–93. Both New York Yankee third-baseman Red Rolfe and Chicago Cub first-baseman Ripper Collins wrote columns for the *Daily Worker.* On the sports stars and the Popular Front, see Gerald Horne, *Black Liberation/Red Scare: Ben Davis and the Communist Party* (Newark: University of Delaware Press, 1994), pp. 61–3, 154–5; and Hutchinson, *Blacks and Reds,* pp. 217 n. 9. Frances Farmer, *Will There Really Be a Morning?* (New York: Dell, 1972). In some cases, left-wing agents built alliances between stars and the left: this was certainly the case with jazz impressario John Hammond, who worked with Count Basie, Benny

Goodman, and Billie Holiday, and seems true of George Evans, a Hollywood agent who encouraged Frank Sinatra's Popular Front affiliations. See John Hammond, *John Hammond on Record: An Autobiography* (New York: Summit Books, 1977); and Kitty Kelley, *His Way: The Unauthorized Biography of Frank Sinatra* (New York: Bantam, 1986), p. 106. See also Jon Wiener, "When Old Blue Eyes Was Red," in his *Professors, Politics and Pop* (London: Verso, 1991).

87. Axel Madsen, *Stanwyck: A Biography* (New York: Harper, 1994), p. 278. Lela Rogers paraphrased in Otto Friedrich, *City of Nets: A Portrait of Hollywood in the 1940s* (New York: Harper & Row, 1986), p. 303.

88. Paul Buhle has offered the most persuasive typology of Popular Front film genres in his "The Hollywood Left", pp. 101–19. For *film gris*, see Thom Andersen, "Red Hollywood," in Suzanne Ferguson and Barbara Groseclose, eds, *Literature and the Visual Arts in Contemporary Society* (Columbus: Ohio State University Press, 1985), pp. 141–96. See also Brian Neve, *Film and Politics in America: A Social Tradition* (London: Routledge, 1992); Bernard Dick, *Radical Innocence: A Critical Study of the Hollywood Ten* (Lexington: University of Kentucky Press, 1989); and George Lipsitz, *A Rainbow at Midnight: Labor and Culture in the 1940s* (Urbana: University of Illinois Press, 1994), pp. 279–302. Susan Smulyan, *Selling Radio: The Commercialization of American Broadcasting, 1920–1934* (Washington, D.C.: Smithsonian Institution Press, 1994) pp. 114–16; Gertrude Berg, *Molly and Me* (New York: McGraw-Hill, 1961). On the narrative form of the domestic drama, I am indebted to Judith Smith's paper on Lorraine Hansberry at the 1995 American Studies Association convention. See also George Lipsitz, *Time Passages: Collective Memory and American Popular Culture* (Minneapolis: University of Minnesota Press, 1990), for the continuation of these working-class narratives in early television.

89. The Ford narrative is constructed from *Friday*: 24 January 1941; 27 September 1940 was a special issue on anti-Semitism; 14 February 1941; 7 March 1941; 28 February 1941; 9 May 1941; September 1941, pp. 22–3.

90. *Friday*: 10 May 1940; 30 May 1941; 18 April 1941; 22 March 1940; 29 March 1940; 12 April 1940.

91. *Friday*: 11 April 1941; 25 July 1941; 22 March 1940; 26 April 1940; 14 June 1940; 24 May 1940; 26 April 1940; 17 January 1941; 19 April 1940; 22 March 1940; 14 March 1941.

92. *Friday*: 4 April 1941, pp. 24–5.

93. Benjamin Stolberg, "Muddled Millions: Capitalist Angels of Left-Wing Propaganda," *Saturday Evening Post* 213.33, 15 February 1941, p. 92. See the similar attack in Eugene Lyons, *The Red Decade: The Stalinist Penetration of America* (Indianapolis, Ind.: Bobbs-Merrill, 1941), p. 380.

Notes to 4

1. Edmund Wilson, *The Shores of Light: A Literary Chronicle of the 1920s and 1930s* (1952; rpt. Boston: Northeastern University Press, 1985), p. 496.

2. Sinclair Lewis, "Manhattan at Last," *Saturday Review*, December 1925, reprinted in Barry Maine, ed., *Dos Passos: The Critical Heritage* (London: Routledge, 1988), pp. 71, 68. Matthew Josephson, *Infidel in the Temple: A Memoir of the Nineteen-Thirties* (New York: Alfred A. Knopf, 1967), pp. 66, 68.

3. John Dos Passos, *The Major Nonfictional Prose*, Donald Pizer, ed. (Detroit, Mich.: Wayne State University Press, 1988), p. 134.

4. John Dos Passos, *The Best Times: An Informal Memoir* (New York: New American Library, 1966), p. 205. John Dos Passos, "Sacco and Vanzetti," *New Masses* 3, November 1927, p. 25, reprinted in Dos Passos, *Major Nonfictional Prose*, p. 99.

5. The *Time* cover was in part the work of Robert Cantwell, a young radical novelist working in the Luce empire: Townsend Ludington, *John Dos Passos: A Twentieth Century Odyssey* (New York: E.P. Dutton, 1980), p. 352. Jean-Paul Sartre, "John Dos Passos and *1919*," in his *Literary and Philosophical Essays* (New York: Collier, 1962), p. 103.

6. Dos Passos's break with the Communist Party and with the *New Masses* occurred during the March 1934 controversy over the Communists' role in disrupting a Socialist Party memorial meeting for the Austrian socialists at Madison Square Garden. He joined an open letter condemning the Communists and was denounced by the editors of the *New Masses*. Nevertheless,

Dos Passos remained active and visible on the left until his 1937 trip to Spain, where his search for a friend, José Robles, who had been executed by the Communists, led to a break with his non-Communist left associates. Nevertheless, though critics usually read *The Big Money* as critical of the left, its popularity among Popular Front audiences indicates that it was not generally seen as opposed to the left. On the Second American Writers' Congress, see Virginia Spencer Carr, *Dos Passos: A Life* (Garden City, N.J.: Doubleday, 1984), p. 379.

7. Though Dos Passos affiliated himself with the radical right and its anti-Communism, he was never a true conservative, in the sense of having a deep commitment to tradition, family, and religion: he remained a militant atheist. If the world Dos Passos lived through had not been so dramatically divided between Communism and anti-Communism, his politics might not have been seen to change at all (something he himself claimed). He began as a left-leaning anarchist and ended as a right-leaning libertarian.

8. Unless otherwise noted, references to *U.S.A.* are to the single-volume Modern Library edition: John Dos Passos, *U.S.A.* (New York: Modern Library, n.d. [1938]). However, since each novel is paginated separately, I will cite the title and page of the novel: Dos Possos, *The 42nd Parallel*, p. 385.

9. Dos Passos, *The Big Money*, p. 450. Dos Passos, *Major Nonfictional Prose*, p. 243.

10. Dos Passos, *The Big Money*, pp. 432–3, 431, 436. Dos Passos, *Major Nonfictional Prose*, p. 147.

11. Dos Passos, *The Big Money*, p. 437.

12. Dos Passos, *Major Nonfictional Prose*, p. 115. Much of critical discussion of *U.S.A.* has revolved around the place of history in the trilogy. In 1960, he renamed his works "contemporary chronicles," suggesting that "in this sort of novel the story is really the skeleton on which some slice of history the novelist has seen enacted before his own eyes is brought to life" (pp. 238–9). Barbara Foley, one of the best contemporary critics of Dos Passos, has persuasively demonstrated the ways history provides the formal structure of the novels, and suggests that his practice is less that of the traditional historical novel than a precursor of the documentary non-fiction of Norman Mailer and the postmodern historical fiction of E.L. Doctorow. See Barbara Foley, "From *U.S.A.* to *Ragtime*: Notes on the Forms of Historical Consciousness in Modern Fiction," *American Literature* 50, March 1978, pp. 85–105; "History, Fiction, and Satirical Form: The Example of Dos Passos' *1919*," *Genre* 12, Fall 1979, pp. 357–378; and "The Treatment of Time in *The Big Money*: An Examination of Ideology and Literary Form," *Modern Fiction Studies* 26, Autumn 1980, pp. 447–67.

13. Dos Passos, *The 42nd Parallel*, pp. 25, 108–9.

14. Dos Passos, *Nineteen-Nineteen*, p. 241; Dos Passos, *The Big Money*, p. 19.

15. John Dos Passos, "A Great American," *New Masses* 3, December 1927, p. 26, reprinted in Dos Passos, *Major Nonfictional Prose*, pp. 104–5. Dos Passos, *Nineteen-Nineteen*, pp. 178–84.

16. T.K. Whipple, "Dos Passos and the U.S.A.," in Andrew Hook, ed., *Dos Passos: A Collection of Critical Essays* (Englewood Cliffs, N.J.: Prentice-Hall, 1974), pp. 89, 92. The debate over Dos Passos's "Marxism" began with Matthew Josephson's review of *Nineteen-Nineteen* as "a Marxist epic" and the counterargument by Horace Gregory, Alfred Kazin, and Edmund Wilson that *U.S.A.* was conceived under the influence of Veblen. See Josephson, "A Marxist Epic," *Saturday Review*, March 1932, and Gregory, "Dos Passos Completes His Modern Trilogy," *New York Herald Tribune Books*, August 1936, both reprinted in Maine, ed., *Dos Passos*, pp. 106–8, 130–34. By 1938, Dos Passos himself was writing to a graduate student that his work was "more likely to stem from Whitman (and perhaps Veblen) than from Marx . . . The Marxist critics are just finding out, with considerable chagrin, that my stuff isn't Marxist. I should think that anybody with half an eye would have noticed that in the first place." Townsend Ludington, ed, *The Fourteenth Chronicle: Letters and Diaries of John Dos Passos* (Boston: Gambit, 1973), p. 516. The contemporary consensus is that Veblen rather than Marx is the key to Dos Passos's thinking: see Fred Pfeil, "Montage Dynasty: A Market Study in American Historical Fiction," in his *Another Tale to Tell: Politics and Narrative in Postmodern Culture* (London: Verso, 1990); however, two important attempts to re-Marx Dos Passos are Foley's provocative parallel between *Nineteen-Nineteen* and the *Eighteenth Brumaire* in her "History, Fiction, and Satirical Form," and Stanley Corkin's attempt to see parallels between Dos Passos and the Frankfurt School's Hegelian Marxism: Corkin, "John Dos Passos and the American Left: Recovering the Dialectic of History," *Criticism* 34.4, Fall 1992, pp. 591–611.

17. Dos Passos, *Major Nonfictional Prose*, pp. 82, 126. Hacker quoted in Paul M. Buhle, *A Dreamer's Paradise Lost: Louis C. Fraina/Lewis Corey (1892–1953) and the Decline of Radicalism in the United States* (New Jersey: Humanities Press, 1995), p. 118. By the early 1940s, Corey's sense of impending doom had been replaced by a somewhat stunned acknowledgement of the New Deal's resurrection of capitalism in such works as Louis Hacker's own *The Triumph of American Capitalism: The Development of Forces in American History to the End of the Nineteenth Century* (New York: Simon and Schuster, 1940), and Thomas C. Cochran and William Miller's *The Age of Enterprise: A Social History of Industrial America* (New York: Macmillan Company, 1942). Whereas Corey had attacked the "state capitalism" of the NRA in 1934, the later books, which include Corey's own *The Unfinished Task: Economic Reconstruction for Democracy* (New York: Viking, 1942), had more sanguine views of the emerging New Deal economic order. Hacker had been a leading Marxist economic historian, the chair of the American Marxist Association, and sections of his book had been published in the short-lived intellectual journal, *Marxist Quarterly*. By 1940, however, he was concluding that "capitalism was a success" and that he was "not really fearful of American state capitalism" (pp. 434–5); and when the book was reprinted in 1947, he claimed that it was "an effort at a reply to the Marxian analysis." (See the preface to the 1947 Columbia University Press edition.) This was not entirely true: despite the fact that Hacker's conclusions are those of a disillusioned anti-Stalinist, his account of the rise of American capitalism bears the imprint of the amalgam of Beard, Veblen and Marx that dominated Popular Front history-writing. Cochran and Miller's *The Age of Enterprise*, which charts the course of American history "from a business point of view," also bears this imprint. Americans "have been primarily a business people," they argue. "To get attention in industrial America, a school, a mechanical invention, a cure, or a game had to be presented, as Veblen said, as a 'business proposition'" (p. 2). Cochran was, along with his friend Kenneth Burke, an editor of the Popular Front magazine *Direction*: see Burke's review of *The Age of Enterprise* in *Direction* 6.1, Spring 1943, p. 3.

18. Josephson, *Infidel in the Temple*, p. 183. See Matthew Josephson, *The Robber Barons: The Great American Capitalists, 1861–1901* (1934; rpt. New York: Harcourt, Brace and World, 1962); and David E. Shi, *Matthew Josephson: Bourgeois Bohemian* (New Haven, Conn.: Yale University Press, 1981), pp. 155–66, 253–9.

19. Dos Passos, *Major Nonfictional Prose*, p. 123; Carr, *Dos Passos*, p. 335. A number of Dos Passos's sources have been identified: see Donald Pizer, *Dos Passos's U.S.A.: A Critical Study* (Charlottesville: University Press of Virginia, 1988), p. 196, n. 22. Just as Ferdinand Lundberg sued Welles for copyright infringement, at least one of Dos Passos's sources felt he had been plagiarized.

20. Dos Passos, *The Big Money*, p. 526; Dos Passos, *The 42nd Parallel*, pp. 328, 27; Dos Passos, *The Big Money*, p. 433. These simple divisions obscure the fact that several figures themselves represent the divisions: Ford is both robber baron and mechanic-inventor; Bryan shares elements of Debs and of Wilson; and even Hearst is both robber baron and populist politician. I will return to the other two sets of portraits: the writers—John Reed, Randolph Bourne, Paxton Hibben, and Thorstein Veblen; and the artists—Isadora Duncan and Rudolph Valentino.

21. Whipple, "Dos Passos and the U.S.A.," p. 89. Georg Lukács, *The Historical Novel* (1937; rpt. London: Merlin Press, 1962).

22. Foley, "The Treatment of Time in *The Big Money*," pp. 456–8. Foley, "From *U.S.A.* to *Ragtime*," pp. 92–3.

23. See Pizer, *Dos Passos's U.S.A.*, for a discussion of Dos Passos's sources; the source for Mary French is suggested by Dee Garrison, *Mary Heaton Vorse: The Life of an American Insurgent* (Philadelphia: Temple University Press, 1989), p. 159.

24. Maine, ed., *Dos Passos*, pp. 91–2. Edmund Wilson, review, *New Republic*, March 1930, reprinted in Maine, ed., *Dos Passos*, pp. 84–7. Dos Passos, *The Big Money*, pp. 217, 268.

25. Dos Passos, *The Big Money*, pp. 462, 525.

26. Dos Passos, *The Big Money*, p. 561.

27. The Wilson letter (July 1939) is reprinted in Maine, ed., *Dos Passos*, p. 214. He repeats the complaint in a 1949 letter, also reprinted in Maine, ed., *Dos Passos*, p. 242. Sartre, "John Dos Passos and *1919*," p. 100. Dos Passos, *The Big Money*, pp. 164, 209. Dos Passos "invented only one thing, an art of story-telling," Sartre wrote (p. 95), and Sartre's account of that art

remains the starting point for the most interesting formal discussions of *U.S.A.*'s narrative discourse. Pizer, *Dos Passos's U.S.A.*, offers a useful synthesis of such work. See Brian McHale, "Talking U.S.A.: Interpreting Free Indirect Discourse in Dos Passos's *U.S.A.* Trilogy," *Degrés* 16, 1978, pp. cl–c7; 17, 1979, pp. d1–d20, which argues persuasively that American writers who have exploited colloquial speech have been preoccupied by the sense that "the technical language of those most intimately involved with a particular aspect of reality must model that reality more faithfully than neutral language" (p. c5), and goes on to note that Dos Passos's discourse emphasizes this "technical register"—the language shared by characters of common class or situation- rather than "idiolect"—the distinctive style of a particular character. His conclusion that the thematic coherence of the formal devices is found in Dos Passos's "deterministic vision of human existence" is, however, a disappointing short-circuit of the formal analysis.

28. Dos Passos, *Major Nonfictional Prose*, pp. 81, 117. Wilson in Maine, ed., *Dos Passos*, p. 213. Dos Passos, *The Big Money*, p. 100.

29. Dos Passos, *Major Nonfictional Prose*, p. 81. Dos Passos, *The Big Money*, p. 486.

30. Dos Passos, *Major Nonfictional Prose*, pp. 123–4.

31. John Dos Passos, "Whom Can We Appeal To?", *New Masses* 6, August 1930, p. 8, reprinted in *Major Nonfictional Prose*, pp. 132–3. As I noted earlier, Dos Passos's concept of the writer as technician bears striking resemblances to Kenneth Burke's account of the "complete propagandist," Antonio Gramsci's theory of intellectuals, and Walter Benjamin's discussion of the "author as producer." All of these were attempts to theorize a new cultural politics, which takes shape in the Popular Front and breaks from the politics of proletarian culture. Dos Passos's earliest formulation of the "word-slinging organism" occurred in a 1926 response to his friend Mike Gold's call for a proletarian literature.

32. Dos Passos, *Nineteen-Nineteen*, p. 211. Malcolm Cowley, *Exile's Return: A Literary Odyssey of the 1920s* (1934; rpt. New York: Penguin, 1976), pp. 207, 217. James Rorty, *Our Master's Voice: Advertising* (New York: John Day, 1934).

33. Dos Passos, *The 42nd Parallel*, pp. 205–6, 246, 249, 255.

34. Dos Passos, *The Big Money*, p. 131. Dos Passos, *Major Nonfictional Prose*, p. 150, 81.

35. Dos Passos, *The Big Money*, p. 558.

36. Dos Passos, *The Big Money*, p. 556. Dos Passos's map and character list is reproduced in Pizer, *Dos Passos's U.S.A.*

37. Dos Passos, *The Big Money*, pp. 126, 125.

38. Alfred Kazin, *On Native Grounds: An Interpretation of Modern American Prose Literature* (New York: Reynal & Hitchcock, 1942), p. 352.

39. Dos Passos, *Major Nonfictional Prose*, p. 245. Dos Passos, *The Big Money*, p.40, 144.

40. The trilogy's abortions include those of Annabelle (*The 42nd Parallel*, p. 198); Emiscah (*The 42nd Parallel*, pp. 387–8); and Mary French (*The Big Money* pp. 148 and 447). Anne Elizabeth Trent is pregnant when she dies in a plane crash. Though Mac, J. Ward Moorehouse, and Charley Anderson do father children, the only major woman character who has a child that lives is Eveline.

41. Dos Passos, *The Big Money*, pp. 131, 439.

42. Dos Passos, *The 42nd Parallel*, p. 212. On the Eleanor Association, see Lisa M. Fine, *The Souls of the Skyscraper: Female Clerical Workers in Chicago, 1870–1930* (Philadelphia: Temple University Press, 1990), pp. 151–65; she also discusses Dos Passos's Janey Williams, pp. 146–7. I am indebted to Jeanne Lawrence for drawing my attention to the Eleanor Association.

43. Dos Passos, *The Big Money*, p. 555.

44. Ludington, ed., *The Fourteenth Chronicle*, p. 408.

45. Carr, *Dos Passos*, p. 300. Dos Passos, *Major Nonfictional Prose*, p. 150.

46. Dos Passos, *The 42nd Parallel*, p. 79.

47. Pizer, *Dos Passos's U.S.A.*, p. 198 n. 15; I owe the account of the excision of the Ike Hall narrative to Pizer. John Dos Passos, "Migratory Worker," *Partisan Review* 4.2, January 1938, p. 16–20. John Dos Passos, "Tin Can Tourist," *Direction* 1.1, December 1937, pp. 10–12.

48. Dos Passos, *The Big Money*, p. 439.

49. Dos Passos, *The 42nd Parallel*, pp. 104, 102. Dos Passos, *Nineteen-Nineteen*, p. 427. Dos Passos, "Migratory Worker," pp. 16, 20.

50. The first edition of *The 42nd Parallel* opened with an epigraph from *American Climatology*,

which was cut in the three-volume edition of *U.S.A.* Too often it is assumed that the First World War is the imaginative center of *Nineteen-Nineteen*; however, in his introduction to the 1932 republication of *Three Soldiers*, Dos Passos summed up the meaning of 1919: "The memory of the spring of 1919 has not faded enough. Any spring is a time of overturn, but then Lenin was alive, the Seattle general strike had seemed the beginning of the flood instead of the beginning of the ebb, Americans in Paris were groggy with theatre and painting and music; Picasso was to rebuild the eye, Stravinski was cramming the Russian steppes into our ears, currents of energy seemed breaking out everywhere as young guys climbed out of their uniforms, imperial America was all shiny with the new idea of Ritz, in every direction the countries of the world stretched out starving and angry, ready for anything turbulent and new, whenever you went to the movies you saw Charlie Chaplin." Dos Passos, *Major Nonfictional Prose*, p. 146.

51. Dos Passos, *The 42nd Parallel*, pp. 118–19. Dos Passos, *The Big Money*, p. 354.

52. Carr, *Dos Passos*, p. 331. Dos Passos, *The Big Money*, pp. 165, 426, 332, 333, 553.

53. Dos Passos, *The Big Money*, p. 476. Lawson quoted in Ludington, *John Dos Passos: A Twentieth Century Odyssey*, p. 379. Dos Passos's hostility to film stars can be seen in the Valentino portrait in *U.S.A.* and in the James Dean portrait in *Mid-Century*.

54. Dos Passos, *The 42nd Parallel*, pp. 87, 396–8. Dos Passos, *Nineteen-Nineteen*, pp. 130–32, 427–31.

55. Dos Passos, *The Big Money*, pp. 435, 437, 461, 463.

56. Pfeil, "Montage Dynasty," p. 171.

57. Dos Passos, *The 42nd Parallel*, pp. 25, 81, 245, 302.

58. Dos Passos, *The Big Money*, p. 107.

59. Dos Passos, *The Big Money*, p. 524.

60. Dos Passos, *The 42nd Parallel*, pp. 307, 245.

61. Dos Passos, *The 42nd Parallel*, p. 13.

62. Dos Passos, *Nineteen-Nineteen*, pp. 256, 266, 367. Dos Passos, *The 42nd Parallel*, p. 406. Dos Passos, *Nineteen-Nineteen*, p. 171.

63. Dos Passos, *The 42nd Parallel*, p. 175. The closest thing to a political awakening one finds in the trilogy is when Anne Trent momentarily transcends her racism and impulsively defends a woman striker from the police.

64. Dos Passos, *The 42nd Parallel*, p.83. Ludington, ed., *The Fourteenth Chronicle*, p. 460. John R. Dos Passos, *The Anglo-Saxon Century and the Unification of the English-Speaking People* (New York: G.P. Putnam's Sons, 1903), pp. 192, vii. Ludington, ed., *The Fourteenth Chronicle*, pp. 447–8, 449, 451.

65. Dos Passos, *Nineteen-Nineteen*, p. 423. Moreover, Compton is the least developed of the major characters, the only one to have only a single narrative segment.

66. Dos Passos, *The Big Money*, p. 470.

67. Dos Passos, *The Big Money*, p. 515.

68. Dos Passos, *The Big Money*, p. 462. John Dos Passos, "The Making of a Writer," *New Masses* 4, March 1929, p. 23, reprinted in *Major Nonfictional Prose*, p. 116.

Notes to 5

1. Edmund Wilson, "The Literary Class War," May 1932, reprinted in his *The Shores of Light: A Literary Chronicle of the 1920s and 1930s* (1952; rpt. Boston: Northeastern University Press, 1985), pp. 534–9. "Books in Review," *Literary America* 4.2, Winter 1936, p. 106. See also Philip Rahv, "The Literary Class War," *New Masses*, August 1932, pp. 7–10.

2. I am greatly indebted to the recent resurgence of excellent scholarship on aspects of proletarian literature, including Alan M. Wald, *Writing from the Left: New Essays on Radical Culture and Politics* (London: Verso, 1994); Barbara Foley, *Radical Representations: Politics and Form in U.S. Proletarian Fiction, 1929–1941* (Durham, N.C.: Duke University Press, 1993); Paula Rabinowitz, *Labor and Desire: Women's Revolutionary Fiction in Depression America* (Chapel Hill: University of North Carolina Press, 1991); Walter Kalaidjian, *American Culture between the Wars: Revisionary Modernism and Postmodern Critique* (New York: Columbia University Press, 1993); James F. Murphy, *The Proletarian Moment: The Controversy over Leftism in Literature* (Urbana: University of Illinois Press, 1991); James D. Bloom, *Left Letters: The Culture Wars of Mike Gold*

and Joseph Freeman (New York: Columbia University Press, 1992); Cary Nelson, *Repression and Recovery: Modern American Poetry and the Politics of Cultural Memory, 1910–1945* (Madison: University of Wisconsin Press, 1989); Douglas Wixson, *Worker-Writer in America: Jack Conroy and the Tradition of Midwestern Literary Radicalism, 1898–1990* (Urbana: University of Illinois Press, 1994); Constance Coiner, *Better Red: The Writing and Resistance of Tillie Olsen and Meridel Le Sueur* (New York: Oxford University Press, 1995); and Paul Lauter, "American Proletarianism," in Emory Elliott, Cathy N. Davidson, Patrick O'Donnell, Valerie Smith, and Christopher P. Wilson, eds, *The Columbia History of the American Novel* (New York: Columbia University Press, 1991). I have two quarrels with this fine work: first, it often identifies too closely with the project of canon reconstruction, and thus fails to address the significance of proletarian literature in US cultural history generally. And second, with a few exceptions, it tends to accept a restrictive chronological definition of proletarian literature, ending in 1941 or 1942 and concentrating on the early years of the 1930s. Since literary movements and avant-garde aesthetics leave an imprint on a writer's career, the most powerful manifestations of a new aesthetic may not emerge until much later. I am also indebted to Marcus Klein, *Foreigners: The Making of American Literature* (Chicago: University of Chicago Press, 1981); to Thomas J. Ferraro, *Ethnic Passages: Literary Immigrants in Twentieth Century America* (Chicago: University of Chicago Press, 1993); and to Leslie Fiedler's classic readings of twentieth-century US literary history: *Waiting for the End: The Crisis in American Culture and a Portrait of Twentieth Century American Literature* (New York: Stein and Day, 1964) and *Love and Death in the American Novel* (1960; rpt. New York: Stein and Day, 1975). Fiedler's deep ambivalence about Popular Front culture made him one of the last polemicists (dismissing Dos Passos, proletarian literature, and Popular Front writing) and the first historian (recognizing the significance of the plebeian writers and their ghetto tales).

3. Even Terry Eagleton's fine "Proletarian Literature," in Francisco García Tortosa and Ramón López Ortega, eds, *English Literature and the Working Class* (Sevilla: Publicaciones Universidad Sevilla, 1980), pp. 5–10, begins from definition. Both Walter B. Rideout, *The Radical Novel in the United States, 1900–1954: Some Interrelations of Literature and Society* (New York: Hill and Wang, 1956), and Foley, *Radical Representations*, attempt to define proletarian literature as a genre or collection of subgenres and begin with the debates over the definition of proletarian literature. Foley ends up with a formal definition, seeing proletarian literature as several sub-genres sharing a didactic, propagandist form and an explicitly revolutionary perspective; consequently, she excludes such works as *Call It Sleep* (p. 324n) and *Lawd Today* (p. 203n) from the genre because their left-wing politics are not explicit.

4. Two novelists associated with the "proletarian" label wrote eloquent critiques of this sort of literary taxonomy: see Josephine Herbst's letter to David Madden, quoted in the introduction to his collection, *Proletarian Writers of the Thirties* (Carbondale: Southern Illinois University Press, 1968); and Benjamin Appel, "Labels," in David Madden, ed., *Tough Guy Writers of the Thirties* (Carbondale: Southern Illinois University Press, 1968).

5. I draw the notion of a formation from Raymond Williams's late essays, particularly "The Future of Cultural Studies" and "The Uses of Cultural Theory," in his *The Politics of Modernism: Against the New Conformists* (London: Verso, 1989).

6. Michael Gold, "A Proletarian Novel?" *New Republic*, 4 June 1930, p. 74. The phrase "mushroom mags" comes from Fred R. Miller, "The New Masses and Who Else," *The Blue Pencil* 2, February 1935, pp. 4–5, quoted in Daniel Aaron, *Writers on the Left: Episodes in American Literary Communism* (New York: Harcourt, Brace and World, Inc., 1961), p. 296. Philip Rahv's famous 1939 indictment of proletarian literature as "the literature of a party disguised as the literature of a class" is misleading. Though he was right to understand the proletarian movement as a literary formation, not as "the literature of a class," he overestimates the centrality and ubiquity of the Party. It was the literature of a movement, which included Party and non-Party "communists." As I noted above, many American radicals invented their own "communisms" in these years, both in dialogue and dissent with the Party's "communism." Most estimates suggest that only a quarter of the members of the John Reed Clubs were members of the Communist Party, and they were the part of the proletarian movement most closely connected to the Party. For the most part, the so-called "fellow travelers" *were* the radical movement, even in the early years of the depression. Philip Rahv,

"Proletarian Literature: A Political Autopsy," in his *Literature and the Sixth Sense* (Boston: Houghton Mifflin, 1970).

7. Quoted in Eric Homberger, *American Writers and Radical Politics, 1900–1939: Equivocal Commitments* (Basingstoke: Macmillan Press, 1986), p. 126. Mike Gold, "Go Left, Young Writers!," January 1929, reprinted in Michael Folsom, ed., *Mike Gold: A Literary Anthology* (New York: International Publishers, 1972), pp. 188–9. See also David Peck, "'The Tradition of American Revolutionary Literature': The Monthly *New Masses*, 1928–1933," *Science and Society* 42.4, Winter 1978–79, pp. 385–409. For treatments of Gold, see Bloom, *Left Letters*; and Rachel Lee Rubin, "Reading, Writing and the Rackets: Jewish Gangsters in Interwar Russian and American Narrative," Ph.D diss., Yale University, 1995.

8. Folsom, ed., *Mike Gold*, p. 14.

9. *True Story* quoted in Ann Fabian's excellent "Making a Commodity of Truth: Speculations on the Career of Bernarr MacFadden," *American Literary History* 5.1, Spring 1993, pp. 63, 59.

10. Quoted in Moses Rischin, *The Promised City: New York's Jews, 1870–1914* (New York: Harper and Row, 1970), p. 131. Folsom, ed., *Mike Gold*, p. 65.

11. John Dos Passos, *The Major Nonfictional Prose*, Donald Pizer, ed. (Detriot, Mich: Wayne State University Press, 1988), p. 117. Joseph North, ed., *New Masses: An Anthology of the Rebel Thirties* (New York: International Publishers, 1969), pp. 20–21. See also Wixson, *Worker-Writer in America*, pp. 146–7, for reactions to the *New Masses*.

12. On the JRC conventions, see Aaron, *Writers on the Left*, pp. 223–30, 280–82; and Homberger, *American Writers and Radical Politics*, pp. 119–140. The source of the numbers is Orrick Johns, "The John Reed Clubs Meet," *New Masses*, 30 October 1934, pp. 25–6.

13. Rabinowitz, *Labor and Desire*, p. 187 n.14. Coiner, *Better Red*, p. 148. Aaron quoted in Wixson, *Worker-Writer in America*, p. 287. Arthur C. Ferrari, "Proletarian Literature: A Case of Convergence of Political and Literary Radicalism," in Jerold Starr, ed., *Cultural Politics: Radical Movements in Modern History* (New York: Praeger, 1985), p. 180. See also Murphy, *The Proletarian Moment*, p. 57.

14. Matthew Josephson, *Infidel in the Temple: A Memoir of the Nineteen-Thirties* (New York: Alfred A. Knopf, 1967), p. 363. Freeman quoted in Aaron, *Writers on the Left*, pp. 228–9.

15. Malcolm Cowley, *The Dream of the Golden Mountains: Remembering the 1930s* (New York: Penguin Books, 1981), pp. 146, 136–7. Other accounts of the John Reed Clubs by outsiders include Albert Halper's brief tale of Diego Rivera's lecture to the New York Reed club; it is interesting for its depiction of the sectarian struggles between the Communist Party and the group around Jay Lovestone with whom Rivera was involved, but is hardly representative. Halper says it was the only meeting he ever attended. Halper, *Good-bye, Union Square: A Writer's Memoir of the Thirties* (Chicago: Quadrangle Books, 1970), pp. 93–7. Howard Fast recalls going to half a dozen meetings of the New York Reed club, but didn't connect with them: "they were," he says, "college people and college graduates." Howard Fast, *Being Red* (Boston: Houghton Mifflin, 1990), p. 54. Edward Dahlberg, *The Confessions of Edward Dahlberg* (New York: George Braziller, 1971), pp. 286–9.

16. Joseph North, *No Men Are Strangers* (1958; rpt. New York: International Publishers, 1976), p. 108. Jerre Mangione, *An Ethnic at Large: A Memoir of America in the Thirties and Forties* (New York: G. P. Putnam's Sons, 1978), p. 121–2. Le Sueur quoted in Bettina Drew, *Nelson Algren: A Life on the Wild Side* (New York: Putnam, 1989), p. 77. See also Dahlberg, *Confessions of Edward Dahlberg*, pp. 286–9; and Horace Gregory, *The House on Jefferson Street: A Cycle of Memories* (New York: Holt, Rinehart, and Winston, 1971), pp. 182–3. Like Mangione, Gregory says his attendance was infrequent, and he felt like an "odd man out." Nevertheless, like Mangione, he was one of the instructors in the Reed club writers school. Alan Wald notes the unreliability of Gregory's autobiography: Wald, *Writing from the Left*, p. 75.

17. For the details of the Reed club writers school, see Homberger, *American Writers and Radical Politics*, p. 130. Mangione recalls teaching a course on book reviewing, and quitting after two weeks, "embarrassed by the presumption such teaching implied": *An Ethnic at Large*, p. 122. For the Reed club artists, see Helen Harrison, "John Reed Club Artists and the New Deal: Radical Responses to Roosevelt's 'Peaceful Revolution'," *Prospects* 5, 1980, pp. 241–68; and Patricia Hills, *Social Concern and Urban Realism: American Painting of the 1930s* (Boston: Boston University Art Gallery, 1983), pp. 15–16.

18. William Alexander, *Film on the Left: American Documentary Film from 1931 to 1942*

(Princeton, N.J.: Princeton University Press, 1981), pp. 6, 11. Alan M. Wald, *The New York Intellectuals: The Rise and Decline of the Anti-Stalinist Left from the 1930s to the 1980s* (Chapel Hill: University of North Carolina Press, 1987), pp. 76–7. Arnold Rampersad, *The Life of Langston Hughes. Volume I: 1902–1941. I, Too, Sing America* (New York: Oxford University Press, 1986), p. 215. On the Rebel Arts Group, see their magazine *Arise*, February 1935.

19. On Rexroth and the SF club, see Linda Hamalian, *A Life of Kenneth Rexroth* (New York: Norton, 1991), pp. 67, 69. On the Carmel club, see Rampersad, *Langston Hughes, Volume I*, 278–84, 291–3; Ella Winter, *And Not to Yield: An Autobiography* (New York: Harcourt, Brace and World, 1963), pp. 180–215; and Orrick Johns, *Time of Our Lives: The Story of My Father and Myself* (New York: Stackpole Sons, 1937), pp. 302–34.

20. On Siqueiros and the Hollywood club, see Laurance P. Hurlburt, *The Mexican Muralists in the United States* (Albuquerque: University of New Mexico Press, 1989), pp. 205–6, 284 n. 36; Homberger, *American Writers and Radical Politics*, 131; Wixson, *Worker-Writer in America*, p. 395; and Rampersad, *Langston Hughes, Volume I*, p. 236. On the Japanese Proletarian Artists League, see Karl G. Yoneda, *Ganbatte: Sixty-Year Struggle of a Kibei Worker* (Los Angeles: UCLA Asian American Studies Center, 1983), pp. 44, 56–7.

21. On the Chicago club, see Homberger, *American Writers and Radical Politics*, p. 131; Michel Fabre, *The Unfinished Quest of Richard Wright* (New York: William Morrow and Company, 1973), pp. 94–117; Drew, *Nelson Algren*. Conroy's line about the Chicago post-office school is in Jack Conroy, "A Reminiscence," in David Ray and Robert Farnsworth, eds, *Richard Wright: Impressions and Perspectives* (Ann Arbor: University of Michigan Press, 1973), p. 32.

22. Richard Wright, *American Hunger* (New York: Perennial Library, 1979), pp. 67, 73.

23. Wright, *American Hunger*, pp. 65, 63, 64, 67, 69.

24. Wright, *American Hunger*, pp. 125, 93.

25. Wixson, *Worker-Writer in America*, p. 114, makes the important point that the midwestern radicals knew each other only by mail; Conroy never met his co-editor of *Rebel Poets* (p. 142) and did not meet either Wright or Le Sueur until the Chicago Reed club convention.

26. Stephen Halpert, ed., *A Return to Pagany: The History, Correspondence, and Selections from a Little Magazine, 1929–1932* (Boston: Beacon Press, 1969).

27. On Macleod, see Alan Wald, *The Responsibility of Intellectuals: Selected Essays on Marxist Traditions in Cultural Commitment* (New Jersey: Humanities Press, 1992), pp. 102–7.

28. William Carlos Williams, "Comment," *Contact* 1.3, October 1932, p. 131. William Carlos Williams, "An American Poet" (1937) has been reprinted in North, ed., *New Masses: An Anthology*, pp. 233–9. William Carlos Williams, "What Is Americanism? A Symposium on Marxism and the American Tradition," *Partisan Review and Anvil* 3.3, April 1936, pp. 13–14.

29. Gold quoted in Murphy, *The Proletarian Moment*, p. 134. "Proletarian Portrait" was the title of a Williams poem of 1935. William Carlos Williams, *The Farmers' Daughters: The Collected Stories* (New York: New Directions, 1961), p. 32. N.L. Rothman, "Review," *Saturday Review of Literature*, 26 June 1937.

30. Paul Mariani, *William Carlos Williams: A New World Naked* (New York: W.W. Norton, 1981), pp. 345–6. *New Republic*, 11 October 1933. On *Anvil*, see Jack Conroy and Curt Johnson, eds, *Writers in Revolt: The Anvil Anthology, 1933–1940* (New York: Lawrence Hill, 1973). For Conroy's biography, see Wixson, *Worker-Writer in America*.

31. For the sales and reception of *The Disinherited*, see Foley, *Radical Representations*, pp. 89, 103, 133–5.

32. Jack Conroy, "The Worker as Writer," in Henry Hart, ed., *American Writers' Congress* (New York: International Publishers, 1935), pp. 83, 86. Foley, *Radical Representations*, p. 48n. The Anvil League advertisement is in *Anvil* 9, January–February 1935. There is an apparent and revealing discrepancy in Conroy's account of the origin of *Anvil* itself. The first issue suggests that the magazine grew out of a split in the Rebel Poets between Conroy (and his young Communist collaborators) and the older left-wing socialist poets Ralph Cheyney and Lucia Trent. However, Conroy's subsequent accounts of the origin of *Anvil* do not mention the split with Cheyney, instead stressing the split between himself and the leaders of the New York Rebel Poets, Philip Rahv and William Phillips, who went on to edit *Partisan Review*.

33. Michael Gold, "A Letter to the Author of a First Book," in his *Change the World!* (New York: International Publishers, 1936), pp. 215–20.

34. Jack Conroy, review of *Jews Without Money*, *Earth* 1.2, May 1930, p. 12.

35. Wixson's *Worker-Writer in America* is not only a brilliant biography of Conroy, but includes the most persuasive reading of *The Disinherited* (though he unfortunately sets it against the conventional or orthodox proletarian novel, rather than seeing it as one of the modes of proletarian fiction): see p. 214 on the "worker narrative", and pp. 227, 244, 340–49, 426.

36. Estelle Gershgoren Novak, "The *Dynamo* School of Poets," *Contemporary Literature* 11.4, 1970, pp. 526–39. *Challenge* 1.1, March 1934, p. 39.

37. Rampersad, *Langston Hughes: Volume One*, p. 215; Langston Hughes, *I Wonder as I Wander: An Autobiographical Journey* (1956; rpt. New York: Hill and Wang, 1964) pp. 213–14.

38. Henry Hart, ed., *American Writers' Congress* pp. 105, 113, 147–8. Langston Hughes, *The Ways of White Folks* (1934; rpt. New York: Vintage, 1971), pp. 188, 248.

39. Hughes, *The Ways of White Folks*, pp. 110, 53. There are several collections of the Simple stories, most recently Langston Hughes, *The Return of Simple* (New York: Hill and Wang, 1994). On Harrington, see Oliver W. Harrington, *Why I Left America and Other Essays* (Jackson: University Press of Mississippi, 1993); and M. Thomas Inge, *Dark Laughter: The Satiric Art of Ollie Harrington* (Jackson: University Press of Mississippi, 1993).

40. On Le Sueur, see Coiner, *Better Red*, pp. 72–140; Rabinowitz, *Labor and Desire*, pp. 97–100, 114–24; and Linda Ray Pratt, "Woman Writer in the CP: The Case of Meridel Le Sueur," *Women's Studies* 14, 1988, pp. 247–64. For a brief account of *Midwest*, see Harry T. Moore, "Preface," to Madden, ed., *Proletarian Writers of the Thirties*, p. vi.

41. Elaine Hedges, "Introduction," to Meridel Le Sueur, *Ripening: Selected Work, 1927–1980* (Old Westbury, N.Y.: Feminist Press, 1982), pp. 8–9; Meridel Le Sueur, *The Girl* (Cambridge: West End Press, 1978), p. 149.

42. B.A. Botkin, "Regionalism and Culture," in Henry Hart, *The Writer in a Changing World* (n.p.: Equinox Cooperative Press, 1937), p. 156. Meridel Le Sueur, "Proletarian Literature and the Middle West," in Hart, ed., *American Writers' Congress*, pp. 138, 137. McWilliams gives an important early summary in the pamphlet *The New Regionalism in American Literature* (Seattle: University of Washington Book Store, 1930). See also Norman MacLeod's account of the Southwest as a region in *Front* 1, December 1930, and Constance Rourke, "The Significance of Sections," *New Republic*, 20 September 1933, pp. 148–51.

43. Meridel Le Sueur, *Harvest Song: Collected Essays and Stories* (Albuquerque, N. Mex.: West End Press, 1990), p. 64. "O Prairie Girl, Be Lonely" is collected in Le Sueur, *Ripening*.

44. Benjamin Appel, "The 'Message' Novel," *The Writer* 57.2, February 1944, p. 35. Benjamin Appel, "Miss America and the Look-Back Boys," *Literary Review* 17.1, Fall 1973, p. 13. See also John E. Hart, "From Hoodlum to Fascist: Benjamin Appel's 'Brain Guy' Trilogy," *South Dakota Review* 28.1, Spring 1990, pp. 80–89.

45. Benjamin Appel, "Labels," in Madden, ed., *Tough Guy Writers of the Thirties*, p. 13. Benjamin Appel, "The 'Message' Novel," pp. 35–8.

46. *The New Tide* 1, October–November 1934.

47. Carlos Bulosan, *America Is in the Heart: A Personal History* (1943; rpt. Seattle: University of Washington Press, 1991), pp. 193–4.

48. Kalaidjian, *American Culture Between the Wars*, p. 59. Harvey Klehr, *The Heyday of American Communism: The Depression Decade* (New York: Basic Books, 1984), p. 350. Cowley in "Thirty Years Later: Memories of the First American Writers' Congress," *American Scholar* 35.3, Summer 1966, pp. 513, 496. Cowley, *The Dream of the Golden Mountains*, p. 272. For the reassessment of proletarian literature in the mainstream reviews and quarterlies, see Kenneth Burke, "Symbolic War," *Southern Review* 2, Summer 1936, pp. 134–47; and the reply by Allen Tate in *Southern Review* 2, Autumn 1936, pp. 363–72. V.F. Calverton, "Proletarianitis," *Saturday Review of Literature* 15.11, 9 January 1937, pp. 33ff.; C.I. Glicksberg, "Proletarian Fiction in the United States," *Dalhousie Review* 17, April 1937, pp. 22–32; Alan Calmer "Portrait of the Artist as a Proletarian," *Saturday Review of Literature* 16.14, 31 July, 1937, pp. 3ff.; Harold Strauss, "Realism in the Proletarian Novel," *Yale Review* 28, 1938, pp. 360–74; Philip Rahv, "Proletarian Literature: A Political Autopsy," *Southern Review* 4, Winter 1939, pp. 616–28; R.W. Steadman, "A Critique of Proletarian Literature," *North American Review* 247, Spring 1939, pp. 142–52; and L. Robert Lind, "The Crisis in Literature," *Sewanee Review* 47, 1939, pp. 35ff., 184ff., 345ff., 524ff.; *Sewanee Review* 48, 1940, pp. 66ff., 198ff.

49. See Hart, ed., *American Writers' Congress*; Hart, ed., *The Writer in a Changing World*; and Donald Ogden Stewart, ed., *Fighting Words* (New York: Harcourt, Brace and Company, 1940).

50. Drew, *Nelson Algren*, p. 104. Hamalian, *A Life of Kenneth Rexroth*, p. 99. Mangione, *An Ethnic at Large*, p. 124.

51. Appel, "Miss America and the Look-Back Boys," p. 31. Ruth Lechlitner, "anti-war and anti-fascism," *Carleton Miscellany* 6.1, Winter 1965, p. 81. Judy Kutulas, "Becoming 'More Liberal': The League of American Writers, the Communist Party, and the Literary People's Front," *Journal of American Culture* 13.1, 1990, pp. 71–80, and Judy Kutulas, *The Long War: The Intellectual People's Front and Anti-Stalinism, 1930–1940* (Durham, N.C.: Duke University Press, 1995) are informative, but they accept the received wisdom about the Popular Front: that it was not radical and that the main interest of the organization did not lie in its cultural activities but in the internal struggles between Communists and non-Communists. The best source on the League is the memoir by Franklin Folsom, *Days of Anger, Days of Hope: A Memoir of the League of American Writers, 1937–1942* (Niwot: University Press of Colorado, 1994).

52. *Challenge* 2.1, Spring 1937, p. 41.

53. On Ellison and the League, see Folsom, *Days of Anger, Days of Hope*, pp. 201, 209. On *The Negro Quarterly*, see Jerry Gafio Watts, *Heroism and the Black Intellectual: Ralph Ellison, Politics, and Afro-American Intellectual Life* (Chapel Hill: University of North Carolina Press, 1994), pp. 41–3. On the magazines of the 1950s, see Wald, *Writing from the Left*, pp. 85–99.

54. Damon Knight, *The Futurians: The Story of the Science Fiction "Family" of the 30's That Produced Today's Top SF Writers and Editors* (New York: John Day, 1977); Frederik Pohl, *The Way the Future Was: A Memoir* (New York: Ballantine, 1978), pp. 60–102. On the Harlem Writers Club and the Harlem Writers Guild, see Harold Cruse, *The Crisis of the Negro Intellectual* (New York: William Morrow, 1967), pp. 213–220; and Phillip M. Richards, "Foreword," to Julian Mayfield, *The Hit and the Long Night* (Boston: Northeastern University Press, 1989), pp. vi–vii.

55. On the Central Distribution Agency, see Douglas Wixson, "Red Pens from the Village: *The Anvil* and *The Left*, Midwestern Little Magazines of the Early 1930s," *Midamerica* 11, 1984, p. 49. On the Book Find Club, see Folsom, *Days of Anger, Days of Hope*, pp. 96–7. On Progress Publishing, see *Direction* 2.4, July–August 1939, p. 19.

56. Leah Levenson and Jerry Natterstad, *Granville Hicks: The Intellectual in Mass Society* (Philadelphia: Temple University Press, 1993), p. 196. Bernard Smith, *A World Remembered, 1925–1950* (New Jersey: Humanities Press, 1994). Lieber quoted in Rampersad, *Langston Hughes: Volume One*, p. 281. See also Wixson, *Worker-Writer in America*, pp. 584–5; and Halper, *Good-Bye, Union Square*, pp. 47, 49, 206. Henry Hart, "Contemporary Publishing and the Revolutionary Writer," in Hart, *American Writers' Congress*, p. 161. Many left-wing writers explored the economics and politics of publishing. Isidor Schneider wrote about the first major strike in publishing in the October 1934 *Literary America*, and contributed a series of essays about the business of writing to the *New Masses*. The first major scholarly studies of the relation between American literature and the book trade were products of the Popular Front literary world: William Charvat, *The Profession of Authorship in America, 1800–1870* (n.p.: Ohio State University Press, 1968); and Malcolm Cowley, *The Literary Situation* (New York: Viking Press, 1954).

57. Benjamin Appel, "My Generation of Writers," *Tomorrow* 10.6, February 1951, pp. 5, 6.

58. Folsom, ed., *Mike Gold*, p. 189.

59. Kenneth Burke, "Symbolic War," p. 147.

Notes to 6

1. Irwin Granich [Michael Gold], "Towards Proletarian Art," *Liberator*, February 1921, reprinted in Michael Folsom, ed., *Mike Gold: A Literary Anthology* (New York: International Publishers, 1972), pp. 64–5.

2. Alfred Kazin noted that "the Thirties in literature was the age of the plebes—of writers from the working class, the lower class, the immigrant class, the non-literate class, from Western farms and mills—those whose struggle was to survive. When you thought of the typical writers of the Twenties, you thought of rebels from 'good' families—Dos Passos,

Hemingway, Fitzgerald, Cummings, Wilson, Cowley." Kazin, *Starting out in the Thirties* (Boston: Little, Brown, 1965), p. 12.

3. On the *Saturday Evening Post*, see Jan Cohn, *Creating America: George Horace Lorimer and the Saturday Evening Post* (Pittsburgh, Pa.: University of Pittsburgh Press, 1989). Anzia Yezierska, *Red Ribbon on a White Horse* (1950; rpt. New York: Persea Books, 1981), p. 81. Keneth Kinnamon and Michel Fabre, *Conversations with Richard Wright* (Jackson: University Press of Mississippi, 1993), p. 83. Russell Leong, "Toshio Mori: An Interview," *Amerasia* 7.1, 1980, p. 95. See also Marcus Klein, *Foreigners: The Making of American Literature* (Chicago: University of Chicago Press, 1981), who draws a line between the "modernists" and the "barbarians," the "foreigners," the ghetto writers who remade American literature. The American makers of the modernist movement thought of themselves as a "dispossessed *social* aristocracy" (p. 11): indeed, Eliot, Pound, Stevens, Cummings, Moore, Hilda Doolittle, Dos Passos, Stein, and others were from old American stock, from families that were or had been wealthy. Instead of Cowley's account of a generation disillusioned with commercialism, Klein sees a group displaced from its "rightful" place in US society. Thus, the anti-Semitism and racism of the modernists was not a lamentable capitulation to the social conventions of the day, but a key part of their sense of history. Pound, who suggested that "one could write the whole social history of the United States from one's family annals," was able to encompass US history in an "anecdote" of a Philadelphia neighbor of his youth who "was not only a gentleman but the fine old type. And his son is a stockbroker, roaring himself hoarse every day in the Wheat Pit . . . and *his* son will look like a Jew, and his grandson . . . will talk Yiddish. And this dissolution is taking place in hundreds of American families" (p. 15). Klein's debunking of American modernism in order to establish an alternative tradition of "foreigners" is powerful and persuasive. But he cedes too much by abandoning the term "modernism." The social origins of modernism lie in the dilemmas facing writers of subaltern racial and ethnic formations: the dilemmas of double audiences and cultural clashes. The Yiddish, Scandinavian, and German theaters in the US were more "modern" than the English language stage, Werner Sollors reminds us, and before Harriet Monroe's *Poetry* opened its pages to Eliot and Pound, there was a Yiddish avant-garde in poetry. As Terry Eagleton once argued, the characteristic modernist finds language a material force, a foreign object, because he or she is not fully enfranchised within the dominant language, the dominant stories. The works of the tenement writers thus constitute subaltern modernisms, formations organized around the avant-garde "little magazines" and manifestos of the Harlem and Chicago Renaissances, and of the proletarian literature movement.

4. Michael Gold, *Jews without Money* (1930; rpt. New York: Carroll & Graf: 1984), p. 84.

5. Gold, *Jews without Money*, pp. 86, 244, 309. The Messiah passages are on pp. 159, 190, 184. I am indebted to the superb reading of *Jews without Money* in Rachel Lee Rubin, "Reading, Writing and the Rackets: Jewish Gangsters in Interwar Russian and American Narrative," Ph.D. diss., Yale University, 1995, pp. 145–219. See also James D. Bloom, *Left Letters: The Culture Wars of Mike Gold and Joseph Freeman* (New York: Columbia University Press, 1992); and Richard Tuerk, "*Jews without Money* as a Work of Art," *Studies in American Jewish Literature* 7.1, 1988, pp. 67–79.

6. For the *Bud* stories, see Sau-Ling C. Wong, "Tales of Postwar Chinatown: Short Stories of *The Bud*, 1947–1948," *Amerasia* 14.2, 1988, pp. 61–79. This is only a sampling: see also the discussions in Thomas Gladsky, *Princes, Peasants, and Other Polish Selves* (Amherst: University of Massachusetts Press, 1992), pp. 81–135; Alexander Karanikas, *Hellenes and Hellions: Modern Greek Characters in American Literature* (Urbana: University of Illinois Press, 1981), pp. 80–92.

7. Melvin P. Levy, "Michael Gold," *New Republic*, 26 March 1930, pp. 160–61. Michael Gold, "A Proletarian Novel?," *New Republic*, 4 June 1930, p. 74. Henry Roth, "On Being Blocked & Other Literary Matters: An Interview," *Commentary*, August 1977, p. 35. On the realist aesthetic of the critics, see James F. Murphy, *The Proletarian Moment: The Controversy over Leftism in Literature* (Urbana: University of Illinois Press, 1991). The Gold controversy has often been discussed: see Edmund Wilson, *The Shores of Light: A Literary Chronicle of the Twenties and Thirties* (1952; rpt. Boston: Northeastern University Press, 1985), pp. 536–9; Murphy, *The Proletarian Moment*, pp. 129–30; Tuerk, "*Jews without Money* as a Work of Art," pp. 69–70. The *Call It Sleep* controversy lasted from 12 February to 5 March, 1935 in the *New Masses*. See also Murphy, *The Proletarian Moment*, pp. 131–3. Barbara Foley, *Radical Representations: Politics and Form in*

U.S. Proletarian Fiction, 1929–1941 (Durham, N.C.: Duke University Press, 1993), turns this on its head by defending an aesthetic of didacticism. Though this is powerful in reassessing several explicitly didactic and propagandist works, she ends up underemphasizing the ghetto pastorals with their lack of explicit politics: see her notes on *Call It Sleep* (p. 324n) and *Lawd Today* (p. 203.n). By reading these books simply as proletarian *Bildungsroman*, her propagand-ist aesthetic finally renders a negative judgement on them: they are not radical enough (pp. 316–20).

8. Kenneth Burke, letter, *New Masses*, 26 February 1935, p. 21.

9. Di Donato quoted in Mike Gold, "Change the World," *Daily Worker*, 13 June 1939, p. 7. See also Milton Meltzer, "'The Job' Haunts Pietro di Donato, Good Bricklayer and Fine Novelist," *Daily Worker*, 1 May 1939, p. 7.

10. Granville Hicks, *The Great Tradition: An Interpretation of American Literature since the Civil War* (New York: International Publishers, 1935), p. 314. Alfred Kazin, *On Native Grounds: An Interpretation of Modern American Prose Literature* (New York: Reynal and Hitchcock, 1942), pp. ix, 371. Kazin, *Starting out in the Thirties*, p. 13.

11. Richard Wright, "Blueprint for Negro Writing," *New Challenge* 2.2, Spring 1937, p. 58. Michael de Capite, "The Story Is Yet to Be Told," *Common Ground* 1.1, Autumn 1940, pp. 29–36.

12. Raymond Williams, "Working-Class, Proletarian, Socialist: Problems in Some Welsh Novels," in H. Gustav Klaus, ed., *The Socialist Novel in Britain* (Brighton: Harvester, 1982), pp. 114, 118.

13. On Olsen, Constance Coiner, *Better Red: the Writing and Resistance of Tillie Olsen and Meridel Le Sueur* (New York: Oxford University Press, 1995), p. 146. John Fante, "Bill Saroyan," *Common Ground* 1.2, Winter 1941, p. 64. Similarly, Conroy's attempts to write an autobiography were foiled by his inability, in his words, to "get out of Monkey Nest." Douglas Wixson, *Worker-Writer in America: Jack Conroy and the Tradition of Midwestern Literary Radicalism, 1898–1990* (Urbana: University of Illinois Press, 1994), p. 2. Alfred Kazin said memorably of James Farrell: "If all writers remember longest what they learned in their youth, Farrell's work suggests that he remembered nothing and learned from nothing but his youth." Kazin, *On Native Grounds*, p. 383.

14. Daniel Fuchs, *Summer in Williamsburg* (1934) in his *Three Novels* (New York: Basic Books, 1961), pp. 263, 12, 375–6.

15. H.T. Tsiang, *And China Has Hands* (New York: Robert Speller, 1937), pp. 32, 103, 159.

16. Robert Forsythe [Kyle S. Crichton], *Redder than the Rose* (New York: Covici Friede, 1935), pp. 81–7. Raymond Williams, *Writing in Society* (London: Verso, n.d.), pp. 233–4.

17. Conroy quoted in Foley, *Radical Representations*, p. 295 n. 13. Jerre Mangione, *An Ethnic at Large: A Memoir of America in the Thirties and Forties* (New York; G.P. Putnam's Sons, 1978), p. 299. See Foley, *Radical Representations*, pp. 286, 295–6, for the way the genre of the proletarian sketch, adopted from Soviet Proletcult, influenced the work of Gold and Conroy; see also David Peck, "Joseph North and the Proletarian Reportage of the 1930s," *Zeitschrift für Anglistik und Amerikanistik* 33.3, 1985, pp. 210–20.

18. Leong, "Toshio Mori," p. 94. Richard Wright, "Alger Revisited, or My Stars! Did We Read that Stuff?" *PM*, 16 September 1945, p. 8. Gold, *Jews without Money*, pp. 190, 187. James T. Farrell, *Young Lonigan* in *Studs Lonigan: A Trilogy* (New York: Modern Library, 1938), p. 35. Wixson, *Worker-Writer in America*, pp. 35, 39–40, explores Conroy's debt to dime and pulp fiction; there are direct references to the pulps in Jack Conroy, *The Disinherited* (1933; rpt. New York: Hill and Wang, 1963), pp. 70, 73; and Jack Conroy, *A World to Win* (New York: Covici Friede, 1935), p. 347.

19. Tsiang, *And China Has Hands*, p. 32. Richard Wright, *Lawd Today* (1963; rpt. Boston: Northeastern University Press, 1986), p. 150.

20. Edmund Wilson's collection of depression journalism was first titled *The American Jitters* (1932) and later retitled *The American Earthquake* (1958). Gilbert Seldes's narrative of the depression was entitled *The Years of the Locust* (1933).

21. Billie Holiday with William Dufty, *Lady Sings the Blues* (1956; rpt. New York: Avon Books, 1976), p. 32. A Popular Front version of the stockbroker narrative was Orson Welles's portrayal of the ruined banker in Archibald MacLeish's play, *Panic*.

22. Pietro di Donato, *Christ in Concrete* (Indianapolis, Ind.: Bobbs-Merrill, 1939), pp. 97–8, 188.

23. Tillie Olsen, *Tell Me a Riddle* (1961; rpt. New York: Dell, 1976), p. 19. Conroy, *The Disinherited*, pp. 65–6. Marita Bonner, *Frye Street and Environs: The Collected Works* (Boston: Beacon Press, 1987), pp. 153, 156, 211.

24. Fuchs, *Summer in Williamsburg*, pp. 374, 376–7. Di Donato, *Christ in Concrete*, p. 137. For an important discussion of the problems in representing working-class communities, see Williams, "Working-Class, Proletarian, Socialist," pp. 116–17.

25. Gold, *Jews without Money*, p. 178. Bonner, *Frye Street and Environs*, p. 102.

26. Henry Roth, *Call It Sleep* (1934; rpt. New York: Cooper Square Publishers, 1970), pp. 117–36. Richard Wright, *Native Son* (New York: Harper and Brothers, 1940), pp. 208, 216.

27. Gold, *Jews without Money*, pp. 180, 62.

28. Bell quoted in David P. Demarest, Jr, "Afterword," to Thomas Bell, *Out of this Furnace* (1941; rpt. Pittsburgh, Pa.: University of Pittsburgh Press, 1976), p. 418. On Fast, see Alan Wald, *The Responsibility of Intellectuals: Selected Essays on Marxist Traditions in Cultural Commitment* (New Jersey: Humanities Press, 1992), pp. 92–101; and Priscilla Murolo, "History in the Fast Lane," *Radical History Review* 31, December 1984, pp. 22–31.

29. Fuchs, *Summer in Williamsburg*, 373. Fuchs, *Homage to Blenholt* (1936) in his *Three Novels* (New York: Basic Books, 1961), p. 297. Gold, *Jews without Money*, p. 309.

30. Kenneth Burke, *The Philosophy of Literary Form: Studies in Symbolic Action* (1941; rpt. Berkeley: University of California Press, 1973), pp. 296, 299. See also Kenneth Burke, "Symbolic War," *Southern Review* 2, Summer 1936, pp. 134–47. On allegory, see Michael Denning, *Mechanic Accents: Dime Novels and Working-Class Culture in America* (New York: Verso, 1987), pp. 73–4. My account has also been deeply influenced by Alfred Habegger, *Gender, Fantasy, and Realism in American Literature* (New York: Columbia University Press, 1982), pp. 111–12; and Fredric Jameson, *The Political Unconscious: Narrative as a Socially Symbolic Act* (Ithaca, N.Y.: Cornell University Press, 1981), who suggests that realistic novelists, "shepherds of Being," have an aesthetic and narrative commitment to the solidity and permanence of the social world. In a brief aside, Jameson notes that "a curious subform of realism, the proletarian novel, demonstrates what happens when the representational apparatus is confronted by that supreme event, the strike as the figure for social revolution, which calls social 'being' and the social totality itself into question, thereby undermining that totality's basic precondition: whence the scandal of this form, which fails when it succeeds and succeeds when it fails, thereby evading categories of literary evaluation inherited from 'great realism'" (p. 193).

31. Coiner, *Better Red*, p. 178. Olsen quoted in Deborah Rosenfelt, "From the Thirties: Tillie Olsen and the Radical Tradition," *Feminist Studies* 7.3, Fall 1981, p. 389. Tillie Olsen, *Yonnondio: From the Thirties* (1974; rpt. New York: Delta, 1989), pp. 4, 6, 20, 47–8, 111, 125, 21, 132.

32. Vernon Louis Parrington, "The Beginnings of Critical Realism in America" in his *Main Currents in American Thought: An Interpretation of American Literature from the Beginnings to 1920* (New York: Harcourt, Brace and Company, 1930), p. 325. Harold Strauss, "Realism in the Proletarian Novel," *Yale Review* 28, 1938, pp. 361–2. Kazin, *On Native Grounds*, pp. 371, 363–99.

33. William Empson, *Some Versions of Pastoral* (1935; rpt. New York: New Directions, 1974), pp. 6, 11, 15, 16, 20, 17. The one American who commented on Empson's interpretation of proletarian literature was Kenneth Burke, whose scattered comments on proletarian literature invoke both naturalism and pastoralism. See Burke, *The Philosophy of Literary Form*, pp. 422–6. However, it was a younger leftist American critic—Leo Marx—who was to reinject the pastoral in discussions of American culture. For his illuminating reconsideration of Empson, see Marx, "Pastoralism in America," in Sacvan Bercovitch and Myra Jehlen, eds, *Ideology and Classic American Literature* (Cambridge: Cambridge University Press, 1986).

34. Kazin, *On Native Grounds*, pp. 386–7. Richard Wright, "How 'Bigger' Was Born" (1940) in his *Native Son* (New York: Harper Perennial, 1966), p. xxvii.

35. Richard Wright, *Lawd Today* (1963; rpt. Boston: Northeastern University Press, 1986), p. 189. Arnold Rampersad, "Foreword," to Wright, *Lawd Today*, p. 5.

36. Margaret Walker, *Richard Wright: Daemonic Genius* (New York: Warner Books, 1988), p. 62. Wright, *Lawd Today*, pp. 154, 10, 101, 165, 124, 125, 95, 168, 175.

37. Wright, *Lawd Today*, pp. 137–62.

38. Richard Wright, "Between Laughter and Tears," *New Masses*, 5 October 1937, pp. 22–5. Farrell, "Introduction," to his *Studs Lonigan*, p. xii. See also Wright's introduction to Nelson Algren, *Never Come Morning* (New York: Harper and Brothers, 1942), which directly addresses "Mr. and Mrs. American Reader"; and Algren's own 1962 preface, reprinted in *Never Come Morning* (New York: Four Walls Eight Windows, 1987). For a gothic reading of the proletarian novel, see Leslie Fiedler, *Love and Death in the American Novel* (1960; rpt. New York: Stein and Day, 1975), pp. 481–2, 499–500.

39. Edward Dahlberg, "Portrait of the Gangster," *New Masses*, 24 February 1934, p. 24. Robert Sklar, *City Boys: Cagney, Bogart, Garfield* (Princeton, N.J.: Princeton University Press, 1992), p. 8. Charles Eckert, "The Anatomy of a Proletarian Film: Warner's *Marked Woman*," in Bill Nichols, ed., *Movies and Methods: Volume II* (Berkeley: University of California Press, 1985), pp. 420–24.

40. Fuchs, *Summer in Williamsburg*, pp. 331–4. Tsiang, *And China Has Hands*, p. 79. Gold, *Jews without Money*, pp. 37, 309.

41. Fuchs, *Summer in Williamsburg*, pp. 242, 380. Fuchs, *Homage to Blenholt*, pp. 66–7, 48, 302. I am indebted to the superb interpretation of the figure of the gangster in the works of Fuchs and Gold, as well as those of Isaac Babel, Samuel Ornitz, and Venyamin Kaverin, in Rubin, *Reading, Writing, and the Rackets*.

42. Daniel Fuchs, *Low Company* (1937) in his *Three Novels* (New York: Basic Books, 1961), p. 179.

43. Dashiell Hammett, *Red Harvest* (1929; rpt. New York: Vintage, 1972), pp. 4, 7. See Carl Freedman and Christopher Kendrick, "Forms of Labor in Dashiell Hammett's *Red Harvest*," *PMLA* 106.2, March 1991, pp. 209–22.

44. James T. Farrell, *Literature and Morality* (New York: Vanguard Press, 1947), p. 89.

45. For a discussion of Himes's thrillers, see Michael Denning, "Topographies of Violence: Chester Himes' Harlem Domestic Novels," *Critical Texts* 5.1, 1988, pp. 10–18.

Notes to 7

1. Woody Guthrie, *Pastures of Plenty: A Self-Portrait* (New York: HarperCollins, 1990), p. 42.

2. Robert Warshow, *The Immediate Experience: Movies, Comics, Theatre and Other Aspects of Popular Culture* (New York: Atheneum, 1971), pp. 34–45. Leslie A. Fiedler, *Waiting for the End: The Crisis in American Culture and a Portrait of Twentieth Century American Literature* (New York: Stein and Day, 1964), p. 61. The young Fiedler saw *The Grapes of Wrath* as a sentimental novel of social protest along the lines of *Uncle Tom's Cabin*, "marred by social piety and turgid symbolism": Fiedler, *An End to Innocence: Essays on Culture and Politics* (Boston: Beacon Press, 1955), p. 192; the older Fiedler has abandoned his New Critical disdain for such popular mythic power.

3. See Carey McWilliams, *Factories in the Field: The Story of Migratory Farm Labor in California* (1939; rpt. Santa Barbara: Peregrine Smith, 1971), p. 211–63. Lowell K. Dyson, *Red Harvest: The Communist Party and American Farmers* (Lincoln: University of Nebraska Press, 1982), pp. 84–93; Vicki L. Ruiz, *Cannery Women, Cannery Lives: Mexican Women, Unionization, and the California Food Processing Industry, 1930–1950* (Albuquerque: University of New Mexico Press, 1987), pp. 49–51; Juan Gómez-Quiñones, *Mexican American Labor, 1790–1990* (Albuquerque: University of New Mexico Press, 1994), pp. 131–41; Dorothy Healey, *Dorothy Healey Remembers: A Life in the American Communist Party* (New York: Oxford University Press, 1990), pp. 42–55; Cletus Daniel, *Bitter Harvest: A History of California Farmworkers, 1870–1941* (Berkeley: University of California Press, 1981), pp. 105–257; Jerold S. Auerbach, *Labor and Liberty: The La Follette Committee and the New Deal* (Indianapolis, Ind.: Bobbs-Merrill, 1966), pp. 177–96.

4. Mike Quin's "Mexican Hands" was published in 1933 in the John Reed Club's *Partisan* and reprinted in his *On the Drumhead* (San Francisco: Pacific Publishing, 1948). Arnold Rampersad, *The Life of Langston Hughes. Volume I: 1902–1941. I, Too, Sing America* (New York: Oxford University Press, 1986), pp. 290–91. One of the Communist organizers, Dorothy Healey, later wrote that Steinbeck's *In Dubious Battle* was "the best fictional description ... of a Communist-led agricultural strike." Healey, *Dorothy Healey Remembers*, 45. James Cagney was Red-baited as early as 1934 for his financial support of the farmworkers' strike: see Robert

Sklar, *City Boys: Cagney, Bogart, Garfield* (Princeton, N.J.: Princeton University Press, 1992), p. 46.

5. See Milton Meltzer, *Dorothea Lange: A Photographer's Life* (New York: Farrar Straus Giroux, 1978). On *The Plow*, see William Alexander, *Film on the Left: American Documentary Film from 1931 to 1942* (Princeton: Princeton University Press, 1981), pp. 93–109.

6. McWilliams, *Factories in the Field*, p. 10. Meltzer, *Dorothea Lange*, pp. 92–106, 155, 182. The text of *Their Blood Is Strong* is reprinted in Warren French, ed., *A Companion to The Grapes of Wrath* (New York: Viking Press, 1963).

7. On the textile strikes and Wiggins, see Jacquelyn Dowd Hall, James Leloudis, Robert Korstad, Mary Murphy, Lu Ann Jones, and Christopher B. Daly, *Like a Family: The Making of a Southern Cotton Mill World* (Chapel Hill: University of North Carolina Press, 1987), pp. 214–15, 226–9; and Doug DeNatale and Glenn Hinson, "The Southern Textile Song Tradition Reconsidered," in Archie Green, ed., *Songs about Work: Essays in Occupational Culture for Richard A. Reuss* (Bloomington: Indiana University Press, 1993). On the Gastonia novels, see Candida Ann Lacey, "Striking Fictions: Women Writers and the Making of a Proletarian Realism," *Women's Studies International Forum* 9.4, 1986, pp. 373–84; Sylvia Jenkins Cook, *From Tobacco Road to Route 66: The Southern Poor White in Fiction* (Chapel Hill: University of North Carolina Press, 1976), pp. 85–142; John Reilly, "Images of Gastonia: A Revolutionary Chapter in American Social Fiction," *Georgia Review* 28, 1974, pp. 498–517; Barbara Foley, *Radical Representations: Politics and Form in U.S. Proletarian Fiction, 1929–1941* (Durham, N.C.: Duke University Press, 1993); and Paula Rabinowitz, *Labor and Desire: Women's Revolutionary Fiction in Depression America* (Chapel Hill: University of North Carolina Press, 1991).

8. See Robin D.G. Kelley, *Hammer and Hoe: Alabama Communists during the Great Depression* (Chapel Hill: University of North Carolina Press, 1990), for a superb account of Alabama Communists. See Rampersad, *Life of Langston Hughes: Volume I*, pp. 223–33, for Hughes's southern trip; see Douglas Wixson, *Worker-Writer in America: Jack Conroy and the Tradition of Midwestern Literary Radicalism, 1898–1990* (Urbana: University of Illinois Press, 1994), pp. 409–11 for Conroy's trip. John L. Spivak, *A Man in His Time* (New York: Horizon Press, 1967), pp. 165–241. See Alan M. Wald, *Writing from the Left: New Essays on Radical Culture and Politics* (London: Verso, 1994), pp. 152–61, on the representations of black struggles by radical white writers. One can see the Scottsboro cultural struggle represented in Nancy Cunard's famous anthology of 1934, *Negro*. See Brenda McCallum, "The Gospel of Black Unionism," in Green, ed., *Songs about Work* for the importance of the jubilee gospel quartets for black CIO organizers.

9. On Harlan, see John W. Hevener, *Which Side Are You On? The Harlan County Coal Miners, 1931–1939* (Urbana: University of Illinois Press, 1978). Malcolm Cowley, *The Dream of the Golden Mountains: Remembering the 1930s* (New York: Penguin Books, 1981), pp. 51–76. On the NMU singers, see Archie Green, *Only a Miner: Studies in Recorded Coal-Mining Songs* (Urbana: University of Illinois Press, 1972), pp. 77–88, 419–35.; Julia S. Ardery, ed., *Welcome the Traveler Home: Jim Garland's Story of the Kentucky Mountains* (Lexington: University Press of Kentucky, 1983).

10. For a fine study of the African American migration narratives, see Farah Jasmine Griffin, *"Who set you flowin'?": The African–American Migration Narrative* (New York: Oxford University Press, 1995).

11. Edwin Berry Burgum, *The Novel and the World's Dilemma* (New York: Oxford University Press, 1947), pp. 285, 283–4.

12. Edmund Wilson, *The Shores of Light: A Literary Chronicle of the Twenties and Thirties* (1952; rpt. Boston: Northeastern University Press, 1985), p. 499. My account of the making of *The Plow That Broke the Plains* is taken from Alexander's excellent *Film on the Left*, pp. 93–112. James N. Gregory, *American Exodus: The Dust Bowl Migration and Okie Culture in California* (New York: Oxford University Press, 1989), suggests that about 6 percent of the Southwestern migrants were from the Dust Bowl. Indeed, the majority of migrants were not farmers; blue-collar workers were the group overrepresented in the ranks of the migrants (pp. 11, 15–17).

13. Otis Ferguson, reprinted in *The Film Criticism of Otis Ferguson* (Philadelphia: Temple University Press, 1971). Irving Lerner, "*The Plow That Broke the Plains*," reprinted in Herbert Kline, ed., *New Theatre and Film 1934 to 1937: An Anthology* (San Diego, Calif.: Harcourt Brace

Jovanovich, 1985), pp. 313–16. Kenneth Burke, *The Philosophy of Literary Form: Studies in Symbolic Action* (1941; rpt. Berkeley: University of California Press, 1973), p. 81.

14. Meltzer, *Dorothea Lange*, p. 101. Robert DeMott, "Introduction," to John Steinbeck, *Working Days: The Journals of The Grapes of Wrath, 1938–1941* (New York: Penguin 1990), p. xxvii.

15. McWilliams, *Factories in the Field*, p. 303. Michael Ciment, *Conversations with Losey* (London: Methuen, 1985), p. 70. Zanuck produced the film from Nunnally Johnson's screenplay, and John Ford directed it. Collins served as a technical advisor on the film. DeMott, "Introduction," p. xxix. Robert DeMott notes that Collins' skeptical reaction to the CIO organizing led Steinbeck to change his mind about heading the Steinbeck Committee, though he lent his name to it (p. 149).

16. Gregory, *American Exodus*, pp. 58–62. Jackson J. Benson, *The True Adventures of John Steinbeck, Writer* (1984; rpt. New York: Penguin, 1990), p. 304. John Steinbeck, *Their Blood Is Strong*, reprinted in French, *A Companion to* The Grapes of Wrath, pp. 85, 56, 57.

17. Will Geer, "Early Woody," in Harold Leventhal and Marjorie Guthrie, eds, *The Woody Guthrie Songbook* (New York: Grosset and Dunlap, 1976), p. 13. The standard biography is Joe Klein, *Woody Guthrie: A Life* (New York: Alfred A. Knopf, 1980).

18. Gregory, *American Exodus*, pp. 224–5, 20–21.

19. On Guthrie's California years, see Klein, *Woody Guthrie*, pp. 77–136; Guthrie, *Pastures of Plenty*, pp. 15–32; Al Richmond, *A Long View from the Left: Memoirs of an American Revolutionary* (New York: Dell Publishing Co., 1972), p. 280. See Klein, *Woody Guthrie*, pp. 139–69 for Guthrie's work in New York in the spring of 1940.

20. Wilfrid Mellers, *A Darker Shade of Pale: A Backdrop to Bob Dylan* (New York: Oxford University Press, 1985), p. 51. *Dust Bowl Ballads*, Victor P-27 and P-28, included twelve sides; they have been reissued with two unissued sides from the same recording session on Rounder CD 1040. The original liner notes by Guthrie have been reprinted in Guthrie, *Pastures of Plenty*, pp. 41–5. Steinbeck quoted in Richard A. Reuss, "Woody Guthrie and His Folk Tradition," *Journal of American Folklore* 83, 1970, p. 280.

21. Alan Lomax, Woody Guthrie, and Pete Seeger, *Hard Hitting Songs for Hard-Hit People* (New York: Oak Publications, 1967), p. 215. Woody Guthrie, "Songs of the Migratious Trail," *Direction* 3.3, March 1940, p. 6.

22. Klein, *Woody Guthrie*, p. 123. Guthrie notes the influence of Robinson's ballad in his "Songs of the Migratious Trail," p. 7. Note also the parallels between Pretty Boy Floyd's and Tom Joad's encounter with the deputy sheriff. Guthrie recorded "Pretty Boy Floyd" at the *Dust Bowl Ballads* recording session, but it was not included in the Victor album; it has been included in the recent CD release.

23. The Carter Family version, "Can't Feel at Home," was recorded 25 May 1931 and appeared on Victor 23569 and Bluebird B-6259; both Mainer's Mountaineers and the Monroe Brothers recorded popular versions of "This World Is Not My Home" in the mid 1930s: Bluebird B-6088-B and Bluebird B-6309. See Bill C. Malone, *Country Music U.S.A.* (Austin: University of Texas Press, 1985), pp. 122–3; and Neil V. Rosenberg, *Bluegrass: A History* (Urbana: University of Illinois Press, 1985), p. 34.

24. Guthrie, "Songs of the Migratious Trail," p. 6. Guthrie, *Pastures of Plenty*, p. 42.

25. McWilliams, *Factories in the Field*, pp. 132–3. Carlos Bulosan, *America Is in the Heart: A Personal History* (1946; rpt. Seattle: University of Washington Press, 1991), p. 199. *The New Tide* 1, October–November, 1934. For Bulosan's biography, see E. San Juan, Jr, "Introduction," to Carlos Bulosan, *On Becoming Filipino: Selected Writings* (Philadelphia: Temple University Press, 1995); Susan Evangelista, *Carlos Bulosan and His Poetry: A Biography and Anthology* (Quezon City: Ateneo de Manila University Press, 1985); and P.C. Morantte, *Remembering Carlos Bulosan* (Quezon City: New Day Publishers, 1984).

26. Bulosan, *On Becoming Filipino*, p. 138.

27. Bulosan, *America Is in the Heart*, pp. 189, 124.

28. Bulosan, *America Is in the Heart*, pp. 261, 139, 214, 128.

29. Fante, quoted by Carey McWilliams in his introduction, to Bulosan, *America Is in the Heart*, p. xviii. Morantte, *Remembering Carlos Bulosan*, pp. 51–63; Evangelista, *Carlos Bulosan and His Poetry*, p. 9. Bulosan, *America Is in the Heart*, pp. 176, 222. The first incident is discussed in Dorothy Bintang Fujita Rony, "'You Got to Move Like Hell': Trans-Pacific Colonialism and

Filipina/o Seattle," Ph.D. diss., Yale University, 1996, p. 220–25; for the murder of the historical Virgil Dunyungan (Bulosan's Dagohoy), see Chris Friday, *Organizing Asian American Labor: The Pacific Coast Canned-Salmon Industry: 1870–1942* (Philadelphia: Temple University Press, 1994), pp. 145–8.

30. Bulosan, *America Is in the Heart*, p. 304. For the structure of the Filipino migrant community, I am indebted to Rony, "'You Got to Move Like Hell'", pp. 157–65.

31. Bulosan, *America Is in the Heart*, pp. 98, 130–37, 155, 204–5.

32. Bulosan, *America Is in the Heart*, pp. 113, 128, 155, 258.

33. Bulosan, *America Is in the Heart*, pp. 228–43, 235. Alice and Eileen Odell were based on Sanora and Dorothy Babb; Sanora Babb was a well-known left-wing regionalist writer who had written a novel about migrant workers, *Whose Names Are Unknown*, which was not published. A section of it appears as Sanora Babb, "From 'Whose Names Are Unknown,'" *Michigan Quarterly Review* 29.3, Summer 1990, pp. 353–71. Note also Bulosan's meeting with the proletarian novelist "Laura Clarendorn" whose novel featured a Filipino protagonist: she is Clara Weatherwax, the author of *Marching! Marching!* (p. 238).

34. Bulosan, *America Is in the Heart*, pp. 153, 205.

35. Bulosan, *America Is in the Heart*, pp. 324, 311–13, 326.

36. See Maria Montes de Oca Ricks, "Ernesto Galarza," in Francisco A. Lomelí and Carl R. Shirley, *Chicano Writers: Second Series*, Dictionary of Literary Biography Vol. 122 (Detroit, Mich.: Gale Research, 1992), pp. 89–101; David G. Gutiérrez, *Walls and Mirrors: Mexican Americans, Mexican Immigrants, and the Politics of Ethnicity* (Berkeley: University of California Press, 1995), pp. 155–68; *Photo-History* 2, July 1937. Mario T. García, *Memories of Chicano History: The Life and Narrative of Bert Corona* (Berkeley: University of California Press, 1994), pp. 117, 227–9; and Gómez-Quiñones, *Mexican American Labor*, pp. 235–42. For critical readings of *Barrio Boy*, see Ramón Saldívar, *Chicano Narrative: The Dialectics of Difference* (Madison: University of Wisconsin Press, 1990), pp. 154–70; José David Saldívar, *The Dialectics of Our America: Genealogy, Cultural Critique, and Literary History* (Durham: Duke University Press, 1991), pp. 138–43; and Renato Rosaldo, *Culture and Truth: The Remaking of Social Analysis* (Boston: Beacon Press, 1989), pp. 155–60.

37. Ernesto Galarza, *Barrio Boy* (Notre Dame: University of Notre Dame Press, 1971), pp. 132, 134, 229, 228.

38. Galarza, *Barrio Boy*, pp. 145–6. Rosaldo, *Culture and Truth*, p. 159.

39. Galarza, *Barrio Boy*, pp. 113, 166–8, 111, 179, 127, 239–40, 265.

40. Galarza, *Barrio Boy*, pp. 202, 229.

41. Galarza, *Barrio Boy*, pp. 46, 206–7, 256.

42. Gregory, *American Exodus*, pp. 139–71. Klein, *Woody Guthrie*, pp. 198–204; David King Dunaway, *How Can I Keep From Singing: Pete Seeger* (New York: McGraw-Hill, 1981), pp. 78–106.

43. Evangelista, *Carlos Bulosan and His Poetry*, pp. 20–23. See E San Juan, Jr, *Carlos Bulosan and the Imagination of the Class Struggle* (Quezon City: University of the Philippines Press, 1972); Frank Chin, Jeffrey Paul Chan, Lawson Fusao Inada, and Shawn Hsu Wong, eds, *Aiiieeeee! An Anthology of Asian–American Writers* (Washington, D.C.: Howard University Press, 1974); and Emma Gee, ed., *Counterpoint: Perspectives on Asia America* (Los Angeles: UCLA Asian American Studies Center, 1976).

44. García, *Memories of Chicano History*, pp. 225–7.

Notes to 8

1. I am particularly indebted to Wilfrid Mellers, *Music in a New Found Land: Themes and Developments in the History of American Music* (New York: Oxford University Press, 1987); Christopher Small, *Music of the Common Tongue: Survival and Celebration in Afro-American Music* (New York: Riverrun Press, 1987); Charles Keil and Steven Feld, *Music Grooves* (Chicago: University of Chicago Press, 1994); and Michael Chanan's two books: *Musica Practica: The Social Practice of Western Music from Gregorian Chant to Postmodernism* (London: Verso, 1994), and *Repeated Takes: A Short History of Recording and Its Effects on Music* (London: Verso, 1995). See also Joseph Lanza, *Elevator Music: A Surreal History of Muzak, Easy-Listening, and Other Moodsong* (New York: Picador USA, 1995).

2. For the fullest version of the caricature, see R. Serge Denisoff, *Great Day Coming: Folk Music and the American Left* (Urbana: University of Illinois Press, 1971). However, even the sympathetic histories focus on these aspects: see Robbie Lieberman, "*My Song Is My Weapon*": *People's Songs, American Communism, and the Politics of Culture, 1930–1950* (Urbana: University of Illinois Press, 1989); Robert Cantwell, *When We Were Good: The Folk Revival* (Cambridge, Mass.: Harvard University Press, 1996); Barbara L. Tischler, *An American Music: The Search for an American Musical Identity* (New York: Oxford University Press, 1986).

3. Seeger quoted in David King Dunaway, *How Can I Keep from Singing: Pete Seeger* (New York: McGraw-Hill, 1981), pp. 118, 319. *Music Front* was the title of a journal published by the Pierre Deygeter Club.

4. Marc Blitzstein, untitled ["In America..."], Orson Welles Manuscripts, Lilly Library, Indiana University, Box 5, f22.

5. The phrase "proletarian opera" is from a press release to *Unison*: Orson Welles Manuscripts, Lilly Library, Indiana University, Box 5, f22. Memoirs of the *Cradle*'s opening night include: Marc Blitzstein, "Out of the Cradle," *Opera News* 24.15, 13 February 1960, p. 10; Howard Da Silva, liner notes to Marc Blitzstein, *The Cradle Will Rock*, Composers Recordings Inc., SD 266, 1964; John Houseman, *Run-Through: A Memoir* (New York: Simon and Schuster, 1972), pp. 245–79; Orson Welles, *The Cradle Will Rock: An Original Screenplay* (Santa Barbara, Calif.: Santa Teresa Press, 1993); Archibald MacLeish, "Foreword," to Marc Blitzstein, *The Cradle Will Rock: A Play in Music* (New York: Random House, 1938).

6. Blitzstein quoted in Robert J. Dietz, "The Operatic Style of Marc Blitzstein in the American 'Agit-Prop' Era," Ph.D. diss., University of Iowa, 1970, p. 213. Blitzstein quoted in WPA press release, 11 June 1937, Orson Welles Manuscripts, Lilly Library, Indiana University, Box 5, f21.

7. Virgil Thomson, "In the Theatre," *Modern Music*, January–February 1938, pp. 112–14. The original cast recording was Marc Blitzstein, *The Cradle Will Rock*, Musicraft No. 18, 1938. The symposium is noted in *New Masses* 26.14, 15 March 1938, p. 3.

8. Robert H. Zieger, *The CIO, 1935–1955* (Chapel Hill: University of North Carolina Press, 1995), pp. 34–9, 54–65.

9. Zieger, *The CIO*, p. 62. Hallie Flanagan, *Arena* (New York: Duell, Sloane, and Pearce, 1940), p. 202. On the Memorial Day massacre, see Jerold S. Auerbach, *Labor and Liberty: The La Follette Committee and the New Deal* (Indianapolis, Ind.: Bobbs-Merrill Company, 1966), pp. 121–8; and Raymond Fielding, *The American Newsreel, 1911–1967* (Norman: University of Oklahoma Press, 1972), pp. 281–3.

10. *Daily Worker* interview quoted in Eric A. Gordon, *Mark the Music: The Life and Work of Marc Blitzstein* (New York: St Martin's Press, 1989), p. 146. For the amateur performances of *The Cradle*, see Gordon, *Mark the Music*, pp. 174, 165. Letter from the CIO in the Orson Welles Manuscripts, Lilly Library, Indiana University, Box 1, November 1937–April 1938.

11. For the influence of Foster, see Gordon, *Mark the Music*, p. 131.

12. *Music Vanguard* 1.2, Summer 1935, p. 94. For a fine discussion of Blitzstein's debt to the Composers Collective, see Carol J. Oja, "Marc Blitzstein's *The Cradle Will Rock* and Mass-Song Style of the 1930s," *The Musical Quarterly* 73.4, 1989, pp. 445–75. For the history of the Composers Collective, see Gordon, *Mark the Music*, pp. 86–116; Richard A. Reuss, "The Roots of American Left-Wing Interest in Folksong," *Labor History* 12, Spring 1971, pp. 259–79; Carol J. Oja, "Composer with a Conscience: Elie Siegmeister in Profile," *American Music* 6.2, Summer 1988, pp. 159–80; Aaron Copland and Vivian Perlis, *Copland: 1900 through 1942* (New York: St Martin's, 1984), pp. 222–30; David K. Dunaway, "Unsung Songs of Protest: The Composers Collective of New York," *New York Folklore* 5, Summer 1979, pp. 1–19; and David K. Dunaway, "Charles Seeger and Carl Sands: The Composers' Collective Years," *Ethnomusicology* 24.2, May 1980, pp. 159–68.

13. *Music Vanguard* 1.1, March–April 1935. Dunaway, "Charles Seeger and Carl Sands," p. 166.

14. Blitzstein quoted in Copland and Perlis, *Copland*, p. 223. Marc Blitzstein, "The Case for Modern Music: II. Second Generation," *New Masses*, 21 July 1936, pp. 28–9. The fullest treatment of the influence of Brecht, Weill, and Eisler on Blitzstein is Dietz, "The Operatic Style of Marc Blitzstein," pp. 138–83.

15. Gordon, *Mark the Music*, pp. 100–15, 125–6. Albrecht Betz, *Hanns Eisler: Political*

Musician (Cambridge: Cambridge University Press, 1982), pp. 143–9, 165–9. James K. Lyon, *Bertolt Brecht in America* (Princeton, N.J.: Princeton University Press, 1980), pp. 6–20. Eva Goldbeck, "Principles of 'Educational' Theatre," *New Masses*, 31 December 1935. Ronald Sanders, *The Days Grow Short: The Life and Music of Kurt Weill* (New York: Holt, Rinehart and Winston, 1980), pp. 217–55. Marc Blitzstein, "Weill Scores for Johnny Johnson," *Modern Music* 14.1, November–December 1936, pp. 44–6.

16. Blitzstein, untitled ["In America . . ."], pp. 1–2.

17. Aaron Copland, "Marc Blitzstein," in Elie Siegmeister, ed., *The Music Lover's Handbook* (New York: William Morrow, 1943), p. 762. Virgil Thomson, *A Virgil Thomson Reader* (New York: E.P. Dutton, 1981), p. 301.

18. Blitzstein, *The Cradle Will Rock: A Play in Music*, p. 23. Brecht quoted in Minna Lederman, *The Life and Death of a Small Magazine (Modern Music, 1924–1946)* (Brooklyn: Institute for Studies in American Music, Brooklyn College, 1983), pp. 66–75. Marc Blitzstein, "As He Remembered It—The Late Composer's Story of How 'The Cradle' Began Rocking," *New York Times*, 12 April 1964, sec. 11, p. 13.

19. Blitzstein, *The Cradle Will Rock: A Play in Music*, pp. 138, 106. Marc Blitzstein, "Author of 'The Cradle'," *Daily Worker*, 3 January 1938, p. 7. Edith Hale, "Author and Composer Blitzstein," *Daily Worker*, 7 December 1938, p. 7.

20. Virgil Thomson, *The State of Music* (New York: William Morrow, 1939), pp. 136–7, 158–9. Marc Blitzstein, "The Case for Modern Music: III. Technique and Temper," *New Masses*, 28 July 1936, p. 28.

21. Blitzstein, "Author of 'The Cradle'," p. 7. The phrase "labor battle song" was used by Brooks Atkinson, "Marc Blitzstein's 'The Cradle Will Rock' Officially Opens at the Mercury Theatre," *New York Times*, 6 December 1937, p. 19. Blitzstein, *The Cradle Will Rock: A Play in Music*, p. 150. Mellers, *Music in a New Found Land*, p. 420.

22. Thomson, *A Virgil Thomson Reader*, p. 301. Blitzstein, *The Cradle Will Rock: A Play in Music*, p. 139. Blitzstein, "The Case for Modern Music: II. Second Generation," p. 29.

23. R.D. Darrell, "Blitzstein Brings New Tunes to Music," *New Masses*, 28 December 1937, p. 27. Oja, "Marc Blitzstein's *The Cradle Will Rock*", pp. 461–73. Blitzstein, *The Cradle Will Rock: A Play in Music*, p. 136.

24. See Robert Snyder, "The Paterson Jewish Folk Chorus: Politics, Ethnicity and Musical Culture," *American Jewish History* 74, September 1984, pp. 27–44; Ruess, "The Roots of American Left-Wing Interest in Folksong," p. 267; Dunaway, "Unsung Songs of Protest: The Composers Collective of New York," p. 5; Mark Slobin, *Tenement Songs: The Popular Music of the Jewish Immigrants* (Urbana: University of Illinois Press, 1982), pp. 46–7; and Arthur Liebman, *Jews and the Left* (New York: John Wiley and Sons, 1979), pp. 304–7.

25. Robinson quoted in Oja, "Marc Blitzstein's *The Cradle Will Rock*," p. 458. Oja, "Composer with a Conscience: Elie Siegmeister in Profile," 166. Earl Robinson, liner notes to Paul Robeson, *Ballad for Americans and Carnegie Hall Concert, Volume 2*, Vanguard VSD-79193, 1965. The three Timely 78s by the New Singers are: 1) the Eisler/Brecht "United Front," sung by Mordecai Baumann with the New Singers, directed by Lan Adomian, and Marc Blitzstein on piano; and Maurice Sugar's "The Soup Song," sung by Felix Groveman with the New Singers and Blitzstein on piano; 2) the "Internationale" sung by the New Singers, with Blitzstein on piano; and Eisler's "Forward but Not Forgotten," sung by Baumann with the New Singers; and 3) the Eisler/Brecht "In Praise of Learning," sung by Baumann with the New Singers and Blitzstein on piano; and the Eisler/Brecht "Rise Up" sung by Baumann with the New Singers and Blitzstein on the piano. The three Timely 78s by the Manhattan Chorus are: 1) "Hold the Fort," with Baumann as lead singer; and "Solidarity"; 2) Maurice Sugar's "Sit Down"/"Write Me Out My Union Card" and Joe Hill's "Casey Jones"; and 3) "We Shall Not Be Moved"/"Join the Union"; and "On the Picket Line." As this book was going to press, these Timely recordings were rereleased on *Songs for Political Action: Folkmusic, Topical Songs and the American Left, 1926–1953*, Bear Family BCD 15720 JL, 1996.

26. *No for an Answer* has not been published; parts of the original production appear on the cast recording: Marc Blitzstein, *No for an Answer (Excerpts): An American Opera*, Keynote No. 105, 1941, reissued as JJA-19772. Subsequent citations are to this recording; the liner notes include sections of the libretto and Blitzstein's own commentary. I am also indebted to the analysis of *No for an Answer* in Dietz, "The Operatic Style of Marc Blitzstein", pp. 254–85, 326–39.

27. Copland, "Marc Blitzstein," p. 763.

28. Mellers, *Music in a New Found Land*, p. 420.

29. Copland, "Marc Blitzstein," p. 763. Thomson, *A Virgil Thomson Reader*, pp. 300–301.

30. It ran for 1,108 performances, closing on 22 June 1940. The road version finally closed in Los Angeles in May 1941. Gerald Bordman, *American Musical Revue: From "The Passing Show" to "Sugar Babies"* (New York: Oxford University Press, 1985), p. 109. See also *PM*, 23 June 1940 which gives a figure of 1,105.

31. Bordman, *American Musical Revue*, pp. 108–9. R. Serge Denisoff, *Great Day Coming*, p. 67. Edward Pessen, "The Great Songwriters of Tin Pan Alley's Golden Age: A Social, Occupational, and Aesthetic Inquiry," *American Music* 3.2, Summer 1985, p. 194.

32. Schaffer quoted in Harry Goldman, "When Social Significance Came to Broadway: 'Pins and Needles' in Production," *Theatre Quarterly* 7.28, Winter 1977–1978, p. 26.

33. On Friedman and the Shock Troupe, see Jay Williams, *Stage Left* (New York: Charles Scribner's Sons, 1974), pp. 79–86, 157–71. Another Shock Troupe member, Earl Robinson, was one of the two pianists for the *Pins and Needles* runthrough.

34. Friedman quoted in Harry Goldman, "Pins and Needles: An Oral History," Ph.D. diss., New York University, 1977, p. 71. Rubinstein quoted in Goldman, "When Social Significance Came to Broadway," p. 27. Harold Rome, "Foreword," Harold Rome Papers, Yale University Music Library, Box 40 F285.

35. Rubinstein quoted in Goldman, "Pins and Needles: An Oral History", p. 74. For the legal conflict with Actors Equity, see Harry and Theresa Goldman, "Pins and Needles," *Performing Arts Review* 7.3, 1977, pp. 356–77. *Pins and Needles* opened with nineteen numbers. To this, *Pins and Needles 1939* added five numbers and cut three; *New Pins and Needles* added ten numbers and cut thirteen. There were other smaller changes within each edition; though no one has catalogued all of the show's numbers, there seem to have been between forty and fifty, including several that were only part of the road show.

36. Other sketches satirizing the American right included "The Harmony Boys" on native fascists, "The General Is Unveiled" (an early ballet), "What This Party Needs" (on the Republican party), "We'd Rather Be Right," and the song "Call It Unamerican."

37. Morgan Y. Himelstein, *Drama Was a Weapon: The Left-Wing Theatre in New York, 1929–1941* (New Brunswick, N.J.: Rutgers University Press, 1963), p. 81. Himelstein and Goldman, "Pins and Needles: An Oral History," both chart the changes in the show's anti-fascist numbers.

38. Several of *Parade*'s sketches were published in *New Theatre*, June 1935. Himelstein, *Drama Was a Weapon*, p. 136.

39. See Pessen, "The Great Songwriters of Tin Pan Alley's Golden Age"; Harold Meyerson and Ernie Harburg, *Who Put the Rainbow in the Wizard of Oz?: Yip Harburg, Lyricist* (Ann Arbor: University of Michigan Press, 1993); Deena Rosenberg, *Fascinating Rhythm: The Collaboration of George and Ira Gershwin* (New York: Dutton, 1991); and Edward Jablonski, *Harold Arlen: Happy with the Blues* (1961; rpt. New York: Da Capo, 1986).

40. Philip Furia, *The Poets of Tin Pan Alley: A History of America's Great Lyricists* (New York: Oxford University Press, 1990), p. 15. See also Peter Van Der Merwe, *Origins of the Popular Style: The Antecedents of Twentieth-Century Popular Music* (Oxford: Clarendon Press, 1989); and Charles Hamm, *Yesterdays: Popular Song in America* (New York: Norton, 1979).

41. Millie Weitz, "Nobody Makes a Pass at Me" / Kay Weber and Sonny Schuyler, "One Big Union for Two," Decca 23060. Ruth Rubinstein, "Chain Store Daisy" / Kay Weber and Sonny Schuyler, "Sing Me a Song with Social Significance," Decca 23061. These are collected on IJA-19783. There was also a Bluebird recording of "Sing Me a Song With Social Significance" and "Chain Store Daisy" featuring the popular singers Nita Carol and Alan Hoit; and a Brunswick recording (8077) of "Sunday in the Park" and "Doin' the Reactionary" by the Will Hudson/Eddie De Lange Orchestra. I have also consulted Harold Rome, *Pins and Needles: Twenty-Fifth Anniversary Edition of the Hit Musical Revue*, Columbia CK 57380.

42. Harold Rome, "Sing Me a Song with Social Significance," Mills Music, 1937.

43. Goldman, "Pins and Needles: An Oral History," p. 206 n. 10.

44. Labor Stage, *Pins and Needles*, Theater program (1938), pp. 18, 16. On the ILGWU plays, see Colette A. Hyman, "Workers on Stage: An Annotated Bibliography of Labor Plays of the 1930s," *Performing Arts Resources* 12, 1987, pp. 171–96.

45. Slobin, *Tenement Songs*, pp. 61, 202–5.

46. Zieger, *The CIO*, p. 86. Rose Pesotta, *Bread upon the Waters* (1944; rpt. Ithaca, N.Y.: ILR Press, 1987), pp. 395, 350, 333, 359. For *I Hear America Singing*, see *Friday*, 21 June 1940.

47. Himelstein, *Drama Was a Weapon*, pp. 75–84; and Goldman, "Pins and Needles: An Oral History," p. 140. See also Louis Schaffer's pamphlet, *Stalin's Fifth Column on Broadway: A Cue to Theatre People* (New York: Rand School Press, 1940).

48. Tucker and Alfasa quoted in Goldman, "Pins and Needles: An Oral History," pp. 202–3.

49. Goldman, "Pins and Needles: An Oral History," pp. 117, 107. Goldman, "When Social Significance Came to Broadway," p. 36. See also Liebman, *Jews and the Left*, pp. 270–78, on the ethnic divisions in the ILGWU.

50. Alfasa and Harary quoted in Goldman, "Pins and Needles: An Oral History," pp. 118, 238.

51. Harold Rome, "Sunday in the Park," Mills Music, 1937. For the popular recording of "Sunday in the Park," see Joel Whitburn, *Pop Memories 1890–1954: The History of American Popular Music* (Menomonee Falls, Wis.: Record Research, 1986), p. 220.

52. "Ellington's Silver Jubilee in *Downbeat*," reprinted in Mark Tucker, ed., *The Duke Ellington Reader* (New York: Oxford University Press, 1993), p. 266; Edward Kennedy Ellington, *Music Is My Mistress*, (Garden City: Doubleday & Company, 1973), pp. 180, 460. Barry Ulanov, *Duke Ellington* (1946; rpt. London: Musicians Press, 1947), p. 245.

53. Barry Singer, *Black and Blue: The Life and Lyrics of Andy Razaf* (New York: Schirmer Books, 1992), p. 208. See also Eileen Southern, *The Music of Black Americans: A History* (New York: Norton, 1983), pp. 427–34.

54. Reuben and Dorothy Silver, interviewers, "Langston Hughes: Playwright," *Artist and Influence* 13, 1994, p. 118. See also Martin Duberman, *Paul Robeson* (New York: Alfred A. Knopf, 1988), p. 231; and Arnold Rampersad, *The Life of Langston Hughes. Volume I:1902–1941. I, Too, Sing America* (New York: Oxford University Press, 1986), pp. 328–9.

55. For the radical black theater, see *New Theatre* 2.7, July 1935; Herbert Kline, ed., *New Theatre and Film: 1934–1937: An Anthology* (San Diego: Harcourt Brace Jovanovich, 1985), pp. 112–26; Michael Gold, "At Last, a Negro Theater?," *New Masses*, 10 March 1936, p. 18; Malcolm Goldstein, *The Political Stage: American Drama and Theater of the Great Depression* (New York: Oxford University Press, 1974), pp. 161–71. For *Mulatto*, see Rampersad, *The Life of Langston Hughes. Volume I*, pp. 312–14.

56. Mark Naison, *Communists in Harlem during the Depression* (Urbana: University of Illinois Press, 1983), pp. 36–7; Klaus Stratemann, *Duke Ellington Day by Day and Film by Film* (Copenhagen: JazzMedia ApS, 1992), places the Harlem Revels Solidarity Ball on 22 March 1930 (p. 26), and notes a Scottsboro benefit in 1935 (p. 129). For the 1932 Scottsboro benefit, see Naison, *Communists in Harlem*, p. 72; and John Hammond, *John Hammond on Record: An Autobiography* (New York: Summit Books, 1977), p. 65. Edward Morrow, "Duke Ellington on Gershwin's 'Porgy'," *New Theatre* 2.12, December 1935, pp. 5–6, reprinted in Tucker, ed., *The Duke Ellington Reader*, pp. 114–18, with a reply from the office of Ellington's manager. *Chicago Defender* quoted in John Edward Hasse, *Beyond Category: The Life and Genius of Duke Ellington* (New York: Simon and Schuster, 1993), p. 246. Ellington was criticized by some figures on the left, notably the jazz critic and producer John Hammond, who had organized the 1932 Scottsboro benefit: in 1935, he wrote that Ellington "consciously keeps himself from thinking about such problems as those of the southern share croppers, the Scottsboro boys, intolerable working and relief conditions in the North and South, though he is too intelligent not to know that these all exist." John Hammond, "The Tragedy of Duke Ellington, the 'Black Prince of Jazz'," November 1935, reprinted in Tucker, ed., *The Duke Ellington Reader*, pp. 118–20.

57. Hammond, *John Hammond on Record*, p. 155. Rampersad, *The Life of Langston Hughes: Volume I*, pp. 356–65, 384. *Don't You Want to Be Free?* and *Limitations of Life* have been reprinted in James V. Hatch, ed., *Black Theater, U.S.A.: Forty-Five Plays by Black Americans, 1847–1974* (New York: Free Press, 1974), pp. 262–77, 655–7. "Negro Artists to Present Social Revue Sunday Night," *Daily Worker*, 6 May 1938, p. 7.

58. Tucker quoted in Goldman, "Pins and Needles: An Oral History," p. 118. Stanley Green, *Ring Bells! Sing Songs! Broadway Musicals of the 1930s* (New York: Galahad Books, 1971), pp. 166–7. Whitburn, *Pop Memories*, pp. 73, 160. Rome was briefly involved in *Sing for Your*

Supper, the most ambitious musical production of the Federal Theatre Project, opening in April 1939. He contributed lyrics under the pseudonym Hector Troy. Though the show closed after three months when the Federal Theatre Project funds were eliminated, one of its songs, Earl Robinson and John LaTouche's "The Ballad of Uncle Sam," became a Popular Front anthem when Paul Robeson sang a revised version, "Ballad for Americans" on CBS radio. Ned Lehac, "The Story of *Sing for Your Supper*," in Glenn Loney, ed., *Musical Theatre in America* (Westport, Conn.: Greenwood, 1984).

59. Goldstein, *The Political Stage*, p. 203. Nancy Lynn Schwartz, *The Hollywood Writers' Wars* (New York: Alfred Knopf, 1982), pp. 164–6. *Friday*, 24 January 1941, pp. 22–3. Edward Eliscu, "Hollywood Produces *Meet the People*," *Direction* 3.4, April 1940, pp. 7–9. John Gassner, "Stage," *Direction* 4.2, February 1941, pp. 8–9. Earl Mills, *Dorothy Dandridge: A Portrait in Black* (Los Angeles: Holloway House, 1970), pp. 59–62. David W. Stowe, *Swing Changes: Big Band Jazz in New Deal America* (Cambridge: Harvard University Press, 1994), pp. 71–2. "The Same Old South" has been reissued on *The Chronological Count Basie and His Orchestra, 1940–1941*, Classics 623, 1992. *Meet the People* was made into an MGM musical, produced by Yip Harburg and featuring Lucille Ball as a Broadway star who goes to work in a shipyard; MGM eliminated the black actors.

60. Rampersad, *The Life of Langston Hughes. Volume I*, pp. 389–95. Arnold Rampersad, *The Life of Langston Hughes. Volume II: 1941–1967. I Dream a World* (New York: Oxford University Press, 1988), pp. 10, 18.

61. Henry Blankfort was active in California Popular Front organizations throughout the 1940s, including the Hollywood Democratic Committee and the Progressive Citizens of America; he was a cousin of Michael Blankfort, a left-wing screenwriter who had been an assistant director of the Theatre Union's *Stevedore* and a *New Masses* drama critic. Ellington quoted in John Pittman, "The Duke Will Stay on Top!," reprinted in Tucker, ed., *The Duke Ellington Reader*, p. 149. Tucker is unable to identify the source of the clipping (other than San Francisco in August or September 1941); since John Pittman was a leading African American Communist and a writer and managing editor for the San Francisco *People's World*, it seems the likely source.

62. Gunther Schuller, *Early Jazz: Its Roots and Musical Development* (New York: Oxford University Press, 1968), p. 339–40. Jablonski, *Harold Arlen*, pp. 63–4.

63. Only sections of *Jump for Joy* have survived; there is no complete score, script, or recording. The surviving recordings were collected on Duke Ellington, *Jump for Joy*, Smithsonian R 037 DMM 1–0722, 1988; Patricia Willard's essay accompanying the recording is the most detailed account of the show. The original program is reprinted in Ellington, *Music Is My Mistress*, pp. 177–9. See also Duke Ellington, *The Blanton-Webster Band*, RCA 5659–2-RB, 1986; and *The Duke Ellington Carnegie Hall Concerts, January 1943*, Prestige 2PCD-34004–2, 1977.

64. Ellington, *Music Is My Mistress*, pp. 175–96; Willard, annotations to Ellington, *Jump for Joy*, pp. 13, 15, 16, 19.

65. Willard, annotations to Ellington, *Jump for Joy*, p. 17.

66. Ellington, *Music Is My Mistress*, pp. 175–6; *Variety* quoted in Stratemann, *Duke Ellington Day by Day*, p. 170. The incident about dialect is told in Willard, annotations to Ellington, *Jump for Joy*, p. 11. Davis quoted in Ulanov, *Duke Ellington*, p. 242. For a brief account of the place of *Jump for Joy* in Los Angeles's black community, see Bruce M. Tyler, *From Harlem to Hollywood: The Struggle for Racial and Cultural Democracy, 1920–1943* (New York: Garland Publishing, 1992), pp. 109–13.

67. Pittman, "The Duke Will Stay on Top!," p. 150.

68. Ellington, *Music Is My Mistress*, p. 181. John Hammond, "Is the Duke Deserting Jazz?" (1943), reprinted in Tucker, *The Duke Ellington Reader*, p. 173. Almena Davis, "Duke Ellington Fascinates Interviewer as He Takes 'Downbeat' Writer to Task" (1941), reprinted in Tucker, ed., *The Duke Ellington Reader*, p. 145.

69. Ellington, *Music Is My Mistress*, p. 180. Willard, annotations to Ellington, *Jump for Joy*, p. 20. Brian Priestley and Alan Cohen, "Black, Brown & Beige," in Tucker, ed., *The Duke Ellington Reader*, p. 198.

70. Duke Ellington, "We, Too, Sing America" (1941), reprinted in Tucker, ed., *The Duke Ellington Reader*, p. 147. The radio broadcast is noted in Stratemann, *Duke Ellington Day by Day*, p. 166.

71. Roi Ottley, *New World A-Coming* (Boston: Houghton Mifflin, 1943), p. 291. Duberman, *Paul Robeson*, p. 249; August Meier and Elliot Rudwick, *Black Detroit and the Rise of the UAW* (New York: Oxford University Press, 1979), p. 105. See also Herbert Garfinkel, *When Negroes March: The March on Washington Movement in the Organizational Politics for FEPC* (New York: Atheneum, 1969).

72. Stowe, *Swing Changes*, pp. 69–70. Stratemann, *Duke Ellington Day by Day*, p. 171.

73. Ellington, *Music Is My Mistress*, p. 183. Stratemann, *Duke Ellington Day by Day*, p. 242, 257, lists a number of these including the Negro Freedom rally (6 June 1943), the Negro Labor Victory Committee's Tribute to Negro Servicemen (27 June 1943), the Paul Robeson Birthday Party (16 April 1944), and the Joint Anti-Fascist Refugee Committee benefit (14 May 1944). See also Stowe, *Swing Changes*, pp. 69–70; Gordon, *Mark the Music*, pp. 217.

74. James Farmer, *Lay Bare the Heart: The Autobiography of the Civil Rights Movement* (New York: Plume, 1986), p. 167. Duke Ellington, "No Red Songs for Me," *New Leader*, 30 September 1950, pp. 2–4.

75. Morrow, "Duke Ellington on Gershwin's 'Porgy'," p. 115. Hasse, *Beyond Category*, p. 369. Rex Stewart, *Boy Meets Horn* (Ann Arbor: University of Michigan Press, 1991), p. 211. Gunther Schuller, *The Swing Era: The Development of Jazz, 1930–1945* (New York: Oxford University Press, 1989), p. 141.

76. Morrow, "Duke Ellington on Gershwin's 'Porgy'," pp. 116–17. Ellington, *Music Is My Mistress*, p. 180.

77. Gordon, *Mark the Music*, pp. 309–16; Thomson, *A Virgil Thomson Reader*, p. 301. Ellington, *Music Is My Mistress*, p. 185; on *Beggar's Holiday*, see also Bernard Eisenschitz, *Nicholas Ray: An American Journey* (London: Faber and Faber, 1993), pp. 85–8; and John Houseman, *Front and Center* (New York: Simon and Schuster, 1979), pp. 188–96.

78. Rampersad, *The Life of Langston Hughes. Volume II*, p. 250.

79. Sidney Finkelstein, *Jazz: A People's Music* (New York: Citadel Press, 1948), pp. 267, 257.

80. Callender quoted in Stuart Nicholson, *Billie Holiday* (Boston: Northeastern University Press, 1995), p. 153. See also Bernard F. Dick, *Radical Innocence: A Critical Study of the Hollywood Ten* (Lexington: University Press of Kentucky, 1989), p. 76; Stowe, *Swing Changes*, pp. 138–9; and Krin Gabbard, *Jammin' at the Margins: Jazz and the American Cinema* (Chicago: University of Chicago Press, 1996), pp. 120–22.

81. See Marc Blitzstein, *Regina*, London 433 812–2, 1992, with libretto.

Notes to 9

1. Martin McCall, "Billie Holiday at Best in New Recordings," *Daily Worker*, 29 July 1939, p. 7. McCall is identified as Margulis in Ronald D. Cohen and Dave Samuelson, *Songs for Political Action: Folk Music, Topical Songs and the American Left, 1926–1953*, p. 12, a book which accompanies a collection of recordings with the same title, Bear Family BCD 15720 JL.

2. Martin Williams, *The Jazz Tradition* (New York: Oxford University Press, 1993), p. 86. John Hammond, "Foreword," Liner notes to Billie Holiday, *The Golden Years*, Columbia C3L 21, 1962.

3. Williams, *The Jazz Tradition*, p. 85. Michael Brooks, Liner notes to *The Quintessential Billie Holiday. Volume 8 (1939–1940)*, Columbia CK 47030, 1991.

4. Gunther Schuller, *The Swing Era: The Development of Jazz, 1930–1945* (New York: Oxford University Press, 1989), p. 543. Irving Howe and Lewis Coser, *The American Communist Party: A Critical History* (1957; rpt. New York: Frederick A. Praeger, 1962), p. 365–6. For a powerful critique of the "natural instincts" position, see Robert O'Meally, *Lady Day: The Many Faces of Billie Holiday* (New York: Arcade Publishing, 1991), p. 154.

5. Lisa Appignanesi, *The Cabaret* (New York: Universe Books, 1976), p. 12. Josephson quoted in Whitney Balliett, *Barney, Bradley and Max* (New York: Oxford University Press, 1989), p. 43. See also Peter Jelavich, *Berlin Cabaret* (Cambridge, Mass.: Harvard University Press, 1993).

6. Balliett, *Barney, Bradley and Max*, p. 44. *Direction* 2.1, January–February 1939, p. 27. In the mid thirties Leon Josephson had been active in the German anti-Nazi underground, and HUAC inquisitors later hounded both Josephsons, claiming that Leon was a Comintern agent. There have been persistent unsubstantiated claims that Café Society was financially backed by

the Communist Party itelf. See Helen Lawrenson, *Whistling Girl* (Garden City, N.Y.: Doubleday, 1978), pp. 86–98. Harvey Klehr, *The Heyday of American Communism: The Depression Decade* (New York: Basic Books, 1984), p. 376. My discussion of Café Society owes much to my conversations and correspondence with David Stowe, who also lent me a copy of Barney Josephson's FBI file. See his forthcoming essay, "Barney Josephson and Cafe Society: The Politics of Culture in the Popular Front," delivered at the American Studies Association Convention, 1994.

7. James Gavin, *Intimate Nights: The Golden Age of New York Cabaret* (New York: Grove Wiedenfeld, 1991), p. 26. Appignanesi, *The Cabaret*, p. 91. Gordon quoted in Balliett, *Barney, Bradley and Max*, pp. 24–5.

8. Quotation from "TAC," *Direction* 2.3, May–June 1939, p. 35. Malcolm Goldstein, *The Political Stage: American Drama and Theater of the Great Depression* (New York: Oxford University Press, 1974), pp. 157, 197–203. "TAC," *Direction* 1.9, November–December 1938, pp. 22–3; "Cabaret TAC," *TAC* 1.7, February 1937, pp. 16–17. Michael Ciment, *Conversations with Losey* (London: Methuen, 1985), p. 54. See also Eric A. Gordon, *Mark the Music: The Life and Work of Marc Blitzstein* (New York: St Martin's Press, 1989), pp. 176–7. Cabaret TAC was a model for other Popular Front cabarets: in the spring of 1938, Nicholas Ray organized and staged the Washington Political Cabaret [Bernard Eisenschitz, *Nicholas Ray: An American Journey* (London: Faber and Faber, 1993), p. 47], and the Motion Picture Artists Committee (MPAC) in Hollywood created the cabaret revue *Sticks and Stones* [Goldstein, *The Political Stage*, p. 203; Larry Ceplair and Stephen Englund, *The Inquisition in Hollywood: Politics in the Film Community, 1930–1960* (Berkeley: University of California Press, 1983), p. 115].

9. John Hammond and James Dugan, "Swat that Jitterbug," *TAC* 1.6, January 1939, p. 11. See also Ralph Ellison, "TAC Negro Show," *New Masses* 34, 27 February 1940, pp. 29–30.

10. O'Meally, *Lady Day*, p. 133. Billie Holiday with William Dufty, *Lady Sings the Blues* (1956; rpt. New York: Avon, 1976), p. 84. Holiday says that she "dug it right off," but most biographers note her initial hesitation. Josephson quoted in Kitty Grime, *Jazz Voices* (London: Quartet Books, 1983), pp. 165–6.

11. John Chilton, *Billie's Blues: The Billie Holiday Story, 1933–1959* (1975; rpt. New York: Da Capo, 1989), p. 68. Wilson quoted in O'Meally, *Lady Day*, p. 152. O'Meally, *Lady Day*, pp. 131, 140.

12. Again, O'Meally is an exception, taking Holiday's political stance seriously, arguing that "'Strange Fruit' . . . gave direct expression to her identity as an African American of political consciousness." O'Meally, *Lady Day*, p. 136.

13. On Johnson, see Mark Naison, *Communists in Harlem during the Depression* (Urbana: University of Illinois Press, 1983), p. 201; and Gerald Horne, *Black Liberation/Red Scare: Ben Davis and the Communist Party* (Newark: University of Delaware Press, 1994), p. 58.

14. Charles and Angeliki Keil also note that "many white ethnics were making their way into the jazz world during the 1920s—Bix Beiderbecke, Frank Teschmaker, Gene Krupa, Benny Goodman, Mez Mezzrow, Wingy Manone, Max Kaminski: the long list contains a great many German, Jewish, Irish, and a few Polish names—but the impulse to form 'polka bands' might be considered a parallel response to the jazz wave." Charles Keil and Angeliki V. Keil, *Polka Happiness* (Philadelphia: Temple University Press, 1992), p. 30.

15. Artie Shaw, *The Trouble with Cinderella: An Outline of Identity* (1952; rpt. New York: Da Capo, 1979), p. 37. Thomson's 1943 article is cited in Frederic Ramsey, Jr., "Trumpet for America," *Direction* 6.3, November 1943, p. 7.

16. Toshio Mori, *Yokohama, California* (Caldwell: Caxton Printers, 1949), p. 76. For a fine discussion of "Bei Mir Bist Du Schoen" and "Beer Barrel Polka," see Victor Greene, *A Passion for Polka: Old-Time Ethnic Music in America* (Berkeley: University of California Press, 1992), pp. 127–35.

17. Ralph Ellison, *Shadow and Act* (1964; rpt. New York: New American Library, 1966), pp. 26, 28, 163. Ellison quoted in Michel Fabre, "From *Native Son* to *Invisible Man*: Some Notes on Ralph Ellison's Evolution in the 1950s," in Kimberly Benston, ed., *Speaking for You: The Vision of Ralph Ellison* (Washington, D.C.: Howard University Press, 1990), p. 202.

18. Jerry Wexler and David Ritz, *Rhythm and the Blues: A Life in American Music* (New York: Alfred Knopf, 1993), pp. 17, 33, 24, 37.

19. One key exception is David Stowe, *Swing Changes: Big-Band Jazz in New Deal America* (Cambridge, Mass.: Harvard University Press, 1994), pp. 50–72, 230–39. I am indebted to

Stowe's work on the "swing-shaped" culture of the period, and to conversations with him about the politics of swing. Two other historians who have written on the jazz left are Eric Hobsbawn, *The Jazz Scene* (New York: Pantheon Books, 1993), pp. 218–22, 292–3, 322, 344; and Horne, *Black Liberation/Red Scare*, pp. 62, 102, 108–10, 120, 250, 352 n. 54.

20. Naison, *Communists in Harlem during the Depression*, pp. 70, 105. John Hammond, *John Hammond on Record: An Autobiography* (New York: Summit Books, 1977), p. 65.

21. Naison, *Communists in Harlem during the Depression*, pp.43, 100. Arnold Rampersad, *The Life of Langston Hughes. Volume I: 1902–1941. I, Too, Sing America* (New York: Oxford University Press, 1986), p. 162. Margaret B. Wilkerson, "Excavating Our History: The Importance of Biographies of Women of Color," *Black American Literature Forum* 24.1, Spring 1990, pp. 81–4.

22. Naison, *Communists in Harlem during the Depression*, pp. 197, 212. Ross Firestone, *Swing, Swing, Swing: The Life and Times of Benny Goodman* (New York: Norton, 1993), p. 211. *New Masses*, 11 January 1938, p. 26. Horne, *Black Liberation/Red Scare*, p. 61. Stuart Nicholson, *Billie Holiday* (Boston: Northeastern University Press, 1995), p. 122. Jo-Carroll Silvers quoted in Kitty Kelley, *His Way: The Unauthorized Biography of Frank Sinatra* (Toronto: Bantam Books, 1986), p. 110.

23. Horne, *Black Liberation/Red Scare*, pp. 107–8, 120, 155. See also Chilton, *Billie's Blues*, p. 103; and Martin Duberman, *Paul Robeson* (New York: Alfred A. Knopf, 1988), p. 283.

24. Gerald Horne, "The Red and The Black: The Communist Party and African–Americans in Historical Perspective," in Michael E. Brown, Randy Martin, Frank Rosengarten, George Snedeker, eds, *New Studies in the Politics and Culture of U.S. Communism* (New York: Monthly Review Press, 1993), p. 214. Horne, *Black Liberation/Red Scare*, p. 259. Gary Giddins, *Celebrating Bird: The Triumph of Charlie Parker* (New York: Beech Tree Books William Morrow, 1987), p. 113. Dizzy Gillespie with Al Fraser, *To Be, or Not . . . to Bop: Memoirs* (Garden City, N.Y.: Doubleday, 1979), p. 287. Both Scott and Horne were listed in *Red Channels: The Report of Communist Influence in Radio and Television* (New York: American Business Consultants, 1950).

25. Gillespie, *To Be, or Not . . . to Bop*, p. 291. The Basie recordings are on *The Chronological Count Basie and His Orchestra 1940–1941*, Classics 623; and *The Chronological Count Basie and His Orchestra 1941*, Classics 652; see also Albert Murray, *Good Morning Blues: The Autobiography of Count Basie* (New York: Random House, 1985), pp. 250–51; Duberman, *Paul Robeson*, p. 177; Michel Fabre, *The Unfinished Quest of Richard Wright* (New York: William Morrow, 1973), p. 237. Jon Wiener, "When Old Blue Eyes Was Red," in his *Professors, Politics, and Pop* (London: Verso, 1991), pp. 263–9.

26. Gillespie, *To Be, or Not . . . to Bop*, p. 80.

27. See John Chilton, *Sidney Bechet: Wizard of Jazz* (New York: Oxford University Press, 1987), pp. 144, 151; Willie "the Lion" Smith, *Music on My Mind: The Memoirs of an American Pianist* (Garden City, N.Y.: Doubleday, 1964), p. 236; Roy Porter, *There and Back* (Baton Rouge: Louisiana State University Press, 1991), p. 50; Gillespie, *To Be, or Not . . . to Bop*, p. 80; see also Bill Coleman, *Trumpet Story* (Boston: Northeastern University Press, 1991), pp. 129–30.

28. Stowe, *Swing Changes*, p. 91.

29. Carter quoted in Firestone, *Swing, Swing, Swing*, p. 80. Gillespie, *To Be, or Not . . . to Bop*, pp. 405–6. For an overview of the color line in swing, see Stowe, *Swing Changes*, pp. 121–33, 230–9. Scott DeVeaux, "The Emergence of the Jazz Concert," *American Music* 7.1, Spring 1989, pp. 6–29.

30. See Stowe, *Swing Changes*, pp. 65–9, 232, for the debates in the *Daily Worker*. See also Muriel Reger, "The Negro in Relation to Jazz," *Direction* 2.1, January–February 1939, pp. 21–2, for an attack on jazz and defense of black classical artists; and the "Jazz vs. Folk Music" debate between Elie Siegmeister and Russell Ames: *Direction* 4.1, January 1941, pp. 20–21. On Smith, see Jerre Mangione, *An Ethnic at Large: A Memoir of America in the Thirties and Forties* (New York: G. P. Putnam's Sons, 1978), pp. 113, 226–32. James Lincoln Collier, "The Faking of Jazz," *New Republic*, 18 November 1985, pp. 33–40. For persuasive replies to Collier, see John Gennari, "Jazz Criticism: Its Development and Ideologies," *Black American Literature Forum* 25.3, Fall 1991, pp. 449–523; and Whitney Balliett, *Goodbyes and Other Messages: A Journal of Jazz, 1981–1990* (New York: Oxford University Press, 1991), pp. 246–7.

31. For the Keynote story, see Joe Klein, *Woody Guthrie: A Life* (New York: Alfred A. Knopf, 1980), pp. 196–7; Gordon, *Mark the Music* p. 204; Hammond, *John Hammond on Record*,

pp. 213–19; Arnold Shaw, *Honkers and Shouters: The Golden Years of Rhythm and Blues* (New York: Macmillan, 1978), pp. 329–31; and Balliett, *Goodbyes and Other Messages*, pp. 189–92.

32. House Committee on Un-American Activities, "Testimony of Hazel Scott Powell," 81st Cong., 2d sess., 22 September 1950, p. 3619. House Committee on Un-American Activities, "Hearings Regarding Communist Infiltration of Minority Groups—Part 3: Testimony of 'Josh White'," 81st Cong., 2d sess., 1 September 1950, p. 2836. White quoted in Chilton, *Billie's Blues*, p. 104. For a representative statement, note Nat Hentoff's comment that some jazz musicians "were caught up in the Camp Unity-type of 'popular front' of the 1930s and 1940s, but nearly always as rather guileless followers, not as originators of ideas or actions," *The Jazz Life* (1961; rpt. New York: Da Capo, 1975), p. 96.

33. Lena Horne and Richard Schickel, *Lena* (Garden City, N.Y.: Doubleday, 1965), pp. 116, 117–18. Gillespie, *To Be, or Not . . . to Bop*, p. 287.

34. Horne, *Black Liberation/Red Scare*, pp. 352 n. 54, 108; Stanley Dance, *The World of Earl Hines* (1977; rpt. New York: Da Capo, 1983), pp. 183–6; Balliett, *Goodbyes and Other Messages*, pp. 48–51; Hammond, *John Hammond on Record*, pp. 245 and passim; *New Masses*, 13 October 1936. Gordon, *Mark the Music*, p. 217.

35. Unidentified musician quoted by Chilton, *Billie's Blues*, p. 67.

36. Gail Lumet Buckley, *The Hornes: An American Family* (New York: Plume, 1987), p. 144. Murray, *Good Morning Blues*, p. 250. Rampersad, *The Life of Langston Hughes. Volume II*, pp. 18, 46, 47, 73. Duberman, *Paul Robeson*, p. 284. Horne and Schickel, *Lena*, p. 117.

37. Schuller, *The Swing Era*, p. 806. Hammond quoted on the jukebox market in Grime, *Jazz Voices*, p. 159. Wilson quoted in Chilton, *Billie's Blues*, p. 26.

38. Sidney Finkelstein, *Jazz: A People's Music* (New York: Citadel Press, 1948), p. 216. For descriptions of Café Society, see Balliett, *Barney, Bradley, and Max*, pp. 39–53; Balliett, *Goodbyes and Other Messages*, pp. 48–51, 235–6; Hammond, *John Hammond on Record*, pp. 159–62; Nicholson, *Billie Holiday*, pp. 108–21; Lawrenson, *Whistling Girl*, pp. 86–98; and Bill Coleman, *Trumpet Story* (Boston: Northeastern University Press, 1991), pp. 123–5, 140–41. Coleman played trumpet in Wilson's band. I am indebted to David Stowe for the recording of Eddie Heywood and His Orchestra, *Jazz at the Cafe Society, N.Y. in the 40s*, Commodore CCK 7010, 1989.

39. For Holiday's biography, see Nicholson, *Billie Holiday*; and Donald Clarke, *Wishing on the Moon: The Life and Times of Billie Holiday* (New York: Viking, 1994). However, O'Meally, *Lady Day*, offers the most persuasive understanding of her apprenticeship and training.

40. For Holiday's recordings and recording sessions, see *The Quintessential Billie Holiday*, Columbia; *Billie Holiday*, Commodore CCD 7001; and Phil Schaap, "Discography," in Nicholson, *Billie Holiday*, pp. 254–83.

41. Dan Morgenstern, Liner notes to Louis Armstrong, *Portrait of the Artist as a Young Man, 1923–1934*, Columbia C4K 57176, p. 50. Holiday quoted in Clarke, *Wishing on the Moon*, p. 48. Schuller, *The Swing Era*, p. 536.

42. Gordon, *Mark the Music*, p. 189. Hazel Scott, "The Yanks Aren't Coming"/"Mene, Mene, Tekel," 78 rpm, TAC 3, probably 1940. Bill Chase, "All Ears," *Amsterdam News*, 31 August 1940, p. 11. Nicholson, *Billie Holiday*, p. 122; Duberman, *Paul Robeson*, p. 283; Horne, *Black Liberation/Red Scare*, pp. 108, 120; Chilton, *Billie's Blues*, p. 103. Nicholson suggests that "The Yanks Aren't Coming" was the subtitle of a Lewis Allan song, "Over Here," pp. 120–21.

43. Helen Oakley Dance, "Irene Kitchings," in Stanley Dance, *The World of Earl Hines*, p. 181. See also Sally Placksin, *American Women in Jazz: 1900 to the Present. Their Words, Lives, and Music* (n.p.: Wideview Books, 1982), pp. 109–12.

44. Holiday with Dufty, *Lady Sings the Blues*, p. 168. Schuller, *The Swing Era*, p. 538.

45. Gabler quoted in Clarke, *Wishing on the Moon*, p. 170.

46. Christopher Small, *Music of the Common Tongue: Survival and Celebration in Afro-American Music* (New York: Riverrun Press, 1987), p. 202. Finkelstein, *Jazz*, p. 40. Holiday quoted in O'Meally, *Lady Day*, p. 41.

47. Herzog quoted in Clarke, *Wishing on the Moon*, pp. 188–91.

48. Holiday with Dufty, *Lady Sings the Blues*, p. 105.

49. O'Meally, *Lady Day*, p. 21. Holiday with Dufty, *Lady Sings the Blues*, pp. 88–91. Herzog quoted in Clarke, *Wishing on the Moon*, p. 191.

50. For the accounts of Holiday's "protective" attitude, see Scott quoted in John White,

Billie Holiday: Her Life and Times (New York: Universe Books, 1987), p. 45; and Horne and Schickel, *Lena*, p. 116. On Scott, see Linda Dahl, *Stormy Weather: The Music and Lives of a Century of Jazzwomen* (New York: Pantheon, 1984), p. 72; Charles V. Hamilton, *Adam Clayton Powell, Jr.: The Political Biography of an American Dilemma* (New York: Atheneum, 1991), pp. 107, 163, 165, 195–6; and Coleman, *Trumpet Story*, p. 123.

51. Horne and Schickel, *Lena*, p. 3. See also Buckley, *The Hornes*; James Haskins with Kathleen Benson, *Lena: A Personal and Professional Biography of Lena Horne* (New York: Stein and Day, 1984); "Downbeat Baby," *Friday*, 13 June 1941, pp. 38–9.

52. Nicholson, *Billie Holiday*, p. 158. Balliett, *Barney, Bradley and Max*, p. 53. The Pegler quotation comes from a clipping in Barney Josephson's FBI file.

53. Horne and Schickel, *Lena*, p. 115. Horne quoted in White, *Billie Holiday*, p. 79. See also the Hollywood Writers' Mobilization radio program in which both Scott and Horne starred, "Something about Joe." Arch Oboler and Stephen Longstreet, eds., *Free World Theatre: Nineteen New Radio Plays* (New York: Random House, 1944), pp. 176–87.

54. White quoted in Chilton, *Billie's Blues*, pp. 103–4.

55. Francis Davis, *The History of the Blues* (New York: Hyperion, 1995), p. 171. Bruce Bastin, *Red River Blues: The Blues Tradition in the Southeast* (Urbana: University of Illinois Press, 1986), p. 323. White is mentioned only in passing in Robbie Lieberman's study of the left-wing folksong movement, *"My Song is My Weapon": People's Songs, American Communism, and the Politics of Culture, 1930–1950* (Urbana: University of Illinois Press, 1989); and he is hardly noticed by either of the major treatments of the folk revival: Robert Cantwell, *When We Were Good: The Folk Revival* (Cambridge, Mass.: Harvard University Press, 1996), and Neil V. Rosenberg, ed., *Transforming Tradition: Folk Music Revivals Examined* (Urbana: University of Illinois Press, 1993).

56. The best sources on White's life are Dorothy Schainman Siegel, *The Glory Road: The Story of Josh White* (1982; rpt. White Hall, Va.: Shoe Tree Press, 1991); Robert Shelton and Walter Raim, *The Josh White Song Book* (Chicago: Quadrangle Books, 1963); David Moore, Liner notes to Josh White, *Complete Recorded Works 1929–1940*, 3 volumes, Documents, DOCD-5194, DOCD-5195, DOCD-5196, and to Josh White, *Complete Recorded Works 1940–1941*, Document DOCD-5405; Cohen and Samuelson, *Songs for Political Action*; Bastin, *Red River Blues*, pp. 167–71, 322–4; Robert Santelli, *The Big Book of the Blues: A Biographical Encyclopedia* (New York: Penguin, 1993), pp. 447–8; and Ray M. Lawless, *Folksingers and Folksongs in America: A Handbook of Biography, Bibliography and Discography* (New York: Duell, Sloan and Pearce, 1960), pp. 233–35. For White's recordings, see White, *Complete Recorded Works*. For a discography, see Robert M.W. Dixon and John Godrich, *Blues and Gospel Records 1902–1943* (Essex: Storyville Publications, 1982). On Leadbelly's ARC recordings, see Charles Wolfe and Kip Lornell, *The Life and Legend of Leadbelly* (New York: HarperCollins, 1992), pp. 156–60. On Blind Willie Johnson, see Mark A. Humphrey, "Holy Blues: The Gospel Tradition," in Lawrence Cohn, ed., *Nothing but the Blues: The Music and the Musicians* (New York: Abbeville Press, 1993); on Carr and Blackwell, see Mark A. Humphrey, "Bright Lights, Big City: Urban Blues," in Cohn, ed., *Nothing but the Blues*.

57. Duberman, *Paul Robeson*, p. 391.

58. Bastin, *Red River Blues*, pp. 323–4. For an account of Lomax's Delta recordings of Waters and House, see Alan Lomax, *The Land Where the Blues Began* (New York: Pantheon Books, 1993).

59. The Lomax recording of Broonzy, Memphis Slim, and Williamson has been released as *Blues in the Mississippi Night*, Rykodisc RCD 90155. A "semi-fictionalized" version of the interview was published in a Popular Front journal as Alan Lomax, "I Got the Blues," *Common Ground* 8.4, Summer 1948, pp. 38–52. Michael K. Honey, *Southern Labor and Black Civil Rights: Organizing Memphis Workers* (Urbana: University of Illinois Press, 1993), p. 130.

60. Jacquelyn Dowd Hall, James Leloudis, Robert Korstad, Mary Murphy, Lu Ann Jones, and Christopher B. Daly, *Like a Family: The Making of a Southern Cotton Mill World* (Chapel Hill: University of North Carolina Press, 1987), pp. 341–2.

61. Dolores Janiewski, "Flawed Victories: The Experiences of Black and White Women Workers in Durham during the 1930s," in Lois Scharf and Joan M. Jensen, *Decades of Discontent: The Women's Movement, 1920–1940* (Boston: Northeastern University Press, 1987), pp. 96, 101. On the Southern Negro Youth Congress, see Robin D.G. Kelley, *Hammer and Hoe: Alabama*

Communists During the Great Depression (Chapel Hill: University of North Carolina Press, 1990), pp. 200–19; and Junius Irving Scales and Richard Nickson, *Cause at Heart: A Former Communist Remembers* (Athens: University of Georgia Press, 1987), pp. 119–20, 162–8.

62. Jackson quoted in Robert Cohen, *When the Old Left Was Young: Student Radicals and America's First Mass Student Movement, 1929–1941* (New York: Oxford University Press, 1993), pp. 222–3. Stuart Bruce Kaufman, *Challenge and Change: The History of the Tobacco Workers International Union* (Urbana: University of Illinois Press, 1987), p. 95. Honey, *Southern Labor and Black Civil Rights*, p. 274. For the history of Local 22 in Winston-Salem, see Bob Korstad, "Those Who Were Not Afraid: Winston-Salem, 1943," in Marc S. Miller, ed., *Working Lives: The Southern Exposure History of Labor in the South* (New York: Pantheon Books, 1980); Robert Korstad and Nelson Lichtenstein, "Opportunities Found and Lost: Labor, Radicals, and the Early Civil Rights Movement," *Journal of American History* 75.3, December 1988, pp. 786–811; and Karl Korstad, "Black and White Together: Organizing in the South with the Food, Tobacco, Agricultural and Allied Workers Union (FTA-CIO), 1946–1952," in Steve Rosswurm, ed., *The CIO's Left-Led Unions* (New Brunswick, N.Y.: Rutgers University Press, 1992).

63. Bastin, *Red River Blues*, pp. 205, 257, 266.

64. Brenda McCallum, "The Gospel of Black Unionism," in Archie Green, ed., *Songs about Work: Essays in Occupational Culture for Richard A. Reuss* (Bloomington: Special Publications of the Folklore Institute, No. 3, Indiana University, 1993). Kip Lornell, *"Happy in the Service of the Lord": Afro-American Gospel Quartets in Memphis* (Urbana: University of Illinois Press, 1988), p. 27. Humphrey, "Holy Blues," pp. 137–8.

65. Bastin, *Red River Blues*, pp. 217–20, 169. Hammond, *John Hammond on Record*, pp. 154–9.

66. For Richardson, see Eugene Gordon, "A People's Theatre in Harlem," *Daily Worker*, 7 August 1939, p. 7; and Rhonda Hanson, "United Public Workers: A Real Union Organizes," in Ann Fagan Ginger and David Christiano, eds, *The Cold War against Labor* (Berkeley, Calif.: Meiklejohn Civil Liberties Institute, 1987), pp. 173–4.

67. Ellison, *Shadow and Act*, p. 242, 250. The phrase "vernacular musicking" is from Small, *Music of the Common Tongue.*

68. In March 1940, White had recorded *Harlem Blues* for Musicraft: it was his first recording session in more than four years. He sang both urban blues standards like "Careless Love" and the Leroy Carr/Scrapper Blackwell blues "Prison Bound," and the spiritual "Motherless Children." Musicraft was a Popular Front independent label that recorded African American folk music: a year earlier, in April 1939, they had recorded Leadbelly's first album, *Negro Sinful Tunes.*

69. Lawrence Gellert, *"Me and My Captain" (Chain Gang Songs): Negro Songs of Protest* (New York: Hours Press, n.d. [1939]). Lawrence Gellert, "Negro Songs of Protest in America," *Music Vanguard* 1.1, March–April 1935, pp. 3–13; "Four Negro Songs of Protest from the Collection of Lawrence Gellert," *Music Vanguard* 1.2, Summer 1935, pp. 68–70. For Gellert, see Bastin, *Red River Blues*, pp. 64–7; John H. Cowley, "Don't Leave Me Here: Non-Commercial Blues: The Field Trips, 1924–1960," in Cohn, *Nothing But the Blues*, pp. 267–9; and John Cowley, "Shack Bullies and Levee Contractors: Bluesmen as Ethnographers," in Green, *Songs about Work*, p. 135. See also Bruce Conforth's liner notes to the Gellert recordings: *Negro Songs of Protest*, Rounder 4004; *Cap'n, You're So Mean: Negro Songs of Protest, Volume Two*, Rounder 4013; and *Nobody Knows My Name: Blues from South Carolina and Georgia 1924–1932*, Heritage HT 304.

70. Shelton and Raim, *The Josh White Song Book*, pp. 24, 106, 154.

71. Josh White and His Carolinians, *Chain Gang*, Columbia C-22, 1940 (4 78-rpm disks with lyrics on liner notes), rereleased on White, *Complete Recorded Works Volume 4.*

72. Richard Wright, "Notes on Jim Crow Blues," Liner notes to Josh White, *Southern Exposure: An Album of Jim Crow Blues*, Keynote 107 (3 78-rpm disks), 1941. *Southern Exposure*, without the Wright liner notes, was rereleased on White, *Complete Recorded Works Volume 4.*

73. Kelley, *Hammer and Hoe*, pp. 209–10.

74. Paul Oliver, "'Sales Tax on It': Race Records in the New Deal Years," in Stephen W. Baskerville and Ralph Willett, *Nothing Else to Fear: New Perspectives on America in the Thirties* (Manchester: Manchester University Press, 1985), p. 208. See also Paul Oliver, *Blues Fell This Morning: Meaning in the Blues* (Cambridge: Cambridge University Press, 1990). For the "Crow

Jane" songs, see Jeff Todd Titon, *Early Downhome Blues: A Musical and Cultural Analysis* (Chapel Hill: University of North Carolina Press, 1994), p. 166.

75. Many of White's political songs of the 1940s have been rereleased on *Songs for Political Action.* This collection also includes Brownie McGhee's Encore recording of "Black, Brown and White."

76. For an account of the early careers of Terry and McGhee, see Bastin, *Red River Blues,* pp. 254–71, 324–9. Howard Taubman, "Folk Songs on the Firing Line," *Negro Quarterly* 1.2, Summer 1942, pp. 182–3; Cohen and Samuelson, *Songs for Political Action,* pp. 15–16. Horne, *Black Liberation/Red Scare,* p. 238. *Ammunition* 2.10, September 1944, p. 36.

Notes to 10

1. Orson Welles, "Theatre and the People's Front," *Daily Worker,* 15 April 1938, p. 7.

2. Irving Howe and Lewis Coser, *The American Communist Party: A Critical History* (New York: Frederick A. Praeger, 1962), p. 365. Alfred Kazin, *Starting out in the Thirties* (Boston: Little, Brown and Company, 1965), p. 119.

3. Larry Ceplair and Stephen Englund, *The Inquisition in Hollywood: Politics in the Film Community, 1930–1960* (Berkeley: University of California Press, 1983), p. 447, list Welles as one of about seventy key activists in Hollywood. For Chaplin and the Popular Front, see Charles Maland, *Chaplin and American Culture: The Evolution of a Star Image* (Princeton, N.J.: Princeton University Press, 1989), pp. 159–278; for O'Neill and the left, see Joel Pfister, *Staging Depth: Eugene O'Neill and the Politics of Psychological Discourse* (Chapel Hill: University of North Carolina Press, 1995), pp. 105–85.

4. Letter from SAC to the Director, 26 September 1949, in Federal Bureau of Investigations, "Orson Welles," Bufile 100–23438. I am grateful to James Naremore for lending me the Welles FBI file: see also his "The Trial: The FBI vs. Orson Welles," *Film Comment,* January–February 1991, pp. 22–7.

5. Pauline Kael, "Raising Kane," in *The Citizen Kane Book* (New York: Limelight Editions, 1984), pp. 26–8. Richard Pells, *Radical Dreams and American Visions* (New York: Harper and Row, 1973), p. 289. FBI, "Welles," p. 5 of the introduction to exhibits.

6. Welles, "Theatre and the People's Front," p. 7. Kazin, *Starting out in the Thirties,* p. 119. Orson Welles, "The Nature of the Enemy," Mss. of 22 January 1945 speech in Orson Welles Manuscripts, Lilly Library, Indiana University, Box 4 f26.

7. John Houseman, "Again—A People's Theatre; The Mercury Takes a Bow," *Daily Worker,* 18 September 1937, p. 7. John Houseman's three-volume autobiography includes: *Run-Through: A Memoir* (New York: Simon and Schuster, 1972); *Front and Center* (New York: Simon and Schuster, 1979); and *Final Dress* (New York: Simon and Schuster, 1983). The closest thing to Welles's autobiography is Orson Welles and Peter Bogdanovich, *This Is Orson Welles* (New York: HarperCollins, 1992). There are many biographies of Welles: I have drawn primarily on Barbara Leaming, *Orson Welles: A Biography* (1985; rpt. New York: Penguin, 1986); Frank Brady, *Citizen Welles: A Biography of Orson Welles* (New York: Charles Scribner's Sons, 1989); and Simon Callow, *Orson Welles: The Road to Xanadu* (New York: Viking, 1995). The best critical study of Welles remains James Naremore, *The Magic World of Orson Welles* (1978; rpt. Dallas, Tex.: Southern Methodist University Press, 1989). Bret Wood, *Orson Welles: A Bio-Bibliography* (New York: Greenwood Press, 1990) is an indispensable account of the Mercury productions. See also "Special Issue on Orson Welles," *Persistence of Vision* 7, 1989, in which an earlier version of this chapter appeared.

8. Annette T. Rubinstein, "The Cultural World of the Communist Party: An Historical Overview," in Michael E. Brown, Randy Martin, Frank Rosengarten, and George Snedeker, eds, *New Studies in the Politics and Culture of U.S. Communism* (New York: Monthly Review Press, 1993), pp. 240, 248. Houseman, *Run-Through,* p. 257.

9. Harold Cruse, *The Crisis of the Negro Intellectual* (New York: William Morrow and Company, 1967), p. 520.

10. Orson Welles, "The Self-Conscious Theatre," *Saturday Review,* 8 February 1941, p. 12. Mordecai Gorelik, *New Theatres for Old* (1940; rpt. New York: Samuel French, 1947), pp. 4, 408.

See also Ira A. Levine, *Left-Wing Dramatic Theory in the American Theatre* (Ann Arbor: UMI Research Press, 1985).

11. Wendy Smith, *Real Life Drama: The Group Theatre and America, 1931–1940* (New York: Alfred Knopf, 1990), p. 272. See also Elia Kazan, *A Life* (New York: Alfred A. Knopf, 1988); Thomas H. Pauly, *An American Odyssey: Elia Kazan and American Culture* (Philadelphia: Temple University Press, 1983); Harold Clurman, *The Fervent Years: The Group Theatre and the Thirties* (1945; rpt. New York: Da Capo, 1975); Robert Sklar, *City Boys: Cagney, Bogart, Garfield* (Princeton, N.J.: Princeton University Press, 1992); Arthur Miller, *Time Bends: A Life* (New York: Grove Press, 1987).

12. Gorelik, *New Theatres for Old*, p. 337. Michael Ciment, *Conversations with Losey* (London: Methuen, 1985), p. 20. See also David Caute, *Joseph Losey: A Revenge on Life* (London: Faber and Faber, 1994); and Bernard Eisenschitz, *Nicholas Ray: An American Journey* (London: Faber and Faber, 1993).

13. The Living Newspaper, "*Injunction Granted*," *Minnesota Review*, New series 1, Fall 1973, p. 99. See also the articles accompanying the *Minnesota Review* text: Arnold Goldman, "Introduction"; Joseph Losey, "Prefatory Note"; and John Fuegi, "Russian 'Epic Theatre' Experiments and the American Stage." Hallie Flanagan, *Arena: The Story of the Federal Theatre* (1940; rpt. New York: Limelight Editions, 1985), p. 72. See also John O'Connor and Lorraine Brown, *Free, Adult, Uncensored: The Living History of the Federal Theatre Project* (Washington, D.C.: New Republic Books, 1978), pp. 76–87.

14. Hughes quoted in Doris Abramson, *Negro Playwrights in the American Theatre, 1925–1959* (New York: Columbia University Press, 1969), p. 80. See also E. Quita Craig, *Black Drama of the Federal Theatre Era* (Amherst: University of Massachusetts Press, 1980); and Rena Fraden, *Blueprints for a Black Federal Theatre, 1935–1939* (Cambridge: Cambridge University Press, 1994). On Hughes's drama, see Leslie Catherine Sanders, *The Development of Black Theater in America: From Shadows to Selves* (Baton Rouge: Louisiana State University Press, 1988), pp. 62–119.

15. See Ethel Pitts Walker, "The American Negro Theater," in Errol Hill, ed., *The Theatre of Black Americans* (New York: Applause, 1987); and Harold Cruse, *The Crisis of the Negro Intellectual* (New York: William Morrow and Company, 1967), pp. 206–24.

16. Glenda E. Gill, "Canada Lee: Black Actor in Non-Traditional Roles," *Journal of Popular Culture* 25.3, Winter 1991, pp. 79–89.

17. Houseman, "Again—a People's Theatre," p. 7.

18. Houseman, "Again—A People's Theatre," p. 7. Lawrence Levine, "William Shakespeare and the American People: A Study in Cultural Transformation," in his *The Unpredictable Past: Explorations in American Cultural History* (New York: Oxford University Press, 1993).

19. Clurman, *The Fervent Years*, pp. 215–16. Houseman, *Run-Through*, p. 410.

20. Houseman quoted in Callow, *Orson Welles*, p. 368. Houseman, *Run-Through*, p. 338.

21. FBI, "Orson Welles." Meltzer is identified as Welles's chief advisor in Tom Pettey, letter to Herb Drake, 5 May 1942, Orson Welles Manuscripts, Lilly Library, Indiana University. Richard Wilson, letter to Howard Cheney, 10 December 1942, Orson Welles Manuscripts, Lilly Library, Indiana University. Robert Meltzer, letter to Orson Welles, 3 March 1941, Orson Welles Manuscripts, Lilly Library, Indiana University.

22. Emil Pratt, "Orson Welles and Citizen Kane," *New Masses*, 4 February 1941, pp. 26–7. "Orson Delivers," *Friday*, 17 January 1941, pp. 24–5. Orson Welles, "*Citizen Kane* Is Not about Louella Parson's Boss," *Friday*, 14 February 1941. "Mrs Citizen Kane," *Friday*, 13 June 1941.

23. Mercury press release quoted in Leaming, *Orson Welles*, p. 170. Unnamed critic quoted in Houseman, *Run-Through*, p. 317. *Catholic World* quoted in Richard France, ed., *Orson Welles on Shakespeare: The W.P.A. and Mercury Theatre Playscripts* (New York: Greenwood Press, 1990), p. 105. Welles quoted in Callow, *Orson Welles*, p. 324. Welles and Bogdanovich, *This Is Orson Welles*, pp. 32–3, 298–9. Welles quoted in Brady, *Citizen Welles*, p. 212.

24. Orson Welles, "Survival of Fascism," Speech at Modern Forum, Wilshire Ebell Theater, 4 December 1944, p. 4, in Orson Welles Manuscripts, Lilly Library, Indiana University, Box 5 f12. Welles, "The Nature of the Enemy," p. 3.

25. Welles, "The Nature of the Enemy," p. 4.

26. Houseman, "Again—a People's Theatre," p. 7. Kazin, *Starting out in the Thirties*, p. 119.

27. *With Orson Welles*, Turner Network Television, 1990: this was a version of the 1980 BBC production, *The Orson Welles Story*, directed and produced by Alan Yentob and Leslie Megahey.

28. Welles quoted in Naremore, *The Magic World of Orson Welles*, p. 12.

29. "Interview with Orson Welles," *Cahiers du Cinéma*, 1958, translated and edited in Terry Comito, ed., *Touch of Evil* (New Brunswick, N.J.: Rutgers University Press, 1985), pp. 205–7.

30. Alfred Hitchcock, "Introduction," to Eric Ambler, *Intrigue* (New York: Knopf, 1943). Joel Hopkins, "An Interview with Eric Ambler," *Journal of Popular Culture* 9, Fall 1975, p. 286. For a more extensive discussion of the Popular Front spy thriller, see my *Cover Stories: Narrative and Ideology in the British Spy Thriller* (London: Routledge and Kegan Paul, 1987), pp. 59–90.

31. John Howard Lawson, *Film: The Creative Process* (New York: Hill and Wang, 1964), p. 126.

32. Screenplay quoted in Wood, *Orson Welles: A Bio-Bibliography*, p. 157.

33. Welles quoted in Naremore, *The Magic World of Orson Welles*, p. 117.

34. Lloyd quoted in Richard France, *The Theatre of Orson Welles* (Lewisburg, Pa.: Bucknell University Press, 1977), pp. 55, 106.

35. Welles, "The Nature of the Enemy," p. 13. Jean Rosenthal, *The Magic of Light* (New York: Theatre Arts Books, 1972), p. 22.

36. Walter Benjamin, "The Work of Art in the Age of Mechanical Reproduction" [1936] in *Illuminations* (New York: Schocken Books, 1969), pp. 242–3. Kenneth Burke, "The Rhetoric of Hitler's *Battle*," in his *The Philosophy of Literary Form: Studies in Symbolic Action* (1941; rpt. Berkeley: University of California Press, 1973), pp. 191–2. See also "Anthony in Behalf of the Play" and "Growth among the Ruins" in the same collection.

37. Welles's experience in the Federal Theatre and in radio's world of "sustaining" programming led him to argue that Hollywood too should have its "experimental" studios: "It is too bad that there is no money spent in Hollywood for experiment. If you take any other large industry—General Electric, chemistry, automobiles—you spend at least ten per cent— maybe twenty per cent—of your profits on a laboratory where experimentation is done. There is not one cent spent by anybody in Hollywood for experiment." Orson Welles, lecture to motion picture students of New York University, 20 October 1942, p. 2, in Orson Welles Manuscripts, Lilly Library, Indiana University, Box 5 fl.

38. Welles quoted in Naremore, *The Magic World of Orson Welles*, p. 13. Hadley Cantril, *The Invasion from Mars: A Study in the Psychology of Panic* (1940; rpt. New York: Harper and Row, 1966), pp. 47–63.

39. Cantril, *The Invasion from Mars*, p. 157. Cantril's elaborate attempt to explain why working people and poor people were more likely to be frightened is based on an unexamined metaphor, the word "insecurity," which insecurely conflates economic and psychological insecurity. At one point, Cantril writes that the answers to one question "reflect the basic insecurity of over half the population." The question from the Gallup Poll, however, only asked how long the respondent could survive without relief if he or she lost their job. The rest of the explanation depends on an elaborate opposition between "critical ability" and "susceptibility-to-suggestion-when-facing-a-dangerous-situation." "Critical ability" is defined as "a general capacity to distinguish between fiction and reality or the ability to refer to special information which is regarded as sufficiently reliable to provide an interpretation." For Cantril, "critical ability" knows no escape: "If critical ability is to be consistently exercised, it must be possessed by a person who is invulnerable in a crisis situation and who is impervious to extraneous circumstances." Behind this argument lay a deep contempt for working-class culture: "Dull lives may be cheered with bright clothing or gaudy furniture, harassed breadwinners may become fixtures at the local beer hall, worried housewives may zealously participate in religious orgies, repressed youths may identify themselves for a few hours with the great lovers or gangsters of the silver screen. There are many socially accepted ways of escape from the responsibilities, worries, and frustrations of life—the movies, the pulp magazines, fraternal organizations, and a host of other devices thrive partially because their devotees want surcease from their woes." Though Cantril explicitly distances himself from those who "condemn 'the masses' in wholesale fashion," his conclusions echo them. Cantril, *The Invasion from Mars*, pp. 155, 130, 117, 149, 161.

40. Sylvia Holmes is quoted in Cantril, *The Invasion from Mars*, pp. 53–4.

41. Eckhard Breitinger, "The Rhetoric of American Radio Drama," *Revue des langues vivantes* 44, 1978, pp. 229–46. Archibald MacLeish, *The Fall of the City: A Verse Play for Radio* (New

York: Farrar & Rinehart, 1937), pp. 31–3; my quotation follows the radio broadcast, which differs slightly from the published text.

42. Archibald MacLeish, "Air Raid," in his *Six Plays* (Boston: Houghton Mifflin, 1980), pp. 102, 120. Douglas Coulter, "Preface," to his collection, *Columbia Workshop Plays: Fourteen Radio Dramas* (New York: Whittlesey House, 1939), p. xvi.

43. Pritt, "Orson Welles and Citizen Kane," p. 27.

44. John Dos Passos, *The Big Money*, in *U.S.A.* (New York: Modern Library, n.d. [1938]), pp. 476–7. Edward A. Ross, "How to Smash Hearst," *Champion of Youth*, in FBI, "Welles," exhibit 94. For the League and *Citizen Kane*, see Charles Glenn, "News, Views, Gossip from Filmland Capital," *Daily Worker*, 21 January 1941, p. 7; and Charles Glenn, "Hollywood Writers Say No to War Maneuvers," *Daily Worker*, 23 January 1941, p. 7. Molly Castle, "'Citizen Kane': Tops from Every Angle," *US Week* 1.8, 3 May 1941, p. 17.

45. Cedric Belfrage, "Orson Welles' *Citizen Kane*," *The Clipper* 2.3, May 1941, pp. 13, 12. Muriel Draper, "Citizen Welles," *Direction* 4.5, Summer 1941, p. 11. John Howard Lawson, *Film: The Creative Process* (New York: Hill and Wang, 1964), p. 139.

46. "Interview with Orson Welles," *Cahiers du Cinéma*, p. 204. Welles quoted in Callow, *Orson Welles*, p. 494.

47. Welles and Bogdanovich, *This Is Orson Welles*, pp. 114, 490, 130.

48. Many critics have missed this, separating the film's formal techniques from its content. "There are far too many trick camera angles," Joy Davidman argued in *The New Masses*, "too many fantastic combinations of light and shadow, indicating an incomplete translation of Welles' famous stage technique into screen terms. Frequently he lets his showmanship run away with him, preferring to astound rather than to convince." For formalist critics, this showmanship was the heart of the film. "All Welles's tricks, as they are often contemptuously called—the lightning mixes, the stills which come to life, the complex montages, the elasticity of perspective, the protracted dissolves, the low-angle camera movements—are what still gives the film any interest," Peter Wollen argued in a classic interpretation of *Citizen Kane*. "Nobody, after all, has ever made high claims for its 'novelistic' content, its portrayal of Kane's psychology, its depiction of American society and politics in the first half of the twentieth century, its anatomy of love or power or wealth. Or, at any rate, there is no need to take such claims seriously." Davidman, "Citizen Kane," *New Masses*, 13 May 1941, p. 28. Peter Wollen, "Introduction to *Citizen Kane*," in his *Readings and Writings* (London: NLB, 1982), p. 60.

49. Welles and Bogdanovich, *This Is Orson Welles*, p. 74. Welles told Barbara Leaming a similar story, except that he played himself in a "March of Time" show about *The Cradle Will Rock*: Leaming, *Orson Welles*, p. 628. The incident he remembers may actually be the 22 March 1935 "March of Time" show, in which he recreated part of his stage performance of *Panic*.

50. Welles, "*Citizen Kane* Is Not about Louella Parson's Boss."

51. Wollen, "Introduction to *Citizen Kane*," p. 52.

52. Robert Carringer, *The Making of Citizen Kane* (Berkeley: University of California Press, 1985), pp. 50–51, 75. R.H. Winnick, ed., *Letters of Archibald MacLeish, 1907–1982* (Boston: Houghton Mifflin, 1983), p. 275.

53. On the Luces' financial involvement with the Mercury, see Houseman, *Run-Through*, pp. 304–5. "Marvelous Boy," *Time* 31.19, 9 May 1938, pp. 27–31.

54. Winnick, ed., *Letters of Archibald MacLeish*, p. 293.

55. Welles quoted in Callow, *Orson Welles*, p. 497.

56. Quoted in Callow, *Orson Welles*, p. 338.

57. Carringer, *The Making of Citizen Kane*, pp. 81, 105.

58. Welles and Bogdanovich, *This Is Orson Welles*, p. 74. *Variety* quoted in Callow, *Orson Welles*, p. 549. "Orson Welles," *Life*, 26 May 1941, pp. 108–16. The key figure seems to have been *Life* editorial assistant Richard Pollard, to whom Welles wrote: "If anybody is responsible for 'Citizen Kane' being released, I think it is you . . . You have been so interested that it is difficult for me to remember you are not with us in the Mercury Theatre. I wish you were." Orson Welles, letter to Richard Pollard, 15 May 1941, in Time Inc. Archives.

59. Mary McCarthy, "February 1938: Elizabethan Revivals," in her *Sights and Spectacles, 1937–1956* (New York: Farrar, Straus and Cudahy, 1956), p. 17.

60. For accounts of the "middlebrow" culture of modern times, see Joan Shelley Rubin, *The Making of Middlebrow Culture* (Chapel Hill: University of North Carolina Press, 1992); James

Sloan Allen, *The Romance of Commerce and Culture* (Chicago: University of Chicago Press, 1983); and Joseph Horowitz, *Understanding Toscanini: How He Became an American Culture-God and Helped Create a New Audience for Old Music* (Minneapolis: University of Minnesota Press, 1987).

61. Pierre Bourdieu, *Distinction: A Social Critique of the Judgement of Taste* (Cambridge, Mass.: Harvard University Press, 1984), pp. 329, 326, 323. The classic critique of middlebrow culture is Dwight Macdonald, "Masscult & Midcult," in his *Against the American Grain: Essays on the Effects of Mass Culture* (New York: Random House, 1962).

62. See also Beverley Houston, "Power and Dis-Integration in the Films of Orson Welles," *Film Quarterly* 35.4, Summer 1982, p. 9, who notes that "for 'people,' of course, read 'women'."

63. Davidman, "Citizen Kane," p. 28. Victor S. Navasky, *Naming Names* (New York: Penguin Books, 1981), p. 227.

64. Welles quoted in Naremore, *The Magic World of Orson Welles*, p. 116. W.A. Swanberg, *Luce and His Empire* (New York: Charles Scribner's Sons, 1972), p. 221.

65. Welles, "Survival of Fascism," pp. 23, 25.

66. Welles, "Survival of Fascism," p. 25. Welles was an editorial writer for the monthly *Free World* and published a dozen short articles between October 1943 and December 1945. Dolivet is discussed in most of the Welles biographies, but a somewhat more detailed account appears in Michael Straight, *After Long Silence* (New York: W.W. Norton, 1983), pp. 252–8. Welles and Dolivet worked together from 1943 until their estrangement over *Mr. Arkadin* (which Dolivet produced) in 1955.

67. Welles, "The Nature of the Enemy," p. 21.

68. Welles interviewed in *On Orson Welles*. Mark Naison, *Communists in Harlem during the Depression* (Urbana: University of Illinois Press, 1983), pp. 140–88. Roi Ottley, "The Negro Theatre 'Macbeth'," *Amsterdam News*, 18 April 1936. The text of *Macbeth* is reprinted in France, ed., *Orson Welles on Shakespeare: The W.P.A. and Mercury Theatre Playscripts* ; a brief film of the production is included in the WPA newsreel *We Work Again*, 1937. See also France, *The Theatre of Orson Welles*.

69. De Paur quoted in O'Connor and Brown, *Free, Adult, Uncensored*, p. 122. See also Craig, *Black Drama of the Federal Theatre Era*, pp. 154–71.

70. For the Welles-Ellington collaboration, see Duke Ellington, *Music Is My Mistress* (Garden City, N.Y.: Doubleday, 1973), pp. 239–41; and Klaus Stratemann, *Duke Ellington Day by Day and Film by Film* (Copenhagen: Jazzmedia ApS, 1992), pp.193–5. See also Billie Holiday with William Dufty, *Lady Sings the Blues* (1956; rpt. New York: Avon, 1976), pp. 93–4. Welles would continue to feature jazz on the radio. In 1944, he wrote "My new radio program is theoretically 'popular,' which is to say that my sponsors maintain a traditional fondness for Hit Parade arrangements, and big lush orchestrations... However, they will tolerate ... a small combination of fine instrumentalists playing real jazz for a 'spot' or 'novelty.'" Orson Welles, letter to Miss Morden, 4 February 1944, Orson Welles Manuscripts, Lilly Library, Indiana University.

71. Welles quoted in Robert Stam, "Orson Welles, Brazil and the Power of Blackness," *Persistence of Vision* 7, 1989, p. 102. Tom Pettey, letter to Herb Drake, 5 May 1942, Orson Welles Manuscripts, Lilly Library, Indiana University. Tom Pettey, letter to Herb Drake, 7 April 1942, Orson Welles Manuscripts, Lilly Library, Indiana University. See also Catherine Benamou, "*It's All True* as Document/Event: Notes towards an Historiographical and Textual Analysis," *Persistence of Vision* 7, 1989, pp. 121–52.

72. Welles's *It's All True* footage can be seen in at least three productions: Rogério Sganzerla's Brazilian television program *Brasil*; the American Film Institute documentary *It's All True: Four Men on a Raft*, produced by Fred Chandler, 1986; and *It's All True*, directed by Myron Meisel and Bill Krohn with Richard Wilson, 1993.

73. Richard Wright, letter to John Houseman and Orson Welles, 19 May 1940, in Orson Welles Manuscripts, Lilly Library, Indiana University. Hearst review quoted in John Houseman, "*Native Son*," in his *Entertainers and the Entertained: Essays on Theater, Film, and Television* (New York: Simon and Schuster, 1986), p. 42. John Gassner, "Stage," *Direction* 4.5, Summer 1941, p. 43. Samuel Sillen, "Bigger Thomas on the Boards," *New Masses*, 8 April 1941, p. 27. The published version of the play by Richard Wright and Paul Green was *not* the version Welles staged: for an account of the stageplay, see Houseman, "*Native Son*," pp. 32–42; and

"Native Son," in Burns Mantle, ed., *The Best Plays of 1940–41* (New York: Dodd Mead, 1941), pp. 29–63.

74. Keneth Kinnamon and Michel Fabre, eds, *Conversations with Richard Wright* (Jackson: University Press of Mississippi, 1993), p. 40. John Gassner, *Producing the Play* (New York: Dryden Press, 1941), p. 431. Gassner, "Stage," 42.

75. Gassner, "Stage," p. 43.

76. The Sleepy Lagoon Defense Committee, *The Sleepy Lagoon Case* (Los Angeles: Mercury Printing, 1943), pp. 19, 11. Welles may have financed the pamphlet under the name "Mercury Printing Company." See also Carey McWilliams, *North from Mexico: The Spanish-Speaking People of the United States* (1948; rpt. New York: Greenwood Press, 1968), pp. 228–33; Joint Fact-Finding Committee on Un-American Activities in California, *Second Report: Un-American Activities in California* (Senate of the State of California, 1945), pp. 174–97; and Joint Fact-Finding Committee on Un-American Activities in California, *Fourth Report: Communist Front Organizations* (Senate of the State of California, 1948), p. 375.

77. "Memorandum of a meeting of the Emergency Entertainment Industry Committee, Radio Sub-Committee," attached to Pauline Lauber, letter to Orson Welles, 16 July 1943, Orson Welles Manuscripts, Lilly Library, Indiana University. William Robson, "Open Letter on Race Hatred," in Erik Barnouw, ed., *Radio Drama in Action: Twenty-Five Plays of a Changing World* (New York: Rinehart & Company, 1945). Orson Welles, letter to Davidson Taylor of CBS, 21 September 1943, Orson Welles Manuscripts, Lilly Library, Indiana University. Howard Koch, letter to Orson Welles with script of *Snowball*, 1943, Orson Welles Manuscripts, Lilly Library, Indiana University.

78. Oliver W. Harrington, *Why I Left America and Other Essays* (Jackson: University Press of Mississippi, 1993), p. 103. The text of Welles's first Woodward broadcast on 28 July 1946 was reprinted as "Orson Welles Smashes at Southern Bigots in Radio Talk," *Los Angeles Sentinel*, 15 August 1945, pp. 1, 20. Five of Welles's broadcasts dealt with the Woodward case: 28 July; 5, 11, 18, and 25 August, 1946. Welles and Bogdanovich, *This Is Orson Welles*, pp. 398–9. I am grateful to Jane Levey for lending me copies of materials about the Woodward case.

79. "Interview with Orson Welles," *Cahiers du Cinéma*, p. 204.

80. On *Touch of Evil*'s scripts, see John Stubbs, "The Evolution of Orson Welles's *Touch of Evil* from Novel to Film," in Comito, ed., *Touch of Evil*, pp. 183–4. See also William Anthony Nericcio, "Of Mestizos and Half-Breeds: Orson Welles's *Touch of Evil*," in Chon A. Noriega, *Chicanos and Film: Representation and Resistance* (Minneapolis: University of Minnesota Press, 1992).

81. Welles and Bogdanovich, *This Is Orson Welles*, pp. 309, 308. The two shots are #277 and #256 in the published continuity script: Comito, ed., *Touch of Evil*, pp. 100–106, 91–6.

82. "Interview with Orson Welles," *Cahiers du Cinéma*, p. 212.

83. Kazan, *A Life*, pp. 273, 134–5.

Notes to 11

1. Michael Wilmington, "*Dumbo*," in Danny Peary and Gerald Peary, eds, *The American Animated Cartoon: A Critical Anthology* (New York: E.P. Dutton, 1980), p. 78; for Art Babbitt's dissent, see John Grant, *Encyclopedia of Walt Disney's Animated Characters* (New York: Harper and Row, 1987), p. 172.

2. Robert Feild, *The Art of Walt Disney* (New York: Macmillan, 1942), pp. 2–3. Paul Hollister, "Walt Disney," *Atlantic Monthly* 166, December 1940, p. 689. Pare Lorentz, *Lorentz on Film: Movies 1927 to 1941* (New York: Hopkinson and Blake, 1975), pp. 148, 150.

3. Bert Cochran, *Labor and Communism: The Conflict That Shaped American Unions* (Princeton, N.J.: Princeton University Press, 1977), p. 160.

4. Harvey Deneroff, "'We Can't Get Much Spinach!' The Organization and Implementation of the Fleischer Animation Strike," *Film History* 1, 1987, pp. 1–14. Testimony of Herbert Sorrell, "Jurisdictional Disputes in the Motion Picture Industry," Hearings before the House Special Subcommittee on Education and Labor, 80th Congress, pp. 1875–6.

5. Shamus Culhane, *Talking Animals and Other People* (New York: St Martin's Press, 1986), pp. 186–7.

6. Bob Casino, "Interview with Disney Animator: Willis Pyle," *Toy Values Monthly*, October 1991, p. 28. Testimony of Herbert Sorrell, pp. 1234–6.

7. Feild, *The Art of Walt Disney*, p. 282. Leonard Mosley, *Disney's World* (New York: Stein and Day, 1985), pp. 190–96.

8. Authors' interviews with Bill Pomerance, June 1991 and June 1992.

9. Richard Schickel, *The Disney Version: The Life, Times, Art, and Commerce of Walt Disney* (New York: Simon and Schuster, 1968), pp. 248–9.

10. Authors' interview with Mary Eastman, 24 June 1992. Jack Kinney, *Walt Disney and Assorted Other Characters: An Unauthorized Account of the Early Years at Disney's* (New York: Harmony Books, 1988), p. 137. Casino, "Interview with Disney Animator," p. 28.

11. Kinney, *Walt Disney and Assorted Other Characters*, p. 137.

12. Testimony of Walter E. Disney, "Communist Infiltration of Hollywood Motion-Picture Industry," House Committee on Un-American Activities, 82nd Congress, pp. 282–5.

13. Schickel, *The Disney Version*, p. 258. Testimony of Herbert Sorrell, p. 1905.

14. Testimony of Herbert Sorrell, p. 1875.

15. Testimony of Herbert Sorrell, p. 1907. "Men Who Draw Walt Disney's Animated Cartoons Report Their Own Strike," *PM*, reproduced in M.B. Schnapper, *American Labor: A Pictorial Social History* (Washington, D.C.: Public Affairs Press, 1972), p. 545. "Who's Afraid of Big Bad Walt?," *Friday*, 25 July 1941.

16. "Communist Infiltration of Motion-Picture Industry," House Committee on Un-American Activities, 82nd Congress, Appendix, p. 536.

17. Testimony of Walter E. Disney, p. 283.

18. Testimony of Walter E. Disney, p. 283. "Disney's Proposed Layoffs May Again Tie Up His Cartoon Plant," *Variety*, 13 August 1941.

19. Interview with Bill Pomerance. "Film Cartoonists Reach Out to S.A. to Picket Junket by Disney," *Variety*, 3 September 1941. For a discussion of Disney's Latin American trip, see Eric Smoodin, *Animating Culture: Hollywood Cartoons in the Sound Era* (New Brunswick, N.J.: Rutgers University Press, 1993), p. 147.

20. "Cartoonists and Disney Settle," *Variety*, 30 July 1941. Nancy Lynn Schwartz, *The Hollywood Writers' Wars* (New York: Alfred A. Knopf, 1982), pp. 204–7.

21. Testimony of Herbert Sorrell, p. 1913. "U.S. Labor Conciliator Steps In to Hasten Disney-Cartoon Peace," *Variety*, 2 July 1941. Schickel, *The Disney Version*, p. 261. Casino, "Interview with Disney Animator," p. 28. Testimony of Walter E. Disney, p. 284. Testimony of Charlotte Darling Adams, "Investigation of Communist Activities in the Los Angeles Area," House Committee on Un-American Activities, 83rd Congress, p. 2311.

22. John Canemaker, "Vlad Tytla: Animation's Michelangelo," in Peary and Peary, eds, *The American Animated Cartoon*, p. 87. Melendez quoted in Charles Solomon, *Enchanted Drawings: The History of Animation* (New York: Knopf, 1989), p. 71.

23. Solomon, *Enchanted Drawings*, p. 71; Culhane, *Talking Animals and Other People*, p. 236.

24. Greg Ford and Richard Thompson, "An Interview with Chuck Jones," *Cambridge Animation Festival '85*, London 1985, p. 5. John D. Ford, "An Interview with John and Faith Hubley," in Peary and Peary, eds, *The American Animated Cartoon*, p. 183. Hurtz quoted in Leonard Maltin, *Of Mice and Magic: A History of American Animated Cartoons* (New York: New American Library, 1987), p. 323.

25. Testimony of Charlotte Darling Adams, p. 2313.

26. Ford, "An Interview with John and Faith Hubley," p. 184.

27. Quoted in Maltin, *Of Mice and Magic*, p. 324.

28. Authors' interviews with Edwina Hammond Pomerance, June 1991 and June 1992.

29. Interview with Edwina Hammond Pomerance. The Biberman talk on social realism was repeatedly brought up in the HUAC hearings, when Bernyce Polifka Fleury, Eugene Fleury, Charlotte Darling Adams, and Zachary Schwartz testified against their former comrades. See Testimony of Bernyce Polifka Fleury, "Communist Infiltration of Hollywood Motion-Picture Industry," House Committee on Un-American Activities, 82nd Congress, pp. 1777–8; Testimony of Eugene Fleury, "Communist Infiltration of Hollywood Motion-Picture Industry," House Committee on Un-American Activities, 82nd Congress, p. 2067. Testimony of Charlotte Darling Adams, pp. 472–3. Testimony of Zachary Schwartz, "Investigation of Communist

Activities in the New York City Area," House Committee on Un-American Activities, 83rd Congress, pp. 1448–9.

30. Interview with Edwina Hammond Pomerance. Ford, "An Interview with John and Faith Hubley," p. 190.

31. John Hubley, "The Writer and the Cartoon," in *Writers' Congress: Proceedings of the Conference Held in October 1943 under the Sponsorship of the Hollywood Writers' Mobilization and the University of California* (Berkeley: University of California Press, 1944), pp. 105–11.

32. Hubley, "The Writer and the Cartoon," p. 110.

33. Hubley, "The Writer and the Cartoon," p. 111. Phil Eastman, "New Techniques and Uses," in *Writers' Congress*, pp. 122–6. John Hubley, "Beyond Pigs and Bunnies: The New Animator's Art," *American Scholar* 44.2, Spring 1975, pp. 213–23.

34. For *Tuesday in November*, see John Houseman, *Front and Center* (New York: Simon and Schuster, 1979), pp. 124–7.

35. Schwartz quoted in Maltin, *Of Mice and Magic*, p. 326. Jack Zeller, "Films for Unity," *Film News* 7.3, December 1945, p. 10. International Union, United Automobile, Aircraft and Agricultural Implement Workers of America, *Proceedings . . . Second Annual Education Conference*, Detroit, 1945, p. 86. Stills from the film were reproduced in the UAW's monthly magazine, *Ammunition* 2.8, August 1944, pp. 16–17, and Harburg and Robinson's song was printed in *Ammunition* 2.10, September 1944, p. 12.

36. "UAW-CIO Film Production Expands," *Film News* 6.6, June 1945, p. 8.

37. See *Ammunition* 5.1, January 1947, p. 35, and 5.2, February 1947, pp. 32–7.

38. Ford, "An Interview with John and Faith Hubley," p. 185. *Post* review quoted in Solomon, *Enchanted Drawings*, p. 211.

39. Ring Lardner, Jr, Maurice Rapf, John Hubley, and Phil Eastman, "'Brotherhood of Man': A Script," *Hollywood Quarterly* 1, July 1946, pp. 353–9. John Hubley and Zachary Schwartz, "Animation Learns a New Language," *Hollywood Quarterly* 1, July 1946, pp. 360–63.

40. Solomon, *Enchanted Drawings*, p. 210. Roger Keeran, *The Communists and the Auto Workers Union* (Bloomington: Indiana University Press, 1980), p. 261. Larry Ceplair and Steven Englund, *The Inquisition in Hollywood: Politics in the Film Community, 1930–1960* (Berkeley: University of California Press, 1983), pp. 196–7.

41. Hurst quoted in Solomon, *Enchanted Drawings*, p. 221.

42. Interview with Bill Pomerance.

43. Thom Anderson, "Red Hollywood," in Suzanne Ferguson and Barbara Groseclose, eds, *Literature and the Visual Arts in Contemporary Society* (Columbus: Ohio State University Press, 1985), pp. 183, 187.

44. Melendez quoted in Solomon, *Enchanted Drawings*, pp. 215–16, 220.

Notes to 12

1. League of Professional Groups for Foster and Ford, *Culture and the Crisis: An Open Letter to the Writers, Artists, Teachers, Physicians, Engineers, Scientists, and Other Professional Workers of America* (New York: Workers Library Publishers, 1932), pp. 29–30.

2. A.L. Kroeber and Clyde Kluckhohn, *Culture: A Critical Review of Concepts and Definitions* (1952; rpt. New York: Vintage Books, n.d.), p. 3. Warren Susman, *Culture as History: The Transformation of American Society in the Twentieth Century* (New York: Pantheon Books, 1984), pp. 153–4, 164.

3. Susman, *Culture as History*, p. 84. Note also the influential essay by the editors of *Cahiers du Cinéma*, "John Ford's *Young Mr. Lincoln*" (1970), translated in *Screen* 13.3, 1972. My own essay of 1986 began to explore Marxist cultural studies in the United States, but it remained too dismissive of the Popular Front tradition: see "'The Special American Conditions': Marxism and American Studies," *American Quarterly* 38.3, 1986, pp. 356–80.

4. The *Culture and the Crisis* authors have generally been identified as Lewis Corey, Malcolm Cowley, Matthew Josephson, Sidney Hook, and James Rorty.

5. Sidney Hook, *Towards the Understanding of Karl Marx: A Revolutionary Interpretation* (New York: John Day, 1933), pp. x, 130, 188.

6. Perry Anderson, *Considerations on Western Marxism* (London: NLB, 1976), p. 53.

7. Anderson, *Considerations on Western Marxism*, p. 56.

8. Eastman quoted in William L. O'Neill, *The Last Romantic: A Life of Max Eastman* (New York: Oxford University Press, 1978), p. 129. John P. Diggins, *Up from Communism: Conservative Odysseys in American Intellectual History* (New York: Harper and Row, 1975), pp. 17–73.

9. Max Eastman, *Marx, Lenin and the Science of Revolution* (London: George Allen and Unwin Ltd, 1926), pp. 32, 46, 62.

10. Eastman, *Marx, Lenin and the Science of Revolution*, p. 221.

11. Max Eastman, "The Doctrinal Crisis in Socialism," *Modern Quarterly* 5.4, Winter 1930–31, pp. 426–9.

12. Eastman, *Marx, Lenin and the Science of Revolution*, pp. 159, 160.

13. Hook, *Towards the Understanding of Karl Marx*, p. 115.

14. Hook, *Towards the Understanding of Karl Marx*, pp. 69, 95, 76. Sidney Hook, "Marxism, Metaphysics, and Modern Science," *Modern Quarterly* 4.4, May–August 1928, pp. 388–94: this was Hook's review of Eastman.

15. Sidney Hook, review of Max Eastman, *Karl Marx's Capital and Other Writings*, *Modern Monthly* 7.4, May 1933, pp. 248–50.

16. Max Eastman, "If Marx Had Studied under Dewey," in his *Art and the Life of Action* (New York: Knopf, 1934). For the major exchanges, see *Modern Quarterly* 4.4, May–August 1928, pp. 388–94; *Modern Quarterly* 5.1, November 1928–February 1929, pp. 85–7, 88–91; *Modern Quarterly* 5.4, Winter 1930–31, pp. 422–50; *Modern Monthly* 7.4, May 1933, pp. 210–13, 248–50; *Modern Monthly* 7.5, June 1933, pp. 290–93, 320; *Modern Monthly* 7.6, July 1933, pp. 348–51; *Modern Monthly* 7.7, August 1933, pp. 447–48; *Modern Monthly* 7.8, September 1933, pp. 510–12; *Modern Monthly* 7.9, October 1933, p. 576.

17. Leon Samson, *Toward a United Front: A Philosophy for American Workers* (New York: Farrar and Rinehart, 1933), pp. 5, 16, 261–2.

18. Sidney Hook, "The Anatomy of the Popular Front," *Partisan Review* 6.3, Spring 1939, p. 40. In subsequent accounts, Hook and others claimed that their opposition to the Popular Front was due to the fact that it was a false front, dominated and manipulated by the Communist Party and made up of "fellow travelers." Hook's 1939 essay, however, makes it clear that he understood the Popular Front as a broad popular movement of whom the Communist Party was simply the "most vociferous supporter" (p. 44): "Who are they? Among the groups left or center—the Social-Democrats, Communists, Laborites, Farmer-Laborites, some Socialists, and the liberals and progressives of indeterminate hue who sleep in a different political bed every election day. All, practically, but the Bolshevist-Leninists, who have learned nothing and forgotten nothing since October 1917" (p. 32).

19. Sidney Hook, *Reason, Social Myths and Democracy* (1940; rpt. New York: Harper Torchbook, 1965), p. 141. Sidney Hook, *Out of Step: An Unquiet Life in the 20th Century* (New York: Harper and Row, 1987), pp. 160, 600–601.

20. Edmund Wilson, *To the Finland Station: A Study in the Writing and Acting of History* (1940; rpt. Garden City: Doubleday, 1953), pp. 194, 189.

21. For a contemporary socialist consideration of pragmatism, see Cornel West, *The American Evasion of Philosophy: A Genealogy of Pragmatism* (Madison: University of Wisconsin Press, 1989).

22. William Cain, "An Interview with Irving Howe," *American Literary History* 1.3, Fall 1989, p. 559.

23. James Rorty, *Our Master's Voice: Advertising* (New York: John Day, 1934), pp. 32, 30. See also his pamphlet about radio, *Order on the Air* (New York: John Day, 1934); and the discussion of Rorty in Robert McChesney, *Telecommunications, Mass Media and Democracy: The Battle for the Control of U.S. Broadcasting, 1928–1935* (New York: Oxford University Press, 1993). Rorty was a close political associate of Sidney Hook and followed him to the political right.

24. Kenneth Burke, *Permanence and Change: An Anatomy of Purpose* (New York: New Republic, 1935), p. 93.

25. Fredric Jameson, "The Symbolic Inference; or, Kenneth Burke and Ideological Analysis," *Critical Inquiry* 4, Spring 1978, p. 512. Frank Lentricchia, *Criticism and Social Change* (Chicago: University of Chicago Press, 1985), p. 66. In an earlier essay, I took issue with Lentricchia's characterization of Burke as a Western Marxist, accepting the received view of Burke as a non-Marxist liberal theorist of symbolic action, a view that Lentricchia's

interpretation does not fundamentally contest. Paul Jay's illuminating essay on Burke argues persuasively that the parallels between Burke and contemporary critical theory are less interesting than the way Burke responds to the crisis of the 1930s. However, I am not persuaded that Burke's response to his time is best charted through his changing treatments of Marx and Freud, as Jay suggests. Indeed, both Lentricchia and Jay cite the 1950s revisions of Burke's books of the 1930s; neither seems aware of the substantial changes made in the later editions. See Denning, "'The Special American Conditions'," p. 359. Paul Jay, "Kenneth Burke and the Motives of Rhetoric," *American Literary History* 1.3, Fall 1989, pp. 535–53. Burke's politics and self-censorship were discussed in a special issue of *Communication Studies* 42.3, Fall 1991: see Edward Schiappa and Mary F. Keehner, "The 'Lost' Passages of Kenneth Burke's *Permanence and Change*," pp. 191–8; Philip C. Wander, "At the Ideological Front," pp. 199–218; Don M. Burks, "Kenneth Burke: The Agro-Bohemian 'Marxoid'," pp. 219–33; and James Arnt Aune, "Burke's Palimpsest: Rereading *Permanence and Change*," pp. 234–7.

26. Kenneth Burke, "Curriculum Criticum," in his *Counter-Statement*, 2nd edition (1953; rpt. Chicago: University of Chicago Press, 1957), p. 215.

27. Kenneth Burke, *Permanence and Change: An Anatomy of Purpose*, 2nd revised edition (Los Altos, Calif.: Hermes Publications, 1954), p. xv.

28. Burke, *Permanence and Change* (1935), p. 338 and (1954), p. 263; (1935), p. 344 and (1954), omitted; (1935), p. 345 and (1954), revised to read "Once a cooperative way of life . . .," p. 268.

29. Kenneth Burke, *Attitudes toward History*, 2 vols (New York: New Republic, 1937) and *Attitudes toward History*, 2nd revised edition (Los Altos, Calif.: Hermes Publications, 1959): (1937), vol. 2, p. 206 and (1959), omitted; (1937), vol. 2, pp. 234–5; (1959), omitted. Frank Lentricchia opens his study of Burke by pointing out the centrality of the section in which this passage occurred.

30. Burke, *Attitudes toward History* (1937), vol. 2, p. 114.

31. Kenneth Burke, *The Philosophy of Literary Form: Studies in Symbolic Action* (1941; rpt. Berkeley: University of California Press, 1973), p. xx. Kenneth Burke, *A Grammar of Motives* (1945; rpt. Berkeley: University of California Press, 1969), p. 442.

32. Kenneth Burke, "Literature as an Equipment for Living," *Direction* 1.4, April 1938, p. 13. Burke, *The Philosophy of Literary Form*, pp. 304, 109.

33. Paul Jay, ed., *The Selected Correspondence of Kenneth Burke and Malcolm Cowley, 1915–1981* (New York: Viking, 1988), p. 202. For Burke's discussion of Strachey's Marxism, see *Permanence and Change* (1935), pp. 286–94. For Burke's discussion of Bentham, Marx, and Veblen, see Kenneth Burke, *A Rhetoric of Motives* (1950; rpt. Berkeley: University of California Press, 1969), pp. 90–132.

34. Burke, *Attitudes toward History* (1937), vol. 2, pp. 234–5. Burke, *The Philosophy of Literary Form*, p. 305.

35. Burke, *Attitudes toward History* (1937), vol. 2, p. 233.

36. Burke, *Attitudes toward History* (1937), vol. 2, p. 233.

37. Burke, *The Philosophy of Literary Form*, p. 26n. Burke, *Attitudes toward History* (1937), vol. 1, p. 129.

38. Burke, *Attitudes toward History* (1937), vol. 2, p. 71. Burke, *Permanence and Change* (1935), p. 148.

39. Burke, *Attitudes toward History* (1937), vol. 2, pp. 68, 44–5. Burke, *The Philosophy of Literary Form*, p. xix.

40. "Thirty Years Later: Memories of the First American Writers' Congress," *American Scholar* 35.3, Summer 1966, p. 506.

41. "Thirty Years Later," p. 506.

42. "Thirty Years Later," pp. 507–8.

43. "Thirty Years Later, p. 506. Matthew Josephson, *Infidel in the Temple: A Memoir of the Nineteen-Thirties* (New York: Alfred A. Knopf, 1967), p. 371. Malcolm Cowley, *The Dream of the Golden Mountains: Remembering the 1930s* (New York: Penguin Books, 1981), p. 227.

44. Lentricchia, *Criticism and Social Change*, pp. 101, 86.

45. James T. Farrell, *Yet Other Waters* (New York: Vanguard Press, 1952), p. 123.

46. Kenneth Burke, "The Writers' Congress," *The Nation*, May 1935, p. 571.

47. Jay, *The Selected Correspondence of Kenneth Burke and Malcolm Cowley*, p. 232. The account of the University of Washington affair is on pp. 305–13.

48. The Hook-Burke exchange can be found in *Partisan Review* 4.1, December 1937, pp. 57–62; and *Partisan Review* 4.2, January 1938, pp. 40–47.

49. Boorstin's testimony is reprinted in Eric Bentley, ed., *Thirty Years of Treason: Excerpts from Hearings before the House Committee on Un-American Activities, 1938–1968* (New York: Viking, 1971), pp. 601–12.

50. On Matthiessen as cultural historian, see Leo Marx, "The Teacher," *Monthly Review* 2.6, October 1950, p. 207. F.O. Matthiessen, *American Renaissance: Art and Expression in the Age of Emerson and Whitman* (New York: Oxford University Press, 1941), p. xv. Caroline Ware, "Introduction," to Ware, ed., *The Cultural Approach to History* (New York: Columbia University Press, 1940), pp. 3–16. On Ware, see Ellen Fitzpatrick, "Caroline F. Ware and the Cultural Approach to History," *American Quarterly* 43, June 1991, pp. 173–98. On Rourke, see Joan Shelley Rubin, *Constance Rourke and American Culture* (Chapel Hill: University of North Carolina Press, 1980).

51. Jonathan Arac, *Critical Genealogies: Historical Situations for Postmodern Literary Studies* (New York: Columbia University Press, 1989), p. 167.

52. For *Common Ground*, see William C. Beyer, "Louis Adamic and *Common Ground*, 1940–1949," and John L. Modic, "Louis Adamic and the Story of *Common Ground*," both in *Louis Adamic: Simpozij Symposium* (Ljubljana: Univerza Edvarda Kardelja v Ljubljani, 1981).

53. The first use of the term "ethnicity," according to Werner Sollors, was in the sociological studies of Lloyd Warner in 1941. Werner Sollors, *Beyond Ethnicity: Consent and Descent in American Culture* (New York: Oxford University Press, 1986), pp. 21–4. John Collier and Saul K. Padover, "An Institute for Ethnic Democracy," *Common Ground* 4.1, Autumn 1943, p. 5. Langston Hughes, "White Folks Do The Funniest Things," *Common Ground* 4.2, Winter 1944, pp. 42–6. M. Margaret Anderson, "Letter to the Reader," *Common Ground* 4.3, Spring 1944, p. 92.

54. Anderson, "Letter to the Reader," p. 93.

55. Carey McWilliams, *Brothers under the Skin* (Boston: Little, Brown and Company, 1943), pp. 14–16.

56. McWilliams, *Brothers under the Skin*, p. 317.

57. McWilliams, *Brothers under the Skin*, p. 77.

58. Gary Gerstle, *Working-Class Americanism: The Politics of Labor in a Textile City, 1914–1960* (Cambridge: Cambridge University Press, 1989), p. 318. See also Steve Fraser and Gary Gerstle, eds., *The Rise and Fall of the New Deal Order, 1930–1980* (Princeton, N.J.: Princeton University Press, 1989).

59. Carey McWilliams, *The Education of Carey McWilliams* (New York: Simon and Schuster, 1979), pp. 114–15.

60. For a selection of Cox's writings and a biographical account, see Herbert M. Hunter and Sameer Y. Abraham, eds, *Race, Class and the World System: The Sociology of Oliver C. Cox* (New York: Monthly Review Press, 1987).

61. Oliver Cromwell Cox, *Caste, Class and Race: A Study in Social Dynamics* (1948; rpt. New York: Monthly Review Press, 1970), pp. 486, 331–2.

62. Cox, *Caste, Class and Race*, p. 322.

63. Cox, *Caste, Class and Race*, p. 510.

64. Paul Sweezy, "Foreword," to Hunter and Abraham, eds, *Race, Class and the World System*, p. xi.

65. For a fine discussion of the "mass culture" debate, see Andrew Ross, *No Respect: Intellectuals and Popular Culture* (New York: Routledge, 1989). For the argument that American Communist critics "were squarely in the emerging pattern of the mass culture critique," see Paul R. Gorman, *Left Intellectuals and Popular Culture in Twentieth-Century America* (Chapel Hill: University of North Carolina, 1996), p. 132. My discussion of the debate over mass or popular culture can be found in "The End of Mass Culture," *International Labor and Working-Class History* 37, Spring 1990, pp. 4–18; and "The Ends of Ending Mass Culture," *International Labor and Working-Class History* 38, Fall 1990, pp. 63–7.

66. Bettina Berch, *Radical by Design: The Life and Style of Elizabeth Hawes* (New York: E.P. Dutton, 1988), p. 74.

542   *Notes to Pages 457 to 470*

67. Elizabeth Hawes, *Why Is a Dress?* (New York: Viking, 1942), pp. 2, 7, 160.
68. Elizabeth Hawes, *Fashion Is Spinach* (New York: Random House, 1938), pp. 295–6.
69. Hawes, *Why Is a Dress?*, pp. 149, 29, 75.
70. Hawes, *Why Is a Dress?*, p. 8. Elizabeth Hawes, *Hurry Up Please Its Time* (New York: Reynal & Hitchcock, 1946), p. 2.
71. Sidney Finkelstein, *Jazz: A People's Music* (New York: Citadel Press, 1948), pp. 157–8. In 1958, however, George Steiner did note that Finkelstein, "one of a small yet interesting group of American Marxists," was one of the "theoreticians and practical critics whom anyone seriously concerned with literature would be wrong to ignore." Steiner, *Language and Silence: Essays on Language, Literature and the Inhuman* (New York: Atheneum, 1967), pp. 315, 317. See also Maynard Solomon's discussion of Finkelstein in Solomon, ed., *Marxism and Art: Essays Classic and Contemporary* (New York: Vintage, 1974).
72. Finkelstein, *Jazz*, pp. 98, 231.
73. Finkelstein, *Jazz*, pp. 223, 194–7, 33, 50, 43.
74. Finkelstein, *Jazz*, p. 28.
75. On James, see Paul Buhle, *C.L.R. James: The Artist as Revolutionary* (London: Verso, 1988); and Kent Worcester, *C.L.R. James: A Political Biography* (Albany: State University of New York Press, 1996). For his US writings, see Scott McLemee and Paul LeBlanc, eds, *C.L.R. James and Revolutionary Marxism, 1939–1949* (Atlantic Highlands, N.J.: Humanities Press, 1993).
76. C.L.R. James, *American Civilization* (Cambridge: Blackwell, 1993), p. 36.
77. James, *American Civilization*, p. 138.
78. James, *American Civilization*, pp. 166, 173, 227.
79. Irving Louis Horowitz, ed., *Power, Politics and People: The Collected Essays of C. Wright Mills* (New York: Ballantine Books, 1963), p. 256.

Notes to Conclusion

1. Bob Dylan, "11 Outlined Epitaphs," Liner notes to his *The Times They Are A-Changin'*, Columbia CS 8905, 1964.
2. Fredric Jameson, *Postmodernism, Or, The Cultural Logic of Late Capitalism* (Durham, N.C.: Duke University Press, 1991), p. 209.
3. Stuart Hall, "Gramsci's Relevance for the Study of Race and Ethnicity," in David Morley and Kuan-Hsing Chen, eds, *Stuart Hall: Critical Dialogues in Cultural Studies* (London: Routledge, 1996), p. 423.
4. Clancy Sigal, *Going Away: A Report, A Memoir* (1961; rpt. New York: Dell, 1970), pp. 294, 504, 60, 181.
5. Sigal, *Going Away*, pp. 241, 141. He considers going to the University of Minnesota, one of the centers of the newly formed American Studies movement.
6. Steve Fraser and Gary Gerstle, "Introduction," to Fraser and Gerstle, eds, *The Rise and Fall of the New Deal Order, 1930–1980* (Princeton, N.J.: Princeton University Press, 1989), p. xix. Other accounts of the decline of New Deal populism include Jim Sleeper, *The Closest of Strangers: Liberalism and the Politics of Race in New York* (New York: Norton, 1990); Thomas Byrne Edsall with Mary D. Edsall, *Chain Reaction: The Impact of Race, Rights, and Taxes on American Politics* (New York: Norton, 1992); and Michael Kazin, *The Populist Persuasion: An American History* (New York: Basic Books, 1995). I am indebted to Nikhil Singh's critique of this populism in his "'Race' and Nation in the American Century: A Genealogy of Color and Democracy," Ph.D. diss., Yale University, 1995.
7. Harriette Arnow, *The Dollmaker* (1954; rpt. New York: Avon, 1972), p. 245. See also Susan Willis, "A Literary Lesson in Historical Thinking," *Social Text* 3, Fall 1980, pp. 136–43.
8. Sigal, *Going Away*, p. 311. Arnow, *The Dollmaker*, pp. 156, 479.
9. Arnow, *The Dollmaker*, pp. 22, 23, 501.
10. Sigal, *Going Away*, p. 159.
11. *People's World* quoted in Elia Kazan, *A Life* (New York: Alfred A. Knopf, 1988), p. 566.
12. Maurice Isserman, letter to *The Nation*, 13 December 1986, p. 658. This was part of a debate over Jesse Lemisch, "I Dreamed I Saw MTV Last Night," *The Nation*, 18 October 1986.
13. Jameson, *Postmodernism*, p. 24. For contemporary reviews of the revival of the thirties,

see David R. Peck, "'The Orgy of Apology': The Recent Reevaluation of the Literature of the Thirties," *Science and Society* 32.4, Fall 1968, pp. 371–82; and David Peck, "Salvaging the Art and Literature of the 1930s: A Bibliographical Essay," *Centennial Review* 20.2, Spring 1976, pp. 128–41. See also Alan Wald, "The Legacy of Daniel Aaron," in his *Writing from the Left: New Essays on Radical Culture and Politics* (New York: Verso, 1994), pp. 13–27; and Paul Buhle, ed., *History and the New Left: Madison, Wisconsin, 1950–1970* (Philadelphia: Temple University Press, 1990).

14. Tillie Olsen, *Yonnondio: From the Thirties* (1974; rpt. New York: Delta, 1989), pp. 133, 48. Donald Pizer, ed., *John Dos Passos: The Major Nonfictional Prose* (Detroit, Mich.: Wayne State University Press, 1988), p. 118.

Index